Skating In America
(1921-1996)

The 75th Anniversary History of the
United States Figure Skating Association

by Benjamin T. Wright
USFSA Historian

Colorado Springs, Colorado – 1996

CREDITS

Design and Layout: Barnstorm Design/Creative of Colorado Springs, Colo.

Printing: Sport Graphics of Indianapolis, Ind.

Photography: Courtesy of World Figure Skating Museum and Hall of Fame, William Udell and Paul Harvath.

Cover photography: Mike Below of Colorado Springs, Colo.

It is not for the historian to speculate on the future. However, a reading of this History will show that as the United States Figure Skating Association ends its 75th year and looks forward to its 100th Anniversary in 2021, it does so in a strong condition, not only financially but also in the strength of its member clubs and their membership.

There are, of course, challenges to be met: the possibility of over-exposure, especially through the media, including television, which could result in a decline in public interest and support; the continuing commercialization of the sport and the consequent blurring or obliteration of the distinction between those who participate in skating for reasons other than material gain and those who do so for a living; and the continuing decline in the standards of performance in the sport. However, with a conscientious and forward-looking leadership, the Association can look ahead with confidence to the future with the knowledge that it too will evolve and change as the sport does, and that it will maintain its pre-eminent position as the National Governing Body for the sport in the United States.

It should also be noted that the comments and opinions set forth in the text are strictly those of the author and do not in anyway reflect the policies or positions of the USFSA on the matters discussed.

It is only appropriate to express my appreciation to those persons who have supported the project of the preparation of the History and who have encouraged and assisted in its completion. Among them are Morry Stillwell, the current USFSA President, Jo Lawless, Chairman of the 75th Anniversary Committee and Beth Davis, Curator of the World Figure Skating Museum. Finally, my heartfelt thanks go to my wife Mary Louise, without whose help and constant support, the History would never have been completed.

Benjamin T. Wright

USFSA Historian

Belmont, MA   *May 1996*

While the United States Figure Skating Association (USFSA) is 75 years old in 1996, it is not, either by European or North American standards, considered to be an "old" national association, although its antecedents go back just as far as those in other countries. The honors belong in Europe to the National Ice Skating Association of the U.K., founded in 1879 as the

The Formative Years
(1886-1920)

National Skating Association of Great Britain, and in North America to the Canadian Figure Skating Association (CFSA), founded in 1888 as the Amateur Skating Association of Canada (ASAC).

Figure skating in the United States had a rudimentary form of organization as early as 1864, when the first Championship of America was held at Troy, N.Y., and was won by the legendary Jackson Haines. Thereafter, various abortive efforts were made up to the 1880's to form a national governing body, led largely by the major skating clubs in Boston, New York and Philadelphia. The oldest skating club in the United States still in existence today is the Philadelphia Skating Club and Humane Society, founded in 1849.

Jackson Haines

Finally, in 1886, the first national association was founded, the National Amateur Skating Association (NASA). This body consisted largely of skaters from the Eastern part of the country and especially from the New York City area. NASA continued to conduct the Championship of America in the so-called American Style throughout its life. Although national in name, it was essentially regional or local in nature and eventually expired in 1905. The Championships of America continued until 1909 under the auspices of the New York Skating Club, founded in 1863.

After the turn of the century, the sport began to move away from the American Style, which concentrated on small intricate figures, with the drawings on the ice being paramount, much as was the case with the "special figures" performed in Europe at the time. The freer style of skating, originally carried to Europe in the 1860's by Jackson Haines, returned

Irving Brokaw

to North America and quickly became the dominant form in which the majority of active skaters participated.

The first exhibition of the so-called International Style of skating in North America was held in 1908 at the Cambridge (Mass.) Skating Club, founded in 1898 and still in existence today. Demonstrating the new type of skating were Irving Brokaw of New York, who had been Champion of America in 1906, and who would subsequently have a major hand in the foundation of the USFSA, and Karl Zenger, the Champion of Germany in 1906. J. Frank Bacon of Cambridge, himself an American champion in 1893, demonstrated the old style. The event was organized by George H. Browne of Cambridge, the founder and headmaster of the Browne & Nichols School in 1883, who was an ardent skater, author and judge. While on sabbatical leave, he traveled to Switzerland to learn the new style which was originally called the Continental Style to distinguish it from the English Style, which was similar in form to the American Style.

The Continental Style had its genesis in the pioneering exhibitions throughout Europe of Jackson Haines of New York in the late 1860's. Essentially, the International Style, as it quickly became known, is the freer form of skating we know today, with open positions of the arms and legs and covering the entire ice surface. The English and American styles were rigid with the arms by the sides, the legs straight, and performed in a very small area. Probably the distinguishing aspect between the old and new styles was the use of music for the performance of free skating as had been done by Haines.

George H. Browne (1857-1931) is generally considered to have been the "father" of modern figure skating in the United States and is remembered by the memorial trophy in his name for the Men's Championship of the United States, presented by The Skating of Boston in 1931. Browne was one of the founders of the USFSA and its first Secretary in 1921-1922. Irving Brokaw of New York, on the other hand, was the first leading exponent of the International Style in the United States.

Brokaw represented his country in the figure skating events of the Olympic Games held in London in 1908, the only American to do so, placing sixth. He was elected an Honorary President of the USFSA in 1922, after having served as a Vice President of the Association in its first year, while serving again as a Vice President from 1923 to 1924. He was not thereafter active in the Association, although he remained an important influence in the affairs of the Association. His only title in the International Style was in the Waltz in 1920 with Mrs. Gertrude Cheever Porter. Perhaps his most notable contribution to the sport was his book **The Art of Skating**, published in two editions in 1910 and 1926, which remains to this day one of the basic references for the early history of the sport. Brokaw passed away in 1939 and was posthumously elected to the United States Figure Skating Hall of Fame in 1976. After his death, a memorial trophy in his name was presented by his three daughters for the Junior Men's event of the National Championship.

George H. Browne

The next attempt to establish a national association resulted in the formation of the International Skating Union of America in 1907. The name, which would be confused with that of the present international federation today, was not a problem then, since the international federation was generally known by its German name, the "Internationale Eislauf-Vereinigung" (IEV). The ISU of A, as it was called, was a unique body. It included among its members the Amateur Skating Association of Canada, as well as the Western Skating Association of Canada, and three regional associations in the United States: the New England, Eastern and Western Skating Associations. It was in effect, an "association of associations," a format which would continue in speed skating and was the governing body of the skating sports (speed and figure) for all of North America. It was the direct ancestor of the USFSA, as will be seen.

According to Browne, the first formal competition in the International Style held in the United States was a local one at Lexington, Mass., in 1911. The winners were Thomas M. Vinson, the father of Maribel Vinson, and Edith Rotch, the sister of Charles M. Rotch. Vinson had been an American Style skater and was second in the American Championship in 1893. He later was a long-time judge for the USFSA. In the Ladies event, Theresa Weld made her first appearance in competition.

Jeanne Chevalier and Norman Scott

The dual nature of the ISU of A having jurisdiction over skating in both Canada and the United States, quickly resulted in friendly and vigorous competition across the border under its sponsorship (which continues today between the successor organizations.)

It was the now defunct (once again) discipline of Fours (two ladies and two men) which was the initial competitive vehicle for the friendly exchange between the two countries. In 1913, the first international competition in North America, for Fours, was held in Ottawa for the cup presented by HRH the Duke of Connaught, the son of Queen Victoria, then the Governor General of Canada. The cup was competed for by the Minto Skating Club of Ottawa and The Skating Club of Boston, with the former coming out on top. Actually, it would not be until 1941 in Philadelphia that an American Four would be successful in the North American Championship for the cup. The next year, 1914, a return match was held between the two clubs, for the Ellis Memorial Trophy, named for a charitable institution supported by the Boston club, which was the winner of a competition in which the four team members skated both Singles, Pairs and Fours. Essentially, this was a very early form of team event.

The first National Championships in the International Style were organized under the auspices of the ISU of A in 1914 in New Haven, Conn. They were actually called the International Championships of America and consistent with the charter of the sponsoring organization, were open to both Americans and Canadians. The four titles (Men, Ladies, Pairs and Waltz) were evenly divided between them. The Men's event was won by Norman Scott of Montreal, who with his partner Jeanne Chevalier also won the Pairs event. The Ladies title went to Theresa Weld of Boston, who also won the Waltz event with her partner Nathaniel Niles.

Because of World War I, no further championships were organized until 1918, as the war was winding down, this time in New York City. The winner of the Ladies title was Mrs. Rosemary Beresford of England, who defeated Theresa Weld. At the time, citizens of the British

Theresa Weld and Nathaniel Niles

Commonwealth countries could compete in the championships of all the nations of the Empire, so Mrs. Beresford was eligible to participate, although she actually represented the New York Skating Club. The Men's event went to Niles, who with Miss Weld also won the Pairs event, the first of what would be nine championships for them in Pairs. Also added were Junior Singles events, which would remain in the championship structure thereafter. The winners were Sherwin Badger and Mrs. Clara Rotch Frothingham, another sister of Charles M. Rotch, both from Boston.

No championships were held in 1919, but they were again organized in 1920 in New York, and in 1921 in Philadelphia. Following the formation of the USFSA in 1921, there was considerable confusion over the years concerning the status of these first four nationals. Some expressed the opinion that they should be considered as North American Championships, and others that they were in fact open National Championships. The matter was not finally settled until 1940, when a resolution of the Executive Committee was adopted declaring the Championships of 1914, 1918, 1920 and 1921 to be considered as National Championships, with the North American Championships to have first been held in 1923. As a result, while the 1996 National Championships are in fact the 75th organized by the USFSA, they are the 79th overall, since there has been no further break in the series even during World War II.

Oscar L. Richard

The 1920 championships held in New York represented the first appearance of a younger generation of skaters, with 19-year-old Sherwin Badger of Boston becoming the Men's champion, defeating Niles, the defender from 1918. Theresa Weld, now 27, regained her Ladies title and also won the Pairs and Waltz events with Niles. The winner of the Junior Men in 1920 was the legendary Oscar L. Richard of New York, no "spring chicken" at the age of 67. He lived to the ripe old age of 93, passing away in 1948. He was elected an Honorary Vice President of the USFSA in 1941, and is perhaps best known for his donation of trophies for the "most outstanding free skating performance" in the Senior and Junior Men's events and for the "most artistic free skating performance" in the Senior and Junior Ladies events at the Nationals.

The 1921 championships in Philadelphia saw all the Senior champions retain their titles, and the now Mrs. Blanchard and Niles added the Fourteenstep title to their collection while retaining their Pair and Waltz titles. The Junior Ladies champion was Beatrix Loughran of New

York. There was a good entry in 1921 with 29 entrants in seven events, not bad for those days. There had been 25 entries in 1920.

It is an interesting footnote in history that the International Skating Union of America never obtained membership in the international federation, although in 1914 it had formally adopted the rules of the latter body governing figure skating. On the other hand, the Amateur Skating Association of Canada had joined the IEV in 1894, just two years after its founding in 1892, in order to bid for and ultimately to hold the World Championship in Speed Skating for Men in Montreal in 1897. It would remain the only official World Championship in either discipline held in North America for 33 years, until 1930. Perhaps the ISU of A felt that the membership of the ASAC in the IEV was sufficient. Curiously, George Browne of Cambridge tried to form an independent national association and to obtain membership in the IEV in 1914, but this effort was defeated by the strong opposition of the leading skating officials from New York, on the grounds that the ISU of A was itself seeking such membership. The effort, of course, turned out to be fruitless due to the outbreak of World War I and the complete cessation of the operations of the IEV for seven years until 1921.

Another milestone, in addition to the establishment of national championships, occurred in 1920, when the Olympic Games were revived in Antwerp, Belgium. Two winter sports, figure skating and ice hockey, were included on the program. At the preceding Games at Stockholm in 1912, figure skating had not been included, although as noted, the sport had been included in the 1908 Games at London (indoors, of course).

For the 1920 Games, it was decided to send a figure skating team, consisting of the top two skaters who were still active from the 1918 Championships of America, since no championships were held in 1919. These were Theresa Weld and her partner Nathaniel Niles. No officials were nominated because the ISU of A was not a member of the IEV and therefore had no referees or judges recognized internationally outside North America.

The invitation issued by the Belgian Olympic Committee was sent only to the victorious nations of World War I, with the defeated countries, which also happened to be among the strong nations in skating at the time, being excluded. The IEV, under the leadership of its President, Viktor Balck of Sweden, declined to participate in the organization of the figure skating events at Antwerp, at first threatening to disqualify all who participated. The IEV finally permitted the competition to proceed without penalty. It was the strong opinion of General Balck, that all skating nations should be included, which in part accounted for the seemingly long delay in reorganizing the IEV after World War I. Its first post-war Congress was not held until 1921, when all the former member nations could participate, having restructured in most cases their national governing bodies under new political regimes.

Competition in the figure skating events of the Games was spirited and close, and reflected the differences in style between the Americans and the Europeans (which would be seen again in 1948). Notable, as well, was the emergence from retirement of Ulrich Salchow of Sweden, the legendary 10-time World Champion between 1900 and 1911 and the defending Olympic champion (from 1908). He placed a creditable fourth, at the age of 42, behind his compatriot, Gillis Grafström. Theresa Weld placed third overall to win the first Olympic medal in figure skating for the United States. She won the free skating and had placements from the judges ranging from first to last. Some of the judges felt that her free skating was too risqué, with her skirt flying up to her knees in the jumps, a fact that she personally recounted to the author. Niles placed sixth in the Men's event, and he and Miss Weld were fourth in the Pairs. No Canadians entered figure skating events, but their hockey team won the gold medal, with the United States team second.

Thus, by 1920, two fundamental "pillars" for a national association had been established: the holding of national championships on a regular basis, and the tradition of sending the best skaters to participate in the major international championships and especially in the Olympic Games.

In any event, with the end of the War and the revival of prosperity in North America, the stage was set for appearance on the scene of a new and independent national association to represent the figure skaters of the United States.

Following World War I, in the era which would be known as the "Roaring Twenties," interest in recreational activities and sports increased rapidly. Skating activity in the new International Style was no longer confined to the few established and leading clubs, such as Boston, New York and Philadelphia, although they were clearly the leaders, but was actually

The Beginning
(1921-1922)

practiced around the northern part of the country, including the Twin Cities of Minneapolis and Saint Paul, Minn., and Chicago. In the Northeast, country clubs and municipalities maintained outdoor ice surfaces, while at the same time, indoor skating rinks began to appear. Instructors and books of instruction, such as those written by Browne and Brokaw, were more readily available, as were new and improved skates, generally based on the model originated by Jackson Haines. As a result, the "devotees of the art," as Browne called them, began to move for the reorganization of figure skating under the control of figure skaters and independent of speed skaters and hockey players.

The International Skating Union of America and its member associations had served the sport well under the leadership of Brokaw who had served as Chairman of its Figure Skating Committee. However, overall authority for the sport did not reside in the figure skaters, but rather in the speed skaters.

There was also a pulling apart of the member associations of the ISU of A, with the two from Canada, the Amateur Skating Association of Canada and the Western Skating Association, especially wishing to go their own ways.

Actually, the creation of a new national association was not accomplished in the form of a complete separation of the new body from the old. Rather, what happened was the creation of a new member association (a subsidiary, if you will) of the ISU of A, to which the control of amateur figure skating on ice throughout the United States was delegated. This fact would be of importance following the demise of the ISU of A in 1927 and its replacement with the Amateur Skating Union of the United States, as will be seen.

The initiative for the creation of the new association came from the figure skating side, led by Paul Armitage of New York, who had succeeded Irving Brokaw as the Chairman of the Figure Skating Committee of the ISU of A. He presented the proposal to the meeting of the International

Skating Union of America, held at Lake Placid, NY on February 10-11, 1921, which unanimously adopted the enabling resolution on the 11th. It is worthwhile to record the actual text of the resolution, since it forms the basis for the existence and authority of the USFSA over the sport to this day:

"Resolved, that from and after March 31, 1921, the control of figure skating throughout the United States be vested in the United States Figure Skating Association of the I.S.U. (of America), and that it be recognized as the sole governing body over all matters pertaining to amateur figure skating throughout the United States, with full power to elect and appoint its officers and officials and prescribe rules and regulations, appoint judges, assign dates of meetings and rule upon the status of figure skaters and take such steps as it deems for the best interest of the sport, not inconsistent, however, with the articles of affiliation between the I.S.U. and both the A.A.U. of the United States and the Amateur Skating Association of Canada."

The reference to the Amateur Athletic Union (AAU) in the resolution reflected the fact that the ISU of A had itself in 1908 entered into "Articles of Alliance" with the AAU, in which the latter recognized the authority and jurisdiction of the ISU of A over the skating sports, both speed and figure. Comparable agreements were entered into by both the USFSA and the ASU with the AAU in later years for the same purpose. Right up to the passage by the United States Congress of the Amateur Sports Act in 1978, the USFSA appointed and sent delegates to the meetings of the AAU, pursuant to such agreement. In that year, by the mandate of Congress, the hegemony of the AAU over amateur sports in the United States was transferred to the United States Olympic Committee (USOC).

Despite the deadline of March 31 for the transfer of jurisdiction contained in the resolution, no action appears to have been taken to implement it until April 4, 1921, when a meeting of the "Eastern figure skaters" was held in New York City to "form and organize" the United States Figure Skating Association. Happily, the 1921 Championships of America had already been held in Philadelphia on February 25-27 under the sponsorship of the ISU of A, so there was no immediate urgency in taking further action. Actually, it is quite possible that the participation of many of the "Eastern figure skaters" in the Championships was one reason for the delay.

The principal actions taken at the April 4 meeting included the following: (a) the acceptance of the grant of jurisdiction made by the ISU of A and the agreement to form the USFSA; (b) the appointment of a committee to draft a proposed Constitution and By Laws for the Association, to be submitted to an adjourned meeting to be held on April 16, just 12 days later; and (c) the acceptance of applications of clubs for membership. These clubs, which were seven in number, became, therefore, the charter member clubs of the Association:

Beaver Dam Winter Sports Club (Mill Neck N.Y.)

The Skating Club of Boston

Chicago Figure Skating Club

New York Skating Club

Philadelphia Skating Club and Humane Society

Sno Birds of Lake Placid (N.Y.)

Twin City Figure Skating Club [1]

A. Winsor Weld

All the above clubs, with the sole exception of the Sno Birds of Lake Placid, are members of the Association today.

It is worth noting that the composition of the ad hoc committee (as we would call it today), included Joseph Chapman and John L. Evans from Philadelphia, Paul Armitage and James A. Cruikshank from New York, A.Winsor Weld and Nathaniel W. Niles from Boston, Karl Engel from Chicago, Hugh A. Whytock from Salt Lake City, W.P. Fuller from San Francisco and Chris I. Christenson from Saint Paul, truly a blue ribbon group, representing the leaders of the sport at the time.

The meeting also adopted guidelines, as the "sense" of the meeting, for the future structure of the new association: that there be two forms of membership — clubs and individuals; that there be a (Governing) Council, consisting of representatives of the member clubs and individual members; that no initiation fees be charged, and that the dues would be $15 per year for clubs and $2 per year for individuals; and that as soon as the organization of the Association was completed, application be made to join the Internationale Eislauf-Vereinigung (IEV).

Obviously, the task of preparing the necessary documents and charter for the Association turned out to be a greater one than the 12 days contemplated for their presentation and approval permitted, so the adjourned meeting of April 16 was never held. No record of it has been found. However, the date of April 4, 1921, can probably be considered as the actual founding date of the Association, since all the required resolutions were adopted, even though the "formal" organization did not take place until later in the year.

The next action that we see is a letter from the "ad hoc" committee, dated June 15, 1921, extending an invitation to clubs to join the new association and to appoint delegates to the Governing Council (which now had its present name), to participate in a meeting to be held in the "near future to formulate plans for stimulating figure skating during the coming season." The invitation was signed by nine of the original 10 members of the committee, of which A. Winsor Weld had been appointed the temporary chairman at the April 4 meeting.

[1] The name was changed in 1929 to Figure Skating Club of Minneapolis.

Since skating in those days was definitely a winter sport, being practiced to a considerable extent out of doors, no further action took place until the new season was actually under way. Finally, a meeting was called and held in New York City on Dec. 3, 1921, to complete the organization of the Association. Mr. Weld served as chairman.

At the meeting, the Constitution and By Laws were duly adopted and officers elected. The original slate of officers consisted of five, as follows:

> President – A. Winsor Weld, Boston
>
> First Vice President – Irving Brokaw, New York
>
> Second Vice President – Hugh A. Whytock, Salt Lake City
>
> Secretary – George H. Browne, Cambridge (Mass.)
>
> Treasurer – John L. Evans, Philadelphia

The officers were members of the Governing Council, together with delegates from the clubs. It was the only governing body established at the beginning. Six standing (or permanent) committees were created and chairmen appointed, as follows:

> Executive – Paul Armitage, New York
>
> Standards and Tests – Joel B. Liberman, New York
>
> Competitions and Rules – James A. Cruikshank, New York
>
> Amateur Status and Allied Questions – A. Winsor Weld, Boston
>
> Membership Elections – Charles E. F. McCann, New York
>
> Publication and Publicity – Irving Brokaw, New York

As can be seen, an "Executive" Committee was formed, but it was just another standing committee, and its membership included only one officer, Dr. Whytock. As the Association grew, the Executive Committee did eventually evolve into an elected governing body, with at large members, which was redesignated in 1980 as the Board of Directors.

Dr. Whytock of Salt Lake City was a remarkable person, attaining the age of 98. Originally from Minneapolis, he was an active skater for 93 years. An Honorary member of the Utah FSC, he was the "grand old man of figure skating" in Utah and was actively skating and helping youngsters on the ice through the spring of 1963, prior to his death in the early fall of that year.

Additional clubs elected to membership at the December 1921 meeting included the following:

> Cambridge (Mass.) Skating Club
>
> *The Country Club (Brookline, Mass.)
>
> *Merion Cricket Club (Pa.)
>
> *Minnesota Skating Association (Minneapolis)
>
> New Haven Skating Club
>
> *Uptown Skating Club (New York)

The clubs elected to membership in 1921 were all considered as charter members at the time of the 25th Anniversary in 1946, with those indicated above by an asterisk(*) having either resigned or disbanded by that time. The Beaver Dam Winter Sports Club, which was founded in 1916, resigned from the Association in 1941, but returned to membership 20 years later in 1961. The two country clubs (TCC and Merion) which are very famous in the golf world, resigned before World War II and have never returned.

The objects of the Association were set forth in the new Constitution as follows: "(1) To improve, encourage, and advance Figure Skating in all its branches. (2) to provide standards therein. (3) To prescribe tests and rules for the holding of competitions and meets, and to appoint referees and judges therefor. (4) To pass upon and determine the amateur status of any figure skater. (5) To publish and disseminate information concerning figure skating by bulletin, paper, book or otherwise. (6) Generally to take all steps necessary to regulate figure skating throughout the United States."

Except for some rather significant changes over the years with respect to eligibility, the objectives generally look familiar and have been perpetuated well in the succeeding versions of the charter documents of the Association. Our founding fathers built well.

A vital action also taken at the December 1921 meeting was the decision to send representatives to the forthcoming meeting of the ISU of A, to be held on Dec. 10, just a week later, in Pittsburgh, to insure that the control over the sport was fully vested in the new Association. At that meeting, Articles of Alliance were drawn up and executed, by which the ISU of A recognized the USFSA as being the sole governing body over amateur figure skating in the United States, while at the same time, the USFSA, which became an allied member of the ISU of A, recognized the ISU of A "as having sole control of ice skating throughout America." While at the time it was felt that "all possibility of divided responsibility or dual control (over figure skating) is happily avoided," only a few short years in the future, the question of that control would become very much an issue between the Association and the successor body to the ISU of A, the Amateur Skating Union (ASU) of the United States.

It did not take the new association long to begin the task of carrying out its responsibilities. The first meeting of the Executive Committee was held on Feb. 5, 1922, at the Iceland Rink in New York City. The Committee as initially appointed consisted of just five members, with Paul Armitage of New York as the chairman. Strictly speaking, the meeting was really the organizational meeting of the Association and the chairmen of the various standing committees appointed just a little over a month before made reports, among them Amateur Status, Competitions, Membership and Standards and Tests. The principal business was, obviously, the organization of the first National Championships to be sponsored by the USFSA to be held in early March in Boston. As part of that organization, it was also necessary to appoint judges, which was done by the Committee with a total of 27 being appointed from seven clubs. The clubs with the largest number were The SC of Boston and the New York Skating Club, each with nine. Two judges were appointed from the Twin City SC of St. Paul, Minn., and one from the Chicago SC, representing the Midwest.

The outline of the test structure was also adopted, based upon the schedule of the New York SC, to which was added a Junior or introductory test as used at The SC of Boston. The idea behind the schedule was that each two tests in the structure would constitute one of the International tests, so a skater progressing through the schedule would have to learn only one figure embodying entirely new principles in each test.

A principle was also established that competitions under the auspices of the USFSA had to be organized by a member club, and that the existing regional skating associations could not do so independently. This decision was a result of a request from the Minnesota Skating Association, which was not a member club of the USFSA, to hold a figure skating tournament. This issue would arise again many years later when Inter-Club Councils, which were not Association members, wished to organize competitions. It was also decided that entrants in the National Championships had to be either U.S. citizens or residents for one year.

Amateur Status rules also were adopted, containing the basic definition of an amateur, as had originally been adopted by the Amateur Athletic Union (AAU). The actual text was as follows:

"An amateur is a person who participates in Figure Skating for the sake of the pleasure afforded by the occupation itself and not for any pecuniary gain, being a person for whom the pursuit is solely a recreation and in no sense a business." As the rules started out, there was no provision for the reinstatement of a person "who has knowingly or with intent been a professional." The matter of registration of all skaters was considered but not acted upon, and there would be no registration (for a fee) for another 30 years.

A Committee of Records was established, with Mrs. Rosalie Knapp of New York as the first chairman. The mandate of the Committee was to "keep records of all tournaments, and any other writings and papers concerning skating history in the making." Here was the genesis for the ultimate creation of the Museum many years later.

Also approved was the publication of "monthly papers or bulletins to be sold for a regular subscription price," which, of course, was the beginning of **Skating** magazine. The first dues income from the member clubs was reported, totaling $172 from 12 clubs and one individual (Mr. Joseph K. Savage of New York, who paid $2).

With respect to the 1922 National Championships, many of those who had been responsible for the organization of the prior championships under the ISU of A were still involved, so that all was accomplished efficiently and with dispatch. The Championships included Junior singles events, as had been the case in 1918, 1920 and 1921. In the Senior events, all the champions from 1921 successfully defended their titles: Sherwin Badger in the Men, for his third; Theresa Weld, now Mrs. Blanchard, in the Ladies, also for her third, and with Nathaniel Niles of Boston in the Pairs, for their fourth. The Waltz competition was in those days a somewhat

Sherwin Badger

informal affair and was not recognized as a national "championship," nor were official medals awarded to the winners. Rather, it was a national "competition," and was often won by couples, the partners in which had not skated together on a regular basis. This was the case in 1922, when Beatrix Loughran of New York won in partnership with Edward Howland of Boston. It was, strictly speaking, the first National Senior title for Miss Loughran, who had won the Junior Ladies in 1921. A Fourteenstep event had also been added in 1920, and was won in 1922 for the second time by Mrs. Blanchard and Niles. The two Junior singles titles were both won by Boston skaters, Louis Washburn and Helen Stantial. There were over 30 entries in the seven events, almost exactly the same number as had competed in 1921 in Philadelphia. It was a successful start to what would be an unbroken series of National Championships, up to those in San Jose, Calif., in 1996.

Having determined that the International Skating Union of America was not a member of the Internationale Eislauf-Vereinigung, the USFSA quickly moved to apply for membership in the latter body, which was granted in 1923. At that time, membership in the IEV was only granted to associations which had jurisdiction over both sports, i.e., speed and figure skating, but despite this requirement, membership was extended to the USFSA. It thereby became the first national association representing just one sport to become a member. The Council of the IEV advised the USFSA that it would enjoy the same voting rights (i.e., one vote) as other members, but only until a national association for speed skating might be formed in the United States and became a member, at which time the vote at Congresses of the IEV would be halved between the two associations, if they did not in fact merge. This decision of the Council was not supported by the Constitution of the IEV and was objected to by some, but the seeming importance of there being a member from the United States obviously overcame the objections.

The first annual meeting can properly be said to have been the Governing Council meeting held in April 1922, at the Bar Association of the City of New York (42 West 44th Street), with New York City remaining the site of the meeting until 1946. Eleven clubs were represented, quite a good number, considering there were only 15 member clubs in all. The Governing Council acted upon such matters as the medals and judging forms, called "blanks," for tests and competitions and the awarding of the 1923 Nationals to the New Haven SC. The test schedule recommended by the Executive Committee was approved. The Council also adopted a strong statement to the effect that "a professional in any other form of sport is ineligible to compete in any event sanctioned by the Association." An amendment to the Constitution was also adopted, which required a two-thirds vote of all the members of the Association represented at a meeting, in order for amendments to the Constitution and By Laws to be adopted, to which was added a 20 day notice requirement.

It is difficult from the viewpoint of 75 years later to accurately determine the number of members or even of active skaters included in the member clubs of the Association, especially since some of them were essentially recreational in nature, with large "temporary" or seasonal memberships. Of the 13 clubs becoming members in 1921, a very rough estimate can be made that their total membership was under 2,000 and, of that, the active competitive skaters would have been less than 100.

Despite its relatively modest size, the Association was well established right from the beginning and quickly moved forward in carrying out its object to "improve, encourage and advance" figure skating in the United States.

Under the active and energetic leadership of President Weld, who would serve until 1925, the new Association took immediate action in several critical areas to "stimulate" the growth of figure skating. One of the first initiatives was to create a North American Championship. In view of the long-term friendly relations with our neighbors across the border to the North, stimulated

Initial Progress
(1923-1927)

by the Connaught Cup competitions which had started in 1913, it was only natural for the new association and the Amateur Skating Association of Canada to act together to create what would be the first regular International Competition in the "standard" disciplines (Singles and Pairs), with Fours being added as a separate event for the Connaught Cup.

The North American Championships were to be biennial in nature (every two years), alternating between the two countries. In the first competition, held in Ottawa, Ontario, in 1923, the honors were evenly divided. Sherwin Badger won the Men, Theresa Weld Blanchard, the Ladies, Dorothy Jenkins and A.G. McLennan of Ottawa the Pairs, and the Minto Skating Club Four, consisting of Elizabeth Blair, Florence Wilson, Philip H. Chrysler and C.R. Morphy, the Fours. There were 13 entries. An informal waltz competition was also included, won by Florence Wilson of Ottawa and Joel B. Liberman of New York.

As a footnote to the competition: Nathaniel Niles, the partner of Mrs. Blanchard in the Pairs, skated with a sprained ankle, as reported in **Skating** magazine (in the very first issue). "The fact that, in spite of his disability, he persisted in carrying out the doubles program, is a striking tribute to his good sportsmanship." In commemoration of this fact, the Canadian hosts had a small silver medal made, which attested to his courage and which was duly presented to him. (That medal was one of the first artifacts received by the World Figure Skating Museum from Niles' late brother David S. Niles.) Mrs. Blanchard and Niles placed second in the competition.

The founding of **Skating** magazine in 1923 was another significant step forward, as it provided a medium of communication among the member clubs of the Association, an essential bulwark of any member-type organization. From the beginning, the two persons who were primarily responsible for the publication of the magazine were Nathaniel Niles and Mrs. Theresa Weld Blanchard. "Tee," as she was known, served as the editor of the magazine jointly with Niles from 1924 to 1931. When he passed away at the early age of 45, she was the sole editor until 1963, a remarkable tenure of 40 years, entirely as an unpaid volunteer. The magazine in the beginning was edited and published from her home. After retiring as the active editor, Tee continued to serve the magazine as editor emeritus up to the time of her death in 1978 at the age of 84. By then, the editor had become a full-time employee.

Tee was really the "heart and soul" of figure skating in the United States during her life. From her long competitive career, both nationally and internationally, she had vast contacts around the world, and much was written in the magazine about international activities right from the beginning. She was also a "one woman" placement bureau for former competitive skaters seeking teaching positions in the United States, and by way of a confirmation of that effort, was the first chairman of a Professionals Committee of the Association from 1937 to 1947.

Right from the beginning, the financial problems of the magazine can be seen in the reports of the annual meetings, with annual deficits being recorded and assumed by the Association. This pattern has continued throughout the years, despite periodic efforts to upgrade the publication, such as the two size changes made in 1966 and 1993. None-the-less, the magazine has had an unbroken publishing life, and is just two years younger than the Association itself. It will observe its own 75th anniversary in 1998. After being published out of Tee's house, the tiny staff shared office space with The Skating Club of Boston and ultimately became part of the Central Office of the Association, when that facility arrived in Boston in 1950.

Time after time, when magazine deficits were discussed at the Governing Council and Executive Committee meetings, the decision to continue publication despite them was made, a recognition of the importance of such a communications medium to the life and strength of the Association.

It should also be noted that the magazine from 1941 until 1968 also was the official publication of the CFSA and contained the results of the Canadian qualifying competitions and Nationals, as well as lists of tests passed and club news. For one season, from 1941 to 1942, the magazine was the official magazine of the Roller Skating Rink Operators Association (RSROA) and included roller skating news and competition results.

A small, yet important event also took place in late 1922, when the Executive Committee authorized the purchase of a die and the striking of a standard medal for the National Championships. The die and medals were made by Dorrety of Boston, a well known jeweler in Boston. The arrangements for the medal and its design were carried out by George H. Browne. The medal, which shows only a Winged Victory and the letters "USFSA," became in effect the first seal or "logo" of the Association. There is nothing on it to indicate that it was related to skating.

The design graced the cover of **Skating** magazine from 1923 to 1936, when a pictorial cover was introduced. It was also used on the cover of the Rulebook from 1940 to 1956. The medal was used for the Nationals from 1923 until 1956 and also was used for the North Americans in 1925, with the appropriate lettering being added on the top or on a bar on a ribbon from which the medal was suspended. Medals then were pinned on, and did not carry a ribbon for placing around the neck, as is the case today. Such emblems form an important part of the image or persona of organizations which involve the general public. Simple and dignified as it was, the old medal stood the test of time well.

Another important decision in 1922 was the creation of figure skating tests, which, with the addition of tests for Pairs and Dance in later years, are really the backbone of progress in skating, measuring as they do proficiency at various points along the way, and, in modern times, serving as the basis of eligibility for qualifying competitions. The test structure adopted was unique, in that it provided for eight tests in compulsory figures and a Junior (later Preliminary) Test, with free skating also in the Seventh and Eighth Tests. The comparable tests of the older established associations, such as the British and Canadian, were usually only three or four in number, and for figures only, yet covered the entire schedule of figures (41 in all). Each test was a "monster" to take and pass, which was also true of the figure tests later adopted by the International Skating Union (ISU). The CFSA converted from a four test schedule to that of the USFSA in 1941.

Joel Liberman of New York, Chairman of the Standards and Tests Committee of the Association, in an article also in the first issue of **Skating**, gives the reasons for the USFSA schedule as follows: "We found that it was impossible except in the rare instance of a few persons with exceptional aptitude for figure skating to cover their tests in a reasonable number of years, and even those few had exceptional opportunities in the way of time or instruction or both...and finally the national committee decided to break away from the older tables and while retaining all the figures, a fewer number was allotted to each test, and the number of tests increased."

In the beginning, the tests from Junior through Third could be judged by judges appointed by the member clubs themselves, while the judges for the higher tests were appointed by the Standards and Tests Committee from the approved list of (competition) judges each year. Medals were provided, with a bronze for the First Test, a Silver for the Fourth Test and a Gold (provided by the Association) for the Eighth Test, with suitably numbered bars being provided for the tests in between. Again, Dorrety of Boston made the test medal, which carried the words "USFSA of the ISU of A." The test medal still had that wording on it for many years after the ISU of A was long gone, perhaps an early example of economy or belt tightening in the 1930's.

That the tests quickly became popular and an integral part of the activities of the member clubs can be seen in the original report in the same article by Mr. Liberman, that 163 tests were passed in 1923 by the members of just four clubs, with the New York SC having a total of 81 and

The SC of Boston a total of 66. We do not know, unfortunately, how many tests were actually taken.

The first Eighth or Gold Tests were passed in 1924 by none other than Nathaniel Niles and Mrs. Blanchard, who took it together. Tee always said that Nat was "No.1" and that she was "No.2." The "explosion" in the number of tests taken and passed and especially in the Gold tests, did not occur until long afterwards, following World War II, with the Gold test being limited to those who were active competitors at the National Senior level. Interestingly, Sherwin Badger, a five-time National Champion, and the title holder in 1924, never passed the test.

The second meeting of the Executive Committee was held in October 1922, in New York City, with representatives of the standing committees for Amateur Status, Competitions, Membership, and Standards and Tests present. The Committee confirmed the prior action of the Governing Council that the 1923 Nationals would be held at New Haven. Since then, it has been the Executive Committee and its successor body, the Board of Directors, rather than the Governing Council, that have assumed the duty of the awarding the major championships sponsored by the Association. The Waltz and Fourteenstep events were described as "contests" with two rounds: an initial round by all couples in a border pattern, followed by a final round performed by each couple separately in a two- or three-lobed eight pattern. It was at this meeting that the Howe Trophy for Fours was accepted. Also approved was the schedule of tests.

The second annual meeting, again in April 1923 in New York, saw present just one Individual member (out of seven), and nine clubs, with six being listed as "not present or represented." It was at this meeting that a completely new Constitution and By Laws were adopted, which really represent the basis of the current By Laws, both in substance and in form. The meeting also approved the award of the 1924 Nationals to Philadelphia, as well as the concept of the payment of expenses for exhibitions, entering competitions or serving as judges at competitions. Eligibility for entry in the National Championships was also defined by requiring all entrants to be members of the Association.

Having pioneered in its participation in the Olympic Games of 1920, the Association was quick to plan to send a team to the 1924 Games, participation in which was approved by the 1923 Governing Council meeting. Organized by the French, it had been decided by the International Olympic Committee (IOC) to include winter sports in the quadrennial observance of the modern Olympics, with the summer Games being held in Paris. The winter sports were organized in Chamonix and were called the "International Sports Week 1924." They were not officially designated as the First Olympic Winter Games until a meeting of the IOC in 1926. Nonetheless, they were clearly thought of as being Olympic in nature at the time. In **Skating** magazine, the events were described as the "Winter Sports Division of the 1924 Olympic Games."

A team was selected consisting of Mrs. Blanchard, Beatrix Loughran, Sherwin Badger and Nathaniel Niles, with Henry W. Howe of New York as a judge. As it turned out, neither Badger, who was married in January, nor Howe could go. Charles M. Rotch of Boston was appointed as the replacement for Mr. Howe, but no one was selected to replace Badger. The Chamonix Games began the remarkable international competitive career of Beatrix Loughran, who placed second behind the ultimate winner, Herma Szabo-Plank of Austria. It was the second U.S. medal and what would be the first of three for her, the most (so far) earned by any U.S. figure skater in the Olympics. Mrs. Blanchard placed fourth, while in the Men, Niles again placed sixth, as he had in 1920. He and Mrs. Blanchard also placed sixth in the Pairs, an event which saw the Olympic debut of Andrée Joly and Pierre Brunet of France, who were third, and would later enjoy distinguished teaching careers in the United States. Mr. Rotch was not invited to serve as a judge, but instead, he was made the referee of the Ladies and Pairs events.

Beatrix Loughran

Miss Loughran went on to the World Championships for Ladies in Oslo, Norway, the first skater from the United States to enter a World Championship, and placed third, the first World Championship medal earned by a U.S. figure skater. The German champion, Ellen Brockhöfft, who had not participated at Chamonix, placed second, behind Mrs. Szabo-Plank, who won her third title. The other members of the Olympic Team did not elect to skate at Oslo and returned home instead.

Another unusual and somewhat innovative idea was also adopted in 1923, which was to have an Association carnival at the end of each skating season under the auspices of a different member club each year. The purpose of the carnival as announced at the time was "to give an opportunity for all the figure skaters of the country to become better acquainted, to talk over the events of the season just passed and to discuss plans for the future. Not alone will these carnivals serve to give all attending an enjoyable time, but also will serve in spreading the interest in figure skating and obtaining converts to the sport."

The first Association carnival was held in Boston in 1924, and it was continued in 1925 in Philadelphia and in 1926 in New York City. These shows were gala affairs and included all the top skaters of the day, including many from Canada. Those professionals who still did exhibitions were prominently featured, with even the legendary Charlotte doing a pair in 1926 with Baron von Petersdorff. Willie Frick of Boston did his candle dance and a pair routine with his wife, Cathleen Pope.

The Association carnival was not held after 1926, perhaps because the three cities involved, which were the principal centers of the sport at the time, had their fill of it. They wished to return to their own shows, which they did with outstanding success all through the 1930's up to World War II.

At the National Championships of 1923, held in New Haven, a Junior Pairs event was included for the first time, the winners being Mrs. Ruth Chapman and her husband Joseph Chapman of Philadelphia. The latter had been one of the founders of the Association and had been the USFSA Secretary in 1923-24 and would be the USFSA Treasurer in 1925-27. The Senior champions, Sherwin Badger, Theresa Weld Blanchard and Blanchard and Niles all retained their titles.

The 1924 Nationals were held at Philadelphia, with all the Senior champions retaining their titles, as in 1923. The championships had grown considerably, with 43 entries in nine events. The winner of the Junior Ladies was Maribel Vinson of Boston, the first step on a long competitive road which would continue until 1937.

The 1924 Governing Council meeting saw a modest increase in the number of clubs represented, to 12, but the minutes of the meeting show that more than 2,800 members were represented by them, with three clubs (Cambridge, Providence and Merion) being listed as having "over 600" members. A small footnote mentions that "owing to the destruction by fire of the New Haven Arena, the National Championships (of 1925) have been given to New York and the International (North Americans) to Boston." It is a curious fact that rinks seemed to burn down in those days, since the original Boston Arena had also been destroyed by fire in 1918. Perhaps it was the fact that ammonia was the principal refrigerant and added to the fire hazard.

There still seemed to be concern about what medals to award to the Waltz and Fourteenstep competitions at the Nationals, and the decision was made that the winners would receive the standard medal in the small (or Junior) size, but that no third place medals would be awarded unless there were at least five entries. It was noted also that the cost of publishing **Skating** magazine was "about $1,000," and that the "income is considerably less than this amount."

The Fall meeting of the Executive Committee for 1924 was held at New York in October, which has been the month for the Fall meeting ever since, and also the annual meeting of the

Executive Committee and its successor body pursuant to the By Laws. The perennial discussion of the deficit of the magazine continued, as it would for the next 50 years. A decision was also made that the complete record of the results of the National Championships would be published in the magazine, an obligation which has been faithfully adhered to by the magazine ever since in its role of being an official publication "of record."

The 1925 Nationals were held in New York and saw new champions crowned in the Men, Badger having retired. Nathaniel Niles won his second title after seven years, and Beatrix Loughran dethroned Mrs. Blanchard, who retained her Pair title with Niles.

The second North American Championships were held in Boston in 1925 and Mrs. Blanchard and Niles won their first and only North American Pairs title. Beatrix Loughran, who had won her first national title a month earlier at New York, won the Ladies event, defeating Cecil Smith of Toronto, the Canadian Ladies champion, with Mrs. Blanchard third. In the Men, Melville Rogers of Ottawa won his first title, defeating Niles and placed second with his wife, Gladys in Pairs.

The 1925 Governing Council meeting was held in New York in June, and it was reported that the cash balance was $415.85. There was a discussion over the merits of requiring tests to be passed by all judges (unanimous), since apparently some clubs in holding tests had passed them by a majority only. It was approved that those who had passed such tests by a majority only "may keep their medals," but in the future all tests would have to be passed unanimously. This requirement would be changed to a majority basis many years later. There was also a report by the Special Committee on Judging, which consisted of Henry Howe, chairman, Mrs. Paul Armitage, Rosalie Knapp and Mrs. Blanchard. The concern of the committee was not with the eligibility of persons to

Henry W. Howe

become judges, but rather with defining the standards of the sport, that is, of "judging," in effect a forerunner of the Skating Standard Committee of today. Also noted was concern with the failure of the ISU of A to observe their agreement with the USFSA, which granted to the latter complete control (in the United States) over figure skating.

The Fall 1925 meeting of the Executive Committee, also held in New York, was primarily concerned with such technical matters as the methods for the drawing of compulsory figures at Nationals, which under the then IEV rules were very complicated. The idea of groups of figures from which the draws would be made had not yet been thought of.

Also in 1925, A. Winsor Weld of Boston, the first President, decided to step down after four years in office, having shepherded the fledgling organization through its early growth, and was succeeded by Henry W. Howe of New York. Weld was elected an Honorary President, only the second person so honored, together with Irving Brokaw of New York. It is quite appropriate that one representative from New York and one from Boston have been the only persons so elected, when the contributions of the two centers to the founding of the Association are considered. Actually, no other persons would be elected to an Honorary office until Oscar L. Richard of New York was elected an Honorary Vice President in 1941.

Mr. Weld was not active thereafter in the affairs of the Association, although he subsequently served as Secretary and then President of The Country Club (of Brookline, Mass.). He passed away in 1956 and was posthumously elected to the United States Figure Skating Hall of Fame in 1976.

At the 1926 National Championships in Boston, Nathaniel Niles was the defending champion, having accomplished the feat in 1925 of regaining a title he had last held in 1918.

Chris Christenson

Among his competitors was Chris I. Christenson of Saint Paul, Minn., who had been third in 1924 and fourth in 1925. It was quite common in those days for the competitors in one event to serve as judges in another, and Christenson judged three events in 1926, including the Senior Ladies. He had also served as a USFSA Vice President in 1924-25, a busy man indeed. In the competition, Christenson defeated Niles in both figures and free skating to win the National title at the age of 50, the oldest of all the Senior Men's champions by a wide margin. Niles, however, regained the title in 1927 at New Haven and New York (the competition being divided between the two cities). Christenson went on to a long career as a judge and booster of the sport in his native state, but was not active in USFSA affairs in his later years, other than as a judge.

Already mentioned has been the discipline of Fours, as represented in the Connaught Cup competitions. In 1922, Henry Howe presented a trophy for competition in the discipline, which was the first National Championship trophy to be the permanent property of the club winning the competition three times. The offer of the trophy contained an unusual provision of "the reward for winning in any year being the right to compete for the Connaught Cup in Canada in that year," to quote the minutes. In the 1923 Nationals, the first time the Fours event was held, the Boston Four had to withdraw at the last moment due to illness of one of its members, so the New York Four, consisting of Grace Munstock, Clara Hartman, Paul Armitage and Joel Liberman was the only entry. In 1924, there was an actual competition, with the same New York Four winning over a Four from Philadelphia, but in 1925 the New York Four was again the only entry, as a result of which the New York Skating Club was awarded the trophy for permanent possession.

It is a curious fact that the USFSA records of the national title holders credit the New York Four with winning the title in both 1924 and 1925, but not in 1923. Perhaps it was poetic justice that the Howe trophy did not disappear completely, but was ultimately redonated as a permanent trophy when the event was revived 10 years later. Under today's rules, of course, the Four would have been credited with but one win. The provisions of having a sole entry skate to a standard and be awarded a title, as in England, never was applied in the United States. The rule that there must be at least two entries for a competition to be held is of long standing.

In 1927, the first major change in the relationships of the fledgling Association to the other governing bodies of the ice sports took place. The International Skating Union of America, with the departure of the Amateur Skating Association of Canada and the Western Skating Association of Canada, dissolved, with a new successor body, the Amateur Skating Union of the United States (ASU) being formed. The ASU included as members the former regional associations and allied members of its predecessor. The new association did not consider itself strictly a speed skating group, but as the successor of the ISU of A with respect to "ice skating" in the United States, which included both speed and figure skating. Accordingly, the new association asked the USFSA to transfer to it its membership in the IEV, with the agreement that the ASU representatives would vote in all matters relating to figure skating in accordance with the wishes of the USFSA. To this, the USFSA agreed, and the membership was finally given to the ASU in 1928, with it remaining the ISU member until 1965.

Unfortunately, the agreement of co-operation never worked out as contemplated, and presented problems for the USFSA in its relationships with the IEV until World War II. The ASU was never represented at any Congress between 1927 and 1938, other than by a proxy, which was usually given to the speed skating representative of the NSA of Great Britain. Matters of interest to the USFSA were not acted upon by the proxy carrier, who generally voted in the interests of his own association. It was never thought to be intentional on the part of the ASU, but rather a lack of interest on its part in the activities of the IEV. Racing rules in the United States and in the rest of the world were completely different from one another. Those of the ASU provided for pack style or mass starts, while those of the IEV provided for pairs only competing against each other, with times governing the final result. As a consequence, there were few ASU competitors really interested in competing abroad, other than in the Olympic Winter Games (in which speed skating made its debut in 1924). The fact that the USFSA itself had no vote or representative present at ISU meetings gave it much less "clout," and problems resulted during the 1930's with skaters coming to the United States for exhibitions. Despite these problems, the USFSA began to do well in competitions abroad as a new generation of younger skaters appeared on the scene and replaced those who had been the leaders since before World War I.

During the 1920's, the growth of the Association is difficult to track due to the absence of adequate records. Financial reports are referred to in the minutes of the annual meetings but cannot be found. For example, in the minutes of the Governing Council meeting of 1926, it is mentioned that a "favorable report" was given by an auditing committee of the Treasurer's report, a balance of $541.54 being shown. In contrast, by 1932, the long-term Treasurer, Heaton R. Robertson of New Haven, reported the cash balance on hand was "approximately" $9,000.00.

The 1927 National Championships were unique, in that they were held for the first day in New Haven and, as is stated in **Skating** by Richard L. Hapgood of Boston, "the conclave hauled up tent-pegs and moved to New York City, where the final clean up of competitive strife was held at the New Madison Square Gardens and Iceland." In the Ladies, Beatrix Loughran successfully defended her title, with Maribel Vinson now second. In the Men, as noted, Niles won his third championship, with Roger Turner of Boston, the 1926 National Junior champion, second, and the defender, Chris Christenson, fourth. Mrs. Blanchard and Niles won their ninth and last Pair title, while in the Junior Pairs, Maribel Vinson and Thornton Coolidge were the winners, with Suzanne Davis of Boston, the Junior Ladies winner.

The 1927 North American Championships were held at Toronto with form being maintained, but with the younger or new generation of skaters being in evidence. Melville Rogers of Ottawa retained the title he had first won in 1925, while right behind him was Sherwin Badger. Now of New York, he had returned to competition in singles after a three-year layoff, followed by Roger Turner and Montgomery Wilson of Toronto, both of the new generation. Nathaniel Niles, who was the 1927 National champion over Turner, could do no better than fifth. In the Ladies, Beatrix Loughran retained her title, while next were Constance Wilson and Cecil Smith of Toronto, followed by Maribel Vinson, all three of them of the new generation. In the Pairs, Constance and Montgomery Wilson were third, the start of an illustrious career in that discipline for them. The winners were Marion McDougall and Chauncey Bangs of Ottawa, followed by Mrs. Blanchard and Niles.

The 1926 and 1927 Governing Council meetings, again in New York, drew what would seem to us today, quite a modest number of delegates, with 11 clubs being represented in 1926 and only nine in 1927. In actual numbers of persons present, according to the minutes, there were 18 in 1926 and 23 in 1927.

In 1926, there was a discussion that the size of the Executive Committee, which was 16 in number, should be reduced to five or seven members, since under the revised Constitution, it "shall have in charge the general management and conduct of the Association." After discussion, the size of the committee remained unchanged. One fascinating exchange in 1926 deserves repeating: "Mrs. (Rosalie) Knapp (of New York) stated that contestants had expressed to her the desire to see their marks as soon after the competition as possible and further stated that some method ought to be worked out whereby the comparative marks should be sent to each competitor. Mr. (Joel B.) Liberman (of New York) stated that in the years this had been done we were unusually fortunate in having an interested skater who worked out comparative tables, placed them on tracing cloth and struck off blue prints. A complete record would take a week of one person's time, but if a professional draftsman were instructed how to make it up the job could be continuously given to him."

Subsequently, in 1927, the suggestion was adopted that "photostats of the judging cards be made and bound together," i.e., into a protocol. There is no mention, however, of distributing them. How the world has changed since. Interestingly, some of the very blue prints and photostats referred to are still in the archives of the Association in the Museum.

The 1926 Executive Committee meeting was held in November in New York. It confirmed that the Association would continue its membership in the IEV, despite the apparent dissatisfaction with that body. Also considered was an Intermediate class of competition (what would eventually in the 1930's become the Novice event), but no action was taken other than to increase the difficulty of the compulsory figures to be skated in the Junior class. The publication of a new booklet to include "all existing competition rulings" was approved. A special edition of the magazine in December 1925 had contained the Constitution and By Laws and the competition and test rules. This would now be replaced with small pocket-sized booklets covering the various separate areas. These would remain in use until the first Rulebook was published in 1939.

The 1927 Governing Council meeting also voted that the committee chairmen who were not members of the Executive Committee, could attend its meetings which were being held on a formal basis in both the spring and fall, just as today.

An important principle of membership in the Association was adopted: "that this Association presupposes that the clubs forming its membership shall continue as active skating organizations with their members practicing the art of Figure Skating under their auspices and that if any club ceases to function for a period of one year as above outlined that its membership in the Association cease."

The 1927 Fall Meeting of the Executive Committee was held as usual in New York City in November. It was noted that there would be no Association carnival in view of the fact that "certain entertainments" were to be held to raise funds for the Olympic Team. It was also voted that lists of judges be compiled for tests which would be divided into two classes: the first class containing the names of judges appointed for tests up through the Fourth test (later to be called

Low Test judges), and a second class containing the names of judges for tests up through the Seventh test (later to be called High Test judges). The Eighth or Gold test would still have to be judged by National judges, or as they are known today, Gold Figure Test judges. The committee also voted to enter into negotiations with the successor body to the ISU of A, the ASU, with the intention of the Association becoming a full member of the latter, subject to the proviso that the Constitution and By Laws of the ASU require that the vote of the ASU when it became a member of the IEV would be cast on figure skating matters "in such manner" as the USFSA desired.

The appearance on the scene of a new (and younger) generation of skaters, which would be the "second" when speaking in terms of the life of the Association, was readily apparent at the 1927 North American Championships at Toronto, where a mixture of the old and the new was present.

International Recognition
(1928-1932)

The youth movement picked up speed during the 1927-28 season, and for the first time, a full Olympic Team was sent to the 1928 Winter Games at St. Moritz. The team was selected on the basis of the results from 1927, since the 1928 Nationals followed the Worlds and Olympics. In the Men, there were Niles, Turner and Badger, while in Ladies it was Loughran, Vinson and Blanchard. In Pairs, Blanchard and Niles would be going to their third Olympics, and with them was a new pair of Sherwin Badger with Beatrix Loughran. Miss Loughran had skated Pairs in the 1927 Nationals with Raymond Harvey of New York, later her husband, placing second, while Badger had not previously competed in Pairs. Joel B. Liberman of New York was sent as a judge. Henry W. Howe, also of New York and second President of the USFSA, went along as a spectator. Little did he realize that he would be pressed into service as a judge for the Ladies when the traditional St. Moritz thaw caused the compulsory figures of the two Singles events to be held at the same time.

Sherwin Badger and Beatrix Loughran

The team did very well in the competition. Beatrix Loughran placed third in the Ladies for her second Olympic medal, behind two other new generation skaters, Sonja Henie of Norway and Fritzi Burger of Austria. She was closely followed by Maribel Vinson in fourth place, while Mrs. Blanchard was 10th, out of 20 entrants, still a creditable showing. In the Men, Turner and Badger were down the line, placing 10th and 11th, respectively, with Niles 15th. It was Badger's first Olympics. In the Pairs, he and Beatrix Loughran

Roger Turner

placed fourth, in their first major competition together, behind the winners Andrée Joly and Pierre Brunet of France, and two Austrian Pairs, Lily Scholz and Otto Kaiser and Melitta Brunner and Ludwig Wrede. Mrs. Blanchard and Niles were ninth out of 13 Pairs.

This time, unlike 1924, most of the Olympic Team went on to the World Championships, which in those days were often divided between various cities. In 1928, the Men's event was held in Berlin, while the Ladies and Pairs were in London. In the Men, Turner and Niles placed fifth and 10th, while Badger elected to stick with the Pairs event a week later. The Men's winner for the fourth time was Willi Böckl of Austria. Surprisingly, when asked right after the 1928 season for recommendations for a teaching position at the New York Skating Club, he offered himself for the job. Soon he arrived in the United States to begin a long and distinguished career in that capacity.

In the events at London, Beatrix Loughran also decided to limit herself to Pairs. The only entry in the Ladies was Maribel Vinson, who surprised everyone by taking second place behind Sonja Henie, defeating the Olympic silver medalist, Fritzi Burger, in the process. In the Pairs, Loughran and Badger placed fifth, with Mrs. Blanchard and Niles, seventh.

At the 1928 Nationals, the youth movement simply took over, with Roger Turner winning the first of what would be seven Men's titles. Maribel Vinson won the Ladies, for the first of nine titles, while she and Thornton Coolidge of Boston won the Pairs, ending the long reign of Mrs. Blanchard and Niles.

While abroad for the Olympic Games, Henry Howe had worked tirelessly with the IEV to obtain the award of the World Championships of 1930 to the United States. As previously noted, only one World Championship, the 1897 Men's Speed Skating at Montreal, had been held on the North American continent. American skaters were long overdue for such an event. The award of the event was finally made in 1929, to the Skating Club of New York,

Maribel Vinson

which had joined the Association that year as a successor club to the former New York Skating Club. The IEV also informed the USFSA that Mr. Howe had been approved as the referee for the championships and Mr. Liberman as the U.S. judge. The championships were to be held at Madison Square Garden.

Charles T. Church

Having served for three years and completed the two major tasks of organizing an Olympic Team in 1928 and obtaining the 1930 World Championships for the United States, Henry Howe stepped down in 1928 and was succeeded by Charles T. Church, also from New York, as the third USFSA President. It would be Church's obligation during his two years in office to carry out the principal task of organizing the 1930 World Championships, which he did well, together with Howe. Church retired in 1930, but was not active in the affairs of the Association thereafter, and passed away in 1953.

The 1928 Governing Council meeting was again held in New York City in April. This time there were 11 clubs represented with more than 2,400 members. One Individual member was present and six guests. The Treasurer's report noted that there was a balance remaining to the credit of the Association of $397.37. The deficit of the magazine was reported as "about $900." The creation of a permanent Judges Committee, with Henry Howe as the first chairman, was approved. Up to that time, there had been a temporary special committee to prepare lists of judges eligible to serve at the National Championships, with test judges still the responsibility of the Standards and Tests Committee. Now all matters concerning judges were to be consolidated under one permanent committee.

Dialogue continued, just as it does today concerning eligibility. This time, the question was what penalties would be imposed for infractions of the amateur rules. It had already been recognized in 1926 that the payment of reasonable expenses for serving as a judge at a competition held under Association auspices was appropriate. There was an interesting stipulation imposed, which required the secretary of the judge's club to approve the expense report.

The 1928 Fall Meeting of the Executive Committee was held in New York in November. At the beginning, the Committee was originally just five in number from 1921 to 1923, then six for one year 1923-1924, 10 for another year 1924-1925, 12 from 1925 to 1927 and 15 for 1928-1930, with all the members being elected at the same time, essentially at-large. On this occasion, most of the standing committees made no report. Niles reported for the magazine on efforts to obtain additional subscriptions through the clubs, and that five issues were published instead of three, it having been an Olympic year. The magazine deficit was $948 for the year. Also reported was the receipt of a donation of movie film of the 1928 Olympic Winter Games, by Raymond Harvey of New York, perhaps the first time that the Association was the recipient of historical memorabilia.

The receipt of reimbursement from the American Olympic Association of $2,450 towards the expenses of the 1928 Olympic Team was reported as an unexpected and pleasant surprise, in view of the previously firmly announced position of the AOA that the sports were on their own.

At the same time it was reported that the IEV membership of the Association had been transferred to the ASU as previously agreed upon. One proposal the USFSA wanted to make to the IEV was reported, which was to shorten the Men's free skating from five minutes to four minutes, something that would eventually get done by half, i.e., to four and one-half minutes. An apparent strong dissatisfaction with the prior action of the Governing Council to abolish the National Championships for the Waltz and Fourteenstep and to replace them with a Dance competition with two parts, consisting of the conventional Waltz and an original Dance was reported. An attempt was made to overturn the decision of the Council by the Executive Committee, an unprecedented action, which was ruled out of order by the chairman, who ruled that actions of the Governing Council could only be changed by it and not by the Executive Committee. An unofficial vote was still taken to ascertain the attitude of the members of the Committee and the officers with respect to the Governing Council action, which was eight in favor and six against. The heat of this issue is readily apparent, since the names of those voting and how they voted are expressly recorded in the minutes of the meeting published in Skating magazine. While the issue was not a major one, the ruling was, since it established once and for all the ultimate authority of the Governing Council as the highest governing body of the Association.

The 1929 Nationals at New York City saw the Senior champions all successfully defending their titles. However, no one from the USFSA journeyed to the World Championships of that year to London for the Men, where the legendary Gillis Grafström won his third and last title, or to Budapest for the Ladies and Pairs.

It was also at the 1929 Nationals that the traditional Waltz and Fourteenstep (some times called Tenstep) competitions were discontinued, and a Dance event was added, consisting that year of a Waltz and an Original Dance. The Waltz was revived as a separate event in 1930 and continued until 1935, but the Fourteenstep competition was not. The latter had first been contested in 1920, with Mrs. Gertrude Cheever Porter and Irving Brokaw of New York the first winners.

Mrs. Porter would in 1932 donate the Porter trophy for the Senior Ladies event of the Nationals, which remained in use until 1971. It was replaced by the Owen Memorial trophy, presented by F. Ritter Shumway, The Skating Club of Boston and Mrs. Porter in memory of Maribel Vinson Owen and her two daughters, Laurence and Maribel (Junior), who were killed in the air accident at Brussels in 1961. The small replica trophies of the Porter trophy were a very distinct and visible memento of the title, and were also seen for the other Senior events, during the time when such items could still be purchased in sterling silver without costing a fortune.

The 1929 North American Championships were held in Boston and were really a battle between Roger Turner and Maribel Vinson with Thornton Coolidge in Pairs on the one hand, with Connie and Montgomery (Bud) Wilson of Canada, on the other. The latter won all three titles, which was an unusual sweep, but they also had done the same in the Canadian Championships.

What marks this particular championship, however, is that an even number of judges (four) was used on each event for the first time: two each from the United States and Canada. This system (eventually with six judges) would survive and work well until the mid-1950's, when the ISU finally blew the whistle on it, since an even number of judges was a technical violation of ISU rules. It is curious that the IEV (ISU after 1945) never paid any attention to the use of an even number of judges for so many years, even though the North American Championships were considered as an International Competition under ISU Rules. On the basis of participation in it, many judges and referees had earned credit for appointment or promotion as international officials.

The 1929 Governing Council meeting returned to New York and finally, we see an increase in the number of clubs represented, to 15, plus six individual members. The President of the Amateur Skating Union of the United States (ASU), William Carroll Hill of Boston, was present as a guest, reflecting a policy which would be followed in later years of inviting the leaders of the principal skating-related organizations in North America to the meeting, such as the Canadian Figure Skating Association (CFSA), the Professional Skaters Guild of America (PSGA), which became in 1995 the Professional Skaters Association (PSA), and the Ice Skating Institute of America (ISIA).

This year, the Treasurer reported a balance on hand of $2,844.72, and at the same time reported that $3,146.02 had been received, and $301.30 spent. The magazine deficit was reported as approximately $1,500.

The Council acted upon technical rules, one of which was "the present optional method used by judges in marking school figures on a basis of four for print, three for form, two for repetition and one for size, should be made obligatory." The rule specified that in assigning a mark, the order of importance was print, carriage and movement, repetition and size, but without assigning any values to them. Another proposal concerning free skating was that "each element under the title 'Program,' composition, variety and difficulty, and that each element under the title 'Performance,' carriage, movement and control shall be marked separately." The questions required an actual ballot, just as is seen in the Governing Council today. Both proposals were defeated by a slight margin.

The 1929 Executive Committee meeting was held in New York as usual, in October. In those days it was a one day meeting only. The famous 'cash balance' was reported as $1,182.42, after the payment of the usual magazine deficit. The meeting report was filled with plans for the forthcoming 1930 World Championships in New York, including such items as the IEV gold medals for first prizes having been ordered from G.W.A. van Laer of Amsterdam, an IEV Council member apparently charged with the responsibility for supplying them. Also noted was the ordering of an official English translation of the IEV rules (which were in German). Also reported was the holding of an Association Carnival in New York in January 1930 with 12 numbers, including groups from Ottawa and Toronto. A contribution of $6,500 from the sponsoring organization of the carnival, the New York Music Week Association, was needed in order to insure Association participation, which gives an idea of the value then placed on such participation. The carnival was to be a month before the Worlds, so the foreign skaters would not appear in it. The event represented an early example of Association co-operation with a non-skating organization in putting on such a production.

Despite the crash of the stock market in late 1929 and the onset of the Great Depression, the 1929-30 season was a major high point for the Association. The World Championships in New York were followed by several successful club carnivals in which the foreign visitors took part. These carnivals served to promote greater interest in the sport. In turn, this was of help to member clubs in surviving the rigors of the economic downturn.

A side effect of the Worlds being abroad, in so far as Europe was concerned, was the decision of the IEV to inaugurate Ladies and Pairs events in the European Championships, the oldest ISU Championship which had been only for men since 1891. Fritzi Burger of Austria, the runner-up to Sonja Henie in the 1929 Worlds chose not to come to the Worlds in 1930 because, as she told the author, her father had said to her: "Why not be the first European Ladies Champion (the competition was in her home town of Vienna), rather than to travel all that distance just to be second again to Sonja." Despite the fact that some of the top European skaters did not come, (among them, Gillis Grafström the defending champion, who suffered an injury in training) the championships, while not large in numbers, were of a high standard, with Americans and Canadians giving a good showing.

In the Men, Karl Schäfer of Austria won his first World title, with Roger Turner of Boston a surprising second, on the strength of his excellent compulsory figures. Another unexpected medalist was Georg Gautschi of Switzerland, third, followed by Montgomery Wilson of Canada and Ludwig Wrede of Austria, who was a former World champion in Pairs and also competed in that event in New York with Melitta Brunner. The rest of the field included three Americans, James L. Madden of Boston, Gail Borden, II of New York and William J. Nagle of Brooklyn.

There is a story about the Men's event which was related to the author by Richard L. Hapgood of Boston, who was a reporter for the **Boston Transcript**, and who was himself an excellent skater and judge. He traveled from New York to Boston after the competition with the Austrian judge and asked him why he had given Schäfer 11 sixes (6.0) out of 12 (the other being a 5.9) in the compulsory figures, to which the judge, Mr. Julius Edhoffer, replied that he "always gave a six to the best figure."

The Ladies event was smaller in number than the Men's (six entrants to eight), with Sonja Henie of Norway easily winning her fourth title. Second was Cecil Smith of Canada in a mild upset over Maribel Vinson, third, and Constance Wilson of Canada, the North American Ladies champion, fourth. Cecil had been Canadian Ladies champion in 1925 and 1926, but with the arrival on the scene in that country of Constance Wilson had not been able to regain the title. Her silver medal in New York must have been most enjoyable. In fifth place was Melitta Brunner of Austria, who would also compete in the Pairs with Wrede, followed by Suzanne Davis of Boston. It is a curious trivia of history that Constance Wilson always did very well in the North American Championships, but was usually defeated in the Worlds and Olympics by those she had beaten in the former competition.

The Pairs event saw Andrée Joly, now married, and her husband Pierre Brunet win their second World title, with Brunner and Wrede, second, and Beatrix Loughran and Sherwin Badger of New York, third, followed by Constance and Montgomery Wilson of Canada, the North American champions, fourth, with the indefatigable Mrs. Blanchard and Nathaniel Niles, sixth. Later in 1930, Badger was elected as President of the USFSA. Curiously, the Brunets were World champions in Pairs only in the even-numbered years (1926, 1928, 1930 and 1932).

All the carnivals reported in **Skating** magazine in which the foreign skaters participated both before and after the Worlds are described with such words as "America's Greatest Skating Carnival - Sonja Henie's First American Exhibition" (New York); "a capacity audience witnessed a most brilliant carnival" (New Haven); "Boston's Finest Carnival;" "a most tremendous success" (Philadelphia). It is no different today with the presence of the World or Olympic champions in a club carnival (there are very few left) or in a series of exhibitions. They insured success, especially at the gate.

Almost forgotten in all the "hoopla" about the Worlds, the foreign visitors and the subsequent carnivals, were the Nationals of 1930. Coming a month after the Worlds, they were held in Providence, Rhode Island for the first time. They would be held there twice more, in 1974 and 1995. The Senior singles title holders, Roger Turner and Maribel Vinson successfully retained their crowns, but in Pairs, for the first time since 1918 a team not from The SC of Boston won, with the Beatrix Loughran and Sherwin Badger (he was, of course, a former Bostonian) taking the title. In the Junior Men's event the name of Bruce Mapes (for whom the Mapes jump - the flip - was named), husband of Evelyn Chandler, the Junior Ladies champion of 1929, is found. Another legendary name in the

Junior men's event in 1927 and 1928 is that of Roy Shipstad of St. Paul, Minnesota, later of "Ice Follies" fame, third in both years, while in 1931 Robin Lee, also from St. Paul, first appears, third in his first Nationals.

At the 1930 Annual Meeting of the Association, a revised Constitution and By Laws were adopted, with the provision, which is still in effect, that the power of appointing the chairmen and members of all committees be delegated to the President. In exercising this power for the first time, Mr. Badger, the new President, appointed the chairmen of the committees, but delegated the power to appoint the members of the committees to the respective chairmen.

Sherwin C. Badger

Badger, in becoming the fourth President, established some remarkable firsts: At the age of 29, he was the youngest President ever elected; the first and only President to be a National champion and Olympic medalist (also in pairs at Lake Placid in 1932) at the same time.

The 1930 Fall meeting of the Association was held in New York in late October. Mentioned specially was a donation from The SC of Boston of $500 from the proceeds of its carnival in 1929. The balance on hand was reported as $4,500. Advanced to Maribel Vinson and Roger Turner was the sum of $500 each to defray in part their expenses in traveling to the 1931 World Championships in Berlin, upon which Turner offered to forego the sum voted to him, so that Vinson could receive $1,000. It was the first specific grant of such funds to competitors to participate in the World Championships.

Completely revised competition rules were announced, which brought together for the first time, the important rules of the IEV, the Association and the agreement with Canada for the North American Championships. The principal change cited had to do with the National Junior singles events, which imposed the passing of the Fourth Test as a requirement for entry, with the local organizing committee also being empowered to limit the number of entries to eight, by eliminating any entrants which had not passed the test. Among the reasons cited for the qualifying test requirement was that "in recent years, the number of entries for these competitions has been so large that the events have been unwieldy. The competitions were fair neither to skater or judge, for no skater can put forth his best effort throughout an event lasting several hours and no judge can mark with any degree of precision when his eyes and mind have become bewildered by the multitude of school figures executed by 10 or more skaters, nor can he compare with accuracy the free skating of all entries." Here we see the perennial concern about overly large events, which remains an ongoing problem today.

The momentum created by the 1930 Worlds in skating in the United States carried over into the next season, with a decision being made to send a small team to the 1931 World

Championships in Berlin. It was a good move, actually, since it was already known that the 1932 Olympic Winter Games would be held at Lake Placid, N.Y., and a "ranking" and further experience in the prior Worlds would be of value in the following year. The team consisted of Roger Turner, Maribel Vinson and her second pair partner, George (Geddy) Hill. Thornton Coolidge, with whom she had twice won the National championship, had moved to New York in 1929 and their partnership broke up. No judge was sent, but W.L. Hildburgh, an American living abroad, who had served as a representative for the ASU at IEV meetings, acted on behalf of the Association as a judge in all three events.

In the Men, Turner retained his runner-up position, this time being pressed by Ernst Baier of Germany, while Hill placed 11th. Vinson was fourth, with the legendary Hilde Holovsky of Austria, only age 13 and soon to pass away from the flu in 1933, second and Fritzi Burger, third. In the Pairs, Vinson and Hill placed fifth.

All this time, with interest heightened by all the publicity, the Nationals (the only major competition then) was growing substantially. In 1931 at Boston, there were 50 entries, with nine in Junior Men and 11 in Junior Ladies, while in 1922 there were just 30 entries, with five each in the Junior events.

At the 1931 Annual Meeting of the Association in New York, there were 18 clubs represented out of a total of 22, with the total number of members being listed in the minutes as almost 3,400. Unfortunately, there is no way to determine today the actual total membership of the Association then. There was no registration, and the clubs simply reported their approximate membership for the purpose of the number of votes to which they would be entitled in the Governing Council. Actually, between 1929 and 1935, only 12 new clubs joined the Association, a reflection of the impact of the Depression on recreational activities, such as sports.

The year 1931 was also marked by the deaths of three of the founders of skating in North America; George H. Browne of Cambridge, Mass., Henry W. Howe of New York and Louis Rubenstein of Montreal, who had been a Champion of America and Canada, and a long-time Secretary-Treasurer and later President of the Amateur Skating Association of Canada.

For the 1932 Nationals, a very unusual trophy was presented. The Henry Wainwright Howe Memorial Trophy for Pairs carries as its handles Mr. Howe's skates with which he had won the National Waltz title in 1923 with Mrs. Howe. The trophy had been designed by Gail Borden, II, a member of the Skating Club of New York and himself an active competitor and former National Junior champion, and had been made possible by donations from the membership of the Association, an expression of the high regard in which Mr. Howe had been held.

Another permanent trophy was donated in 1931 by The Skating Club of Boston in memory of George H. Browne. The three trophies, the Browne, the Porter and the Howe, plus the first

Howe trophy for Fours, became the symbols of the National championships and can be seen in many programs and in publicity over the years. Two of them, the Browne for the Men and the Howe for the Pairs are still active today, but no longer travel for safety reasons. They reside in dignified splendor in the World Figure Skating Museum in Colorado Springs. The names of the winners are added each year, so that they remain up-to-date.

The 1931 Fall Meeting of the Executive Committee took place in New York City. The report in **Skating** carried headlines, which cited three major actions: the 1932 Olympic Team would be selected at the National Senior Championships; the Junior championship eligibility was raised to the Fifth test; and National Novice Championships were to be inaugurated in 1932. Noted was the amount ($3,906.05) raised for the Henry Howe Memorial Trophy, which was quite a tribute to Mr. Howe's memory. A By Law amendment was also proposed, which provided that a quorum for the holding of a meeting would be one-half of the total number of members (inclusive of the officers, who were not strictly then members of the committee, which by now was 20).

One interesting rule change was a confirmation of the procedure by which the four couples to enter the final round of the Waltz competition were to be selected. It was by a vote of the judges, with the four couples receiving the highest number of votes being retained, and ties having to be skated off. There was no provision for selecting the finalists on the basis of the placements in the initial round, if one can believe it. Perhaps this procedure reflected the essentially informal aspect of the earlier Waltz competitions, although by the 1930's, it was serious business.

With the Olympic year of 1932 approaching, there was great excitement in the country, especially since both the Winter and Summer Games were to be held in the United States, even without the overwhelming deluge of media coverage that would be the case today, as was seen in 1980, 1984 and 1996, although the coverage in the print media, as we would call it today (the newspapers and magazines), was extensive for that day. Because of the dates for the Games in Lake Placid, in early February, the unusual decision was taken to divide the National Championships, with the Senior events to be held in New York at Iceland, the famous home rink of the Skating Club of New York, in late December 1931, except for the Pairs, which was held at the (new) Madison Square Garden. The Dance, Waltz, Junior and new Novice Singles events were also to be held in New York at Iceland, but in late March. The events in December were, in effect, the Olympic trials for the 1932 team and were carried out to capacity audiences in the famous fourth floor rink with its electric ice maker on top of the old Madison Square Garden building (not so old then, but now long gone).

All the defending champions retained their titles, Roger Turner and Maribel Vinson in Singles and Beatrix Loughran and Sherwin Badger in Pairs. The United States was allowed four entrants in both Men and Ladies and two in Pairs. Alternates were also designated and just one judge, Charles M. Rotch of Boston, a manager, Joel Liberman, New York, an assistant manager, Richard Hapgood of Cambridge, Mass., and a chaperone, Mrs. Blanchard, going to her fourth Olympic Winter Games. The second-place pair of Maribel Vinson and George Hill, as it turned out, did not compete, because "Geddy," as he was called, had some academic difficulties at Harvard, which would not let him go. They were replaced by Gertrude Meredith and Joseph Savage of New York, who placed seventh, which was remarkable in itself, since Savage was also the chief referee for the Speed Skating events (he had been the first President of the ASU) and did both.

For the early Olympic Winter Games, starting in 1924, no funding to cover the expenses of a team was provided by the American Olympic Association (later the United States Olympic Committee). It was incumbent upon the USFSA itself to raise the necessary funds. This position was made abundantly clear in 1927 by the head of the AOA , General Charles Sherrill, to Joseph K. Savage of New York, when "he was officially informed that the entry of a Figure Skating Team depended upon whether the expense be borne by the sport itself and that no part of the expense would be paid by the Olympic Committee." The necessary funds were raised and a team was duly sent.

In the Games themselves, the U.S. team acquitted itself well, coming home with two medals for the first time: Maribel Vinson was third in Ladies, behind Sonja Henie of Norway and Fritzi Burger of Austria; and Beatrix Loughran and Sherwin Badger were second in Pairs in a very close competition, in which they very nearly unseated the defending champions, Andrée and Pierre Brunet. The best Turner could do was sixth, largely because he was not up to his usual standard in the figures, a bit of a come down from his two runner-up finishes in the two previous World Championships of 1930 and 1931. The Men's event marked the end of the long reign of Olympic champion Gillis Grafström of Sweden, who was defeated by his much younger rival, Karl Schäfer of Austria. Third was Montgomery Wilson from Canada for the first Olympic medal for that country.

Following the Games, the 1932 World Championships were held for the first time in Canada at Montreal. Grafström did not compete, having suffered a minor injury, but all the other foreign competitors participated, with Schäfer and Henie retaining their titles and the Brunets regaining theirs, since they had not participated in 1931, in accordance with their usual even-year pattern. The U.S. team did less well than at the Olympics with only one medal in the Pairs where Loughran and Badger placed third, behind the Hungarian pair of Emilia Rotter and Laszlo Szollas. Theresa Weld Blanchard and Nathaniel Niles were entered in the Pairs event, since Hill was still absent, placing eighth in what would be their last competition, since Niles passed away later in the year at the age of 45. They had a remarkable run, with their first competition having been in 1914.

Nathaniel Niles had a strong influence on the early years of the USFSA, and actually had been offered the presidency in 1921, but had deferred to Mr. Weld. He also, with his long-time partner Theresa Weld Blanchard, established **Skating** magazine on a sound footing, at least editorially, if not financially. He had also been an outstanding tennis player, ranked in the top 10 for many years and was the 1908 collegiate champion.

In the Men's singles at Worlds, the third U.S. entrant was the third place finisher from the prior year's National Junior event, Robin Lee of St. Paul, Minnesota. At the age of 12, he certainly was one of the youngest ever to represent the United States in a World Championship. He placed ninth.

As planned, the Junior and the new Novice Singles events, together with the Dance events of the Nationals, were duly held separately in New York in late March, with Lee winning the Men's event. The first Novice champions, names unknown today, deserve to be mentioned, when the ongoing controversy, 64 years later, of whether or not the Novice events should remain in the main Nationals is considered. They were Samuel Ferguson and Valerie Jones, both from New York. George Hill, finally released from purgatory by his college, showed up to win the Dance event (then an Original Dance) with Clara Rotch Frothingham, who had been the National Junior Ladies champion of 1918, performing a Tango, so his season was not entirely lost.

Following the various competitions, there again ensued a very successful round of club carnivals featuring the foreign stars with four of them within one week of one another; New York, New Haven, Boston and Philadelphia, almost reminiscent of the World Tour of today. Grafström, who had remained in North America after the Olympics, was able to skate in the carnivals, performing his famous Swedish mazurka program in national costume which, through the generosity of his widow, Mrs. Cecile Grafström, now is a major exhibit in the World Figure Skating Museum in Colorado Springs. A notable part of the carnivals was the appearance of two very young girls from Great Britain who had also participated at the age of 11 in the Olympic and World Championships: Megan Taylor and Cecilia Colledge. Little was it known then that they would be the dominant skaters of the late 1930's after the retirement of Sonja Henie. The carnival at New York was actually an Association carnival.

With summer skating inaugurated at Lake Placid in the summer of 1932, a beneficial use of the Olympic Arena, the first summer carnival was held there that year. It would be a forerunner for summer shows and "pops" concerts at many other summer centers which would follow the lead of Lake Placid, such as that at St. Paul, Minn.

The 1932 Governing Council meeting closed what had been a very busy season, with 20 clubs represented, reflecting a total of over 3,200 members. There were seven member clubs not represented. The cash balance on hand had now reached the substantial number of $9,000. Happily, the annual deficit for the magazine had declined to about $670. It is notable that, throughout all the years and over and over again as reported in the minutes, the importance of the magazine to the Association and the firm resolve to keep it going was maintained, despite the annual deficits which would, of course, in later years, be quite substantial; although the numbers reported would not be large today, they were then. Also reported were the number of tests passed during the year, with the report being divided between men and women. The grand total was 137, with 79 being passed by women and 58 by men. Also voted was a rule that the winners of the National Novice events could not compete again in the event, a limitation which already applied to the Junior level.

At the end of the 1932 season, Sherwin Badger, perhaps exhausted by his dual role as Association officer and competitor, stepped down as President and was succeeded by Charles M. Rotch as the fifth occupant of the chair.

By the 1932-1933 season, with just 11 years of existence behind it, the Association had experienced modest growth which, of course, had been adversely affected and slowed by the Great Depression. There were 27 member clubs with approximately 4,500 members located in 10 different states.

Expansion Westward
(1933-1936)

The Association was still largely an Eastern organization. Based on the Sectional divisions later adopted, of the 27 member clubs, 17 were from the East, eight from the Midwest and two were from the Pacific Coast. Of the Eastern clubs, four were country clubs with outdoor ice only. Several of them, notably The Country Club (TCC) of Brookline, Mass., a charter member and the Brae Burn Country Club of West Newton, Mass., would remain members for many years without ever having an active participation in or having used programs from the USFSA, although they maintained their outdoor rinks, which TCC does to this day.

The advent of indoor artificial ice rinks on the Pacific Coast did not really get underway until the early 1930's, when financial resources were once again available for recreational purposes. However, the increase in the number of such rinks and of activity in the sport was very rapid. By 1930, skating on the Pacific Coast was still rink skating, not club skating, but by 1931 there were three clubs on the Coast: the Seattle Skating Club, the Spokane Figure Skating Club and the St. Moritz Ice Skating Club, then in Oakland and later in Berkeley. However, the first Pacific Coast club officially to join the Association was the Skate and Ski Club of San Francisco, closely followed by the Los Angeles FSC, both in 1933.

In 1934, two more Pacific Coast clubs joined: the St. Moritz ISC, still a member today, and the Yosemite Winter Club. The latter skated on natural outdoor ice in the Yosemite National Park. A California Skating Association had been formed by 1932 and sponsored the first formal competition in figure skating in California at Yosemite, the California State Outdoor Championships of 1933. There also was an indoor championship started the same year in San Francisco. Obviously, because the jurisdiction of the USFSA was clearly national in scope, the CSA was not legally empowered to sanction figure skating events on its own. The programs for the competitions included Intermediate and Juvenile events (long before their time elsewhere) and also included classes for "amateur woman-professional partner" and amateur man-professional partner." The President of the CSA, Don Tressider, the Yosemite director and later a President of Stanford University, took the position that progress in Western skating demanded sponsorship by the CSA rather than by the USFSA. The Association position was clearly set forth by former President Weld, who stated at the Executive Committee meeting in 1933 that he felt "the situation to be most complicated, involving considerable danger to the USFSA if district associations were given permanent power to control figure skating." A resolution was promptly adopted calling for a committee to investigate the situation in California with the mission of devising ways and means for the control and governing of figure skating in that district that would be satisfactory to the CSA, the USFSA and the ASU.

Before that could happen, however, it was necessary to bring the California clubs "into the fold" and the leaders of the Association were quick to do so, dispatching ambassadors to the Coast to visit the new clubs and to invite them to join the Association. The first to go was the Association Secretary, Richard L. Hapgood of Cambridge, Mass., who went to the Coast in late 1933 to investigate and to do "missionary work," visiting San Francisco, Oakland, Los Angeles and Yosemite. Fortunately, he was able to persuade the Coast clubs to become "law abiding citizens of the USFSA world," as it was put on the subject in the 1946 Anniversary booklet. Actually, the Association essentially permitted the various competitions and activities started by the CSA to continue but, obviously, in accordance with the Constitution, By Laws and Rules of the USFSA. Later, Mrs. Theresa Weld Blanchard, Roger F. Turner, and Heaton R. Robertson, the Treasurer, would visit the Coast to judge tests and competitions there.

In any event, skating on the Pacific Coast grew rapidly under the benign umbrella of the USFSA so that, by 1941, there were 25 member clubs and the Nationals of 1942 were awarded to the St. Moritz ISC, completing an effort first started by Alex Young, Jr., of San Francisco, as early as 1937, when he had attended the USFSA Annual Meeting. Due to the War, however, it would not be until 1947 that the Championships finally reached the Pacific Coast.

With the increased interest and activity in the sport, certainly to some degree influenced by the appearances of the foreign skaters in carnivals in 1930 and 1932, and strongly pushed after 1936 with the arrival on our shores of Sonja Henie of Norway, the need for additional competitive opportunities quickly became apparent.

As a result, the three Sectional Championships were all inaugurated in the 1930's. The Midwesterns were the first in 1933 and the Pacific Coast's the second in 1936. The Eastern Section, despite the fact that it had the most skaters, was the last of the three to do so in 1938. The Sectional Championships were not at the outset qualifying competitions. That would come much later, after World War II. Nor were they of the same standard as the National Championships. Up until 1967, the Sectional classes were one level lower than those at the Nationals, i.e., the

Sectional Senior class skated the compulsory figures and duration of free skating specified for the National Junior class.

It should also be noted that there was a model for the new championships, the Middle Atlantic Championships, inaugurated in 1921 just before the Association was founded, held under the auspices of the Middle Atlantic Skating Association of the ISU of A. The Middle Atlantic Championships are the oldest continuous figure skating competition in the country and are still held today under the auspices of The Skating Club of New York. Because they predate the Association, there is a famous rule still in the book which states: "Nothing herein contained shall affect the established method of conducting the Middle Atlantic Championships."

The first Midwestern Championships were held in St. Louis in 1933 with Senior events only. There were just three judges, Mrs. Blanchard, Mr. Robertson and Chris Christenson of St. Paul, Minn., with four entries in Men, six in Ladies and two in Pairs, plus an informal Waltz competition. The winners were Robin Lee in the Men's, Ann Haroldson of Duluth, Minn., in the Ladies and Edith and Arthur Preusch of Minneapolis, who won both the Pairs and the Waltz.

The first Pacific Coast Championships were held at Yosemite, out of doors, in 1936, this time with a fairly complete slate of events, including Senior and Junior Singles and Pairs, Novice Singles, plus a Waltz competition. Two names stand out in the summaries; Eugene Turner of Los Angeles, the winner of the Senior Men and Robert Scott of St. Moritz ISC, the winner of the Junior Men. They would be the first National champions from the Pacific Coast. The winner of the Waltz competition with his partner, Frances Wright, was Howell Janes of St. Moritz ISC, who would later have a distinguished career as a judge and referee at the World level.

The Eastern Section finally got around to joining the parade in 1938 when the first Eastern Championships were held at Lake Placid. Here, too, Senior and Junior events in Singles and Pairs were offered and there was also a Juvenile Girls, as well as Waltz and Fourteenstep competitions. The Men's winner was Roger Turner, the former National champion while in the Ladies, Katherine L. Durbrow of New York was the winner, thereby setting a unique record, as she had been the runner-up in the 1933 Midwesterns, representing St. Louis. Certainly, she is the only person to have competed in two of the first three Sectionals. The Pairs went to Grace and James Madden, who had been the National champions in 1934.

At the beginning of the Sectionals as qualifying competitions, because of the fact noted above that they were a class lower than the Nationals, there was still no qualification requirement, either in competition or test-wise, for the National Senior events while for the National Junior event, the Sixth (figure) test had become the only requirement. Qualifying from the Sectional was first applied only to the National Novice level with a long and complicated rule, but essentially the requirements were the Fourth or Fifth Test and having placed in the first four in the Sectional

Junior, or having won the Sectional Novice. If there has been any area in which the rules have been changed more often than anywhere else, it is in the rules for qualifying for competition, which are still being changed almost annually, even today.

Maribel Vinson and George Hill

The 1933 Nationals were held at New Haven, with Maribel Vinson and Roger Turner retaining their Senior Singles titles. The Championships also marked the first title in Pairs for Maribel and her partner, George E.B. Hill. In the Dance event, the winners were Suzanne Davis and Frederick Goodridge of Boston. The Waltz competition had become a separate event again in 1930 and had been won three times in a row from 1930 to 1932 by Mrs. Edith Secord of New York, with two different partners, Joseph K. Savage in 1930 and 1932 and Ferrier T. Martin in 1931. This time the title went to Ilse Twaroschk and Fred Fleischmann of New York. In the Novice events, Polly Blodgett of Boston won the Ladies with Joan Tozzer, also of Boston, second. The Junior Men's winner was William Swallender of Minneapolis, later a well known coach, who was lost in 1961 in the Brussels crash.

No one from the United States journeyed to the 1933 World Championships at Stockholm for the Ladies and Pairs and at Zurich for the Men. Sonja Henie and Karl Schäfer retained their titles, while Emilia Rotter and Laszlo Szollas regained the Pair title. It was a return to the normal pattern of minimal or little U.S. participation in the World Championships in the non-Olympic years, which can be well understood, when the difficulties of travel (by ship) in those days is considered.

The 1933 North American Championships held at New York were also notable for the absence of Maribel Vinson and Roger Turner, as well as of Beatrix Loughran and Sherwin Badger. As a result, the defending champions, Montgomery Wilson and Constance Wilson-Samuel, again took all the titles. There was, however, one significant aspect to the Championship. That was the revival of the Connaught Cup competition for Fours as a part of the North American Championships, which had last been held in 1923, with the famous Minto Skating Club Four of Prudence Holbrook, Margaret Davis, Melville Rogers and Guy Owen retaining the cup and winning their first North American title. The only U.S. Four entered was from Boston and included Theresa Weld Blanchard, Suzanne Davis, Richard L. Hapgood and Fred A. Parmenter. From then on, the Fours event remained a part of the North American Championships until 1949.

The 1933 Governing Council meeting was held at New York as usual, again in early April, with 20 clubs represented, reflecting over 4,200 members. There were seven clubs not represented. The Treasurer's report reflected a cash balance on hand of $6,316.53. The total number of sanctions granted for exhibitions was 39. The magazine deficit was stated as possibly amounting to $400, but would probably be less. The total number of subscribers was reported as about 1,000 out of a possible total membership of the Association of 5,000 or 6,000 members. It was suggested that more clubs should take advantage of the (optional) club subscription plan, either by adding $1.00 to the annual dues as was done by The Skating Club (New York), or by deducting $1.00 from the annual dues as was done by The SC of Boston. For the first time, the Association had advanced at the start of the year the sum of $500 to the magazine in anticipation of the deficit.

Discussed for the first time was the matter of clubs contributing a certain percentage of the net profits of their carnivals or other exhibitions to the Association when there was paid attendance. Thus was born the idea of sanction fees, which would in subsequent years constitute a major portion of the income for the Association. At the same time, it was voted to pay the travel expenses of the officers to the meetings of the Governing Council and Executive Committee.

The Fall Meeting of 1933 was held at The Country Club in Brookline, Mass., a departure from New York City. The meetings of the Executive Committee, which were really the Board of Directors of the Association, were becoming increasingly important, with much of the essential legislation concerning technical matters being decided by it in the form of rule changes. The receipt of $125.88 from The SC of Boston, representing 10 percent of the net profit from its 1933 carnival, was the first such assessment fee paid (voluntarily) to the Association. The matter of violations of the amateur status rules in California was discussed, and it was reported that the USFSA rules in that regard would definitely be followed in the future. Added to the Amateur Status Committee was Alex Young, Jr., of San Francisco, who would pass upon questions of amateur status on the Coast and also grant sanctions for exhibitions. Word was also received from the IEV that exhibitions in a foreign country or by a foreign skater in the United States required the consent of both of the associations involved, which would have a direct effect on the flow of skaters back and forth between Canada and the United States. Ultimately, joint rules were developed by the two associations to facilitate the process, while at the same time observing the requirements of the IEV rule. This would lead by 1937 to the establishment of the Carnival and Exhibition Sanctions Committee to administer the granting of sanctions. In 1933, permission for exhibitions in Canada by U.S. skaters had to be obtained either from the President or the Chairman of the Amateur Status Committee.

It was also in 1933 that a significant move was made by just one person, which would change the way in which the United States viewed and participated in international competition.

Having graduated from Radcliffe College, Maribel Vinson decided to spend the season of 1933-1934 abroad, based in England, with a view towards entering both the European and World Championships, since she was also a member of the National Skating Association of Great Britain. The then ISU Rules permitted a non-European to enter the European Championships, which are an ISU Championship, if the person was a member of a European member association of the ISU. This prerogative would survive until after World War II. By going abroad, Maribel gave up the defense of her two National titles, and her pair with Geddy Hill was temporarily put on ice. It was a bold decision and was concurred in by Maribel's long time teacher, Willie Frick. Thus was born the idea of foreign training, with the view of trying to compete with the Europeans on equal terms on their own ground on a more regular or even annual basis. The United States still had never won a World or Olympic title, although there had been a few silver and bronze medals along the way.

Maribel's success in the two Championships probably was a little less than she had hoped for. Perennially, she had always been regarded as a leading contender for the highest honors, but her performances in competition never quite reached the heights achieved in training, as evidenced by the fact that she won but one Ladies Championship of North America in 1937, after Constance Wilson-Samuel had retired, although she had competed in the event continuously, with one exception since 1929.

In the European Championship at Prague, Maribel placed third, behind Sonja Henie and the dual speed and figure skating star, Liselotte Landbeck of Austria; while in the 1934 World Championships at Oslo, the best she could do was fifth, with the appearance on the scene of a new representative of the next generation which would dominate the late 1930's, Megan Taylor of Great Britain, who placed second to Henie. Curiously, Gail Borden, II, of New York, took a leaf from Maribel's book and showed up at the Men's championship at Stockholm, he too being an NSA member, placing eighth.

At the same time as these foreign exploits, there was yet another visit by several of the top European skaters to take part in what had become a very well recognized and established tour of club carnivals. The visitors were Sonja Henie and Karl Schäfer, the reigning World champions, who were accompanied by the 12-year-old Hedy Stenuf of Austria, who would herself make a considerable splash in the American skating pond a few years later. Hedy and Karl did a Pair called the "Devil Dance," which was very well received. The carnivals were once again a success, both financially and otherwise, and kept the interest in the sport on the rise. These were strictly amateur shows but were of a high standard and were held in the large arenas. In many respects they were the forerunners of the touring professional shows to appear on the scene after 1936.

The 1934 Nationals were held in Philadelphia and were one of the largest up to that time, with more than 70 entries in 11 events. With Maribel away, Suzanne Davis, also of Boston, won the Ladies event, in which she created quite a sensation in the compulsory figures by wearing shorts, which merited a photograph and a brief article in **Skating** magazine, in which Mrs.

Blanchard said, "For the first time in our Nationals a lady competed in shorts and they were greeted with much praise!" The shorts were, by today's standards, quite conservative. The Pair title went to Grace and James Madden, while Roger Turner won his seventh straight Men's title, but youth was right on his heels, with Robin Lee, now representing New York, a close second. It also must be noted that the representatives of The SC of Boston won seven of the 11 titles, the highest total won by any club at a Nationals before or since. Three of the remaining four titles went to the Skating Club, New York and the only one left, the Novice Men, to a lone Midwestern representative, Oliver E. Haupt, Jr., of St. Louis, Mo.

Suzanne Davis

The 1934 tour of European skaters was repeated in 1935 with a different cast of characters, this time including Maxi Herber and Ernst Baier of Germany, the new European Pair champions, Vivi-Anne Hultén of Sweden, who had been a World Silver medalist and was the current Bronze medalist, and Idi Papez and Karl Zwack of Austria, the European Pair champions of 1933.

While the two tours of 1934 and 1935 had their bright side, there was a dark side as well. Some of the demands made by the visitors upon their host clubs were excessive, if not improper and also probably were violations of the strict amateur status rules of both bodies. Further, promoters became involved, which further complicated the issue. Protests made by the USFSA to the IEV were unavailing and were rejected. Unfortunately, the Amateur Skating Union, which was the IEV Member from the United States, did not support the USFSA protest, which was made on its behalf by the NSA, a fact which resulted in a further deterioration of relations between the ASU and the USFSA. The issue was explosive enough that informal discussions actually took place among the representatives of the English speaking members of the IEV, with a view towards their withdrawal from that body and the formation of a new international federation, which would not be dominated by the vested interests of certain Continental IEV members in Europe. A third successive tour planned for 1936 between the IEV and the ASU, without the participation of the USFSA, fortunately never got off the ground.

The 1934 Governing Council meeting was back at the old stand in New York at the Bar Association, with 26 clubs represented and six clubs not represented. The clubs represented reflected over 3,200 members, although the number is probably low as some clubs did not report actual numbers but just the minimum number needed to obtain the maximum number of delegates. The President, Mr. Rotch, reported upon the 1934 Nationals at Philadelphia: "...commented on the large number of entries as a desirable indication of the growth of interest in the sport, but pointed out that this had necessitated the postponement of the Men's Senior school figures until the morning of the second day, obliging the competitors to skate three hours of school figures in the morning and the free skating in the (same) evening. This he regarded as too fatiguing a contest. For the future he recommended dividing the various events of the championships into two groups and running them off at different times in different places." Here was the "germ" of the same discussion that continues today concerning the content of the Nationals, and especially the Novice events.

There is also a report by the Treasurer which is revealing. Heaton Robertson stressed the Association's urgent need for additional money over and above its ordinary receipts, which he placed at about $700 a year. He indicated that the Association's ordinary expenses averaged annually around $500, but there were extraordinary expenses in 1933-1934 which had reduced the cash balance (i.e., the assets or capital) by about $1,600, and it was the second year of a similar reduction in cash. He predicted that unless radical steps were taken to secure more revenue for the Association from carnivals, the cash balance would be wiped out in three or four years if the Association continued on its present basis of the services it is rendering to its member clubs. (Sounds familiar, doesn't it?)

After serving for two years as President, Charles Rotch himself stepped down in 1934 and Sherwin Badger reassumed the office for an additional year, so that he was in the middle of the entire controversy involving the foreign skaters. He again retired in 1935, and Mr. Rotch returned to the Presidency for two more years until 1937.

However, there would be a major event in 1936 in the United States which would change the face of the sport forever: the professional debut of Sonja Henie, the three time Olympic champion.

Charles M. Rotch

In the summer of 1935, another form of overseas training was carried out, when four young skaters from Boston and their teacher spent the summer in England. At that time, the rinks in England were major training centers for all the top European skaters and many of the leading coaches who would later emigrate to the United States. The skaters were Bernard Fox, then the National Novice champion; Joan Tozzer, his future pair partner and the Novice Ladies champion of 1934; and two young sisters, Margaret and Jennie McKean. The teacher was Willie Frick, who, while on an earlier sojourn in England in 1933, had taken and passed all the tests of the NSA, including its First Class or Gold Test. The results of this hard work can be seen in the 1936 Nationals, when Fox won the Junior title and with Joan, the Junior Pair title, while she was runner-up in the Junior Ladies.

There were five judges for the Junior Ladies: two each from Boston and New York and one from New Haven. Naturally, the New York judges voted for Katherine Durbrow, the ultimate winner and the two Boston judges for Tozzer, while the New Haven judge placed Durbrow first and Tozzer fourth. This pattern would be seen many times during the next three years, with the on-going close rivalry between New York and Boston skaters, especially in the Ladies. Just as is the case today, there was no accountability then on the part of the judges for their performance or for such obvious bias and it was often the hapless fifth judge who had to keep the panel honest.

The 1934 Fall meeting of the Executive Committee took place in New York as usual in October. The Treasurer, Heaton Robertson, reported the cash balance as a $4,976. An amateur status rule was passed which provided that no amateur skater could appear in a movie and receive compensation, directly or indirectly, nor may such a person allow his or her name or title to be used, even if receiving no compensation. This was the beginning of the rule known as "capitalizing on one's athletic fame" as a form of professional activity, whether or not being compensated for such activity. It would last right up to modern times, gradually being whittled down to essentially the rule of today, which permits such activities as long as they are carried out under contracts approved by the Association. The motivation for the adoption of the rule can be traced to a California situation, where there had been instances of skaters appearing as extras in films, and the rule was intended to reconfirm the intention of the Association to enforce strictly the principles of amateurism.

A list of official judges had finally been published in the magazine in 1934, which showed 79 Low Test judges from 14 clubs, and 71 High test judges from nine clubs. The High Test judges, who could also judge Low Tests, were listed twice, so the pool of judges available for Low tests was actually 150. The magazine situation was clearly stated, with receipts of $1,648.22, expenditures of $2,213.63, making a deficit of $565.41.

It was at the 1935 Nationals at New Haven that one of the monuments of the older generation

Robin Lee

fell, when 15-year-old Robin Lee, representing New York, defeated 34-year-old Roger Turner, to win what would be the first of five consecutive Senior Men's championships. Maribel Vinson, however, recaptured her Senior Ladies title with ease and also took back the Pair title with her partner George Hill, in both cases defeating the defending champions from 1934. In the Novice Men, the winner was Bernard Fox of Boston, while the Junior Ladies was won by Polly Blodgett, with Ardelle V. Kloss, later Mrs. Lloyd B. Sanderson of New York, third. The Waltz title went to Nettie Prantel and Roy Hunt of New York, who were also one-half of the New York Four which won that title, the other half being Ardelle Kloss and Joseph Savage. They succeeded to the title won in 1934 by the Boston Four of Mrs. Blanchard, Suzanne Davis, Frederick Goodridge and Richard Hapgood, in the first competition in the discipline since 1924.

At the 1935 North Americans in Montreal, Maribel still could not defeat Constance Wilson-Samuel in Ladies, but she and Hill did win the Pairs, upsetting the defending champions, Mrs. Wilson-Samuel and Montgomery Wilson, who retained his Men's title over Robin Lee.

Despite the loss of his Men's title in 1935, Roger Turner was far from finished, and he actually was recalled to active duty in 1937 to fill in for an injured Robin Lee at the North American Championships in Boston. There, by reason of his excellent compulsory figures, he placed second to Montgomery Wilson, in what could well be considered his finest hour, defeating as he did several of the young hot shots of the day. Roger was also determined to try for a third Olympic Team in Pairs at the Nationals of 1936, where Senior events, like those of 1932, were held in December 1935 at Iceland and Madison Square Garden in New York. Roger had taken up pairs in 1933-1934 with Polly Blodgett, herself an excellent singles skater and the National Junior Ladies champion of 1935. They had won the National Junior Pair title in 1934 and were fourth in the Senior Pairs event in 1935. In the Nationals, which actually were formally designated as the "Olympic Trials," they placed second to Vinson and Hill and fully expected to be named to the Olympic Team as the second Pair. This was not to be, with the slot being awarded to Grace and Jim Madden, the 1934 champions, who did not compete in the trials due to a leg injury sustained by Madden shortly before. This decision, which has been repeated on occasion since, was always resented by Turner, who felt that he and Blodgett had fairly earned the spot. It reflects the essential problem of such selections, when not based on actual competition, in which the ultimate result is not pleasing to everyone, a "no-win" situation. Later, Turner turned his hand to Dance and placed fifth in the Senior Dance event in 1946 with Betty Davis, his last competitive effort.

Roger Turner had been a Vice President of the USFSA in 1930-1932, and was Chairman of the Standards and Tests Committee from 1934 to 1940. His actual signature was on the blue test certificates issued then, which became collector's items for those who collected

Second New York Four
Joseph Savage, Ardelle Kloss, Nettie Prantel and Roy Hunt

skating autographs. What is remarkable is Turner's tenure as a National Judge from 1927 to 1982, when he stepped down and was made an Honorary National Judge: a span of 55 years, probably the longest length of service of any one in that position. He died in 1993 at the age of 92, and was one of the legends of American skating during his time. He was elected posthumously to the United States Figure Skating Hall of Fame in 1994.

The 1935 Governing Council Meeting was again held in New York City, but this time at the Metropolitan Club, with 21 clubs representing just under 3,900 members. There were 10 clubs not represented. It was noted that the 1935 Nationals at New Haven had netted the Association $100, which was 10 percent of the net profit accruing to the New Haven SC. The carnival and competition assessment was finally made mandatory, with clubs being required to submit reports of their gross receipts, expenditures and net income. Eventually, the assessment for carnivals would be applied to the gross receipts, rather than to the net profit and accordingly at a much lower rate. Separate fixed fees were also imposed for the issuance of sanctions.

Despite Mr. Robertson's dire warnings the previous year, he reported in 1935 that the cash balance was up to $6,876.95, as against $4,976.00 the prior year. The number of sanctions had increased to over 60, with more than 20 involving Canadian skaters. Total dues from the 33 member clubs amounted to $477.00.

A revision of the amateur status rules permitted the reinstatement of professionals, with a five-year waiting period from the last professional act being imposed.

The 1935 Fall Meeting of the Executive Committee took place in New York in October, with Mr. Robertson reporting that the cash balance on hand had reached the magnificent sum of $7,684.67. In the membership area, it was the sense of the meeting that clubs seeking admission should give evidence of a serious intention to foster figure skating by means of sessions at rinks, and that clubs should not be admitted for the sole purpose of sponsoring carnivals. The reconfirmation by the ASU of its agreement with the USFSA, under which the USFSA was recognized as the sole governing body of the sport was also reported.

The 1936 Olympic Winter Games marked the first major effort of the USFSA to send a full team abroad, with four Men, four Ladies and two Pairs being selected, plus a manager, an assistant manager and a chaperone, as well as one judge, Charles M. Rotch. As it turned out, the results were somewhat disappointing, being as follows: Men – 12th (Lee), 13th (Erle Reiter, Minneapolis) and 22nd (Hill), with James Madden, the fourth man not participating, due to a re-occurrence of the injury which had kept him out of the Trials, although he and his sister Grace did compete in the Pairs; Ladies – 5th (Vinson), 12th (Audrey Peppe, New York), 21st (Louise Weigel, Buffalo) and 22nd (Estelle Weigel, Buffalo); Pairs – 5th (Vinson-Hill) and 11th (Madden-Madden).

Mr. Rotch judged all three events, truly a Herculean task and not even permitted by the rules today, especially when it is considered that in Singles 12 figures were skated, 25 Men and 23 Ladies, plus 18 Pairs. The compulsory figures of just one Singles event took two days, all of it outdoors.

Open marking was used for the first time, which meant that the marks were displayed after each figure. While this speeded up the accounting process, the results were still not known for many hours after the end of the competition, since they were calculated by hand. This required multiplying each mark by the factor for the figure in question, then adding up the points earned for each judge, skater by skater; adding together the free skating marks and multiplying them by the appropriate factor, and adding that total to that for the figures, and finally applying placements or ordinals. Despite all this work and time, no computers would appear on the scene to do the job for another 35 years.

The titles went to Karl Schäfer, Austria, winning his second title; Sonja Henie, Norway, winning her third; and Maxi Herber and Ernst Baier, Germany, winning their first. Actually, the highest place by a North American in the Games was the fourth place in Men of Montgomery Wilson of Canada, with Baier gaining a surprising second.

It can only be conjectured, but it is conceivable, that the relatively poor showing of the North Americans was due in part to their having to skate out of doors, which was not their normal training medium, although all of them did some outdoor training for just that reason. This theory, however, is not supported by the results seen in the following World Championships held indoors at Paris, where a much reduced team participated, as is quite typical for the Worlds following an Olympics, even then. This time, there was only one U.S. Lady, Audrey Peppe, who placed 13th. In the Men, Lee placed 8th and Reiter 11th, while in Pairs, Vinson-Hill placed 5th and the Madden's 6th. Again the best place for a North American was the fourth place in Pairs of Louise Bertram and Stewart Reburn of Toronto. The Olympic champions all won their respective

World titles. Henie and Schäfer announced their intention to turn professional, after dominating the scene for 10 years in her case and seven in his, truly marking a watershed in the sport at the time and the opening of the door to the next generation.

Charles Rotch had the distinction of serving as an active official at the Olympic level while also serving as President of the USFSA, just as had his predecessor Henry Howe in 1928, Sherwin Badger as a competitor in 1932 and later Benjamin Wright as a referee in 1975. Mr. Rotch served one more year until 1937, when he stepped down and was succeeded by Joseph K. Savage of New York. He was not thereafter active in the Association, other than as a National judge, but continued to serve as President and Governor of The Skating Club of Boston until his death in 1964.

Joseph K. Savage

Another notable development in 1936 was the complete revision of the Dance events in the Nationals into a Single event, which was in effect a Silver Dance event: the four Dances were skated in two rounds, first one couple at a time in the initial round, with four finalists repeating them, skating in a final round flight of four, which was quite a judging problem.

Dance events had been held in the Nationals right from the beginning in 1914, with the Waltz and the Fourteenstep as separate and essentially informal competitions. The Waltz competition continued right up through 1935, except that in 1929 it was combined with the first Dance championship for an Original Dance. The Fourteenstep competition lasted until 1928 and was discontinued thereafter. The Dance championship for the Original Dance was retained from 1929 to 1934 in that form and the new event, with the Silver Dances, would be in effect until 1942. The first champions in 1936 were Marjorie Parker and Joseph Savage of New York. It is interesting that Savage was the runner-up in the Dance with three different partners: Parker in 1937, Katherine Durbrow in 1938, and with Nettie Prantel in 1939, the latter two years when he was also President.

The 1936 Governing Council meeting was held at the Hotel Madison in New York City, with 31 clubs represented, seven of them by proxies, the largest attendance to date. There were eight clubs not represented, which gives an idea of the growth of the Association up to that time. The passing of 33 tests by 270 candidates during the year were reported and the number of subscribers to the magazine was said to be 1,969, up from 1,450 the prior year. With respect to membership, the concept of the "probationary" member club for one year was introduced, with such clubs lacking only a vote in the annual meeting but being able to enjoy all the rights and privileges of a full member club. A clarification was also announced that amateurs could not skate in carnivals in which there was a preponderance of professionals or which were controlled by them or rink managers. But they could skate in carnivals with professionals controlled by a member club. There would be much fine tuning of this rule over the years, with percentages being specified for permitted and non-permitted participation (such as one professional to four amateurs and the like, but not one on one, a pair, for example). All of this seems silly to us today, but it was not then, with the ideal of the strict amateur being very much the policy at the time.

The 1936 Fall Meeting of the Executive Committee was held in New York City, as usual, at the Bar Association in October. The famous cash balance was reported as $7,261.48 and the deficit of Skating magazine, believe it or not, as $22, but "not including the magazine's share of the joint office expense" (with The SC of Boston). One interesting item reported by the Professionals Committee (Mrs. Blanchard) was that a central bureau of information on professionals had been established and that 325 professionals were listed on the Committee's records. The report also stressed the necessity of offering guarantees of salary as a basis for hiring professionals, which was indeed a standard practice by clubs until well after World War II. Another decision was to use the open system of marking at the Nationals and North Americans.

The arrival on the scene in 1936 of Sonja Henie as a professional and her impact upon the American public is a well known story not directly involving the USFSA, except to the extent that she popularized the sport and the impetus that she gave to the touring ice shows, which would soon supersede the traditional form of club carnival. There was one footnote to her arrival worth mentioning. The Boston carnival was specially revived for an additional performance two weeks after its closing to serve as a vehicle for her professional debut in the United States, together with Jack Dunn of Great Britain, an excellent free skater, who had placed sixth in the 1936 Olympics.

Karl Schäfer delayed his American debut as a professional until 1937, when he starred in a touring show with Maribel Vinson called "Gay Blades," with a cast which included Guy Owen of Ottawa (subsequently Maribel's husband), Fran Claudet, also from Ottawa, and Freddy Mesot of Belgium, as well as the comedian, Freddy Trenkler. This show can be considered as the forerunner of the "Ice Capades," a touring show initiated in 1940 by a group of the major rink owners in the Eastern part of the United States.

It was also in 1936 that "Ice Follies" started its run, under the leadership of Eddie Shipstad and Oscar Johnson of St. Paul, Minn., with Roy Shipstad, Eddie's younger brother as the star. These two shows, together with "Holiday on Ice," founded by Morris Chalfen of Minneapolis, and the "Sonja Henie Ice Review," operated on her behalf by Arthur Wirtz of Chicago dominated the ice show business in the United States for the next 25 years. Many of the retiring USFSA champions found employment in them after their competitive careers were over.

Thus an entire new era in skating was launched, which despite the hiatus of World War II would set the pattern for years to come.

The summer of 1936 saw some new and rather fundamental initiatives, as summer skating, begun at Lake Placid on a formal basis following the Olympic Games of 1932, had grown almost exponentially! The originator of the program had been H.L. "Jack" Garren, who had been the builder and later the manager of the Olympic Arena. Lake Placid was then and remains today

Consolidation and Growth
(1937-1941)

one of the leading centers for summer skating in the United States.

The first such initiative was the holding of a Judges' School at Lake Placid, the first ever organized in the country. It was held for two days in July 1936 and covered the figures and free skating comprehensively, just as is done in the many schools held today. It was, however, a distinct novelty then. The school also included instruction on open marking, which as we have seen had been adopted by the IEV in 1936 and was introduced into North America in 1937. The school was conducted by Mrs. Blanchard and Dick Hapgood of Boston and Joel Liberman of New York, under the supervision of Charles Rotch, then the Chairman of the Judges and Judging Committee of the Association. Unfortunately, the report on the school does not mention how many were in attendance, but it must have been a sizable number as four separate groups are mentioned as being required for the on-ice instruction in figures!

The second initiative had to do with Dance and was made by Maribel Vinson, who, although not a Dance competitor herself, had been appointed the first Chairman of the Dance Committee in 1936, and really deserves the credit for the revision of the rules for competition in dance and the subsequent establishment of standard tests. She also organized at Lake Placid a Dance Conference in August 1936, at which the four then standard Dances were demonstrated, followed by an informal competition in them, which attracted 22 couples. Thus was born the annual Lake Placid Summer Dance Competition, which has continued to today. It is worthwhile to quote from Maribel's conclusions as contained in her report:

"As for the dancing itself, much of it was good, but we found certain fundamental mistakes very common. First of all, American ice dancers, even the best ones, do not hold their partners correctly. The ladies are as much at fault as the men. They either have a careless, sloppy hold for their left arm, or bend their right too much, or else pull away from their partners. Correct position is the basic requisite for ice dancing." Sound familiar?

Maribel herself would remain in competition for one more season, and finally won the 1937 North American Ladies title in Boston, although she lost the Pair title with George Hill to the new young, strong pair from Toronto, Veronica Clarke and Ralph McCreath, fine representatives of the next generation, which can be considered the third from the start of the Association. In the Ladies, the other five competitors were all of the "new" guard, with Veronica Clarke placing an unexpected second, while McCreath was third in the Men, in which Montgomery Wilson won his fifth straight title, as we have seen, over Roger Turner.

Harry E. Radix

The 1937 Nationals were held in Chicago at the invitation of the Chicago FSC and its President Harry E. Radix, which was another "first" – the first time the National Championships were held away from the Atlantic seaboard, as it is described in the report, which goes on to say that there were a record number of entries, and notes the participation of a contingent from the Pacific Coast, who, for the first time, made their presence felt, placing second in the Junior Men, with Eugene Turner of Los Angeles, and winning the Novice Men with Robert Scott of Oakland. The latter was the first National title won by a representative from the Pacific Coast, the forerunner of many more in the future. Maribel won her ninth Ladies title, her sixth Pair title with Hill, while Robin Lee won his third Men's title.

The season of 1937 marked the end of Maribel's competitive career. After but one season in a touring show she turned to a teaching career, first in St. Paul and then subsequently in Berkeley, California, and Boston, until her most untimely death in the air accident in 1961, which also took the lives of her two daughters, for whom she was also the coach. She was one of the founders of the Professional Skaters Guild of America (PSGA), and in her relatively short life, earned great respect as a skater and teacher. Her three definitive books of instruction are now collectors' items and are still as valid today as they were when written. Vinson was elected to the United States Figure Skating Hall of Fame in 1976.

As footnotes to the championships, it can be noted that the Junior Pairs event was won by Ardelle Kloss and Roland Janson of New York. Ardelle would later be one of the leading World Championship judges for the United States, while Janson would serve as the first Executive Secretary of the USFSA from 1947 to 1949.

Harry Radix was a longtime benefactor of the sport and donated two trophies for the Dance championship of the United States, the second of which, still in competition today, is of gold. He also donated the famous "Radix pins," presented to the place winners at the Nationals, Olympics and World Championships, for which he provided in his will in perpetuity. Harry was an Olympic Team Manager in 1952 and 1956 and served on the Executive Committee of the Association from 1935 to 1965.

For his very special contributions to the sport, he was elected an Honorary Member of the USFSA in 1963, one of only four persons so honored other than the past Presidents. He passed away in 1965.

The 1937 Governing Council meeting was held at the Hotel Madison in New York City in early May. President Rotch was not present due to illness and Vice President Savage conducted the meeting. There were 25 clubs represented. The cash balance remained steady at $7,030.82. Reported was the passing of 414 tests by 346 candidates. The Amateur Status Committee, which was still in charge of issuing carnival and exhibition sanctions, reported that more than 100 had been issued, covering many hundreds of skaters. The magazine was reported as having about 2,300 subscribers, an increase of 300 over the prior year. An amendment was proposed to the Constitution and By Laws, deleting the provision permitting a mail vote (of the delegates to the Governing Council representing the clubs, who actually were appointed and served for one year) for the making of amendments. The concept of a rotation of the membership of the Executive Committee was discussed, with a formal plan to be submitted at the next meeting, which would provide for three-year terms for the at-large members. A proposal to raise dues was defeated. It was at this meeting that the Carnival and Exhibition Sanctions Committee was created, with the Association Secretary as the chairman, and consisting of the members of the Amateur Status Committee as members, with the responsibility "to sanction, fix dates of carnivals, schedules and to make all arrangements in connection thereto." It was also at this meeting that President Rotch retired from office and was succeeded by Joseph K. Savage of New York.

The 1937 Fall meeting of the Executive Committee was held at New York in October. Now the cash balance had reached its highest size ever, $11,746.55. Despite this largesse in hand, the question still was raised of gaining additional revenue by assessing clubs on the basis of their membership, rather than by taxing carnival revenue, which had been the principal source of revenue. No action was taken, but the issue of raising additional revenue would remain an ongoing topic of discussion, and this time was referred to a Ways and Means Committee to study, of which former President Sherwin Badger was the chairman. The Amateur Status rules were further tightened to disqualify as amateur persons receiving compensation for services performed at a rink, including coaching, instructing or exhibiting and, if no compensation was received, the disqualification was for the duration of the activity and 90 days thereafter. This was the basis for the subsequent definition of a "temporarily restricted amateur." The same restriction was also to be applied to persons acting as designers or salesmen of skates, clothing or other sporting goods. The meeting also changed the carnival assessment to be either 10 percent of the net profit or 2 percent of the gross receipts after taxes, whichever was greater.

Just a month later, at the end of November 1937, a special meeting of the Executive Committee was convened at the clubroom in Iceland of the Skating Club, New York. Among the matters considered was the matter of appointing an Executive Secretary or an Assistant Secretary, with a search to be made for a suitable candidate, the need for "paid assistance to relieve the officers and committees of routine work" being recognized.

In 1938, as a result of the original initiative of Maribel Vinson, a single USFSA Dance Test was adopted, consisting of the four standard dances, Waltz, Fourteenstep, Tango and Foxtrot, with the provision that for the Waltz, the Continental (now American), Reverse and Three-Lobed Eight Waltz would be skated, in effect, six dances in all. The passing of the test was required for those seeking to enter the National Dance Championship. The scale of marks to be used was on the basis of zero to 10, with a passing mark of six in each dance from each judge being required, divided on a minimum of three between accurate timing and performance.

Because of the great interest in the new test and the numbers of couples taking it, the Single test was quickly expanded in November 1939 into three tests; a Bronze Dance Test to be effective immediately, consisting of two dances, the Continental Waltz and the Fourteenstep, the retention of the existing Silver Dance Test, and a new Gold Test, to be effective with the 1940-1941 season, to include the Blues, Kilian, Viennese Waltz, Rocker Foxtrot and Three-Lobed Waltz. All three tests were to be judged on the same basis as the original test, this time with a passing mark for the Bronze of six, for the Silver of seven, and for the Gold of eight (out of 10).

In 1938, it can be said that the new generation took over, with so much promise, as would be demonstrated for two years, only to be abruptly cut off by the War. Truly a "lost" generation skating-wise.

In the 1938 Nationals, held at the new rink in Ardmore, Pa., of the Philadelphia Skating Club and Humane Society, with Maribel Vinson having retired and gone on to the touring show with her future husband, Guy Owen and Karl Schäfer, the Ladies title went, somewhat unexpectedly, to Joan Tozzer of Boston, primarily by reason of her outstanding compulsory figures, defeating Audrey

Joan Tozzer and Bernard Fox

Peppe of New York, second, her teammate, Polly Blodgett, third, the 1937 runner-up, and Jane Vaughn of Philadelphia, fourth. The "swing" judge this time was Egbert Cary, Jr. of Philadelphia, himself a National Junior champion in 1924, who voted for Joan over Audrey and placed Jane second. Joan also won the Pairs event with Bernard Fox, defeating Grace and Jim Madden. In the Juniors, it should be noted that Eugene Turner of Los Angeles won the Men, while in the Novice, the two winners were Gretchen Merrill of Boston and Arthur

Vaughn, Jr. of Philadelphia, the brother of Jane, all of whom would later be Senior Champions. The 1938 Nationals was the largest up to that time, within excess of 84 entries, with the two Novice singles events alone drawing 20 entries each.

The 1936-1937 season also saw the return of foreign skaters to North America touring the carnival circuit in both the United States and Canada. Cecilia Colledge of Great Britain, the 1937 World Ladies champion, toured Canada but did not come to the United States, while Karl Schäfer, the two-time Olympic Champion and seven-time World champion and Melitta Brunner, both from Austria, made the tour in the United States as professionals. The major club carnivals during the three years 1937-1939 were generally held in the major arenas in the cities of the clubs to full houses. In fact, the success of its carnival during the period was a major factor in the decision of The SC of Boston to build its own rink in 1938, only the second in the country after Philadelphia.

In 1938, the visitors were Felix Kaspar of Austria, the World champion for 1937 and 1938 and Hedy Stenuf, formerly of Austria. Kaspar was an incredible free skater, with the highest and longest jumps ever seen up to then. There is little doubt in the minds of those who saw him that had the technique then been known, he probably could have easily performed triple or even quadruple jumps! His famous Flying Axel Paulsen jump was usually more than four feet in the air and 25 feet long from the take off to landing! Typically, Kaspar had no set program, usually skating to a medley of Viennese Waltzes, as had Schäfer, making it up as he went along. There is a famous story about an occasion at a competition when his record was left on a radiator and melted, to which he said, "no problem, just put on a Waltz and I will be fine," or words to that effect.

Kaspar left Austria after the German take over in 1938, emigrating to Australia, where he remained as a coach during the War before moving onto the United States. He was a coach in this country for many years thereafter in Hershey, Minneapolis and Boston, among other places, and, lastly, in California, before retiring to Florida. He is today (1996) the senior living former World champion while Cecilia Colledge holds that honor among the Ladies.

The 1938 Governing Council meeting was held at the Hotel Lincoln in New York in April. The untimely death of Gillis Grafström of Sweden, at the early age of 45, was noted. He had been a three-time Olympic and World champion and was well remembered for his visit to the United States in 1932 when he earned his fourth medal, a Silver, in the Lake Placid Olympics and appeared in the subsequent club carnivals. The meeting was attended by the representatives of 25 clubs, with the cash balance having dropped back to $8,755.56. Magazine subscriptions were described as "about" 3,000, up 500 from the prior year, and that there would be a "profit" for the year, excluding its share of office expense. There were 34 carnivals and 71 exhibitions sanctioned covering more than 150 skaters. There were 582 tests passed by 486 candidates, showing the "upward" curve of activity which would characterize the growth of the Association over the next years.

The meeting also approved replacing the 24 members of the Executive Committee (all elected at the same time for a one-year term), with 15 members at large, elected in rotation in groups of five for three-year terms, with the officers and standing committee chairmen, who now became voting members of the Committee, being elected and appointed for one-year terms. The at-large group of 15 would remain that size until 1949. The "wrinkle" in the revision was that a member was not eligible for one year to be reelected after the end of a three-year term. The Carnival and Exhibition Sanctions Committee became a standing committee.

Eligibility for Novice and Junior events at Nationals was revised to provide that no entry would be accepted for the Novice class of any skater who had passed the Fifth Test and that no entry would be accepted for the Junior class of any skater who had not passed the Fifth Test, as it was rather clumsily stated in the rule.

For the first time, a special meeting of the Executive Committee following the Governing Council meeting was reported. This meeting would in due course precede the Governing Council meeting and would become a major one for making new rules and in preparing for the next season, which in those days involved the awarding of the next major competitions. This time the 1939 Nationals went to St. Paul. Among the bidders was the St. Moritz ISC of Berkeley, Calif.; the New Haven SC; the Hershey FSC and the Cleveland SC. Thus can be seen the first sign of very active interest and competition for the holding of the Nationals, which would later rotate between the Sections and would be the subject of spirited bidding right up to today. The meeting also approved the hiring of an Executive Secretary, but no action on that score would actually be taken until after World War II!

In 1939, the Nationals were held at Saint Paul, Minn., with Robin Lee winning his fifth straight Senior Men's title. Joan Tozzer retained her Ladies in almost a carbon copy of the 1938 result, with Mr. Cary of Philadelphia once again the key to victory. She and Fox retained their Pair title, while Vaughn and Merrill both moved up to take the Junior titles, in historic back to back wins in consecutive years of the Novice and Junior events. Bernard Fox had done it in 1935 and 1936, but this was the first time it was done in both Men and Ladies. Sandy McDonald and Harold Hartshorne of New York won what would be the first of three titles in Dance.

In the 1939 North Americans at Toronto, Montgomery Wilson of Canada won his sixth straight title, as the last "survivor" of the previous

Four Lady Champions – Suzanne King, Joan Tozzer, Maribel Owen, and Tee Blanchard.

generation, with Mary Rose Thacker from Winnipeg the unexpected winner of the ladies over Tozzer, but the latter with Fox won the Pairs over Ralph McCreath of Canada, the defender from two years before, but with a new partner, Norah McCarthy.

There has been endless speculation ever since as to what these skaters could or would have done in the World championships of that year, for none of the North American winners journeyed to the Worlds. The Ladies were contacted in Prague less than a week later, and the Men and Pairs in Budapest another week after that. The only American representative at the Worlds was Hedy Stenuf, who had continued to train in her native

Harold Hartshorne and Sandy McDonald

Austria and placed second behind two-time champion Megan Taylor of Great Britain, in the absence of the injured Cecilia Colledge, with Daphne Walker of Great Britain third. In the Men, Graham Sharp and Freddy Tomlins of Great Britain placed first and second, so that the British took four of the six medals in the two Singles events!

Mary Rose Thacker of Canada, who would win a second North American Ladies title in 1941 remains a virtual unknown today, and yet she and Tozzer were two of the finest exponents of the compulsory figures of their day or of any other day, for that matter, and would no doubt have done very well against Colledge and Taylor had they ever had the opportunity to compete against them.

There was a curious result in the Fours competition, with the North American title going to one Canadian Four and the Connaught Cup to the second place Canadian Four, because the deed of the gift of the Cup required that all members of a winning Four be from the same club. In the case of the winners, the Caley sisters, Dorothy and Hazel, were from The Granite Club of Toronto, while Ralph McCreath and Montgomery Wilson were from the Toronto Skating Club. The Cup winning Four consisted of Gillian Watson, Ruth Hall, Sandy McKechnie and Donald Gilchrist, all from the Toronto SC. The U.S. Four from New York was third.

Montgomery Wilson of Canada retired from competition after the North Americans in 1939 and shortly thereafter commenced a teaching career in Saint Paul, where his first pupil was Mary Louise Premer. After service in World War II in the U.S. Army, in which he earned a Bronze Star, he returned to Saint Paul in 1945. Shortly thereafter, he went to Boston in 1946, with summer skating in East Lansing, Mich., where he remained as one of the leading coaches of skating in the country until his own untimely death in 1964. Wilson was elected to the World Figure Skating Hall of Fame in 1976.

In the usual foreign tour of the club carnivals in 1939, the visitors were Freddy Tomlins and Daphne Walker of Great Britain. Tomlins had also been an excellent speed skater and was another strong free skater. Using the spinning style of jumping, with the feet close together, which was the characteristic technique of the British skaters, he traveled long and far in the air, but not very high, unlike Kaspar, but his double salchow jump was measured at more than 18 feet from the take off to landing. Sadly, Freddy, who served in the Royal Air Force, was lost in the War, actually the highest ranking skater to lose his life in that conflict.

The 1939 Governing Council meeting was held at New York at the Hotel Lincoln in April, with 25 clubs represented. Noted was the death of the Honorary President Irving Brokaw. President Savage reported that the most important matters to be settled during the coming year were the reduction of expenses, the increase of income and in magazine circulation, the providing of instruction and means of qualifying new judges, and the 1940 Olympics. The Treasurer reported that income and expenditures for the past year were "about even" and the cash balance was $8,794.15, so that the financial position of the Association was about the same as at the end of the prior year. It was reported that 789 tests had been passed by 654 candidates and that sanctions had been issued for 50 carnivals and 60 exhibitions involving more than 235 skaters. Also noted was the issuance of 10 sanctions for competitions, including the Sectionals and the Nationals. At that time, there were only a few of what we call today "non-qualifying" competitions, such as the Middle Atlantics, the Philadelphia District, the Lake Placid Summer competitions and a few state championships. The increase in new member clubs was reported as 16, so there was a total of 71, including those on a probationary status. It was also agreed that in the processing of applications for probationary membership that it was "advisable to study the financial and other relations between a club and a rink, in order to ascertain whether a club is controlled or dominated by a rink." The magazine subscriptions had increased by about 1,100 over the prior year, as compared with 400 and 480, respectively, for the prior two years. There were also more than 500 professionals on file and the Professionals Committee was continuing to assist clubs and professionals to get "together on work."

For the first time the amount of an operating budget was reported in the amount of $6,740, excluding any Olympic-related expenses.

In the area of competitions, the question of criticism of the marks of judges in competitions by skaters, their professionals and others were considered. As a result, a resolution was passed to the effect that the "clubs are requested to take necessary steps to prevent and stop criticism by their professionals in connection with competitions!" The requirement of citizenship to enter competitions was reconfirmed with respect to the North Americans at the request of Canada. There already were some foreign skaters in the United States who wished to compete, the best known being Hedy Stenuf of Austria, who would enter the 1940 Nationals, under the then USFSA rule of citizenship or residence in the U.S. for one year. A special meeting of the Executive Committee was held after the Governing Council meeting for the purpose of awarding the 1940 Nationals. The principal question was whether or not all the events should be held together, rather than split, as they had been in 1932 and 1936. The decision was to hold them together and the sponsoring club selected at the Fall Meeting was the Cleveland SC.

The Fall 1939 meeting of the Executive Committee was held in New York City at The Skating Club, Inc., New York, as it was called then, in early November. The Treasurer reported the cash balance as $10,663.80 and also that the Association showed a "profit" for the year of "about" $900 in its operations. For the magazine, a profit was reported of $1,000, as compared to $550 the prior year. Also reported was the move to 1 Telford Street and the hiring of a managing editor (Winfield A. Hird). Without the late summer test results being included, the passing of 242 figure tests and 103 dances were reported. The expansion of the dance tests into three categories (Bronze, Silver and Gold) was also reported.

There was a "footnote" to the relations with the ASU concerning friction between figure skating clubs and speed skating organizations. Mr. Savage, who was former President of the ASU, reported that body had "rescinded the resolution previously passed which provided for the formation of figure skating clubs by speed skating organizations." It was yet another evidence of the fact that the ASU was not content to leave figure skating matters entirely to the USFSA! Such "organizations" were usually regional or state associations, which formed the membership of the ASU rather than individual clubs. As a means of fostering greater cooperation, Mr. Savage proposed that member clubs permit their skaters to give exhibitions at duly sanctioned race meets.

The curious idea of a touring USFSA show, ostensibly to assist local clubs, was debated, but no action was taken. The majority of the Executive Committee was of the opinion that a touring show was not feasible, and the idea was dropped. Certainly, that remains true today, unless there is an energetic independent promoter who is willing to run such a tour, as is done with such great success by Tom Collins with his Tour of World Champions. The carnival assessment fee was revised to be just 2 percent of the gross receipts from the sale of tickets, after deduction of Federal and state ticket taxes. Also clarified was that a professional could skate with an amateur in a Pair, Trio or Four in the case of accident, illness or other emergency.

The 1940 Olympic Winter Games had been assigned to Japan, and no trials were contemplated, so a 1940 Olympic team had been selected in April 1939, on the basis of the results of the 1939 Nationals, although by the fall, with the start of World War II, the majority of the Figure Skating Committee of the AOA had voted against sending a team to the 1940 Games, wherever held. The members of this "lost" team, like that of the United States for the 1980

Summer Games in Moscow, are just as much Olympians as those fortunate enough actually to compete in the Games, having earned that right, but never having that honor. The team consisted of Robin Lee of Saint Paul and Oliver Haupt, Jr. of Saint Louis, in the Men; Joan Tozzer of Boston and Audrey Peppe of New York, in the Ladies; and Joan Tozzer and Bernard Fox from Boston, in the Pairs. A judge was also to be sent but was never selected, nor were any team managers.

With the start of the War in Europe in September 1939, the European-based IEV, as it had also in 1914 upon the start of World War I, completely shut down. There would be no World or European Championships for seven long years until 1947, and the Olympic Winter Games of 1940 and 1944 were also canceled.

Heaton R. Robertson

Canada was in the War in 1939, but the United States did not enter the conflict until two years later in December 1941, so efforts were made to keep skating going, including the regular competition schedule. In that connection, there was also a change in the leadership of the Association in 1940, when Joseph Savage of New York stepped down and was succeeded by Heaton R. Robertson of New Haven, Conn.

Savage had a very distinguished career in the sport, both as an administrator and skater, with the presidencies of two governing bodies and National Championships in Dance and Fours to his credit. He continued an active career as a committee chairman, a referee and judge in later years and he actually stepped directly from the chair to the chairmanship of the Competitions and Rules Committee, in which position he served for the entire War, until 1945. To a large measure, he was responsible for the continuance of active competition in the country during that period. He also served as Chairman of the Amateur Status Committee from 1945 to 1948 and as Chairman of the Judges and Judging Committee from 1950 to 1951. It was not uncommon in those days for the Past Presidents to be put right back to work in committee assignments after their terms of office and many of them served with distinction in such capacities. Today, there is a tendency to ignore this reservoir of knowledge and experience and to regard them as retired, once they have completed their terms of office. Savage ultimately passed away in 1956.

The 1940 Nationals were held in Cleveland, Ohio, at the Cleveland Skating Club, another member club which had built its own rink. Despite the War, this was also a large championship with 91 entries, including 25 in Novice Ladies. The major story of the competition was in Senior Ladies and Pairs, with the return to the United States and the entry of Hedy Stenuf in both events, with Lloyd "Skippy" Baxter as her partner in the Pairs, both representing the Chicago FSC. Hedy was originally from Austria and had visited the United States with Karl Schäfer in 1934. By 1936, she was representing France, and placed sixth in the European Championships of that year. In

1937, still representing France, she was fourth in both the Europeans and Worlds. In 1938, now representing the U.S., she was the Bronze medalist in the Worlds at Stockholm, behind Megan Taylor and Cecilia Colledge of Great Britain. In 1939, she was the Silver medalist in the Worlds at Prague behind Taylor. Actually she was the only U.S. entry in the Worlds of 1938 and 1939.

The competition between Hedy and defending champion Joan Tozzer was a classic confrontation of styles, but the figures still "ruled" and it was Joan's superiority in that discipline which still then accounted for two-thirds of the total score, that earned her a narrow victory, by three judges to two. In the Pairs, Joan and Bernard Fox retained their title more easily over Stenuf and Baxter, four judges to one. In the Men, it was Ollie Haupt and Baxter against

Hedy Stenuf and "Skippy" Baxter

Eugene Turner of Los Angeles. Haupt was a dynamic free skater, while Baxter was an incredible jumper, and actually is known to have performed in practice during his career some of the triples, but the new Men's Champion, Robin Lee having retired, was Turner, winning the first Senior National title for the Pacific Coast, with Haupt, second and Baxter, third. The elements of program and choreography versus strong athletic ability came in to play in both events and made the decisions of the judges that much more difficult. The ultimate results were a source of controversy for some years thereafter.

Eugene Turner

Another National title that moved west for the first time was Fours, which had not been held between 1935 and 1939, with the New York Four of Nettie Prantel, Marjorie Parker, Joseph Savage and George Boltres having won in that year. The new champion Four was from the Saint Paul FSC, known as the first Saint Paul Four, led by Lyman Wakefield, Jr., Janette Ahrens, Mary Louise Premer and Robert Uppgren, all four of whom would have distinguished careers in the future, Lyman as an Association officer and World judge, Mary Louise as a National and World judge for more than 50 years, and Janette and Bob, National medalists as a Senior Pair and she in Senior Singles. Another winner in 1940 was Ramona Allen of Oakland in the Junior Ladies, who would also serve as a National and World judge for more than 50 years.

One pair that was not able to compete in the 1940 Nationals was Betty Lee Bennett and John Kinney from Seattle, who were the National Junior Pair champions in 1939. They were suspended for six months for skating in unsanctioned carnivals at Seattle and Yakima, Wash., after sanctions had been denied to them by the local sanctions officer. The suspensions, while only for six months at the most, were long enough to keep them out of the Nationals. They never did return to amateur competition, demonstrating the practical severity of such actions which have been very rare in the Association's history.

First Saint Paul Four – Robert Uppgren, Janette Ahrens, Mary Louise Premer and Lyman E. Wakefield, Jr.

The 1940 Governing Council meeting was held at New York in April, with the Executive Committee meeting following. There were 45 clubs represented, including four probationary, which could have delegates present, but did not have a vote. One action taken by the meeting was to authorize the annual publication of an Association Yearbook, which would include in one volume such items as the current list of judges, Association officials, committee lists, member clubs, and minutes of the Governing Council and Executive Committee meetings. The first yearbook appeared in December 1940, and there were three issues published, but the publication died in the War in 1944 and was never revived after the War. Much of what was in it (except for the minutes) can be found today in the annual Directory.

It was reported that the "cash balance" (the favorite measure of success then, as we have seen) was $12,690, with revenues of $11,705 and expenses of $7,490, with most of the latter being the cost of producing the magazine. This rather rudimentary measure does give some idea of the size of the Association at the time. There was a revision to the eligibility requirements for the Sectional and National Championships: Sectional Juniors are those who have passed the fourth and not the sixth test, and Novices those who have passed the second but not the fourth test. For the Nationals, the requirement for Juniors was to have passed the sixth test and for Novices to have passed the fourth test. Also applied to the National Junior was the limitation that only the top eight in figures would free skate, a rule which had applied to the National Novice since 1939.

The Executive Committee, at its meeting following the Governing Council, acted only upon the awarding of the 1941 Nationals and North Americans, with the former going to Boston and the latter to Philadelphia, provided the holding of the champion was acceptable to the CFSA, which was, of course, already a combatant in the War, which the U.S. had not yet entered. The California clubs and Boston were the bidders for the Nationals, while Philadelphia, New York, Chicago and Lake Placid were the bidders for the North Americans. It was at this meeting that the recommendation was made that the 1942 Nationals go to the Pacific Coast, but (as we shall see), the War intervened.

A very rare, special meeting of the Governing Council was held in mid-July 1940 in New York, at which 23 clubs were represented. The sole action taken was to amend the object's clause of the Constitution, with the key language being added "generally to take all steps necessary to regulate Figure Skating throughout the United States...provided that none of the income of the Association enures to the private profit of any of its constituent member clubs, the members thereof, or any of its individual members." This amendment reflected the requirements of the Internal Revenue Service for the initial recognition by it of the Association as a nonprofit organization.

The fall 1940 meeting of the Executive Committee was held at New York, and took another corollary action to that relating to the Yearbook, which was to authorize the annual publication of an Association Rulebook, which would combine in one volume all the rules hitherto published separately in small booklets of varying sizes and shapes! The first rulebook appeared in January 1941, and has been published annually ever since, except between the years 1971 and 1979, when the rulebook was published only every two years with a supplement, again much like the current Directory, being published in the year in between.

The 1940-1941 season can be considered as the last "normal" one for the skaters of the United States, before the country was plunged into the global conflict following Pearl Harbor. The Sectionals were held as usual, with good entries, and the Nationals were held at the SC of Boston, which has a seating capacity of no more than 1,100, yet were a very successful Championships. The ice was painted a pale green, the better to see the figures, one of the first times that technique was used at a major championship, and there were no hockey lines. Eugene Turner returned to defend his Senior Men's title, but he was also entered in the Pairs with Donna Atwood, who was also in Junior Ladies. Turner entered Dance with Elizabeth Kennedy. Although the Philadelphia Skating Club and Humane Society with Jane and Buddy Vaughn and Bill Grimditch won the Harned Trophy for the club earning the most points, in effect the "team" championship, which had been first presented by Bedell H. Harned of New York, a former USFSA officer, in 1939, the Los Angeles FSC was a solid third behind the Skating Club, New York, strictly as a result of the efforts of Gene and company!

Not only did Gene retain his title over Vaughn, but he and Atwood also won the Senior Pairs and Donna herself won the Junior Ladies, while Gene and his dance partner Elizabeth Kennedy almost made it a "triple" by placing a close second to the defending champions in the Dance, Sandy McDonald and Harold Hartshorne of New York. One of the sensations of the competition was the free skating of Bill Grimditch, who won the Junior men. His performance was so outstanding that he was added to the team for the following North American Championships in his home rink in Ardmore, Pa., where he placed a very creditable third.

Jane Vaughn of Philadelphia won the Senior Ladies in a close competition with Gretchen Merrill of the host club, and her brother Arthur, or Buddy as he was known, was the runner-up to Turner. While the Men's events were down in numbers, there were 76 entries in the 1941 Nationals, with 14 in the Dance.

Surprisingly, despite their own participation in the War, the Canadians wanted to have the North American Championships continue, and they were accordingly held in Philadelphia. As the reporter of the event says in her report, "Never before in this great biennial event have we seen so many young skaters on each team. These youngsters kept up with the seasoned skaters and standards were high throughout." This was the "lost" generation, with one or two exceptions of skaters who persevered during the War and went to greatness afterwards. One of them was Barbara Ann Scott of Ottawa, then the Canadian Junior Ladies champion at the age of 14, who placed sixth. Another was Ramona Allen, the 1940 National Junior champion, who placed eighth.

The Men's event was the story of the Championships, an epic battle between Eugene Turner and Ralph McCreath of Toronto for the vacant title. At that time, the events were judged, as has been previously noted, by an even number of judges, three from each country. In this case, Turner built up a substantial lead over McCreath in the figures and the title seemed to be his. However, McCreath pulled out all the stops in the free skating and closed the gap to the point where there was an ordinal tie, three judges, obviously the Canadians, for McCreath and three judges, obviously the Americans, for Turner, so that the title had to be decided on total points, with McCreath the winner by 1575.8 to 1575.0. The event demonstrated the inherent problem with a two-nation competition and the natural bias that was inherent in the judging system used, which sadly would ultimately lead to the demise of this wonderful event in 1971. McCreath also won the Pairs with his new partner Eleanor O'Meara, defeating Atwood and Turner. Eleanor was also the runner-up in the Ladies to Mary Rose Thacker of Winnipeg, who retained her title.

The honor of the United States was successfully defended, however, by the Saint Paul Four, of Janette Ahrens, Mary Louise Premer, Robert Uppgren and Lyman Wakefield, Jr., which won the North American title and the Connaught Cup, by defeating the Toronto Four of Therese McCarthy, Virginia Wilson, Donald Gilchrist and Michael Kirby. It was the first ever success for an American Four over a Canadian Four for either the Championship or the Cup. Gilchrist would go on to a distinguished career in the CFSA, of which he was the President, as well as in the ISU, where he served on the Figure Skating Technical Committee and as a member of the Council, and as a World Championship Referee for many Worlds, European and Olympic Championships. He actually was the first Canadian elected to office in the ISU.

Following the competitions, the usual rounds of club carnivals went on in both countries, sort of a "last hurrah" before everyone went off to war. This time the stars were home grown with the Canadians and Americans crossing the border to skate in each other's shows.

The 1941 Governing Council meeting was held in New York at the new Weston Hotel, at which it would remain for the next several years, in April. For the first time, the spring meeting of the Executive Committee preceded the Governing Council meeting, as it has ever since. With the minutes being recorded in detail in the Yearbook, we can now see exactly the number of clubs represented. There were 32 with delegates present reflecting more than 3,600 members and another 35 represented by proxy, with more than 2,700 members, for a total of 67 clubs with more than 6,300 members. The new president, Heaton R. Robertson of New Haven was in the chair, and in his report cited such unfinished business as amendments to the Constitution, the matter of geographical representation on committees, the publication of additional booklets on carnival information, competition information and judges and judging, and the design of a suitable emblem (logo). Also mentioned was a "definite ruling of what is permissible in skating the repetition of the inside back take off, in order that judges may not be inclined to differ radically on this point!" This shows how important then the compulsory figures were in the activity of the Association.

The Treasurer's report recorded the balance on hand as $14,363.04, which was all in an account in a bank in New York, there being no investments as such in those days. The Association operated on a strict cash basis. Expenses were reported as $5,803.24 and income as $6,295.28. For the magazine, a balance sheet was submitted, which reflected net assets of $4,128.05, principally in cash and inventory of publications. A profit and loss statement was also provided, which showed total income of $10,866.22, expenses of $10,418.99 and a net income of $447.23. The income from subscriptions was $6,702.00 and from advertising $4,031.44.

The holding of the first Gold Dance tests in the summer of 1941 was proposed by the Dance Committee. There were some "housekeeping" amendments to the Constitution and By Laws, one of which was that the officers and committee chairmen would take office September 1, which created an awkward interregnum of several months following the Governing Council meeting. Eventually, the By Laws would be changed to provide for the new officers and committee chairmen to take office immediately following the conclusion of the Governing

Council meeting. Another amendment provided for the creation of Sectional Committees as standing committees, based upon the Sectional divisions of the country as determined for the purpose of competition. Although the Sectional Committees did not last, being discontinued in 1980, the geographical definition of the sections was added to the By Laws and therefore can only be changed by the Governing Council and not by the Competitions Committee, as was originally the case.

The Executive Committee, at its meeting before the Governing Council meeting worked primarily on the amendments to the Constitution and By Laws. At its meeting following Governing Council, the Committee awarded the 1942 Nationals to the St. Moritz ISC of Berkeley, Calif. The matter of the placement of the Sectional Championships was referred to the new Sectional Committees for action, a duty which those committees carried out in the future, and which, after the committees were abolished, the Vice Presidents, together with the Vice Chairmen of the Competitions Committee have been primarily responsible for.

The 1941 fall meeting of the Executive Committee was held at the New Weston in New York in October. Procedures covering internal accounting were approved, with respect to which, the treasurer asked that "all those to whom appropriations are voted keep a careful check on their expenditures so that they do not unwittingly exceed their appropriations." Certainly, in those trying times, the matter of fiscal responsibility and of living within one's income was very much in the minds of the financial officers.

It was also at this meeting that the change to a marking scale of zero to 10 was first proposed, along with the "modified open system" of marking, in which all the marks were displayed at the end of an event, rather than after each skater. Also approved was the appointment of a Summer Skating Committee, which was to formulate standards for the operation of summer sessions in exchange for the official cooperation of the USFSA. It is hard for us today to realize that summer sessions had to be officially sanctioned by the Association in order for them to be able to hold competitions and tests. The Summer Skating Committee was a special committee from 1941 to 1957 and a standing committee from 1957 to 1964, when it was finally discontinued.

As can be seen by all the meeting activity, the War was not an overriding factor in the operations of the Association, except for the lack of international competition, and that the concerned officers and committee chairmen were acting with their usual energy and dedication.

With the War at hand, which greatly affected skating around the world, perhaps it is also a good time to review the state of the sport in 1941, 20 years after the founding of the Association.

In just 20 short years, very rapid advances had been made, except possibly in Dance. There were improved skates, with a closed toe, white boots and short dresses for the Ladies, and the

The War Years
(1941-1945)

athletic technique in free skating had now reached an ability to handle double revolution jumps routinely, which were virtually unheard of in 1921. Pairs had increased in difficulty, with overhead lifts at full extension, such as the "Baier" (otherwise the Lasso) lift, beginning to be seen. Death spirals (backward outside only) were now a regular part of the programs, but there still was not much in the way of solo athletic difficulty done by the individual partners. Dance, on the other hand, being just about ready to enter the "Compulsory Dance" era, with new dances coming in from Great Britain primarily to be added to the original two dances of the Waltz and Fourteenstep, but was still in its rudimentary stages as a competitive discipline. Fours was still popular to a degree, but would soon die off, due to the difficulties of training and ice time. Figures, on the other hand, were probably at the highest level they would ever reach in the period of the late 1930's up to 1939, and the inevitable decline in them would soon begin after the War, which, of course, was matched by still further rapid advances in free skating athletic difficulty.

It is also useful at this point to look at the structure of the Association. When founded, there was no board of directors at all in the modern sense, just the then five officers (there were only two Vice Presidents). There were six standing (now permanent voting) committees only: Amateur Status, Publications, Records and Tests, all since discontinued, plus Competitions and Membership, still around today. In 1928, a Finance Committee was added, which for many years was responsible primarily for the budget. As the tests had become more popular and a greater number of judges were needed for that activity, rather than just for competitions, as had been the case in the beginning, a separate committee to administer the training, appointment and supervision of the judges was obviously needed. Mr. Henry Howe, a Past President, was the first chairman of the Judges Committee, while the first chairman of the Finance Committee was A. Winsor Weld, another Past President, which perhaps demonstrates the importance attached to these two new committees.

It was not until 1938 that the chairmen of the standing committees, by reason of that office, became voting members of the then Executive Committee, although they were then, and still are today, appointed by the President and not elected. This anomaly still exists. Actually, as previously noted, the Executive Committee itself was merely just another standing committee, and its chairman, of course, did preside over the fall meetings, rather than the President, although these regular meetings included the officers and committee chairmen. The Executive Committee did not really take on its role of being the "board of directors" until 1931, when the original provision of it having its own chairman was abolished, so that thereafter, the President presided over all meetings. Initially only five in number, the Executive Committee "grew" steadily, already being 10 in number by 1924 and 24 by 1937, all elected at large.

Finally, in 1938, the Executive Committee was restructured to include 15 at large members, elected in three rotating groups of five for three-year terms, with the provision that those elected were not eligible for re-election until after one year off. Those elected were not divided into groups by Sections. This revision came many years later (in 1971). The original idea of the at-large members was to serve as a "pool" or resource for future officers and committee chairmen, and to provide a special service or function as needed, but they were not selected on any geographical basis or distribution.

By 1941, the Treasurer still "proudly" reported only the cash balance at the end of the season as the measure of success, which in 1941 was $14,363.64. There were obviously no assets or savings, and the Association was run strictly out of a checking account. Figures for income and expense are few and far between for those early years! However, an idea of the size of the Association by 1941 can be obtained, with there having been a total of 91 clubs elected to membership by that year, reflecting an approximate total of 7,000 members, so we can extrapolate the numbers to a total active skating membership of around 10,000. The largest clubs were still those consisting of recreational skaters on outdoor rinks; Cambridge, Mass., Beaver Dam, N.Y., and Yosemite, Calif., with 400, 315 and 330 members respectively, while the strongest clubs were still Boston (listed as "over" 100), New York (262) and Philadelphia (300). There were, however, some newcomers to the strong ranks, notably St. Moritz ISC at 376 and Chicago at 210. Of the states at the 1941 annual meeting, there were 21 represented, with three from the Pacific Coast: California, Oregon and Washington.

Much of the above-mentioned information comes from the annual Yearbook, first published in 1940, with its companion publication, the Rulebook. Up to that time, other than for **Skating** magazine, there had been no national publications which contained the reports of the meetings and the committee lists, lists of clubs and the like, nor any compilation in one publication of the rules. Previously, small (3 x 5 inch) booklets had been issued for the major rules, such as for competitions and tests. These little booklets were of all different sizes, so a

Rulebook, which brought them all together into one was a vital need, yet it is surprising that it took so long to produce it. The Yearbook, on the other hand, while a good idea and now seen in a modern version called the "Directory," did not last for more than three seasons, due to poor sales during the War, after which its contents were incorporated into the Rulebook, and report books for the annual meetings of the Governing Council and Executive Committee began to be issued after the War. The Rulebook, on the other hand, has always been a "best seller" for the Association.

In general, the effects of the War on the sport were what one would expect, and with the War effort and rationing, obviously non-essential activities were curtailed. With the men at war, the sport was left to the ladies and the older folks primarily, a pattern still with us perhaps as a result of the conflict. Many rinks were closed, although the major ones in the larger urban centers seem to have survived. Skating was, after all, a good recreational activity for those on the homefront. What is surprising is the amount of competition that still took place. The Sectionals and Nationals were never canceled and continued right through the War, although there were no Senior Men's events at Nationals between 1944 and 1946. By way of contrast, the CFSA after 1942 continued National Junior and Novice events only, and the Senior events were canceled. In fact, the three Sectionals in the U.S. of 1942 held up remarkably well, for example: Easterns - 127 entries, Midwesterns - 59 entries; and Pacific Coast - also 59 entries. In the Easterns of that year there were 30 entries in the Novice Ladies alone, and the three Dance events totaled 43 entries. Of course, when the Men's Singles events are examined, the effect of the War can be seen: in Easterns - 21; Midwesterns - 15; and Pacific Coast - 10. On the other hand, there were Pairs and Dance events in all three Sectionals which also included Men. The judges in these competitions, which, with but a few exceptions, had been largely men in the past, were now composed more of women, a trend that has continued to today to the extent that men judges are now in a small minority on most competition judging panels. The same can be said for the referees, almost always men in the past, and now largely women. Of course, during the war some of the "senior citizen" men judges, of which there were a fair number, continued to serve.

It was in the 1941-1942 season that the first real impact of the War was felt, when it was necessary to transfer the 1942 National Championships from the Pacific Coast, where they would have been held for the first time, back to the Midwest. When reports were received that the parents of many possible competitors were unwilling to send their children to the Pacific Coast, due to the wartime conditions there, which included martial law and the forced evacuation by the Army of Japanese-American citizens to internment camps. The St. Moritz Ice Skating Club of Berkeley, Calif., which had originally been awarded the Championships, offered to give up the event in the interest of insuring that the Championships included entries from all parts of the United States and that the events would be of a truly championship caliber.

The St. Moritz club relinquished the Championships with the understanding that they would be the preferred choice for the 1943 event, if conditions permitted. It was not, however, until 1947 that the Championships finally reached the Pacific Coast at Berkeley, while the 1942 Championships were, through the efforts of Walter S. Powell of St. Louis, and his newly formed Midwestern Committee, transferred to the Chicago FSC. The "hysteria" was probably somewhat overblown, however, since the Pacific Coast Sectional Championships for 1942 were successfully held at Seattle without any significant diminution in the number of entries.

Doris Schubach and Walter Noffke

The 1942 Nationals were well attended, with 71 entries in nine events. The St. Paul Four had no competition and skated an exhibition. Jane Vaughn, now Mrs. Sullivan, of Philadelphia, successfully defended her title, again defeating Gretchen Merrill of Boston, while Bobby Specht of Superior, Wis., representing Chicago, became the new National Champion, Eugene Turner having gone off to war in the Air Corps. The Senior Pair event was won unexpectedly by the virtually unknown pair of Doris Schubach and Walter Noffke from Springfield, Mass., whose coach was Doris' father, Gustave Schubach, although they had indeed won the Junior title in the previous year and are one of the few pairs to accomplish the back to back Junior-Senior double. They defeated the more experienced pair of Janette Ahrens and Robert Uppgren of St. Paul. The Dance event for the first time went to a couple from Philadelphia, Edith Whetstone and Alfred Richards, who defeated the defending champions Sandy McDonald and Harold Hartshorne of New York. It was the beginning of the "youth" movement in Dance which would come to full flower after the War. Jane Sullivan's husband was a young lieutenant in the Army Air Corps, who was at the time of the Nationals stationed at his alma mater West Point, as an instructor.

Riggs Sullivan would go on to become a Major General in the Air Force, serving as Commandant of Cadets of the new Air Force Academy after service in heavy bombers during the War and in SHAEF and the Strategic Air Command after it. Bobby Specht entered the Air Corps and after the War went on to a long and distinguished career as the principle male star of Ice Capades, both as a Single and as a Pair with Donna Atwood.

Club carnival activity dwindled during the War. Yet the new touring professional ice shows kept going, perhaps because of their entertainment value to a general public dedicated to the war effort and suffering the constraints applied to their life styles as a result. It is remarkable, however, that summer skating continued to flourish, with such centers as Lake Placid, St. Paul, Sault Ste. Marie, Colorado Springs, Rochester (Minnesota) and two famous centers in Canada, Schumacher and Kitchener, Ontario, remaining open.

Two significant decisions were made which affected the 1941-1942 season. The first was the acceptance of **Skating** magazine as the official publication of the Roller Skating Rink Operators Association (RSROA), which while it was the trade association of the roller rink owners and operators, it was also the de facto national governing body of artistic roller figure skating in the United States. The magazines of that season reflect this relationship, with considerable roller coverage in them. In addition, USFSA officials served in the major roller championships. Unfortunately, the relationship did not last, due to the organization of a rival association, the Amateur Roller Skating Association (ARSA). With Joseph Savage as President, it obtained recognition from the Amateur Athletic Union (AAU) and sought to replace the RSROA as the national governing body. There was then no overall governing body to resolve the dispute, which continued for many years thereafter. The ARSA held National championships in 1942, and Edward LeMaire of New York, a former National Junior champion in Singles and Pairs on ice was proclaimed the National roller champion. The USFSA again assisted the new organization by providing judges, but the relationship with the RSROA in the magazine was discontinued, since the USFSA itself was also allied with the AAU. These were the days of the strict interpretation of amateur status, and the RSROA was a professional organization, although it must be said that in its administration of amateur roller skating, it served the best interests of the skaters, as can be demonstrated by the fact of the ultimate merger of the two rival bodies many years later into the United States Federation of Amateur Roller Skaters (USFARS) and the recognition of the latter by the international federation, the "Fédération Internationale de Patinage á Roulettes" (FIPR), now called the FIRS. Actually, the inclusion of roller news in the magazine for that one war time season was a positive thing for the Association. It is to be regretted that it was not continued, when the similarities between the two sports are recognized, as well as the later success of many roller skaters in competition on ice, right up to today.

The second decision to affect the 1941-1942 season was the change of the marks to be used in tests and competitions to a scale of 0 to 10 from the traditional international scale of 0 to 6. The larger scale of marks had already been implemented in the new schedule of Dance tests already adopted in 1939. The theory behind the change was to provide a greater range of marks for the use of the judges, thereby enabling them to make more accurate decisions. The old scale went back to the early days of the IEV, having been adopted in 1895, and was based on the triple repetition of compulsory figures. The adoption of the larger scale did not at the time have any significant effect on skating competition in the United States, especially with the IEV being completely shut down and there being no International Competitions, other than the North Americans. Although the CFSA also adopted the new scale of marks, the IEV scale was still used in the North Americans. The latter was judged on the "full" open system, with the marks being displayed after each performance, while in National and Sectional competitions, a modified open system was used, which involved the displaying of the marks only at the end of each part of an event.

As it turned out, the 0 to 10 scale of marks did not accomplish the purpose intended. Judges marked right up to the top of the larger scale in free skating especially, and did not use the full range of the marks, just as they do today! With the increased competition internationally that came after the War, the two North American skating countries became more and more "out of sync" with the rest of the world, especially their judges, and a return to the old scale of 0 to 6 was finally made in 1959. A "noble" experiment that was a failure!

The 1942 Governing Council meeting was held at the Hotel New Weston in New York in April, and was very well attended despite the War, with 34 clubs represented by delegates. It should be noted, however, that the delegates who traveled the furthest distance were Charles Peffers of the Oakland FSC and Howell Janes of the Glacier FSC, both in California. It probably took them five days to cross the continent in one direction, with five more on their return; so their dedication was outstanding. Of course, with the Nationals of 1942 having been transferred from the Pacific Coast, they were very interested in preserving the position of the Coast clubs for the future award of the championships, once the situation permitted it. The bulk of the California clubs (10) were represented by Janes as their proxy. There were 19 clubs in all represented by proxy. President Robertson spoke in his report of all of the new publications that had been issued and the improvement in the quality and financial situation of the magazine, and cites them as concrete evidence of the effort on the part of everyone concerned that they represented. Heaton goes on to say, "…years of work by this Association, though not in a field of very large numbers, has been guided only by the purest and most unselfish of motives, and so has created a lasting monument to fair sportsmanship, fair – mindedness and integrity. Our young skating people, quite over and above their health and their pleasure, have developed character; and the force, for example, amid bitter disappointment to take it – and come back again to win." Not bad thoughts for today!

Among the rule changes adopted, was the division of the National Dance championship into Junior and Senior divisions, the raising of the passing mark for the Eighth (Gold) Figure Test, a new rule barring the relatives of professionals from judging their pupils, and the approval of summer sessions, at which USFSA standards would be observed. The required standards were spelled out, one of which was the "assurance of good ice," and another was the availability of "recognized professional instructors" in sufficient numbers to handle the demand for lessons. Each session had to be sponsored by a member club! The sessions sanctioned were: Colorado Springs, Lake Placid, Rochester, Minn., Sault Ste. Marie, Mich., and St. Paul, Minn. The Executive Committee met before the Governing Council and recommended that, if at all possible, the 1943 Nationals should be held, but deferred action on their award until the Fall meeting. Offers to conduct the championships without being a bidder for them were received, but the feeling was that they should go to the Pacific Coast if possible.

At the Fall 1942 meeting of the Executive Committee, held at the New Weston in New York, the 1943 Nationals were awarded to The Skating Club, New York. A decision was made to limit the qualifiers for the Novice Singles to those placing first, second or third in the Sectionals. The three Sectional championships were all awarded, the Easterns to New Haven, the Midwesterns to Cleveland and the Pacific Coasts to Berkeley. Unfortunately, the North Americans would not be held, with the CFSA deciding not to hold them due to the wartime conditions. Resignations from the Executive Committee were received from William Wardman of Colorado Springs and John J. Allen, Jr. of Oakland, due to their being in military service, Wardman in the Marines and Allen in the Navy, but the resignations were not accepted and the two gentlemen were granted leaves of absence instead.

There was considerable discussion about the status of the member clubs, which, obviously, in some instances had lost ice or were otherwise behind in the payment of their dues. The procedure which was adopted provided for the automatic suspension of a club failing to pay its dues within 30 days of a request from the Treasurer, with such a club being reported to the Governing Council for expulsion if the dues remained unpaid. However, at the Fall meeting of the Executive Committee, it was decided that clubs which had lost their ice be retained as members whether or not their dues were paid. A recommendation was also made to tighten up the system on which a club was assigned to a specific level of dues depending upon the size of its membership, which some clubs had sought to get around by paying their dues for the lowest bracket at the beginning of the year and then later sending additional funds stating that their membership had increased. An important rule was adopted which provided that a competitor who was a full member of more than one club, could represent only one and the same club during the skating year. The rule also provided that "no competitor shall be permitted to acquire residence in a place other than that of the skater's actual legal, business or college residence merely for the purpose of representing or skating for some club or organization located at or near such place." How times have changed!

Also announced was the removal of the magazine office from 1 Telford Street to 30 Huntington Avenue, in Boston, where it would remain until moving to 575 Boylston Street in 1961.

For the 1942-1943 season, the change approved by the Executive Committee was implemented in the structure of Dance competition, with the creation of a Junior Dance event in the National Championships, in which the Silver compulsory dances would be skated, with the Senior Dance event skating the Gold compulsory dances, plus two Silver Dances. For the 1943 event, the dances were the "Continental" (American) Waltz in the initial round and the Three-Lobed Waltz in the final round, together with the Blues, Quickstep and Westminster Waltz. Thereafter, in future years, the Gold dances would be drawn from the Blues or "Iceland" Tango, Quickstep or Kilian and Westminster or Viennese Waltz. The only test requirement for both Senior and Junior events was the Silver Dance Test, although the Gold Dance Test had been established in 1940. However, it had not been until 1943 that the first complete Gold Test had been passed by Sandy McDonald of New York, and the second such test was not passed until 1944 by her partner Harold Hartshorne. They had been the National Dance champions from 1939 to 1941! As is true today, the dances in the test could be passed separately, and in the summer of 1941, the first major summer test session in the Gold Dance Test was held at Lake Placid, with eight candidates taking the Blues, two the Viennese, three the Kilian, and two the Quickstep, of which six candidates passed the Blues and two the Kilian. It is amusing to read from the report that "it was found advisable for at least one judge to skate the dance with each candidate." This amply demonstrates just how hard it was to pass the Gold Dance Test, so it can be very well appreciated why the complete Gold Test as a requirement for Senior Dance Competition did not come into effect until the 1973-1974 season! Another small effect of the War was an announcement that the USFSA would not "for the duration" present Gold Test medals to the successful candidates!

It was also in the 1942-1943 season that the New England Championships were established. In addition to the Middle Atlantic Championships, there were other local or regional competitions already in existence, such as the California championships previously mentioned, and others, such as the Philadelphia District and the Northwest. The latter was first held in 1941 and was open to Canadians. These competitions, which we would call "non-qualifying" competitions today, continued to grow despite the War and demonstrated the need for greater opportunities for competition outside of the Sectionals and the Nationals. The New Englands addressed that need in the Northeast corner of the country and were an immediate success.

It is an historical fact that an earlier championship of New England had been held in 1915, under the auspices of the New England Skating Association (NESA), which would later be one of the regional member associations of the Amateur Skating Union (ASU) and responsible for speed skating in the area. The winner of the Ladies event in 1915 was none other than Miss Theresa Weld, who defeated Mrs. Clara Rotch Frothingham. The 50th anniversary of the event was observed at the 1965 New England Championships at The Skating Club of Boston, with both ladies present, wearing their original medals!

The 1943 Nationals were held in New York City, with the Figures, the new Junior Dance and the Novice Singles being held at the Iceland rink, home of the Skating Club of New York, and the free skating in Madison Square Garden; always a rewarding experience for the younger skaters to compete in such a large and famous arena. The author served as the announcer and remembers well the excitement in the air. Due to the wartime conditions, entry in the Novice Singles was limited to the first three finishers in the Sectionals, a reduction of one from the existing requirement, which was in fact very complicated! The rule provided that the first and second place winners from the prior year could not re-enter, but those who placed third through seventh in the prior two years could, plus the first four from the Sectional Junior (remember that the level of National Novice was the same as Sectional Junior then), the Sectional Novice winner (one level lower), and finally a winner of a State, Association or District championship in which National Novice Figures or higher were skated. Got it?

Jane Vaughn Sullivan and "Buddy" Vaughn

The Championships drew 62 entries in 10 events, and while the Mens' events were small, there was still a high order of competition. The winner of the Senior Men was Arthur "Buddy" Vaughn, Jr., the brother of Jane from Philadelphia, who defeated Arthur Preusch, Jr. from St. Paul. "Buddy" Vaughn had been the National Novice and Junior champion in 1938-1939, one of those "back-to-back" achievements, thereby becoming the first man to win all three National Singles titles. On the Ladies side, Gretchen Merrill of Boston finally won her first Senior title, with strong competition from Dorothy Goos of New York, the 1942 Junior Ladies champion, who was a very powerful free skater. Coincidentally, Gretchen was the exact counterpart of Vaughn, having won the Novice and Junior Ladies in the same years that he had. She was not, however, the first lady to win all three Singles titles, that honor belonging to Joan Tozzer of Boston, who had been Novice champion in 1934, Junior Champion in 1937 and Senior champion in 1938.

Doris Schubach and Walter Noffke of Springfield retained their Senior Pair title, with Walter coming out of Navy training for the purpose. The runners-up again were Janette Ahrens (who was also third in the Senior Ladies) and Bob Uppgren of St. Paul, with Dorothy Goos and Edward LeMaire of New York, the 1942 Junior champions, third. There is an amusing story about the latter. Eddie LeMaire, sadly killed in the air accident in 1961, often said that he had no problem lifting Dorothy, but much more of one keeping his feet on the ice when she went up in the air! In 1943, Eddie won the Junior Men's event. In Senior Dance, skating the Gold Dances for

Gretchen Merrill

the first time, the winners were Marcella May and James Lochead, Jr., of San Francisco, taking that title to the Pacific Coast for the first time. Marcella later went on to a long and distinguished career as a World Championship judge. The new Junior Dance event was won by Dorothy Glazier and Lyman Wakefield, Jr., representing Boston. Lyman was from St. Paul and was serving in the Navy in the Boston area, while continuing to skate at The SC of Boston. Appropriately, The SC of New York won the Harned Trophy for the club earning the most points, with Boston and St. Paul second and third.

Another impact of the War was a requirement that all supplies of critical metals and other materials in private hands be turned in for re-use in the war effort. In those days, the pictures printed in magazines were on lead and zinc plates mounted on wooden blocks. **Skating** magazine had a substantial supply of these "cuts," as they were called, in metal filing cabinets. Before disposing of them, the decision was made by Mrs. Theresa Weld Blanchard, the editor, to see if they could be used to make a "picture" book covering the previous 20 years. Accordingly, proofs were pulled and the best were selected and ultimately published in a booklet the same size as the magazine, called **Skating Through the Years**. The booklet was, in effect a 20th Anniversary survey of the Association and magazine and sold well enough to merit a second updated edition in 1957. Such a booklet could well be done again, using the substantial photograph archives of the magazine. The author was privileged to have worked on both editions for Mrs. Blanchard.

The 1943 Governing Council meeting was held at New York in March, in order to coincide with the National Championships the same weekend. Among the rule changes adopted was the addition of semi-final rounds in Dance competitions, and the display of the judges' marks for figures only at the end of each figure. Skaters holding the Eighth (Gold) Test were no longer eligible to enter the Junior Singles, while for entry in the Senior events, the Seventh Test was required. There were complicated rules adopted concerning eligibility to enter National Novice Singles. For example: "Those placing 3 ,4, 5, 6 or 7 in National Novice Singles during the second previous skating season and the first four in Sectional Junior Singles held during the previous skating season are no longer eligible to compete in National Novice Singles." It was also provided that a Sectional Novice winner did not have to pass the Fourth Test in the period between the Sectionals and the Nationals in order to compete in National Novice Singles. Got all that?

Another significant event occurred during the 1942-1943 season, when the Southern California Inter-Club Association was founded in 1943 to hold the first annual Southern California Inter-Club Championships in Westwood. The Association was the first association of figure skating clubs in the United States and has served as the "model" for the many such associations and councils that have followed. The founding clubs were the All Year FSC of Westwood, the Arctic Blades FSC of Paramount, the Blade and Edge Club of Pasadena, and the Los Angeles FSC. The Association hosted the USFSA annual meeting in 1953, 1965, 1971 and 1980 and also hosted the Pacific Coast and Southwest Pacific Championships and many judges' schools and seminars. Its special and unique activity perhaps is the organization in 1965 of a Central Judges Bureau through the efforts of Norman Fuller of the Arctic Blades FSC. The Bureau assigns judges and trial judges to the test sessions of the member clubs. Among those who have had a key role in the Association have been Sidney MacSween of the Blade and Edge Club, Robert McLeod of the Arctic Blades Club and Betty Sonnhalter, also of Arctic Blades FSC, who served as the Secretary of the Association for over 35 years. The apparent key to the success of the Association has been that it has never imposed any rules or regulations which would affect the internal operation or jurisdiction of a club, and ever since its founding has had a remarkable record of harmony and cooperation, which is quite unique in the country. Actually, as the Southwest Pacific Regional became an ever larger competition, permission was obtained to use "group divisions" of the Lower Singles events, which was later adopted by the USFSA and applied to all the Regionals throughout the United States.

The 1943-1944 season was perhaps the "depths" of the War; when would it ever end? The German and Japanese "empires" were at their maximum expansion, and the invasion of the European continent had not yet taken place. Despite all this and the incredible wartime production of military hardware going on, skating continued to "boom," with more clubs joining the Association; in 1941 – 11; in 1942 – 9; none in 1943 and in 1944 – 6, for a total up to then of 106. The number of tests passed, which now included many individual dances, was over 2,300 a year, with the majority of them being taken in the various summer sessions held around the country, which were in those days sanctioned (i.e., licensed) by the Summer Skating Committee, established in 1941. With greater administrative responsibilities, the "Sectional" structure of the Association was emerging. Because of its special situation and distance from the then Eastern skating centers, a Pacific Coast committee was established in 1938, the Midwestern committee in

1941, as we have seen and an Eastern committee in 1942.

Two other important new committees were also created during the War, a Judging Standards committee in 1943 and a Public Relations committee in 1944. The former was an "ad hoc" committee headed by Heaton Robertson of New Haven, the immediate Past President, with the specific mission of the preparation of a booklet, now forgotten, called the "Evaluation of Errors in School Figure," which was for its time a very definitive work on the subject. Figures then loomed large on the horizon, and in competition constituted 60 percent of the score. Public Relations was formed as a special committee, although later, in 1964, it became a standing committee, lasting until 1987, when it was discontinued and the public relations function was moved in to Headquarters. As the sport had grown in the country, the need for a public relations effort quickly became apparent, at that time primarily through the print media, as a supplement to the magazine.

There was also a change of administration in 1943, when Heaton Robertson of New Haven stepped down as President after three years of leading the Association through the first part of the War. He was succeeded by Walter S. Powell of Saint Louis. Heaton continued his efforts in judging, and served as chairman of the Judges committee from 1945 to 1947, as well as chairman of the Eastern committee from 1943 to 1945. A remarkable intellect, he was perhaps best remembered for his "nurturing" and teaching of new young judges. He had been a competitor many years in the Junior Men's event of the Nationals, often coming on or going off the ice to serve as a judge or referee at the same competition. He was a skilled mathematician, and one story about him reflects that. At a competition he was judging, at the end of the free skating, he asked for a few moments to transcribe his marks. It was found that he had started out with too high a range, so he had just kept right on marking above the then maximum mark of 10.0, and after the event, in virtually a few seconds, he transposed his entire set of marks down to within the maximum permitted. Fortunately for him, the modified open system was being used! During his final years, Heaton was elected an Honorary Vice President (in 1951) of the USFSA, only the second person so honored, the other being Oscar L. Richard of New York. He passed away in 1953 and was posthumously elected to the United States Figure Skating Hall of Fame in 1976. After his death a memorial trophy in his name was presented by the members of the Association for the Novice Ladies event of the Nationals.

In 1945 and 1946, as the chairman of the Judges committee, Robertson made a comprehensive revision of the judges' lists, weeding out many who had been inactive, were over age or incompetent. Actually, quite a few judges (including the author) came back from overseas at the end of the War to find themselves dropped from the lists, and when Heaton was asked

Walter S. Powell

why, he replied, "…you did no judging, you were inactive," as if there had been an opportunity to do so in the Philippines in 1944-1945!

To curtail the number of entries in the Novice classes at Nationals, an idea which can be regarded as somewhat "penny-wise and pound-foolish" in hindsight, since the lower classes should be the last to be curtailed and the number of entries was not as yet unmanageable! Authority was also granted to the referees of Sectionals to limit the number to free skate in Junior, Novice and Juvenile Singles to 15, instead of 20. The 1944 Nationals were held at Minneapolis and drew 45 entries, the smallest number so far during the War. There was no Senior Men's event, and in the Junior and Novice Men, there was a total of only 10 entries. The

Donna Jean Pospisil and Jean-Pierre Brunet

Pairs and Dance events were also small, with eight in the former and only seven in the latter. Gretchen Merrill won her second title, Doris Schubach and Walter Noffke, still in the Navy, their third and Marcella May and James Lochead, Jr., their second. The latter also skated in Senior Pairs and placed third, while Lochead won the Junior Men, quite a busy competition for them!

However, the interest in the championships was really focused on the lower events. In Junior Pairs, the winners were Donna Jean Pospisil and Jean-Pierre Brunet from New York, who defeated Karol and Peter Kennedy from Seattle. Donna Jean had been a champion in roller skating and Jean-Pierre was the son of Andrée and Pierre Brunet, while in Novice Men, the winner was Richard Button, of Englewood N.J., representing Philadelphia, with Jean-Pierre, second. It is a nice historical footnote that one of the judges of the Novice Men, in her first Nationals, judged the same event in the 1994 Nationals at Detroit, exactly 50 years later. That judge was Mary Louise Premer of St. Paul. Another judge on the same panel was Jane Vaughn Sullivan, the former National Ladies champion, who was by now an active National judge. While Pospisil and Brunet may not be remembered today, Dick Button obviously is, and his debut on the National scene in 1944 represents the start of his fabulous career, as we will see.

The 1944 Governing Council meeting was held in New York at the Hotel New Weston. The Secretary, Harry Keighley of Illinois, reported that there were 96 member clubs in good standing, with 17 whose dues were still unpaid and 14 whose dues were unpaid and "whose existence was doubted." The 96 clubs were divided, 40 in the East, 31 in the Midwest and 25 on the Pacific

Coast. He also indicated that they comprised 13,000 members, with about 50 percent in the East, 30 percent in the Midwest and 20 percent on the Coast. Also voted was a ruling that any arrangements between instructors and amateurs for lessons at reduced rates under restrictive conditions, such as payments to be made by the amateur after turning professional, were "contrary to the amateur spirit" and a violation of the amateur status rules.

The Executive Committee, at its meeting, delayed the award of the 1945 Nationals to its Fall meeting. It is amazing today to consider that the award of such a major event would not be made until less than six months before the event was to be held! The publication of a new Rulebook was authorized, since it had not been published in 1943. With the demise of the Yearbook, the information formerly contained in that publication was incorporated into the Rulebook, except that the meeting minutes and reports were no longer published, and would in the future be found only in the Report books for the meetings themselves, with a "Report of Action" being sent out to the clubs.

By the beginning of the 1944-1945 season, the War could be seen to be winding down, with victory in Europe at least only a matter of weeks or months away. So the wartime "mentality" had begun to wane and people were beginning to look towards a return to normal life and pursuits, including skating. In the three Sectionals in 1945, the number of entries had begun to rise again: Easterns - 83; Midwesterns - 67; and Pacific Coast - 71. The 1945 Nationals again returned to New York, Iceland and Madison Square Garden, and drew 86 entries. There was actually a Fours event with three Fours entered! With the agreement of the CFSA, the Ladies event of the North American Championships was also held in New York immediately following the Nationals.

The Vice Chairman of the organizing committee for the Skating Club of New York was Anne Harvey, better known to us today as Anne (Gram) Gerli, still active as a judge, Governing Council delegate and Nominating Committee member, a testimony to her long dedication to the sport. Lyman Wakefield, Jr., by now a Navy Lieutenant Commander, returned this time in Junior Pairs, and was the winner with Betty Jean Higgins, representing Boston, defeating another young promising pair of Yvonne Sherman and Robert Swenning from New York. Lyman had now demonstrated his versatility by winning National titles in three different disciplines, Fours, Dance and Pairs. During his college days, he had also been a collegiate champion in Singles. He too went on to serve as an Association officer, World and National judge.

Gretchen Merrill of Boston won her third straight title, defeating Janette Ahrens of St. Paul, while in the Pairs, the "next" generation arrived with a bang, when Donna Jean Pospisil and Jean-Pierre Brunet of New York, won the title over Ann and Michael McGean from Cleveland, with Marcella May and James Lochead, Jr., of San Francisco again third. The "youth" movement continued in the Dance, with Kathe Mehl and Robert Swenning of New York defeating the defending champions, May and Lochead in the Senior event, with Anne Davies and Carleton C.

Hoffner, Jr., of Washington DC, third, while Patsy Jones and Walter H. Bainbridge, Jr. also from Washington, DC, won the Junior event. Dick Button continued his march up the ladder with an easy win in the Junior Men over McGean and Swenning, while Eileen Seigh, representing Philadelphia, won the Junior Ladies, defeating Yvonne Sherman. As can be seen it was the common practice in those days for the young skaters to compete in one or more disciplines.

A new trophy was presented for the first time at the 1945 Nationals, the Oscar L. Richard Trophy for the most artistic free skating performance by a lady in the Senior and Junior Singles events, "without reference to acrobatics or the purely athletic features involved in free skating," to be decided by a panel of three non-skating judges, consisting of an artist, a sculptor and a musician, of national reputation. The first winner was Janette Ahrens of St. Paul, and Mr. Richard, aged 90 and an Honorary Vice President of the Association, presented the trophy himself. The Richard Trophy for Ladies and its counterpart for Men, first awarded in 1947, proved controversial and were regarded as a "consolation" prize, if the recipient was not also the winner of the championship, since the criteria used by the panels of judges were obviously not based on the same principles used by the official judges in awarding the championship titles. While a nice idea, the award of trophies for special events or categories have never proven satisfactory, and in this case, the Richard trophies were eventually discontinued in 1956.

The North American Ladies immediately followed and turned into a close battle between Barbara Ann Scott of Ottawa and Gretchen Merrill of Boston, the respective National lady champions of their countries. Gretchen probably gave away any chance of winning in the figures, when she placed the paragraph loop on a line in the ice, a classic error, which when a figure is not properly lined up, really magnifies the mistake for the judges. There were eight Ladies in the event, four from each country, and the Americans succeeded in taking the second, third and fourth places, with Merrill, Ahrenes and Margaret Grant, from St. Paul. The usual six judges were used, with Barbara Ann winning by four judges to two. This title was the "launching pad" for the distinguished career of Barbara Ann in European, World and Olympic competition just two years later. The event was carried out in one day, with the figures (eight in all) being skated at Iceland in the morning and the free skating the same evening in Madison Square Garden. On this high note, the competitive season ended, and soon thereafter the War itself, so that "normal" activities could be expected in 1945-1946, hopefully including the revival of International competition abroad.

The 1945 Governing Council meeting was held at the New Weston in New York, "as usual," in April. It was reported that there were now 114 clubs, of which 12 were probationary and 13 inactive. Among the actions taken was a reorganization of the Constitution and By Laws to include many of the "Miscellaneous Rulings" of the Governing Council and Executive Committee, which had grown to quite a large collection, with some of them obsolete. Some, mostly of a procedural nature, were retained, but eventually, in later revisions, they would all either be incorporated into the Constitution and By Laws or otherwise dropped. The Executive Committee at its meeting awarded the 1946 Nationals to Chicago.

The 1945 Fall meeting of the Executive Committee was held in New York in late October. Among the rules adopted was one requiring certification that a skater is receiving a standard education must accompany all entries in the Sectional and National championships. A rule providing that a former professional who had been reinstated remained ineligible to compete (other than in closed club competitions not requiring a sanction) was also approved. The death in September of John B. Thayer, of Philadelphia, an Association Treasurer in 1943-1945 and an Executive Committee member 1938-1941 was noted.

All in all, the Association and the sport had come through the War both stronger and larger than before it, and had expanded into a truly national organization, with active clubs and skaters across the country, and perhaps only the Southeastern portion still awaiting development.

The chapter title is a phrase often applied to the period indicated, when American skaters were dominant in international competition, in Singles at least, if not also in Pairs and Ice Dancing (after 1950). The temptation to use it here was too great to resist.

With World War II over in 1945 and expectations high for an early resumption of

The "Golden Age" of American Skating Begins (1946-1948)

international competition, there was every expectation among both the Americans and Canadians that they would soon be sending teams abroad. Unfortunately, due to the collapse of Europe after the War, it would be another year before the World and European Championships were revived and the International Skating Union (now known by its English acronym - "ISU") re-organized. So the season of 1945-1946 was something of a waiting game.

The three Sectional Championships were held as usual, and the number of entries still reflected the effects of the War, as many were still in service until 1946. The Easterns had 77 entries, the Midwesterns 57 and the Pacific Coast 80. In the Nationals itself, again held in Chicago there were 75 entries. The Men's events were still small, with only 16 entries in the three classes but the Senior Men's event was revived and drew five entries. Gretchen Merrill of Boston won her fourth straight title, again defeating Janette Ahrens of St. Paul. Donna Jean Pospisil and Jean-Pierre Brunet of New York retained their Senior Pair title.

There is a sad postscript to the career of this young and very promising pair. After the 1946 Nationals, they retired when Jean-Pierre withdrew from competitive skating to concentrate on his education, although he did compete in Fours in 1948. In August of 1948, Jean-Pierre was killed in a single vehicle accident when the jeep he was driving overturned near Boyne City, Mich., the summer home of his parents, Andrée and Pierre Brunet. He was just short of his 18th birthday. A fund for a memorial trophy in his memory was implemented by skaters at Lake Placid which culminated in the Jean-Pierre Brunet Memorial Trophy for the Novice Men's National Championships. The fortitude with which his parents carried on their careers as teachers of skating was remarkable, especially with Pierre being the coach of the three Heisses (Carol, Nancy and Bruce). The impact of the loss of their only child upon them was readily apparent to all who knew them. One can only speculate what Jean-Pierre might have accomplished in life. Prior to his death, he had been admitted to the Massachusetts Institute of Technology (MIT) on a full scholarship. His untimely death would be recalled in 1961, when other young promising skaters were lost in the air accident at Brussels, Belgium.

Anne Davies and Carleton Hoffner

The 1946 Nationals reflected a strong statement by the next and first post-War generation of young skaters who had been coming up through the ranks during the War years. In the Senior Men, Dick Button, representing Philadelphia, easily won what would be the first of seven titles defeating James Lochead of Berkeley, the 1944 Junior champion. Dick thus completed an unprecedented three-year sweep of the Novice, Junior and Senior titles in consecutive years, an accomplishment never achieved by anyone else. In the Senior Dance event youth took over with Anne Davies, just 14 years of age and Carleton C. Hoffner, Jr. representing Washington, taking the title over Lois Waring of Baltimore and Walter H. ("Red") Bainbridge, Jr. of Washington, to start what would almost become a dynasty in Dance by the Washington club over the next few years. The quality of the compulsory dances of Davies and Hoffner was such that upon completion of their Kilian, the audience refused to permit the competition to continue until they did an encore, certainly an unprecedented occurrence in competition.

The year 1946 also marked the 25th Anniversary of the Association, and while no special events were scheduled in observance, a booklet was published called "The First Twenty-Five Years" of the USFSA. An unusual format was followed, with each of the former Presidents of the Association (there were eight of them, including Walter Powell, who retired from office that year) writing a brief summary report of his administration. The booklet, which was prepared by Mrs. Theresa Weld Blanchard, contained much vital information and has been a most valuable resource for the current work.

President Powell, in his report in the Anniversary booklet, cites various accomplishments achieved during the wartime period, including efforts to establish uniform judging standards and programs to educate judges, and skaters. He also refers to the remarkable increase in interest in summer skating, with seven centers being on the approved list of the USFSA for 1946. Such centers were authorized to conduct test sessions, judging schools, dance conferences, carnivals, pop concerts and the like.

By 1946, 115 clubs had joined the Association since the beginning, with 112 members in 1946, consisting of 41 from the East, 44 from the Midwest and 27 from the Pacific Coast. The report is again completely silent on the status of the Association with respect to the size of the membership. There is a clue in the report on the magazine by Mrs. Blanchard, in which it is indicated that subscriptions were in excess of 8,000 in 1946, so it can be speculated that the total membership of the Association was on the order of 10,000. Financial information shows that the Association had at the end of the 1945-46 season, assets (the former famous "cash balance") of $34,012, revenues of $8,720 and expenses of $3,400. A modest increase in (club) dues for the larger clubs was adopted but a proposal to "assess all members of member clubs with a head tax," i.e., what is now know as the "registration fee," was defeated. This was a hot issue for several years, until a fee was finally approved in 1950 at the princely sum of 50 cents! Historically, increases in the amount of the registration fee have been like pulling teeth ever since, very difficult to obtain, and usually lagging behind the need.

The 1946 Governing Council meeting was held again at the Hotel New Weston in New York in early May. The earlier action taken concerning the right to compete of former professionals (in any sport), was narrowed to professionals in ice and roller skating only. A new schedule of dues was approved, with the amount payable for a club with over 250 members being raised to $50.00. An Individual membership, which included a subscription to the magazine, was still a bargain at $5.00. The fees for taking tests were raised, with an Eighth Test at $5.00 and the Gold Dance Test $1.00 per dance. The old fee had been just 50 cents, as a registration fee for each test, regardless of level. Only the Preliminary (the former Junior) Test and the Bronze Dance Test remained at that level.

Also voted was the right of a member club to appeal to the Membership Committee with respect to any alleged unfair practices employed against it, as for example, by another club or a rink. In that regard, in 1948 a Rink Cooperation Committee would be set up to act as a liaison between member clubs and rinks and to aid in the resolution of disputes. At long last, the 1947 Nationals were finally awarded to the St. Moritz ISC of Berkeley, Calif. Sanction fees for qualifying competitions were also updated, with that for the Nationals being $125.00 which included the judges boxes and forms. A further revision was made in the judging system to be used at the National and Sectional championships. No announcement was to be made of the marks during or after the figures, and the judges would not be told how they had marked the figures before judging the free skating. The figure marks would be computed and the eight finalists would be posted in alphabetical order. Remember that this was still when the final result was based upon the combined total of all the marks of a judge for both figures and free skating. However praiseworthy the attempt was to insulate the judges from bias and influence, such a system, needless to say did not last very long, especially since the skaters wanted to know what their marks were and where they had placed.

It was at this meeting that a Trophy Committee was established, as a sub-committee of the Competitions Committee. The responsibilities assumed by the committee were to draw up a standard deed of gift and to keep track of the trophies which were still traveling. At a luncheon following the end of the meeting, as part of the observance of the 25th Anniversary of the Association, three of the living Past Presidents (Charles T. Church, Joseph K. Savage, and Heaton R. Robertson) were present, while the other two (Sherwin Badger and Charles Rotch) sent their regrets. Representing the late Henry W. Howe, was his widow, Mary Barton Howe and representing her father, A. Winsor Weld, was Theresa Weld Blanchard. Honorary Vice President Oscar L. Richard was also present (at the age of 90).

Henry M. Beatty

Having completed a tough three years as President, keeping the Association going despite the War, Walter Powell stepped down and was succeeded by the first of the "Cleveland" Presidents, Henry M. Beatty. Walter would remain very active in the international side of the Association until his untimely death in 1961, and much of the success of the United States skaters in international competition was due to his efforts. He became the first chairman of a new International Committee in 1946, serving until 1952. More importantly, however, he was the first representative of the USFSA ever elected to office in the ISU. It is hard to imagine today, that the USFSA (and the CFSA), had no representatives in the ISU for the first 50 years of its existence. It was strictly a European operation, and as has already been noted, there was concern about that fact during the 1930's. Powell was elected to the ISU Council in 1947, serving until 1961, when he was succeeded by Henry M. Beatty, who served in turn until 1967. Hank was followed by John R. Shoemaker of San Francisco in that year, who became the Vice President for Figure Skating just a few weeks later, when the new ISU President, Ernst Labin of Austria, died unexpectedly. Jack is, so far, the only USFSA representative to serve as an officer of the ISU, until 1980. He was succeeded as an ISU Council member by Charles DeMore of Cleveland, who served until 1994, when Claire Ferguson was elected at the Boston Congress as the first woman Council member from the United States and the third ever, the first having been Sonia Bianchetti of Italy and the second, Joyce Hisey of Canada. The USFSA will have held a seat on the ISU Council for a total of 51 consecutive years by 1998 (when the next elections will take place).

The Fall meeting for 1946 of the Executive Committee was held at New York in late October with President Beatty presiding for the first time. At the meeting the entries for the first post-War World Championships at Stockholm were approved. The North American Championships were also to be revived at Ottawa with a Dance event to be added. Added to the prior action of raising the test fees was the requirement for the payment of a registration fee of $1.00 by foreign amateurs and professionals taking tests. While reciprocity between Canadian and U.S. tests was retained (up through the Sixth), a skater could only obtain the appropriate medal by actually taking the test in the other country, so that a skater taking a test in Canada could only obtain the Canadian medal and the medal for the same test in the U.S. by taking and passing the test in the U.S. It was also decided that dancers who had taken and passed the five dances in the Gold Dance Test (Kilian, Blues, Viennese, Westminster and Quickstep) would be deemed to have passed the complete test. The test had formerly included the Carroll Tango up until 1944. New dances would be added in the future until the Test by the mid-1950's had seven dances, with the Three-Lobed Waltz and Argentine Tango being added. Then in 1956, it was cut to four dances, but a free dance program (of three minutes) was added.

The 1946-1947 season represented the return to normal international competition around the world. In those days, as had been the case in 1934 when Maribel Vinson had entered it, the European Championships were open to non-Europeans who belonged to a European Member of the ISU. There was then no formal World Team and any selections made of persons to enter the ISU Championships were based upon the results in the prior year's Nationals since the Nationals were held after the Worlds until 1958. As a result, it was the Executive Committee of the Association that selected the skaters to enter the 1947 World Championships to be held at Stockholm, Sweden. The committee did in effect select a team with one Man, three Ladies and three Pairs, consisting of Dick Button as the Man, Gretchen Merrill, Janette Ahrens and Eileen Seigh as the Ladies and Pospisil-Brunet, Karol and Peter Kennedy and Doris and Walter Noffke, the former champions, now married, as the Pairs. Selected to serve as judges and also as delegates at the ISU Congress, which was to be held immediately following the Championships, were two former Presidents, Sherwin Badger and Joseph Savage.

The make-up of the contemplated delegation demonstrated the intent and will of the USFSA to make its presence felt in the Championships in the future. By the time the Championships rolled around, however, the composition of the group had materially changed.

In fact, the first post-War championships which saw the impact of the North Americans were the European Championships at Davos on the great outdoor rink there, the largest of its kind in the world. Two Americans, Gretchen Merrill and Roberta Jenks Scholdan elected to enter the Ladies, while the Canadians were represented by Barbara Ann Scott. Roberta, now the wife of the future Broadmoor coach, Edi Scholdan, had placed fifth in the 1946 Nationals and had really entered on her own, but with the blessing of the Association, and did quite well, earning 13th place out of 20. As it turned out, the Ladies event was again a close battle between Barbara Ann Scott and Gretchen Merrill, with the leading European competition coming from Daphne Walker of Great Britain, and they finished in that order. It was the high spot of Gretchen's career. At Davos, Col. Harold G. Storke, then serving with the American occupation forces in Vienna and a judge from the SC of Boston, was called upon to serve as a judge for the United States, while Donald Cruikshank of Canada served for the CFSA. It was a generous gesture on the part of the International Skating Club of Davos, the organizing club, to invite non-European judges to serve. For Col. Storke it was the start of a distinguished career as a judge internationally. He would return home and continue his activity as a judge and referee, becoming the Chairman of the USFSA Competitions Committee in 1951 serving to 1954 and Chairman of the Amateur Status Committee from 1957 to 1960. He was later Secretary of the Association and was serving in that office at the time of his death in 1961.

The skating at Davos was outdoors, which was new to the North Americans. In the early years following the War it should also be remembered that many of the Continental European skaters, had had only limited training opportunities for some years before the revival of competition, plus the difficulties of the rationing of food and the war damage to their cities, including skating rinks, in some cases. This is not intended to denigrate in any way from the achievements of the North Americans and the Europeans still presented formidable competition and were very successful themselves, especially in such disciplines as Pairs and later in Ice Dancing. It should also be noted that the German and Japanese skaters did not return to competition until 1951, although the Austrians and the Italians were allowed to come back in 1948.

Dick Button

It is difficult to apply an appropriate adjective to the impact of Dick Button's free skating on the Europeans who were seeing it for the first time. It was a revolution compared with what they were used to before the War. Here was a young, very strong and athletic skater performing jumps and spins of great difficulty with comparative ease. The Europeans just did not know how to handle it. In the competition, Hans Gerschwiler of Switzerland, who had placed fifth in the last European Championships before the War in 1939, gained a big lead over Button in figures, and just managed to hold on to it in the free, to eke out a 3 to 2 decision from the five judges. A Danish judge placed Button first, together with Lyman Wakefield of the U.S. Ulrich Salchow, the former ten time World champion and ISU President, was so unhappy with the result, that he presented to Dick one of his own trophies, by way of a consolation prize. Salchow described Dick's free skating as follows: "Button was a real master in free skating. He showed that he was a skater of great courage and grand form; also that he is on the way to become a real artist. Not more acrobatic than necessary, manly in style, powerful, simple and natural."

In the Ladies, Barbara Ann Scott of Canada easily dominated the competition, repeating her European win over the same two competitors, with Daphne Walker, of Great Britain second this time and Gretchen Merrill third. Eileen Seigh was fourth, with a "Button style" performance in the free skating, which earned her third place in that division, while Janette Ahrens finished sixth. A completely unknown pair from Belgium, Micheline Lannoy and Pierre Baugniet with no prior pre-War record, won the Pair title in a close competition with Karol and Peter Kennedy, while the Noffke's finished sixth. The silver medal of the Kennedy's was the first ever earned by an American Pair in the Worlds, the best previous places having been the bronze medals won by Beatrix Loughran and Sherwin Badger in 1930 and 1932. All in all, it was a very successful re-entry into World level competition for the North Americans, with Canada winning one gold and the U.S. two silver medals out of nine.

The 1947 Nationals followed the Worlds and were inevitably somewhat of an anti-climax but were noteworthy in several respects. It was the first time that the championships were held on the Pacific Coast, at long last fulfilling the commitment made in 1942. A reporter said, "…the efforts begun in 1937 were realized in 1947. Since it took 15 years to move the Nationals from the Atlantic seaboard west to Chicago in 1937, our ten-year effort (it would have been five years had the war not intervened) seems extraordinarily successful." It was a big championship, with 83 entries in 11 events, including Fours. Button and Merrill retained their titles, while the Pairs crown went unexpectedly to a young pair from New York, Yvonne Sherman and Robert Swenning, the Junior champions from the prior year, who defeated the Kennedys. Swenning won the Junior Men, while Yvonne also won the Junior Ladies event after six tries and two runner-up finishes. She had invariably been placed high in the figures and then could not hold the lead against stronger free skaters, so her triumph was a popular one.

The Dance event saw Lois Waring and Red Bainbridge turn the tables on the defending champions, Anne Davies and Carleton Hoffner in another close competition, while former champion Marcella May with a new partner, Frank Davenport, finished third. In Fours, what was known as the "second" Saint Paul Four, of Janet Gerhauser, Marilyn Thomsen, John Nightingale and Marlyn Thomsen, won what would be the first of three titles over a four from St. Louis.

Lois Waring and "Red" Bainbridge

Finally, at the end of March, the long 1946-47 competitive season ended with the revival of the full North American Championships at Ottawa, Ontario, to which a Dance event was added, but with the Silver Dances being skated at the request of the Canadians since they were not yet ready to do the Gold Dances. Unfortunately, there was no competition for Fours.

Dick Button won his first Men's title over the competitor who would become his closest rival throughout the rest of his competitive career, Jimmy Grogan, representing the St. Moritz ISC, then age 15, whose only prior experience at the National level before 1947 had been a seventh place in the 1946 Novice Men. Grogan had previously placed third in the Senior Men at the 1947 Nationals behind John Lettengarver of St. Paul.

In the Ladies, Barbara Ann Scott retained her title, with Janette Ahrens second and the young Junior champion, Yvonne Sherman third. Gretchen Merrill, after her long and exhausting stay abroad, elected not to enter. In Pairs, the Canadians Suzanne Morrow and Wallace Diestelmeyer were the winners defeating Sherman and Swenning and the Kennedys to maintain the Canadian supremacy in that event. The Dance title went to Waring and Bainbridge over Davies and Hoffner. There was only one Canadian couple entered as the Canadian champions, Margaret Wilson Roberts and Bruce Hyland had had to withdraw due to illness on his part. The trophies and medals were presented by the Governor General of Canada, Field Marshal Earl Alexander of Tunis, a famous wartime general who honored the championships with his presence. The Ottawa crowd was very fair and even expressed their displeasure at the marks awarded to Barbara Ann by the Canadian judge from Ottawa when compared to those which he had awarded to Eileen Seigh.

The 1947 meeting of the Governing Council was held for the first time outside New York City at the Edgewater Beach Hotel in Chicago, where it would remain until 1953. The report noted that a Midwestern city provided a better opportunity geographically for more clubs to be represented in person by their delegates. There was a lengthy discussion in the Executive Committee meeting of establishing a permanent office for the Association with a salaried Executive Secretary to handle the routine work of the officers and committee chairmen. The Secretary reported that there were 104 member clubs, with 39 in the East with 6,300 members; 39 in the Midwest with 4,700 members and 26 on the Pacific coast with 3,600 members, so that the total membership was on the order of 14,600. A modest deficit for the year was reported, despite $8,000 spent to send skaters and judges to the World and European Championships the first post-War impact of such participation. The addition of Gold Dance events to the Sectionals was also recommended.

With respect to **Skating** magazine it was reported that there were 8,830 subscriptions, an increase of 500 over the prior year. Sales of booklets were at 4,000. The passing of 1,002 Figure and 609 Dance tests was reported, of which 10 were Gold Figure and 11 were complete Gold

Dance, so the rapid rise in the numbers of such tests being passed had already begun. There were seven summer sessions approved and four judges schools were announced, so the post-War activity continued to increase as normalcy returned. Sanction fees for exhibitions were increased, at $5.00 for a single exhibition; $10.00 for a series of exhibitions and $15.00 for carnivals. The per diem amount for expenses was raised to $15.00 but only $10.00 while en route.

The Sunday luncheon following the meeting was honored by the presence of Avery Brundage, then the President of the U.S. Olympic Committee, as it was now called. Brundage spoke of the anticipated difficulties that would be encountered in traveling to and from the 1948 Olympic Winter Games, and urged all planning to attend to make their plans early.

There was one more major (non-skating) event in the 1947 season of great importance to the USFSA: the first post-War ISU Congress held in June in Stockholm. The Congress had had to be postponed from the original February date due to lack of sufficient delegates for a quorum. As a result, Messrs. Badger and Savage did not go and were replaced at the Worlds by Lyman Wakefield, and by Walter Powell at the Congress.

There were three major decisions made which affected the USFSA. The first was the adoption of a dual or split membership permitting separate members for speed and figure skating from the same country. As a result, the USFSA became once again a Member of the ISU, for figure skating with the ASU remaining the Member for speed skating. The same was true for the CFSA, which became the Canadian figure skating Member, together with the ASAC for speed skating. The second action was the appointment of an ad hoc committee to establish standards and rules for international competition in ice dancing. Originally, Clarence L. ("Larry") Parker of Washington, D.C., was appointed from the United States but he had to withdraw due to illness and was replaced by William O. Hickok, IV,

William O. Hickok, IV

from Harrisburg Pa., his successor as Chairman of the USFSA Dance Committee. The other members were Reginald Wilkie from Great Britain and Marcel Nicaise from Belgium. The committee was to bring its proposals to the 1951 Congress. The third decision was the reduction of the number of compulsory figures to be skated in Championships from 12 to six. The 1947 Worlds had been run under the 1939 Regulations with the larger number of figures having to be skated. The change was prophetic and the first chink in the armor of the dominance of figures. The change was to the benefit of the skaters from North America, who were not noted for their figures. Salchow, while praising Button's free skating said of his figures, "Button knows very well in his school figures all the easy and the more difficult elements, but he has neglected the great art of a smooth but powerful change of feet. The inside back changes of feet were not very good. The strivances to trace as close as possible brought him in a wrong position. The turns were otherwise excellent."

The 1947-1948 season really was completely taken up with the run up to and the participation in the Olympics and Worlds to be followed by the Nationals which would be held for the first time at Colorado Springs. The Olympic Team was selected in advance in accordance with the then practice and consisted of three Men, three Ladies and two Pairs. The designated manager was Harry N. Keighley of Evanston, Ill. and the judge was to be Sherwin Badger of New York. In addition to the Team, Lois Waring and Red Bainbridge were also designated to demonstrate ice dancing at the Games as well as elsewhere in Europe if official demonstrations could be arranged.

One of the selected ladies, Janette Ahrens (the others were Gretchen Merrill and Eileen Seigh) declined by reason of her impending marriage. Accordingly, it was decided to conduct a tryout to select a third lady, which was held at Chicago in December 1947 with the winner being Yvonne Sherman of New York. She was already a member of the Team in Pairs with Bob Swenning (the other pair being the Kennedys).

The European Championships of 1948 were held at Prague before the Olympics and Dick Button decided to enter, as did John Lettengarver who with Jimmy Grogan were the other two men on the Olympic team. Barbara Ann Scott returned to defend her title and Roberta Scholdan also repeated her entry of the prior year. This time, Dick defeated Hans Gerschwiler of Switzerland, the defending champion, with relative ease. His figures were considerably improved, and Dick lead in points and Hans in placings. Under today's scoring system, Dick would have won the figures. Lettengarver was fifth. Col. Storke was called upon again to serve as a judge from the United States in the event. In the Ladies, Barbara Ann also won easily, while Scholdan finished 18th. Just as the Championships were ending the Communist takeover of the Czech government took place. Dick and Barbara Ann just made it out of Prague before the airport was closed. Dick's victory represented the first time an American man had ever won an international title, other than the North Americans, or competed in a European Men's event. 1948 would be last time the North Americans had the opportunity to compete in the European Championships since thereafter non-Europeans were barred from the event. There has been occasional debate at ISU Congresses on the subject, since the Europeans, being an ISU Championship (the Men's event is the oldest, having first been held in 1891) and the argument was that all ISU Championships should be open to all ISU Members.

The Olympic Winter Games, the first since 1936, soon followed at St. Moritz, Switzerland, the site of the 1928 Games. Typically, inclement weather was a material factor in the Games, just as it had been 20 years earlier, snow, too warm, too cold, etc. This time, Button clearly won the figures on the strength of his better paragraph loop and skated an excellent program to win his first and the first ever for North America, Olympic title. His free skating was described as including "five double jumps and jump-spin combinations." Lettengarver skated equally as well in the free skating, placing second in that part, to finish fourth, while Jimmy Grogan placed sixth.

In each of his competitions, Dick Button always did something new. He was the first to do a Double Axel Paulsen jump, the first to do three consecutive double loop jumps in combination, and the first to do a flying camel spin called, obviously, the "Button camel." While not the originator, he did very high and spectacular flying sit, Axel sit and jump sit spins. These had been developed by his coach, Gustave Lussi and first performed by two of Dick's Philadelphia SC & HS predecessors and colleagues, Buddy Vaughn and Bill Grimditch. Finally, in 1952, Dick topped it all by doing the first triple jump in competition, the loop. He also revolutionized the competitive garb worn by the men, which up to then, had invariably been a short jacket and black tights. Instead he went for black trousers and a white mess jacket, which was more suitable for his athletic style.

Barbara Ann Scott added the Olympic gold medal to her collection while the American girls did not fare so well, with Yvonne Sherman sixth, Gretchen Merrill eighth, and Eileen Seigh 11th, largely due to their placements in the figures. The Kennedys could not repeat their success of the prior year in the Pairs, and finished sixth with Yvonne Sherman and Robert Swenning placing fourth. Because of the schedule with the Ladies and Men's events essentially back to back, Col. Storke was called in to judge the Ladies while Bernard Fox, who had replaced Sherwin Badger did the Men and Pairs. Lois Waring and Red Bainbridge, together with two British couples and a Belgian couple, demonstrated the dances and yet despite the enthusiasm of the public for their performances it would be another 28 years before Ice Dancing would make it into the Games in 1976.

The Canadians also did well at the Games. In addition to Barbara Ann's gold medal, Suzanne Morrow and Wallace Diestelmeyer placed third in Pairs, so the North Americans again won three medals out of nine, but this time, two of them were gold. The Belgian pair of Micheline Lannoy and Pierre Baugniet repeated their win of the prior year, to win the second ever Olympic medal for Belgium, the prior one having come also at St. Moritz in 1928, with Robert van Zeebroeck's Bronze in the Men. No German or Japanese competitors participated and the Soviets would not appear on the scene until 1956. However, the Austrians were back and did well. Eva Pawlik was second in all three major championships while Edi Rada, who would later be a leading coach in Canada, placed third in the Europeans and Olympics. He had pre-War experience, having been fourth in both the 1939 Europeans and Worlds.

The 1948 World Championships were held at Davos and the results almost seemed routine, with Button, Scott and the Belgians all winning, but for the United States at least it was a first. By winning the Worlds, Dick Button had completed an unprecedented "Grand Slam" of his own Nationals, the North Americans, Europeans, Olympics and Worlds, so he was a "quintuple" titleholder, all at the same time, as was, of course, Barbara Ann! Lettengarver and Grogan were fourth and fifth while Sherman was sixth with both Merrill or Seigh having withdrawn, perhaps because of disappointment from their relatively poor showings at St. Moritz. The Kennedys did better at Davos placing fourth, defeating Sherman and Swenning who were fifth. While the rivalry between them was keen, the Americans and Canadians were very much aware that they were in a sense a team in carrying forward North American skating against their European counterparts.

Before leaving Europe, an International Dance Conference was held in London, at which a British couple and Waring and Bainbridge again demonstrated, and the ad hoc committee of which Bill Hickok was a member, essentially reached general agreement on the rules and especially on the diagrams, steps and timing for the standard compulsory dances to be proposed to the ISU. In 1949, Bill Hickok would be elected to the newly established Ice Dance Technical Committee of the ISU, serving until 1951 and again from 1953 to 1957, when his service was cut short by his untimely death. He really was the "father" of modern ice dancing in America. He was succeeded by F. Ritter Shumway of Rochester, N.Y. in 1957 who served to 1959, when he was not re-elected because he was not an ISU Championship Judge in Dance, a requirement imposed on eligibility for membership on the committee. Ritter was followed by Harold Hartshorne of New York who served from 1959 to 1961, when he too was cut short in the midst of his career by the Brussels air accident. The fourth USFSA representative to serve on the Dance Committee was H. Kendall Kelley of Cleveland, from 1961 to 1967. There was an almost unbroken tenure of Americans on the committee from 1949 to 1967 (except for 1951-1953), and surprisingly there has been no USFSA member of the committee since.

The National Championships followed at Colorado Springs, the first of what would be an extraordinary string of very successful National, World and World Junior Championships at that famous venue. Following the opening in 1938 of the Broadmoor Ice Palace (a former riding hall) at the Broadmoor Hotel, a new resident skating club had been formed there. Originally called the Pikes Peak Figure Skating Club, it became a member of the Association in 1939 and was assigned along with the State of Colorado to the Pacific Coast Section. Only two years later, the club hosted the 1941 Pacific Coast Championships and after the War, hosted that event again in 1947. Prior to the 1947-1948 season the club had been renamed the Broadmoor Skating Club and transferred with the state to the Midwestern Section. Based upon its prior record and experience, the award of the 1948 Nationals to the club under the leadership of William Wardman and Carl

W. Chamberlin, was well justified. The Championships were also strongly promoted by the City of Colorado Springs through its Chamber of Commerce, as part of their "Pikes Peak Winter Festival," which also included the NCAA Ice Hockey Championships and a ski meet at Pikes Peak. The policy of the Broadmoor Hotel had always been to support sports, going back many years under the management of Spencer Penrose and Charles L. Tutt and later William Thayer Tutt. It can be safely said that without the generous and unstinting support of the hotel these major events would never have been the great successes that all of them were.

Dick Button and Gretchen Merrill retained their National Senior titles, while the Kennedys defeated Yvonne Sherman and Robert Swenning for the Pair crown. Third in the Senior Pairs were Harriet Sutton and Lyman Wakefield of St. Paul. The latter was also an active judge, but still managed to continue his remarkable competitive career. Lois Waring and Red Bainbridge retained their Dance title, again defeating Anne Davies and Carleton Hoffner, with another strong couple of Irene Maguire and Walter Muehlbronner of New York, third. Davies and Hoffner also won the Junior Pairs.

There was another development during the 1947-48 season of significance for the future of the Association which was the hiring of a full time Executive Secretary. The need had become increasingly apparent as the Association had steadily increased in size and by 1947 had "in excess of 15,000 figure skaters," as stated in the announcement of the appointment in the magazine. The significant increase in international activity following the War, was another reason for the need for a permanent office. The first holder of the position was Roland G. Janson of New York, a long-time member of The Skating Club of New York, who had been National Junior Pair champion in 1937 with Mrs. Ardelle Sanderson. He had also been a teacher of skating and had produced and directed carnivals. Later, he had been the manager of the Iceland rink atop Madison Square Garden, the home of the New York club. His office was located at 5101 39th Avenue, Long Island City, N.Y., and was in effect the first permanent Association office, although it should be pointed out that there had been an office in Boston for **Skating** magazine for many years. As previously mentioned, the magazine had first been published out of Mrs. Blanchard's home at 57 Hedge Road, Brookline, Mass., from its beginning in 1923 to 1936, then in joint quarters with The Skating Club of Boston at 236 Huntington Avenue, Boston until 1939, when it moved to 1 Telford Street, Brighton, on the property of the Boston club. It remained there until 1942, when it returned to 30 Huntington Avenue in Boston. These addresses were then the Association's in effect, since Mrs. Blanchard was really the heart and center of the organization during all those years.

The 1948 Governing Council meeting returned to Chicago in late April with the Treasurer reporting that there were 107 member clubs, of which 16 had a membership of over 250, 13 had between 150 to 250 members, 13 had 100 to 150, 31 had 50 to 100, and 34 less than 50 members. Following the recent trend of updating all fees and prices, the price for the Rulebook was raised to $2.00 per copy, but $1.50 for lots of 50. The passing of Oscar L. Richard was noted and a scroll was to be prepared in his memory and presented to The SC of New York, its current name.

The Finance Committee presented an annual budget and the necessity of increasing income was cited, since the Association was operating at about $1,000 annual deficit. This is the first apparent report of a formal budget being submitted for approval by the Governing Council, although budgets had certainly been prepared prior to the War on a more informal basis by the Executive Committee.

The 1948 Fall meeting of the Executive Committee was held at the New Weston in New York in October, right about on the dates used today of the 9th and 10th. The principal business was a (first) meeting of the new International Committee (created in 1946 and becoming a standing committee in 1949), which was to determine and recommend the basis for the selection of the World and Olympic Teams for 1948. Essentially, selection was to be based upon the finish in the last National Championships held prior to the World (and Olympic) Championships, but also to include the winners of the Junior Singles, in addition to the first, second and third in the Senior Singles and Pairs. It was also reported that sufficient funds had been raised to cover all the expenses of the Olympic Team. The sum of $750 was contributed to the expenses of the defending World champion (Dick Button), and the same amount for a judge.

The 1949 Nationals were awarded to the Broadmoor SC of Colorado Springs and the North Americans to Philadelphia. There was a detailed explanation by the chairman of the Competitions Committee of the award to the Broadmoor two years in a row (in 1948 and 1949). Both Boston and the Broadmoor submitted bids for the 1949 event. Broadmoor's bid included a flat guarantee to the Association plus a division of the net proceeds after the deduction of a flat sum for the rink expenses. Boston, on the other hand agreed to take care of all expenses and to turn over all net profit to the Association. Despite this generosity, it was the opinion of the Competitions Committee that to show the event to so small an audience made it appear doubtful that the gross income would do no more than cover the expenses and would not justify making the award to Boston for geographical considerations. Obviously, a defense of the decision appeared to be necessary, in view of the award of the championship to the same club two years in a row. This was, of course, before the Sectional rotation of the Nationals was implemented.

An additional category of figure judge, called Intermediate, was included in the classes of judges with a Low Test judge now eligible to judge up through the Second Test, the new Intermediate Test judge up through the Fourth Test, and the High Test judge up through the Seventh Test.

The summer session activity was reported with nine sessions being sanctioned, one in the East (Lake Placid), four in the Midwest (Colorado Springs, Rochester, Sault Ste. Marie and St. Paul), and four in the Pacific Coast (Berkeley, Bremerton, Pasadena and Tacoma). A total of 560 tests were passed during the summer, including 11 Gold Figure and 20 Gold Dance. Fifteen judges schools were held, nine dance conferences and 53 pop concerts or carnivals. In the overall picture, a total of 2,722 tests were passed, consisting of 1,580 figure tests and 1,142 dance tests with a total of 13 Gold Figure Tests. Of the 1,097 member clubs, 55 held tests during the season.

The relatively short period between the end of the War and 1949 can be considered as one of the most important in the history of the Association, converting it from a small somewhat local organization into a major player and power on the international skating scene, bringing it into the modern era.

When contrasted with the previous two seasons from 1947 to 1949, the next few seasons seem "quiet" by comparison, yet the beat went on, much as it does today, leading up to the next Olympic year in 1952. The "rhythm" of the sport is still even today directly affected by the peaking of public interest at the time of the Olympic Games. That interest was in the past

On to Oslo
(1949-1952)

reinforced by the fact that the Summer and Winter Games were held in the same year, although not in the same country since 1936. Whether that phenomenon will continue in the future remains to be seen, since the change in 1992 to separate the Winter and Summer Games from each other by two years. Despite the fact that the World Championships are older and considered by the ISU to be more prestigious, they are held annually, and lack the "glamour" and attraction of the Olympics, which are held only every four years.

A further step forward in the development of Ice Dancing domestically was the adoption of a new schedule of Dance tests, effective in 1949, consisting of four tests, with a Preliminary Dance Tests being added, as well as several new dances. The "Continental Waltz" was replaced with the "American Waltz" and the new dances added were the Swing Dance, Dutch Waltz, Fiesta Tango, European Waltz, Rocker Foxtrot, Paso Doble and Argentine Tango.

Two of the new dances were of U.S. origin, the Dutch Waltz and Fiesta Tango having been invented in 1948 by George Muller, formerly of Germany, but a teacher of dance for many years in several clubs around the country, including Boston. The Swing Dance was invented by Hubert Sprott of Canada in the same year. The other dances were all of British origin and had been known there since before the War.

A further revision to the dance structure was made in 1949-1950, when the requirement was imposed that for the final round of both Gold and Silver Dance competitions, six dances would be skated! Happily, this endurance test would not last long, as finally, free dancing was introduced to the competition structure at the Gold level with the competitions of 1952.

At the same time, the 1949 Congress of the ISU approved in total the rules and standards proposed by the ad hoc dance committee and established a permanent Technical Committee for Ice Dancing, as we have seen. The first Chairman of the Committee was Marcel Nicaise of Belgium, with Reg Wilkie of Great Britain, the first British champion in Ice Dancing (as it is called in the

ISU), with his partner Daphne Wallis, and Bill Hickok as the first members. The stage was thus set for the first international competition in the discipline under the new rules in 1950.

December 1948 had also marked the 25th anniversary of **Skating** magazine, and Mrs. Blanchard described its beginning as "something evolved, a little wobbly to be sure, but the birth of a great idea. The new infant would have perished very suddenly had it depended for its life blood on circulation figures and advertising revenue." She goes on to say that the "original aim to spread knowledge of figure skating and to distribute official information and rulings among Association members was somewhat modified with the publication of the Rulebook. In recent years the tendency has been to direct the magazine more to non-competitive and beginning skaters, to make it light and instructive in an elementary way and to carry just the really essential official items. During its early years **Skating** received valuable monetary backing from the ever-growing list of member clubs and its deficits, which re-occurred with unfailing regularity, were met out of the Association treasury." These words are prophetic and could well apply to the magazine of today!

Harry N. Keighley

In 1949, President Henry M. Beatty of Cleveland retired from office and was succeeded by Harry N. Keighley of Evanston, Ill. Hank was far from finished in his active career, continuing to serve the Association and later the ISU. He was perhaps best know as the perennial Referee of the National Championships, serving consecutively from 1946 through 1957 and again in 1960 and 1961. He was also Chairman of the Competitions Committee once again in 1949-1950 and 1954-1955, of the Judges Committee from 1951 to 1954 and of the International Committee in 1954-1955. He was also a World Championship Referee, serving at eight Worlds and one Olympics. A major contribution by him was his organization of the very successful World Championships held at Colorado Springs in 1957, 1959, 1965 and 1969. It is also not generally known that he was the motivating force behind the establishment in 1961 of the Memorial Fund, following the Brussels air accident, and was the first chairman of the Memorial Fund Committee in 1961-1962. Following the death of Walter Powell in that accident, he succeeded him as a member of the ISU Council, serving until 1967. Hank was already working on the next World Championships to be held at Colorado Springs at the time of his death in 1972. He was posthumously elected to the United States Figure Skating hall of Fame in 1977.

The major championships of 1949 were notable for the reappearance of some familiar faces but some new young skaters were also present, a situation which would continue right up to the present day. The USFSA has always supported, whenever possible, the cause of youth at the highest levels and in this year, the previous year's Junior winners were also selected. Several of the 1948 team either had retired or elected not to enter. Among them were John Lettengarver and Eileen Seigh, who had turned professional, and Gretchen Merrill, who elected not to go to Worlds, but did defend her National title. In the Pairs, Yvonne Sherman and Bob Swenning had retired, although Yvonne continued on in Ladies Singles. Replacing them were Anne Davies and Carleton Hoffner, perhaps better known as dancers, but also the Junior Pair Champions of the prior year. Two new men, Hayes Alan Jenkins, from Akron, the 1948 Junior Champion, and Austin Holt from Berkeley, who had been fourth in the Senior Men, and two new ladies, Andra McLaughlin of New York, fifth in the 1948 Senior Ladies, and Virginia Baxter of Detroit, the Junior Ladies Champion, were also on board, so the on-going "changing of the guard," so common in the immediately post-Olympic year, was in full operation! Most of the new arrivals were well known as excellent free skaters.

Yvonne Sherman

In the World Championships themselves, which were held at Paris, Dick Button easily retained his title, defeating Ede Kiraly of Hungary, who had been third in 1948, and Edi Rada of Austria. Jimmy Grogan placed fourth, Hayes Alan Jenkins, sixth, and Austin Holt, seventh. In the Ladies, Barbara Ann Scott was gone, and a new champion was crowned, Alena ("Aja") Vrzanova of Czechoslovakia, who had been fifth in 1948. By reason of her good figures and a new "lease on life" in free skating from her new coach, Gus Lussi, Yvonne Sherman placed a solid second, ahead of Jeannette Altwegg of Great Britain, while Andra McLaughlin and Virginia Baxter placed sixth and seventh. Eva Pawlik of Austria, who had won the European Ladies and was the presumed favorite, had to withdraw after the figures, in which she had placed second. In Pairs, Ede Kiraly and his partner Andrea Kekessy of Hungary, who had been second in 1948, won the title vacated by Lannoy and Baugniet, with the Kennedys regaining second place and another silver medal, while Anne Davies and Carleton Hoffner were a surprising third, over another experienced pair from Hungary, Marianne and Laszlo Nagy, who were the European runners-up. The medal count this time was four, consisting of one gold, two silver and a bronze, one better than the previous high of three in 1930 and the best showing by the Americans in a Worlds to date!

The North American Championships followed the Worlds at Philadelphia, and resulted in rare clean sweep of all five titles by the U.S. skaters, with Button retaining the Men's title,

Second Saint Paul Four – Marlyn Thomsen, Marilyn Thomsen, Janet Gerhauser and John Nightingale

Yvonne Sherman winning the Ladies, the Kennedys the Pairs, Waring and Bainbridge retaining the Dance title, and a revived Fours event going to the second St. Paul Four of Gerhauser, Thomsen, Thomsen and Nightingale. The classic split between the Canadian and U.S. judges can again be seen in the Pairs, with Marlene Smith and Donald Gilchrist of Canada, having three firsts from the Canadian judges and the Kennedys the other three from the U.S. judges, but two of the latter placing the Canadians third, which cost them the title. The other contesting pair was another dance couple doing Pairs, Irene Maguire and Walter Muehlbronner, third. Gretchen Merrill did enter the North Americans and after placing a close second in the figures dropped to fourth, a preview of the Nationals to come.

The 1949 Nationals returned to Colorado Springs and were again a great success, with 80 entries. Dick Button won his fourth straight title, over Grogan and Jenkins, while Yvonne Sherman won her first title, dethroning Gretchen Merrill, whose six-year reign thus came to an end. The Kennedys took the Pairs, followed by Maguire and Muehlbronner, and Davies and Hoffner, while Waring and Bainbridge retained their Dance title and also won the Junior Pairs. Maguire and Muehlbronner also placed second in Dance, followed by Carmel and Ed Bodel from Berkeley.

There was still a tendency then for skaters to compete in more than one event, and the demands of pair skating had not yet reached a point that dancers could not handle it, and with their often better unison, they sometimes fared very well. At that time, the Senior Pairs had to skate their free skating twice (there was no short program), the first time for familiarization and no marks, and the second time for the "money." In the Senior Pairs, Maguire and Muehlbronner were the clear "winners" in the first skating, but could not do it twice in a row and lost the title to the Kennedys in a 3 to 2 decision. The Novice Ladies' Champion was a young skater from Boston, Tenley Albright, while the Novice Men's Champion was Hugh C. Graham, Jr. of Tulsa, both of whom would be heard from in different ways in the future.

It was also in 1949, that the Executive Committee was again enlarged to include 18 at large members, with six being elected for three-year terms in rotation. The former limitation on service that a retiring member was not eligible for re-election for one year was dropped. The at large group would remain at 18 until 1957, when it was reduced to 12, in two groups of six, for two year terms, until 1959, when it was returned to 18, but in two groups of nine for two-year terms. This format remained in effect until 1961, when a further change was made to 18 at large members, all elected at once for a one-year term! Got it? No doubt there were seemingly valid reasons for all this "churning," but in hindsight, the various changes seem a little silly!

Karol and Peter Kennedy

The 1949 Governing Council was back in Chicago at the Edgewater Beach Hotel in May. There were 33 clubs represented by 71 delegates and 23 clubs by proxies, representing "approximately" 53 percent of the membership. It has always been essentially impossible to get any firm handle on the exact number of skaters actively involved in the Association, beyond the number registered (after 1950) but an old "rule of thumb" was that for each active skater, there were at least two other persons (parents mostly) involved.

An "innovation" at the meeting was the submission by the various chairmen of the committees of reports in writing in advance (described then as "mimeographed" copies), which were sent to the clubs with the call of the meeting. Thus was born the famous or "infamous" Report Book, the bane of the existence of all who have served as committee chairmen. The meeting approved a new schedule of figure tests, which was graded gradually upward by increasing the total factors of each test. The new preliminary test added "straight skating" of short strokes, forward and backward, with correct take-offs from one foot to the other. The loop figures were spread over enough tests to maintain their continued practice.

The meeting reflected the first attempt at what would become a concerted campaign to assess all members of clubs with a "head tax" (registration fee). The proposal was defeated, but would return again in the following year and was finally passed in 1950. The principle of an additional assessment fee for carnivals in which World, Olympic or National (Team) skaters appeared, of one percent of the gross receipts, was also adopted.

A reflection of the impingement of the new medium of television into sports was reflected in the fact that a Television Committee was established with Henry Beatty as the chairman. The committee would last only one year, but would be revived in 1961, with Carl W. Gram, Jr., as the chairman, a time when the interest of television in acquiring the rights to broadcast the National Championships was becoming a significant factor in the finances of the Association.

Lois Waring and Mike McGean

The season of 1949-1950 might well be called the "Year of the Dance," since it was in 1950 that the first International Competition in Ice Dancing was held, at the same time as the 1950 World Championships at Wembley Stadium outside London. Red Bainbridge had retired to concentrate on his education. He would later "turn professional," as we said in those days, and Lois Waring had acquired a new partner and future husband in Michael McGean from Cleveland, a member of a well known skating family from that important center in the Midwest.

Selected to go to this first competition were Lois Waring and Michael McGean, Irene Maguire and Walter Muehlbronner, the runners-up in the 1949 Nationals and Carmel and Ed Bodel, the bronze medalists, with Bill Hickok as the USA judge. In those days, there was no prohibition on a member of an ISU Technical Committee serving as a judge, as there is today, so the entire committee served as judges, and there even was a second Belgian judge and one Czech judge on the panel of five.

Lois and Mike won the competition relatively easily over Sybil Cooke and Robert Hudson of Great Britain, although they were placed fifth by Reg Wilkie, so obviously, there still was some work to do to obtain standardization in the judging side! Third were Maguire and Muehlbronner and fifth were the Bodels, certainly a strong first showing for American ice dancing. However, that first win, while not as yet a World Championship (that would come in 1952), still remains the only one achieved by dancers from the United States up to today (1995). Lois and Mike went on to win the National title that year at Washington, D.C., her fourth and his first.

This first International competition in ice dancing included free dancing for the first time, and right from the beginning it was controversial, just as it is today! Free dancing would not, however, be added to the Nationals until 1952. The reporter of the 1950 International Competition stated it as follows: "Just what is meant by free dancing, and how is it different from pair skating? Some couples skated programs that were quite indistinguishable from pairs, while others interpreted the requirement as a program primarily of sequences of steps similar to those used in the ice dances. That there was no agreement among the judges as to the respective merits of the two types of programs was evident from the considerable variations in the placings."

There would be a second International Ice Dancing Competition held at Milan in 1951, together with the World Championships of that year, to which Lois and Mike returned to defend their title, but this time, they could do no better than third, behind the two very strong British couples, Jean Westwood and Lawrence Demmy, the winners, and Joan Dewhirst and John Slater. These two couples would engage in many very close competitions over the next few years, establishing the almost total dominance of the new discipline by the couples from Great Britain, which would last until the early 1960's. Two new U.S. couples also went to Milan, Carol Peters and Daniel Ryan from Washington, DC, the Silver Dance (Junior) champions from 1950, who placed fourth and Virginia Hoyns and Donald Jacoby, representing Philadelphia, who were fifth.

Another major "milestone" in 1949 was the award to Dick Button of the James E. Sullivan Memorial Trophy, presented to the outstanding "amateur" athlete in the country by the Amateur Athletic Union (AAU), then the "superpower" of sport in the United States. The AAU was the National Governing Body (NGB) for nine different sports and an organization with which the USFSA had been "allied" for the purposes of Olympic representation, as the term was used, virtually since its founding. Dick was the first figure skater and the first winter sports athlete ever to win the prestigious trophy, which was in memory of an early AAU President. So far, he remains the only figure skater ever to have been so honored, although several speed skaters have won the trophy since, including Eric Heiden, Bonnie Blair and Dan Jansen. Quite a few people thought that Dick should have won in 1948, and although a year "late," the award to him was a high honor indeed, both for himself, as well as for the sport in the United States.

It was also in 1949 that the decision was made to transfer the office of the Association to Chicago, but Roland Janson had found it impossible to make the move and had resigned. As a result a new Executive Secretary was hired, Miss Irene W. Baldwin, the former Executive Secretary of the Chicago FSC. The new office was at 450 East Ohio Street in Chicago, and with President Keighley also from the Chicago area, support of and coordination with the office was readily available.

Also in 1949, the schedule of figure tests was revised, transferring several figures from one test to another, although the Eighth Test remained unchanged. The new schedule was "graded gradually upward by increasing the total factors of each test" and a new Preliminary Test (replacing the former Junior Test) was added. This action required coordination with the CFSA, which had adopted the USFSA test structure in 1941, so that reciprocity between the two test systems could be maintained. Full interchangeableness between the test schedules of the two associations was eventually done away with in 1970, as the schedules and judging systems between the two countries evolved in different directions, but a vestige of it still remains, which permits Gold medalists of one association to take the Gold Medal Test, in Figures, Pairs and

Dance of the other association, without having to take all the prior tests. This is really the last vestige of the cooperation between the two associations, other than in sanctions, which was such an important part of the activities of the USFSA until the demise of the North American Championships in 1971. Since then, unfortunately, the two associations have generally gone their separate ways and the friendly relations across the border are no longer of such great importance as they were in the past when the sport was smaller.

There was a continued modest decline in the number of clubs in the Association, so that by 1950, the number was down to 103 from two years prior, with 39 from the East, 41 from the Midwest and 25 from the pacific Coast. Some of the attrition can be attributed to the War. With revenue somewhat reduced and with the increased demands of international skating, actions taken at the 1950 Governing Council meeting included the establishment of the registration fee of 50 cents, and the extra one percent carnival assessment for those in which National and World level skaters appeared, as already mentioned.

Also implemented was an Interim Probationary Membership for clubs, which enabled a new club to become a member of the Association between meetings of the Governing Council. Such clubs were then eligible for election as probationary members at the next Annual Meeting, and after one year in that category, were eligible for election as full members. Basically, such clubs could do everything a full member club could, except to hold competitions and to send delegates to the Governing Council meetings. The former limitation would eventually also be eliminated. The Probationary Membership had been originally implemented in 1936.

Elected as the first Honorary Member of the USFSA in 1949 was Herbert J. Clarke of Great Britain, the President of the ISU, in recognition of his 25 years of service to that organization. "H.J.," as he was called, had been a long time friend of U.S. figure skating. He is, so far, the only foreign non-member ever elected to honorary membership in the Association. It was also in 1949 that two deaths occurred of persons who had made significant contributions to the Association. The

first was of Paul Armitage of New York, who can really be considered as a "founder." He was Chairman of the Executive Committee from 1921 to 1925, and also a member of the first New York Four, together with Clara Hartman, later his wife, Grace Munstock and Joel Liberman, the first National champions in Fours in 1924. The second was Sandy McDonald, also from New York, who had been the National Dance champion with Harold Hartshorne from 1939 to 1941, and, as we have seen, the first USFSA Gold Medalist in Dance. Her death was most untimely, at a relatively early age. She was a Canadian, originally from Nova Scotia and later from Edmonton, to which she returned in 1946.

Herbert J. Clarke

The 1950 Nationals in Washington, DC were successful. Button, Sherman and the Kennedys all retained their titles, while Waring and McGean won the Dance. Also in the Championships were Tenley Albright, of Boston, who won the Junior Ladies, and Carol Heiss, of New York, who was fourth in the Novice Ladies, from both of whom much would be heard in the years ahead. The practice then popular of skating in more than one event continued. Irene Maguire and Walter Muehlbronner were second in both Senior Pairs and Dance, while Anne Davies and Carleton Hoffner were third in both events. Janet Gerhauser and John Nightingale from St. Paul won both the Junior Pairs and the Fours, the latter with the Thomsen twins, for their third title.

The 1950 Governing Council meeting was held at Chicago in May, and it was at this meeting that the new registration fee of 50 cents was finally approved. The resolution for adoption pointed out that the present cash surplus was considered inadequate in the view of the Executive and Finance Committees to warrant deficit financing, and further that the surplus should be built up by at least $10,000, in view of the heavy demands for international skating, and to keep a safe reserve for contingencies. Curiously, at the same time, the new one percent additional sanction assessment for carnivals with World level skaters in them was dropped, perhaps because it was felt that the registration fee would replace it from a revenue standpoint.

At the meeting, the death of Clarence L. "Larry" Parker of Washington, D.C., was noted with a memorial resolution. Parker had been a chairman of the Dance Committee and a member of the Executive Committee.

The Fall 1950 meeting of the Executive Committee was held at the New Weston in New York. An initial proposal was made to provide for a majority pass only (two of three judges) for tests, rather than the existing unanimous requirement. While not adopted then, the idea would take root and eventually become the rule. Also approved was the requirement for an annual written examination to be required of all referees and optional for judges. A "temporary" rule was adopted which based selection for the 1951 Worlds on the results of both the 1950 and 1951 Nationals, since the latter were to precede the Worlds, which was not usually the case in those days. It would not be long before the Nationals would precede the Worlds on a regular basis, with selection for the latter being based on the former. The complicating factor in the equation in 1951 was the presence of the North American Championships in the schedule in the odd-numbered years, which made the "window" for the Nationals between the North Americans and the Sectionals rather small.

The year 1950-1951 was the first with the new registration fee and for the first time, actual numbers are available, which at least give an idea of the active membership of the Association. For the year ending in 1950, the revenue of the Association was $9,596, the expenses were $7,828 and the assets were $45,208, up almost $10,000 from 1946. By the end of the year in 1951 there were 114 clubs, a slight increase over the prior two years, and there were 13,616 registered members. The revenue of the Association for that year was $15,704, expenses were $13,095, while assets were $50,208; so it can be demonstrated that a steady, but modest increase in the number of members and in the net value of the Association was under way, this still being well before the future television era.

The structure and operations of the Association were becoming more clearly defined along Sectional lines. As a result of the "California" situation in the mid-1930's, a Pacific Coast Sectional Committee had been established in 1938, with Henry F. Swift of San Francisco as the first chairman. It was followed in 1941 by a comparable Midwestern Committee, the first chairman of which was Walter S. Powell of St. Louis. The third and last Sectional Committee formed was that for the East, in 1942, the first chairman of which was Past President Sherwin C. Badger. The committees were directed to "collect and disseminate information to encourage the advancement of figure skating in all its branches and to promote harmony and progress among members and clubs in their respective sections." The latter obligation was really the one that counted! Curiously, the Sections have never been defined either in the Constitution or later in the By Laws, but only in the Competition Rules, for the purposes of entry into the Sectional and later the Regional Championships. This has meant that revisions to the Sections has been accomplished through the Competitions Committee by a simple majority vote, rather than by the Governing Council by a two-thirds vote, which would seem to be unwise, but which has, in practice, worked well. Finally, in 1952, a third Vice President was added, with each Vice President being automatically the Chairman of his or her respective Sectional Committee. As will be seen, the Sectional Committees were eventually abolished in the major re-organization of the Association that took place in 1980 as a consequence of the Amateur Sports Act of 1978. The changes adopted also provided that the First Vice President must come from the same Section as the President, for the purposes of the succession. This provision, however, did not last long, and was soon changed in 1956 simply to provide that the Vice Presidents "in their order" would succeed. This meant that they had to be designated and elected as First, Second and Third, and there were no criteria applied, either based upon seniority or geography as to the order in which they would serve, that decision essentially being left to the Nominating Committee.

After but one year in Chicago, the permanent office of the Association was moved to Boston in 1950, where it would remain until 1979. It had separate office space in the same building as **Skating** magazine at 30 Huntington Avenue, even on the same floor, but across an air well, so that the occupants in one office could see (and wave to) those in the other! The new office manager, who was initially designated as an "Assistant" Secretary and in 1952 would reassume the title of Executive Secretary held by her predecessors, was Virginia Badger Bremer, the sister of Sherwin Badger and herself a National Junior Ladies champion in 1928. Ginny had been the Circulation Manager for the magazine, so the move across the air well was not a difficult one for her. When the permanent office had first been contemplated, a special committee was formed to provide general supervision and guidance, the first chairman of which in 1947 was Thomas A. Dean of Chicago. In 1950, Theresa Weld Blanchard became the chairman of what eventually came to be called the "Central Office Committee." The committee remained in existence until 1977, just prior to the move of the Association to Colorado Springs in 1979, and in its time was a valuable resource for the office staff. (One cannot help but wonder, with the complexity of the Headquarters operation today, whether such a committee should not be revived, since oversight responsibility for the Headquarters operation is too great a burden to impose upon the officers.) Thus, finally, the offices of the Association were consolidated in one place, and as time went on, the integration of their functions increased, especially after the retirement of Mrs. Blanchard as Editor of the magazine in 1963.

In 1951, for the first time in quite a few years, the National Championships were held early, at the end of January in Seattle, and before the World Championships in Milan, Italy. As a result, the World Team could be selected on a current basis, not from the results of the prior year. The effect was that quite a turnover could be seen in the Team, although it continued to be led by a now "veteran" Dick Button.

Sonya Klopfer

Yvonne Sherman and Gretchen Merrill were gone, while in the Men, the most promising young bronze medalist of 1950, Richard Dwyer, had departed for the professional ranks and the Ice Follies, at a very young age. It was a major loss, since his potential for the future in international competition had been obvious. He enjoyed a long and distinguished career in the Ice Follies, eventually succeeding Roy Shipstad as "Mr. Debonair." He would be elected to the World Figure Skating Hall of Fame in 1993.

The new Ladies champion was Sonya Klopfer from New York, with Tenley Albright, second and Virginia Baxter third. In the Men, it was Button, Jimmy Grogan and Hayes Alan Jenkins in that order, with it being the closest competition of Dick's career. Being busy in college on an "honors" program, he had not trained too diligently for his defense so that the gap between him and Jimmy Grogan had virtually disappeared, both in figures and in free skating. Dick only retained his title by the smallest of margins and a 3 to 2 decision by the judges. In the Pairs, it was the defending World Champions, the Kennedys as the winners, with Janet Gerhauser and John Nightingale second, both Irene Maguire and Walter Muehlbronner and Anne Davies and Carleton Hoffner not returning. Lois Waring and Michael McGean having retired (as it turned out, temporarily), the Dance title went to Carmel and Ed Bodel, with Virginia Hoyns and Donald Jacoby, who had been fourth in the 1950 Silver Dance, second, ahead of Carol Peters and Daniel Ryan. In the Novice Ladies, Carol Heiss of New York was the winner.

The Milan Worlds in 1951 were a memorable one for several reasons. Dick Button had buckled down to work after Seattle and retained his title, his fourth, over Grogan, who placed second, with Hayes Jenkins fourth, Dudley Richards of Boston, the 1951 National Junior Champion, fifth and Donald Laws, the 1950 Junior Champion, seventh. In those days, the United States often enjoyed the luxury of four entries in the Singles, something no longer possible today. In the Ladies, Jeannette Altwegg of Great Britain won on the basis of her superior figures, with Sonya Klopfer, third, Tenley Albright, sixth and Andra McLaughlin of New York, seventh. Although Andra had twice won the Richard Trophy at the Nationals, her relatively weak figures had kept her out of the medals, despite her outstanding free skating. Placing 11th was Frances Dorsey, the 1951 National

Jimmy Grogan

Junior Ladies champion. In the Pairs, the Kennedys were defeated in a close competition by Ria Baran and Paul Falk of Germany, who also were the World champions in Roller Pair skating, with the appearance for the first time in the Worlds after the War of the German skaters. The Kennedys had arrived late on the scene, due to carnival commitments in the United States and had to skate almost immediately upon arrival, so perhaps "propeller lag" (there being no jet aircraft yet), got to them! Gerhauser and Nightingale placed eighth and Austin and Anne Holt, who had been fourth in the Nationals, placed 11th.

The season was not yet over, as the 1951 North Americans were still to be skated, this time at Calgary, Alberta, which would become a major venue in the future. The Canadian challenge was not as strong as in prior years, with skaters from the United States again sweeping all the titles: Button in the Men, Klopfer in the Ladies, the Kennedys in Pairs and the Bodels in the Dance. No Fours event was held. Of the 12 available medals, the U.S. took nine of them, with the best Canadian place being the Silver medal of Suzanne Morrow of Toronto in the Ladies, with Tenley Albright third. It is an historical note that the panels of judges were all men, with one exception, Mary Louise Premer of St. Paul, who judged all four events. Actually, in the prior two North Americans since the War, there had been only one woman on the panels of judges each year, Margaretta Drake from Chicago in 1947 and Marge Ridgely of Baltimore in 1949. Although the rules now provided for the Gold Dances to be skated, and the first Gold Dance Tests had been held in Canada in 1950, the Silver Dances were still used in the Dance event by agreement between the two associations.

The North Americans were run according to prevailing ISU Rules, except for the number of judges, which meant that the Open System of judging was used, involving the display of the judges' marks after each performance. The Open System had come in internationally in 1936, and was used by the USFSA at the Nationals until 1946, when the Modified Open System was adopted, which provided for the display of all the marks after the end of each part of an event. The Open System returned in 1973 for the Nationals and the Senior events of the Sectionals and Regionals, while the Modified Open System itself was replaced in 1990 by the old Closed System, in which no marks are displayed at all. The Open and Modified Open Systems, despite their merits, have fallen victim to the demands of time, as the classes in the qualifying competitions have continued to increase in size. From the standpoint of the judge, the Modified Open System is probably the best, but efforts to have it adopted by the ISU were unsuccessful. The public demand for the Open System continues to make it the system of choice for those events which are televised.

The 1951 Governing Council meeting was held at the Edgewater Beach Hotel in Chicago. There were now 114 member clubs, 42 in the East, 44 in the Midwest and 26 on the Pacific Coast. It was confirmed that appearances on television of amateur skaters had to be approved by the Public Relations Committee (which had been created in 1944 as a special committee), the then sanction body. The Association made clear early on in the game that the rights to televise were the property of the Association and under its control, a wise decision.

The continued issue of competitor and coach conduct was revisited and a very strong rule was adopted to the effect that "if an entrant in a competition or a candidate for a test, or a relation or trainer of an entrant or candidate, shall express himself in a highly improper manner concerning the conduct or the result of a competition or test, or concerning the conduct or qualification of an official or judge, the entrant or candidate concerned may be suspended from skating in competitions or tests for such period as may be decided" by a committee consisting of the President, the chairmen of the Competitions and Rules, Standards and Tests, Dance, Judges and Judging and the chairman of the appropriate Sectional Committee. Invariably, such rules are a reaction to a particular instance. There were at that time some parents especially who objected to the results of the competitions in which their children were involved, so that a rather punitive and somewhat subjective rule seemed to be in order at the time. The Executive Committee, at its meeting following the Governing Council meeting, awarded the 1952 Nationals to the Broadmoor SC, which represented the third time in five years that club had been given the responsibility of organizing them. This experience would be a major factor in the future award of the World Championships to the Broadmoor, for the first time in 1957.

The fall 1951 meeting of the Executive Committee was held for the second time outside New York City, at the Broadmoor Hotel in Colorado Springs (the other time having been in 1933 at The Country Club in Brookline, Mass., at the invitation of former President Weld, who was then the President of TCC). A decision was made to hold an Olympic Tryout to select the 1952 Olympic Team, which was awarded to Indianapolis, with all net revenues to go to the USFSA for the benefit of the team. With the first World Championship in Ice Dancing also to be held in 1952, a Dance Tryout was included in the program at Indianapolis. The meeting also recognized the principle of paying the expenses of the officers and standing committee chairmen to attend meetings of the Governing Council and Executive Committee. The miscellaneous ruling which had approved the principle of the payment of such expenses went back to 1941, and the new revision had the effect of limiting such support to the officer and the chairmen of the standing committees only, leaving out the chairmen of the special committees. There was not, as yet, any intention of paying the expenses of the at large members of the Executive Committee to attend such meetings.

It was at this meeting that the addition of a third Vice President, one for each Section was proposed, and if the President became incapacitated for any reason the Vice President for his Section would serve in his place. The provision of designating the three Vice Presidents as First, Second and Third, for the purposes of the succession, would come later. It was also voted that sanctions for the holding of tests, judging schools, conferences, and the like, could only be issued to member clubs.

Prior to the 1952 season and the Olympic Winter Games of that year, the full Olympic Tryout to select the Team was held, as noted above, due in part to the rapid turnover involved in the composition of the World Teams of the immediately preceding years, and also because the Nationals of 1952, which had been awarded to Colorado Springs were back on the old schedule of coming at the end of the season after the international competitions. Only Dick Button, as the defending Olympic champion was excused from participating in the Tryout. The Tryout in Dance for team members was the first in that discipline, which was to be held at the Worlds for the first time as a full fledged championship event (the first two years of 1950 and 1951 having been International Competitions only). The panel for the competition in Singles included Henry Beatty as the Referee, and Kendall Kelley, Walter Powell, Joseph Savage, Mary Louise Premer and

Benjamin Wright, as the judges, which can be seen included no less than five past or future Presidents of the USFSA, with Mary Louise the only lady and the future wife of one of them!

In the Men, Jimmy Grogan won easily, in what may have been the best performance of his career, freed as he was of the pressure of having to compete against Dick Button. Hayes Jenkins and Dudley Richards were second and third, with Ronnie Robertson, representing the Broadmoor SC, and the 1950 National Novice champion, fourth. In the Ladies, Sonya Klopfer won in a very close competition with Tenley Albright, who won the figures. The result was 3 to 2, with the younger members of the panel in the minority, but their judgment was vindicated when Tenley reversed the result in the Olympics. Third was Virginia Baxter from Detroit. In the Pairs, it was the Kennedys and Gerhauser-Nightingale, while in Dance, Lois Waring and Michael McGean, who would be married later in the year, returned to defeat Peters and Ryan.

The 1952 Olympic Winter Games were held at Oslo, Norway, in an urban setting, with the free skating held in the center of the gigantic Bislett Stadium inside its famous speed skating track. The figures were held on an outdoor artificial ice rink called Jordal Amphi. In the Ladies, Tenley Albright surprised all by placing a close second to Jeannette Altwegg of Great Britain, with Sonya Klopfer and Virginia Baxter fourth and fifth behind Jacqueline du Bief of France. In the Men, it was Button retaining his title, and doing the triple loop for the first time in competition, with Grogan and Jenkins third and fourth behind Helmut Seibt of Austria. There were many who were of the opinion that Seibt should not have been in the medals, because of his relatively poor free skating, which was proven correct in the later Worlds at Paris. In the Pairs, Baran and Falk, continuing in the tradition of German pair skating set by Maxi Herber and Ernst Baier before the War, won the Gold medals, over the Kennedys, who earned the second Silver medal in Pairs at the Olympics for the United States, the other having been in 1932 by Loughran and Badger. Janet Gerhauser and John Nightingale placed sixth. With two medals and eight finishes in the top six it was a most successful Olympics for the United States. Button's feat is really quite remarkable, as he was still pursuing an honors program in college (he eventually graduated in 1952 cum laude), and had to complete and forward his honors thesis from abroad, at a cost in postage, with which his father was not happy! The last time that the United States had won two medals at the same Games was in 1932 at Lake Placid.

The World Championships followed the Olympics as usual at Paris, with the only major withdrawal being that of Jeannette Altwegg, who elected not to defend and retired. The battle for the Ladies developed into a good one between du Bief and Albright, but the latter became ill with bronchitis and had to withdraw, after placing second in figures, with Klopfer and Baxter claiming the silver and bronze medals. In the Men, Button won what would be his fifth and last title, with Grogan gaining a well deserved second over Jenkins, with Seibt quite properly fourth. Dudley

Richards, who had not skated in the Olympics, finished fifth. In the Pairs, the Falk's repeated their Olympic win over the Kennedys, with Gerhauser and Nightingale fifth. In the first World Championship in Ice Dancing, Carol Peters and Daniel Ryan placed third, with the Bodels, who had missed the Tryout, fourth. Carol Johns and Jack Jost from Baltimore, who had been third in the Tryout, placed eighth. They had the unusual distinction of being double Gold Medalists in both Singles and Dance. Unfortunately, Lois Waring suffered an injury in practice, so she and McGean were unable to compete. The dances skated were the Rocker Foxtrot, Westminster, Quickstep and Argentine Tango, and free dancing was skated in the final round, which Mrs. Blanchard commented as having lifts and spins that should have been omitted. The ultimate winners were Jean Westwood and Lawrence Demmy of Great Britain. Lawrence once told the author that their program was essentially a revised version of that with which they had won the British Junior Pair Championship a few years before! So, in the Worlds, the medal count went up to a total of seven out of 12, with a most rare sweep of the medals in the Men for the U.S., which had not been done since the Austrians in 1928.

There was an unfortunate incident at the Worlds, when Peter Kennedy allegedly assaulted a press photographer after the Pair event, an act which resulted in his suspension indefinitely by both the ISU and the USFSA, thereby effectively ending his competitive career and that of his sister Karol. The suspension by the USFSA was also based upon the additional circumstance that the Kennedys had skated an exhibition without proper sanction at Garmisch, Germany, following the Worlds.

The 1952 Nationals were held at Colorado Springs late in March, and here, unfortunately, there were drop outs, with Sonya Klopfer and Virginia Baxter declining to compete, as a result of which they were suspended, since they had made the commitment as members of the World and Olympic Teams to participate in the Nationals. However, the suspensions were, in fact, lifted shortly thereafter, after satisfactory explanations for their absence were received.

A curious rule adopted in 1947 was still in effect at the 1952 Nationals, requiring two performances in the Senior Singles events and in the Senior and Junior Pairs, and the Fours events, with the first being without marks. As we have already seen, it could be costly if a competitor could not perform equally well both times. The competitors were also permitted to furnish to the judges a brief written description of the free skating program prior to the first skating. This system, which was a uniquely American device, was retained until 1953, and nothing like it would be seen again until the introduction of the short program 20 years later.

For the first time in the Nationals, free dancing was included in the Gold (Senior) Dance event, but still with three compulsory dances being skated in the final round, in addition to the four skated in the initial round, truly a "grind!" Lois Waring and Michael McGean regained the title they had last held in 1950, and the day after the Nationals ended, were married at The Broadmoor. Dick Button closed out his distinguished career with his seventh title, equaling the record of Roger Turner set between 1928 and 1934. Jimmy Grogan was again second, for the seventh time in major competitions – four Nationals, two North Americans and one Worlds. Hayes Alan Jenkins was third. In the Ladies, Tenley Albright claimed what would be the first of five Senior Ladies titles, defeating Frances Dorsey of Seattle, in the absence of Klopfer and Baxter. The Kennedys retained the Pair title, their fifth and last, their suspensions not yet having been imposed. Carol Heiss moved up to Junior Ladies champion and would be ready for her debut internationally the following year, as would Ronnie Robertson who won the Junior Men. The Novice Men's winner was Tim Brown, representing Baltimore, who would in a few years be the close rival of David Jenkins, third in the Junior Men in 1952.

The 1952 Governing Council meeting was again held at the Edgewater Beach Hotel in Chicago, but it was voted in the future to rotate the meetings between the Sections, with the 1953 meeting to be held on the Pacific Coast.

It was at the 1952 meeting, a medallion designed by Mrs. Clara Rotch Frothingham of Boston was accepted for a plaque to be presented to the winners of the National trophies for which there were no replicas. The medallion, mounted in a Lucite block, has also been presented to the outgoing Presidents, in recognition of their service to the Association. Mrs. Frothingham had also designed the unique emblem of The SC of Boston. She was a former National Dance champion and was one of the first National Dance judges appointed when that class of judge was established in 1938. Also, in 1952, the position of "Chief Accountant" was formalized, although it had been a requirement for competitions to have such an official since 1948, with the first appointments being made by the Executive Committee to that position. Obviously, there had been "secretaries" (as they were called abroad) or accountants for competitions since the beginning, but it was on an informal basis and it had been the responsibility of the host clubs to provide them. The new position, being an official one, meant that the Chief Accountants were appointed in the same manner as Referees and Judges, and recognized as officials, with the same eligibility for reimbursement of their travel and living expenses. As recommended by the Executive Committee, a mandatory examination was instituted, to be taken by Referees on an annual basis for the retention of appointment.

Another major change approved was a recodification to incorporate into one section of the Rulebook the basic rules relating to the standards of skating, or as they were more formally called "regulations governing the manner of performance and the marking of figure skating," or the Skating Standards Regulations (SSR), as they became known in 1960. The responsibility for setting up such rules and keeping them up to date with current international standards was placed in the hands of a special committee consisting originally of the chairmen of the Tests,

Competitions, Judges and International Committees, with one of them being appointed chairman. In the beginning, the chairman was usually the chairman of the Tests Committee, although later, the duty was more often assigned to those involved with the ISU. The committee was expanded in 1962 to include the chairman of the Dance Committee, and in 1965 to include the ISU Representative, as well as those USFSA persons who were serving as ISU officeholders.

There was also a change in the "cycle" of the issues of the magazine, with the "volume" being changed to eight issues on a calendar year basis (January to December) instead of on a seasonal basis, from November to May. The reason for the change was a practical one, which was to have the two Fall issues (November and December) reach all subscribers as they were published. Since many clubs then opened their seasons late in the autumn (from the standpoint of the publication schedule), renewal orders could not be collected and sent in until the publication schedule was well under way. This resulted in most subscribers receiving the first two or three issues of the new volume well after they were originally published.

Originally, there had been only three issues a season from 1923 to 1927; five in 1927-1928, due to its being an Olympic year; four from 1928 to 1933; five again in 1933-34; six from 1934 to 1943; five once again in 1943 to 1945, due to the War; six again from 1945 to 1947 and eight until 1978, when there were nine, and finally ten in 1979 until 1994, when the magazine went to a bimonthly publishing schedule of six issues, plus a supporting bimonthly newsletter between the issues of the magazine. However, the latter are really "magazines" and have continued to be numbered in consecutive order in the appropriate "volume," which by 1995 was number 72. Of course, the change made in 1952 presented a problem for those persons who had complete sets of the magazine, since up to then the volumes had usually been bound by season and not by year.

Finally, in 1952, there was a further "changing of the guard," with Harry Keighley stepping down and being succeeded by H. Kendall Kelley, the second of the "Cleveland" Presidents. As was the tradition and generally accepted practice then, Harry continued in the active service of the Association, as Chairman of the International Committee from 1952 to 1955, of the Dance Committee from 1955 to 1956 and again from 1959 to 1962, and of the Judges Committee from 1968 to 1971. He also served as Third Vice President from 1956 to 1958, the only Past President to serve as a Vice President after his term of office, other than Sherwin Badger and Charlie Rotch, back in the 1930's, when they were "swapping" the chair between them! The special function which Harry carried out from 1965 to 1976, was as chairman of the USFSA Olympic Committee, a special committee primarily concerned with the raising of funds in support of the Olympic teams.

H. Kendall Kelley

He also served as chairman of a USFSA-PSGA Liaison Committee from 1964 to 1967. Harry passed away in 1983, and was posthumously elected to the United States Figure Skating Hall of Fame in 1993.

The 1952 fall meeting of the Executive Committee was back in New York, this time at the Hotel Vanderbilt, with 23 of the 33 members of the committee present. The so-called conduct rule was broadened to provide for the suspension of any person or club for violation of any rule of the USFSA, or for conduct which was considered injurious to the sport or contrary to the interests of the USFSA. It was another rather subjective rule, which was adopted in the atmosphere of the suspensions of Sonya Klopfer and Virginia Baxter, which had been followed by the suspension in June 1952 of the Kennedys.

The selection rule for Worlds was broadened to include in the "zone" of consideration, the top five in Senior Singles and top two in Junior Singles in the "most recent" Nationals. For Pairs, it was the top four, plus the Junior Pair winners, and for Dance, it was the top six in the Gold Dance. The number of figure tests taken during the year was reported as 2,297, up from 2,088 the prior year and to 1,587 passed, up from 1,469. In Dance, dances passed increased from 1,873 to 2,208. There were 12 Eighth Tests passed out of 47 taken, and 50 Gold Dances out of 162 taken.

The number of sanctioned summer sessions was now up to 15, with six in the east, six in the Midwest, and three on the Pacific Coast. Figure and Dance judges' schools were conducted at five summer centers: Colorado Springs, Lake Placid, Rochester, Seattle and Tacoma.

The first sign of support for the clubs organizing the Sectionals was seen in a decision of the Association to underwrite any cash losses to the extent of $250 each! It was also at this meeting that the authorization for an official accountant to run the accounting rooms at the Nationals and Sectionals was approved.

While it can be said that the "Golden Age" was still continuing, the year 1953 could well have another heading, being the "year of the break through" (for the ladies, that is). In all organizations, there are major "milestones," and the USFSA was no exception. From the standpoint of international skating, these "milestones" can be summarized, as follows:

Break Through for the Ladies (1953-1956)

1923 – The Association obtains membership in the IEV; 1924 – an Olympic team is sent to the first Olympic Winter Games in Chamonix, France; 1930 - the World Championships are held in the United States for the first time (in New York); 1932 - the Olympic Winter Games are held in the United States, also for the first time (at Lake Placid); 1948 - an American wins the World

Tenley Albright

and Olympic championships for Men for the first time (Dick Button); 1950 - an American pair wins the World title for the first time (Karol and Peter Kennedy); and in 1953 - an American wins the World Championship for Ladies for the first time (Tenley Albright). There would be many future milestones, of course, but the "break through" in 1953 was an enormous one, although in hindsight, it does not seem so important today, when all the World Lady champions that the United States has had since that first one, are considered. Yet, what they achieved was all built on that initial success.

With the North American and National Championships again following the Worlds, which would be held out of doors on the giant rink at Davos, Switzerland, the team had to be selected by the International Committee, without the benefit of the results of a current competition being available for the purpose. There were some large "gaps" to be filled. Button, Klopfer, Baxter, the Kennedys, Gerhauser-Nightingale, Waring-McGean, among others, were all gone. There were essentially no top Senior pairs left, and in the end, none were selected, clearly illustrating the inherent problems of basing selections on "ancient history," as it were, being the results of the Nationals of the prior year.

Even without any Pairs, a large team was selected, consisting of four Men, four Ladies and three Dance couples, under the then rather liberal rules of the day. Nonetheless, this still resulted in there being only 15 Men, 19 Ladies, 10 Pairs and 12 Dance couples in the Championships, a modest entry by today's standards. On the Men's side, the competition was really among the Americans themselves, since Jimmy Grogan had returned, with the obvious hope of succeeding to the title left vacant by his long time rival, Dick Button. With the retirement of Helmut Seibt of Austria, the leading European was Carlo Fassi from Italy, the new European champion, who would subsequently enjoy a long and very distinguished teaching career in the United States and in his native Italy. In the Ladies, with the retirement of Jacqueline du Bief of France, the leading opposition came from Valda Osborn of Great Britain, the new European Ladies champion, and Gundi Busch of Germany. On the U.S. Team, there were also two young "powerhouses," the National Junior champions of 1952, competing in the Worlds for the first time, Ronnie Robertson at age 15 and Carol Heiss at age 13.

Hayes Alan Jenkins

As is sometimes the case when a perennial runner-up finally has the opportunity to obtain the top rung, after the retirement of the former winner, another challenger appears on the scene to take the laurels. Such was the fate of Jimmy Grogan in the 1953 Worlds. Despite a strong effort in the figures, which he won fairly decisively, he could not hold off the challenge of Hayes Alan Jenkins in the free skating, placing third in that part and lost the title to him by a narrow 5 to 4 margin, to finish as World Silver medalist for the third straight time. Ronnie Robertson placed a solid fourth behind Fassi with a strong free skating program for which he earned second place in that part. Dudley Richards, the fourth U.S. skater placed sixth.

In the Ladies, Tenley Albright won the figures and the free skating relatively easily, to win her first World title and the first for the United States, defeating Gundi Busch and Valda Osborn in that order. Carol Heiss was fourth overall, and was third in the free skating. The other Americans, Margaret Anne Graham, placed seventh, and Miggs Dean from Detroit, 16th. The Dance event, saw another medal for the

United States, when Carol Ann Peters and Daniel Ryan placed third, with the other two couples, Virginia Hoyns and Donald Jacoby fifth, and Carmel and Ed Bodel seventh. As a result, the "medal count" was again four for the U.S. — two Gold, one Silver and one Bronze.

The North American Championships were held following the Worlds, but before the Nationals, so it was again necessary to search for pairs to enter the event. Chosen at the last minute were Carole Ann Ormaca and Robin Greiner from Fresno, Calif., the 1953 Pacific Coast champions, and Margaret Anne and Hugh C. Graham, Jr., from Tulsa, who had been runners-up in the Midwesterns. These two pairs did surprisingly well, placing second and third behind the ultimate winners, Frances Dafoe and Norris Bowden from Toronto. Hayes Jenkins and Tenley Albright both won their first North American titles, and the Dance event was won by Carol Ann Peters and Daniel Ryan.

Carol Ann Peters and Daniel Ryan

In the 1953 Nationals winding up the season, Ormaca and Greiner won the Senior Pair title in their first entry in a Nationals. Theirs is a curious story. They had been runners-up twice in the Pacific Coast Junior Pairs event in 1950 and 1951 but had not entered the Nationals. In 1952, Robin Greiner skated with another partner, Gail Patnott and finished fourth in the Pacific Coast Senior Pairs. Renewing his partnership with Ormaca for 1953, they won the Pacific Coast Senior Pairs event, were second in the North Americans and the new National Champions, all in the space of one year!

Hayes won his first National title and Tenley her second, with Ronnie Robertson and Carol Heiss, second, respectively. Margaret Anne Graham was third in the Ladies, her brother Hugh was fourth in the Men, and together they were runners-up in Pairs! The winner of the Junior Men, after placing fourth in the figures, was David Jenkins, the younger brother of Hayes. The 1953 Nationals were the first in which an Association-certified Chief Accountant was in charge of the accounting room, and the author was privileged to have served in that capacity.

Among the rule changes implemented in 1953, were the addition of a free dance to the Silver Dance event, with eight couples to qualify for the final round. Curiously, this would last but six years, and was dropped after 1959 and would not return to the event until 1977. However, in 1973, an original set-pattern dance had replaced the compulsory dances in the final round, and would be retained when the free dance was put back in. The "OSP," as it was called, was added to the Gold Dance event in 1971. The Silver Dance event had been inaugurated in 1943 as the National "Junior" Dance event, but was renamed in 1946 as the National "Silver" Dance event. This term, as well as "Gold" and "Bronze," were used for the qualifying competition Dance events until 1979, when the terms "Senior, Junior and Novice" replaced them.

It was also in 1953 that a decision was made to implement an examination for judges, the taking of which annually would be a requirement for retention on the active list. At the same time, in June 1952, a special committee had been created called the Skating Standards Committee, with the responsibility for setting up and maintaining the basic rules relating to the standards of skating in a separate section of the Rulebook, to be called the "Skating Standards Regulations (SSR)." Essentially, the committee was required to follow the actions of the ISU at its biennial Congresses in changing rules relating to the standards of skating and see that they were implemented in the United States.

By 1953, there were 119 member clubs and 16,788 registered skaters. The Finance Committee had already noted that the principal source of income for the Association was now from the registration fees, and the dues of member clubs had accordingly been reduced slightly in 1952, to $10 for every 50 members, and not more than $50 for any club! Another aspect of the improving financial situation was the fact that over 6,000 skaters had participated at 14 summer sessions sanctioned by the Association. A Summer Skating Committee had been created as early as 1941, with the responsibility for "sanctioning" (i.e., licensing) summer sessions which wished to advertise that they were approved by the Association for the purpose of conducting test sessions and holding judges' schools, as well as carnivals and exhibitions. The committee would last until 1964, when skating had become much more of a year around activity and summer sessions had become merely an extension of the seasons of the sponsoring clubs.

At the 1953 Governing Council meeting, which was held at the Hotel Huntington in Pasadena, Calif., for the first time on the Pacific Coast, the Past Presidents, of which there were then eight still living, were recognized for their service to the USFSA and presented with the National medallion in Lucite. On the same occasion, which was the 30th Anniversary of Skating magazine, Theresa Weld Blanchard was also honored for her service as editor, as well as for her "immeasurable contributions to the sport," as it is stated in the report. The deaths of Heaton Robertson, a Past President and Honorary Vice President, and of Past President Charles T. Church also were noted.

Reported to the meeting was the fact that individual registrations had increased by 1,600 over the prior year. For the Nationals, the so-called "double skating" in Senior Singles, Pairs and in Junior Pairs was eliminated, and the entries in Junior and Novice Singles were limited to three from each Section (instead of four) with all entrants doing the free skating.

The Tests Committee reported that for the first six months of the season, 1,083 figure tests were taken with 69.8 percent passed, while 1,134 dance tests were taken with 63.5 percent passing. Also reported were the first ISU Dance Tests taken in the United States, at Philadelphia in May 1953.

Following the end of the competition season of 1953, what might be called the first "World Tour" occurred. Exhibitions by the champions had, of course, been common for many years, but in the case in point, a formal invitation was issued by the National Skating Union of Japan for Hayes Jenkins and Tenley Albright to skate a series of exhibitions in Japan, which they did, accompanied by Dr. Hollis Albright, Tenley's father, and Past President Harry Keighley of Chicago. Coincidentally, Jack Jost from St. Louis, who was then serving in the U.S. Army in Japan, had been invited to enter the Japanese National championship and had been the winner of the Senior Men's event; so he too was included in the exhibitions, which took place at Tokyo, Osaka and Nagoya.

The trip was important to the re-establishment of friendly relations in skating between Japan and the United States, which had been cultivated especially by Mrs. Blanchard with the first Japanese skaters to enter the Olympic Winter Games in 1932 and again in 1936. It also provided the Japanese with the incentive to improve the quality of their skating to the end that they could return to international competition and make a creditable showing. Actually, when Japan was permitted to return to competition by the ISU in 1951, they sent one lady, Etsuko Inada, and one man, Ryusuke Arisaka, to Milan, where they had placed 21st and 11th, respectively. Inada had been the youngest skater in the 1936 Olympics, placing 10th. After that first post-War effort, the Japanese would not return to the Worlds again until 1957. Hayes and Tenley were really "role models" for them, and miles of footage was taken by the diligent Japanese cameramen, since they performed their competitive programs in the exhibitions, with the film being used later for instructional purposes.

During the 1953 and 1954 seasons, a series of articles appeared in Skating magazine in which the activities and responsibilities of each of the major standing committees of the Association were explained, and a short biographical sketch of the current chairman of each committee was included. This series has, so far as is known, only appeared once, and it could well be revived in the future, since it provides to the general membership insight and knowledge of the functions of the USFSA.

The committee structure of the Association is really where the action is, although in the modern era of commercialism in the sport, the business decisions, and there are obviously many more of them, have to be made by the staff at the Headquarters, working with the present Executive Committee. In 1953-1954 there were 12 standing committees with 223 members and nine special committees with 124 members. By contrast in 1993-1994, there were 17 permanent committees (11 voting and 6 non-voting) with 547 members, 14 special committees also with 223 members and three ad hoc special committees with 37 members. Of course, it should be noted that the total number of committee members is lower than the totals indicated, since many persons serve on more than one committee.

Still, the expansion in the size of the committee membership is much larger than the actual growth of the membership as measured by the number of registered skaters. The latter has been rather slow and modest over the years, although the number of member clubs has grown substantially. Of the three sections, the largest number of clubs and skaters continue to be in the East, followed by the Midwest, with the Pacific Coast the last and smallest. Actually, the size of the Eastern Section is about the same as the Midwest and Pacific Coast combined. This was just as true in 1954 as it was in 1994, with the demographics remaining essentially the same over the years, despite the expansion of the sport into the Southeastern and Southwestern parts of the country.

By the same token, the number of referees and judges has also experienced a substantial increase, and actually today, there seems to be a shortage of judges, even with the decline in the testing activity in the figures. In 1953-54, there were 29 Referees, 19 Chief Accountants (a new position, as previously noted) and 735 Judges. In 1993-94, there were 204 Referees, 107 Accountants and 1,044 Judges. Again, it should be noted that the totals do not reflect the actual number of persons, since many on the lists hold multiple appointments. As can be seen, the number of Referees and Accountants has increased, keeping pace with the significant increase in the number of qualifying and non-qualifying competitions over the past few years. On the other hand, the number of judges has increased far less, only about 50 percent from the 1954 figure, which tends to support the view that there are not enough of them to properly meet the demands. The increase in registration figures for the same years is from 16,788 to 49,573 or just under 300 percent in 50 years.

The 1953 fall meeting of the Executive Committee was held in Chicago at the Edgewater Beach Hotel, the first time that meeting had been held in the Chicago area, which later would be its regular site near the airport from 1955 through 1977. At the meeting it was noted that 6,000 skaters had participated in the 14 sanctioned summer sessions, over twice the number reported for 1952. On the other hand, carnival activity and income was down. Since there were still inactive clubs, it was the sense of the meeting that such clubs could remain members, as long as they held annual meetings and paid their dues, but after two years, they would lose their jurisdiction over their area, or what we call today, their "principal skating headquarters."

The 1953-1954 season was another in what seemed at the time the "perils of Tenley," as distinguished from the "perils of Pauline"! Again, the World Championships preceded the Nationals. The team selected was once more made up of four Men, four Ladies, two Pairs, and three Dance couples. The championships were held at Oslo, Norway, the site of the 1952 Olympic

Winter Games. Hayes Jenkins returned to defend, accompanied by Jimmy Grogan, back for another try, plus Hayes' younger brother David, the 1953 National Junior Champion. In Ladies, Tenley returned, but Carol Heiss was unable to compete due to a leg injury, so the other U.S. skaters were Frances Dorsey of Seattle, Margaret Anne Graham and Miggs Dean.

While Hayes defended easily, for his second title, Tenley ran into unexpected difficulty, with a fall in the free and lost her figure lead to Gundi Busch of Germany, who thereby became the first German woman to win Worlds. Dorsey was fifth, Graham, 11th and Dean 15th. Grogan once again was second, for the fourth time, with David Jenkins fourth, and Robertson, fifth.

In the Pairs, Frances Dafoe and Norris Bowden of Canada won their first title, while Ormaca and Greiner were fourth, with the Grahams, fifth. In the Dance, Carmel and Ed Bodel were third, gaining their first medal in the Worlds, with Virginia Hoyns and Donald Jacoby, fifth and Phyllis Schroeder Forney and Martin Forney from Hershey, sixth. So the medal count remained at four, with one Gold, two Silvers and one Bronze.

Carmel and Ed Bodel

The Nationals of 1954 were held at Los Angeles, returning again to the Pacific Coast. Carol Heiss returned to competition and placed second to Tenley, who won her third title. Hayes retained his title, but Jimmy Grogan was gone, having turned professional to join the Hollywood Ice Revue and to serve as a partner to Barbara Ann Scott. As a result, brother David wound up second in a modest upset over Ronnie Robertson. Ormaca and Greiner won their second Pair title, and the Bodels their second Dance title. Among other winners to be watched in the future were Tim Brown, representing Los Angeles, the winner of the Junior Men and Catherine Machado, also from Los Angeles, winning the Junior Ladies. The winners of the Silver Dance were Sidney Foster and a future USFSA President, Franklin Nelson, representing Boston, although she was from Fargo, N.D. and he from Tulsa, Okla. They were students at Radcliffe and Harvard, respectively.

Fourth in the Senior Men was Hugh C. Graham, Jr., also from Tulsa, who would be Franklin's predecessor as President in the 1980's. In the Ladies Novice event, the Heaton R. Robertson Memorial Trophy was presented for the first time, having been funded by donations from the skating public. At the same time, the purchase of standard medals for the Sectionals and a three-year supply of the National medals had also been authorized by the Executive Committee the prior fall.

The 1954 Governing Council meeting was held at the Hilton Hotel in Chicago, and represented the beginning of the rotation of the meeting between the Sections, which has been followed ever since. The President reported that the total number of registered skaters had again increased, and was estimated to reach a total of about 19,000, as compared with 18,500 the prior year and 16,600 two years before. However, the number of clubs losing their ice had also increased and fewer clubs had joined the Association. This was also reflected in the number of figure tests taken, which had declined by 15 percent, although there was an increase of 33 percent in the number of Dance Tests, primarily in the lower levels.

It was also in this year that the educational requirements for entry into competition for those under age 18 were tightened, essentially requiring that a certificate of educational status be obtained from the local school authorities and filed with the Competitions Committee prior to the start of the competition season. The intent was to insure that all school-age competitors were fully in compliance with the education laws in their own states. More than 350 skaters filed the necessary certificates and no applicant was denied entry into competition. However, the requirement to file the separate educational certificate did not last and was transferred in 1960 to the entry blank for competitions, with only the competitor's home club making the certification. This had the effect of weakening the requirement, although it still remains in the rules today, but is generally not strictly enforced.

The fall 1954 meeting of the Executive Committee was held for the first time in Cleveland. The matter of the majority pass in tests was revisited, but no action was taken, although there was some sentiment for it, if at the same time a minimum passing mark requirement was retained, which would permit a test to be failed if one judge went below the minimum. This would indeed eventually become the rule for both Figure and Dance tests. The idea of Pair Tests was also presented for the first time, but such tests would still not be implemented for several years. Also created were two classes of Dance Referee, National and Sectional, as was already the case in Singles and Pairs.

The 1954-1955 competitive season was an important one, as is always the case with the year prior to an Olympics, and with the Nationals still following at the end of the season, the results in it would be the basis for the selection of the Olympic and World Teams for 1956. No separate tryout, as had been held in 1951, was planned. The big "question," obviously, was whether Tenley Albright could regain her World title at Vienna. Gundi Busch, the 1954 champion had turned professional, also to join the Hollywood Ice Revue and Valda Osborn of Great Britain had also departed for the professional ranks, so Tenley's competition would come primarily from her own teammate Carol Heiss and two Austrian girls, Hanna Eigel and Ingrid Wendl.

On the Men's side, the European competition for Hayes Jenkins in his second defense, would be from the rising young French skater, Alain Giletti, and the Czech skater, Karel Divin, but the principal opposition would come from Ronnie Robertson and Hayes' brother David.

The championship was held on the enormous natural ice surface of the Weiner Eislauf Verein (WEV) in the center of Vienna, where this venerable skating club had its base since 1867. The weather conditions, especially for the figures, were difficult, with wind and extreme cold. Despite these problems, Hayes Jenkins successfully defended his title, with Ronnie Robertson second and David Jenkins, third, for another sweep of the medals by the Americans and the second time for a non-European skating nation. Only three times before, in 1927, 1928 and 1952, had such a sweep occurred, with three Austrians on the podium the first two times, and three Americans the third time (Button, Grogan and Hayes Jenkins).

In the Ladies, Tenley Albright regained the title she had lost in 1954, with Carol Heiss second and Hanna Eigel third. The author remembers well, that when Tenley left for Europe to seek to regain the title, there were just two people at the airport to see her off, her father and the author. Of course, when she returned as the World Ladies' Champion once again, there was large delegation there from the press and her club, to greet and to congratulate her, plus those same two who had been there when she left. How fickle is fortune! Thus, in the 1955 Worlds, the "medal count" had now reached five, with two Gold, two Silver and a Bronze!

In the Pairs, Dafoe and Bowden retained their tile, with Ormaca and Greiner again fourth. In the Dance there was another medal sweep, by the British, then the dominant country in the discipline. The Bodels were fourth, with a new couple of Joan Zamboni (the daughter of Frank Zamboni, the inventor of the ice resurfacer) and Roland Junso, fifth. In the prior year's Nationals, each had skated with a different partner. Roland was third in the Gold Dance and Joan second in the Silver Dance, so their new partnership was a very new one and they did very well in their first Worlds.

The North Americans followed the Worlds at Regina, Saskatchewan, and were before the Nationals, with the U.S. skaters winning three of the four titles. Frances Dafoe and Norris Bowden of Canada again won the Pairs, defeating Carole Ormaca and Robin Greiner, right behind whom was the promising young Canadian couple of Barbara Wagner and Robert Paul. The Bodels won the Dance, with Zamboni and Junso second, while Hayes Jenkins and Tenley Albright retained their titles. David Jenkins and Carol Heiss were both second. Ronnie Robertson did not compete at Regina, having returned from the exhibition tour after the Worlds with bronchial pneumonia. Nonetheless, the U.S. skaters took nine of the 12 medals. Only in Pairs was Canada supreme, and they would remain so for another seven years.

The 1955 Nationals returned to Colorado Springs and The Broadmoor, with all the Senior champions from 1954 retaining their titles. Third in the Senior Ladies was Catherine Machado, from Los Angeles, a fine free skater, who had placed 10th in the Worlds, but had not entered the North Americans. Carol Heiss's younger sister Nancy won the Junior Ladies, while in the Junior Pairs, Maribel Y. Owen, the daughter of Maribel Vinson Owen, was the winner with Charles (Chuck) Foster, the brother of Sidney, representing Boston. It was just 28 years since young Maribel's mother had won the Junior Pairs with Thornton Coolidge in 1927. Chuck would go on to become the Secretary of the U.S. Olympic Committee and a World Championship Referee.

Strictly speaking, the Association had never had a "logo," as we would say today, or a trademark, the National medal having been its symbol, appearing on the cover of **Skating** magazine, the Yearbook and Rulebook. It was proposed in 1955 that a new National medal be designed, to be used after the present inventory was used up in one year, with a contest to be conducted for that purpose. The final design accepted was submitted by the maker of the original medal, Dorrety of Boston, which had supplied them since the first Nationals under the USFSA in 1922. The new medal featured a map of the United States overlaid with the letters "USFSA" but still with no skate on it, although the medal itself at least had a winged skate on the top. The main part of the medal, which was rectangular, would become the emblem or symbol of the Association and the new medal first replaced the old one on the cover of the Rulebook for 1956-1957. The new medals were first used at the 1956 National Championships in Philadelphia. There would be several other medal and logo design changes in the future, but the original medal had lasted for 33 years!

At the 1955 Governing Council meeting, which was held at Buffalo, New York, it was reported that the number of member clubs had reached 120 with 18,880 registered skaters. Specifically mentioned were appropriations of $400 to purchase films of the 1955 Nationals; $200 "for use in starting a Skating Museum or Historic Collection" and $250 for the purchase of dies for the new medal. The filming of the Nationals by Howard Craker from Los Angeles would continue for many years, and today forms a valuable chronicle of the sport. Here, for the first time, is seen the "gleam" of the idea for a museum, for even then, the amount of historical memorabilia stored in the Association offices was growing rapidly.

A new schedule of Dance Tests was also inaugurated, adding two new tests to the structure, a Pre Silver and a Pre Gold. The two new tests were created out of the same 20 dances currently in the old tests, as in the surveys made preceding the adoption of the new schedule, many clubs had objected to the addition of new dances. The Gold Dance Test would now require a three minute free dance. It was noted that 862 figure tests and 1,485 dance tests (which, of course, included individual dances passed) had been taken during the first six months of the year. The numbers reflected a modest decline, due in part to the tightening-up of the test standards and the resulting improvement in the quality of the tests taken.

The year 1955 again represented a change in the Presidency, with Kendall Kelley retiring, after serving for three years. He was succeeded by the first President from the Pacific Coast, Kenneth L. Brown, from Berkeley, Calif. Ken Kelley would continue in an active role, serving as a member of the ISU Ice Dance Technical Committee from 1961 to 1967. In the Association, he was the Chairman of the Competitions Committee from 1955 to 1957, of the Judges Committee from 1957 to 1960, the International Committee from 1960 to 1962, and the Dance Committee from 1962 to 1965. He passed away in 1980.

Kenneth L. Brown

The Fall 1955 meeting of the Executive Committee returned to Chicago, back at the Edgewater Beach Hotel. A complete revision of the amateur status rules was approved, which basically brought together, various miscellaneous rulings, and covered clearly the various types of activities which could result in disqualification or restriction temporarily, such as use of name and photograph, rink attendants, designers and models, unsanctioned events, tryouts and solicitation of employment and agreements with professionals. The tryout rule was a tough one, as it meant a skater who tried out for a professional show and did not get the job was still ineligible for one year!

Harry Radix, chairman of the Olympic fund raising for the 1956 Team, reported that over $10,000 had been received in contributions, with more to come, and he expressed the certainty that the budget would be met by such volunteer means.

The Olympic season of 1955-1956 came close to being the "peak" of the "Golden Age," although the Olympic year of 1960 perhaps is a close second. The Olympic Winter Games were to be held at Cortina, Italy, in the Dolomite Alps, just south of the Austrian border. The figure skating would still be held in an outdoor but artificially refrigerated stadium. The Olympic Team consisted of three Men, three Ladies and two Pairs, while for the Worlds at Garmisch, Germany, the alternates for the Singles and Pairs and three Dance couples were added.

The plans for the Team contemplated air travel on an "Olympic Flight" from New York, with all the team on board, a practice that became a major issue five years later. However, the major news item was the injury suffered by Tenley Albright in practice just two days after their arrival in Cortina. In seeking to avoid other skaters who were being photographed, she fell and spiked herself in the ankle, a severe puncture wound. Upon the arrival of her father two days later, he took over and managed to get her back on the ice after three days, so that she had 10 more days of recovery before the competition started. Actually, by the time the free skating was held, she had not done a run through of her program for 20 days! Despite the pain and discomfort encountered from the strapping necessary, since the injured ankle was on her landing foot, she managed to compete.

At the same time, the media had taken up the idea that there was a personal rivalry between her and Carol Heiss, which was not in fact the case, other than that they were strong competitors, with Carol being the younger by four and one-half years. The affair had all the overtones of the old Boston-New York controversy of the late 1930's! Unfortunately, some of those involved in a non-skating capacity with the skaters did not help matters by their statements to the press. The Ladies event was judged by 11 judges, only the second time such a large panel was used, the other having been the Pairs event in 1948. Tenley won the figures decisively and also won the free skating over Carol Heiss, while the third U.S. skater, Catherine Machado, placed third in the free skating to finish in eighth place overall. Only the U.S. judge, Kendall Kelley placed Carol first, after tying her and Tenley in the free skating.

Ronnie Robertson

In the Men, the Americans achieved an Olympic sweep of the medals, matching those in the Worlds of 1952 and 1955. This was the second time it had occurred in the Olympics, the other having been by Sweden in 1908 in the Men, led by Ulrich Salchow. Hayes Alan Jenkins added the Olympic Gold medal to his collection, with Ronnie Robertson and David Jenkins, second and third, respectively. Ronnie did defeat Hayes in the free skating, but Hayes wound up the winner with six of the nine judges. It was the high point for the U.S. skaters in the Olympic Games, with five out of six medals in Singles.

In the Pairs, there was a big upset and controversy, when Sissy Schwarz and Kurt Oppelt of Austria defeated the World Champions, Frances Dafoe and Norris Bowden of Canada on total ordinals, 14 to 16, each of them having four first place ordinals, but Dafoe-Bowden having two third places from the German and Hungarian judges. The remaining first place went to the third place pair, Marianne and Laszlo Nagy of Hungary (from the Hungarian judge, naturally). The U.S. pairs were Ormaca-Greiner, fifth and Lucille Ash and Sully Kothman from Colorado seventh, who had been the runners-up in the 1955 Nationals to make the Team. Unfortunately, the national bias of some of the judges was fairly apparent and would require drastic action by the ISU to correct it, which was ultimately taken in 1957 in the form of the suspension for life of two of the Austrian officials.

The World Championships were held in Germany for the first time since 1938, at Garmisch-Partenkirchen, the site of the Olympic Winter Games of 1936. The Pairs event was a repetition of the Olympics, with Dafoe and Bowden again losing to Schwarz and Oppelt, this time by a four to five margin, although they had skated much better than at Cortina. Carole Ormaca and Robin Greiner, took yet another fourth place, their third, while Ash and Kothman were sixth. In between were Barbara Wagner and Robert Paul of Canada. In the Dance, there was yet another British sweep of the medals, with new champions, Pamela Weight and Paul Thomas succeeding Jean Westwood and Lawrence Demmy. Joan Zamboni and Roland Junso placed fourth, Carmel and Ed Bodel sixth, and Sidney Foster and Franklin Nelson, the 1954 Silver Dance champions, seventh.

In the Ladies, Carol Heiss performed well in the figures to defeat Tenley Albright for the first time in that event by five judges to four, thereby setting up her ultimate victory in the free skating, to win her first World title. Both of them skated very well in the free and it was really a matter of style to choose between them. Catherine Machado was third in the free skating to place sixth in the final. It is a credit to both Carol and Tenley, that neither of them ever made any excuse for the results, Tenley, her injury or Carol, the media fuss, plus the fact that her mother was seriously ill with cancer and would die soon after the competition season. They exemplified the ideal of sportsmanship in their performances and demeanor throughout a long and very stressful competition season.

Carol Heiss

The 1956 Nationals were held at Philadelphia and here, yet another controversy erupted, when the USFSA received from the representative of a foreign skating association a protest claiming that excessive expenses had been demanded in connection with exhibitions which were to have been skated abroad by Ronnie Robertson. There was also an active rumor that Ronnie had signed a contract with Ice Capades prior to the Nationals, which was in those days an obvious "no no." He was permitted to skate, but the results were not to be made official until the protest had been disposed of. Eventually, at the spring meeting of the Executive Committee in May, it was announced that an investigation made by the Association had produced insufficient evidence on which to press charges, and accordingly, Ronnie was awarded his second place medal and the Oscar L. Richard Trophy, which he had also won by reason of his free skating performance. In fact, Ronnie did turn professional shortly thereafter and joined the show.

In the Championships, Tenley retained her title, defeating Carol, who had the misfortune to skate a rocker not up to her standard and to get too far behind. Machado was third. In the Men, it was the same order of Hayes Jenkins, Robertson and David Jenkins, with Tim Brown, fourth. Ormaca and Greiner won their fourth straight pair title, with Ash and Kothman second, and

Maribel Owen and Chuck Foster third. The Dance title went to Joan Zamboni and Roland Junso, who defeated the defending champions, Carmel and Ed Bodel. The Junior Pairs were won by Nancy Rouillard and Ron Ludington from Boston, with Ron also placing fourth in the Men's Novice. Ron had been a competitive roller skater, with only two years on the ice up to that time, and was the North American champion of the RSROA in 1952. He also had passed the first Gold Free Skating Test on rollers. Such tests would not be seen in the USFSA until 1977.

The years 1955 and 1956 also saw the passing from the scene of two stalwart founders, in the persons of Joel B. Liberman in 1955 and of Past President Joseph K. Savage in 1956, both from New York. While never President, Joel had served in almost every other major Association position, including Secretary from 1924 to 1928 and from 1931 to 1932, and especially as the Chairman of the Judges Committee from 1939 to 1945. He had been a judge at the 1928 and a referee at the 1932 Olympic Games, as well as at innumerable World, North American and National Championships. He also was a member of the first New York Four, which had been the first National Champions in 1924.

Joe Savage had enjoyed a very diverse career, not only in skating, having been the first National Champion in Dance in 1936, but also as an official in both speed skating and roller skating. He had the unique distinction of having served as President of three different governing bodies in the three sports, the USFSA, the Amateur Skating Union and the Amateur Roller Skating Association. The loss of both of these men was a severe one, not only to the Association, but also to skating in New York, where they had both been "pillars" of The Skating Club of New York since before World War I.

At the 1956 Governing Council meeting, which was held at Berkeley, Calif., the third "leg" of the new rotation, a new definition of an amateur was accepted, the principal provision of which was that an amateur is a "person who participates in any capacity in this sport without receiving or seeking material gain;" still the classic definition of the "simon pure" athlete. Strict amateurism would die hard, despite the ongoing changes in the economic aspects of the sport.

The Judges Committee was split into two separate committees, one for Dance Judges and one for Figure Judges. This strange dichotomy would last until 1967, when the two committees would, unlike Humpty Dumpty, be put back together again. Actually, it was a jurisdictional issue, with the Dance Committee claiming jurisdiction over all aspects of dancing, not just the standards, but also the tests, competitions and officials. The question of the jurisdiction between the so-called "standards" committees, such as Dance and later Singles and Pairs on the one hand, and the operating committees, such as Competitions and Tests, on the other, still causes confusion and remains an issue today.

At the same meeting, a bid was initiated to the ISU for the award of the 1957 World

Championships for The Broadmoor at Colorado Springs. The Worlds had been held up to then but once in the United States, in New York in 1930. The bid, which had the full backing of Thayer Tutt of the Broadmoor Hotel was a strong one, despite two limitations, the altitude of Colorado Springs (6,000 feet) and the small size of the Broadmoor Ice Palace.

Perhaps because of the interest in the Olympics, test activity during the 1955-1956 season enjoyed a major increase. In just a six-month period, 994 figure tests were taken, compared with 862 in the prior year, and 2,181 dance tests, compared with 1,485 the year before. At that time, the test activity reported to the meetings of the Executive Committee and Governing Council were in six month segments.

Also noted was the trend then for private rinks to be closed or sold, coupled with an increase in the number of rinks built and operated by municipalities and educational institutions, nothing really different than today, with the "ups and downs" of the sport in public interest being thus reflected. Ritter Shumway, then Chairman of the College Figure Skating Committee, stated that "…the greatest opportunity that opens before us for expanding interest and participation in figure skating lies in the shadows of the ivied walls of our educational institutions." Classic Ritter, who was after all an ordained minister, but completely true then and still true in 1995, especially with Title IX to cope with!

The 1956 Fall meeting of the Executive Committee was held at the Drake Hotel in Chicago. The death of Honorary President A. Winsor Weld was noted with a memorial resolution. Another death reported was that of Carl W. Chamberlin of Colorado Springs, who was the general chairman of the 1957 World Championships to be held at the Broadmoor. He had also been an Executive Committee member. Despite his death, the organization of the Championships was still carried out very well, largely through the efforts of Thayer Tutt of the Broadmoor Hotel and Henry Beatty, representing the Association.

The Sanctions Committee reported revenue for the year of $9,045, an increase of $2,414 over the preceding year, much of which was due to a $2,500 exhibition fee received from the Ed Sullivan Show, at which the U.S. Olympic Champions had appeared. A resolution of thanks to Mr. Sullivan for his presentation of the event in the interest of the Olympics was adopted.

So it was that the Association turned to the next four years with anticipation and high hopes.

With the 1956-1957 season, there were several new "milestones" to consider! The first was the award in 1955 of the 1960 Olympic Winter Games to Squaw Valley, Calif., the second to be held in the United States and the first since 1932. USFSA President Ken Brown was a member of the Organizing Committee and would have a major role in the preparations for the Games, one of the controversial aspects of which, unrelated to

The "Golden Age" Ends
(1957-1960)

skating, would be the omission of a bobsled run, despite the fact that the event had previously been held at every Winter Games from 1924 through 1956.

Another and much more immediate milestone was the award by the ISU Council at its 1956 meeting of the 1957 World Championships to the United States, the USFSA and the Broadmoor SC, the first in the United States since 1930, and from the North American viewpoint, 25 years since the Montreal championships of 1932.

A further and what could be considered as a "negative" milestone, were two significant changes in the format of the North American Championships. The first and major one was the use of an uneven number of judges, and the second and lesser one being a return to the 0 to 6 scale of marks from the scale of 0 to 10 that had been in use in the North Americans since 1945.

Another milestone was the death in September 1956 of Herbert J. Clarke of Great Britain, the first Honorary member of the USFSA and the former President of the ISU, and the death in October 1956 of Honorary President A. Winsor Weld, who was generally considered to be the "founder" of the USFSA.

As is almost always the case with the first year following an Olympics, there were major changes in the ranks of those still competing. Both Hayes Alan Jenkins and Tenley Albright retired, he to attend Harvard Law School and she to attend Harvard Medical School, a somewhat rare case of Olympic Champions pursuing their education and careers outside of professional skating. Hayes would go on to a long and distinguished career as a counsel for the Goodyear Tire and Rubber Company, while Tenley would join her father and brother as a surgeon. Among others in Singles that also left the competitive ranks were Ronnie Robertson, as we have seen, and Catherine Machado. Still around as the next "new" generation, were David Jenkins, Carol Heiss and Tim Brown. In Pairs, Carole Ann Ormaca and Robin Greiner had retired, as had Lucille Ash and Sully Kothman. In Dance, however, Joan Zamboni and Roland Junso, and Carmel and Ed Bodel were still active.

The schedule for the 1957 competitive season was unusual in that the North Americans preceded the Worlds, with the Nationals still bringing up the rear at the end of the season after the Worlds. The North Americans which were held at Rochester, N.Y., was therefore a very important competition for the potential members of the World Team. The competitors to represent the U.S. at the North Americans and Worlds were selected in advance by the International Committee, following the procedure then required by the competition schedule. Included in those selected were many that were known to have retired, just in case they changed their minds, one of whom was Tenley Albright, who did not make a final decision until somewhat late in the game!

In mid-1954, the ISU Council, through the new President, Dr. James Koch of Switzerland, had taken notice of the fact that the North American Championships were "not being carried out in accordance with the Regulations of the ISU," which was coupled with the request that the "necessary measures" be taken to insure that the next North Americans would be held in accordance with ISU Rules. The ISU took the position that the North Americans were an International Competition, even if only between the skaters of two ISU Members. This directive obviously engendered a lot of discussion across the border in North America, to the extent that no action was taken to change the 1955 North Americans, which were held under the old rules.

The USFSA and the CFSA both claimed that the championships had originally been approved in the 1920's by ISU President Salchow on the basis that they were not an "International" event in the real sense, but merely a team event between two associations only. This opinion had been confirmed in 1933 by Herbert J. Clarke, then the Vice President of the ISU, saying that the championships were "really not international events but are merely bi-national." Of course, the facts of the matter were that the North Americans had indeed been regarded as an International Competition by the participating associations, skaters and officials, with the quality of the event advancing to the point that the holders of the titles found them of great value to their competitive campaigns abroad. The championships had also been used since the beginning as a training ground for officials, and often represented the activity upon which their nominations for appointment as referees and judges by the ISU was based. There were very few International Competitions being organized then outside of Europe, and even there, in only a few resort areas, such as St. Moritz and Davos, Switzerland.

As a result, the two associations eventually had to bow to the inevitable and made the necessary changes in the rules requested. The uneven number of judges initially provided that the greater number would be from the host country, and also that the referee from the host country would be the Senior Referee in general charge of the competitions. The scale of marks was also returned to 0 to 6. As it turned out, the change to an uneven number of judges, especially, would spell the beginning of the end of the North American Championships, although they would last for another 14 years until 1971.

David Jenkins

The argument in favor of there being an even number of judges was well made by Dick Hapgood, a former USFSA Secretary, in which he stated, "...prior to the adoption of the even number of judges, there was always the feeling that in close contests, the judges would divide by countries and that the skater with the minority of the judges had the cards stacked against him. With three judges from each country, the competitors, their families, and the spectators all felt that everyone had a fair chance and that no contest would be decided solely by which country had a majority of judges." In general, this had been true, although "manipulation" of even that supposedly fair system could be seen in such famous competitions as the 1941 Men and the 1949 Pairs events. With the uneven panels of judges, it would be all "down hill" from then on.

The championships were organized by the Genesee FSC under the leadership of F. Ritter Shumway, actually the second major competition organized by that brand new club, which became a USFSA member in 1955. In 1956, when a fire destroyed the rink in Baltimore scheduled to hold the 1956 Eastern Championships, Ritter and Genesee picked up and ran the competition on very short notice at the rink of the Rochester Institute of Technology (RIT), of which Ritter had been one of the donors. That competition was a "prelude" for the 1957 North Americans and also for the 1959 Nationals, all of which were extremely well run. Ritter Shumway, would later be President of the USFSA from 1961 to 1964. The compulsory figures and dances of the North Americans were held at the RIT rink and the free skating in Rochester's War Memorial arena.

In the competition itself, David Jenkins and Carol Heiss became the new Singles Champions, with Barbara Wagner and Robert Paul of Toronto, who had been third in 1955 and were the new Canadian Champions, winning the Pairs. Geraldine Fenton and William McLachlan, she from Hamilton and he from Toronto, won the Dance for the first title in that category for Canada, a recognition of the rapid advances that had been made in Canada in dance in a relatively short period of time. Carole Jane (Yarmila) Pachl, an emigrée from Czechoslovakia, and now from Toronto and the Canadian Ladies Champion, was second to Carol, with her counterpart, Charles Snelling, from Toronto, second to David. In the Pairs, Maria and Otto Jelinek, from Oakville, Ontario, also refugees from Czechoslovakia, placed second, with Nancy Rouillard and Ron Ludington from Boston, the 1956 Junior Pair Champions, third. In Dance Joan Zamboni and Roland Junso were second, but closely followed by Sharon McKenzie and Bert Wright from Los Angeles, a new couple, who had been fourth in the 1956 Gold Dance in their first trip to the Nationals. Bert had been second in the Silver Dance in 1955 with another partner.

Nancy Rouillard and Ronald Ludington

In training, it had been Carol Heiss's practice to run through her complete free skating program twice, back to back, with essentially no rest period in between. This was a decision of her coach, Pierre Brunet, which certainly paid off in the actual competition, where her speed was invariably commented upon. At Rochester, when she came off the ice after finishing a flawless free skating performance, she said to the author, who was the Chief Accountant at the championships, "Well, I could do it again!" David Jenkins did equally well in the free and was a worthy successor as champion to his brother, who was on hand to see him compete. Third was Tim Brown, an excellent skater of the figures, while fourth was Donald Jackson, of Oshawa, another name that would be heard from in the future.

The 1957 Worlds were a major logistical problem in selecting, assembling and transporting the European skaters and officials to far off Colorado. The European Championships were held at Vienna, from where the selected competitors, accompanying persons and officials were transported in one group by air to the United States. The ISU itself undertook to make and carry out the necessary arrangements, which were accomplished in flawless style, largely through the efforts of Georg Häsler, the Honorary Secretary of the ISU, in coordination with Thayer Tutt of the Broadmoor Hotel on the "receiving" end. Despite the long travel distance required, there were 11 countries represented with 17 entries in the Men; 20 in the Ladies; 5 in the Pairs; and 11 in the Dance. Only the Pairs suffered by comparison, but even in Garmisch in 1956, there had been only 11 pairs, of which the majority had not returned. Notable among the nations represented were Australia and Japan, the latter for the first time since 1951.

Clearly, the films taken and the research carried out by the Japanese after the 1953 tour by Hayes Jenkins and Tenley Albright had paid off, as the Japanese entries did better. Yuko Araki, a tiny 12-year-old girl, was a "carbon copy" of Tenley, even to the gestures and other mannerisms, placing 19th. The other Japanese lady competitor, who placed 17th, was Junko Ueno, age 13, who would go on to compete in two Olympic Games and later would become a World Championship Referee for Japan, as well as a National Judge for the United States. The latter rank was earned during two sojourns here while her husband, Hiroshi Hiramatsu, was assigned to the office of one of the main Japanese trading companies in New York. Junko has been very much involved in the organizing of all the major competitions held in Japan during the past 20 years. Her mother,

Kinuko Ueno, was also a World Championship Judge. There were three Japanese men, two of whom, Kazuo Ohashi and Hideo Sugita, would become World Championship Referees and officers of the National Skating Union of Japan (NSUJ). They placed 14th and 15th, respectively, while the other Japanese entrant, Yukio Nishikura, was 13th. During the 1957 Worlds, the Japanese continued their diligent photographing of everyone and everything. The delegation was led by Prince Tsuneyoshi Takeda, a cousin of the Emperor, the President of the NSUJ, and later a member of the International Olympic Committee. He can really be regarded as the founder of modern figure skating in Japan.

Tim Brown

In the Men's Championship, David Jenkins was the winner, but the surprise of the events was the strong showing of Tim Brown, who placed second, with Charles Snelling of Canada, third. Tom Moore, from Seattle, the 1955 National Junior Champion, placed fifth, with the 1956 Junior Champion, Robert Lee Brewer, from Pasadena, eighth. In the Ladies, Carol Heiss successfully defended her title, with two Austrian girls, Hanna Eigel and Ingrid Wendl, second and third, followed by Carole Jane Pachl of Canada. Carol's sister Nancy, the National Junior Ladies Champion in 1955, placed eighth, perhaps the first time two sisters had competed in the same World Championship event, although the Weigel sisters, Louise and Estelle, from Buffalo, had done so in the 1936 Olympic Winter Games, placing 21st and 22nd, respectively.

While the Pair event was small in number, the competition was keen, with Barbara Wagner and Robert Paul of Canada, regaining for Canada the title previously held by Frances Dafoe and

Norris Bowden. The young German pair of Marika Kilius and Franz Ningel were second, with the Jelinek's third and Rouillard-Ludington fourth. In the Dance, June Markham and Courtney Jones of Great Britain maintained the British supremacy, but for the first time, two North American couples were second and third; Geraldine Fenton and William McLachlan of Canada were second and Sharon McKenzie and Bert Wright of the United States were a solid and surprising third, followed by Joan Zamboni and Roland Junso in fourth.

From the United States standpoint, it was a most successful championship, not only in its organization, but also in the medals, with four, two Gold, one Silver and one Bronze. It was confidently predicted by all present in 1957 that the championships would soon again return, which they indeed did in 1959, 1965, 1969 and 1975, not to mention three World Junior Championships in 1985, 1990 and 1994, for a total of eight ISU Championships in all, the second largest number (after Davos, Switzerland with 10) held at the same site and in the same arena.

The 1957 Nationals were held back in Berkeley, Calif., and again hosted by the St. Moritz ISC. For Carol Heiss and David Jenkins, it would be their first National titles, one of the rare occasions when two World Champions were not yet the champions of their own country while winning their World crowns, which, of course, Carol actually did it twice! Nancy Rouillard and Ron Ludington won their first Senior Pair title, and Sharon McKenzie and Bert Wright easily won the Dance title, with the new partnership of Andrée Anderson from Buffalo and Donald Jacoby from Rochester, placing second and the defending champions Joan Zamboni and Roland Junso, third. Tim Brown, with Susan Sebo, from Berkeley, also were sixth in Dance, while he was the runner-up to David Jenkins in the Senior Men.

Sharon McKenzie and Bert Wright

Another death occurred in 1957, which was a severe blow to the world of ice dancing, that of William O. Hickok, IV of Harrisburg, Pa., a former Chairman of the USFSA Dance Committee, and a member of the Ice Dance Technical Committee of the ISU. Elected to succeed him on that committee at the 1957 ISU Congress was F. Ritter Shumway, from Rochester, at that time the Chairman of the USFSA Dance Committee.

At the 1957 Governing Council meeting, which was held at the Edgewater Beach Hotel in Chicago, a constitutional change was also adopted, reducing the number of at large members of the Executive Committee from 18 to 12, in two groups of six, elected for two-year terms. The reduction would only last until 1959, when the number was raised back to 18, in two groups of nine for two-year terms. Also for the first time, expense reimbursement to the extent of "two-thirds payment of first-class round-trip airplane fare" was extended to the at large members. Up to that time, expense reimbursement had only been made to the officers and chairmen of the standing committees, a "miscellaneous ruling" of the Governing Council, as they were called, since before the War.

Also at the meeting, the Summer Skating Committee was made into a standing committee, in recognition of the continued expansion and growing importance of summer skating, which was the time period during which the majority of the tests were taken. The Executive Committee also authorized that an Association "trading" pin be obtained, to be made available to skaters and officials participating in international competitions and otherwise to be available for purchase by the public. This was the first time that recognition of this important custom (of trading pins) was made officially and supported by the Association. In the years since, there have been many such pins made and distributed in a great variety of shapes, sizes and quality. Also official pins for the members of the World Team and for those on the National Team participating in international competitions have been provided, most of them being retained and proudly worn as treasured keepsakes by those receiving them.

Although the custom of special commemorative pins being struck for major championships seems to have declined in recent years, due largely to their high cost, in the years following the War, such pins or special badges were issued for almost every major championship and were highly prized. Today, some of them are truly "collector's items" and are of considerable value, and there have even been books published containing photographs of them for collectors. It is perhaps those issued by the Broadmoor for its many championships that stand out the most as a collection.

The Governing Council meeting also approved a clarification concerning the director of a corporation which owns or operates a rink, providing that such a director, if receiving no compensation for services, would not be deemed a paid employee of the rink and therefore ineligible.

The meeting also noted the death of William O. Hickok, IV, with a memorial resolution. Bill had also been an Association Vice President as well as a World Championship Referee in ice dancing. His contribution to the foundation of modern ice dancing has already been reported herein.

The test reports reflected a turn around in the number of tests taken; up 26 percent for figure (1,256) and 4 percent for dance (2,226), but on the other hand the passing percentages were down, by 3 percent for figure and 2 percent for dance, which indicated a general tightening of the standards. The Publications Committee was discontinued and replaced with a Publications Advisory Committee, which would itself be discontinued in 1963.

The 1957 Fall meeting of the Executive Committee took place in Chicago, and ongoing projects were discussed, among them the creation of Pair Tests and further clarification of the amateur status rules to bring them into line with those of the ISU, ASU and USOC, always a complicated process, since the latter were usually a "moving target." As a "footnote" to history, it was also voted to remove the restriction placed on the amateur status of Willi Boeckl, the former World Champion and teaching professional at The SC of New York, so that he could become a judge. Willi was now retired and had been a World judge for his native Austria while still a competitor.

The next two seasons, 1957-1959 would basically be the ongoing "run" toward 1960 and the Olympic Winter Games of that year at Squaw Valley. While some of the "veterans" of the international scene were remaining in competition, a new "crop" of younger skaters were also making their way into the picture.

As the 1957-1958 season was starting, the report to the Executive Committee that fall showed a remarkable increase in the number of tests taken: 3,176 in Figures and 5,527 in Dance. Interest was clearly high. Finally, an official USFSA pin was adopted, consisting of a small reproduction in "oxidized" silver of the National medal, but without the winged skate on the top.

Again, the season was "backwards" as usual, with the Worlds preceding the Nationals. The former were to be held at Paris, France, and the latter at Minneapolis. The World Team was again selected on the basis of the previous year's results. The unique aspect of the Championships was that all four defending champions from the previous year came back to defend their titles, and all were successful in doing so. Also notable was the arrival on the scene for the first time of competitors from the Soviet Union, three Men and two Pairs only. There had been no Russian or Soviet skaters in the Worlds since 1914, so these skaters were the first to appear since before the Bolshevik Revolution of 1917! Some speed skaters had competed in ISU Championships after World War I, but no figure skaters. With the strong tradition and excellence of Russian skating in St. Petersburg before World War I, it is indeed incredible that no one came out into the international arena for 44 years! The Soviet men did not do much, being 17th, 20th and 21st, but the two pairs would. They were Nina and Stanislav Zhuk, who placed eighth and Liudmila Belousova and Oleg Protopopov, who placed 13th. Stanislav Zhuk would later be the leading pair coach in the Soviet Union, while Belousova and Protopopov would make a remarkable record in the future and virtually revolutionize modern pair skating. The American pairs were Nancy and Ron Ludington, now married, who placed fifth, and Mary Jane Watson and John Jarmon, from Colorado Springs ninth.

In the Men, David Jenkins successfully defended his title, with Tim Brown again second, but the two young Frenchmen, Alain Giletti and Alain Calmat, were creeping up and placed third and fifth, respectively, with Donald Jackson of Canada, fourth. The other two Americans, Robert Lee Brewer, the National Junior Champion of 1956, and Tom Moore, were 10th and 12th. Actually, it was apparent that after the top few the quality of the U.S. representatives was not as high as those of the immediate past, a portent for the future after 1960.

Carol Heiss won her third straight World Ladies title, with two Austrians, Ingrid Wendl and Hanna Walter, again second and third. Her sister Nancy placed sixth, with the two other U.S. skaters, Carol Wanek, from New York, the National Junior Ladies Champion of 1957, ninth and Claralyn Lewis from Colorado 10th. In the Dance, the U.S. representatives did a little better, with Andrée Anderson and Donald Jacoby, third, and Claire O'Neill and John Bejshak, from Baltimore, the National Silver Dance Champions the prior year, eighth. The medal count was four, two Gold, one Silver and one Bronze, not bad, but one could not but wonder how the U.S. would do after Jenkins, Heiss, Brown and company retired.

At the Nationals in Minneapolis, the results were fairly "routine" with David Jenkins, Carol Heiss and the Ludington's all retaining their titles, while Anderson and Jacoby, the runners-up in 1957, won their first title, Sharon McKenzie and Bert Wright having retired. Tim Brown, the Men's silver medalist, continued also to do Dance with Susan Sebo and placed third. Ron Ludington had also taken up Dance and won the Silver Dance event with Judy Lamar, from Boston, the daughter of a Harvard football coach. Third in the Senior Pairs was the new partnership of Maribel Owen and Dudley Richards. Dudley, who had enjoyed a distinguished career in Singles, and had been a member of the World Team from 1951 to 1953, had

Andrée Anderson and Donald Jacoby

done a Pair with Tenley Albright in 1950-1951, and they had actually won the Eastern Senior Pairs in that year, but the pair had abruptly ended after a fall and a minor injury to Tenley, with Dr. Albright deciding singles only was the thing for her in the future, probably a wise decision! Maribel Owen's sister Laurence, the Eastern Senior Ladies Champion, was third in the Junior Ladies event, with Barbara Ann Roles, from California, the new champion.

Following the Nationals, the second Japanese Tour took place, this time with Carol Heiss, Tim Brown and the Ludingtons, accompanied by Mr. and Mrs. Henry M. Beatty, as the representatives of the USFSA. They did three exhibitions in Tokyo, as well as in Fukuoka, Osaka and Nagoya. This second tour was as popular and as well received as that four years earlier and did much to promote greater interest in skating in Japan. Both tours, had, of course, the approval and full cooperation of the Occupation Forces and Government of Japan under General MacArthur.

At the 1958 Governing Council Meeting in Boston, the presence was noted of the then CFSA President, Richard McLaughlin, from Oshawa, Ontario, the start of a continuing tradition of the Canadian President attending the USFSA meeting on a regular basis each year and the USFSA President attending the CFSA annual general meeting, the "AGM," as they call it, in exchange. Each President presents a short report of the "state" of his or her Association, and these exchanges have been most informative and of value and have been a means of maintaining the long and friendly relations between the two associations, which can be traced back to before World War I, as well as to their joint membership in the International Skating Union of America in the early days of the USFSA.

Attendance at the Boston meeting was unusually large, with 81 clubs being represented, 43 by delegates and 38 by proxy.

Efforts continued to enforce the amateur status rules and in the Chicago area there had been a "mass" suspension for one year of skaters for participating in an unsanctioned carnival run by the Michael Kirby Ice Skating Schools. With the founding later of the Ice Skating Institute of America, the trade association of the rink owners and operators, relations with them affecting the registered skaters of the Association who participated in their programs, would be an ongoing problem for the Association, not fully resolved until 1974.

A major step forward was taken with the establishment in 1959 of Sub-Sectional Championships as qualifying events for the Eastern and Pacific Coast Sectional Championships. In each Section three Regions were created: for the East, New England, North and South Atlantic, and for the Pacific Coast, Central Pacific, Northwest and Southwest Pacific. The skaters qualifying for the Sectionals would be the top four places, plus the winner of a Sub-Sectional in the prior year. However, such championships for the Midwestern Section would not be established until 1962. The decision not to start Sub-Sectionals in the Midwest in 1959 was a curious one. The professed reasons were that they were not needed, plus the long travel distances and consequent expense that would be required. On the other hand, in the 1958 Sectionals, the Midwesterns were actually the largest, with 132 entries and the largest event of 25 in Novice Ladies. The Pacific Coasts were the smallest, with 99 entries and the largest event the Juvenile Girls with 17 entries. The Easterns were in the middle, but almost as large as the Midwesterns, with 124 entries, the largest event being 19 in the Bronze Dance. All three Sectionals had added Juvenile singles fairly early, the Easterns in 1942, the Pacific Coasts in 1938, an outgrowth of their experience in the California State Championships, and the Midwesterns in 1949. The purpose was to promote skating at the lower levels, since Novice Singles were and still are the lowest National event. There was an age limit for the Juveniles of 13, the only event carrying one, except for Veterans Dance which had first begun in the East in 1950 with an age limit of 35.

The Gold Dance Test was revised to include just the Compulsory Dances, with a new and separate Gold Free Dance Tests being inaugurated. Free Dance had been part of the Gold Dance Test, just as free skating was part of the Eighth Figure Test, only since 1955. Two additional tests had already been added to the schedule of Dance Tests in 1955, the Pre Silver between the Bronze and Silver, and the Pre Gold between the Silver and the Gold. At the same time, Pair Tests were in preparation and would be inaugurated in October 1958. There was a "race" to see which pair would be the first to earn the coveted Gold Pair Test. Two pairs, both from the Boston area, took their Gold Tests on the same day, with Maribel Owen and Dudley Richards becoming the first Gold medalists and Nancy and Ron Ludington the second, although they were the first to pass the Silver Pair Test.

There was a report on the appointment of judges, which shows the problems of increasing the judging corps. There had been 31 nominations for Low Test judge, of which 17 were appointed, for Intermediate Test judge, eight out of 11, and for High Test, four out of five, so that of 47 nominations, only 29 were approved. In some instances, the clubs were not following through in making recommendations or if they did, they were without the required supporting information. Clearly, a greater effort was needed to create more judges, and this was in 1958! It is still the same today!

Another "minor" financial milestone was achieved, when the registration fee was raised to $1.00 from 50 cents, "in order to present a balanced budget for the forthcoming year" as it was stated in the report of the meeting.

Howard D. Herbert

The year 1958 also marked the end of the tenure in office of Kenneth Brown, of California, who stepped down after three years as President and was succeeded by Howard D. Herbert from New Jersey. Ken stepped in as Chairman of the Competitions Committee in 1958 and served for one year. At the same time, he was a key figure in the organization of the Squaw Valley Olympics, being instrumental in bringing in computers, both for use in disseminating information, as well as for the calculation of results. While not as active thereafter in the Association as some of his predecessors, he did remain a member of the Executive Committee until 1967. He passed away in 1988.

The Fall 1958 meeting of the Executive Committee was held at the Edgewater Beach in Chicago. It was noted that 21 summer sessions had been sanctioned for 1958, a substantial increase. Also noted was the continued rise in the number of tests taken, especially in Dance, up 20 percent (to 6,615), while figure tests taken were up slightly (to 3,195). A special exemption was granted to the Lakewood Winter Club of Tacoma permitting the club to hold Sixth, Seventh and Eighth Tests, although the rink size was sub-standard. A revised rule was adopted in 1958 requiring an ice surface for the free skating of at least 125 by 75 feet, actually a rather small surface. If the waiver had not been granted, apparently, it would not have been possible to hold high tests in some of the Northwest Region clubs, such as Lakewood. The waiver was for a two-year period. It is interesting to note that the same dimensions mentioned above remain the minimum standard today, with the total square feet (9,375) still stated in the rule just as it was in 1958!

At the meeting there was discussion of the application of Federal Excise taxes to club dues, and of proposed legislation which would enable clubs to seek exemption. The Association did not then have its famous "501(c)(3)" exemption as a non-profit and charitable organization, but the interested parties, chiefly Delaplaine McDaniel of Philadelphia and Thedore Patterson of Boston, remained the "watchdogs" of the situation and provided assistance to the clubs when needed.

With Sub-Sectionals (ultimately redesignated as "Regionals" in 1965) having been approved to start in 1959, the first six such championships went well, with those on the Pacific Coast (Central Pacific, Northwest Pacific and Southwest Pacific) having an average entry of 58, with the largest being the Southwest Pacific with 63. In the East (New England, North Atlantic and South Atlantic), the North Atlantics were the largest with 65 entries and the South Atlantics the smallest with 27, the average of the three being 44. In those areas which had already had non-qualifying Sub-Sectionals in the past, such as California, New England and the Northwest, the entries were higher than in areas, such as South Atlantic, where such competitions had been few and far between. Clearly, however, the need for the new level of qualifying competition had been demonstrated. For comparison, the figures for the first Sectional Championships based on the new system were; Eastern - 98; Midwestern - 107; and Pacific Coast - 96. The error in the decision to postpone the inauguration of Sub-Sectionals for the Midwestern Section was readily apparent!

The year 1959 saw the return, happily, of the World Championships to Colorado Springs and the Broadmoor. It was most unusual for a championship to be held once again at the same venue in such a relatively short period of time, as it has always been the policy of the ISU to follow an informal "rotation" of its events around the World, wherever possible. Apart from the obvious success of the 1957 Championship as a reason for the award of the 1959 Worlds to the USFSA and the Broadmoor SC, there was another very practical one. With the 1960 Olympic Winter Games scheduled for Squaw Valley, Calif., in accordance with an IOC policy, a "pre-Olympic" competition must be held in each sport at the site of the Games to test the facilities. While no such competition was originally scheduled for figure skating, one was arranged in 1959 for speed skating. The "test" competition for figure skating ultimately were the 1960 Pacific Coast Championships, held at Squaw Valley at the beginning of January, just a few weeks before the Games.

Another charter flight was arranged from Europe to bring the competitors and officials to Colorado Springs for the championships. Accompanying them on the same flights over and back was a group of speed skaters, who went on to Squaw Valley for the speed skating competition there, then returning to the Springs for the flight back to Europe through New York. The speed skating delegation included some very famous skaters and champions, such as Lassi Parkinen of Finland, the World Champion of 1947 and at the time the substitute ISU Council member for speed skating, Juhani Järvinen, also from Finland, the reigning World Champion, who set a World record in the 1,500 meters on the Squaw Valley track, and the legendary Evgeni Grishin of the Soviet Union, already the winner of two Gold medals in 1956, who would win two more in the 500 and 1,500 meter races in the Squaw Valley Olympics.

In 1959, the National Championships were finally scheduled to precede the Worlds, as they have ever since. This enabled the World Team to be selected on a current basis, rather than on a year old record. For similar reasons to those for the award of the Worlds, the 1959 Nationals were awarded to the Genesee FSC of Rochester, N.Y., and really to Ritter Shumway, in recognition of the success of the 1957 North Americans there and Ritter's proven organizational ability. The North American Championships were also scheduled for after the Nationals and before the Worlds, in Toronto, following the usual rotation between the two countries, so for once, the competitive schedule was in the "right" order!

The Genesee club proudly reported that almost 14,000 spectators attended the championships, "almost double the number at any previous Nationals" over the three sessions scheduled in the War Memorial arena, consisting of a Friday evening, Saturday and Sunday afternoons. The schedule for the Nationals in those days usually provided for the championships to end on a Sunday afternoon, but, of course, that would all change with the advent of television on a regular basis, still five years away. Also, the programming of the events had been "carefully balanced so that every major session would include at least one example of each form of skating." This often meant that a lower class would be paired with a Senior class, such as Novice or Junior Ladies with Senior Men, which enabled the Juniors and the Novices to perform in the main arena. It is unfortunate that today that opportunity has generally been denied to them, with the Juniors and the Novices usually competing in what is nothing more than a practice rink and sometimes not getting into the main arena at all. Such is life with television!

David Jenkins, Carol Heiss and Nancy and Ron Ludington all continued their "march" towards Squaw Valley by retaining their titles, while Andrée and Donald Jacoby, now married, won their second title in the Gold Dance. Carol's sister Nancy was now the runner-up in the Senior Ladies, with Barbara Ann Roles third; while in the Senior Men, Tim Brown was again the silver medalist, with Robert Brewer third. In the Senior Pairs, after the Ludingtons were Gayle and Karl Freed from Indianapolis, followed by Maribel Owen and Dudley Richards. The Ladies Junior winner was Laurence Owen, with Gregory Kelley from Boston, the Junior Men's winner. (When contemplating the rising success of these young skaters in 1959, one cannot help but be reminded that they were lost ahead of their time just two short years later.) In the Gold Dance, Judy Lamar and Ron Ludington placed third and were nominated for the World Team as a result, as were the runners-up in the event, Margie Ackles and Charles Phillips, Jr. from California. Tim Brown and Susan Sebo were still in the Gold Dance event and placed fourth. In the Men's Novice, Monty Hoyt from Denver and Scott Allen from New York, were one and two, respectively, and Gary Visconti from Detroit was eighth, all of whom would soon be heard from in the 1960's. A footnote to the championships was that the Broadmoor SC won the Harned Trophy for the club with the most points in a close competition with The SC of Boston. It was the third time the Broadmoor had won the coveted trophy, its prior wins having come in 1952 and 1955, both years in which the championships were held at the Broadmoor.

In the North Americans at Toronto, Carol Heiss, Barbara Wagner and Robert Paul, and Geraldine Fenton and William McLachlan, all routinely defended the titles they had won in 1957, but there was a new Men's Champion. Since David Jenkins did not enter, due to the demands of his schedule in medical school in Cleveland, the winner was Donald Jackson of Oshawa, Canada, who defeated Tim Brown, the 1958 World runner-up, on the basis of his excellent free skating. He had, however, been able to stay close to Brown in the figures. Under the scoring system then long in use, the marks of each judge were added together, after having the appropriate factors applied to them, so that a final ordinal was arrived at for each skater by each judge for the combined total of the factored figure and free skating marks. The figure results were, obviously, a major factor in deciding a championship, since they were 60 percent of the total score, and the strong free skaters had to stay with the strong figure skaters as best they could, in order to have a chance. The system would change after 1980 to one involving the use of factored placements for each part of a competition to determine the result, thereby eliminating the final ordinal for each judge.

The World Championships were again a resounding success. They were part of the "Rush to the Rockies" celebration in the State of Colorado, in commemoration of the 100th Anniversary of the first settlement of the Territory in 1859. Despite the fact that Carl Chamberlin, who with William Wardman had been one of the organizers of the various championships held at the Broadmoor up to 1957, had passed away in the fall of 1956, Henry Beatty of Cleveland had stepped in as general chairman and the organization was once again carried out without any real hitches. There were many memorable events off the ice, and the Governor of the State and the Commandant of the Air Force Academy were among the guests, with tours of the new Academy and parties there being hosted by Jane Vaughn Sullivan, the former National Ladies Champion, whose husband, Brigadier General Riggs Sullivan was the Commandant of Cadets.

This time, the entries were down a little from 1957 with 13 Men, 15 Ladies, 8 Pairs and nine Dance couples, for a total of 45, again from 11 countries. The Soviet skaters did not come, due to visa difficulties, and there was but one representative from an Eastern Bloc country, Czechoslovakia, with Karol Divin fifth in the Men. The same two Soviet Pairs from 1958 had entered the 1959 Europeans at Davos, with the Zhuks placing second and Belousova-Protopopov, seventh, so presumably they would have done well in Colorado.

Although he was defeated in the figures by his long time rival, Tim Brown, David Jenkins managed to successfully defend his World title, with his very strong free skating, with Donald Jackson of Canada, also passing Brown, who wound up third. There was an interesting comment in the report about the figures, which stated that "they were generally of a low standard, with the Europeans being hampered by the fact that their blades were hollow ground for skating on outdoor ice, which is much harder than indoors. When on the softer indoor surface, it was extremely difficult for these competitors to prevent themselves from double tracking." On the other hand, the free skating was of the highest quality. It is hard to imagine from this distance in time, just how good Jenkins and Jackson were in free skating, and it is believed that they would have done equally as well today. David did many of the triple jumps then, and Jackson was not far behind him in that department. Among other content, Jackson did "delayed double Salchow, double Lutz, triple Salchow and Axels in both directions," while David did "two double Axels in succession, triple Salchow and triple loop and a spectacular flying camel into a back sit spin." The styles of the two skaters could not have been more different, but each was a master of his craft in his own way.

In the Ladies, Carol Heiss was completely dominant, both in figures and free. It is sometimes forgotten just how good she was in figures, which she skated with speed. Apart from her, the figure standard was low for the rest of the ladies as well. One European observer was quoted as saying, "Abominable! Why don't they learn to keep their heads up?" The Austrians again had a representative on the podium, with Hanna Walter, second, but there was a new face on the scene in Sjoukje Dijkstra, from the Netherlands, a strong free skater who was third. The legendary Ina Bauer of Germany was fourth and Barbara Roles fifth in her first Worlds. Sjoukje had been 12th in the 1957 Worlds, climbing from 21st and last in 1955, but by 1959 she was the European Ladies Silver medalist behind Walter. She and her compatriot, Joan Haanappel, the European Bronze medalist, who had to withdraw in Colorado after the figures due to illness, were the first skaters from The Netherlands to achieve World rank, and Sjoukje, who trained in England with Arnold Gerschwiler, would eventually compile an outstanding record, including the Olympic Gold in 1964.

In the Pairs, Barbara Wagner and Robert Paul of Canada won their third straight title, with a new German combination of Marika Kilius and a new partner, Hans-Jürgen Bäumler placing second, while Nancy and Ron Ludington took third in a close competition with Maria and Otto Jelinek of Canada. Maribel Owen and Dudley Richards were sixth. In the Dance, Courtney Jones of Great Britain also had a new partner in Doreen Denny, and was unbeatable, for his third title and her first. Courtney is generally considered to be the greatest male ice dancer ever, and at the time of his 1959 win, he and Doreen had only been skating together a few months. The surprise in the event were Andrée and Donald Jacoby, who placed second over the runners-up from the previous two years, Geraldine Fenton and William McLachlan of Canada. Margie Ackles and Charles Phillips were fourth and Judy Lamar and Ron Ludington ninth.

At the year end meeting of the Governing Council, which was held at the Benjamin Franklin Hotel in Seattle, Washington, only the third time on the Pacific Coast, several rule changes were made. One was to create two classes of Accountant, National and Sectional. Another was the return to the marking scale of 0 to 6; and another was the transfer to the International Committee of the responsibility for the selection of participants in the North Americans. It was also voted to return the number of at large members of the Executive Committee to 18 from 12, as previously mentioned.

There had also been a small "hassle" with the ISU, which had put out a Judges Handbook for Figures, based largely on the USFSA booklet "Evaluation of Errors in Figures," but without proper credit being given to the latter. At the 1959 Congress, the error was recognized and subsequent issues of the handbook reflected the proper credit. Since then, all USFSA publications have been or should be properly copyrighted!

F. Ritter Shumway

A decision at the 1959 ISU Congress at Tours, France, involved a rule change which affected eligibility for election to the Figure Skating and Ice Dance Technical Committees, on the latter of which Ritter Shumway had been serving since 1957 as the successor to Bill Hickok. The Congress adopted a requirement that the members of the two committees had to be at least World Championship Referees or Judges. In the mid-1950's a more formal system for the evaluation and discipline of judges had been developed as an outgrowth of the scandal involving the Austrian officials, which had resulted in their suspension. The theory was that since the Technical Committees would serve as the "jury" in such cases, their members should be "peers" of those who might be subject to disciplinary action. Ritter was a National Referee and Judge in the United States, but did not hold any ISU appointment, so he was declared ineligible to be a candidate for re-election, a decision which he, being the sporting gentleman he was, did not protest, but graciously withdrew in favor of Harold Hartshorne from New York, who did have the required qualifications and was accordingly elected to the Dance Committee. On the face of it, not to have permitted Ritter to have been a candidate was clearly unfair, but such is the way of the ISU sometimes! However, he became the new First Vice President of the USFSA at its meeting, a prophetic choice as it would turn out.

Also at the USFSA meeting, a further suspension for one year of skaters for appearing in another Michael Kirby Ice Studio show which was unsanctioned was approved, with the problem of such acts remaining essentially unresolved, and unfortunately, with no effort apparently being made to negotiate any reasonable solution.

In addition, the size of the team for the 1960 Olympic Winter Games was announced as being three Men, three Ladies and three Pairs. (The addition of Ice Dancing was still 16 years away, although an effort on the part of the ISU to make it an Olympic medal event had started as early as 1948.) The maximum number of entries in Worlds was also reduced to the same levels, with each ISU Member being entitled to two entries and to a third if they had a skater in the first 12 in the prior year. It was the first significant step taken to tighten the entry requirements, essentially to the detriment of the stronger nations, that has been ongoing in various forms ever since!

The 1959 Fall Meeting of the Executive Committee was held in Chicago, and finally, the majority judging of tests was approved, to be effective with the 1961 Rulebook (in 1960), with the proviso that any mark below the minimum passing mark (by any judge) would still fail the test.

Also noted was the death in September of Lieutenant General Oscar W. Griswold, who had been the director of the Broadmoor Ice Palace from 1950 to 1959. The commanding general of the XIVth U.S. Army Corps in the Pacific Theater during World War II, Gen. Griswold had played a significant role in the organizing of both the Worlds of 1957 and 1959, as well as of the Nationals of 1952 and 1955. They used to say that he was the only person able to control the "skating mothers" in the rink, and his three stars were helpful to the maintenance of discipline in the rink! Another death noted was that in May 1959, of Sir Samuel Hoare, Viscount Templewood, a long time member and former President of the NSA of Great Britain and a cabinet minister in the British Government before and during the War. He was probably the highest government official to actually have been an active skater and proudly held the British Second Class Test, which he passed when he was over the age of 50.

With the Olympic Winter Games to be held in February, the Nationals were scheduled for the end of January, 1960, as has been the case in the Olympic year since the competition schedule was "put in order" with all the qualifying competitions "moving up" by a month. The Sub-Sectionals were usually at the end of the preceding November or in early December, followed by the Sectionals in late December or early January. There have actually been instances of competitions starting or being held on New Year's Day of the Olympic year!

The 1960 Nationals were held at Seattle, nine years after their prior appearance there in 1951, and it would be on the basis of the results there that the Olympic and World Teams would be chosen. The two Teams are actually separate from each other, although at the point of original selection, the personnel is very much the same, depending upon the number of entries permitted in the respective events. The team managers or "leaders," as they are called in the ISU, are different, as are the judges selected, so there is a "changeover" between the "managements" of the Teams after the Games. Very often the World Team is considerably different from and smaller than the Olympic Team, due to the inevitable "drop outs" that occur after the Games, so it has been the practice to designate several alternates, just in case.

In the Ladies, Carol Heiss won her fourth and last title in the Senior Ladies, with Barbara Ann Roles and Laurence Owen second and third. David Jenkins came out of medical school long enough to win his third Senior Men's crown, with Tim Brown again second and Robert Lee Brewer from Los Angeles third in a rare tiebreaker on total points with Bradley Lord from Boston. The Senior Pairs went to the Ludingtons, with Maribel Owen and Dudley Richards, the runners-up. In the Dance, the Jacobys having retired, the Gold Dance title went to Margie Ackles and Charles Phillips, Jr., with Marilyn Meeker and Larry Pierce from Indianapolis second and Yvonne Littlefield and Roger Campbell from Los Angeles third.

As a result, the Olympic Team looked like this: Men - Jenkins, Brown, Brewer; Ladies - Heiss, Roles, Owen; Pairs - Ludingtons, Owen-Richards, Ila Ray and Ray Hadley, Jr. The Squaw Valley Games were a success, although the venue was very small and remote, and for the spectators, it meant staying as far away as Reno, Nev., and "commuting" daily up into the mountains, which when there was a heavy snow, presented many problems. In some respects, the Games were a precursor of those at Lake Placid in 1980 from the transportation standpoint. Blyth Arena, where the figure skating was held, was covered and with artificial ice and had a seating capacity of 8,500. It was open on one end, which made the figures sometimes difficult when the wind was blowing in the open end. It would not be until the 1964 Games that figure skating would finally "go indoors" permanently!

A rare recognition was extended to the figure skaters when Carol Heiss was selected to recite the Olympic Oath on behalf of all the athletes, the first time that a lady athlete had been accorded this honor. The final Olympic Torch bearer was a speed skater, Ken Henry, the Gold Medalist in the 500 meter race in 1952. The Pairs competition opened the Games and Barbara

Wagner and Robert Paul of Canada, fully demonstrated their mastery of the discipline in a unanimous (by all judges) win over Marika Kilius and Hans-Jürgen Bäumler of Germany, for the first Olympic Gold medals in Pairs for Canada. The Ludingtons won the Bronze medal, with the Jelineks close behind. Maribel Owen and Dudley Richards did not skate as well as they could and wound up 10th, with the Hadleys 11th. The Soviet pairs reappeared for their first Olympics and the first for any Russian since 1908, with Nina and Stanislav Zhuk sixth and Liudmila Belousova and Oleg Protopopov ninth. There were 13 pairs in all, including one from Australia and one from South Africa, with the latter being the last entry of South Africans in a World or Olympic Championship until 1992, with the exception of the World Juniors of 1977.

In the Men, the surprise winner of the figures was Karol Divin of Czechoslovakia, with Tim Brown not having a good day and placing fifth. David Jenkins managed to place second in the figures, and so was ahead of his principal rival in the free skating, Donald Jackson of Canada, fourth in that category. The young French skater, Alain Giletti was third, as he was also in the free skating, yet wound up fourth in the final result! In the free, Jenkins and Jackson were 1-2, with Brown fourth, and Divin no better than fifth. So in the final result, Jenkins won the Gold medal, Divin the Silver and Jackson the Bronze, Brown was fifth and the third U.S. man, Robert Lee Brewer was seventh. It was David's last competition and his finest hour, as he would not enter the Worlds and returned directly to medical school. His performance in the Nationals could well have been his best, however, as in that competition he was well behind Brown in the figures and had a lot of ground to make up, just as he did against Divin in Squaw Valley. His free skating was very much ahead of his time, as he did all the triples then known, except the Lutz and Axel, but his double Axel and the flying spins, just as had been those of his brother Hayes, were outstanding.

By winning the Olympics, David put himself and his brother Hayes into the record books forever, being the only brothers to win Olympic Gold and back to back at that! What a joint record they had: two Olympic Gold medals, seven World Gold medals, three North American Gold medals, and eight National Senior Men's gold medals, one Olympic Bronze medal, and three World Bronze medals, plus innumerable others, in all colors! However, a third person would soon be added to the incredible legacy of the Jenkins family, when Hayes and Carol Heiss were married in New York in April 1960, bringing to the collection her one Olympic Gold medal, five World Gold medals, two North American Gold medals, four National Senior Ladies Gold medals, and one Olympic Silver medal, plus many more, including several won for speed skating! Hayes has been quoted as saying in jest that Carol went to the 1960 Worlds at Vancouver just to have one more Worlds than he! It is doubted that there can be a more outstanding family in sport. David went on to become a physician and a leading gastro-enterologist in Tulsa, Okla., Hayes as a corporate lawyer, as we have already noted, and Carol, after bringing up three children, a very successful coach and today the representative of the USFSA to the United States Olympic Committee. Not forgotten in all this is Hayes and David's older sister, Nancy Sue, with whom Hayes did pairs and dance, winning the Midwestern Senior Pairs in 1948 and the Midwestern Senior Dance in 1947 and 1948. Despite a debilitating illness, Nancy has carried on a full life as a wife and mother, and in fact, their mother, Mrs. Sarah Jenkins, was herself a long time and active judge.

In the Ladies, the soon-to-be bride, Carol, skated conservatively and well to add the Olympic Gold to her Silver medal from 1956. Runner-up was Sjoukje Dijkstra from The Netherlands, with Barbara Ann Roles skating very well to earn the Bronze, while Laurence Owen placed sixth.

As is so often the case with respect to the Worlds following the Olympics, there were many changes in the team. There have often been opinions expressed that the Worlds should not be held in the Olympic year, something the IOC would like, partly because of the "drop outs," but the post-Olympic Worlds are really the "kick off" for the next quadrennial, and often young and promising skaters are seen who would not otherwise have the opportunity to be there. This was the case in the Men in 1960, since David Jenkins retired, but Tim Brown and Robert Brewer also decided not to go, leaving the U.S. with no men at all. Virtually at the last minute, however, Bradley Lord and Gregory Kelley, both from Boston, who had been fourth and fifth respectively in the Nationals, were called upon to represent their country. They went and did well! In the Ladies, Carol Heiss returned to defend, and was accompanied by her Olympic teammates, Barbara Roles and Laurence Owen. In the Pairs, all three Olympic pairs went to Vancouver, while the Dance couples selected, Margie Ackles and Charles Phillips, Marilyn Meeker and Larry Pierce, and Yvonne Littlefield and Roger Campbell were all on hand.

The Vancouver Worlds were the first held in Canada since 1932 and were very well organized by the British Columbia Section of the CFSA. The Sections in the CFSA are essentially regional associations in their own right, with jurisdiction over all local matters, with general supervision being provided by the CFSA headquarters. As a result, the organizing skills of the Canadians have been outstanding, and there has not really been any major international event held across the border that has not been a success, at least technically and esthetically, if not financially! Vancouver was no exception. The ISU President, Dr. James Koch from Switzerland was on hand (he did not go to the Olympics, since he was not a supporter of the Games, choosing instead to watch the Men's free skating on a tiny black and white television set in the author's home while en route to Vancouver), and generally since then the ISU President has honored figure skating with his presence, whether or not he is the ISU Representative, the official in overall charge who also presents the medals.

The surprise of the championships was in the Men, in which it had generally been predicted that Donald Jackson of Canada was the favorite and logical successor to David Jenkins.

It was not to be, however, as Alain Giletti of France won the figures across the board, in the absence of Divin, who had returned home, and was solid second in free skating to take the title, the first ever for France. Jackson finished second again. In third place was the second French representative, Alain Calmat. The two U.S. representatives, Bradley Lord and Greg Kelley, placed sixth and ninth, respectively. Young as he was (age 20), Alain Giletti was an experienced "veteran" and by 1960 had already been European champion four times, as well as runner-up four times, going back to 1953.

Carol Heiss completed her outstanding career with her fifth Ladies title and her "usual" clean performance, although she did omit her double Axel. Sjoukje Dijkstra was second and Barbara Roles third, while Laurence Owen placed ninth.

In the Pairs, Barbara Wagner and Robert Paul of Canada also finished their competitive career on a high note with their fourth title, but this time, their compatriots, Maria and Otto Jelinek were second, defeating Marika Kilius and Hans-Jürgen Bäumler of Germany. The Ludingtons also closed out their competitive days with a sixth place, while Maribel Owen and Dudley Richards were 10th. The two Soviet pairs, of Nina and Stanislav Zhuk and Liudmila Belousova-Oleg Protopopov were fifth and eighth, respectively.

In the Dance, Doreen Denny and Courtney Jones retained the title they had first won in 1959, with Bill McLachlan and his new partner Virginia Thompson second; the French couple, Christiane and Jean-Paul Guhel third, followed by Margie Ackles and Charles Phillips, fourth and Marilyn Meeker and Larry Pierce, fifth. Yvonne Littlefield and Roger Campbell were eighth.

At the Governing Council Meeting of 1960 at the Broadmoor in Colorado Springs, it was voted that all USFSA Past Presidents should be elected as Honorary members for life. This action confirmed that taken in 1953, when the Past Presidents were recognized for their service. The applicable clause in the Constitution was amended to provide for election by the Governing Council for such term as it saw fit. It also specifically clarified the fact that Honorary Members were not foreclosed from serving in office or in other positions to which elected or appointed. There had been confusion in this regard with many of the Past Presidents actively serving as committee chairman, and in one case as a Vice President, after they left office. They did not, however, have a vote in the Governing Council. The original provision, which went all the way back to 1921, had included the curious limitation that the election of Honorary members would be for one year only! This explains why the four original Honorary officers, two Presidents and two Vice Presidents, were always included in the reports of the nominating committee each year. It also explains why the action in 1949 of the Executive Committee in electing Herbert J. Clarke of Great Britain the first Honorary member was ratified by the Governing Council in 1952, since only the latter body actually had the authority to elect such members!

At the same time, the Constitution was also amended to provide that the immediate Past President would automatically serve for a one-year term on the Executive Committee. Again, the limitation of a one-year term only was eventually removed in 1971, so that the immediate Past President now serves on the Board of Directors and also on the Executive Committee for as long as he or she remains in that position, which has been up to four years in one instance.

Another new Association pin was approved similar in design to the first one, including a map, but this time with a skater over it and the letters USFSA in one corner. It was also smaller and in color, being enameled instead of oxidized silver. The National medal, however, remained unchanged.

It was noted that the number of Member clubs had increased substantially to 165 in 1960, compared to 120 five years earlier. In a portent for the future, it was announced that CBS-TV had proposed to "put the 1961 Nationals on video tape and show the film eight days after the Nationals on a Sunday P.M. sports spectacular," to use the words of the report to the meeting. There was yet another suspension of skaters for appearing in the Michael Kirby Ice Studio show, for the third year in a row! In hindsight, it is incredible that the issue could not be satisfactorily resolved, but it had become a personal vendetta in the Chicago area, with the protagonists polarized from one another. Also at the 1960 Governing Council Meeting, the President of the Professional Skaters Guild of America (PSGA), then Wally Sahlin, was invited to attend, together with the Guild's Executive Secretary, Mrs. Agnes Hutchinson. Wally presented a report to the Executive Committee offering various suggestions that the Guild felt would improve the sport. This too has become a tradition and the PSGA President is a most welcome addition to the annual meeting.

The fall 1960 meeting of the Executive Committee was held at the Sheraton-Blackstone Hotel in Chicago, the meeting in Chicago still not having "settled down" at its airport location in Des Plaines, Ill. Noted were the deaths of Herbert Crispo, Past President of the CFSA and of Hayes R. Jenkins, the father of Hayes Alan and David Jenkins. An agreement with the Columbia Broadcasting System (CBS) to broadcast on television the 1961 Nationals, with a modest rights fee being paid, which was the first national agreement for television, although there had been local television on occasion, for example, the 1956 Nationals in Philadelphia, but that, of course, did not involve any payment. The size of the fee received is unknown, but probably was no more than $10,000 or so.

With the close of the 1960 season, the "Golden Age" came to an end, although at the time, the future held great promise. Little did anyone know what lay ahead.

The 1960-1961 season started routinely enough. There was the usual excitement with new faces on the scene following the retirement of those who had been on top for the past four years and anticipation over who would succeed them.

One rule change had been made and announced, which was a "majority pass" in tests,

Triumph and Tragedy
(1961-1964)

meaning that only two out of three judges were needed to pass a test. The unanimous pass requirement had been in effect since 1923. The provision that a mark below the minimum by one judge would still result in the failure of a test, remained in effect until 1995, when it also was dropped. The rule had the effect of making the passing of tests a little easier, but also was a positive change, since it eliminated the effect of one judge being "off the mark" as it were.

The six Regional Championships were still not that large in size, but they had the effect of decreasing the number of entries in the Sectionals. In 1961, there were 95 entries in the Easterns and 60 in the Pacific Coasts, but that year for the latter was an aberration, since no Juvenile Singles events were held and they would not return to the schedule until 1965. By contrast, in what would be the final Midwesterns before Sub-Sectionals were introduced to the Midwestern Section, starting in 1962, there were 155 entries, including 31 in Novice Ladies. There were no elimination rounds in those days, although the rule providing that in the Sectional Junior and lower classes only the top eight in the figures could free skate had been in effect since 1946. One of the reasons the Midwestern Section had hung back in accepting Sub-Sectionals was the argument that the Midwestern Sectional was the oldest of the three and that the additional competitions would detract from its importance and prestige. Happily, that has never been the case, and the qualifying competitions system, once uniform across the country has proven to be very successful, although of course, there have been various instances of "tinkering" with it, i.e. increasing the number to qualify from each event in the lower competition and the ever present problem of "byes" and who gets them!

The season seemed to have already a sense of "impending doom," as there had been several deaths in the months preceding the Nationals, of people who had played an important role in the early days of the Association. Among them were Henry F. Swift of San Francisco, one of the founders of skating in California; M. Lester Madden of Boston, the father of Jimmy and Grace

Madden, who had been chairman of the Executive Committee of the Association back in 1930 and a long-time officer of The SC of Boston; and Ralph G. Van Name from New Haven, another pioneer in the Association and supporter of the sport, as can be seen by the fact that the New Haven SC held no less than six National Championships between 1914 and 1935.

Then, early in January 1961, the USFSA President, Howard D. Herbert, of Moorestown, N.J., died unexpectedly at the age of 72, the first and only President to die while in office. Herbert probably had been the oldest President up to that time, having taken office at the age of 69. As a result, F. Ritter Shumway, the First Vice President, became the acting President less than a week before the Nationals and three weeks before the fateful day of Feb. 15, 1961. The applicable provision of the By Laws stated that "the Vice Presidents in their order shall perform the duties of the President in his absence, inability or refusal to act." There was no provision in the case of the death of the incumbent, for the automatic succession of the First Vice President to the office of President, so Ritter remained the acting President until the Governing Council meeting of 1961. Only on one other occasion since then has there been an acting President, under completely different circumstances during the Gulf War in the 1990's, as we shall see. In any event, Ritter took immediate charge and exercised outstanding leadership throughout the following crisis.

The 1961 Nationals were held in Colorado Springs, the fourth held at the Broadmoor since 1948, and the "new" guard was very much in evidence, with every Senior title up for grabs, without a defending champion. Despite the dampening effect of the loss of President Herbert, the championships were well organized and well attended, as has invariably been the case at the Broadmoor, with close competition in all the events, especially in the Seniors.

In the Senior Men, the battle was principally between Tim Brown, representing St. Moritz, seeking his first National Senior title, Bradley Lord from Boston, the 1957 Junior Champion, and Gregory Kelley, the 1959 champion, formerly of Boston but now representing his training site, the Broadmoor, where Edi Scholdan was his coach. Tim had been the 1954 Junior Champion and been the runner-up in the Senior Men for the past four years. Once again, the "runner-up jinx" seemed to apply, as Tim could do no better than third, with Bradley the new champion, and Gregory the runner-up. Also in the event, placing fifth, was Bruce Heiss, the brother of Carol and Nancy, both of whom had retired, carrying on the family tradition.

In the Senior Ladies, the contenders were Laurence Owen from Boston, the Junior Ladies Champion in 1959, Stephanie Westerfeld of the Broadmoor, fourth in 1960, Rhode Lee Michelson from Paramount, Calif., the Novice Ladies Champion in 1958 and Karen Howland from Sun Valley, the 1960 Junior Ladies Champion. In all the Senior events it was an entirely new "crop" of skaters, moving up from the Junior level rapidly to fill the "vacuum" in the ranks of the Seniors, a very healthy prospect for the future. In the end, it was Laurence Owen who prevailed, to win the title previously held by her mother and coach nine times. In view of what happened, one cannot but help to link together Laurence and Jean-Pierre Brunet, the talented children of former champions, both of whom never fulfilled the ultimate promise they had displayed. Stephanie Westerfeld finished second and Rhode Lee Michelson just edged out Karen Howland for third on a total point tie breaker, 913.49 to 911.90 points.

In the Senior Pairs, Maribel Owen, or "young" Maribel as she was called, with Dudley Richards, representing Boston, won the title, again one formerly held by her mother six different times with two different partners. Second were Ila Ray and Ray Hadley, Jr., from Seattle, the 1957 Junior Pair Champions, with Laurie and Bill Hickox, from San Francisco, the 1960 Junior Pair Champions third.

The Senior Dance event also had new faces and combinations a characteristic of the dance ever since, with a constantly changing of partnerships from year to year! The new champions were Diane Sherbloom of Los Angeles and Larry Pierce of Indianapolis. Pierce had been the Silver Dance Champion in 1959 with Marilyn Meeker, while Sherbloom had been runner-up in the Silver Dance the same year with Roger Campbell. Second were Dona Lee Carrier with Roger Campbell who had been third in 1960 with Yvonne Littlefield. Patricia and Robert Dineen, representing Lake Placid, who had been the 1960 Silver Dance Champions, had stayed together, been married and placed third! With the depth of its team, which also included Lorraine Hanlon as the new Junior Ladies Champion and Tina Noyes as the new Novice Ladies Champion, the Boston club won the Harned Trophy, repeating at the same time the feat of winning all three ladies titles that had first been accomplished in 1939, when Joan Tozzer, Gretchen Merrill and Betsy Nichols, had done so, although it was New York that had won the Harned Trophy in that year!

After the Nationals, it was on to the North American championships in Philadelphia. The Canadians fielded a very strong team in Donald Jackson, representing Toronto, the defending champion in the Men and the World Silver medalist in 1960, Wendy Griner from Toronto, the Canadian Ladies Champion, who had been 12th in the Olympics and seventh in the Worlds in 1960; Maria and Otto Jelinek, the Canadian Pair champions and World Silver medalists, and in Dance, Bill McLachlan, the defending champion from 1959, with his new partner Virginia Thompson, from Toronto, with whom he had been the World Silver medalist in 1960. Three out of the four top entrants from Canada were the reigning World Silver medalists, and they prevailed in the championships to win the coveted North American titles. They were considered as a very important springboard for the coming Worlds in Prague, just as the European Championships were for those from that continent. On the U.S. side, Tim Brown elected not to go to the North Americans and Worlds, and was replaced by Doug Ramsey from Detroit, who had been fourth in the Nationals and was the National Junior Champion in 1960.

In the Ladies, there was a modest upset of sorts, when Laurence Owen became the Ladies Champion, defeating Wendy Griner, although in fact in the two championships in 1960, they had split the results, with Laurence ahead in the Olympics and Wendy ahead in the Worlds. For Laurence, it was, of course, a title previously held by her mother in 1937. With an uneven number of judges, consisting of three from the U.S. and two from Canada (as required by the ISU mandate since 1957), the majority for Laurence in a 3 to 2 decision, were two Americans and one Canadian, so the specter of "national bias" did not rear its ugly head! In the Men and Pairs, the new U.S. Champions placed second to their Canadian counterparts, while in the Dance, the runners-up were Dona Lee Carrier and Roger Campbell, with the new U.S. Champions, Diane Sherbloom and Larry Pierce fourth behind Paulette Doan and Kenneth Ormsby from Toronto.

1961 World Team

Because of the tight schedule, since the North Americans were held on Feb. 11 and 12, 1961, and the Worlds were scheduled to start in Prague, Czechoslovakia on Feb. 22, it was decided the World team, plus the supporting personnel, including the Team Manager, Deane McMinn from California, referees, judges, coaches and family members would go directly from Philadelphia to New York and depart for Europe on the 14th. They would travel on Sabena Airlines, the Belgian national carrier, to Brussels, connecting to a flight directly to Prague on the 15th. A full team had been selected, consisting of three Men, three Ladies, three Pairs and three Dance couples, reflecting the policy of the USFSA to always send the full complement of entries to which it was entitled at the World and Olympic levels.

Also in the delegation were Walter Powell from St. Louis, ISU Council member and Referee; Harold Hartshorne, from New York, ISU Ice Dance Technical Committee member and Judge and his wife Louise; coaches Billy Kipp from California, Maribel Vinson Owen from Boston, Danny Ryan from Indianapolis, Edi Scholdan from Colorado Springs and his son, Jimmy, Bill Swallender from Detroit, family members, Mrs. Ann Campbell, Mrs. Alvah Hadley, Nathalie Kelley and Sherri Westerfeld, and spectator, Eddie LeMaire, a National judge from New York and his son, Richard, for a total of 34 persons out of a total passenger list of 72 on a Boeing 707 aircraft.

On the morning of Feb. 15, 1961, when on final approach to the Brussels airport, the aircraft was ordered to go around and make another approach, due to the presence of a small airplane on the active runway. While making the turn to do so, the plane crashed near the airport with the loss of all on board. There has never been any official explanation of the cause of the accident, either by the Belgian Government or by Boeing, the manufacturer, and the claims by the families of the victims were settled in accordance with the International Convention which limits the liability of the air carrier in the event of accidental death. There were several theories for the cause of the accident, among them pilot error and the design of the aircraft. Coincidentally, not long after the accident, the particular model of the aircraft was modified by Boeing to add a vertical stabilizer fin under the tail.

Although the majority of the competitors and officials were already in Prague or on their way there, the ISU, through its President, Dr. James Koch of Switzerland, decided to cancel the championships, out of respect for the deceased, despite the urging of the USFSA, through acting President Shumway and others, that they be allowed to go on. The ISU did, however, at its subsequent Congress, re-award the 1962 championships to the Czech federation and Prague.

There were several persons who were to have been involved in the 1961 Championships that were not on board. Among them were Past President Kendall Kelley of Cleveland and Edward Marshall, President of The Skating Club of Boston, who were already in Europe on their way to Prague. Mary Louise Wright, the selected judge for Singles and Pairs, who had withdrawn due to the illness of her mother, Margaret Ridgely, the selected Dance judge, and Montgomery "Bud" Wilson, the coach of Bradley Lord, had been scheduled to go later. Messrs. Kelley and Marshall immediately went to Brussels, where they gave material assistance to the authorities in the difficult task of identification, as well as the making of the arrangements for the repatriation of the remains of the victims.

At the end of March, a special Memorial Benefit show was put on in Boston Garden. Organized by The Skating Club of Boston, which had canceled its annual production of "Ice Chips," the show was directed by Bud Wilson, assisted by Cecilia Colledge, with as many of those from the Worlds who could be obtained, and especially the Canadians, participating. Among those who donated their services were Dick Button, who both skated and served as announcer, David Jenkins from Ice Follies and Barbara Wagner and Robert Paul from Ice Capades. A special message from the President of the United States, John F. Kennedy, was read by his brother Edward M. Kennedy, later the Senator from Massachusetts and also the college roommate of Dudley Richards. The proceeds of the show went to a charitable foundation formed at the suggestion of Past President Henry M. Beatty, originally called the "1961 U.S. World Team Memorial Fund," now simply the "Memorial Fund." Over the years since, the Fund has grown substantially and especially during the long tenure and leadership of Ritter Shumway as its chairman, has provided support, both educational and otherwise to many generations of promising skaters. The show itself was videotaped by CBS-TV, thus preserving this tribute to their teammates and friends by those who skated.

With the cancellation of the Worlds, the season came to an abrupt end, with some of the club carnivals in which the members of the Team would otherwise have participated being either canceled or curtailed. Then in April another unexpected blow occurred with the death of Col. Harold G. Storke of Hull, Mass., the Association Secretary. "Pete" Storke had been an outstanding judge and referee at the Worlds and Olympic both before and after he had returned home from service in the U.S. Army and had subsequently served the Association in many varied ways. One legacy that he left was a complete revision of the Constitution and By Laws which was adopted at the 1961 Governing Council Meeting. The recodification resulted in the merger in 1962 of the Constitution and By Laws into one document, now called just the "By Laws," and the incorporation either into them or into the rules of the many "miscellaneous rulings" of the Governing Council and Executive Committee that had accumulated over the years. These had the force of rules but had not been incorporated into the By Laws formally. It was a major task for which he deserved great credit. There would not be another major revision until 1980, following the passage of the Amateur Sports Act of 1978.

The 1961 Governing Council Meeting was held in New York and was preceded by a memorial service for those lost in the air accident, as well as for the late President and Secretary. The service was presided over by acting President Shumway, himself an ordained minister, and was solemn and heartwarming, although obviously an emotional occasion attended by many of the family members of the deceased.

At the meeting, it was announced that the Memorial Fund already had in hand $4,000 and would receive another $12,724, representing the net proceeds of the benefit show. Henry M. Beatty was appointed to replace Walter Powell as the delegate to the 1961 ISU Congress, at which he was also elected to the ISU Council, succeeding Powell and thereby continuing the U.S. presence on that important body. Kendall Kelley was also elected to membership on the ISU Ice Dance Technical Committee, in replacement of Harold Hartshorne.

Network television was now a reality. With the CBS agreement for the 1961 Nationals, the Television Committee was revived, to handle future negotiations and also sanctions for appearances on television, with Carl W. Gram, Jr. of New York as the chairman. Actually, the CBS film of the 1961 Nationals is the only footage available of those lost in the Brussels air accident, since the Howard Craker film of the championships, which he had made for many years for the Association, disappeared not long after the event.

In the business carried out at the meeting, test fees were raised, as were the dues for member clubs, a periodic exercise. The Association has always exercised restraint, if anything leaning over backwards to hold down such fees and dues if at all possible. It was also at the 1961 meeting that the Constitution and By Laws were finally revised, so that all the collected Miscellaneous Rulings of the Governing Council and Executive Committee were finally eliminated. A category of General Rules (GR) was adopted, which picked up some of them, such as, for example, those relating to expenses. The "GR" are something of a "catchall" including such items as the Code of Ethics, member club proposals, the Skating Standards Committee, finance, budgets, and administration.

Since life must go on, the 1962 Nationals were awarded to The SC of Boston, which would be observing its 50th anniversary in 1962, perhaps in appreciation for the support of that club in organizing the benefit show, and the 1962 Governing Council meeting was awarded to Sun Valley, the first time to a major resort area.

At the 1961 ISU Congress, it was voted that the entries of the USFSA in the 1963 and 1964 Worlds would not need to qualify for the Championships. The qualifying eligibility for the 1962 Worlds was on the basis of the placements earned at Vancouver in 1960. Otherwise, entry was limited as follows: "Each ISU Member may enter one skater, plus a skater placing in the first five in the prior year, and an additional skater if it had any skater among the first 10 places in the prior year, but with a maximum of three in any one event." This is, with some minor modifications, essentially the rule today. The exemption of the U.S. skaters from the rule for two years was of major assistance to the USFSA in its recovery from the loss of the skaters in the air accident and would materially accelerate a return to the podium. It was a very generous gesture on the part of the ISU and was largely due to the strong support received from Dr. Koch.

Despite the passage of many years, the effects of the loss of the skaters and especially of the coaches is still being felt in U.S. figure skating. Especially in Boston, the standard of skating exemplified by those lost has never been fully regained, and National titles for the Boston area skaters have been few and far between since, with a few outstanding exceptions. Perhaps it is too sweeping a generalization, but the air accident represented a major cost to the standard of U.S. figure skating, which has not been fully recovered. In effect, while one generation of skaters was lost, there were two generations of coaches taken away, since many of the top skaters in 1961 would themselves have eventually become coaches.

It was also in the fall of 1961, that the Association made a local move from 30 Huntington Avenue, Boston, to new and larger offices in Copley Square at 575 Boylston Street. The Central office and the magazine were now in one suite of offices rather than separated as they had been at Huntington Avenue since 1950. It was proudly stated in the announcement that the new offices had 2,600 square feet compared to a total of 1,400 square feet in the old office! Included in the furnishings was "a display case for our historical collection and trophies," the "kernel" of the future Museum!

Joining the Association office in Boston in the fall of 1961 was the fourth Executive Secretary, Col. Gerard B. Crook, who had recently retired from active military service in the Judge Advocate General's Corps. He had been a member of the Broadmoor SC, where he had served on the Board, and of the Washington FSC, with service as the Secretary and Vice President of the latter. His daughter Sally was an active ice dancer, who would place third in the National Silver Dance in 1963.

The Fall 1961 meeting of the Executive Committee was held in Chicago at the Edgewater Beach Hotel. The planned incorporation of the Association in Rhode Island was noted, which offered certain legal advantages while not changing the continued operations of the Association under its charter as a non-profit, membership organization. Still being sought was the status of a charitable and educational institution to which gifts and bequest could be made which would be tax deductible. Further contributions to the new Memorial Fund were also announced with the largest being $7,500 from Ice Capades.

As the new season of 1961-1962 started, there was much interest and speculation as to who would be the new top skaters, replacing those that had been lost, since there were obviously no defending National Champions. Some, but not all of those seeking to gain the top level, first had to go through the qualifying structure, which still was one level below that of the Nationals. Among them can be seen the names of those who would be actively competing and representing the U.S. internationally over the next several years: In the East, Albertina Noyes of Boston, Tommy Litz of Hershey, Scott Allen of New York; in the Midwest, Christine Haigler, Gary Visconti, Tim Wood, Darlene Streich and Charles Fetter, Jr., in the Pacific Coast, Cynthia and Ron Kauffman from Seattle, Yvonne Littlefield and Peter Betts, just to name a few.

With Sub-Sectionals now in place in the Midwestern Section, the Midwestern championships for 1962 had stabilized at 90 entries. The Pacific Coasts were at 77 and the Easterns at 92, so although the Coasts were slightly smaller, this reflected and it still does today, their smaller number of clubs and skaters than the other two sections.

The 1962 Nationals came to Boston for the first time since 1941, and what would be, as it has turned out, the last time to date. The events were held at The SC of Boston's rink for the figures and compulsory dances, with the free skating and final rounds of the dance events being held at the McHugh Forum of Boston College. Four practice rinks were used, a luxury not always seen at the Nationals of today. The other rinks in addition to Boston and McHugh were the Watson rink at Harvard University and the North Shore Sports center in Lynn. Returning after two years off, during which time she had married and become a mother, was Barbara Roles Pursley from Southern California, representing the Arctic Blades FSC, in the Senior Ladies, which title she won with relative ease over Lorraine Hanlon of Boston, the 1961 National Junior Ladies Champion. In the Senior Men, primarily by reason of his superior figures, Monty Hoyt from Denver became the new champion, over Scott Allen from New York. Monty had been the National Junior Champion in 1961, and thus completed the rare "Junior-Senior" double of winning the two titles back to back, a feat previously accomplished by Dick Button in 1945-1946.

In the Pairs and Dance, there was another relatively rare "double," when Dorothyann Nelson and Pieter Kollen from Lake Placid, won the Pairs and were second in the Dance, just as Eugene Turner had done in Boston in 1941. The champions in the Dance were Yvonne Littlefield and Peter Betts, representing the Arctic Blades FSC of Paramount, Calif. Peter was originally from Boston, but he and Yvonne continued the strong tradition of excellence in Dance exemplified by their predecessors from Southern California, such as Diane Sherbloom with Larry Pierce, Margie Ackles and Charles Phillips, Jr., Sharon McKenzie and Bert Wright, and Joan Zamboni and Roland Junso. Others winning titles in the 1962 Nationals who would soon be heard from were Christine Haigler from Colorado Springs in the Junior Ladies, Tommy Litz of Hershey in the Junior Men, and Tim Wood of Detroit in the Novice Men.

Barbara Roles Pursley

The 1962 Worlds were held at Prague, as had been promised by the ISU, and are remembered for the "come from behind" win of Donald Jackson in the Men for the first Canadian Men's World title, as well as performing the first triple Lutz in competition. Maria and Otto Jelinek of Canada returned to their original homeland to claim an emotional World title in Pairs. Otto would go on to a long career as a commentator on television and to a distinguished political career in which he became a member of the Canadian Parliament and eventually a cabinet minister.

For the U.S. team, which traveled on separate aircraft, it was a tough test to find the "level" or really the "floor" on which to build back. Actually, the results were not the lowest encountered by a USFSA World Team, since the Association has been sending them. (A team for our purposes is considered as one with an entry in each of the four events, if eligible, of Men, Ladies, Pairs and Dance. The first teams sent were in the Olympic years only – 1920, 1924, 1928, 1932 and 1936 –

before the War, with one exception of 1931, and after the War on an annual basis since 1947.) The results of 1962 can be summarized numerically as follows: Men - 6th, 8th; Ladies - 5th, 10th, 11th; Pairs - 8th, 10th; Dance - 7th, 8th. The fifth place was earned by Barbara Roles Pursley in Ladies, a creditable showing. The new champion was Sjoukje Dijsktra of the Netherlands, with Wendy Griner of Canada, the runner-up. In the Men, it was Monty Hoyt who gained the sixth place. Dorothyann Nelson and Pieter Kollen were seventh in Dance and eighth in the Pairs.

To demonstrate the accomplishments of the young and inexperienced 1962 team, their record can be compared with that of the 1994 team as follows: Men - 7th, 13th; Ladies - 8th (plus 13th in one elimination round); Pairs - 6th, 12th, 17th; Dance - 12th. In 1994, there was no one in the top five places, and it is indeed the lowest year of all! In any event, the travel along the road back had begun and begun well.

The 1962 Governing Council meeting was held in Sun Valley, Idaho, which had skating out-of-doors and was a member club of the Association since 1939. Despite the recreational attractions of this most glamorous of resorts, the delegates worked just as hard and just as long hours as they otherwise would have in a more mundane metropolitan area. Despite the remote location and the difficulty of travel, there were still over 120 persons registered, with 99 clubs registered out of a total of 164. In reporting on the World Team, President Shumway referred to the fact that there were two entrants in the top 10 in each event, certainly a more reasonable goal than the top five! It was also announced that Col. Crook had resigned after only seven months in office. He had during his brief tenure also been the Team Manager for the 1962 World Team. As could have been expected, there were many memorial trophies accepted for events in the qualifying competitions which did not already have trophies, to perpetuate the memory of those lost in the Brussels accident. One change was made to the Constitution, to add the ISU Representative as a voting member of the Executive Committee. Yet again, those USFSA members participating in the Michael Kirby school show in the Chicago area, which was an unsanctioned event, were suspended for one year, as were those in another show sponsored by a skating school run by Harris Legg. This ongoing saga was almost becoming a farce, but the problems it represented would not be addressed and settled for another 12 years!

The Sun Valley meeting became the "model" for later meetings, especially those in resorts, with the inclusion in the activities of organized social events between and after the business sessions, which enabled the delegates to mix, relax and to get to know one another, a very important aspect of all the meetings since. In this case, of course, there was a Western-style barbecue and the skating rink was operating for those who wished to try it and who had remembered to bring their skates. The meeting was generally considered "the best one we have ever had," as quoted in the official report.

With respect to meetings in general, in the fall of 1962, the Executive Committee met for the first time at the O'Hare Inn, near the O'Hare Airport. This reflected a policy of having the Fall or Annual Meeting of the Executive Committee at a relatively central point in the country, with good access by air from both coasts, especially as jet travel became more common in the 1960's. Before then, it was not uncommon to take the overnight train at least from the East Coast! The Executive Committee originally met in New York City from 1922 until 1952, with two exceptions: Brookline, Mass., in 1933 and Colorado Springs in 1951. The first meeting place was the Bar Association of the City of New York on West 44th Street, and later the New Weston Hotel, one of the sites for the meeting that became over the years a "second home" to the members of the body!

The meeting first moved to Chicago in 1953, then to Cleveland in 1954 and back to Chicago in 1955, to remain there until 1977, with the O'Hare Inn the preferred site for the majority of those years. In 1978, with the anticipated transfer of the Central Office to Colorado Springs, the first fall meeting there since 1951 took place in 1978 at the Olympic Training Center, where it has been held ever since up to 1995.

A development beginning in the 1960's, was the growth of International Competitions sponsored by the various ISU Member associations. There had "always" been a few of such competitions, usually held in conjunction with an ISU Championship event, but "stand alone" International Competitions were rare before World War II. After the War, a few of them began. One, for example was the "Coupe de Paris," held in 1950, with the winners being Hayes Alan Jenkins in the Men, Yvonne Sherman in the Ladies and Jennifer and John Nicks in the Pairs. In that competition, Hayes defeated Helmut Seibt of Austria, who would in 1952 be the Olympic Silver medalist under somewhat cloudy circumstances!

In 1962, an International Junior Competition for Junior Ladies was held at Davos, Switzerland, which is probably the first such event in which American skaters participated. The winner was Maidie Sullivan from Colorado Springs, with Christine Haigler, also from the Springs, second, and yet another Broadmoor SC skater, Susan Prange fourth. Third in the competition was Sally-Anne Stapleford of Great Britain, who, since 1992 has been the Chairman of the ISU Figure Skating Technical Committee. Jane Vaughn Sullivan served as the U.S. judge.

The only International Competition held on a regular basis after the War was the Richmond Trophy for Ladies, sponsored by the NSA of Great Britain and inaugurated in 1949, but U.S. skaters did not enter it until 1962 when Carol Noir of New York, the 1960 National Novice Ladies Champion, did so and placed second, behind the ultimate winner, Nicole Hassler of France. The USFSA also had a judge in the event for the first time, Mrs. Jane Vaughn Sullivan, who at that time was living in Paris where her husband was stationed with the Allied Armed Forces in Europe. There were then no funds available from the Association for such events, so that interested participants had to pay their own way, including any judges that might go. The "largesse" of today was unknown and unheard of then! It is hard for us to imagine the competitive season without the large number of International Competitions held today, but back then, there was virtually no participation in them on a regular basis other than in the North Americans and the World and Olympic Championships.

At the fall meeting of 1962, there were several small but significant developments. One was the adoption of a design for a USFSA patch to be worn by skaters going to Championships with a "chevron" indicating the championship and the date. This is the first recognition of the concept of national representation, as distinguished from individual representation, and was the forerunner of the "uniforms" provided today. Also at the meeting, Robert Ellis was appointed as Business Manager, in replacement of Col. Crook. Ellis, came to the Association from The Christian Science Monitor and had a background in both journalism and the law. He would remain with the Central Office and the magazine until 1967.

A highlight of the meeting was the election of Theresa Weld Blanchard as an Honorary member of the Association, the 1962-1963 season being the 40th anniversary of the founding of **Skating** magazine in 1923. Mrs. Blanchard remained as the editor through that season and retired in June of 1963, when she was duly recognized as Editor Emeritus.

As the qualifying competition cycle went on during the 1962-1963 season, generally the Sub-Sectional Championships were providing the proper basis for the process in each section, with a few obvious exceptions. In each section, for example, the total number of entries was as follows: Easterns - 86; New Englands - 65; North Atlantics - 74; South Atlantics - 78. Midwesterns - 84; Eastern Great Lakes - 75; Southwesterns - 39; Upper Great Lakes - 71. Pacific Coasts - 75; Central Pacifics - 75; Northwest Pacifics - 59; Southwestern Pacifics - 82. As can be seen, the Southwestern and the Northwest Pacific Sub-Sectionals were the smallest, so that full balance had still not been achieved between the nine Sub-Sections, with the total number of entries between them being, by Section: Eastern - 217; Midwestern - 198 and Pacific Coast - 216. However, there was nearly a balance between the three Sectional Championships. As time went on, some of the more "remote" areas of the country, especially in the South and Southwest, where skating was little known with few rinks, would gradually "fill in," so that the sport can be found throughout the country today, regardless of location or climate.

The 1963 Nationals were held at Long Beach, Calif., returning to South California for the first time since 1954. Under the rotation of the Nationals site between the three Sections, established after 1949, only the Pacific Coast Section tried to follow the additional rotation of the event between its own three Sub-Sections. Actually, up to this point in time, the Sub-Sections were not defined in the rules, the delineation of them being left to the Chairmen of the Sectional

Committees and the Vice Chairman of the Competitions Committee for each Section. The Regions, as they were called after 1966, were added to the Competition Rules in 1968 and remain there to this day, never having been transferred to the By Laws, although the definition of the Sections had been placed in the By Laws in 1961 in the recodification carried out by the late Col. Storke.

With Barbara Roles Pursley again having retired to have her second child, the Senior Ladies title was open, and this time was decided between two excellent figure skaters, who were not known for their strong free skating. Lorraine Hanlon returned the title to Boston after two short years. She was coached by Cecilia Colledge, the 1937 World Ladies Champion regarded by some as having been the best lady skater of figures of all time. Second was Christine Haigler of Colorado Springs, with Karen Howland of Sun Valley, third. In the Senior Men, Monty Hoyt returned to defend, but he came up against one very strong free skater in Tommy Litz, from Hershey, the ultimate winner, and another skater who was equally good in both disciplines, Scott Allen of New York, who placed second. Monty finished third, ahead of Gary Visconti of Detroit.

The Senior Pairs was won by the brother and sister pair from Colorado, Judianne and Jerry Fotheringill, who just edged out by a 3 to 2 margin, Vivian and Ronald Joseph of Chicago. Third was Pieter Kollen with a new partner Patti Gustafson, representing Lake Placid. The Dance title went to an unexpected winner, Sally Schantz, from Indianapolis but representing Boston and Stanley Urban of Buffalo, who defeated the defending champions Yvonne Littlefield and Peter Betts. The Schantz-Urban combination was another one born out of a "college" connection, since Stanley was a student at Boston College at the time. Down the line can already be seen some of the prominent skaters of the future, with Cynthia and Ron Kauffman winning the Junior Pairs, and Tim Wood placing third in Junior Men.

The 1963 North American championships were held at Vancouver, British Columbia and closely followed the National Championships of the two countries. This time, the Canadian skaters carried out their first sweep of all the titles since 1933. The medal count was: Canada - four firsts, three seconds and one third; the United States, one second and three thirds. Certainly, the impact of the 1961 air accident was still being felt in this friendly competition between the two nations. In the Ladies, Wendy Griner of Toronto was the winner, with Petra Burka, also from Toronto, second. The best U.S. place was Lorraine Hanlon in fourth.

In the Men, Donald McPherson of Stratford, Ontario, was the winner over Tommy Litz, with Scott Allen, third, the best showing for the U.S. In the Pairs, Debbi Wilkes and Guy Revell, from Unionville, won the title, with the Josephs reversing the National result to place third ahead of the Fotheringills. The Dance title went to Paulette Doan and Kenneth Ormsby from Toronto, who would be worthy successors to Bill McLachlan and his two partners at the World level, with Schantz and Urban third.

The 1963 Worlds were held at Cortina, Italy, in the open air stadium that had been the site of the 1956 Olympic Winter Games. On the basis of the exemption previously granted to it by the ISU, the USFSA sent a full team of three Men, three Ladies, three Pairs and three Dance couples. Unfortunately, Tommy Litz could not compete due to an injury and Yvonne Littlefield and Peter Betts could not finish their free dance, due to the failure of one of his skate blades. On the Canadian side, Debbi Wilkes and Guy Revell also could not compete due to an injury suffered by Debbi.

Despite the injuries, the results in 1963 reflected a slow and steady progress back up the ladder: Men - fifth, 11th; Ladies - 10th, 13th, 19th; Pairs - seventh, eighth, ninth; Dance - seventh, eighth, 17th. The fifth this time was Scott Allen in the Men. The 17th in Dance was Littlefield and Betts. By the Shumway criteria, there were again placements in the top 10 (just) in all four events. Sjoukje Dijkstra won her second title, with the top American being Lorraine Hanlon in 10th place. Donald McPherson of Canada won the Men, in an upset over Alain Calmat from France, for the second Canadian Men's title in a row. Marika Kilius and Hans-Jürgen Bäumler of Germany won their first Pairs title, with Liudmila Belousova and Oleg Protopopov of the Soviet Union now second. The top U.S. pair were the Fotheringills, in seventh place over the Josephs. In the Dance, the "break through" continued, when the title again went to Eva Romanova and Pavel Roman of Czechoslovakia, who had finally broken the British "stranglehold" in 1961 in their homeland. Sally Schantz and Stanley Urban placed seventh as the top U.S. couple, with Lorna Dyer and John Carrell, right behind in eighth. Much would be heard from the latter in the next few years.

Following the Worlds, there was yet another International Competition held at Megève, France, in which Joya Utermohlen, from New York, placed first in the Ladies, and Gary Visconti of Detroit second in the Men. In an event for Junior Ladies, second place went to Eileen Zillmer, representing the U.S., but actually from Germany. She would be the first skater to present a problem of dual nationality, having been born in Germany to an American father. Ultimately, she would skate for Germany ("West" Germany, as it was called then, or "FRG," to distinguish it from "East" Germany, or GDR). This competition was unusual for another reason, which was that compulsory free skating moves were included on an experimental basis, consisting of different jumps and spins primarily, a forerunner of the future short program, actually not yet in sight for another 10 years. The International Competitions were beginning to represent a very useful training ground for the young and upcoming skaters who could manage to enter them.

In the Spring, a small but very important announcement was made, to the effect that the Memorial Fund had received "tax-exempt" status, now known in the "trade" as 501(c)(3), which provided not only that donations to the Fund were tax deductible, but also that the Fund was not itself subject to income tax. In the beginning, the Fund was not a formal legal entity, but it eventually became a "Massachusetts Trust," a recognized form of non-profit organization in that state, of which the trustees were the officers of the Association. At the same time, the Association, which had been for most of its existence a voluntary association, was finally incorporated in 1962 under the non-profit statute of the State of Rhode Island, that state being chosen primarily for its minimum reporting requirements, and especially that the annual meetings need not be held in the state of incorporation, which would have been the case with a comparable non-profit corporation in Massachusetts. The incorporation of the Association was part of the update and recodification of the Constitution and By Laws of the Association originally carried out by Col. Storke, and after his death, by John F. Groden of Boston, an attorney and officer of The SC of Boston, who was the Association Secretary from 1961 to 1964, Treasurer from 1964 to 1967 and Chairman of the Memorial Fund Committee from 1963 to 1968. It was John who was instrumental in obtaining Internal Revenue approval of the Fund's tax-exempt status and it was also he who set up the procedures for the making of donations to the Memorial Fund, especially those of a restricted nature, which were designed to protect the integrity of its tax-exempt status. John Groden passed away in 1988.

In furtherance of that objective, the Fund in its earlier years actively sponsored instructional clinics and basic skating programs for the general public. There were also various carnivals and a series of exhibitions held by clubs in support of the Fund, some of which became annual events. The most noteworthy was the annual show of the Cleveland Skating Club, from which many thousands of dollars have gone to the Fund.

The 1963 Governing Council meeting was held at Rockton, Ill., at the Wagon Wheel Lodge with over 200 delegates and guests present. The meeting was described in the report as "the most important annual meeting in the history of the USFSA." Little did the speaker of those words know what was ahead in the distant future of the 1990's, but at the same time, it certainly could have been thought to be the case by those present. It marked the beginning of the relaxation of the strict "Avery Brundage" (of the IOC) rules governing amateur status. One change made it "possible for news reporting of figure skating activities on the part of amateur figure skaters to be carried on with much less restriction than in the past," to quote the report. Another, in the words of Thomas Miller from Rochester, was to "worry about policing their own members without attempting to police those outside the membership."

A program was also initiated to further "standardize" judging in competitions and to approve the quality of judging. There was a considerable difference in the viewpoints between the judges of the East and Pacific Coast on the one hand, and the judges of the Midwest on the other, in such matters as the relative importance in compulsory figures of the turns versus the circles. Seminars were to be conducted and instructional films produced and a "performance history" record was to be established, to "indicate the judge's past performance on the ice with regard to his accuracy, temperament, activity and tact." While an accuracy rating record did come out of the initiative, no formal program by which judges can be held accountable for their performances as such, has ever been implemented, leaving the USFSA virtually alone among the "superpowers" of the skating world in that regard!

Another seemingly minor change adopted in principle was to extend associate membership in the Association to universities, colleges and schools which owned skating rinks and/or carried out programs on their ice for basic skaters.

At the 1963 ISU Congress, a "compulsory program" for Pairs was approved, to be included in the World and European championships in 1964, but not in the 1964 Olympic Winter Games. The program, which would in due course be given the name "short" program, initially was called a connected program, with elements to be skated from six categories of lifts, solo jumps, pair spins, solo spins, spiral spins (death spirals) and step sequences. It was to be 2-1/2 minutes in length. The new program was added, in the words of Henry Beatty, the ISU Delegate, "in the belief that, after long hours of work, a championship should be decided on more than a five-minute program. The double skating of the five minute program had been tried out in Europe for several years and was not popular with skaters, officials, or the spectators."

The Congress also awarded the 1965 Worlds to Colorado Springs once again. One of the major issues facing the ISU in those days was the problem of free access to the site of a championship by all participating countries, which during the "Cold War" era, was far from the case. The attempt to require a guarantee to that effect was dropped, when it was determined that only 23 out of 47 member associations could do so, since, obviously, those that could not had no control over what their governments would do.

At the fall meeting of the Executive Committee in 1963, concern was expressed with the level of funds obtained to support the 1964 Olympic and World Teams. The Memorial Fund donated $10,000 towards the expenses of the Olympic team and $2,000 to the World Team. At the same time, the Fund announced an academic scholarship program, which over the years has been an important part of its support of promising student athletes. The School and College Figure Skating Committee also launched a program to provide certificates to be awarded to figure skaters by their schools and colleges in recognition of their accomplishments in the sport. The program, while a recognition effort, was also designed to increase awareness in the academic community of the achievements of figure skaters. Some colleges had done so in the unique fashion of awarding a varsity letter to the champions who were students at their institutions. Dick Button had a letter from Harvard, and Hayes Jenkins had one from Northwestern. Others receiving such special awards included Dudley Richards, Hugh Graham Jr. and Paul Wylie, all from Harvard.

The 40th anniversary of the magazine was recognized and an appropriate article was included in it in the fall of 1963. The first paid Managing Editor had been Winfield A. Hird, hired in 1939, for an all too brief stay, since he went into the service in 1942 and was killed in the War in 1943. He did a lot in a relatively short time to organize the magazine on a sound business basis and to improve the production, printing and distribution of it. His successor was Edith E. Ray, who arrived in 1941, was one of the original WAVE's in the Navy from 1944 to 1946, and returned to the magazine in the latter year, remaining until 1963. It was also reported that the magazine by 1963 had 9,100 subscribers, and that advertising revenue had doubled from the prior year. The recommendation was also made that a public relations assistant and advisor be hired. Carl Gram, Jr., the Chairman of the Television Committee announced that ABC-TV would televise the 1964 Nationals from Cleveland on its Wide World of Sports program, which heralded the beginning of an ongoing relationship with ABC, which has endured to this day!

The Olympic year of 1963-1964 started with a lot of hope for success in the Olympic Winter Games at Innsbruck and the World Championships to follow at Dortmund, Germany. The latter represented a return of the World Championship to (West) Germany for the first time since 1956, and would take place in the largest stadium in the country, the Westfalenhalle. As a pre-Olympic test, an International Junior Competition took place at Innsbruck in December 1963, with Eileen Zillmer as the only entry. The competition represented one of the first times that computers were used to determine the results in an International Competition, although they had been used at the 1960 Olympics at Squaw Valley. The computers used were gigantic when compared with today's PC's, and were in effect typical IBM main frame machines. The printers were equally large, with paper on a continuous roll, which was almost a foot wide!

With the Nationals now preceding the Games, and with the latter starting at the end of January 1964, the usual "compression" of the competition schedule took place. The Sub-Sectionals were held in November and the Sectionals in December, so that the Nationals could begin in the second week in January, with the exception of the Midwesterns, which actually ended only five days before the Nationals started.

For the second time, Barbara Roles, a mother of two, came out of retirement to try for a place on the Olympic Team. Unfortunately, she was not successful,

Peggy Fleming

placing fifth in the Senior Ladies, thereby ending her career. The battle in the event started with the figures, with Christine Haigler from Colorado Springs coming out on top over the defending champion, Lorraine Hanlon from Boston. In third place was Peggy Fleming from Paramount, Calif., who had been third in the National Junior Ladies in 1963, followed by Tina Noyes from Boston, the 1963 National Junior Ladies Champion. In the end it was the excellent free skating of the two former Junior skaters which prevailed, with Peggy the surprise winner of the championship, although Carol Heiss had predicted as much, with Tina pulling up to second. Christine Haigler came in third and Lorraine Hanlon fourth. Peggy had not followed the "normal" path to the top, never having been the winner of either the National Junior or Novice Ladies in the past, although she had done well in them. She was the first National Senior Ladies champion, although not the last, never to have previously won a National title of any kind.

Scott Allen

The Senior Men's event was equally as exciting, with the question, could Tommy Litz defend? After the figures, it was Scott Allen from New York, first, followed by Monty Hoyt from Denver, the 1962 champion, second, Litz, third and Gary Visconti from Detroit, fourth. Despite a sterling effort by Litz in the free, Scott Allen skated equally as well and retained his lead to win his first Senior Men's title, with Litz second, Hoyt, third and Visconti, fourth. In Pairs, the Fotheringills, Judianne and Jerry, returned to defend, and were strongly challenged by the Josephs, Vivian and Ron, and the Kauffmanns, Cindy and Ron, an unusual case of three brother and sister pairs taking the top three spots in that order.

The Dance title went to Darlene Streich and Charles Fetter, Jr. from Indianapolis, the Silver Dance runners-up from the prior year, over Carole MacSween, the Silver winner of 1963, but with a new partner Robert Munz, Lorna Dyer and Robert Carrell from Seattle retained their third place from 1963.

A "footnote" to the championships was that Carol Noir from New Jersey returned to the Junior Ladies, after having been in the Seniors and even having competed in an International Senior event and won her second National title. She had been the Novice Ladies winner in 1960, second in the Junior Ladies in 1961, fifth in the Senior ladies in 1962 and second in the Richmond Trophy of that year. It is probably the only known instance of a skater "going back down," as it were, to a lower class, but she was after all, still only 15! Also in the championships, the march upwards continued for Tim Wood from Detroit, the Junior Men's winner.

So it was on to the larger "arena" of Innsbruck and the drama of that competition. In the Ladies, Sjoukje Dijkstra of The Netherlands, the Silver medalist from 1960, who had suffered through the cancellation of the 1961 Worlds, finally won her Gold, in a decisive fashion over Regine Heitzer of Austria and Petra Burka of Canada. The surprise, in so far as the Canadians were concerned, was the 10th place of Wendy Griner, who had been the World Silver medalist in 1962 and fourth in 1963. Peggy Fleming, Christine Haigler and Tina Noyes finished sixth, seventh and eighth, a huge improvement over the U.S. placements in the 1963 Worlds.

It was in the Men, however, that it could be truthfully said that the "U.S. was back," when Scott Allen took the Bronze medal behind the ultimate winner, Manfred Schnelldorfer of Germany followed by Alain Calmat of France. Actually, the win of Schnelldorfer was a mild upset, as Calmat had been considered the favorite, having beaten Schnelldorfer in the European Championship just a few weeks before. Tommy Litz placed sixth and Monty Hoyt 10th.

The Pairs event was the "sensational" one of the Games, largely because of the huge press buildup given to Marika Kilius and Hans Jürgen Bäumler of Germany, the World Champions, including alleged activities on their part which seemed to be in violation of the then strict amateur status rules. The Olympic event was the last one shot competition, winner take all in one performance. In a five to four decision, the Olympic Gold went to Liudmila Belousova and Oleg Protopopov of the Soviet Union, with the U.S. and Canadian judges being in the majority. The Josephs again overturned the National result and placed fourth, with the Fotheringills seventh and the Kauffmans eighth.

That was not the end of the story, however! Due to all the allegations of professional acts on their part, Kilius and Bäumler returned their Silver medals in 1966, which were distributed to the original Bronze medal winners, Debbi Wilkes and Guy Revell of Canada. This meant that the Bronze medals went to the Josephs, and were presented to them by the President Emeritus of the U.S. Olympic Committee, Kenneth L. Wilson at the 1966 fall meeting of the Executive Committee. Although the West German Olympic Committee was directed to investigate the allegations, it never produced a report nor took any action, nor did the ISU or the IOC. In the end, the Silver medals were replaced and only in recent years returned to Kilius and Bäumler, but no redistribution was apparently ever made of the other medals from the other two pairs, so it would appear that today there are in effect four Silver medals outstanding for the 1964 Pairs event! The official protocol of the event, obviously, reflects the original result. Using the official result in the format seen for the preceding two years, the Olympic places earned were as follows: Men - third, sixth, 10th; Ladies - sixth, seventh, eighth; Pairs - fourth, seventh, eighth.

The 1964 World Championships at Dortmund were somewhat surprising in that the Olympic champions all elected to enter, since two of the four titles (Men and Pairs) were undefended. Donald Jackson and the Jelineks retired. There was another "sensation" at the outset, when all the skaters from East Germany withdrew in protest of a decision by the West German organizers to announce them by the name of their federation, the "Deutscher Eislauf-Verband," instead of by their country, "Deutschland Ost," which later would be more politely rendered as the "German Democratic Republic" (GDR). In the Olympics, there had still been a combined German team, as had also been the case in 1960. In the Worlds of 1962 and 1963, the East Germans had competed and been announced by country with no difficulty, but Dortmund was a different story, for obvious political reasons.

The 1964 Worlds were also notable for several other reasons, including the use of computers provided by IBM Germany for the Olympics at a Worlds and the demonstration of new compulsory dances, the Rhumba, Silver Samba and Starlight Waltz, demonstrated by Peri Horne and Courtney Jones, and Joan and John Slater of Great Britain. The Silver Samba and Starlight Waltz were accepted by the ISU at its Congress, with the Rhumba replacing the Samba in 1969. The Samba, however, would return once again in 1992. This was the first time that new dances were added to the schedule of International Dances originally accepted by the 1951 Congress.

In the Ladies, the results were very similar to those in Innsbruck, with Dijkstra winning her third title, followed by Heitzer and Burka. This time, however, Christine Haigler came fifth, by virtue of a fourth in figures, with Fleming seventh and Noyes ninth, reversing the Cleveland placements. In the Men, Schnelldofer repeated his win over Calmat, but this time Karol Divin of Czechoslovakia, who had been fourth in the Olympics, slipped passed Allen, after placing second in figures. Allen was fourth, Litz sixth and Hoyt 11th.

The Pairs saw the Olympic result reversed between Kilius-Bäumler and Belousova-Protopopov, again by a five to four decision, with the U.S. and Canadian judges now in the minority. The compulsory program was skated for the second time (it having been first done at the European Championships), with Belousova and Protopopov winning it, but they could not hold their lead and placed second in the end, with Kilius-Bäumler retaining their World title. The local audience, in the presence of the German Chancellor, Ludwig Ehrhard, was very vocal in their support of Kilius and Bäumler. Wilkes-Revell were again third, the Josephs fourth, and the Kauffmans, seventh ahead of the Fotheringills, eighth, again a reversal of the national result.

With the ice dancers now on the scene, Eva Romanova and Pavel Roman successfully defended their title, with three British couples in the next three places, while Lorna Dyer and

John Carrell from Seattle placed fifth. Carole MacSween and Robert Munz were sixth and Darlene Streich and Charles Fetter, Jr. eighth, the reverse of the National result. As a result, the placements of the U.S. skaters at Dortmund were: Men - fourth, sixth, 11th; Ladies - fifth, seventh, ninth; Pairs - fourth, seventh, eighth; Dance - fifth, sixth, eighth. The Shumway criteria of an entrant in the top 10 in each event had been fully met and well exceeded, with an entrant in the top five in each event. While there were no medals in Dortmund, the Bronze medal won by Scott Allen at Innsbruck shone like "Gold" for the U.S. Team! It continued the tradition of the U.S. having won one or more medals in every Olympics from 1948, a record which would remain unbroken through 1994. The U.S. has actually won medals in all the Olympics in which there has been figure skating, with the exceptions only of 1908 and 1936.

With a young and fast-rising team, the prospects for the future looked bright.

While we often think of the Governing Council meeting as the culmination, celebration and end of a season, often it can be regarded as the start of the new season, especially when there are rule changes made which will affect competition and testing in the future. That of 1964 was held at Philadelphia, and fits more into the latter mode than the former.

International Progress
(1965-1968)

One of the initiatives of President Shumway in 1963 had been the creation of a special committee called Rules-Drafting, of which the author was the first chairman, serving in that capacity for 10 years. The purpose of the committee was to serve as a co-ordinating agency for the preparation of rule changes, including the review and recommendation of the specific language of all proposals for changes in the By Laws and Rules. The use of the committee for that purpose was not mandatory, but rather a service available to the committee chairmen for assistance in drafting proposals should they wish to avail themselves of it. However, the committee does have the function and duty of seeing that the rules as a whole are consistent with one another and also had the cross-references needed. This in practice meant that the committee (really the chairman!) was the person who actually prepared the rules portion of the Rulebook for publication. Logically, this led to the committee having the responsibility for the preparation of the formal Report of Action taken by the Executive Committee and the Governing Council at their meetings.

Prior to 1963, such reports were somewhat haphazard and often not complete, being prepared by a volunteer selected for the purpose, to assist the Secretary, who was responsible for the formal minutes. Once the Rules-Drafting Committee took over the function, it became more formal, and a format was developed which has generally been followed ever since. Coupled with the issuance of the Report of Action was the distribution to the clubs and eventually to the delegates in advance of the book of reports for the meetings, both Spring and Fall. The committee remained a special committee until 1980, when it became a permanent non-voting committee. Its name was changed to Rules Committee in 1970.

The committee experienced its first "baptism of fire" at the 1964 Governing Council meeting, which was held at Philadelphia, when two major revisions of two groups of rules, those for Membership and Sanctions, were presented. After much debate, the Membership Rule proposals were referred back to committee, while those for Sanctions were accepted. The process fully demonstrated the obvious need that the presenting chairmen be fully prepared with complete text of the rule changes proposed, because of the strong tendency of the delegates to the Governing Council to "write rules on the floor" as we say, with the attendant confusion and inconsistencies that can thereby creep in. The Rules committee has been and can continue to be a key player in this exercise and can greatly facilitate the desired result. The new Sanctions rules included a clearer recognition of the basic policy of the Association that "profits" from amateur figure skating events should go towards the support of the amateur aspects of the sport.

It was reported to the meeting that all three major championships in 1965, the Nationals at Lake Placid, the North Americans at Rochester, and the Worlds, again back in Colorado Springs, would be seen on television. It was also reported by Harry Radix, Chairman of the USFSA Olympic Committee that the budget for the 1964 Olympic Team of $15,000 had been more than met, with donations in excess of $24,000 having been received toward the expenses of the team, of which more than $13,000 was raised through the sale of Olympic pins.

The meeting also authorized the issuance of a World Team "uniform," consisting of a stadium coat, blazer and practice sweater. It was a modest beginning of what would become a standard practice, with the teams of today receiving a great variety of many items of high quality for their use, and, of course, to enhance their image as being representatives of the country.

The meeting also approved a program offered by the Memorial Fund Committee to aid municipal ice rinks in the development of figure skating instruction. A pilot program was to be administered during the 1964-1965 season in cooperation with the Metropolitan District Commission of Boston, which was the agency responsible for recreational facilities in the area. It was also reported that the Memorial Fund had received $69,000 in contributions, including $5,000 from the Ice Capades Ten Year Club.

With respect to the National Senior Singles events, a restrictive rule in effect since 1957, which prevented a skater who placed lower than sixth in the prior year from re-entering was abolished. Prior to the adoption of the rule originally, the requirements for entry had simply been the Eighth Test and having competed in the National Junior Singles at least once. At this time, there still was no basis for qualifying for the Senior events from the Sectionals, since the Senior Sectional event was, as has already been pointed out, actually a Junior event.

The Amateur Status Rules were also changed to enable the Association to register professionals and what were then called "restricted amateurs," who were persons that were temporarily ineligible for a specified period of time by reason of a violation of the rules, which included, for example, trying out for a professional show.

The Summer Skating Committee and its rules were abolished, on the basis that it was felt that the member clubs had as much control over figure skating in the summer as in the winter, and that the rules and committee were no longer needed. Also approved was a Gold Test pin to be presented by the Association in the future to those passing the Gold Test.

The Council approved a change in the By Laws to change the date when the officers and committee chairmen took office from Sept. 1 to July 1. Up to then, outgoing officers and chairmen had continued to hold office until the later of the two dates. Eventually, the effective date for the assuming of office would be changed in 1967 to immediately following the close of the Governing Council Meeting. On the other hand, the fiscal year of the Association remained Sept. 1 to Aug. 31 until 1968, when it too was changed to the July 1-June 30 period. As part of the re-organization of the effective dates, the registration system was revised to provide for a permanent number, rather than one that changed form year to year, as long as the holder remained a member of the Association. The registration year was also changed to begin on Sept. 1 and to be in effect for the following calendar year, i.e., for 16 months. The former rule had been for the calendar year and three months prior thereto, i.e., for 15 months.

New committees created following the meeting included a PSGA Liaison Committee, similar to that established in the previous year for the ISIA, with its first chairman being Past President Harry Keighley. Another special committee appointed was a Museum Committee, with Past President Kenneth L. Brown as its first chairman, the purpose being to investigate the possibilities of creating a museum to house the retired trophies and other memorabilia in the possession of the Association and stored at the Central Office.

The 1964 meeting also marked the retirement from office as President of F. Ritter Shumway, who stepped down after three tumultuous years, throughout which he had exercised outstanding leadership in bringing the Association back from the depths of the 1961 accident. His service to the Association was far from finished. In order to retain his advice and counsel, a new special committee called Long Range Planning, with Ritter as its first chairman was created. He served in that capacity until 1967, when he was succeeded by the then outgoing President, John R. Shoemaker of San Francisco. The committee, however was disbanded in 1968 and did not return until 1986.

More importantly, Ritter returned to his original love, Dance, when he became the Chairman of the Dance Committee for the second time in 1972, serving until 1975. He also served as Chairman of the International Committee from 1967 to 1970. Most important of all, however, was his service as Chairman of the Memorial Fund Committee from 1970 to 1992, in which capacity he worked diligently to promote the Fund, to increase its assets and to help more worthy skaters. He became the embodiment of the Fund, as he often skated himself with his long-time partner, Harlene Lee, in shows for its benefit. In his earlier days, he had been the Eastern, North Atlantic and Middle Atlantic Champion many times in Veteran's (now Adult)

Dance with a series of partners. In recognition of his unique and outstanding service, he was elected to the World Figure Skating Hall of Fame in 1986. He was also an Honorary member of the USFSA and at the time of his death in 1992 was the Senior Past President, or "001," as the position is more informally known.

John R. Shoemaker

Ritter was succeeded as President by John R. Shoemaker, from San Francisco, the second President from the Pacific Coast. He had previously served as First Vice President in 1962-1963 and as Treasurer in 1963-1964.

The fall 1964 meeting of the Executive Committee was held at Chicago in late October at the Ascot Motel. Noted at the meeting were the deaths of Willie Frick, long-time (since 1920) teacher at The SC of Boston and the coach of many of its finest champions, and of Agnes Hutchinson of Colorado Springs, the Executive Secretary of the Professional Skaters Guild of America since 1949.

Among the actions taken were a complete revision of the Sanctions Rules, including a clearer recognition of the basic policy that the profits from amateur figure skating events should go towards the support of the amateur aspects of the sport. In addition, the basic principle was reconfirmed that a fee must be paid when there is an exhibition for which admission is charged if the exhibition constitutes the major part of the entertainment.

When the 1964-65 season started, the question was what further progress could be made by the young group of skaters that had challenged in 1964 at the Olympics and Worlds? The hope was that a further move upward was both possible and imminent! With the Worlds back at the Broadmoor, the opportunity existed to do well on "home" ice. There were already changes in the cast, with Tommy Litz, the 1963 National Champion having turned professional, while Monty Hoyt and Lorraine Hanlon had also retired, as had Judianne and Jerry Fotheringill, Darlene Streich and Charles Fetter, Jr.

As would soon become the prevailing pattern, an International Competition was the season "opener," with Eileen Zillmer the only entry for the U.S. placing eighth. The policy of sending skaters at Association expense to such events was still a few years away, and actually, in the late spring of 1964, Cecile Rusch, representing Boston, had won an International Junior Competition held at Oberstdorf, one of the first such successes for the USFSA. Another portent for the future was also seen in a Professional competition being held at Lake Placid in December 1964, under the sponsorship of the International Professional Skaters Union (IPSU), with the winners being all former U.S. or Canadian Champions: Sonja Klopfer, Donald Jackson, Maria and Otto Jelinek, and in Dance, Marilyn Meeker and Ron Ludington. The competition was called the "World

Professional Invitational Championship," but the use of the title "World" for professional events had and still has a somewhat different meaning, since there have been on occasion more than one such event being held in the same year!

The 1965 Nationals came to Lake Placid for the first time and were held in the 1932 Olympic Arena. In the Senior Ladies, Peggy Fleming won her second title with relative ease, with Christine Haigler second and Tina Noyes third. In the Men, Scott Allen, the defending champion, was upset by Gary Visconti from Detroit, with the previous year's Junior Champion Tim Wood third. In the Pairs, Vivian and Ronald Joseph of Chicago became the new champions, with Cindy and Ron Kauffman the runners-up. Kristin Fortune, the 1964 Silver Dance Champion with another partner, was the winner of the Senior Dance title with new partner Dennis Sveum from Los Angeles. Second were Lorna Dyer and John Carrell from Seattle.

Gary Visconti

The 1965 North American Championships started just six days later in Rochester, and the United States team was able to regain three of the four titles. Unexpectedly, Lorna Dyer and John Carrell overturning the National result to defeat Fortune and Sveum in Dance. Fourth were Stanley Urban, from Buffalo, now skating with his sister, Susan, while the Canadian Champions Carole Forrest and Kevin Lethbridge were third.

In the Ladies, Petra Burka from Toronto, despite a third place in figures, demonstrated her superiority in free skating by defeating Peggy Fleming, with Valerie Jones, the Canadian Ladies Champion, third. Gary Visconti continued his winning ways in the Men, to take the North American title over Scott Allen, with Donald Knight from Dundas, third. In the Pairs, Vivian and

Vivian and Ronald Joseph

Kristin Fortune and Dennis Sveum

Ron Joseph were the winners, the first American Pair to do so since the Kennedys in 1951. Second were Cindy and Ron Kauffman, with Susan and Paul Huehnergard of Canada third. So the medal count this time was: United States - three Gold and four Silver; Canada - one Gold and four Bronze. Quite a turn around from two years before.

There was little rest for the weary, however, since the World Championships started in Colorado on March 2, just nine days after the end of the Rochester competition. There was always some apprehension among the skaters about going to Colorado Springs to compete because of its altitude of just over 6,000 feet above sea level, with the endless argument of whether one should go early and get acclimated or go in at the last minute and skate before the altitude had an effect. There was no solution to the problem, as it was different for each skater, but the altitude was definitely a factor there, also because the ventilation in the rink was a little old fashioned. Still remembered was Dick Button's "collapse" at the end of his free skating in 1952, but with no ill effects.

The 1965 Worlds at The Broadmoor were again memorable, as all the championships held there have been! Among the lead stories: Could Alain Calmat of France finally win a World title in his 11th year in the event and after two Silver medals and two Bronze medals in the previous four years? Could Liudmila Belousova and Oleg Protopopov win their first Pair title? Could Eva Romanova and Pavel Roman successfully defend their title against the British challenge? Could Petra Burka bring another World title back to North America against the challenge of the Austrians? How would the skaters from the United States do?

Lorna Dyer and John Carrell

Skating on her home ice, Christine Haigler set up an American challenge early in the Ladies, placing second in figures to Burka, with Regine Heitzer of Austria third and Peggy Fleming fourth. In the free skating, Peggy overcame her poor performance of the North Americans and skated a flawless program. As Dick Button wrote in the report, she "skated with extraordinary beauty. Here is a skater who has a unique combination of athletic ability, technical control, great style and immense musicality." By her performance, Peggy pulled up to second, with Christine dropping to fourth. Tina Noyes after a poor showing in the figures did well in the free and pulled up to 10th.

In the Men, Alain Calmat finally achieved his long sought goal, to win his first and only World title, although he had been European Champion three times between 1962 and 1964. He had lost in Moscow to Emmerich Danzer of Austria just before the Worlds, so his win was a most satisfying one for him. Scott Allen again surprised and wound up second after having been fourth in figures. Donald Knight of Canada was third, while Gary Visconti, the National and North American champion, was sixth. Tim Wood, in his first Worlds, was 13th.

In the Pairs, Liudmila Belousova and Oleg Protopopov finally won their first World title, thereby beginning the Soviet "dynasty" in Pairs, that has lasted virtually unbroken, with a few isolated exceptions ever since. Vivian and Ronald Joseph were solid second, while Cindy and Ron Kauffman were sixth, and the third U.S. pair of Joanne Heckert and Gary Clark ninth.

In the Dance, Eva Romanova and Pavel Roman easily retained their title, with their memorable "Sleepy Lagoon" free dance, but Lorna Dyer and John Carrell cracked the British "barrier" and made the podium in third, returning the U.S. to the medals for the first time since 1959, the last time the Worlds had been in Colorado. Just behind them were Diane Towler and Bernard Ford of Great Britain, who would be their greatest rivals and nemesis in the years ahead. Kristin Fortune and Dennis Sveum placed a very creditable fifth, while the Urbans were seventh.

So, once again, the placements had improved markedly: Men - second, sixth, 13th; Ladies - third, fourth, 10th; Pairs - second, sixth, ninth; Dance - third, fifth, seventh, but what was notable was the number of medals - two Silver and two Bronze, the best showing since before 1961. This time, only one entrant was not in the top 10! Was another "Golden Age" about to begin? Perhaps so!

Alain Calmat would retire from competition following the Worlds and go on to become a medical doctor and eventually the Minister of Youth and Sports in the French Government, much as his contemporary Otto Jelinek would do in Canada, while Eva Romanova and Pavel Roman left competition to embark on a professional career.

The Association Annual Meeting for 1965 returned to the Pacific Coast for the first time since 1959 and was held at the Disneyland Hotel in Anaheim, Calif., right next to the original Disneyland. The major change in rules adopted at the meeting was to establish a uniform classification of events from the Regional (formerly the Sub-Sectional) Championships to the Nationals, effective with the 1966-1967 competition season. No longer would Senior Men in the Sectionals qualify for Junior Men in the Nationals or Junior Men in the Sectionals for Novice Men in the Nationals. All entrants in each class of competition would have to qualify each year in their respective classes starting with the Regionals and progressing through the Sectionals to the Nationals. Thus, three men or three ladies in each event would qualify for the next higher one.

At the same time, a new Intermediate class of Singles was added at the Regional and Sectional level, to be one class below Novice and requiring the Third test for entry. The Juvenile events were to be held only at the Regional level, with an age limit of 12 and the Second Test. Comparable rules applied to Pairs, with Senior Pairs having to have passed the Gold Pair Test and Juniors, the Silver. For Dance, two Gold Dances were required, and for Silver, the Silver Dance Test and not more than one Gold Dance. Although a Silver Free Dance was also added, it would not become a requirement for entry into competition until 1969; while for the Senior level, the Gold Dance Test would not be required until 1973 and the Gold Free Dance test until 1981! Another new rule affecting Pairs and Dance was one which permitted dance couples to take the free dance tests as a couple, rather than as individuals, and also Pairs to take the Pair Tests in the same manner, so that the individual status of one partner was unaffected by a failing result.

Also approved was a system of panel judging for the lower (and larger) events of the Sub-Sectionals. Starting in 1966, the system could be used for the Novice and Juvenile events of such competitions. It was an "assembly line" system, which provided for a separate panel of judges (usually three) for each figure, all on the ice at the same time, with the skater going on one end and coming off the other! If there were three figures, as was usually the case, then all nine judges would also judge the free skating. While the system accomplished the purpose of greatly reducing the time required for the skating of compulsory figures, its obvious drawbacks eventually resulted in its discontinuance for use in qualifying competitions in 1977, and its replacement with elimination rounds instead. Vividly remembered by the author was an instance in the 1969 New Englands, when a judge came off the ice after several hours of judging in the system and said "please, no more back double three's," of which he had judged a total of 37 in a row up to that point! He was at the time a World Championship judge from Czechoslovakia, Gerry Bubnik, who was studying for his master's degree at Harvard Law School.

The By Laws were amended to include in the objects of the Association a non-discrimination clause, and the rules were amended to broaden the rights of a professional in another sport, who up to that time was considered to be a professional in skating, in effect granting them all the rights of an amateur except the right to compete.

The concept of a "family" membership was introduced, with reduced fees ($10) for each additional family member (spouse and minor child) of an Individual Member, with one magazine subscription and one Rulebook going to the "first" member for the "full" fee of $15.

Also approved was an amendment to the By Laws to provide for an Honorary membership in the Executive Committee, with the first persons so elected being Edmund C. Bold of Seattle, Harry E. Radix of Chicago and Nelson F. Waters of Alton Bay, N.H. This honor has generally been accorded to those who have served as a member of the Executive Committee (now the Board of Directors) for more than 15 years, as well as an officer and committee chairman. Unfortunately, Harry Radix passed away just a little over three months after his election. He became President of the Chicago FSC in 1930 and organized the Nationals in Chicago of 1937 and 1942. He also served as an Olympic Team manager in 1952 and 1956, but his special legacy was the Radix skate pins, for which he left in his will an endowment to the Memorial Fund which has in part supported the continued presentation of the pins since. Although their cost today is greater than the income available, they are subsidized by the Association. These pins, miniature skates in gold, with a diamond in the toe for the champion, were awarded to the place winners at the Nationals, and also to the place winners in the Worlds, Olympics and North Americans. He also presented trophies for the Senior Dance event of the Nationals. When the first trophy "disappeared," he replaced it with a trophy actually made of gold. He also donated trophies for the Pairs and Dance events in the Midwestern and Pacific Coast Sectionals. He served on the Executive Committee for a total of 24 years between 1935 and 1965, and from 1955 to 1965 was the principle fund raiser for the Olympic Team, as Chairman of the USFSA Olympic Committee.

Also noted was the untimely death of Gretchen Merrill Gay, a former six-time National Ladies champion, who had been a teaching professional in Connecticut in recent years.

One innovation added to the meeting by President Shoemaker was an informal discussion period on Friday afternoon during which the delegates and guests could chat with the officers and committee chairmen regarding any question on USFSA affairs, the forerunner of the later adopted and well received "round table" discussion period.

Although again not reported in the magazine, by 1965 the Association had reached a total of 215 member clubs and 24,388 registered skaters, with total assets of $158,554, total revenues of $97,654 and total expenses of $83,306. The Memorial Fund at the same time, had total assets of $56,714, total receipts of $8,149 and total disbursed amounts of $3,000, a rather modest record for four years after the 1961 accident. There has always been a curious pattern of donations to the Memorial Fund, with there being very little interest in making personal donations on the part of the Executive Committee (later Board of Directors) members, despite fervent pleas in later years by Ritter Shumway, with most of the support coming from the grass roots level.

At the ISU Congress of 1965 in Vienna, a U.S. proposal was adopted, providing that a professional in another sport or someone who is an administrator in a professional sport was not an amateur, despite the fact that the USFSA itself had liberalized its own rules to provided that in the latter case at least, such a person was a Restricted Amateur! Rejected at the Congress was the first attempt to change the ratio between figures and free skating from 60/40 to 50/50. The compulsory connecting pair program, which would be called the "short" program after 1968, was made permanent with three separate groups of seven elements to be drawn in rotation. This Congress finally adopted the principle or policy of the right of free entry into all countries for international competitions or meetings, with the ISU agreeing to cooperate with an organizing member to bring about such right.

The 1965 fall meeting of the Executive Committee, was held in Chicago, back at the O'Hare Inn. A memorial resolution was approved for Harry Radix, and it was noted that the Radix pins would be continued through a bequest by Mr. Radix to the Memorial Fund.

In connection with this meeting, **Skating** magazine for the first time published an actual financial report for the Association, in the form of two "pie" charts showing income and expenses. The financial report is still not published in the magazine today (1995), with only the report of action by the governing bodies now constituting the report of the meetings. For the fiscal year 1964-1965, income was reported of $173,000, and expenses of $158,000. The largest source of income, at 32.7 percent, was the magazine and publications, which included the Rulebook, which has always been a "money maker" for the Association. The next largest source at 31.3 percent, or just over $54,000, was television rights, which is still today the "tail that wags the dog." The third largest category was dues and registration fees at 19.3 percent. On the expense side, 39.1 percent was attributable to "administration" (the Central Office), with another 39.9 percent for the magazine, and the third largest category, administrative for the committees and officials, was at 15.7 percent. The expenses for International participation then were at 5.3 percent, or around $8,400.

The report is revealing, as it shows how much of the costs of operating the Association went then to administration and publications, with only a relatively small amount to the skaters, who were, of course, benefiting on a modest basis from the fledgling Memorial Fund. Obviously, the expenses of officials were an essential part of the competition structure and indirectly benefited the skaters. It is too bad that such a "pie" chart is not published annually, and yet this was the only time (December 1965) that it has ever appeared!

The establishment of the Figure Skating Hall of Fame and Museum at the Broadmoor World Arena (as it was now called) was announced, with the Broadmoor donating the facilities to the USFSA for its use "in preserving and displaying memorabilia of historical interest to the skating world." The ad hoc committee previously formed in 1964 was made a permanent Museum Committee with William R. Haigler of Colorado Springs as its chairman. Unfortunately, no action was taken in the following years to implement the directive, and Haigler passed away suddenly in 1971. In the end, the Museum was transferred back to Boston in 1972, and housed at The Skating Club of Boston until 1975. It was next moved into the Central Office at Sears Crescent in downtown Boston, where there was one room large enough to display the retired trophies and other items of memorabilia that had been collected up to that time.

One technical decision with regard to Dance Tests was a rule change to enable professionals to serve as partners for the Pre Gold and Gold Dance Tests. In a purely administrative move, the Test Rules would be merged together, after having been separate between Figure and Dance since the beginning of the latter before the War!

The Judging Standards Committee also announced that judges seminars would be held at all the qualifying competitions for 1967. Also approved was support for clinics and workshops, the purpose of which would be to teach the techniques of instruction, especially for groups. There has never been enough education which teaches teachers how to teach. All too often young former competitive skaters start out without really any idea of how to do so. The PSGA has done a lot in this area, and it really is their primary responsibility, but the Association has a parallel obligation as well in that area.

One decision taken by the Executive Committee was to pay in full the travel expenses of the World Team for 1966, including uniforms, to which had been added red overcoats. The revision of the Test Rules was also approved, which consolidated into one set of rules all those common to all tests, so that they could be found in one place in the Rulebook, rather than scattered between the Dance and Figure Skating sections. For judges, short seminars were scheduled to be held at all Regional and Sectional Championships, and the mandatory removal of judges who were inactive for more than three years was also approved.

At the beginning of the 1965-1966 season, in an interview published in Skating magazine, President Jack Shoemaker was asked the following question, "In what shape is the USFSA today?" to which he replied in part, "Basically, the USFSA is in good shape. Our competitions are well conducted and show a very high level of skating ability; our World competitors have been placing closer to the top each year and Gold Medals are in sight again...Our financial picture is sound and improving...Public awareness of figure skating is greater than ever before. Television coverage of top level competitions is bringing skating into millions of homes." Sound familiar?

These words were spoken in 1965, 30 years ago, and yet could well be true today. Jack goes on to say that the highest priority for the Association was to increase its membership and number of registered skaters. It is a curious fact that right up to today and despite the exponential growth in interest in the sport, the growth of the Association membership and registrants has been on a very modest rising curve and is almost "flat," when considered apart from those registered in the Basic Skills program. The "magic" formula for increasing membership has not yet been found and was a concern then and should be even more of a concern today. Part of the problem has always been that the Association has never sufficiently addressed ways and means of assisting its member clubs to increase local participation and membership.

The presence of U.S. skaters in International Competitions was still minimal, most often at the Richmond Trophy for Ladies, usually with one U.S. entry, who in 1965 was Wendy Lee Jones of Hershey, Pa., placing fifth. Later in 1966, came one of those rare wins in such an event, when Billy Chapel, then representing the Broadmoor, won the Men's event of the "Grand Prix Internationale de Patinage" at Megève, France.

Cynthia and Ronald Kauffman

The 1966 Nationals returned to Berkeley, Calif., for the first time since 1957, and represented another chapter in the ongoing and spirited rivalry between Scott Allen of New York and Gary Visconti of Detroit, with Allen this time prevailing to win his second Senior Men's title. Chapel was third and in fourth was Tim Wood, also from Detroit, the 1965 Junior Champion. In the Senior Ladies it was all Peggy Fleming who won her third straight title, with her perennial rival Tina Noyes now the runner-up. In the Senior Pairs, with the Josephs having retired to pursue their educations and Ronald eventually becoming a doctor, the new champions were Cynthia and Ron Kauffman from Seattle. In Dance, Kristin Fortune and Dennis Sveum won their second title, reversing the later results of 1965 by defeating Lorna Dyer and John Carrell who were the 1965 North American champions and had placed ahead of them in the 1965 Worlds.

Also seen in the championships were several rising stars of the future, among them Janet Lynn of Rockford, Ill., the Junior Ladies winner and John Misha Petkevich of Great Falls, Mont., the Junior Champion, and in the Dance, the new couple of Judy Schwomeyer from Indianapolis and James Sladky from Syracuse, N.Y., who placed seventh in their first Senior championship after winning the Eastern Senior Dance. Judy was following in the footsteps of her older sister Sandra ("Sandy"), who was already competing in dance at the Senior level with James

Pennington and in the same Nationals placed fourth! Later in life, Sandy S. Lamb would be a leading coach, President of the PSGA and one of the founders of the Special Olympics in which her daughter has been an active and successful participant.

The 1966 Nationals were also notable for the success of Atoy Wilson of Los Angeles in winning the Novice Men, in which he had also been the runner-up in 1965, since Atoy was the first African-American to win a National title. Much of his success can be attributed to his mother, Thelma, a strong supporter of all skaters and especially those of color, a loyal friend to those she chose to honor with her friendship and a "pillar" of skating in Southern California, whose untimely death in 1994 was mourned by all who knew her.

The 1966 World Championships were held at Davos, Switzerland, on the outdoor rink there, as they had been previously in 1948. It would be the last time that the Worlds would be skated entirely outdoors. A new rule went into effect starting in 1967 which required the ISU Championships and the Olympic Winter Games to be held in a "covered and closed" (i.e., indoor) rink, as it was called in the Regulations. (As will be seen, however, the rule was "bent" somewhat for the 1967 Worlds in Vienna.) It is amusing at this late date to read the plea of the reporter of the championships in response to the argument concerning the advisability of holding a competition outdoors and at high altitude, that "skating is indigenous to the outdoors and competitors, as part of their training, should learn to skate under all conditions." Who was the reporter? None other than Dick Button, who had won most of his major championships out-of-doors, outside of North America at least.

It was in Davos that Jack Shoemaker's prediction did indeed come true that "Gold medals were in sight again," and he was there to see it himself! He stated at the conclusion of the events, "The performance of the USFSA skaters in this year's World Championships was outstanding. We won five of the 12 medals awarded – one Gold, one Silver, and three Bronzes and again the United States was the only country to earn the right to three entries and a judge in each class for next year." At that time, the right of a country to have a judge was based on the placements of its skaters from the prior year, with five (out of the nine) judges for an event being in effect "seeded." At the insistence of the smaller countries, this rule would eventually be done away with and all judges would be selected by a blind draw, which has made it much more difficult for the stronger nations to be represented on the panels.

The Gold medal came in the Ladies, in which Peggy Fleming soundly defeated the defending champion, Petra Burka of Canada, who actually wound up third behind Gaby Seyfert of East Germany, who pulled up over Petra in the free skating. Tina Noyes pulled up to ninth, after being 12th in the figures, and Pam Schneider, of New York, the third U.S. entrant, placed 12th. Peggy thus became a worthy successor to Tenley Albright and Carol Heiss as the holder of the

World Championship for Ladies, returning a U.S. skater to the top of the podium for the first time in six years, a period which was in fact much shorter than had been originally predicted back in 1961.

While taking nothing away from Peggy, one reporter stated that Petra had "slimmed herself" out of the title. Petra had been a very strong, consistent and solid skater in the past, but a major loss of weight had apparently affected her superb jumping ability, as well as her confidence, and at Davos with its outdoor conditions and high altitude, her lack of stamina was evident. Peggy, who had almost a 50 point lead in the figures, did not play it safe and for her the altitude was not a problem, since she had been training in Colorado Springs. Her athletic ability, combined with style and musicality were outstanding and she maintained the best traditions of her predecessors. Perhaps it could be said that the "era" of Fleming had begun!

In the Men's event, the new champion was Emmerich Danzer from Austria, who had been the European Champion for the past two years, but was closely challenged by his compatriot Wolfgang Schwarz. This time, Gary Visconti earned the Bronze medal with, by all accounts, the best overall free skating performance, to reverse the National result once again over Scott Allen, who had been third in the figures. Billy Chapel, the third U.S. entry placed 12th.

The Pairs saw the Protopopovs gain their second title, but in a close competition with their teammates, Tatiana Zhuk and Alexandr Gorelik, with Cindy and Ron Kauffman surprising by taking the Bronze medals, the first in Pairs for the U.S. since 1959, and a jump of three places over 1965. The second U.S. pair, Susan Berens and Roy Wegelein, from Los Angeles, placed 11th.

The Dance, with Eva Romanova and Pavel Roman having retired, went to the young British couple of Diane Towler and Bernard Ford, fourth the previous year, with the two American couples, Kristin Fortune and Dennis Sveum and Lorna Dyer and John Carrell, right behind them in second and third place, the first time ever that the United States had two couples on the podium in the Dance event. The third U.S. couple, Susan and Stanley Urban from Buffalo placed 11th.

So the 1965-1966 competition season ended on a high note and there was only the usual administrative work and rule making exercise of the Governing Council Meeting left, which was held in Denver, Colo. One decision coming out of the meeting was to increase the size of Skating magazine from its former 6 x 9 format to 8-1/2 x 11, the theory being that more advertising could be obtained in a "full-sized" format and there would be greater opportunities for broadening the editorial content to include material of interest to the recreational skater. There was even talk of selling the magazine on newsstands. The exercise would last for three years, after which the magazine reverted to its traditional size once again, the experiment having proven to be a dismal failure. Additional advertising was not obtained and the costs of producing the larger size were much higher, so the annual deficits of the magazine continued, but on a larger scale. It remains to be seen whether the second experiment of increasing the magazine's size in 1993 will have the same result or will be successful. It is slightly different, in that now the magazine has six issues, with six other issues which constitute a "newsletter," but in the same size and scope. Obviously, the cost of the newsletter type issues is less, since no color is used in them. The need for a year around magazine is readily apparent in the 1990's, so it may work this time. Certainly it did not work 30 years ago!

At the meeting, it was also announced that Bob Ellis had been appointed Executive Secretary. The Executive Committee also elected as Honorary members of that body, three Past Presidents, Henry M. Beatty, Kenneth L. Brown, and Harry N. Keighley. Another seemingly minor change adopted was to limit the formal trial judging of qualifying competitions to individuals who wish to trial judge events which they needed for promotion. Trial judging had become and still is a "big business" for the organizing committees of the qualifying competitions and especially the Nationals, but it had become unwieldy with many people doing it who were "not going anywhere." So it had to be cut back to a manageable number. On the other hand, as the demand for judges continues to rise and more are needed every year, the trial judging program is absolutely essential, if the Association is to properly serve its constituents. By 1965, the total number of judges in the country had reached 1,114, which, with a total of 215 member clubs, represents an average of a little over five judges per club. Compare this with 1953, when there were 735 judges and 119 member clubs, or an average of a little over six judges per club. Clearly, the increase in the number of judges was not keeping pace with the increase in the number of clubs, and was in fact declining. To date, this trend has not been reversed.

At the same time as the magazine was "enlarged," the Central Office made yet another move in the Boston area, from 575 Boylston Street after five years there to 178 Tremont Street. The former location overlooked Copley Square in the Back Bay of Boston, while the new office overlooked the Boston Common. While not significantly larger, the new space had more separate (but small) offices than the former quarters, which enabled the magazine staff to operate more independently from the Central Office staff. There was also more storage space at 178 Tremont Street. There would be one more move in Boston before the transfer to Colorado in 1979.

In October 1966, the death of Charles B. Blanchard was reported. He was the husband of Theresa Weld Blanchard for 46 years and had always been a faithful supporter of her career in skating, both as a competitor and as editor of the magazine. He himself was involved in literary affairs as an editor at the book publishers, Little Brown and Company.

The 1966 fall meeting of the Executive Committee was held at Chicago. Approved for implementation was a program for skaters below the Preliminary Test level of "badge" or basic skills tests, which were to a large extent modeled on the National Skating Tests of the CFSA, and also on the experience gained in the clinics run by the Memorial Fund in the Boston area, in which "ribbon" tests were used as a measure of progress. These tests would eventually evolve into the Basic Skills program of the Association, which involves a large number of beginner or recreational skaters in the "Skate With US" program.

The Executive Committee approved a rule change to permit the medal winners in the Senior events of the Nationals to reenter the following year without having to qualify through Regional and Sectional Competition. Up to that time, only the titleholder was so exempted. At the same time, the National medal winners would be permitted to enter the comparable Regional or Sectional events, but if such skaters did so, they would have to place in the top three in order to advance. If they did so, they did not replace the next skaters in line, who would also qualify. Sort of a "two-edged sword."

Also approved was a free draw for the starting order of free skating, rather than on the basis of placements in the figures. In Dance, all those in the Sectional Gold and National Dance events could enter the final round and perform their free dance, with the previous eight couple limit in the final round being abolished.

In tests, it was made mandatory that the tests sheets be made available to the test candidates, and the fact that a judge went below the minimum thereby failing a test had to be reported to the judge-in-charge immediately, thereby eliminating what had occasionally been used as a "pocket veto." The ISU Representative was also requested to propose to the ISU the removal of the Starlight Waltz and the Silver Samba from the schedule of International Dances, on the ground that one was too easy (the Starlight) and the other was too hard (the Samba). Only the Samba was dropped but would eventually be restored to the schedule many years later. A memorial trophy was also accepted for the New England Novice Men's event to honor Montgomery "Bud" Wilson, a former North American and Canadian champion and long-time coach at the SC of Boston, who had passed away in 1964.

It was in 1966 that the Program Development Committee was initially established. It was first known by the curious name of "Coordinating Chairman's Committee," with John W. McNair of Baltimore as the first chairman. Its initial mandate was to direct and guide the activities of the ISIA-Liaison, PSGA-Liaison and School and College Figure Skating Committees and to coordinate them (hence the name) with the chairmen of the Amateur Status, Membership and Sanctions Committees. Renamed in one year the Liaison and Program Development Committee, and finally in 1972 taking its present name, the mandate of the committee quickly expanded to have responsibility for all "grass roots" programs, not only their creation and development, but also their promotion, including Basic Tests and Competitions. The committee has come to serve as an "idea" source with the establishment of programs and their initial development, after which they are transferred to the mainstream committees and the rules. An example is the National Collegiate Championships, as well as the Basic Tests and Competitions. The committee has also been involved in the development of therapeutic skating programs for the handicapped, which led to the inclusion of figure skating in the Special Olympics, now handled by a separate special committee. The Program Development Committee became a permanent non-voting committee in 1980. It is a very important committee in the Association, reflecting as it does the principle "outreach" to the general public. The committee also took over the functions of the School and College Figure Skating Committee, which had been in operation from 1950 to 1967.

In the fall of 1966, there is a report in the magazine, describing what was probably the first true Precision Team founded in the country, the "Hockettes" from the Ann Arbor FSC. The team was called a "crack skating chorus," and had 32 members and was cited as already being in its 10th year, which meant that it was founded in 1955. While "group skating" was not new and is found in the ISU Regulations as early as 1909, the form we know today as "precision team skating" was new and a modern development. The article states that a "Hockette must engage in a fixed amount of other figure skating activity for the sake of the Chorus and her status as a regular club member. Strict direction is necessary, but ultimately, it is the group itself who sets the standards. The Hockettes are a success, but, most important, they have learned a basic value of figure skating — the team spirit and club spirit that lie behind that success". Not the best English, but prophetic words that are equally applicable today!

The 1966-1967 competition season was the first in which the levels of the events were the same as the Nationals. This decision toward uniformity in the qualifying competition structure also had a positive "side effect," which was that Senior skaters were now more likely to enter the Sectionals at least and many of them have done so since often for the purposes of training, exposure and evaluation. Examples of this attention to the achievement of excellence have included Scott Hamilton, the World Champion from 1981 to 1984, who was in three of those same four years the Eastern Senior Men's Champion, and Brian Boitano, the 1986 and 1988 World Champion, who did the same, competing as a member of the World Team while still skating in the Pacific Coast Sectional. It has also been a fairly common practice for Pairs and Dance couples to compete in their Sectionals for the same reasons and especially to try out new programs and to obtain the comments of judges. There has seemed to be an idea in figure skating that the less one competes the better, although "competition" should be the name of the game, and those top-ranked skaters who took advantage of the opportunity to enter their Sectional competitions invariably benefited from doing so. Actually in 1967, John Misha Petkevich, Tim Wood and Judy Schwomeyer and James Sladky were all found in their respective Sectionals.

The 1967 Nationals were held in Omaha, Neb., at the "Ak-Sar-Ben" (guess what that stands for spelled backwards) Coliseum and were well run by the FSC of Omaha. In the Senior Men, the "beat" went on, with another epic battle between Gary Visconti and Scott Allen, with Gary coming out on top to take his second National title. Scott placed second, and John Misha Petkevich of Great Falls, Mont., the 1966 Junior Champion, was third. The result went to a "subsequent" majority, that is a majority for second place in this instance, and then to a "greater" majority for second place, with Gary having five seconds and Scott three.

Peggy Fleming easily won her fourth Ladies title, with Tina Noyes again second and Jennie Walsh of Los Angeles third. Janet Lynn of Rockford, Ill., the Junior Ladies Champion of 1966, was right behind in fourth. The Pairs title again went to the Kauffmans, for their second, with Susan Berens and Roy Wagelein of Los Angeles second. In Dance, Lorna Dyer and John Carrell from Seattle, finally made it to the top of the podium for what would be their first and only National Senior title, although they had been the North American Champions already for two years, as well as twice World Bronze medalists! Alma Davenport and Roger Berry from Los Angeles were second and Judy Schwomeyer and James Sladky, third. Roger was the son of one of the pioneer skaters from California, Ernest Berry, who was the Pacific Coast Senior Men's Champion in 1938. The new Junior Ladies Champion was Julie Lynn Holmes from the Arctic Blades FSC in Los Angeles, and the new Junior Pair Champions were Jo Jo Starbuck and Ken Shelley, also from Arctic Blades, all of whom would soon be heard from in the near future. Julie Lynn had also been the Novice Ladies Champion in 1965, for the "back-to-back double" so prized among the younger skaters.

The North American championships of 1967 were held in Montreal, and while a success in themselves, with good skating, encountered many problems. First, the rink to be used, the Maurice Richard Arena, a municipal rink, was shut down when the public works employees of the city went on strike. As a result, the events were transferred to the Town of Mount Royal Arena, where the Ladies figures were held, the McGill University Stadium for the Men's compulsory figures, with the rest of the events being held in the Centre Sportif of the University of Montreal. This was fine, except that the lights went during the Ladies free skating, and when emergency power was finally restored after a 40-minute delay, it was still necessary to use a tiny record player sitting on the barrier to complete the program of Karen Magnussen! Karen wisely took advantage of the delay to have a troublesome skate blade repaired and skated well to place fourth. To top it all off, the temperature dropped to 25 degrees below zero over night, so that all the automobiles of the officials and skaters and their families in the parking lot of the hotel froze up solid, except one, that of the author, which had been kept going over night by periodic trips out to start and run it by the author's wife, Mary Louise.

In the compulsory figure portions of the singles events, held under somewhat adverse conditions on "hockey" ice in very cold buildings, Peggy Fleming took a commanding lead early and held on to it over Valerie Jones of Canada, with Tina Noyes, third and 14-year-old Karen Magnussen of Vancouver fourth. In the Men, Donald Knight was the leader over Scott Allen and defending champion Gary Visconti. In the Pairs, the three American Pairs all placed ahead of their Canadian counterparts in the first three places. The Canadian Pairs were new to international competition and did not yet have the standard of the "dynasty" of World level Canadian Pairs of the previous 10 years. The Kauffmans won their first North American Pair title, with Susan Berens and Roy Wagelein, second and the third-ranked U.S. pair of Betty Jean Lewis and Richard Gilbert from Boston, the National Junior Pair Champions of 1966, third.

In the Dance, Lorna Dyer and John Carrell successfully defended their North American title, with the Canadian couple of Joni Graham and Don Phillips from Kerrisdale, second, followed by Judy Schwomeyer and James Sladky.

In the free skating in the Centre Sportif, Donald Knight won the Men's title for Canada, with Scott Allen holding on the second over Gary Visconti, yet another reversal of the National result between the latter two. Tim Wood was fifth. Peggy won her first and only North American title over Valerie Jones of Toronto, with Tina Noyes third in the problem-plagued free skating.

The "medal count" in the 1967 North Americans was: United States - three Gold, two Silver and four Bronze; Canada - one Gold and two Silver.

The 1967 Worlds were held at Vienna, Austria, considered by some as the "seat" of figure skating. The championship marked the 100th Anniversary of the Wiener Eislauf-Verein, one of the oldest skating clubs in the World, which was still skating on its original site. Although the rules had been changed to require a covered and closed rink, by special dispensation the WEV was permitted to hold the free skating of the championships on the original rink, with the figures being held in the Donauparkhalle, an indoor rink near the Danube Canal. The property of the WEV was huge, and on one end an Intercontinental Hotel had been built, which housed the participants very nicely. Between the hotel and the competition rink was a large practice area. The conditions in the two rinks made for a very interesting event! In the Donauhalle were many birds, which swooped down to the edge of the boards "dive bombing" in their search for food. In the open air competition arena, every form of weather was encountered, from rain to snow to severe cold. In fact, Lorna Dyer of the U.S. caught pneumonia and was unable to attend the banquet, much to her disappointment. Another ailment also struck the U.S. dancers, when Judy Schwomeyer could barely make it through their free dance, under very poor weather conditions. Her problem was described by coach Ron Ludington as a severe case of Worlditis, it being she and partner Jim Sladky's first Worlds. Despite this, they placed eighth overall, a creditable showing, ahead of their teammates, Alma Davenport and Roger Berry ninth, who narrowly defeated them in the Nationals!

In the Dance event itself, Diane Towler and Bernard Ford of Great Britain retained their title, after a strong challenge from Lorna Dyer and John Carrell. Although it is not seen in the placements, the latter earned only the first places of the Canadian and U.S. judges, which would be considered as "continental bias" by the Europeans, but which was not actually the case. There was still in ice dancing then the fundamental difference in style that made the decision making process difficult. The European couples being much more "loose" and less "accurate," while the American and Canadian couples were better skaters, far more accurate in the compulsory dances but less innovative in the free dance, but more in the spirit of the rules as compared to pair skating, with the British couples still supreme in that part of the competition. In the Dance event, in 13th place can be found Liudmila Pachomova and Alexandr Gorshkov of the Soviet Union, in their first Worlds as a couple. Liudmila had first appeared in 1966 with another partner, Viktor Rishkin, who coincidentally also was in Vienna with a new partner, Irina Grishkova, placing seventh. Little did Pachomova-Gorshkov and Schwomeyer-Sladky know then of the battles ahead between them!

The final round of the Pairs event took place in a rainstorm, and there was a memorable moment when at the awards ceremony, the defending champions Liudmila and Oleg Protopopov who won their third title, appeared on the ice for the presentation with an umbrella which they took with them to the podium! The West German pair of Margot Glockshuber and Wolfgang Danne, who had been fourth in 1966, came in second, while Cynthia and Ron Kauffman again placed third. Susan Berens and Roy Wagelein were seventh, while Betty Jean Lewis and Richard Gilbert, the third U.S. Pair, were 13th. With Tatiana Zhuk and Alexandr Gorelik absent, the Soviet presence was a little less strong, except, of course, for the champions. The second Soviet pair of Tamara Moskvina and Alexei Mishin placed sixth, and the third Soviet pair placed eighth. Tamara later became one of the leading Russian Pair coaches along with her husband Igor Moskvin, who was then the coach of the Protopopovs, while Mishin himself has also been a successful coach.

The Men's event in 1967 was really a two-way battle between the two Austrians, Emmerich Danzer, the defending champion, and Wolfgang Schwarz, his closest rival, while right behind them would be Donald Knight of Canada, the new North American champion, and then the two Americans, Gary Visconti and Scott Allen. The local press had a field day, as the U.S. judge, Jane Vaughn Sullivan, whose husband was serving with the U.S. Air Force in Paris, was less than enthusiastic with the skating of Danzer especially, ultimately placing him fifth, with her first place going to Allen. There was a great deal of "commentary" in the tabloid Vienna press, which made life very difficult for her, but she stuck to her guns, although her place did not materially affect the outcome. Danzer retained his title with six out of nine first places. As usual, he had to come from behind the lead of Schwarz in the figures to win. The Canadian judge, Donald Gilchrist, also was not all that impressed with Danzer either, placing him third. When the "dust" or snow finally settled, Danzer was the champion, Schwarz the runner-up and Gary Visconti, third, ahead of Knight, with Allen fifth, thereby overturning the North American result once again! Tim Wood placed ninth.

The Ladies event saw the steady march towards Grenoble in 1968 of Peggy Fleming, who won her second title, despite an unexpected and for her, a rare fall in the free skating on a double Axel. The competition also reflected the appearance on the podium of two strong European challengers in Gaby Seyfert of East Germany and Hana Masková of Czechoslovakia. Gaby was the new European Ladies Champion, having succeeded Regine Heitzer of Austria, who had retired, in what would be the first of a long string of such titles for the Ladies from the GDR, all of whom, would be trained by her mother Uta Muller, as she was herself. In the Ladies event in Vienna, Tina Noyes placed fifth in free skating and finished seventh, with Jennie Walsh, the third U.S. entry placing eighth. Both of them fought back from lower places in figures, which were often then the "bête noir" of the Americans. Only a few were equally as talented in both figures and free with Peggy Fleming being one of them.

Among those present in Vienna were Henry Beatty, the ISU Council member, who was retiring from that position and was there also to introduce the U.S. candidate to be his successor, Jack Shoemaker of San Francisco, the outgoing USFSA President. One of the active members of the local organizing committee was Ernst Labin of Austria, at that time also an ISU Council member. The ISU Vice President for Figure Skating, Jacques Favart from France was also present. All of these men would play a part in the "drama" ahead involving the succession to the Presidency of the ISU, from which Dr. James Koch of Switzerland was stepping down.

Before the ISU Congress of 1967, however, the USFSA Governing Council meeting was held in Buffalo, N.Y., for the second time. One principal matter for discussion was the implementation of Basic Tests, and a collaboration with the American Association of Health, Physical Education and Recreation (AAHPER) was proposed, the implementation of which was placed under the Coordinating Chairman's Committee.

Another "major" action in so far as the individual member was concerned was an increase in the registration fee from $1.00 to $2.00, or 100 percent! Again, however, in recommending the action, there is no mention in the report of the financial status of the Association!

The separate (since 1956) Figure and Dance Judges Committees were once again combined into one Judges Committee, to which was added the Judging Standards Committee originally formed in 1963. The experiment of the separate Judges committees had not proven to be of value with a divergence resulting in the basic standards and procedures to be applied to the appointment of judges, which should be uniform for all types of judges (as would be seen many years later with the addition of precision judges). The functions of the Judging Standards Committee were transferred to what was initially called the Judges Education and Training Section (JETS) of the Judges Committee, with a National Vice Chairman in charge. In 1981, the section would become a subcommittee of the Judges Committee.

Experience has shown that the integration of new activities or functions into the permanent committee structure as quickly as possible is the best way to go, rather than to have an ever-proliferating collection of special or ad hoc committees for special activities. Examples in recent years that can be cited are the National Collegiate championships and the Precision qualifying competitions, including the Nationals. Ad hoc committees are often very useful in the initial effort to get new activities going, the latest example of which are the Adult Nationals, but in the long run, the permanent committees should assume the responsibility for them.

A somewhat controversial decision was taken to add another class of judge between the High test and Silver Dance judges on the one hand and the present National and Gold Dance judges on the other, to be called Gold test and Gold Dance Test judges. There was some objection to the addition of yet another level to climb through, and it has indeed been the case that the addition of more ranks has slowed down the progress of the younger judges through the ranks. On the other hand, the view was that the adding of additional grades would in the end result in better qualified judges who would progress through the ranks in a more orderly manner.

Jack Shoemaker stepped down after three years as President, and was succeeded by Spencer E. Cram, the third of the "Cleveland" Presidents. Jack went on to a distinguished career in the ISU. A former President of the Cleveland Skating Club, Spence was also a National Referee and Accountant. At the time of assuming the Presidency, he planned to move first to Florida and ultimately to Hendersonville, N.C., where in each location he and his wife Jean had enjoyed their other "avocation" of building houses!

The 1967 ISU Congress followed the Governing Council meeting and was held at Amsterdam, the Netherlands. An orderly transition of office took place, with James Koch stepping down as President after 14 years in office, due in large measure to hip surgery which had resulted in the permanent use of crutches, an image which James felt was not a favorable one for an international sports federation president. He was succeeded by Ernst Labin of Austria, with Jacques Favart of France

Spencer E. Cram

continuing in office as Vice President for Figure Skating. Jack Shoemaker was duly elected as the first member of the ISU Council, succeeding Hank Beatty who retired. Jack was the only representative of the USFSA in the ISU at the time, since Ken Kelley, who had been a member of the Ice Dance Technical Committee since 1961, had failed in a bid for re-election in 1965.

Just five weeks after his election, President Labin died unexpectedly, so that in accordance with the ISU Constitution, Jacques Favart became the ISU President and Jack Shoemaker became the Vice President for Figure Skating, a position he would hold with distinction for 13 years until 1980, the only USFSA representative to serve as an officer of the ISU. Jack himself retired in 1980, and surprisingly, again just two months thereafter, Favart died unexpectedly, with the Vice President for Speed Skating, Olaf Poulsen of Norway succeeding him. If Jack had elected to remain in office for one more term, he would have become the President himself, but he always said thereafter that he had no regrets and that the timing of his retirement was right. In fact, he did have some health problems requiring surgery, which could well have made the carrying out the duties of the office difficult, if not impossible. After his retirement, he was elected an Honorary Vice President of the ISU and was the Honorary Chairman of the 1981 Worlds in Hartford, Conn. He passed away in 1988.

In October of 1967, Jack and his wife Edith headed the third U.S. Tour of Japan, at the invitation of the National Skating Union of Japan. The skaters included all four of the National Champions, Gary Visconti, Peggy Fleming, Cindy and Ron Kauffman and Lorna Dyer and John Carrell. In just two weeks, the skaters did eight exhibitions and two clinics for judges in five cities, Tokyo (3), Osaka (2), Fukuoka, Sapporo and Nagoya. The tour again served a dual purpose, to assist in the further development of Japanese skating, and also to improve friendly relations between Japan and the United States. While not repeated since, the tours have lingered in memory on both sides of the Pacific and did much to bring Japanese skating into the modern era.

The fall 1967 meeting of the Executive Committee, which was held in Chicago, continued the progress made in completing the schedule for the Basic Tests and approving the syllabus for them, which had been prepared by teaching professionals Robert and Joan Ogilvie, in cooperation with the Liaison and Program Development Committee, to the end that the tests could actually be launched in 1968 with seminars to be held first to orient and train teachers and judges. There were to be 12 levels or units of proficiency with suitable badges for each one.

The new Judges Education and Training Section of the Judges Committee announced its intention to devote its energies initially to increasing the number of judges, as well as to orienting judges with respect to changes in the rules, by conducting short seminars at all 13 of the qualifying competitions, a practice which has been followed with varying degrees of success ever since.

The Association accepted the revisions made by the ISU at its 1967 Congress to the content of ice dancing competitions, which provided for three compulsory dances and an original set-pattern dance replacing the fourth compulsory dance, to be effective with the 1968-1969 competitive season. Initially, the "OSP," as it came to be called counted for 15 percent of the total score, the three remaining compulsory dances 45 percent and the free dance 40 percent. The OSP was to be judged with just one mark. In the first year in competition, no rhythm or tempo was specified by the ISU, with these basic aspects being left to the choice of the skaters. It almost immediately became apparent that a competition with completely different rhythms was very difficult to evaluate and was "oranges and apples," in so far as the judges were concerned. The decision was then quickly made by the ISU to specify the rhythm in advance. The first time this was done was for the 1970-1971 season, with the Polka the selected rhythm. It would not be until 1977-1978, that the range of tempo to be used was also pinned down. At the 1971 ISU Congress, the use of two marks, composition and presentation, was added and the value of the dance was increased to 20 percent, with the three compulsory dances being at 30 percent and the free dance at 50 percent. This followed an earlier decision by the ISU in 1967 to change the ratio between the compulsory figures and free skating in Singles to 50-50 from 60-40, which had also been accepted by the USFSA. The OSP would remain in a "set-pattern" form until 1990-1991, when it was changed to an original dance without the requirement that it have a repetitive set pattern.

The start of the Olympic year 1967-1968 again began with international competition. The first International Grand Prix de St. Gervais, was held at that French Alpine village in 1967, with Patrick Pera of France the winner. The lone U.S. entrant, Jeff Hall from New York placed seventh. In later years the St. Gervais competition would become a "fixture" on the international circuit, usually being the first Senior International competition for the National Junior Champions of the preceding season. In the Richmond Trophy, the one U.S. entrant, Annetta Baird from Philadelphia placed 10th. Of more importance then was the pre-Olympic competition held at the site of the 1968 Games in Grenoble, France, to which the USFSA sent Tim Wood and John Misha Petkevich, the third and fourth place finishers in the 1967 Nationals. In the competition at Grenoble, Tim placed a close second behind Patrick Pera of France, whom he would soon meet again in the Games themselves, while Petkevich finished eighth in what was his first international competition.

The 1968 Nationals were held in Philadelphia, in the then new building, the Spectrum, with a capacity of 14,800 spectators. It was also decided to use computers to calculate the results. These were again main frame machines called System/360, Model 30, furnished by IBM, with the programs used being based on those developed by Ulrich Barth of IBM Europe in Stuttgart, that had been used in the 1964 Olympics and Worlds. Incredible as it might seem today, the marks were entered into the machine using punch cards. Regular manual accounting on the standard paper forms was also carried out and was still official for the purpose of the final results. It was, however, the first time that computers had been used to calculate the results of a National Championship. It would not be long before the USFSA would follow the lead of the ISU in implementing and making official the use of computers for accounting purposes at its competitions.

In the report in **Skating** magazine, Lynn Thomas writes, "upsets were the story of the week as one national champion was dethroned and five members of last year's World Team failed to place in the top three this year." The pattern was set early, when Tim Wood won the figures, followed by Scott Allen, Gary Visconti and John Misha Petkevich in that order. The "older" guard of Visconti and Allen both skated very well, but were outshone by the "newer" guard. Petkevich won the free skating, earning one 6.0, a very rare occurrence in the Nationals, closely followed by Wood, so that the latter became the new champion, with Visconti hanging on to second, Petekevich pulling up to third and Allen fourth. This presented a dilemma to the International Committee in picking the World and Olympic Teams, which was finally resolved by sending Petkevich to the Olympics and Allen to the Worlds. The figure placements of the two skaters were a material factor in the decision to split the selection.

In the Ladies, Peggy Fleming won her fifth straight title, winning the figures easily and in the free skating earning two marks of 6.0 in a flawless performance, which she finished with greater strength than she had previously shown in the past. Tina Noyes was again runner-up, with 14-year-old Janet Lynn of Rockford gaining the third spot.

The Senior Pairs saw Cindy and Ron Kauffman of Seattle take their third title over Roy Wagelein of Los Angeles with a new partner, Sandi Sweitzer. In third were Jo Jo Starbuck and Ken Shelley, the Junior Champions of the previous year, with Betty Jean Lewis and Richard Gilbert from Boston, fourth. Ken was busy in the 1968 Nationals, just as he would be in the years to come since he also skated Singles, and won the Junior Men's title. He had actually skated Singles the year before as well, but had not made it out of the Sectionals. Fifth in Junior Men was Gordon

Judy Schwomeyer and James Sladky

McKellen, Jr., who had been second the year before, but who would go on to be a champion in the future, while third in Junior Pairs were Melissa and Mark Militano, from Long Island, N. Y., also future champions.

There were new Dance Champions, since Lorna Dyer and John Carrell had retired after the 1967 season. Their worthy successors were Judy Schwomeyer and James Sladky, now representing the Genesee FSC of Rochester, N.Y., with Vicki Camper and Eugene Heffron from Detroit second, and Debbie Gerken and Raymond Tiedemann of New York third. In the continuing effort to add Ice Dancing as an Olympic medal sport, Judy and Jimmy were invited to Grenoble to demonstrate once again what Avery Brundage, the IOC President, chose to call "rhythmic pairs."

Then it was "on to Grenoble" for the Tenth Olympic Winter Games, with hopes high for a better showing than had been the case four years earlier in Innsbruck. As is well known, there is enormous pressure placed on those seeking Olympic medals who have been anointed by the media as "favorites," and often, how such persons handle the pressure is also a measure of their greatness, both as athletes and as persons. While we have not in this narrative placed any great emphasis on the role or activity of officials, on the theory that they are there to serve the sport and the skaters and should be "anonymous" in our subjective judging system, it is worth mentioning that there is just as much pressure on them as well, especially once the media finds out who they are and seeks them out! This was the case in 1968, just as it has been at the Games every time since. In 1968, the judges were Yvonne Sherman McGowan from New York, a former North American and National Ladies Champion and World Silver medalist, and Norman Fuller from Southern California, a successful businessman and also a former competitive skater. In a way, they represented the judging fraternity well, with one being a former champion, World competitor and home maker, and the other, while also a skater, being successful in the business world.

In earlier times, before there was a formal system of judges' education, judges were usually self taught or they were lucky enough to have mentors among present judges to assist and to train them, essentially on a one on one basis. With the inauguration of the Judging Standards Committee in 1963 and its subsequent evolution into the Judges Education and Training Section of the Judges Committee, the education and training of judges had finally been formalized. Many judges' schools are held every year, plus trial judging of qualifying competitions, judges examinations and the like on a continuing basis. Where the system leaves off and what is still lacking is a system of accountability for the performance of judges, in both competition and test judging. In so far as referees and accountants are concerned, a comparable system of education and testing has been established in the Competitions Committee with the creation in 1988 of the Referees and Accountants Education and Training Subcommittee. It should be noted, however, that annual examinations for referees and accountants were initiated in 1955.

The Ladies figures started the figure skating events of the Games with 32 entries and took two days to complete. In the end, Peggy Fleming had a substantial lead over Gaby Seyfert of East Germany, while the battle for third place involved three skaters, Hana Masková of Czechoslovakia, Tina Noyes, and Beatrix Schuba of Austria. In the free skating, Janet Lynn, who had been 14th in figures, placed sixth in free skating to pull up to ninth place overall. Tina faltered a little in the free, placing seventh, to wind up fourth over all, behind Masková, who took the Bronze medal, with Seyfert winning the Silver and Peggy the Gold, for the third Olympic Ladies title for the United States. Schuba, who was third in figures, placed 12th in free skating to finish fifth overall, a pattern which would be repeated over the next few years and which would eventually result in the establishment of the short program for Singles.

While Peggy won, the pressure of being champion, the expectations of her country and the personal desire to skate the performance of her life were a tremendous burden, and she did not achieve the standard she had set for herself in the free skating. However, her style and musicality and other aspects of her skating more than made up for the technical flaws in the athletic content. This phenomenon would be repeated in the future, with such skaters as Scott Hamilton in 1984. It does not in anyway diminish the achievements of the winners, when the pressure placed upon them is considered. What is apparent, however, is that the likelihood today of a long "reign" by a champion is becoming more and more difficult and unlikely, since to the pressures already mentioned have been added to those of a commercial nature.

The Pairs event had 18 entrants, and here too there was great pressure on the favorites, Oleg and Liudmila Protopopov of the Soviet Union, the defending champions and the current World title holders. Tatiana Zhuk and Alexandr Gorelik, also of the Soviet Union, had returned to competition after a year's absence and were the principal and younger threat, since it was the relative "age" of the Protopopovs which made their defense even more intriguing! In the end, they defended the Olympic title with relative ease, receiving first place ordinals from all but one of the nine judges. Zhuk and Gorelik were a solid second, while Margot Glockshuber and Wolfgang Danne of West Germany took the Bronze medal. Cindy and Ron Kauffman finished a somewhat disappointing sixth, after placing fifth in the compulsory program, with a fall in the death spiral and a missed camel spin at the end in the free skating. Sandi Sweitzer and Roy Wagelein placed right behind them in seventh, while the young Jo Jo Starbuck and Ken Shelley finished 13th.

It was in the Men's event, however, that the major upset of the 1968 Games took place, with in this case, the "favorite" faltering in the figures and despite winning the free skating, failed to even make the podium. Emmerich Danzer of Austria had been the World Champion for the preceding two years, with his countryman, Wolfgang Schwarz, as the runner-up. After the figures had been skated by the 28 competitors, Schwarz was on top, as he usually had been in the past, closely followed by Tim Wood, second, Patrick Pera of France, a pupil of Pierre Brunet, a surprising third, with Danzer in fourth, Gary Visconti in fifth and John Petkevich eighth. Despite a valiant effort by Danzer in the free skating, which he won, he still finished fourth in the end, with Schwarz the unexpected Gold medalist. Wood won the Silver and Pera the Bronze. Visconti was in fifth, and Petkevich who was fourth in free skating pulled up to sixth. In the end it was a five to four decision for Schwarz over Wood, which while disappointing, at least promised well for the forthcoming Worlds in Geneva. At least, he had defeated Pera, who had won the Pre-Olympic competition. For the U.S., it was a good, but not spectacular Olympics, with one Gold and one Silver medal, but still a 100 perceent improvement over 1964.

The 1968 Worlds were held soon after the Games at Geneva, the first time in that great city and the second time in Switzerland in the past three years – but this time indoors! Virtually everyone who had competed in the Olympics was on hand, with one outstanding exception, which was Wolfgang Schwarz of Austria, who had promptly retired after his unexpected win in Grenoble. Perhaps he thought that lightning was not likely to strike twice! This meant that the battle for the title in the Men would involve the defender, Danzer, Wood and Pera, with Scott Allen returning to the scene in the place of Petkevich, to renew for what would be for the last time, his rivalry with Gary Visconti. After Tim Wood won the figures over Danzer, the possibility of the first Men's Gold medal in the Worlds since 1959 seemed likely, but it was not to be. In what was at the time a very controversial victory, Danzer managed to win the free skating and retain his title, with Wood second and Pera third. The pleasant surprise of the event was a fourth place for Allen over Visconti, who placed fifth.

The rivalry between Scott Allen and Gary Visconti had been an epic one, going back to 1959 in the National Novice Men, when Scotty was second and Gary eighth. They would meet in National, World and Olympic Competition 14 times over the next nine years, with the final tally being eight wins for Allen and six for Visconti. However, when their competition at the Senior level only is considered, it was a dead heat of six to six with Scott having the last laugh in Geneva.

In the Ladies, with the pressure having been relieved somewhat, yet still there, since to compete in the following Worlds as the Olympic Champion is just like a defense of the latter in effect, Peggy Fleming performed far better than in Grenoble, to win her third World Ladies title, with Gaby Seyfert, second, and Hana Masková, who that year happened to be the European Ladies Champion, third. Beatrix Schuba, on the strength of her strong figures, in which she had placed third, finished fourth overall, after placing 10th in the free skating, with Kumiko Okawa of Japan coming in a surprising fifth ahead of Tina Noyes. Janet Lynn, who had placed 12th in figures, was seventh in free skating to finish ninth.

This was the last competition for Peggy who retired from competition. She has enjoyed a long and distinguished career since, both as a skater, television commentator, wife and mother, and is perhaps the American skater best known to and beloved by the American public. It was she who carried the hopes of the U.S. back to the heights following the 1961 accident and probably did more, except for Sonja Henie herself, to popularize the sport in the United States through the new medium of television. One evidence of her popularity and the respect in which she was held, was her reception at the White House following her return from abroad at the invitation of President Lyndon Johnson.

In the Pairs event, the Protopopovs won their fourth title, with Zhuk and Gorelik again second, but this time, the Kauffmans skated far better than in Grenoble to again take third, as they had in Colorado Springs the prior year. Sweitzer and Wagelein were eighth, and Starbuck and Shelley were 11th.

Worlds after the Olympics in those days was always exciting because the ice dancers were once again on the scene, the event not yet having attained Olympic status. There had been another demonstration of it in Grenoble, the sixth time the discipline had been presented at the Games, and still without success. In the Dance event, Diana Towler and Bernard Ford won their third straight title, in the first British sweep of the medals since 1956. Judy Schwomeyer and James Sladky were fourth, moving up four places from the prior year, with Vicki Camper and Gene Heffron seventh. Back in sixth were Liudmila Pachomova and Alexandr Gorshkov of the Soviet Union, and in eighth Angelica and Erich Buck of West Germany, soon to be a factor on the scene in the future.

So while there would be the usual "downturn" in the post-Olympic year, due to the retirements expected, the 1968-1969 season ahead would be an exciting one, since the World Championships of 1969 were again returning to the Broadmoor in Colorado Springs after four years.

The usual post-competition season activity of the ISU Tour in Europe and the annual meeting of the Governing Council when the "business" of making rule changes for the coming year was traditionally enacted, were duly carried out, with the latter meeting being held in San Francisco for the first time. The Central California Inter-Club Association served as the host, with each of its 10 member clubs assuming separate roles in hospitality and the support for the meetings. One notable report to the meeting was that for the Memorial Fund, which revealed that the assets of the Fund had increased by more than 300 percent since 1965. The Association's the predicted deficit of $10,335 had turned into a modest "profit" of more than $5,000, due in large measure to the increase in registration fees, as well as to a $20,000 return from the 1968 Nationals in Philadelphia. At the same time, the fiscal year of the Association was also changed to commence on July 1st. An increase in the subscription price for Skating to $5.00 was also announced, in a further effort to reduce the substantial annual deficit of the magazine, due in part to the fact that the complete ordinal rankings for all the qualifying competitions had been published, requiring an additional 68 pages.

For the years from 1964 to 1967, these detailed results had been published in full-sized Competition Annuals, which had been sold separately, but the cost of their production had proven prohibitive and the results were therefore returned to the magazine. There is always a problem for an official magazine of a national organization in carrying out its responsibility to be a publication "of record" from the historical standpoint. In that regard, the magazine had always fulfilled that obligation to the fullest extent possible, including as it does, the records, not only of competitions, but also of tests passed. What has been lost from the magazine in recent years, due to the virtually exponential increase in the number of them all year round, are the results of the non-qualifying competitions, which is too bad in a way, as these results are often of great interest. There should be a way somehow, to distribute such information outside the magazine, perhaps in "cyberspace!"

From a technical standpoint, the compulsory Pair program, now to be called the "short" program, was revised to consist of six compulsory moves, as contained in three groups, with one of them to be announced by the ISU one year in advance. Basically, each group contained a lift, solo jump, pair spin, solo spin, death spiral and step sequence. With the influence of the Protopopovs, who invented all of them except the backward outside, to the death spirals included in the groups had been added the backward inside.

The increase in the number of international competitions was also beginning to be seen, with the announcement of the proposed John F. Kennedy International Memorial Winter Games in Lake Placid in 1969 and of the World University Winter Games, also to be held in Lake Placid in 1971. The competitions, however, would not in fact take place until 1970 and 1972.

With the end of the 1960's in sight, the beginning can readily be seen, not only in the rapid increase in the number of international competitions already alluded to, but also in the rise of participation in them by skaters from North America, since the Canadians would be following a parallel track.

Expansion At Home and Abroad (1969-1972)

For example, at the second Grand Prix Internationale de Patinage held at St. Gervais, in what would become its standard time frame of the next to the last week in August, for the first time a U.S. Team was present with excellent results. Jennie Walsh from Los Angeles won the Ladies; Patrick Lalor of Philadelphia and Stephen LeRoy of St. Paul placed fifth and ninth, respectively, in Men; Sheri Thrapp and Larry Dusich from Southern California won the Pairs, and Judy Schwomeyer and James Sladky, the Dance. In the 1968 Richmond Trophy, there were no U.S. entrants, but Eileen Zillmer, who was now representing West Germany, and had formerly represented the U.S. in that event, placed fifth.

The Fall meeting of the Executive Committee for 1968 was held in Chicago at the Marriott Moter Hotel. At the meeting the initial success of the Basic Tests Program was noted, with more than 7,500 already enrolled. The general appeal of the program was attested to by various proposals to film the tests; the need for which as a training tool was recognized.

The responsibility for judges schools was transferred to the Judges Education and Training Section of the Judges Committee (JETS) with an initial program for the holding of three sectional schools by the following spring.

In Dance, a complete revision of the diagrams for the compulsory dances was authorized to be included in the 1970-1971 Rulebook, an overdue revision, since the diagrams had become out of date with the international versions of the same dances.

The Publications Advisory Committee, which had included both USFSA and CFSA representatives, was discontinued, as the CFSA had decided to withdraw its recognition of **Skating** magazine as its official publication. The functions of the former committee were transferred to the Publications Committee. The magazine had been the official publication of the CFSA since 1933 and had faithfully reported Canadian skating news right from the beginning and would continue to do so, but to a much lesser extent than in the past. As time went on, it became increasingly difficult to obtain Canadian news as the former cadre of representatives north of the border gradually eroded away. The CFSA eventually started its own magazine, the **Canadian Skater**, but it did not last and subsequent attempts to maintain a magazine in Canada have not been successful. Even today, despite its size, there is still no official publication of the CFSA that appears on a regular basis.

Plans were announced for what would be the first ISU World Tour in North America in 1969, to include 13 cities in the United States and two in Canada. The limit of 15 exhibitions permitted would remain the standard for the ISU Tour for many years thereafter, with the Tour becoming a standard fixture of the schedule each season following the Worlds on the continent where the Worlds had been held.

Janet Lynn

The 1969 National championships were held in Seattle, with the big question being, who would be the new Senior Ladies champion, now that Peggy Fleming had retired? Among the contenders were three-time runner-up Tina Noyes from Boston, Janet Lynn from Rockford, fourth in 1967 and third in 1968, and Julie Lynn Holmes from Los Angeles, the 1967 Junior Ladies champion and sixth in 1968.

After the figures, the picture was "mixed," with the winner being Dawn Glab, representing Arctic Blades, followed by Tina Noyes, Julie Holmes and Janet Lynn in fourth. It would all come down to the free skating. Because of the pressure, none of the top ladies skated a clean program, but Janet Lynn was the best among them and took the title over Holmes, with Noyes relegated to third on a tie broken by total points, 107.40 to 106.81.

In the Men also, the skating was not of the best, with Tim Wood retaining his title, while John Petkevich, who had been third in figures, pulling up to second, ahead of former champion Gary Visconti. In fourth was Ken Shelley, who again did double duty, by taking second in the Pairs with partner Jo Jo Starbuck, behind the defending champions, Cindy and Ron Kauffman, who won their fourth straight title.

The Dance saw Judy Schwomeyer and Jim Sladky win their second title, with Joan Bitterman and Brad Hislop from Seattle, second, and Debbie Gerken and Raymond Tiedemann from New York, third. The Novice Ladies champion was Dorothy Hamill, representing Rye, N.Y., with Juli McKinstry of Santa Rosa second. Second in the Novice Men was Mahlon Bradley, who would become an orthopedic surgeon and later Chairman of the Sports Medicine Committee of the Association as well as a Team Doctor at the Worlds and Olympics.

The 1969 North Americans were held at Oakland, Calif., and in two of the four events, the results were clear and generally accepted. In the other two, there was controversy and disagreement, which was a forecast of the future and the ultimate fate of the championships. The 1969 version was the 23rd since 1923.

In the Men, Tim Wood was clearly the best and won the title in a unanimous decision over Jay Humphrey of Canada, who was followed by John Petkevich and Gary Visconti. In sixth and last place was Toller Cranston of Canada. It was the same in the Pairs, with Cindy and Ron Kauffman winning their second North American title with another unanimous

Tim Wood

decision over Jo Jo Starbuck and Ken Shelley, with the Canadian pair of Mary Petrie and Robert McAvoy, third. Melissa and Mark Militano from the U.S. were fourth, while Sandra and Val Bezic of Canada were sixth.

In the Ladies, the winner of the figures was Karen Magnussen of Canada, with Janet Lynn second, and Tina Noyes third. Julie Holmes did not do as well as at Seattle and was fourth. In the free skating, Janet Lynn pulled up to first to win the title over Magnussen, while Linda Carbonetto of Canada, who had been fifth in figures, pulled up to third, with Tina, fourth and Holmes, fifth. Janet won by a four to three vote, with the majority being the four U.S. judges on the panel and the minority the three Canadians. The Canadians are convinced to this day that the title was "stolen" from them, although it should be noted that Magnussen had to withdraw from the immediately following Worlds due to shin splints, and she had not skated up to her potential in Oakland. Equally, the U.S. contingent felt that Tina should have been third, and so on! The acrimony was vigorous and strong.

Then came the Dance event, in which Judy Schwomeyer and Jim Sladky were defeated by the virtually unknown Canadian couple of Donna Taylor and Bruce Lennie, who had been 13th in the 1968 Worlds (Schwomeyer-Sladky had been fourth). This time, one U.S. judge did vote for the Canadians, but the result was seen on the U.S. side with the same intensity of feeling as that of the Canadians with respect to the Ladies result! Clearly, the odd number of judges imposed by the ISU, with the majority being from the host country, was not working, and both nationalism and bias had crept into the championships on both sides. It was unfortunate that no action was ever taken by the CFSA and USFSA to attempt to correct the judging situation in the North Americans, such as, for example, requiring the use of one or more "neutral" judges. The medal count in 1969 was U.S. - three Gold, two Silver and two Bronze; Canada - one Gold, two Silver and two Bronze.

The 1969 World Championships again returned to The Broadmoor in Colorado Springs for the fourth time in 12 years, and were as usual an outstanding success, despite the obvious limitations of the arena, with its small seating capacity and lack of ventilation. With the departure of many of the leading skaters in the preceding Olympics, interest was at a high pitch as to who the new champions would be, with only the Pair and Dance titles being defended. There had already been an upset in the 1969 European Championships, when the new young couple from the Soviet Union, Irina Rodnina and Alexei Ulanov defeated the four-time champions, Liudmila Belousova and Oleg Protopopov. Rodnina and Ulanov's only previous appearance in an ISU championship up to then had been a fifth place in the 1968 Europeans.

In the Pair championship, Rodnina and Ulanov won the short program with the Protopopovs holding on to second, followed by Tamara Moskvina and Alexei Mishin of the Soviet Union, third, and Cindy and Ron Kauffman fourth. In the free skating, Oleg and Liudmila did not skate strongly enough to hold on to second, which went to Moskvina and Mishin, but they did stay ahead of the Kauffmans, who had yet another error in the death spiral, just as at Grenoble, which cost them their chance for a medal. Jo Jo Starbuck and Ken Shelley skated all out, having nothing to lose, and actually placed fourth in free skating ahead of the Kauffmans, to pull up from seventh in the short program to sixth overall. The Militanos placed eighth.

So an "era" came to an end, but the contribution of the Protopopovs to modern pair skating will never be diminished. Despite their "seniority" over their competitors, their extraordinary unison and use of choreography and music undeniably makes them one of the greatest pairs of all time. They had just reached the point where the strength and power of much younger rivals was too much for them, especially as the solo content in pair skating increased, a trend which has not always been best for the discipline, with unison still hopefully being the primary criteria.

In the Men, it was Tim Wood's championship all the way, with a string of excellent figures, of which over two thirds received marks well into the 5's. Except for an annoying tendency on the part of the American skaters to leave their centers slightly open, his figures were probably the last time in the Men's event that such quality was seen. His ultimate lead in figures over the European champion, Ondrej Nepela of Czechoslovakia was 125 points, while in the free skating he skated flawlessly, earning three perfect marks for artistic impression! While Nepela could do no better than sixth in the free skating, he held on to second place overall, because his lead over the next competitor was also substantial. In third was Patrick Pera of France, with Gary Visconti fourth ahead of John Petkevich, who despite a second place in free skating, could pull up only two places from his seventh in figures. It was the first Gold medal in the Men for the U.S. since 1959.

In the Ladies, Hana Masková, the Bronze medalist in the prior year, had retired to skate professionally. So it was Gaby Seyfert of East Germany, the Silver medalist, who became the new Ladies champion, although she was defeated in the figures by Beatrix Schuba of Austria, who was able to retain second place, despite a sixth in free skating. Third was Zsuzsa Almassy of Hungary, while Julie Holmes, who was fourth in figures, actually placed second in free skating, but was unable to improve her position, placing fourth overall, but still defeated Janet Lynn, who was fifth in both divisions, and did not reach the standard she had set in the previous two championships. There was no third U.S. lady, since Peggy Fleming had retired. She had been an individually "seeded" skater who could not be replaced with another skater under the then rules of the ISU.

In the Dance, Diane Towler and Bernard Ford of Great Britain won what was their fourth straight title, but it was in this event that the loss of the North American title was costly, as Liudmila Pachomova and Alexandr Gorshkov of the Soviet Union, sixth the previous year, placed second ahead of Judy Schwomeyer and James Sladky, who had been fourth in 1968 and now finished third. The North American champions, Taylor and Lennie, placed eleventh, with both of the other U.S. couples, Gerken and Tiedemann ninth, and Bitterman and Hislop tenth, ahead of them! In truth, however, the battle for second place was not a close one in so far as the judges were concerned, and the Soviet ice dancers were now firmly established as contenders for the future in Dance as well as in Pairs.

The Dance event was the first time the original set-pattern dance was skated, with a wide variety of rhythms and tempi, but in the initial round placements, the positions after the three compulsory dances did not change, nor did they change after the free dance, which has been the prevailing pattern in dance for many years, with the compulsory dance result essentially "calling the shot" for the final. Well remembered by the Americans was the "Peanut Polka" of Judy and Jimmy, a rhythm most suitable for their style, and which would be the forerunner for their later and better known Yankee Polka.

With the 1969 Worlds now history, the championships would not return again to the United States for another six years, consistent with the informal rotation that had developed with Canada, in which the championships came to North America every three years on an alternating basis between the two countries. While this format has not been precisely adhered to in the years since, it has become the general "rule of thumb" followed by the ISU Council in awarding the championships; with in effect, the policy of one year in Europe, one year in Asia if possible, and one year in North America out of every three years. The selection has, however, sometimes been adjusted depending upon the site for the Olympic Winter Games, which have not followed such a rotation.

The 1969 Governing Council journeyed for the first time to Tulsa, Okla., a well deserved award. The Tulsa Figure Skating Club, a member of the Association since 1940, was one of the leading clubs in the Midwestern Section and was also one that had provided and continued to provide leaders for the Association, such as George B. Jenkinson, Jr., who had been Vice President in 1948-1949 and 1959-1962, and Harold T. Leroux, who was Treasurer from 1954 to 1957 and Secretary from 1957 to 1960. The meeting was a small one in attendance, with 41 delegates from 28 clubs, plus the members of the Executive Committee, who were also present for their meeting preceding the Governing Council Meeting.

Henry Beatty, the General Chairman, reported on the success of the 1969 Worlds, with any "profit" from the championships to go directly to the Memorial Fund. Carl Gram, Jr.,who had recently been elected to the Executive Committee of the U.S. Olympic Committee, reported on the success of the first post-Worlds ISU Tour and indicated that a profit to the Association of more than $15,000 would be achieved. Finance Committee Chairman Ted Patterson reported with respect to the burdensome losses incurred by **Skating** magazine, especially during the last three years in the 8-1/2-by-11 format, and the recommendation of the Executive Committee to return to the 6-by-9 size was approved. Also to be studied was the feasibility of the incorporation of a subscription to the magazine in the registration fee for the first registered family member and all single memberships.

Kendall Kelley reported for the JETS on the success of recent judges' schools, especially for lower level judges. He announced that representatives of the JETS would participate in a panel discussion at the annual meeting of the PSGA, a step forward in greater cooperation with the other organizations in the skating world with a responsibility for its standards.

Efforts to "shore up" the somewhat rickety structure of the North American championships included a proviso that the Referee for the Ladies event not be from the same association as the Referee for the Men's event, and likewise, that the Referee of the Pairs not be from the same association as the Referee for the Dance; i.e., an equal division of the four assignments between the two countries. It was a fairly obvious requirement for a bilateral competition, but one not previously formally implemented. In the (in)famous championship of 1969, this division had been followed exactly!

Approved by the meeting under new business was a proposal made by James Poyner, President of the New York Regional Council of Figure Skating Clubs, which essentially permitted any two member clubs to submit proposals for changes in the By Laws and the Rules for action by the Governing Council. Mr. Poyner explained that the intent of the proposal was to make it possible for rule changes which had not received a favorable vote from the appropriate committee or the Executive Committee to be brought to the floor of the Governing Council meeting for vote by the club delegates.

This legislative "tool" has been frequently used since, usually through the offices of the Councils of Figure Skating Clubs, which by 1969 had reached eight in number, with three on the Pacific Coast, four on the East Coast and one in the Midwest. The number of such councils and inter-club associations would substantially increase over the next few years, so that by 1995 there would be 24 of them, broken down as follows: Pacific Coast - five; East Coast - 10; Midwest - nine, representing a majority of the member clubs in the Association. The inter-club councils and associations have been a strong voice on behalf of the member clubs in the Association, and have often served as the means by which qualifying competitions have been organized by a group of clubs working together. Up to date, however, no proposal has ever been made to provide them with an identity or position apart from the clubs they represent, so that they remain true to their prime directive of being responsive to and representative of their constituent clubs.

At the Fall 1969 meeting of the Executive Committee, which was held in Chicago as usual, back at the O'Hare Inn, it was reported that the "moderate but firm growth pattern over the past ten years has escalated into the largest one year gain in registration," from 25,805 in 1968 to 28,358 in 1969. Concern was expressed with respect to the ability of the Association to service the increased membership, especially in the area of tests given and the availability of judges for "this important primary function" of the Association. Much of the increase was attributed to the interest in the Basic Tests Program. This is all very reminiscent of the concern about the same problems in the 1990's. In connection with tests, the USFSA voted to drop the interchangeableness of USFSA and CFSA Tests. At that time, interchangeability was up to and including the Sixth Figure test and the Pre Silver Dance tests (CFSA Senior Bronze), which was also subject to the requirement to pass the applicable CFSA free skating tests, the USFSA not yet having them. Pair tests were not interchangeable. The dropping of interchangeability was implemented in the 1970-1971 Rulebook with the proviso that holders of the Eighth Figure, Gold Pair or Gold Dance Test could, upon application, take the comparable test in the other country without having had to have passed the preceding tests.

It was noted that the Figure Tests Committee had disapproved a PSGA proposal to allow Preliminary and First Test candidates to mark their centers. This change would eventually take place in 1977 for the Preliminary Test only. The PSGA had also proposed that there be free skating tests between the First and Third Test levels. This too was turned down, and yet would also arrive on the scene in 1977, a reflection to their credit of the persistence of the PSGA to pursue an agenda which they thought was best for the sport, which the USFSA did not at first perceive!

Another step forward, as previously noted, was the elimination of the category of a professional in other sports being a professional in skating and the broadening of the rights of the "restricted amateur" to participate in non-qualifying competitions. The category essentially was one of a person who was temporarily restricted for a specified period of time due to a "violation" of the rules covering amateurs. Among the examples were the accepting of gifts in excess of $25 for exhibitions, trying out for a professional ice show, participating in an unsanctioned exhibition (the "Kirby" rule), or being paid for active rink ownership or management, the key element of the rule.

Henry Beatty followed up on his earlier report to the effect that the 1969 Worlds would generate a potential benefit to the Memorial Fund of close to $25,000, the first really substantial revenue to flow from the championships. Although all the prior ones at The Broadmoor had not resulted in any loss to the USFSA, due to the generosity of Thayer Tutt and the Broadmoor management.

The increase in the number of international competitions was cited and it was indicated that some funding for participation in them might be obtained from the USOC, as a part of support for pre-Olympic training. The Association itself still was not supporting financially such participation to any significant extent.

The decision to include a subscription to **Skating** magazine in the registration fee at $5.00, with the fee for subsequent members of the same family being $2.00, was approved. It was pointed out that only one-third of all registered members were receiving the magazine on a voluntary basis. With respect to publications, the proposal to publish the Rulebook only every other year, with a supplement in between was approved and would first be implemented with the Rulebook of 1972-1973, actually published in the Fall of 1971. The two-year Rulebook would last until 1979, when the annual Rulebook was re-instituted. Because the Rulebook was not then loose leaf, but published with a plastic spiral binding, the supplements, which were hard bound and not looseleaf, could not readily be incorporated into the existing book. There was also a significant drop in revenue for the two-year book with many not bothering to obtain the supplement. That probably more than anything contributed to the end of the experiment. At the end of the period, the Rulebook cost $4.00 and the Supplement $2.50.

Since the loose leaf book was started in 1991, it has had the curious feature that when it is removed from its separate binder to be replaced with the next edition, it lacks front and back covers! What has actually happened, starting in 1993, is that there is now also an additional "Directory," which is also hardbound and not loose leaf, so we are back today to exactly what we had 20 years ago, except on an annual basis! The former Supplement and now Directory essentially contain the "back of the book," with all the appropriate lists of officers, committees, officials, clubs, etc., while the Supplement also had a page in the back reporting the changes made in the rules between editions of the full Rulebook itself.

Action was also authorized to protect the logo's and names used by the USFSA, such as "Skating" as a trademark for use in connection with the magazine, and "USFSA." These marks were subsequently approved and are still valid today. Actually, the "shield" design of the USFSA logo with its blue top with a skate in it, and red and white vertical stripes with "USFSA" over them, was first adopted in 1964 and is still in use today.

The end of an "era" was also recorded in October 1969, with the death of Sonja Henie at the age of 59 from leukemia. Her legacy was not only her unique record as a champion figure skater, but also the popularization of the sport, especially following her professional debut in 1936, although perhaps she herself would have regarded the art museum she established in 1968 in her native Oslo with her third husband Neils Onstad as a more lasting one.

Despite the increase in International competition referred to at the Executive Committee meeting, the "season" in that regard was still pretty much limited to the Richmond Trophy in England for Ladies, in which Suna Murray of West Orange, N.J., finished sixth, and to the Grand Prix de St. Gervais, in which the Ladies event was won by Debrah Lauer from Berkeley, Calif., while in the Men's event, James Stuart from New York was second and Gordy McKellen, Jr. of Lake Placid was fifth.

The full qualifying competition structure of nine Regionals and three Sectionals had almost 10 years of experience, the numbers for 1970 demonstrate the success of the system: Easterns - 101 entries; Midwesterns - 92 ; Pacific Coast - 99. The competitions cannot be compared exactly, because of the various optional (non-qualifying) events that could be held, such as Veterans Dance and also in the Regionals, Juvenile Singles. Actually, in the New Englands, a Special Juvenile Singles event was also held, which was for skaters within the proper age limit for Juveniles (under 13), but with one less test, while in the Northwest Pacifics there were even Sub-Juvenile Singles and a Preliminary Dance event and in the Central Pacifics, Pre-Juvenile Singles! In so far as the Regionals were concerned, the total entries were as follows: New Englands - 97; North Atlantics - 119; South Atlantics - 88; Eastern Great Lakes - 106; Southwesterns - 120; Upper Great Lakes - 96; Central Pacific - 123; Northwest Pacific - 143; Southwest Pacific - 165. As can be seen, the Pacific Coast Regionals were by far the largest. What is also very evident is that the vast majority of the entrants are females, with very few males and relatively small numbers of pairs and dance couples. The pattern has prevailed in the sport ever since, and was in effect "magnified" once the qualifying competition structure was settled in.

Prior to that, in the immediate post-War years, this imbalance was not as evident, although, of course, the ladies outnumbered the men even then. This phenomenon was also seen among the officials, with the majority of the judges being women, while the men continued to be the majority of the referees, there being then essentially no women in that category. Actually, of 17 National Referees and 19 Sectional Referees in 1969, not one was a woman, while of 90 National (Figure) Judges, 53 were women, and of 53 National Dance Judges, 36 were from the distaff side. The preponderance of women would substantially increase in all categories of officials over the years, so that today, men are the exception. (There was one World Championship for Men after the 1970's of which the only man on the entire panel of two referees and 10 judges [nine plus a substitute] was the author who served as the referee!)

The 1970 Nationals had 99 entries (remember that an entry in Pairs and Dance counts as one for the purpose of the total number of entries, not as two). Of course, the total number of "persons" participating will obviously be higher. In the Men's event, which had 11 entries, Tim Wood easily defended his title, with John Misha Petkevich second and Ken Shelley third. Ken continued his "dual" effort and he and partner Jo Jo Starbuck succeeded to the title vacated by the Kauffmans who had retired. Melissa and Mark Militano, representing Broadmoor, were second, with Sheri Thrapp and Larry Dusich of Los Angeles, third. In the Dance, Judy Schwomeyer and James Sladky successfully defended their title, with Anne and Harvey "Skip" Millier from Philadelphia, second, and Brad Hislop from Seattle with new partner Debbie Ganson, third. The Milliers had been fourth in 1968 and fifth in 1969 in their two previous appearances in the Senior Dance at the Nationals.

Jo Jo Starbuck and Ken Shelley

In the Ladies, Janet Lynn retained her title, with Julie Holmes second, and Dawn Glab from Arctic Blades third. The only new champions were Starbuck and Shelley, with the other three Senior titles being defended without undue difficulty. There was a mix of experience and youth on the 1970 World Team that would journey to Ljubljana, Yugoslavia, for the World Championships. Today, Ljubljana is the capital of the independent republic of Slovenia.

The championship had many problems of organization, with the lone ISU official on the scene and in charge being Vice President Jack Shoemaker. It was after this championship that Jack insisted that additional ISU officials be present at all ISU championships to supervise the conducting of the competition, such officials first being called "Technical Representatives" and later "Technical Delegates." Today, they are an essential part of any major competition, even at the National level, although the position has not been fully implemented in the United States, as compared with Canada, where the "Tech Rep" is a vital cog in the operation. In the U.S., there still is no definitive manual (called in the ISU the "Memorandum") as a guide to be followed by a local organizing committee for the conducting of championships. As a result, there is a great deal of "re-inventing of the wheel" each year. The lack of such a manual and a clear definition of the role of such an official and the requirement that such an official be present remains an important piece of unfinished business for the Association.

The "story" of the 1970 Worlds was the Dance event which with the retirement of Diane Towler and Bernard Ford of Great Britain, was wide open. The "favorites" included Liudmila Pachomova and Alexandr Gorshkov of the Soviet Union, Judy Schwomeyer and James Sladky of the United States and Angelica and Erich Buck of West Germany, who would be the leading contenders for the World title for the next several years. Judy and Jimmy had held the lead after the compulsory dances, including the original set-pattern dance, but could not hold it in the free dance and wound up second in a 5 to 4 decision. When one of the judges in the majority, from Great Britain, was asked why she had placed them second, she stated that "they were not the North American

Champions," even though Taylor and Lennie of Canada, who had won the North American Dance title in 1969 had retired and were not even in the competition! Thus was started the Soviet "dynasty" in Ice Dancing, which, except for Krizstina Regöczy and András Szallay of Hungary in 1980, Jayne Torvill and Christopher Dean in 1981-1984, and Isabel and Paul Duchesnay of France in 1991, has reigned supreme ever since. The 1970 championship is the closest that an American couple has ever come to winning the World title in Ice Dancing, one which still eludes the representatives of the United States. The other U.S. couples, Ganson and Hislop and the Milliers placed ninth and 10th, respectively.

Julie Lynn Holmes

In the Pairs, Jo Jo Starbuck and Ken Shelley placed fifth, moving up one place from the prior year, while Ken also placed eighth in the Men's event. The Militanos were eighth in the Pairs. The Soviet pair of Irina Rodnina and Alexei Ulanov retained the title, their second, with Liudmila Smirnova and Andrei Suraikin, also of the Soviet Union, second.

In the Ladies, Gaby Seyfert of East Germany retained her title, but now Beatrix Schuba of Austria, who won the figures and placed seventh in the free skating was second. A surprise third was Julie Holmes, third in figures and fifth in free, defeating Janet Lynn, who had a bad day in figures, placing eighth, although she was second in the free skating, to finish sixth overall. Dawn Glab was right behind her in seventh. In the Men, Tim Wood, retained his title, although he lost to Ondrej Nepela of Czechoslovakia in the figures, not being able to repeat his performance of 1969 in that discipline. He excelled once again in the free skating and received three perfect marks, just as he had the year before. John Petkevich was fifth in figures, and despite a second in free skating, did not move up and finished fifth overall.

This was still the era when the figures really counted for more than the prescribed value of 50 percent, primarily because they were judged on more realistic spreads, while the free skating was not, so that the value of the latter in the total points was lower than it should have been. This anomaly was caused by the fact that the marks for the figures were lower, with the real differences between the skaters being more accurately reflected in the marks; while in free skating, with open marking and the audience present, the marks were much higher and with little if any true difference between skaters being reflected in them. The irony of all this is that the part of the competition which was judged the best would be the ultimate cause of the progressive reduction in the value of the figures and the change in the scoring system which occurred in 1980. First there was the "problem" of the good figure skater being over marked in the free skating, which led to the creation of the short program in Singles, and then it was the problem of the good free skater being over marked in the figures, which led to their elimination!

In the final analysis, the 1970 Worlds produced three medals - one Gold, one Silver and one Bronze.

Immediately following the Worlds, a unique and as it turned out, one-time competition was held at Lake Placid, called the Kennedy International Memorial Winter Games. The Kennedy Games figure skating events were part of a larger competition, including other winter sports, but they were in themselves an important milestone for the USFSA, since they were actually the first International Competition (other than the North Americans) held in the United States, which was open to entrants from abroad. There were 10 countries represented, with 30 entries in three events, Men, Ladies and Pairs (there was no dance event). The competition would be a forerunner of the future Skate America competitions.

While the standard of the skating in the Games was not outstanding, it was still of a good quality, with most of the entrants being from the "middle rank" of skaters just below the World Team level. The United States did very well, winning both Singles events, with John Baldwin, the 1969 National Junior Champion, representing the Broadmoor and Gordon McKellen, Jr. of Lake Placid placing first and second, respectively, while in the Ladies, Joanne Darajky of New Jersey, fifth in the Nationals, was the winner, with Jennie Walsh of Los Angeles, third. In the Pairs, the West Germans Brunhilde Bassler and Eberhard Rauch were the winners, with Barbara Brown and Doug Berndt from Denver, the National Junior Pair champions, placing fourth, and Kathy Normile and Gregory Taylor from Buffalo, sixth. In the Men, a young skater from Great Britain named John Curry placed ninth.

Also held in Finland in the middle of the season between the Nationals and the Worlds was the 1970 "Polar" Universiade, which were the sixth University winter games sponsored by the Fédération Internationale du Sport Universitaire (FISU). Two U.S. skaters participated, Jenny Walsh of Los Angeles, second in ladies, and Roger Bass, also from Los Angeles, seventh in Men. They were accompanied by team leader Michael McGean of Dartmouth College, himself a former international champion in ice dancing with his wife Lois. It was the first time Americans had ever participated in the FISU games, which had been held periodically since the 1930's. The involvement in 1970 would provide the basis for future participation in the games of 1972, which were scheduled to be held at Lake Placid, N.Y., between the Olympic Games and the Worlds of that year.

The 1970 Governing Council meeting was held in New York City and represented yet another changing of the guard, with Spencer Cram stepping down, to be succeeded by another Ohioan, Frederick C. LeFevre of Troy. Although Spence was by now living in Hendersonville, N.C., and Islamorada, Fla., not known as centers of skating, he agreed to serve for the season of 1970-1971 as Chairman of the International Committee, a position he had previously held between 1965 and 1967. He was also Chairman of the Nominating Committee from 1970 to 1974, a duty often assumed by a Past President in those days. He also served as Chairman of the Rules Committee from 1973 to 1978 and as Chairman of the Skating Standards Committee from 1975 to 1978. He was elected an Honorary

Frederick C. LeFevre

member of the USFSA upon the occasion of his retirement as President, and is still with us today (1995) as the Senior Past President, or "001." At the meeting, Ritter was also elected an Honorary member of the Executive Committee in recognition of his 23 years of service to the Association.

In the summer of 1970, a team again was sent to St. Gervais, which included Richard Ewell, II, from Los Angeles, who placed fourth, on the strength of his free skating, after a sixth place in figures. The winner was John Curry of Great Britain. James Demogines, also from Los Angeles, placed seventh. In the Ladies, Mary-Lynn Gelderman of New York and Suna Murray of New Jersey placed second and third, behind Cathy-Lee Irwin of Canada; while in Pairs, Sheri Thrapp and Larry Dusich from Los Angeles were second to Sandra and Val Bezic of Canada. There was then no dance event at St. Gervais.

In the 1970 Richmond Trophy competition, there were actually two U.S. entrants, with Dawn Glab of Los Angeles, placing third and Cindy Watson from Tulsa 10th.

At the Fall 1970 meeting of the Executive Committee, which was held in Chicago, again at the O'Hare Inn, the division of the judges' lists into separate test and competition judges was approved, although it was not fully incorporated into the rules until 1971, when the separate categories of competition judges were established, with three on each side, in figure skating, of Junior, Senior and National, and in Dance of Bronze, Silver and National. Up to that time, there had been five categories of figure judges, all eligible to judge both tests and competitions, consisting of Low, Intermediate, High, Gold Test and National. Actually, the original structure in figure skating had been just three levels, Low, High and National, with the Intermediate Test judge being added in 1948. The Gold Test category had been added in 1967. On the dance side, there were also originally three categories, Bronze, Silver and National, with the Gold Dance Test category also being added in 1967. The National judge remained a "dual" category, that is equally qualified to judge both tests and competitions.

It was also during the early 1970's that the ongoing problem of participation by USFSA registrants in activities of the Ice Skating Institute of America (ISIA) became more serious. A skater who participated in an unsanctioned event was restricted for one year, which essentially meant out of competition. There were then four categories under the Amateur Status rules: the Amateur, with full participation; Restricted Amateur (A), someone temporarily restricted who could do everything except compete; Restricted Amateur (B) who was a reinstated skater who could participate fully except in qualifying competitions; and Professional in Skating, who were ineligible except to take tests and perform in sanctioned carnivals and exhibitions. The professional category then included professionals in the other ice sports of speed skating and hockey and also roller skating.

However, the "germ" of future cooperation between the Association and the ISIA was already beginning to thrive, with a recreational team competition being held in New York City in the fall of 1970, sponsored by the SC of Riverdale and sanctioned by the Association with USFSA referees and judges participating.

The 1971 Nationals were held at Buffalo, N.Y., at the end of January and were well organized under the auspices of the Buffalo Skating Club, one of the older clubs in the

Association, having joined in 1929. The Men's event was the only one of the four Senior classes in which there was not a defending champion, with Tim Wood having retired. So it was that John Misha Petkevich of Great Falls, Mont., and Harvard, became the new champion, easily defeating Ken Shelley of Arctic Blades and Gordy McKellen, Jr., of Lake Placid, who were second and third, respectively. Actually, by continuing to compete in more than one event, Ken Shelley was just one of several doing so in Buffalo. Melissa Militano from New York did Senior Pairs (second) and Junior Ladies (first); Sheri Thrapp from Los Angeles did Senior Pairs (fourth) and Senior Ladies (eighth); while Johnny Johns from Detroit, competed in Senior Men (sixth), Pairs (eighth) and Dance (third)! Tenth place in the Men went to Charles Tickner of California.

In the Ladies, Janet Lynn continued her U.S. supremacy by winning her third title, with Julie Holmes, now representing Tulsa, who won the figures, second, while Suna Murray, now from New York, placed third. Fifth was Dorothy Hamill of New York, the 1970 Junior runner-up, in her first Senior competition at Nationals. Juli McKinstry of California, the 1970 Junior Ladies Champion, placed ninth.

The Pair title was retained by Jo Jo Starbuck and Ken Shelley, with the Militanos second and Barbara Brown and Doug Berndt of Denver third. In Dance, Judy Schwomeyer and Jim Sladky still reigned supreme, taking their fourth title and performing their Yankee Polka in the original set-pattern dance, which would eventually be accepted by the ISU in 1975 as one of the standard international compulsory dances. The Novice Men's winner in 1971 was Terry Kubicka from Arctic Blades.

The 1971 North Americans were held at Peterborough, Ontario, and little was it known that this would be the last in the long line of this distinguished event. With Karen Magnussen of Canada in good health, she easily overturned the 1969 loss, winning the Ladies title by a six to one margin, so there was no question of the authenticity of the decision this time. Janet Lynn placed second and Suna Murray third. The CFSA did, however, complain about the absence of Julie Holmes, thinking that she was the U.S. Ladies Champion, which she was not! In the Men's event, John Misha Petkevich won the title over Toller Cranston of Canada, winning the figures and losing the free skating, somewhat of a reversal of form for him. Third was Ken Shelley and fourth was Gordy McKellen, Jr. The modest surprise of the event was that Ron Shaver of Canada finished no better than fifth.

In the Pairs, Starbuck and Shelley added the North American title to their collection, with the Militanos second and the Bezics third. In Dance, it was a U.S. sweep, with Schwomeyer-Sladky finally taking the title that had eluded them in 1969, with the Milliers second and Mary Karen Campbell from Lansing and Johnny Johns from Detroit third. The final medal count was: U.S. - three Gold, three Silver and three Bronze; Canada -one Gold, one Silver and one Bronze.

In April 1972, a meeting of the North American Committee, which was a joint one between the USFSA and CFSA, was held at Toronto, ostensibly to discuss the arrangements for the 1973 North American championships, to be held at Rochester, N.Y. Representing the USFSA, were Charles Foster, the chairman of the committee, Ritter Shumway and Ben Wright. Representing the CFSA were Donald Gilchrist, George Blundun and John McKay. Much to the surprise of the U.S. representatives, the CFSA representative opened the meeting by proposing that the championships be discontinued forthwith, citing, among other reasons: "1. The imbalance of judges between the countries; 2. The timing of the championships (between the National Championships of the two countries and the World Championships); 3. The adverse effect of North American placements on those in the Worlds, resulting in an unwillingness of skaters to compete; 4. No guarantee that the top skaters will compete; and 5. That the championships were no longer of prime importance as a training vehicle for officials in view of the increase in foreign international competitions." Accordingly, there being no other alternative in a bilateral situation and no proposals being made by either side on ways and means of restructuring the championships to accommodate the problems raised, the committee voted to recommend the discontinuation of the championships to their respective associations.

At the same time, Mr. Wright urged that a cooperative effort be made to determine and implement what could be done to hold international competitions on the North American continent in the future, and to that end proposed that a permanent inter-association committee be established, with the committee also to be empowered to consider all matters of mutual interest to the two associations. It was accordingly voted to recommend to the two associations that a "North American Committee" be established, to consist of three members from each Association, with the two Presidents serving ex officio and the chairman being elected by the committee from among its members. With respect to the existing North American Championship trophies, it was agreed that they be recalled from the present holders and returned to the respective association of which they were the property. These were the Weld Trophy for the Ladies, Layman Trophy for the Pairs, and the Trophies presented by the Rochester Institute of Technology and Ritter Shumway for the Dance, going back to the USFSA, with the Rogers Trophy for the Men and the Connaught Cup for Fours going back to the CFSA.

What was not known to the USFSA or its representatives at the time of the meeting was that plans by the CFSA to establish their own International Competition, to be called "Skate Canada," were already well advanced, with sponsorship agreements already in place. So the CFSA had, in effect, no room to negotiate to continue the North Americans, had proposals to do so been made by the other side. It was a "fait accompli." While hindsight is always 20-20 vision, it is clear, in the light of subsequent experience, both with Skate Canada and Skate America, that the championships could readily have been saved and continued, simply by adopting the format developed for the two internationals, by making them "open" or invitational, with foreign officials being used. In any event, it was not to be, and so the 1971 North American Championships were the last.

There had been 24 championships in the 48 years from 1923 to 1971, with one, in 1945, for Ladies only. Looking first at the championships won, the record is as follows:

	Men	Ladies	Pairs	Fours	Dance	Total
Canada	13	11	14	5	5	48
United States	10	13	9	2	8	42

As can be seen, the Canadians had the greater success in the Men, Pairs and Fours, while the United States was superior in Ladies and Dance.

With respect to the total number of medals (1st, 2nd, 3rd) won, the record is as follows:

Canada	23	34	32	10	11	110
United States	44	38	36	10	28	156

Here, the significant difference is in the Men's event and the Dance event, although the United States also has the slight edge in the Ladies and Pairs as well, with only the Fours, of which there were seven competitions, being even. The Dance event had 13 competitions, with the first in 1947.

The 1971 Worlds were held at Lyon, France, with the free skating events being skated in the Palais de Sports, an arena with a temporary ice surface, and Rolba ice resurfacers which scurried around very rapidly, usually leaving poor quality ice in their wake! The practice sessions were held in the modern Patinoire Cours Charlemagne arena right on the bank of the Rhône River which runs through the city. The principal interest was focused on the Men's and Ladies' Singles events. The title in both was vacant, with Tim Wood and Gaby Seyfert of East Germany both having retired. Returning to defend were Irina Rodnina and Alexei Ulanov in Pairs and Liudmila Pachomova and Alexandr Gorshkov in the Dance, both from the Soviet Union.

The Ladies event quickly demonstrated that the compulsory figures were still the deciding factor, with Beatrix Schuba of Austria "in a class by herself" in them, setting a standard similar to that of Jeannette Altwegg of Great Britain 20 years earlier. Her lead was so great, that despite a seventh place in free skating, Trixie still won the title by eight of the nine judges. Once again on the podium, in second place this time, was Julie Lynn Holmes, the only skater to come close to Schuba in the figures, which, despite a fifth place in free skating, also kept her in second. In third was Karen Magnussen of Canada, the new North American Ladies Champion, with a fourth in figures and a second in free to edge out Janet Lynn, the reigning U.S. Ladies Champion, who actually won the free skating. The other U.S. lady, Suna Murray, finished 10th after a poor performance in the figures of 14th, followed by an excellent effort in free skating.

None of the top skaters in the free portion of the event skated completely without error except for Janet Lynn, who was rewarded with two perfect marks. The crowd reaction during the awards ceremony was vociferous in support of Janet, which was finally ameliorated only by a brief appearance by her at the edge of the ice. As the reporter of the championships said, "When Janet received her final ranking of fourth place, the crowd only remembered her sparkling free skating, neglecting to account for half her total, the figures, in which she had placed only fifth. Whistling at the winners and roaring for Janet, the viewers also forgot that she had not received a unanimous first in free skating by the judges. The ensuing situation was unfortunate in that the three winners, were somewhat slighted of their due glory, in spite of justly earning their places."

It was probably at that moment, that figures began to "die," although it would take 19 years for it to actually happen, but the public, media and especially television, simply could not understand an event in which the final result was decided by a largely unseen and essentially unknown part of the competition. The first major step in adjusting the "balance" would occur in the same year, when the short program for singles was adopted by the 1971 ISU Congress in Venice, to become effective for the 1973 season.

In the Men, with the title also open, Ondrej Nepela of Czechoslovakia quickly established his supremacy in the figures to win the title, with Patrick Pera of France, coming second, followed by Sergei Chetverukhin of the Soviet Union, the first Soviet man to make the podium in the Worlds since Nicolai Panin of Russia had done so in 1903! John Petkevich had to settle for fifth place, with a fifth in figures and a fourth in free, behind a new rising young star from East Germany, Jan Hoffman, who was second in the free skating. Ken Shelley placed eighth, after a ninth in figures, not his best performance, while Gordy McKellen, in his first Worlds, placed ninth, despite an 11th in figures and a 10th in free skating! Toller Cranston is found at 11th and John Curry at 14th, just to mention two rising stars.

In the Pairs, Rodnina and Ulanov continued their dominance, with Liudmila Smirnova and Andrei Suraikin, also from the Soviet Union, again second, but the pleasant surprise of the event was the solid third place of Jo Jo Starbuck and Ken Shelley who beat out three German pairs, two East and one West, as well as the third Soviet pair. Melissa and Mark Militano did equally as well, placing sixth, while Barbara Berndt and Doug Brown were 11th.

In the Ice Dance competition, it was again a three-way battle between Pachomova-Gorshkov, the Bucks and Schwomeyer-Sladky. The three couples were so relatively close, that the "politics" of the situation could have had an effect, which in this case resulted in the Bucks taking second and relegating the Americans to third, even though they had no less than three of the nine first place ordinals. Judy and Jimmy had done their usual excellent compulsory dances in which they placed second, and with their Yankee Polka also being described as "fabulous," there was the general feeling that they had once again been "robbed!" They had to skate first in the free dance; there was no "seeded" draw in those days, and their free dance, while more athletic and difficult than that of the Bucks, lacked the style and flow of the latter. But such is the fate of ice dancing; no one is very completely satisfied with the results. In the end, it was the Soviets with five firsts, the Germans with one and the Americans with three, but they also had three thirds and one fourth, so lost the Silver medal by a greater majority of second places, six to five. The Milliers placed ninth and Campbell and Johns, 10th.

In the final analysis, the U.S. had done well in what might have been considered as a slightly "off" year, winning one Silver and two Bronze medals.

The 1971 Governing Council meeting was held at Santa Monica, Calif., with delegates representing 62 member clubs in attendance. Among the actions taken was an amendment to the By Laws to further reconfigure the composition of the at large membership of the Executive Committee, which had been since 1961, one group of 18 all elected together for a one year term. The new provision provided for the election of three groups of six at large members from each Section for a one year term. Also added as a voting member of the Executive Committee was the Chairman of the Olympic Figure Skating Committee, which, when that committee (of the USOC) was discontinued in 1976, would in 1977 become the Olympic Representative, that person who represents the Association on the Board of Directors of the USOC. At the same time, the limitation to a one year term only for the immediate Past President as a voting member of the Executive Committee was dropped, so that such person remains a member for as long as he or she is in that position.

Another action taken, which may seem somewhat esoteric to the uninformed, was an authorization to change the legal status of the Association from a Rhode Island corporation to a Massachusetts Business Trust, the latter being a recognized in the law as a form of non-profit legal entity. The change was made to facilitate the obtaining from the Internal Revenue Service of the required charitable exemption for the Association under Section 501(c)(3) of the Tax Code, since the Memorial Fund was also a Massachusetts Trust and held the same exemption.

Reported to the meeting concerning the financial condition of the Association was that its assets were $279,754, its revenues $263,186 and its expenses were $227,140, for the year ending June 30, 1971.

A three-minute free skating program was added to the Fourth Figure Test, which meant that there was now free skating in four (4th, 6th, 7th and 8th) of the nine figure tests. Also dropped was the use of factors in figure tests.

It was also announced that the offer of The Skating Club of Boston to house the USFSA Museum had been accepted, and that the Museum Committee would be restructured accordingly.

An amount of up to $1,000 was approved at the fall meeting to cover the costs of the transfer from the Broadmoor to Boston.

A memorial resolution was adopted for the late George B. Jenkinson, Jr. of Tulsa, who had passed away in December 1970. George had been a Vice President, Chairman of the Competitions, Membership, Midwestern and Nominating Committees, an International Referee, National Dance Judge and Honorary member of the Executive Committee. It was a long-standing policy of the Executive Committee to honor the memory of those of its deceased members who had also served as officers and committee chairmen of the Association, by the adoption by both it and the Governing Council of appropriate memorial resolutions.

The 1971 ISU Congress held at Venice, in addition to adopting a short program for singles, as previously noted, took several other actions which directly affected the USFSA. One was a redefinition of an International Competition to be one for which the invitations to participate are made by the organizing ISU Member to one or more ISU Members and the entries are made by ISU Members. This made clear that the numerous competitions which were being held in border areas and summer centers (such as Lake Placid), involving U.S., Canadian and perhaps other foreign skaters, were not International Competitions and did not need to be held under ISU Rules or with International judges. This rule has been known ever since as the "Shoemaker rule!" Another basic change made was to determine the starting order for the new short programs from the results of the figures, and for the free skating from the results of the short programs, which corrected the sometimes unfortunate instance of a top ranked skater in the previous part having to skate first in the final free skating.

The sum of $21,000 was donated to Memorial Fund to cover expenses of the competitors in the 1972 Nationals, up to $150 each, the first attempt to assist more than just the top few skaters.

Since 1971 marked the 50th year of the Association, the anniversary was principally observed in three ways. The June 1971 issue of **Skating** magazine was dedicated to it, with a series of articles by the incumbent President Fred LeFevre, Past Presidents Hank Beatty, Harry Keighley, Kendall Kelley, Ritter Shumway, Jack Shoemaker, and Spencer Cram covering the previous 25 years, in a format similar to that followed in 1946. Each Past President wrote as he saw fit about his term of office. In addition, there were several other articles by Dick Button, Bob Sackett, Tenley Albright Gardiner, Michael McGean and Ed Bold writing about their own experiences during the period in question. In addition, a special medal was struck in bronze and silver in a limited edition by the Franklin Mint, with the entire proceeds from their sale accruing to the Memorial Fund. The obverse side showed skaters from each of the four disciplines (Men, Ladies, Pairs, Dance), while the reverse carried the USFSA shield and the 50th Anniversary inscription.

The major event in observance of the anniversary was a gala series of exhibitions for the benefit of the Memorial Fund held at Madison Square Garden in New York City at the end of November 1971. From the past came many of the former champions, including Theresa Weld Blanchard, Sherwin Badger, Roger Turner, Suzanne Davis King, Robin Lee, Joan Tozzer Lincoln, Jane Vaughn Sullivan, Arthur Vaughn, Jr., Dick Button, Yvonne Sherman McGowan, Red Bainbridge, Lois and Michael McGean, Sonya Klopfer, Hayes Alan Jenkins, Tenley Albright Gardiner, Carol Heiss Jenkins, David Jenkins, Monty Hoyt, Yvonne and Peter Betts, Lorraine Hanlon, Scott Allen, Sally and Stan Urban, Darlene Streich and Bucky Fetter, Nancy Ludington Graham, Ron Ludington, Vivian and Ronald Joseph, Cindy and Ron Kauffman, Gary Visconti and Tim Wood, plus the entire 1971 World team and the Ann Arbor Hockettes.

Some, but not all of the former champions took to the ice and showed surprising skill, despite the passage of the years. Dick Button handled the commentary and also announced that highlights of the event would be aired on television at a later date. As the reporter of the event states, "We saw skating presented simply, authoritatively, and classically by the greatest, most talented, young skating athletes of today…and yesterday. The evening's program was closed by the 1971 U.S. Men's Champion, John Misha Petkevich, paying tribute to Theresa Weld Blanchard, America's first lady champion of 1914 and the co-founder of **Skating** magazine. Mrs. Blanchard sat nearby in an open sleigh as John, skating in his usual magnificent fashion in an original program, brought to an end the 50th Anniversary of the USFSA."

Also in November of 1971, the new Owen Memorial Trophy, emblematical of the Ladies Championship of the United States was presented to Janet Lynn on the occasion of the "Skating Spectacular" show sponsored by the Genesee FSC. The original trophy for the Ladies National Championship, the Gertrude Cheever Porter Trophy, in competition since 1933, had "disappeared" after the 1968 Nationals and had not been found, so that it was declared to have been retired and a replacement was provided. Ritter Shumway offered to present a new perpetual trophy and also suggested that the Skating Club of Boston join in the presentation of the new trophy, since so many of those lost in the 1961 airplane accident were from that club, which occurred at the beginning of Mr. Shumway's service as acting President of the USFSA. The new trophy was duly presented to Janet by Mr. Shumway, the President, Ted Buck and Secretary, Henrietta Dane of the Boston club and Professor Hans Christensen of the Rochester Institute of Technology and the creator of the new trophy. There is a curious footnote to this story, which was that the Porter Trophy was subsequently discovered in a box in storage in the Broadmoor World Arena, where it had been sent to Peggy Fleming in 1968, but was never delivered to her! Appropriately, the trophy is now on permanent display in the World Figure Skating Museum on the other side of the Broadmoor from the site of the Arena, now gone and replaced with additional hotel rooms.

With 1971-1972 being another Olympic year, the entire competition schedule was "speeded up," with everything a month early. Despite this acceleration, the modest International Competition schedule was maintained, with yet another team going to St. Gervais and meeting with considerable success. Robert Bradshaw from Los Angeles placed second in the Men, with David Santee of Chicago sixth. In Ladies, Dorothy Hamill of New York and Juli McKinstry of Colorado Springs finished one-two, while in Pairs, Cynthia Van Valkenburg and James Hulick from Los Angeles were second, and Gale and Joel Fuhrman from Rye, N.Y., were third. The record of the U.S. skaters at St. Gervais continued to improve. It was an important win for Dorothy Hamill in her first international competition. The participation at St. Gervais was supported by Olympic Development funds for the first time. In the Richmond Trophy for Ladies, there was but one U.S. entrant, Julia Jean Johnson from Los Angeles, who placed eighth.

The 1972 Nationals returned once more to the Los Angeles area after a nine-year absence, again at Long Beach in the same venue as in 1963. In a significant upset, Ken Shelley dethroned John Misha Petkevich as the National Men's champion by reason of a strong performance in the free skating, coupled with a solid and close second in the figures. John did not skate his best, falling once and two-footing another triple jump. Third was Gordy McKellen. Since Ken also successfully defended his National title in Pairs with Jo Jo Starbuck, their third, he thereby became the first skater at the Nationals to hold two Senior titles at the same time, since Eugene Turner, also from Southern California, had done so in 1941! In the Pairs, Melissa and Mark Militano, representing New York, again placed second, with Barbara Brown and Doug Berndt of Denver again third, the same order as in the previous year.

In the Ladies, the "dual" was between Janet Lynn, the defender and Julie Holmes, who had beaten her in the Worlds three years in a row. Julie again won the figures, but could not hold her lead against Janet's inspired free skating, to again finish second, with Janet winning her fourth title. Third was Suna Murray from New York, with Dorothy Hamill, also from New York, fourth, after placing second in free skating.

In the Dance, Judy Schwomeyer and James Sladky won their fifth title, equaling the previous high since the Dance Championship had been inaugurated in its modern form in 1936, of a total of five by Lois Waring of Baltimore. However, she had won with two different partners, Red Bainbridge in 1947-1949 and with her future husband, Michael McGean in 1950 and 1952, and her titles were not all consecutive, so Judy and Jimmy's five in a row really were a new "record" which also would be equaled by Judy Blumberg and Michael Seibert in 1986. Ann and Skip Millier of Philadelphia were second and Mary Karen Campbell of Lansing and Johnny Johns of Detroit, third. Fifth in the Dance were Jane Pankey and Richard Horne from Wilmington, Del., who were the World Champions in roller ice dancing.

It was at the 1972 Nationals, that the use of the computer to calculate the results was once again used and this time successfully. The earlier effort in 1968 in Philadelphia where IBM set up machines on site and produced incorrect results had made the USFSA understandably suspicious of computers! The creator of the program used, called HAL, was Al Beard of Phoenix, who was then a computer designer for Minneapolis-Honeywell. He began to develop the program in late 1970 or early 1971, as an exercise in learning programming. It was developed in the FORTRAN programming language, which was used on Honeywell computers on time sharing systems. Al was encouraged to go ahead by Chuck Foster, the Competitions Committee chairman, with the assistance and support of Roy Winder, who was then a Vice Chairman of the Competitions Committee for "Special Projects," a position which Al himself has held ever since, and Roy's wife Jean, both of whom were National Accountants. Al first used the program at the Southwest Pacific Regional, running on a time sharing system in Minneapolis, using an 800 number for remote access, with a serial hard copy terminal at site. By the end of the second weekend of the competition (which is usually held over two separate weekends two weeks apart), unofficial computer results were posted for the first time. As Al himself said in a letter to the author, "The USFSA has not been the same since."

With the support of his employer, Al went on to the 1972 Midwesterns to run the program with equally successful results, so that it was inevitable that he would be invited to the Nationals in Long Beach. At each of these championships, Minneapolis-Honeywell donated equipment and the time sharing facilities. Al reminded the author, who was the Referee of the 1972 Nationals, that even though the computer produced results were then "unofficial," with manual accounting still being required for final result verification, the computer results were still used (happily, with no ill effects) for the purpose of making the awards, without waiting for the pencil pushers to come up with them!

An article in **Skating** magazine in March 1972, by Jean Winder, entitled "Hal Hits Nationals," reflects the first use of the name for the program. Of course, it is purely coincidental that two of the three letters in the name happen to be "AL," and that the famous Arthur C. Clarke science fiction classic, "2001," in which there is a runaway computer named "Hal," just happened to have been published a few years earlier!

After more than 10 years of the successful use of the time sharing facilities of Honeywell in Minneapolis and Phoenix for eventually all 13 qualifying competitions, plus the Nationals and later the International and World Championships held in the United States, the decision was made to introduce personal computers in 1984, after a particularly harrowing experience using the Honeywell time sharing system at the 1984 Nationals. As Al relates the story, "Immediately before the start of the live telecast of the Championship Ladies, one of our computers went down and the other required access through a noisy marginal telephone line. We entered marks on only one machine and were in imminent danger of losing our connection to it. Luckily, the results were produced normally at the conclusion of the event so no one knew how close we were to having no computer all." HAL was ported to the PC in time for testing during the 1984-1985 season and the use of the Honeywell machines was discontinued in the 1985-86 season.

Ever since, PC's have been used at all qualifying competitions, and in more recent years, have also fed the marks directly from the scoreboard to the computers, so that results are virtually instantaneous once an event ends. Al Beard has continued to support and guide the program, annually making the necessary changes to it required by the changes in rules. No one has served more faithfully and well than he in this very special and absolutely vital aspect of competitive skating. He is truly the "leader" of all the accountants. Of course the "on line" snooping that took place, with the results of competitions going on at the same time in different parts of the country being downloaded and posted was lost when PC's were introduced. There was also the "mailbox," certainly a forerunner of "e-mail," where questions could be posted and on which Al, watching from afar, would issue admonitions and advice to those working on the front lines!

The 1972 Olympic Winter Games were held at Sapporo on Hokkaido, the Northern island of Japan, a remote location, but with excellent facilities and a very well run Games, the Japanese having had good experience in doing the Summer Games in Tokyo in 1964. The U.S. had a young team, which hoped to challenge for the medals. There were no defending champions from four years earlier, as is usually the case with the Olympics, and the reigning World champions are considered to be the "favorites." As it turned out, "Gold" was not in the cards in 1972, and there would be but one medal, a Bronze, keeping the "streak" alive, but top 10 finishes were common and as a team, the U.S. did well. The irony of the situation was that there were three fourth-place finishes, and as has often been said about the Olympics, the fourth place finisher is usually forgotten. It is perhaps the toughest place for the competitor to finish in, so close and yet so far.

In the Men, Ondrej Nepela of Czechoslovakia won easily on the strength of his figures, although he placed only fourth in free skating. The Silver medal went to Sergei Chetverukhin of the Soviet Union, a classic stylist and despite the lack of a World or European title in his record, probably the best Soviet/Russian male skater of all. He was just a little ahead of his time. He won the free skating after a third place in figures to sew up his Silver medal. In third was the redoubtable Patrick Pera of France, second in figures and eighth in free, but hanging on to pick up his second straight Bronze medal, at the expense of Ken Shelley, fifth in figures and third in free. John Petkevich, with a sixth in figures and second in the free, could pull up only one place to fifth, to just stay ahead of the young Jan Hoffmann of East Germany, who had been fourth in the figures and finished sixth after a 10th in free. Gordy McKellen placed 10th. It almost seemed as if an elevator was in operation, with those in figures who did not free skate well, moving down, but not enough, and those in free skating who had not done well in figures, moving up, but again not enough!

In the Ladies, came the one medal earned by the United States. Beatrix Schuba of Austria, again was totally dominant in figures, to nail down the Gold medal, despite her "usual" seventh or so place in free skating. She still won by all judges. Second was Karen Magnussen of Canada, third in figures and second in free, to hold on for the Silver, over Janet Lynn, fourth in figures and first in free, including one perfect mark, taking the Bronze. She finally turned the tables on Julie Holmes, second in figures, but eighth in free, who placed fourth. Suna Murray, the third U.S. skater, had a disastrous performance in figures, placing 13th, but managed a ninth place in free skating to pull up one place to 12th.

In the Pairs, Irina Rodnina and Alexei Ulanov of the Soviet Union, confirmed their supremacy by taking their first Olympic title, but it was not their best performance, and they were closely pressed by their teammates Liudmila Smirnova and Andrei Suraikin, who actually took three first places. Perhaps, however, Irina was somewhat distracted by the fact that her partner Ulanov had become enamored with Smirnova, which resulted in the breakup of his pair with Rodnina at the end of the 1972 season to skate with Smirnova, whom he eventually married, leaving Irina to find a new partner. Third was the strong East German pair of Manuela Gross and Uwe Kagelmann, as the GDR sports machine was beginning to show its strength in the discipline, just as they had already demonstrated in the Ladies with Gaby Seyfert and now Sonja Morgenstern and Christine Errath, sixth and eighth in the Ladies, respectively. Jo Jo Starbuck and Ken Shelley were a good fourth, but could not break through into the medals. Melissa and Mark Militano placed seventh, while Barbara Brown and Doug Berndt were 12th.

So using our "placing summary" from the 1960's, it was Men - fourth, fifth, 10th; Ladies - third, fourth, 12th; Pairs - fourth, seventh, 12th. The Team Manager of the 1972 Olympic Team was Carl W. Gram, Jr. of New York, who was also serving as the USFSA representative to the U.S. Olympic Committee, and who had done much to obtain Olympic development funds to support the training and competition expenses for the top skaters. Carl was also the Chairman of the Television Committee of the USFSA from 1961 to 1968, responsible for the negotiation with the networks for the sale of the rights to the Nationals, especially. He had also been a Vice President and the Treasurer of the Association. Sadly, he would pass away unexpectedly in 1973, well before his time.

As previously noted, the Seventh World Winter University Games of FISU, also known as the Winter "Universiade," were held at Lake Placid, N.Y., in between the Olympics and the Worlds, and despite the little time to regroup, were well attended. In the figure skating there were 10 Men, 10 Ladies, only two Pairs and six Dance couples, from 10 nations. The U.S. did win the FISU Gold medal predicted by Michael McGean in 1970, when John Misha Petkevich won the Men's event over Vladimir Kovalev of the Soviet Union. Dean Hiltzik from New York was sixth. In 10th and last place was Igor Bobrin of the USSR, a future European champion. In the Ladies, Jennie Walsh from Southern California did it once again, to win the second Gold medal for the U.S., with Julia Jean Johnson, also from Southern California, third, and Louise Vacca from Long Island, a former National Junior Ladies champion, fifth.

In the Pairs, there were but two entries, with Debby Hughes and Phillipp Grout, Jr. from Denver, providing the competition to the experienced winners from the Soviet Union, Galina Karelina and Georgi Proskurin. In the Dance, Debbie Ganson and Brad Hislop from Seattle placed third, while Susan Ogletree from Detroit and Gerry Lane from Boston were fifth. The first two places were controversial, with Elena Zharkova and Gennadi Karponosov of the Soviet Union winning over Diana Skotnicky and Martin Skotnicky of Czechoslovakia. Karponosov would become an Olympic champion just eight years later in the same town in another controversial decision, while Skotnicky would become a leading dance coach, well known for his work with Isabelle and Paul Duchesnay of France and Susanna Rahkomo and Petri Kokko of Finland. In the FISU event, it was the opinion of all (other than the judges!) that the Czech couple should have won! With the excellent showing achieved in the 1972 Universiade, the U.S. in the future would seek to find collegiate competitors to enter, with considerable success.

The 1972 World Championships returned to Canada once again, after 12 years, this time again in the West at Calgary, Alberta. There was the usual "fallout" among the competitors, this time with Julie Holmes turning professional immediately after Sapporo and being replaced by Dorothy Hamill. In the Men, Nepela retained his title, for his second, with Chetverukhin second and Kovalev, third. This time, John Petkevich skated well to place fourth, with Ken Shelley, sixth and Gordy McKellen, seventh. The free skating, however, was won by Toller Cranston of Canada, who had placed ninth in figures, so finished in fifth place.

In the Ladies, without Julie Holmes to challenge her in the figures, Trixie Schuba still piled up a huge lead, but this time could do no better than ninth in the free skating, so was challenged a little more by Karen Magnussen of Canada, who was second in both parts, and Janet Lynn, third in figures and first in free skating, with two more perfect marks. Dorothy Hamill, in her first Worlds, placed eighth in figures and fifth in free to finish seventh, with Suna Murray right behind in eighth place.

In the Pairs event, Rodnina and Ulanov concluded their partnership with yet another title, their fourth, over Smirnova and Suraikin. However, Jo Jo Starbuck and Ken Shelley, after a disastrous short program, including a fall, in which they placed sixth, recovered well and skated brilliantly in the free to place second in that part and wind up third overall, ahead of Gross-Kagelmann. The Militanos were ninth and Brown and Berndt, 14th.

In the Dance, it was once again the three-way battle between Pachomova-Gorshkov, the Bucks and Schwomeyer-Sladky, with the final result in that order, the same as in 1971. The Milliers placed seventh and Mary Karen Campbell and Johnny Johns, 10th. The continuing issue then and now was the tendency of the European dance couples to include more Pair skating elements in their free dance programs, such as lifts and even a "mini"-death spiral (by the Bucks), while the North American couples stuck closer to the rules, used more dance holds and did programs generally true to the ballroom. As has been seen, however, this approach has never been successful, when obviously, the majority of the judges are from Europe and are schooled in that tradition. In retrospect, no U.S. Dance couple deserved more and received less than Judy and Jimmy, and this scenario has been repeated since, with two notable examples, Colleen O'Connor and Jim Millns and Judy Blumberg and Michael Seibert.

The 1972 Governing Council meeting was held in Cleveland, the first time in that city. A memorial resolution was presented by Henry Beatty for Sherwin Badger of Boston, who had been the USFSA President in 1930-32 and 1934-35, as well as a National and North American champion and Olympic Silver medalist, World judge and Honorary member of the USFSA. Almost ironically, at the fall meeting of the Executive Committee, a memorial resolution was presented for Henry Beatty himself, who passed away in August of 1972. Hank had also been a President of the USFSA, from 1946 to 1949, an ISU Council member, World Referee and Honorary member of the USFSA. Also presented was a memorial resolution for Henry Heebner of Philadelphia, who had served as a Vice President, Secretary, committee chairman and referee and judge, who had passed away in May of 1972. There was yet a further death of note, that of H.L. "Jack" Garren of Lake Placid, the long-time builder and manager of the Olympic Arena and founder of the SC of Lake Placid, who passed away just one day before Henry Heebner.

At the Governing Council meeting, delegates from 62 clubs were present. A report on the financial results showed a marked increase of 38 percent in the assets of the Association to $385,039, with revenues also up 20 percent to $319,344, and expenses also rising, but happily at a lower rate of 13 percent.

At the fall meeting of the Executive Committee in Chicago, it was voted to provide that loops would be skated last in all figure tests and that there would be free skating only in the Fourth, Sixth and Eighth Tests. An increase in the fee for the second member of the family of an Individual member from $10.00 to $15.00 was approved. Historically, because as a practical matter, Individual members have no one to represent them, the fees applicable to them have been raised many times unilaterally without regard to the merits of the increase in relation to the value of the benefits received, a classic example of which was an increase in 1994 of 100 percent!

So, the 1968-1972 Olympic cycle came to an end, to start anew in 1973.

With the 1972 Olympics behind them, the top skaters could look forward to the next season with anticipation since, for Singles at least, there would be major changes in the composition of the events. The number of figures was reduced from six to three, and the short program authorized by the 1971 ISU Congress would come into effect. The figures would now be

Cooperation as a Policy
(1973-1976)

worth 40 percent of the total score, the new short program 20 percent and the free skating 40 percent. The short program groups initially included six compulsory elements, basically calling for an Axel, a Double Axel, a jump combination which could include one triple, a flying spin, a spin with change of foot and a step sequence. At the same time, the number of groups for the Pairs short program was increased from three to four, with one group to be drawn annually, excluding the group skated the prior year.

In the ranks of the top skaters, in addition to Julie Holmes, John Misha Petkevich had also retired, as had Jo Jo Starbuck and Ken Shelley, Judy Schwomeyer and Jim Sladky, so only Janet Lynn returned as a defending National champion, the inevitable situation after each Olympic year.

Actually, the first test of the short program took place at the late summer competitions of 1972, with St. Gervais first, to be followed by the new competition for the Nebelhorn Trophy at Oberstdorf, FRG. These two competitions, which were held one week apart at the end of August would eventually become a package as the "Coupe des Alpes," with one team going to both. In this year Oberstdorf came first, although in later years St. Gervais would be in that position, with the team traveling by bus or train from one to the other. While St. Gervais still did not include a Dance event, that discipline was part of the Oberstdorf competition. The shifting of the balance away from the figures was immediately apparent in the success of the U.S. team in both events; Robert Bradshaw of Los Angeles won the Men's event in both, with Terry Kubicka of Arctic Blades, the 1972 National Junior champion second. In the Ladies, Wendy Burge, also from Southern California, the 1972 National Junior Ladies champion, won at Oberstdorf and was second at St. Gervais after a sixth place in figures, but won the free skating. Patricia Shelley, Ken's sister, was sixth at St. Gervais and third at Oberstdorf. Cozette Cady from Troy, Ohio, and Jack Courtney from Wilmington and Gale and Joel Fuhrman from New York exchanged Gold medals in Pairs. The Fuhrmans were the winners at St. Gervais and Cady-Courtney at Oberstdorf. In the Dance event at Oberstdorf, Mary Karen Campbell and Johnny Johns were the winners, so it was a U.S. sweep of all four events at Oberstdorf plus two out of three at St. Gervais. These two competitions would become, in the future, a staple of the international competition schedule.

The effect of the rule changes could also be seen at the Richmond Trophy where the unexpected winner was Dorothy Hamill. After placing fifth in figures, Dorothy won both the short and the long programs to become the first U.S. winner of that prestigious competition. Second was Karin Iten of Switzerland, a disciple of the "Schuba" school (strong figures and weak free), who had defeated Wendy Burge at St. Gervais. Iten won the figures but placed no better than fourth and fifth in the two free skating programs. Juli McKinstry of Santa Rosa finished sixth after placing third in free skating. Fifth in the competition was Dianne de Leeuw of the Netherlands, while ninth was Anett Pötzsch of the GDR, just to look ahead a little. The Richmond competition of that year is also remembered as the one in which the "roof fell in" when a section of the roof dropped on the ice during the skating of Lynn Nightingale of Canada. Happily, Lynn was at the end of the ice at the time and was not injured. Richmond had taken a bomb during World War II, which was probably the cause of the accident, although the 60-year-old building had been recently inspected and found sound.

The 1973 Nationals were held at Bloomington, Minn., a suburb of Minneapolis, a long distance, especially in winter, from the sunny California of the previous year. There was indeed a new cast of characters in the Men's event, in which Gordy McKellen, third in 1972 gained a decisive victory over his competition. Second, following his summer success was Robert Bradshaw, fifth the previous year, while third was the young David Santee of Chicago, the Junior champion of 1971 and eighth in 1972.

Janet Lynn had returned to make one more try to win the elusive World title in the Ladies which she had pursued so diligently since 1968. The first hurdle to that objective was to retain her National title, which she did but not without some difficulty, since she placed second in both figures and in the new short program. In the figures, the leader was Diane Goldstein of Denver, while the winner of the short was Dorothy Hamill. Janet turned it on in the free skating, however, receiving three perfect marks to overtake Dorothy and win her fifth straight title. Juli McKinstry edged past Goldstein to place third to take the third berth on the World Team.

With Jo Jo Starbuck and Ken Shelley having retired, the title in the Pairs went to Melissa and Mark Militano of New York, the runners-up of the previous three years. The young brother and sister pair of Gale and Joel Fuhrman, also from New York, were second. Third place went to Johnny Johns of Detroit with a new partner, Emily Benenson from Wilmington. The winners of the Junior Pairs were Tai Babilonia and Randy Gardner from Southern California. In the Dance there was a small upset of a sort. With Schwomeyer and Sladky gone, the vacant title went to Mary Karen Campbell from Lansing and Johnny Johns of Detroit who defeated the runners-up for the past three years, Anne and Skip Millier from Philadelphia. In third place were the former World roller dance champions, Jane Pankey and Richard Horne from Wilmington and in fourth were Colleen O'Connor and Jim Millns from Rockford, Ill. Johnny Johns had again proved himself a durable competitor by winning medals in both Pairs and Dance.

So it was on to Bratislava (Pressburg, to give it its Hapsburg name), in Slovakia, a part then of Czechoslovakia, not far from Vienna on the Danube river. The Zimny Stadion, or Winter Stadium, earned its name since it was extremely cold, with skylights open at the top through which a little snow occasionally drifted. The hotels were also "borderline" at best. All in all, it was a bit grim; no Western newspapers, no television or radio and so on. This was life behind the "iron curtain." In a sense, the championship itself was also grim. There were two incidents in the Pairs alone which were a cause for concern. The most famous was the failure of the music of Irina Rodnina with her new partner Alexandr Zaitsev, and their refusal to stop, continuing to the end of their program without music, for which they were ultimately marked. Despite this they still won her fifth title and his first. The other incident involved the Militanos, the music of whom started too fast, at which they stopped and restarted but again had to stop, following the shooting of metal staples onto the ice by the audience using rubber bands as slingshots. The ice had to be cleaned and the Militanos skated at the end after all the other pairs. While they did fairly well, the tension of the interruptions was detrimental to their performance and they did not do their best, placing eighth. The Fuhrmans, the other U.S. pair did their best in their first Worlds and finished 13th. As a result of the incident concerning the champions, the rules were subsequently revised to require a skater to stop when directed to do so by the referee when there is a failure of the music or a failure of equipment. In such a case the skater is allowed to either reskate at the end of their group or, if possible, to immediately continue from the point of interruption. The rule, which is known as the "Rodnina" rule would come into play in another famous incident in a European Championship in 1989 involving also the then World champions. One of the not so funny aspects of the two incidents was a subsequent investigation by the authorities to determine whether there had been sabotage of the music system. None was ever reported and the uncertainties of electric power in the Eastern Bloc were much more likely to have been the cause. The runners-up to Rodnina-Zaitsev were her former partner, Alexei Ulanov with his new partner and wife, Liudmila Smirnova, while Manuela Gross and Uwe Kagelmann of the GDR were again third.

There was yet another controversy in the Ladies, this time involving Janet Lynn. After placing second in figures to Karen Magnussen of Canada, Janet had an unexpectedly poor short program in which she placed 12th, missing both her jump combination and the Double Axel. The marks were all over the lot, with the judges having a hard time to decide the severity of the penalties to be imposed for the failures. There were no specific guidelines then and the system of mandatory deductions from the first mark (for required elements) for failures had not yet been added to the rules. There were those who thought the penalties should have been much more severe than they were in some cases. Janet recovered from this disaster and went on to win the free skating, but it was too late, with Karen Magnussen, winning the title on solid performances in all three parts to become the first Canadian lady to win the World title since Petra Burka in 1965. Karen's performance reflected one of the first principles of the new type competition, figures-short-free, which was to be consistent and do well in all three parts. Dorothy Hamill, somewhat ignored in all the turmoil, after an eighth in figures did a businesslike job, with a third in the short program and a second in the free skating, to finish fourth. The Bronze medal went to Christine Errath of the GDR, the new European Ladies champion. Juli McKinstry, the third American lady, finished a creditable ninth.

The Dance event was now down to a two-way battle between Pachomova-Gorshkov and the Bucks, with Schwomeyer-Sladky having departed. The Bucks did the Ravensberger Waltz in the original set-pattern Dance (which would, in 1975, be accepted as a new compulsory dance), but it was not enough and they could not overtake the champions. Mary Karen Campbell and Johnny Johns finished sixth, confirming the National decision over the Milliers who placed 10th, so the fortunes of the U.S. in Dance were down a little.

In the Men, Ondrej Nepela, a native of Bratislava, had been persuaded to continue for one more year to skate in the World championships in his home town. He once again put up his usual lead in figures and held on to win his third title, with a second in both the short program and the free skating. The short program was won by Toller Cranston of Canada but he could do no better than fifth in the free skating, to remain fifth. Gordon McKellen placed seventh and Robert Bradshaw 12th. There was no third U.S. man since the named skater of the prior year, John Petkevich, had retired.

In a sense, despite the Silver medal for Janet Lynn, the 1973 championships were somewhat reminiscent of the record of the U.S. in more recent years, with mixed results and disappointments. From the placement standpoint it was: Men - seventh, 12th; Ladies - second, fourth, ninth; Pairs - eighth, 13th; Dance - sixth, 10th.

The 1973 Governing Council meeting was held in Boston for the second time after 15 years. It was an appropriate location since it was at this meeting that Fred LeFevre stepped down after three years as President and was succeeded by Benjamin Wright of Belmont, a suburb of Boston. Fred continued to serve the Association in many ways, including the chairmanship of the International Committee from 1974 to 1977 and of the Judges Committee from 1977 to 1980. He was also chairman of the Nominating Committee for four years from 1974 to 1977. Perhaps his most important post-presidential service was as chairman of the Grants and Allocations Subcommittee of the Memorial Fund from 1980 to 1988. This is the body which determines the amounts and the recipients of grants from the Memorial Fund to assist with training expenses which Fred carried out with diligence, fairness and tact. The strength of the Memorial Fund owes much to his work in that regard. He ultimately retired to Williamsburg, Va., in 1988, where he passed away rather unexpectedly just after his 80th birthday in 1993. He had also been a National Referee and Gold Test Judge, and was an Honorary member of the Association and of the Executive Committee.

Benjamin T. Wright

Among the business conducted at the meeting was a revision to the Figure Tests to make the free skating portion of the Fourth and Sixth Tests optional, unless the tests were to be used as a qualification for entry in competition. A three-time opportunity to retake the free skating (if failed) without a time limit was also included. The free skating in the Eighth Test remained mandatory.

The gala banquet following the meeting was honored with the presence of Theresa Weld Blanchard, the first National Ladies champion and Dick Button, the first World and Olympic champion from the United States, both of whom made choice remarks directed towards the new occupant of the chair.

Then it was on to the 1973 Congress of the ISU in Copenhagen, where lightning would strike a second time, when the new USFSA President was also elected to membership on the Figure Skating Committee of the ISU by the margin of just one vote over his Soviet rival and later colleague, Valentin Piseev! It was the first time that the Figure Skating Committee had included an American among its members, and was also the first time since 1965 that the USFSA had been represented on both the Council and a Technical Committee. Remarkably, as it seems today, two of the other members of the Committee were a Canadian, Donald Gilchrist and an Englishman, George Marsh, while the new chairman was Sonia Bianchetti of Italy. It was an English-speaking committee which would last in that mode only until 1977. Jack Shoemaker was re-elected as the First Vice President of the ISU, as the other U.S. representative to that body.

At the Congress, the modest progress towards a liberalization of the strict amateur status rules continued, although at a snail's pace. This process has been going on for 25 years and is not over yet. This time, participation in an unsanctioned competition or exhibition was redefined to be a violation of the rules of the ISU Member. Another really major change was the permitting of advertising and sponsorship contracts if made by the ISU Member (the national association), with the display of personal advertising being prohibited during Championships, Competitions and the Olympics. The short program for Singles was expanded to include a seventh element, a spin combination, with the Double Axel becoming mandatory in two of the three groups and the Double Lutz in the other.

The system developed in the U.S. of factoring down was adopted, in which the total points awarded by a judge for the figures were divided by the factor for free skating, with the short program marks being divided by two. The resulting reduced total has added to it the two marks for the free skating, a system which substantially speeded up the obtaining of the final results, especially with manual accounting. Also eliminated were the various tie breaking rules after total points, so that, if the total points were the same, the skaters in question would be tied. These revisions were largely the idea of Jack Shoemaker. The famous old rule of having to receive an average mark of 4.0 in any part of a competition to win a title was deleted. If it had remained in the rules, no one would have been crowned a World champion in Singles since the average of the marks in the figures in most instances was below 4.0.

In the summer of 1973, a team was again sent to St. Gervais and Oberstdorf and, surprisingly, enjoyed almost the same success as in the prior year, winning five of the seven events. There were new faces on the scene which augured well for the future. At Oberstdorf, John Carlow, Jr., from Arctic Blades, the 1973 National Junior champion was the winner, with Charles Tickner from Denver second. Kath Malmberg from Rockford won the Ladies, with Linda Fratianne from Los Angeles second. Tai Babilonia and Randy Gardner, the 1973 National Junior Pair champions from Los Angeles, were the winners in Pairs while in the Dance, Jane Pankey and Richard Horne placed third. At St. Gervais, Tickner was the winner, with Carlow fourth. Fratianne defeated Malmberg to take the Ladies while Babilonia-Gardner were third in the Pairs. It was an auspicious beginning to yet another new generation of skaters. In the Richmond Trophy there were two U.S. entrants; Donna Arquilla of Denver, placing fourth with a second in free skating and Linda Fratianne, who placed eighth. The winner was Dianne de Leeuw, the Dutch-American, representing the Netherlands.

Now, for the first time, the familiar pattern that we know today of international competitions began with the first Skate Canada being held at Calgary. This first Canadian international competition did not include Pairs for several years, since its founder and organizer, George Blundun, was strongly dance oriented and had been elected to the ISU Ice Dance Committee in 1971, the first Canadian to gain membership on that committee. The U.S. did not send its strongest team to Calgary and, actually, some of the old North American caution can still be seen in the selections by the two Associations for their respective international competitions, with rarely the best skaters of one country going to the competition in the other. As a result, Canada won both Singles events with Toller Cranston and Lynn Nightingale, while the Dance went to Hilary Green and Glyn Watts of Great Britain, at that time the World Bronze medalists. The U.S. results in the three events in the first Skate Canada were Terry Kubicka from Arctic Blades eighth in the Men; Juli McKinstry from Colorado Springs fourth in the Ladies, and Anne and Skip Millier from Philadelphia fourth in the Dance. Third in the Dance were Irina Moiseeva and Andrei Minenkov of the Soviet Union, who would soon make a name for themselves in the forthcoming Worlds.

Since 1973 was also the 50th Anniversary of **Skating** magazine, the first issue of which was published in December 1923; there were feature articles in it recounting the inspiration of Theresa Weld Blanchard and Nathaniel Niles in launching the publication so soon after the Association was founded. It may well be that **Skating** is now the oldest periodical in the sport in continuous operation, especially since publication was not interrupted during the War. There are very few magazines today published by the national associations around the world, with all those presently active being independent commercial ventures. It was also in 1973 that Cyril Beastall of England passed away, the long-time editor of **Skating World** (an excellent British magazine), with the inevitable result that the magazine too died. This has often been the pattern of such projects so perhaps the sponsorship by the Association, which was maintained despite annual losses, has had a major role in the magazine's longevity. By this time, the subscription list was up by more than 5,000 to 25,000 and black ink was now seen on the books although, even up to today it is, as our present Treasurer says, a cost center, as distinguished from a profit center.

Under its various editors the magazine has continued to evolve and reflect the ever-changing sport and its constituency. For example, with the increase in the number of international competitions a new column, called "Foreign," which would later become "Ice Abroad" was added, in addition to such basic columns as "People" and "Newsmakers." What is somewhat missed today is the old "Rockers and Counters" column, which reported the news of the clubs, although an abbreviated form of "Club Notes" was retained for some years but has now also disappeared, as did also the "Carnival Merry-Go-Round."

At the Fall Meeting of the Executive Committee, which was held at Chicago at the O'Hare Inn, there took place what was described as a milestone and the major achievement of the current administration, with the approval of the joint policy statements agreed upon between the Association and the Ice Skating Institute of America. Negotiated by the President with his counterpart, Robert Kelton of the ISIA and materially assisted on the USFSA side by E. Newbold

Black, IV, then of New York and Chairman of the Olympic Figure Skating Committee with Walter Muehlbronner, then President of the PSGA as the impartial third party, the statements ended the years of wrangling over unsanctioned events and the participation of USFSA registered skaters in them. The USFSA recognized the role of the ISIA in promoting the activity of ice skating for the recreational skater, so that participation by USFSA members who were also registered with the ISIA in events sponsored by it would not be a violation of the rules of the USFSA. On its side, the ISIA recognized the USFSA as the governing body of the sport of figure skating on ice in the United States and with the same reciprocity with respect to ISIA registrants participating in USFSA events. A mechanism for the resolution of any disputes at the local level was addressed with the revival of the Rink Cooperation Committee, with the three Sectional Vice Presidents serving as the resolvers on the part of the USFSA.

Since then, building on the base thus established, relations with the ISIA have been cordial and ongoing, and there is a real will in both organizations to work together with the PSGA in the overall interests of the sport and of the industry that supports it.

Noted at the Fall Meeting of the Executive Committee was the death of Abbot P. Mills of Washington who had served as a Vice President and Committee chairman. The Committee again authorized the donation to the Memorial Fund of an amount sufficient to provide to each competitor in the Nationals the sum of $150 to assist in defraying travel, training and living expenses. Also approved was the use of computers to process the results for the Nationals, two Sectionals and one Regional.

One action taken by the Executive Committee was to raise the mileage allowance to 12 cents (from 10 cents) and the per diem allowance to $30 (from $25). Also noted was that there were 14 full-time employees at the Central Office, including the magazine staff. Since the 1975 World Championships had been awarded to the United States once again by the ISU, it was also announced that the ISU Tour following the Worlds would be carried out by the International Holiday on Ice Company of Minneapolis (Morris Chalfen). Actually, competitive bids had been solicited from Holiday on Ice, the Ice Follies and the Ice Capades organizations, with Chalfen winning the bid, largely on the basis of a substantial up front guarantee to the Association. Such a guarantee has been a feature of all the contracts for the Tour since. After the death of Chalfen in 1979, the Tour has been produced by his former protegé and colleague, Tom Collins.

The increased international activity continued with skaters going for the first time to the Prague Skate competition in Prague, Czechoslovakia, in November of 1973. Wendy Burge and David Santee each took a Silver medal in their respective events. The Canadians were also doing the same thing and the Ladies winner was Lynn Nightingale, while the Men's winner was Frantisek Pechar of Czechoslovakia. All this activity was unusual in those days due to limited funding, so each new competition entered was an adventure for the skaters and officials with the team leaders and judges now also involved. Today, the whole process of preparation is routinely handled by the National Headquarters.

The 1974 Nationals returned to New England for the first time since 1962 and this time to Providence, R.I., where the championships of 1930 had been held in the old Rhode Island Auditorium, home of the Rhode Island Reds minor league hockey team. This time, with the sponsorship of the **Providence Journal-Bulletin** newspaper, the Nationals were held in the brand new Civic Center in downtown Providence, a part of the renewal of that area which is still going on even today. The chairman of the organizing committee was future President Claire Waters Ferguson, the daughter of Dr. Nelson F. Waters, a former standing committee chairman and Honorary Member of the Executive Committee. It was a well-run championship and very convenient for all concerned, with the principal hotel next door to the main arena.

With Janet Lynn having retired to take up domesticity and to become a mother after a relatively brief professional career, the Ladies championship was up for grabs. Dorothy Hamill, the overwhelming favorite, did not disappoint and won an across the board victory in all three parts and captured her first Ladies title. In the runner-up spot was Juli McKinstry, representing the Broadmoor while in the third position was Kath Malmberg from Wagon Wheel in Rockton, Illinois. In fourth place was Wendy Burge from Los Angeles, who pulled up after a ninth place in the figures and a third in the free skating to take fourth overall.

Gordy McKellen returned to defend his Men's title of the previous year and this time was challenged by young Terry Kubicka from Arctic Blades, the 1972 Junior champion. Third and winner of the figures was Charles Tickner from Denver.

The Pairs reflected the turmoil in that event with not one of the prior year's seven pairs returning intact. Four had split up and the other three had suffered injuries so that only five pairs finally competed, the smallest number in some years. This has often been the prevailing pattern in the discipline since, as Pairs have become more difficult and

Dorothy Hamill

257

more dangerous. Out of the split-ups two new pairs were created, one of which was that of Melissa Militano with Johnny Johns, her brother Mark having turned professional. Melissa and Johnny were clearly superior to the others, winning her second title and his first. This gave Johns a unique double since he had already been the champion in Dance in 1973 with Mary Karen Campbell. Tai Babilonia and Randy Gardner from Los Angeles, the 1973 Junior Pair champions were second, on a fast track towards their ultimate destiny. Erica Susman and Tom Huff from Los Angeles were third, while another new partnership of Cynthia Van Valkenberg and Phillipp Grout, Jr. were fourth.

Anne and Skip Millier remained the perennial runners-up once again in Dance, losing this time to Colleen O'Connor and Jim Millns from Colorado Springs, who had been fourth in 1973 to their second. The Milliers appeared to overstep the bounds a little this time with the introduction of pair type elements into their free dance, resulting in their finishing fourth in that part of the championship. Michelle Ford from Phoenix and Glenn Patterson from Arctic Blades were third, a couple whose free dance was sometimes controversial, although this time it earned them second place in that part and almost won them the Silver medal.

Barbara Smith of Arctic Blades added the Junior Ladies title to her Novice Ladies win of the prior year, the first back-to-back double since Carol Heiss in 1951-1952. In Junior Men, the winner was none other than Randy Gardner of Los Angeles, despite a mishap in which one of his skate blades came off completely during the free skating. However, after repairs he reskated and performed well enough to win the title, becoming one of those few who have won both Junior Singles and Pairs, an increasingly rare feat.

Colleen O'Connor and Jim Millns

The 1974 Worlds were held at Munich, Germany, in the Olympiahalle, which had been the gymnastics hall for the 1972 Olympic Games. There were those involved both in 1972 and at the Worlds in 1974, notably Jim McKay of ABC, who had vivid memories of the terrorist attack on the Israeli team which was very much in their minds less than two years later. In the Munich Worlds, there was also drama and trauma of a much less severe sort.

One interesting facet of the championships was the invitation extended to all the former World champions, one of whom was Anna Hübler Horn who with Heinrich Burger, had been the first World champion in Pairs in 1908. Karen Magnussen had retired so the favorites in the Ladies were Christine Errath of the GDR, the European Ladies Champion, Dorothy Hamill and Dianne de Leeuw of Holland. The local favorite was Gerti Schanderl, skating in her hometown. Karin Iten of Switzerland was the winner of the figures; but with a 14th in the short program and a 17th in the free skating she was out of contention for the medals. She still finished a surprising fifth. Christine Errath was second in figures and won the short so was in the best position going into the free skating. Gerti Schanderl skated just before Hamill in the free and the displeasure of the audience at the marks that she received resulted in an ongoing demonstration, which Dorothy mistakenly thought was aimed at her. Twice, she tried to take her place on the ice to start, but to no avail. Finally, she retreated from the ice to the security of the two team leaders, Doctors Hugh Graham and Franklin Nelson, both future USFSA Presidents. The audience eventually calmed down and began to demonstrate their support for her so she went out and skated the best of all, winning the free skating and with it the Silver medal. Dianne deLeeuw was third, while Kath Malmberg and Juli McKinstry were seventh and eighth, respectively.

There was yet another incident in the Men's competition, also affecting a U.S. skater. This time it was Terry Kubicka in the short program, when the strap under his instep came unhooked and was dragging on the ice. For some unknown reason, the referee failed to take any action until Terry finally stepped on the strap and fell. He was then permitted to reskate but finished in 15th place after another fall. In the free skating he performed well, to place eighth and to finish in 12th place overall. Gordy McKellen made in the free what would have been an early attempt to do a triple Axel but fell, although he skated well otherwise, to finish sixth overall. It should have been Toller Cranston of Canada's championship, but an eighth place in figures doomed him to third place overall. He won both the short program and the free skating to win the small medal then awarded to the best figure skater and the best free skater. To the small medal was attached the unofficial designation of "champion" in that department, although there still was but one World champion, in this instance Jan Hoffmann of East Germany, despite a fifth in the short program, wound up on the top of the podium. Toller was bracketed by two Soviet skaters, Sergei Volkov in second and Vladimir Kovalev in fourth, as the Soviet men continued to build on the legacy of Sergei Chetverukhin.

Happily, the Pairs event was routine with no major mishaps. Rodnina-Zaitsev and Smirnova-Ulanov were again in the top two positions and two more East German pairs third and fourth. The best Melissa Militano and Johnny Johns could do was eighth while Tai Babilonia and Randy Gardener finished 10th. Among the top six pairs, only Sandra and Val Bezic of Canada could crack the Bloc front, with the other five places being taken by three Soviet and two East German pairs. At that time, the depth in the event was extraordinary, with the Soviets and the East Germans being by far the strongest pair skating countries.

The Dance, too, was peaceful and was featured by the memorable original set-pattern dance of Liudmila Pachomova and Alexandr Gorshkov, the Tango Romantica. It would be the third new compulsory dance accepted in 1975. The level of the event may have been enhanced by the fact that the addition of Ice Dancing to the Olympic Winter Games had finally been approved to start in 1976, so the incentive for the top couples to continue for two more years was substantially increased. Here too as in Pairs, the depth in the discipline was very evident. Among those participating were no less than four present and future World champion couples. This was the fifth title for Liudmila and Alexandr but the British were making a modest comeback, with Hilary Green and Glyn Watts second, ahead of Natalia Linichuk and Gennadi Karponosov, another Soviet couple. Fourth were Irina Moiseeva and Andrei Minenkov, yet another Soviet couple. Colleen O'Connor and Jim Millns skated well in their first Worlds to a seventh place finish, while the Milliers were 13th.

The 1974 Governing Council Meeting was held at Seattle, Wash. It too had a little crisis when it was discovered that a group of Soviet skaters had been invited to Expo '74 for exhibitions in Spokane without the prior knowledge of the USFSA which were to be televised. Since the ISU Rules were clear that the authorization for such an event was within the jurisdiction of the USFSA, it was only with the direct intervention of the ISU President, Jacques Favart, by telephone, that the organizers finally recognized their obligations and sought the approval of the Association for the event. The exhibitions were never seen on television.

A memorial resolution was adopted for Jack Hart of Tacoma, a former Vice President, Secretary and committee chairman who had passed away in March. There were some minor technical changes in the rules adopted but the meeting was notable for the presence of Messrs. Robert Kelton of the ISIA and Walter Muehlbronner of the PSGA, two of the "architects" of the policy statements. Both of them emphasized the intention of their organizations to work fully with the USFSA in a spirit of cooperation to the end that all those participating in the sport at whatever level would benefit.

There was a changing of the guard at the Central Office in 1974 when Roy and Jean Winder arrived in Boston to take over, following the departure of Virginia K. Burnham, the daughter of Past President Kendall Kelley, who had served as Business Manager since 1971. Roy assumed the title of Executive Secretary while Jean was an Assistant Secretary. Both of them had been long-time National Accountants. Roy had also served as a standing committee chairman and member of the Executive Committee. As we have already seen, the Central Office was still at 178 Tremont Street in Boston in 1974 and would soon move in 1975 to larger quarters in the Sears Crescent building. Roy and Jean provided much needed leadership to the Central Office and magazine operations, with their own broad background in the sport and Roy was really the first true Executive Secretary rather than merely an office manager.

The 1974 Executive Committee, at its Fall Meeting in Chicago, took some major steps. Among them was the revision of the Junior Singles competition to include three compulsory figures, a short program and free skating. The team trophies at the Nationals and the other qualifying competitions were abolished so that the last competitions for them would be those in the 1974-1975 season. The value and purpose of the team trophies had been gradually eroded over the years as the number of clubs increased and as the honors were spread around among many, rather than a few. It was also voted that the National trophies would be retained by the Museum, shipped to the site of the Nationals for presentation and then returned to the Museum with the winners receiving permanent token trophies. The wear and tear on the trophies, the risk of loss and the cost of their maintenance more than outweighed the value of their being in the possession of the titleholder on a temporary basis. Eventually, once the Museum was established in Colorado, all the permanent trophies would no longer travel although the names of the winners would continue to be engraved on them.

Another action taken was to create a technical committee to review recommendations for the appointment of referees and judges. This committee would eventually become, in 1977, the Judges Review Committee, which is charged with the responsibility for the making of nominations for the appointment of referees and judges by the ISU.

It was also voted that open marking would be used in all events of the National Championships. The schedule of Pair Tests was also revised, with the requirements being updated and a Preliminary Pair Test being added.

It was also decided that all USFSA judges would be appointed for two-year renewable terms coinciding with the publication of the Rulebook and a written examination would be required to be taken at least once during each such term. Initial appointments would be for a term expiring on the date of the first publication of the Rulebook following the date of appointment. It is really publication in the Rulebook (now the Directory) which constitutes official evidence of a judge's appointment, as no certificates or cards are issued reflecting such appointments. The magazine also publishes, for the record, the names of all interim appointments made.

The remarkable run of the U.S. skaters at St. Gervais and Oberstdorf continued in 1974, with the Americans winning five of the seven events and the Canadians the other two. At Oberstdorf, David Santee won the Men, with the young Priscilla Hill from Boston winning the Ladies. Barbara Smith of Burbank, Calif., the 1974 National Junior Ladies Champion, was second. Judy Genovesi and Kent Weigle from Hartford, Conn., the 1973 National Junior Dance champions were the winners in Dance. At St. Gervais, David Santee repeated his Oberstdorf win to complete the rare double of winning both competitions, just as Robert Bradshaw had two years earlier. Barbara Smith reversed the earlier result to win the Ladies, defeating Hill.

The U.S. success continued at the Prague Skate with Terry Kubicka and Kath Malmberg winning both Singles events. Terry was of Czech descent and some of his relatives were there to enjoy his victory, as was the USFSA President, serving as a Referee. Kath Malmberg also entered the Richmond Trophy and placed third. Fourth in that competition was Susan Driano, representing Italy but actually an Italian-American, another of those choosing to skate for another country, based on descent and dual citizenship in the other country. Under ISU rules this could be done provided the member associations of the two countries concerned agreed to such a transfer.

At the second Skate Canada at Kitchener, Ontario, the U.S. came away with three medals. Charles Tickner was third in the Men, Wendy Burge third in the Ladies, and Colleen O'Connor and Jim Millns second in the Dance, to Moiseeva and Minenkov of the USSR, with Genovesi and Weigle fifth. Ron Shaver and Lynn Nightingale of Canada were the winners of the Singles. Another milestone was also reached when U.S. skaters entered for the first time a competition in the Soviet Union, the Moscow Skate sponsored by the Moscow News, an English language newspaper published in that city. There were just two U.S. entries; Juli McKinstry in the Ladies placing fourth and John Carlow, Jr., in the Men, who placed seventh.

There also occurred, that fall, a rare Dance competition at Streatham, outside London called the "Prestige Cutlery" Dance Trophy, an early example of a title sponsor for a figure skating event which would, in later years, become the norm. Michelle Ford and Glenn Patterson, she from Phoenix and he from Arctic Blades, placed fourth, with the winners being Janet Thompson and Warren Maxwell of Great Britain. Warren would eventually emigrate to the United States and serve as chairman of the USFSA Dance Committee from 1993 to 1995. The level of participation of U.S. skaters and the diversity of the competitions being offered was rising rapidly and with it considerable success for the young skaters to achieve recognition and experience in competition abroad.

With the World Championships returning to the United States for 1975 and once again at the Broadmoor, there was a special event in conjunction with the Worlds, which was the first exhibition in the United States of the Gillis Grafström Collection – "Skating In Art" – mounted at the Fine Arts Center in Colorado Springs from January to March 1975. Little was it known then that the collection would return to Colorado in 1979 on permanent loan to the USFSA Museum. The collection included prints, porcelain, silver, books, skates and even music of various periods and styles, demonstrating the broad scope and age of the sport.

The 1975 Nationals were held at Oakland, Calif., at the Oakland-Alameda Coliseum with the St. Moritz ISC as the local organizers. With the Olympic Winter Games just another year away, all the defending champions returned. In both Singles events the defenders found the pressures of doing so considerable, as they did not skate their best in the free skating and were challenged by their young rivals in that department. They relied more on the figures and the short program for their victories. Gordy McKellen won his third Men's title but was second in the free skating to Terry Kubicka, with Charlie Tickner in third place. It was the same in the Ladies, with Dorothy Hamill winning her second title although she was defeated in both the short program and free skating by Wendy Burge, with Kath Malmberg third and Barbara Smith and Priscilla Hill right behind in the next two places.

The defenders in Pairs also had a problem, with Melissa Militano and Johnny Johns having to come from behind to overtake Tai Babilonia and Randy Gardner, first in the short program to take their second title as a Pair, and Melissa's third. Emily Benenson and Jack Courtney from Colorado Springs were third.

At least for Colleen O'Connor and Jim Millns in the Dance, it was clear sailing and they easily won their second title over Judy Genovesi and Kent Weigle, with Michelle Ford and Glenn Patterson third. The Milliers placed fourth. In the Junior Ladies, the winner was Lisa-Marie Allen from Burbank, Calif., who would soon make her presence felt at the Senior level. In the Junior Men in seventh place, was a young man named Scott Hamilton from Bowling Green, Ohio, who would bear watching in the future.

The final award of the Harned Trophy for the club earning the most points was to the Los Angeles Figure Skating Club led by Wendy Burge, Tai Babilonia and Randy Gardner.

The 1975 World Championships in Colorado Springs were really a gala affair done in the true Broadmoor style and probably were the high point of the long line of ISU Championships held at that famous resort. Chuck DeMore of Cleveland had succeeded Hank Beatty as the general chairman and, working closely with Thayer Tutt, produced an outstanding event. For a USFSA President who has a World Championships in his or her own country during his or her term of office, it can be an exhilarating affair but can also have its share of problems to be solved. The 1975 Worlds were no exception to that rule of thumb. At that time, the ISU Rules did not make mandatory the use of flags and anthems at the awards ceremonies. The USFSA had elected not to use them on the principle that skating is an individual sport and the trappings of nationalism and of a particular political system are not appropriate. Once the officials from the Eastern Bloc countries arrived in Colorado Springs and found out no flags and anthems were contemplated, the heat was on, with constant lobbying of the ISU officials as well as the USFSA. In the end, it was readily apparent that to fight the ISU on it was not worth the effort, so it was agreed that flags and anthems would be used. The Broadmoor World Arena staff then had to install, in less than 24 hours, the required hoist for the flags and also to be sure that the necessary anthems and flags were available. These concessions were not, however, extracted without a price which in this case was permission for Judy Schwomeyer and Jim Sladky to demonstrate in the otherwise all amateur exhibition, their Yankee Polka, then under consideration for acceptance as a new compulsory dance. The only problem that arose with the flags was that for the Pairs award ceremony, there was only one East German flag available and there were two GDR Pairs on the podium. Happily, the East German team leader came to rescue and provided a banner which he just happened to have in his luggage. The only difference between the two German flags then was a Communist style seal in the middle of the GDR flag, as was quite common for the national flags of many of the Bloc nations.

It was also at the 1975 Worlds that an international version of the HAL computer program developed by Al Beard for the calculation of the results was introduced, using the Minneapolis-Honeywell timesharing facilities, with complete success. Al himself was the Chief Accountant to insure that things ran properly.

The unexpected absence of Jan Hoffmann of GDR, the defending champion in the Men, due to a non-skating injury that required knee surgery, made the event a wide open one. This was soon seen from the variety of the placements in the various parts of the competition, which were scattered among at least seven different skaters. It was, once again, supremacy in the figures which decided the day, with the strong free skaters being too far down to make up all the lost ground. The new champion, who won the figures decisively, was Sergei Volkov of the Soviet Union, the first skater from the USSR or even from Russia, for that matter, to win the Men's World Championship. Yet he did no better than sixth in the short program and fourth in the free skating but still won the Gold. The runner-up was his teammate Vladimir Kovalev, the new European champion, whose placements were third in figures, fourth in the short and third in the free. Third was John Curry of Great Britain, a skater on the rise, with a second-second and fifth in the three parts. The top American skater was Gordy McKellen, Jr., who finished fifth but with fifth-fifth and seventh. The winner of the short program was Yuri Ovchinnikov, the third Soviet skater who placed sixth overall, while the winner of the free skating was Terry Kubicka, seventh overall, with an 11th in figures and seventh in the short. The winner of the free skating small medal was Toller Cranston, fourth overall, with a third and a second in the short and long. It was a jumble and perhaps reflected the quality of the skating, which was not of a high standard.

On the other hand, the Ladies result was more clear cut. Dianne de Leeuw, the Dutch-American representative of the Netherlands, established an early lead in the figures, held it in the short program and placed second in the free skating to take the title away from the defending champion, Christine Errath of East Germany, who wound up third. She had been sixth in figures, second in the short and fourth in the free. Dorothy Hamill did not start out well, with a fifth in figures and a sixth in the short program, but rallied to win the free skating and retain her Silver medal position for the second straight year. Wendy Burge finished fourth, with a third in free skating, while Kath Malmberg was fifth, with a fourth in both figures and short, but a disastrous 10th in free skating.

The Pairs continued the prevailing Soviet dominance, with Irina Rodnina and Alexandr Zaitsev winning their third title together and Irina's seventh. This time, their perennial rivals Smirnova and Ulanov having departed, the strength of the Soviet team was reduced a little, so that two East German teams, Romy Kermer and Rolf Österreich, and Manuela Gross and Uwe Kagelmann, took the other two medals. The other two Soviet Pairs were fourth and fifth. Melissa Militano and Johnny Johns finished sixth, while Tai Babilonia and Randy Gardner were 10th.

There was an unexpected surprise in Dance with the withdrawal of Liudmila Pachomova and Alexandr Gorshkov, although they were present and were able to demonstrate their Tango Romantica compulsory dance at the exhibition following the championships. Gorshkov had been suffering from a bout with pneumonia which had seriously sapped his strength and prevented the couple from making the preparation needed, although they had retained their European championship earlier. With their streak of five straight World titles ended, the possibility of an American break through was an attractive idea, but it was not to be. The new champions, Irina Moiseeva and Andrei Minenkov were much too strong in the free dance, defeating Colleen O'Connor and Jim Millns, who had been in the lead after the compulsory dances, including the original set-pattern dance. It would not be until 1981 that the original set-pattern dance would become a separate part and in effect the short program for the dancers. Hilary Green and Glyn Watts of Great Britain were third, while the second American couple of Judi Genovesi and Kent Weigle were 12th.

Following the championships, in addition to the demonstrations of the three proposed new compulsory dances, there was also an ISU-sponsored seminar in figure skating (Singles and Pairs), conducted by the Figure Skating Technical Committee for those judges present. The first such official ISU seminars in both figures skating and ice dancing had been held at Bratislava in 1973 and would be continued on a regular basis around the World in the future. It was mandatory that judges attend such a seminar every three (later increased to four) years in order to retain their appointments.

Coming out of the 1975 Worlds and leading into the Olympic year, the U.S. team had the following placements for its efforts: Men - fifth, seventh; Ladies - second, fourth, fifth; Pairs - sixth, 10th; Dance - second, 12th, with two Silver medals. The U.S. was as strong as ever in Ladies but was a little weak in Men and Pairs.

In April of 1975, there took place a competition which had political overtones. The South African Association organized an International Competition in Johannesburg to which 27 skaters from six countries, including four from the United States, agreed to participate. At that time, because of the apartheid policies of the government, South African athletes were banned from almost all international competition, including the Olympics. They had, however, never been thrown out of the ISU despite strong efforts at every Congress for years by the Eastern Bloc countries to expel them. The South African Association had made an informal agreement with the ISU not to enter skaters in the ISU Championships, as long as they were otherwise banned from the Olympic Movement, a commitment which was lived up to by them, with one exception, until 1992.

In order to demonstrate the position of the ISU that politics was not a criteria for participation in sports, Vice President Shoemaker went to South Africa for the competition. The battle was between Charles Tickner, the ultimate Men's winner and Robin Cousins of Great Britain, despite the strong free skating of the latter. The winner in Ladies was Barbara Smith, while, in the Pairs, Emily Benenson and Jack Courtney were second to an Austrian pair, Ursula and Michael Nemec. The competition took place at the Carleton Sky Rink, a new facility on the top of an office building in downtown Johannesburg, with a full-sized surface.

The 1975 Governing Council Meeting, held at the Broadmoor in Colorado Springs for the second time since 1960, was itself an active one. Noted by a memorial resolution was the death, in January, of Dr. Gordon C. Brown of Ann Arbor, Mich., who had been a USFSA Vice President, standing committee chairman, National Referee and Judge. Another death noted was that of Richard C. Clemson of Rye, N.Y., who had been the Vice Chairman for Music of the Dance Committee from 1959 to his death in 1975, a total of 16 years. This position was important, since the person holding it was basically responsible for providing all the music needed for the skating of the compulsory dances in competition. He was the author of **A Guide to Ice Dance Music** as well as of several articles published in the magazine, and accumulated a vast library of records and tapes. Anyone who was a dance referee in those days knew where to go to get the required music. Appropriately, Dick was succeeded as Vice Chairman by Ritter Shumway, another music aficionado who served for 11 years, and who acquired and preserved the original library. Such unsung volunteers are the strength and support of the organization.

Announced at the meeting was the inauguration of the Figure Skating Hall of Fame with the first elections to be completed by the spring of 1976. The idea of Roy Winder and Ted Clarke of Boston, the Hall of Fame would provide the means to honor deserving nominees, both past and present, in three categories: amateur skaters who have been outstanding competitors or who have made noteworthy contributions in style and technique; those who have made noteworthy contributions in a non-skating capacity, through service to a figure skating association; and those who have made significant contributions as professionals in skating. There were to be 27 electors, three from each region, to serve as the panel to vote on the nominations received annually.

By 1975, there were 336 member clubs and 33,656 registered skaters, an increase over the preceding 10 years of 56 percent in the former and of 38 percent in the latter, a pattern which would continue, with the increase in the number of clubs outpacing the increase in the number of skaters. This was also a reflection of the building boom during the 1970's of additional ice rinks riding the popularity primarily of ice hockey. It was what the Bostonians call the Bobby Orr era, as this increase was significant in New England. The financial situation of the Association and the Memorial Fund can be illustrated by comparison with the comparable figures for ten years earlier:

Association	1965-1966	1975-1976	Increase (%)
Total assets	$192,433	$536,509	179
Total revenues	112,681	355,727	216
Total expenses	100,437	273,852	173
Memorial Fund			
Total assets	56,715	247,876	337
Receipts	8,149	151,989	1,765
Disbursed amounts	3,000	131,173	4,272

The Association was beginning to move into the big time. When the agreement for the television rights to the Nationals were renegotiated in 1974, the rights fee went up by 100 percent, from the substantial sum of $35,000 for a three-year contract to the magnificent sum of $70,000 for the same period. The President and the Chairman of the Television Committee were heroes.

Changes made to the By Laws included the adding of a new standing committee for Singles and Pairs, with the consolidation under the Tests Committee of responsibility for figure, Pair and Dance tests, so that the new committee, together with the Dance Committee, would be the two standards committees for their respective disciplines, with the strictly administrative matters residing in the Tests Committee. The jurisdiction of the Membership Committee was expanded to add the responsibility for the changing of names and principal skating headquarters of member clubs. Also approved was an increase of $1.00 in the registration fee for the first member of a family, from $5.00 to $6.00, to reflect an increase in the same amount in the subscription rate for **Skating** magazine.

Accepted with thanks was a donation to the Memorial Fund, from the St. Moritz ISC, of 10 percent of the net income from the 1975 Nationals, in the amount of $4,104.

A recodification was approved of the Skating Standards Regulations (SSR) to consolidate within them all rules common to both tests and competitions, in order to eliminate duplication in the Rulebook and also of rules that have to be changed periodically because of changes approved by the ISU Congress.

In another restructuring it was approved to add Vice Chairmen for Figure and Dance Judges to the Judges Committee for each Region in addition to the existing Sectional Vice Chairmen. This same structure was also eventually implemented in the Competitions Committee in 1984. The additional Vice Chairmen have greatly facilitated the handling of the increase amount of traffic as the number of non-qualifying competitions has escalated.

One controversial issue at the Governing Council was the matter of the fees to be paid with respect to exhibitions or carnivals for the benefit of non-skating related organizations in which members of the World team appeared. The event in question at the time was "An Evening With Champions" produced by Eliot House of Harvard College for the benefit of the Jimmy Fund of the Dana-Farber Cancer Institute in Boston. Since the World team members appearing in the show donated their services, there was a view on the part of the organizers that no fees should be paid. However, the Governing Council approved a fee in such cases of 5 percent of the net amount due to the non-skating related organization, in addition to all regular sanction fees otherwise required.

At the 1975 meeting, the International Committee formalized the practice of announcing the selections of the skaters and officials in International Competitions for the forthcoming season. The competitions chosen were six in number altogether: Nebelhorn Trophy (Oberstdorf) - six skaters, two officials; Grand Prix (St. Gervais) - the same; Prestige Cutlery Awards (Great Britain) - one Dance couple; Skate Canada - four skaters; two officials; Richmond Trophy - two skaters, one official; Prague Skate - two skaters, one official; and Moscow Skate - three skaters, two officials. This made a total of 19 skaters and eight officials (judges), a modest number when compared with the numbers of skaters and officials sent out today, and reflects the scope of the activity at the time.

The 1975 ISU Congress was held at Munich, Germany in June. The major decision taken was the creation of ISU Championships for Juniors who were for Singles, skaters not older than age 16, and for Pairs and Dance couples, not older than age 19 on July 1 preceding the championships. These age limits would later be increased by 1994 in stages to: 18 for ladies in Singles, 19 for men in Singles and 19 for Pairs and Dance couples. The first Junior Championships were scheduled to be held at Megève, France, in March 1976 following the 1976 Worlds at Gothenburg, Sweden. An ISU Championships is not yet a World Championship and reflects the fact that the competition in question is being conducted on an interim or trial basis, with its future permanence to be determined by a later Congress. In the beginning, there was an additional restriction, which was that a skater who had competed in the World, European or Olympic Winter Games (as a Senior) or who had placed first, second or third in a Senior International Competition, could not compete as a Junior. Eventually, all these restrictions would be dropped. With respect to those skaters holding dual citizenship, the rules were revised to require them to select the Association they wish to represent the first time they competed internationally. The amateur status rules were also revised to delete the specific provision that the mere act of signing a professional contract was an automatic cause for disqualification.

The marking system for the short program was changed to provide for two new marks: "required elements" and "presentation." Previously, the short programs had been judged essentially on the same criteria as free skating and used the same marks of "technical merit" and "artistic impression" (in the United States "composition and style"). As a result, there had been problems of properly penalizing failures in the required elements. The new marks provided for a specific scale of deductions from the first mark for such failures. Another important change was the further reduction of the value of the figures from 40 percent to 30 percent with the short program remaining 20 percent and the free skating now 50 percent. Three new compulsory dances were accepted in Dance and, at the same time, the use of vocal music for the original set-pattern dance and the free dance was prohibited (it was already not allowed in Singles and Pairs). In the elections, Jack Shoemaker was returned to office as the First Vice President and Ben Wright was re-elected to the Figure Skating Technical Committee as the two U.S. officeholders in the ISU. George Blundun of Calgary continued to serve on the Dance Committee, and on the Figure Committee there was also Donald Gilchrist of Ottawa, so North America had in fact four representatives. Donald was, at that time, the Consul General of Canada in Los Angeles, an appointment which had required him to step down in 1974 as CFSA President after one year in office.

The prelude to the 1975-1976 Olympic year began in the summer of 1975, with the usual combined team going to Oberstdorf and St. Gervais. While the success of the previous several years was not quite attained, there was one win at Oberstdorf by Lisa-Marie Allen of Burbank, Calif., the National Junior Ladies champion of 1975. She also won at St. Gervais, for yet another double. Ken Newfield from Los Angeles, fourth in the 1975 Nationals, was second at Oberstdorf and won at St. Gervais. Alice Cook from Wilmington and Bill Fauver from Cleveland were second in Pairs in both competitions, while Susan Kelley and Andrew Stroukoff from Boston were fourth in the Dance event at Oberstdorf. The other four events were all won by Canadians, so it was a North American sweep and a good start to the season.

The Fall 1975 Executive Committee Meeting at Chicago reflected the beginnings of the changing scene in the sport, with the Association entering into an agreement with an outside agency to promote commercial licensing, and to serve as the liaison between manufacturers and the USFSA. Unfortunately, the agency produced little or nothing, but the concept of such arrangements was thereby established and would expand in the future, although the various arrangements offered have not proven to be the bonanza expected.

The next step in the infant computer age took place, with the use of computers at all qualifying competitions. Participation in the new ISU Junior Championships was also approved, although there was no formal basis for the selection of the skaters, which turned out to be somewhat haphazard. A proposal to hold a USFSA "Junior Olympics" competition was approved, but nothing came of it until 1995, when the so-called "J-I" (Juvenile-Intermediate) Championships were redesignated as a Junior Olympic event. In another action, the Program Development Committee was authorized to formulate procedures for and to promote Basic Competitions as an expansion of the Basic Tests program. As a footnote to the past, a memorial resolution was adopted noting the death, in July, of Richard L. Hapgood of Boston, who had been the USFSA Secretary from 1932 to 1934 and from 1935 to 1940, Chairman of the Competitions Committee from 1930 to 1932, the first chairman of the Carnival and Exhibition Sanctions Committee in 1937, a National Accountant and a National champion in Junior Pairs and Fours.

In the International Competition realm the beat went on, with the four remaining competitions to which the U.S. had committed to send skaters coming in close succession. At Skate Canada '75 at Edmonton in October, the results were mixed, with a third place in the Men for Terry Kubicka and a third place in the Ladies for Kath Malmberg. In the Dance event, which was then always very strong due to the interest in it of George Blundun, Judy Genovesi and Kent Weigle were fourth, and Susan Kelley and Andy Stroukoff, ninth. Next came the Richmond Trophy, with Barbara Smith taking second and Linda Fratianne of Los Angeles, third.

At Prague in mid-November, the double achieved the prior year was repeated, with Charlie Tickner and Priscilla Hill winning both Men and Ladies. Second in Ladies was Susan Driano of Italy. Finally, there was the Moscow Skate at the end of November, and here it is necessary to note that some unfair judging took place by which the U.S. entrants were rather clearly penalized. The politicization of Soviet and East Bloc judging was then an ongoing problem, which would culminate in the suspension of all the Soviet judges in 1978 for obvious national bias. The main event in question at Moscow was the Ladies, in which Elena Vodorezova of the USSR, a very young and then talented jumper but not much else, after placing fifth in figures, defeated Wendy Burge, who had won the figures and placed third in free skating. As another footnote to history; third in the competition was Karin Enke of East Germany, who would soon forsake figure skating for speed skating and become one of the greatest lady speed skaters of all time. Certainly, her loss at Moscow did not help Wendy in future International and World Championships and raised really for the first time the question of whether the assignment of skaters to international competitions should not also take into consideration the potential risk to them in future major championships. David Santee was fifth in the Men at Moscow and Michelle Ford and Glenn Patterson were seventh in the Dance. Clearly, it appeared that the Moscow Skate was a competition to avoid in the future. Still, the overall record in the six competitions was excellent, with the following places: First - 5; Second - 6; Third - 2; Fourth - 2; Fifth - 1; Seventh - 1; Ninth - 1. All but two of those competing finished in fifth place or higher and, out of a total of 18 places, 13 of them were in the medals, a good standard for the future. It is always important to remember the principles of quality versus quantity in assigning skaters to international competitions.

Noted during the season were the deaths of several prominent skaters from the past, including former World and Olympic champion Karl Schäfer of Austria, and Beatrix Loughran Harvey, former North American and National Champion in Ladies and Pairs and a three-time Olympic medalist.

The 1976 Nationals were back at The Broadmoor in Colorado Springs. It was the third major event the Broadmoor Skating Club had hosted in just a little over a year; the 1975 Worlds, the 1975 Governing Council Meeting and now the 1976 Nationals. The championships marked the U.S. Bicentennial and also the Centennial of the State of Colorado. It was an impressive effort on the part of the club and hotel, which had been recognized at the Governing Council meeting when Thayer Tutt was presented with a silver Paul Revere bowl in recognition of his generous support of competitive figure skating in the United States. In the 1976 Nationals, there were 141 competitors representing 50 member clubs.

At the 1976 Nationals that a new National medal was unveiled and awarded for the first time. The design had been approved at the 1975 Governing Council meeting and was a round medal with the USFSA shield in the middle and suspended from a neck ribbon of red, white and blue stripes.

With both the Olympic and World Teams to be selected, two of the four defending champions were back, except Gordy McKellen, Jr., who had retired to take up a teaching career, and Melissa Militano and Johnny Johns, who had joined the Ice Capades West Company, leaving both the Men's and Pairs titles open.

The title chase in the Men did not start out auspiciously for the eventual winner, Terry Kubicka, who placed third in figures behind Ken Newfield of Los Angeles and David Santee from Chicago. Ken had to withdraw after the short program. Terry was still third after the short program which was won by Charlie Tickner from Denver, so the title was still up in the air. However, Kubicka rallied and won the free and with it the title, with Santee second and Scott Cramer from the Broadmoor pulling up to third.

It was a relatively straight forward defense for Dorothy Hamill in the Ladies. She won her third title without undue difficulty over Linda Fratianne, second and Wendy Burge third, both from Los Angeles. Kath Malmberg, who had been second in the figures, dropped to fourth. Down in 10th place was Suzie Brasher from Utah, then an unknown who would make a name for herself later in the season at the first ISU Junior Championships. Unfortunately, Barbara Smith of Los Angeles, the 1974 Junior Ladies winner and considered one of the favorites for a team berth had to withdraw from the free skating due to a leg injury.

Tai Babilonia and Randy Gardner from Los Angeles, the two times runners-up, won the vacant title in the Pairs decisively over Alice Cook from Wilmington and Bill Fauver from Cleveland, with Emily Benenson and Jack Courtney from the Broadmoor, again third.

The Dance, which was for the first time a competition from which Olympic team status would be decided was all Colleen O'Connor and Jim Millns, representing the Broadmoor, who won for the third straight year, with Judy Genovesi and Kent Weigle of Hartford, second and Susan Kelley and Andy Stroukoff from Boston making it into third over Michelle Ford and Glenn Patterson, the Bronze medalists of the previous two years.

There was a rising young star in the Junior Men by the name of Scott Hamilton, who won that title after being seventh in the prior year. Runner-up to him was 13-year-old Mark Cockerell from Los Angeles, who would also make a name for himself in the forthcoming ISU Junior Championships.

Appointed to manage the two teams were Doctors Hugh C. Graham, Jr. and Franklin S. Nelson from Tulsa for the Olympic Team, and Charles A. DeMore from Cleveland and Paul E. George from Boston for the World Team.

The 1976 Olympic Winter Games were back at Innsbruck, Austria, for the second time, due to the withdrawal of Denver, Colo., as the site, following a negative statewide referendum after the award of the Games to it.

Probably the event with the most interest and also full houses was the first Olympic competition in Ice Dancing, which had finally made the grade as an Olympic medal sport 24 years after it was established as a World Championship. It would be the Soviet Ice Dance dynasty against the rest of the World. Liudmila Pachomova and Alexandr Gorshkov had returned after his illness of the previous season in full form and had won the European championship for the sixth time in preparation for the Games. They went on to win the first Olympic Gold medals. Runners-up, as they had been at the Europeans were the 1975 World Champions, Irina Moiseeva and Andrei Minenkov, while Colleen O'Connor and Jim Millns took the Bronze for the first and so far only Olympic medals for the U.S. in Ice Dancing. They defeated Natalia Linichuk and Gennadi Karponosov, the third Soviet couple, and Krisztina Regöczy and Andras Sallay of Hungary, who stayed on until the next Olympics in Lake Placid in 1980, another famous competition. The other U.S. couples, Judy Genovesi and Kent Weigle and Susan Kelley and Andy Stroukoff placed 15th and 17th, respectively.

The Pairs event was all Soviet and East Germany, with Irina Rodnina and Alexandr Zaitsev winning her second and his first Olympic Gold medals, with the same two East Germany pairs of Romy Kermer and Rolf Österreich and Manuela Gross and Uwe Kagelmann taking the Silver and Bronze medals. Fourth were Irina Vorobieva and Alexandr Vlasov, the third Soviet pair, while the third GDR pair of Kerstin Stolfig and Veit Kempe were sixth. Sandwiched in between this collection of Eastern Bloc athletes were Tai Babilonia and Randy Gardner in fifth place, but with a fourth place in the free skating. Little did they know then that 1976 was to be their only Olympic appearance. Alice Cook and Bill Fauver placed 12th.

Although the U.S. men were not in contention for the medals in the Men, there was an American tinge to the event since John Curry of Great Britain had been training in Colorado with Carlo Fassi, who was also the coach of Dorothy Hamill. John had won the European Championship in a very close decision, coming from behind after figures. In the Olympics, John had to come from behind once again since the figures were won by the 1975 World Champion, Sergei Volkov. He soon faded, winding up fifth. Curry was second in the short program to Toller Cranston, who had been seventh in figures, so the Gold medal was on the line in the free skating. Here Curry skated an absolutely flawless program to become the first British male skater to win an Olympic Gold medal, joining two ladies who had done so, Madge Syers in 1908 and Jeannette Altwegg in 1952. Vladimir Kovalev of the USSR managed to hold on to second place and the Silver medal, despite a third in figures, a sixth in the short and a fourth in the free. Cranston of Canada took the Bronze medal. The top American turned out to be David Santee, who finished sixth, being just edged out for fifth by Volkov. Terry Kubicka, the National champion, placed seventh after an 11th in the figures and a 10th in the short, from which he came back very well with a third in free skating.

The Ladies was a three-way competition between Dianne de Leeuw of the Netherlands, Dorothy Hamill and Christine Errath of the GDR. After the figures, which were won by Isabel de Navarre of the FRG, with Dorothy second, she took control in the short, winning that part, and then went on to skate a flawless free skating to win the fourth Olympic Gold medal for Ladies for the United States. Dianne de Leeuw placed second and Errath third. Right behind them in fourth was Anett Pötzsch of GDR. Wendy Burge finished sixth after a disappointing effort in the free skating, in which she placed ninth. Linda Fratianne was close behind her in seventh. So the placements in Innsbruck in 1976 can be summarized as follows: Men - sixth, seventh; Ladies - first, sixth, eighth; Pairs - fifth, 12th; Dance - third, 15th, 17th. While two medals had been won, with one of them Gold, the overall results for the U.S. showed weakness in the Men and Pairs, and also in the Dance after O'Connor and Millns.

The 1976 World Championships were held at Gothenburg, Sweden, in the "Scandinavium" and, although fairly well organized, were run a bit on the cheap by the rink management, who sought to cut corners wherever possible to save money and thereby to improve the net for themselves. Following the Olympics, both John Curry and Dorothy Hamill announced their intention to retire and not to skate in the Worlds, and John actually returned to England and went on vacation. After much discussion between the USFSA officials on the one hand and the coaches, the skaters and their families on the other, Hamill finally agreed to go to the Worlds, which Curry did as well, after some frantic telephone calls to find him in England and to get him on his way. Their decisions to in effect defend their Olympic wins in the following Worlds turned out to be correct and neither of them can have any regrets for having done so, although their lack of training in between the two competitions made it close for both of them. Curry skated better in Sweden than he had in Austria, to win his first and only World title, as he was again second in figures and third in the short, with Kovalev again his chief challenger. The latter managed to hold second, after a first in figures, a fifth in the short and a fourth in the free. This time, Jan Hoffman of GDR pulled up to third ahead of Cranston, with David Santee, fifth, again ahead of Terry Kubicka, sixth.

Dorothy Hamill, after again being second in the figures in the Ladies to Isabel de Navarre of FRG, won the short and the long to take her first and only World title, with Christine Errath second and Dianne de Leeuw third. The podium was unique, with three World champions, Hamill, 1976, Errath, 1974 and de Leeuw, 1975, sharing the medals. Linda Fratianne did much better than in Innsbruck, with a third in free skating, to wind up fourth, ahead of Wendy Burge, who finished eighth.

The Pairs was the same story with three USSR and three GDR pairs in the top seven, with only Babilonia and Gardner, in fifth, representing the West. It was the eighth title for Rodnina and the fourth for Zaitsev. Alice Cook and Bill Fauver did much better and placed ninth, an improvement of three places over their Innsbruck showing. The World Championship in Ice Dancing also remained the same, with four of the top five couples from the Eastern Bloc. Only Colleen O'Connor and Jim Millns represented the West, in third place although this time, Regöczy and Sallay pulled ahead of Linichuk and Karponosov to place fourth. It was the sixth and last title for Pachomova-Gorshkov. The other two U.S. couples, Genovesi-Weigle and Kelley-Stroukoff, placed thirteenth and eighteenth, respectively. So the placement summary was: Men - fifth, sixth; Ladies - first, fifth, eighth; Pairs - fifth, ninth; Dance - third, 13th, 18th.

The next and new event on the schedule was the first ISU Junior Championships held at Megève, France, in early March, a week after the Senior Worlds in Sweden. A modest U.S. team was dispatched, consisting of Mark Cockerell from Los Angeles, Suzie Brasher from Utah and Lorene and Donald Mitchell from Long Island, N.Y., who had been seventh in the Nationals in (Senior) Pairs and were the 1975 National Junior Pair Champions. Two judges were also sent; Mrs. Anne Gerli from New York and Mrs. Elaine DeMore from Cleveland.

There were 19 entries in the Men's event and, much to the surprise of all, Mark Cockerell was the winner. After a fourth place in figures and a third place in the short program, he won the free skating to take the Gold medal. Down the line in the event were several others who would do well in the future: Brian Pockar of Canada (third), Norbert Schramm of Germany (fourth) and Josef Sabovcic of Czechoslovakia (10th).

The Ladies was equally as surprising, as Suzie Brasher won the figures, was second in the short and won the free, to win the Gold medal. Suzie came from a skating family, the Todds of Indianapolis. Garnet Ostermeier of FRG, yet another German-American skater, was second.

The Mitchells came second in the Pairs, with the Canadian pair of Sherri Baier and Robin Cowan the winners, while Elizabeth and Peter Cain of Australia were third. At that time, the National Junior Pair event did not include a short program, while the ISU Junior did, so the experience of the Mitchells in having skated a short program in the Senior Pair event of the Nationals had served them in good stead. There was no U.S. entry in the Dance, won by Kathryn Winter and Nicholas Slater of Great Britain, he being the son of Joan Dewhirst and John Slater, World Silver medalists in the Dance in the 1950's.

All in all it was a remarkable result, with three medals out of three entries, and two of them Gold. It was just the beginning of a long line of successes for the U.S. in the World Junior Championships, which were promoted to that rank in 1978.

The 1976 Governing Council meeting was a gala affair, held at Washington D.C. and featuring several unique events. The theme for the meeting was set forth by the President in calling the meeting to order, when he suggested that "this be a year of reflection…[which] would give all a chance to remember skating's past masters, honor its present outstanding achievers and consider its future possibilities for development." One of the events was the initial inductions into the USFSA Figure Skating Hall of Fame, for which the first elections were completed that spring. The Hall of Fame was intended from the beginning to encompass all the greats of the past from around the world, not just from the United States and this was reflected in those initially elected. Among them, from the United States, were Sherwin Badger, Theresa Weld Blanchard, Irving Brokaw,

Hall of Fame inductees 1976. Left to right: Dick Button, Tenley Albright, David Jenkins, Peggy Fleming Jenkins, Carol Heiss Jenkins and Benjamin Wright holding the plaque of the absent Hayes Alan Jenkins

Hall of Fame medal

Maribel Vinson, A. Winsor Weld, Jackson Haines, Howard Nicholson, Eddie Shipstad and Oscar Johnson. A special Hall of Fame medal was struck in both Silver and Bronze, with the former being used, suitably dated, as one of the tangible tokens to be presented to new Hall of Fame inductees.

The initial elections to the Hall of Fame also included many of the all-time greats of the sport from outside the United States, such as Axel Paulsen, Norway; Sonja Henie, Norway; Gillis Grafström, Sweden; Karl Schäfer, Austria; Andrée and Pierre Brunet, France; Ulrich Salchow, Sweden; Montgomery Wilson, Canada; Jacques Gerschwiler, Switzerland; Gustave Lussi, Switzerland; Reginald Wilkie, Great Britain; and Edi Scholdan, Austria. Also invited to be present to be inducted in person were six of the Olympic Gold medalists from the United States, of whom five were present: Dick Button, Tenley Albright, Carol Heiss Jenkins, David Jenkins and Peggy Fleming Jenkins. Hayes Alan Jenkins could not be present, being abroad on a business trip, while Dorothy Hamill, the newest and the current Olympic Ladies Champion, did not attend. She also did not attend a reception at the White House for the Olympic medalists who had participated in the Winter Games at Innsbruck, with Colleen O'Connor and Jim Millns, the Bronze medalists in the Ice Dancing, representing the sport.

Also observed at the meeting was a moment of silence and memorial resolutions were adopted for the late Karl Schäfer and Beatrix Loughran Harvey.

The featured speaker at the meeting was Senator John Culver from Iowa, a former Harvard football player and the member of the President's Commission on Olympic Sports, who had been designated by that body to report on figure skating. In his remarks, Senator Culver indicated that the Commission sees the need for some form of highest sports authority to oversee and encourage the growth of amateur athletics, but he emphasized that a federal takeover was not the Commission's intention.

Adopted by the Governing Council were amendments to the By Laws in response to an organizational streamlining of the U.S. Olympic Committee, to provide for a single Olympic Representative to the USOC and to establish an Olympic Figure Skating Committee as a special committee of the USFSA (it had formerly been a committee of the USOC).

In the competition realm, elimination rounds for the Regionals for events with more than 15 entries were to be required. As previously mentioned, a short program for Junior Singles was also to be added. A further revision to the USFSA-ISIA Policy Statements was made which eliminated the requirement that USFSA registered skaters also be registered with the ISIA in order to participate in its activities, there being no formal registration system in the latter organization.

In the final action of the meeting, President Wright stepped down after three years in office and was succeeded by Charles A. DeMore of Cleveland, the fourth President from that city and club. President Wright immediately reassumed the chairmanship of the Hall of Fame and Museum Committee, which he had previously held between 1971 and 1973 and which he still holds today. He also served as chairman of the Central Office Committee from 1976 to 1977, of the Nominating Committee from 1977 to 1981, of the Skating Standards Committee from 1978 to 1983 and ISU Representative between 1980 and 1983. He continued in office as a member of the Figure Skating Committee of the ISU until 1992, serving as Chairman from 1988 to 1992. In addition, he remained

Charles A. DeMore

active as a World Championship Referee until 1993 as well as at the National level as a Referee, Judge and Accountant. He is also an Honorary Member of the USFSA and of the Executive Committee, to which latter position he was elected in 1977.

It had indeed been a memorable three years, highlighted by the adoption of the USFSA-ISIA Policy Statements and the outstanding record of the skaters representing the United States in international competition.

As the new administration settled in the new season was well underway. There was virtually no time for the new officeholders to become familiar with their new positions. They have to hit the rink skating, to coin a phrase.

For 1976-1977 there were five international competitions selected, the same as in the prior

Movement to the West
(1977-1980)

year, but without Moscow. This time the overall results, while generally excellent, did not quite attain the level that had been enjoyed in the immediately preceding years. There were two wins however, of Barbara Smith in the Richmond Trophy and Scott Cramer in the Prague Skate. Other medals won included: Scott Hamilton, a second and a third at Oberstdorf-St. Gervais; Carrie Rugh from Los Angeles, a second and a third, also at Oberstdorf-St. Gervais; Lisa Marie Allen, a second at Prague; and David Santee, a third at Skate Canada, representing a count of eight medals out of 16 places.

The Fall 1976 Meeting of the Executive Committee at Chicago marked new beginnings as the reporter, Mrs. Ruth Jackson of Greensboro, N.C., says, the meeting "...centered on new horizons in cooperation with other organizations concerned with figure skating and proposed rule changes." Actually, the meeting saw the start of a process which would have a significant impact on the future of the Association. A Building Fund was established and, as Mrs. Jackson says, "an ad hoc committee was appointed to investigate the Building Fund's Central Office needs and cost of rental versus ownership, as well as locations for the Central Office, following a review of rising rent costs and the possible sale of the building in which the Central Office is now located." The chairman of the ad hoc committee was Joseph L. Serafine of Chicago.

Also approved, in principle, was the inclusion of up to three PSGA representatives on each USFSA committee, an initial step towards the further integration into the structure of the coaches who, through their President speaking at the Governing Council Meeting, had presented annually many valuable and worthwhile recommendations for changes in the rules. As yet another step in that direction and in view of the probability of the creation of a highest sports authority being considered by the President's Commission on Olympic Sports, it was voted to amend the By Laws to enable non-amateur members of the USFSA to serve on its standing committees. Dues increases from $2.00 to $3.00 per member and from $25.00 to $30.00 for an individual member were also approved. The rules governing gifts for carnivals and exhibitions were broadened to permit the acceptance of merchandise orders as such gifts.

A new free skating test structure, which would be independent of the existing figure tests was also adopted, consisting of Preliminary, Juvenile, Intermediate, Novice and Junior Free Skating Tests. The free skating in the Eighth Test was not changed but free skating was deleted from the Fourth and Sixth Figure Tests, as was the Free Skating Compulsory Moves, which had only just been added to the Third Figure Test in 1975. A Senior Free Skating Test would be added in 1979 and the free skating requirement in the Eighth Figure Test dropped.

Noted at the meeting was the appointment by the ISU Council of Dr. Franklin S. Nelson in May 1976 as a Medical Advisor to that organization. Among the duties of the Medical Advisors are the operation of the doping controls at ISU Championships as well as maintaining them up to date with international standards. The Medical Advisor is also important in supervising the menus to be followed by the organizers of championships. Franklin served as the chairman of the Medical Advisors from 1984 to 1989 and he continues to serve as one of them today, so he will have completed 20 years of service in 1996, the longest of any U.S. representative to hold a position (other than as a judge or referee) in the ISU. The Medical Advisors are appointed by the ISU Council and are not elected, and serve at the pleasure of that body.

Charles Tickner

Authorized for sale by the Museum was a Bronze medal marking the establishment of the Hall of Fame, which would also be available for purchase. The Silver version is used for presentation to new inductees into the USFSA (World since 1984) Hall of Fame.

The 1977 Nationals were held at Hartford, Conn., in the Civic Center and were very successful from the standpoint of support by the public. As usual, following an Olympic year all but one of the defending champions from the prior year had departed: Terry Kubicka and Dorothy Hamill to join Ice Capades, and Colleen O'Connor and Jim Millns to join Toller Cranston's small and select touring company, "The Ice Show," an innovative concept similar to a dance troupe, with only a few skaters and no props or ensemble costumes. This format would become the norm in later years, but in 1976 it was a little ahead of its time with the public being more used to the big extravaganza type shows, such as Ice Capades or Ice Follies. Only Tai Babilonia and Randy Gardner returned to defend the title they had first won in 1976. Despite the departures, the depth of talent in the Men and Ladies was considerable, but less so in Pairs and Dance.

Hopes are always high when titles are vacant, with those close to the top in the past hoping to make it this time. The surprise and yet not completely unexpected winner in the Men was Charlie Tickner from Denver, who had been fourth in 1976 and leapfrogged over both David Santee of Chicago and Scott Cramer of Colorado, the runner-up and third the previous year. Santee won the figures, but Tickner took both the other two parts to win his first title, with Cramer second and Santee third. This time, Charlie did not fail in the free skating as he had in 1976 and had an outstanding performance, with three perfect marks as well.

The result was a little more normal in the Ladies, with the 1976 runner-up, Linda Fratianne, from Los Angeles, coming out on top although she had to be lucky to do it. Winning both the figures and the short program had been Barbara Smith, now out of Colorado, but she could not hold the lead in the free skating which Wendy Burge, also from the Broadmoor, won. Linda actually became the champion with two seconds and a third in the three parts of the competition. This is not to take anything away from her win which was well deserved and showed that consistent performances in all phases would lead to success. She would, in the future, find the figures still an obstacle to that objective.

The Pairs saw Babilonia and Gardner easily win their second title, with a unanimous decision. Second was the completely new partnership of Gail Hamula and Frank Sweiding from the Broadmoor, a completely unknown and new couple although both of them had competed with modest success with other partners. Gail had been ninth in Pairs in 1975 with Phillipp Grout, Jr., from Denver, while Frank was 10th in the same year with his sister, Beth, and second with her in the 1976 Pacific Coast Sectional. A solid third were Sheryl Franks from Lexington and Michael Botticelli from Boston, who had been in the Senior Pairs event for the past two years (seventh in 1975 and sixth in 1976), after a second in the Junior pairs in 1974.

New champions resulted in Dance with Judi Genovesi and Kent Weigle from Hartford, winning appropriately in their home town over Susan Kelley and Andy Stroukoff from Boston and Michelle Ford

Tai Babilonia and Randy Gardner

of Phoenix and Glenn Patterson from Arctic Blades, third. Robert Wagenhoffer, also from Arctic Blades, accomplished a rare double in the Junior events when he won both the Junior Men and the Junior Pairs with his partner Vicky Heasley. Names to remember were Kitty and Peter Carruthers, fourth in Junior Pairs and Brian Boitano, third in Novice Men.

The 1977 Nationals included one controversy not directly involving the USFSA which was precedent-setting, when a local television station decided to broadcast the results showing the performances of the winners in its news segment. ABC-TV, which held the rights from the USFSA and which was broadcasting the championships on "Wide World of Sports" went to court and was able to enjoin the local station (not an ABC affiliate) from broadcasting other than as news the results themselves and then only two hours after the end of the competition. It was a very important decision which preserved the value of the rights, both for the network and for the seller of the rights. Since then, the networks have worked out arrangements which do permit the local stations to broadcast the results more freely, using footage from the originating broadcaster, with appropriate credits being shown.

The 1977 Worlds were held at Tokyo, Japan, the first World Championships in figure skating to be held in that country. Japan had held the 1972 Olympic Winter Games and had organized Worlds in speed skating as early after the War as 1954 and again in 1963. The rink used, Yoyogi Stadium, was actually a swimming pool that had been used for the 1964 Olympic Games, so the ice was less than ideal. Since the ice surface was built over the pool, there was a strange booming sound whenever a skater landed a jump. Attempts to paint the ice met with mixed success and on several occasions the paint came through, to the risk of the skaters. The rink was also extremely cold. There were 93 skaters from 17 countries entered, an excellent showing for a championship held so far away from Europe and North America. Still, Tokyo was a powerful attraction.

There were no defending champions in three of the four events, since John Curry, Dorothy Hamill and Pachomova-Gorshkov had all retired. Returning yet again were Irina Rodnina and Alexandr Zaitsev, seeking their fifth title together and her ninth. This they did with little difficulty, with Irina Vorbieva and Alexandr Vlasov the second Soviet pair in that position. However, a Soviet sweep was prevented by Tai Babilonia and Randy Gardner, who placed third, defeating the new "Mutt and Jeff" pair of Marina Cherkasova and Sergei Shakhrai, a significant improvement over their fifth place of the year before. The latter were a very small and very young girl with a mature and tall man, a difference which was so obvious that it would be reflected in the rules in the future with the judges having to reflect in their marks any obvious lack of unison resulting from such a disparity. The two other U.S. pairs did well in their first appearances at the Worlds, with Hamula and Sweiding placing seventh and Sheryl Franks and Michael Botticelli ninth.

With all three medalists and former champions from 1976 having departed, the Ladies title was open to anyone. For the purposes of perspective, the three ultimate medal winners had been fifth, fourth and ninth in 1976. While Anett Pötzsch of GDR won the figures, she took herself out of the race with a sixth in the short program, although she did place third in the free skating. Second in the figures was Dagmar Lurz of FRG, who also placed third in the short but could do no better than eighth in the free skating. No one would have thought after the short program that Linda Fratianne could win. She had been fourth in figures and had won the short program. While she actually finished second in free skating (to Elena Vodorezova of USSR, who finished seventh due to her poor figures, in which she had been 13th), Linda skated very well and was superior to her two closest rivals, thereby becoming the fifth U.S. lady to win the World Championship for Ladies. These three ladies

Linda Fratianne

would continue to be the closest of rivals for the next three years including the Olympic year of 1980. The other two American ladies, Barbara Smith and Wendy Burge, finished fourth and fifth, respectively, putting three Americans in the top five, a rare achievement. Wendy actually was second in the short program.

The Men was an equally exciting event. Unfortunately, Robin Cousins of Great Britain, who had been third in the Europeans, had to withdraw after the short program due to knee problems. As a result, Vladimir Kovalev of the Soviet Union, who had been second in Europeans, managed to defeat the European champion Jan Hoffmann of GDR, to win by virtue of his slightly better figures. The great moment of the event was when Minoru Sano of Japan pulled up to third by winning the free skating in a dazzling display of flawless free skating. The usually unenthusiastic Japanese were enthralled as Sano became the first medalist in a World Championship for his country. Many wished that Minoru could have been the champion, but a sixth in figures and a fourth in the short prevented him from placing higher. David Santee was a close fourth, again turning the tables internationally on the National Champion, Charlie Tickner, who was a dismal seventh in free skating after a sparkling third in the short program. Scott Cramer, the third American, was ninth, just missing eighth place by one ordinal place.

While Pachomova and Gorshkov were gone, their chief rivals and former champions, Irina Moiseeva and Andrei Minenkov had not and easily won the Dance Championship, with their rivals Natalia Linichuk and Gennadi Karponosov third. Janet Thompson and Warren Maxwell of Great Britain finished second. Just edged out of third place were Krisztina Regöczy and Andras Sallay of Hungary. The two U.S. couples, Judi Genovesi and Kent Weigle and Susan Kelley and Andy Stroukoff were ninth and 12th, respectively, there being no third U.S. couple due to the retirement of O'Connor and Millns.

All in all, it was not a bad Worlds for the young American team: Men - fourth, fifth, ninth; Ladies - first, fourth, fifth; Pairs - third, seventh and ninth; Dance - ninth, 12th, with two medals, one an unexpected Gold. The Men and Ladies were clearly strong and ready to contend for the medals in the future. The Pairs, other than for Tai and Randy, were not so strong and the dancers were on the weak side, a situation which would repeat itself many times in the future. With a few outstanding exceptions, the level of U.S. pair skating and ice dancing would continue to decline over the years.

While the ISU Junior Championships were again held at Megève, France, they were a direct conflict with the 1977 Nationals as a consequence of which the USFSA decided not to send a team, despite the success of 1976. The question of future U.S. participation in the World Junior was very much up in the air unless the dates of the championships were changed. They would be held after the Worlds in 1978 and 1979, before the Europeans in January in 1980 before finally settling in to the prevailing pattern of being held in the first half of December. The U.S. has participated in all of the championships since, starting with 1978, with considerable success. The championships were marred by the complete withdrawal of all the Eastern Bloc entries when a pair from South Africa was entered. As a result, there were but two pairs and the other classes were all smaller as well. It was a purely political decision and had nothing to do with sport. Of the four titles, the Canadians won three of them and the British the fourth.

The 1977 Governing Council meeting was held at Oakland, Calif., returning to the Bay area for the first time since 1968. A memorial resolution was adopted for Theodore G. Patterson of Boston, who had passed away in December 1975. A former Vice President, Secretary, Treasurer and chairman of the Central Office, Eastern, Finance and Memorial Fund Committees, he had also served as an Olympic Team manager in 1952 and 1956 and a World Team manager from 1954 to 1956.

In the financial area, Treasurer Rolf Hessler from Cleveland reported that the Association had been declared an exempt organization under Section 509(a)(2) of the Internal Revenue Code. Such an organization is one that receives less than one-third of its support from investment income and more than one-third from membership fees and other receipts relating to its exempt functions. The exemption required that all organization income be used for the carrying out of exempt functions, with the accumulation of funds not being permitted except for reasonable purposes, one of which was the Building Fund. The exempt status of the Association would again come into play in 1979. The Governing Council approved the increase in Individual Member dues from $25.00 to $35.00 and for the first member (in a family) of a Member Club from $6.00 to $7.00. The increases were primarily designed to offset inflationary costs, which at that time were on the rise.

In the competition area, panel judging at the Regionals was abolished, although it had worked fairly well but had been primarily objected to by judges. In addition, two new categories of competition judge were created, the Senior Competition Judge and Gold Dance Competition Judge, to complete the structure on the competition side. The National Judge still remained at the top in a dual capacity of both a test and competition judge. Also created finally were categories of Honorary Referees and Accountants to match the existing categories of Honorary Judges. It was also voted that the medal winners in the Senior events of the Nationals would have to qualify in their Sectional Championships. These rules would continue to be changed back and forth over the years, and this particular revision was quickly reversed in 1979, so that the medal winners did not need to qualify in their Sectionals. The exemption for the medalists would remain in effect until 1994 when it would be reduced to the champion only. With respect to tests, a new International Dance Test was added to the schedule, consisting of the Starlight Waltz, Ravensburger Waltz, Yankee Polka and Tango Romantica. The first International Dance Tests were taken and passed by Judy and Jim Sladky (now married) at Santa Monica, Calif., on Oct. 1, 1977, the first day the tests were effective. Judy and Jim actually received two perfect marks for their own Yankee Polka. Also added were Adult (over age 35) Dance Tests: A (equivalent to the Gold Dance Test), B (Pre Gold) and C (Silver). The Adult Tests did not require a solo and the passing averages remained the same as for the regular tests.

Electees to the Hall of Fame included from the United States the late Beatrix Loughran Harvey, Henry M. Beatty and Heaton R. Robertson. With the establishment of the Hall of Fame, the Museum Committee was redesignated as the Museum and Hall of Fame Committee, with the name eventually being turned around in 1978.

One highlight of the meeting was the presence and speech of Mrs. John H. (Billy) Mitchell from Vancouver, the first lady President of the CFSA and one who would serve well as a role model for all those ladies aspiring to the chair in the future. It was at this same meeting in 1977 that the USFSA elected its first woman officer in Betty Sonnhalter of Seal Beach, Calif., who served as Third Vice President for 1977-1978, as Second Vice President from 1978 to 1980 and as Secretary from 1981 to 1984. Betty has also served as chairman of the Amateur Status, Nominating, Pacific Coast, Rules and Sanctions Committees, and was elected an Honorary Member of the Board of Directors in 1995.

Betty Sonnhalter

The biennial ISU Congress was held at Paris, at which the major action was to change the term of office from two years to four, effective in 1980, so that those elected in 1977 would serve for three years, with no Congress being held in 1979. Happily, Messrs. Shoemaker and Wright were re-elected to their respective offices and a third American now appeared among the officeholders in George Howie of Wisconsin, elected to the Speed Skating Technical Committee. Dr. Franklin Nelson also continued as a Medical Advisor. The principal change from a technical standpoint was the addition of a short program for Junior Pairs of two minutes maximum duration and also including six required elements in four groups, with one to be drawn annually in the same manner as for the Seniors. The elements were a solo jump, an overhead lift, a death spiral, a solo spin, a pair spin and a step sequence.

The competition season opened with the Coupe des Alpes, with this time St. Gervais going first, followed by Obertdorf which has been the schedule since. In 1977 there was a return to outstanding success. There were now eight events since St. Gervais had added a Dance competition. Robert Wagenhoffer, from Los Angeles, the National Junior champion, won the classic double by taking the Men's events in both competitions. Sandy Lenz, the 1977 National Junior Ladies Champion from Wagon Wheel in Rockton, Ill., placed third in St. Gervais but won Oberstdorf, defeating Reiko Kobayashi of Japan, who had defeated her in the first competition. Gail Hamula and Frank Sweiding of the Broadmoor accomplished an even rarer double in Pairs by winning in both competitions, with Sheryl Franks and Michael Botticelli from Boston right behind in second place in both. The big win was that of Carol Fox and Richard Dalley from Michigan, who had been fifth in the National Senior Dance at St. Gervais, while at Oberstdorf they were second to Jayne Torvill and Christopher Dean of Great Britain, just beginning their rapid rise to the top. As a result, there were six Gold medals, three Silvers and one Bronze out of 10 possible medals. Surely, the best results ever. The new Coupe des Alpes trophy for the National Team scoring the most points in the two competitions was won by the United States.

The success continued at Skate Canada at Moncton, New Brunswick, where the top skaters were sent. Linda Fratianne, the World Ladies champion, won the Ladies with Lisa-Marie Allen, who had been the 1975 National Junior Ladies Champion and fifth in 1977 Nationals second. The winner in the Men was Robin Cousins of Great Britain, returning successfully from knee surgery following the Worlds, with Charlie Tickner second and Scott Cramer third. There was still no Pair event at Skate Canada and, in the Dance, which was won by Janet Thompson and Warren Maxwell of Great Britain, the competition was very strong. Susan Kelley and Andy Stroukoff were seventh and Dee Oseroff from Phoenix and Craig Bond from Sun Valley were 11th. It was again the best showing in Skate Canada up to that time.

In the Prague Skate, yet another and now not so rare double was achieved, with John Carlow, Jr., from Arctic Blades, the 1973 National Junior champion winning the Men and Kathy Gelecinkyj from the Broadmoor, who had been seventh in the 1977 Nationals winning the Ladies. Not to be outdone by this success, Priscilla Hill of Lexington, Mass., fourth in the 1977 Nationals, won the Richmond Trophy. Third was Denise Biellmann of Switzerland, while Jeanne Chapman of Los Angeles, placed seventh. Jeanne was the National Novice Ladies Champion in 1974. She was half Norwegian and had a brief fling in representing Norway in competition, but had subsequently returned to the U.S. competition system.

A new competition had been added in 1977, the Ennia Challenge Cup, held at the Hague in the Netherlands at the end of November. Kathy Gelecinskyj went on to it from Prague and placed fourth, while David Santee won the Men, with Stacey Smith and John Summers from Wilmington, Del., who had been fourth in the 1977 Nationals placing third. Ennia was another of the International Competitions to offer a team trophy for the skaters from the ISU Member (country) earning the most points. The U.S. won the Ennia team trophy in 1977, with Japan second. The Ladies winner was Emi Watanabe, who trained in the United States.

Once the smoke had cleared the record looked like this: First - 11; Second - 5; Third - 3, for a total of 19 medals out of a total possible number of places of 24. While no formal statistics have been maintained on a continuing basis tracking the success of the U.S. skaters in international competition, surely 1977 could well have been the best year of all, or at least close to the top.

The Fall 1977 meeting of the Executive Committee was held at Chicago as usual at the O'Hare Inn. Two matters of significant importance to the USFSA highlighted the agenda. The first was an authorization to acquire land in Colorado Springs adjacent to the Broadmoor Hotel for a National Headquarters building. The land, an acre and a half in size, was zoned for business use and had an abandoned restaurant building on it. Through the generosity of Thayer Tutt and the Broadmoor, the latter acquired the land for $180,000 and resold it to the Association for cost. The next step was to find the financing for the construction of the Headquarters and Museum building.

Ever since Roy and Jean Winder had come to Boston in 1974 and especially after the Central office moved to the Sears Crescent building in 1975, the matter of a permanent headquarters building, either owned or leased, had been under active consideration. Efforts to find such a building in Boston or to build or acquire one had proven fruitless. There were then no governmental sources of industrial financing available and the cost of private or commercial financing was prohibitive. Efforts to obtain the support of the Commonwealth of Massachusetts and the City of Boston in seeking and obtaining financing had fallen on deaf ears despite the fact that the Association was the only national governing body based in the state, where it had been since 1950 and in so far as the magazine was concerned, since 1923. Accordingly, it was necessary to turn elsewhere.

With the United States Olympic Committee already having moved from New York City to Colorado Springs and its impending designation by the Federal Government as the highest sports authority as recommended by the President's Commission on Olympic Sports made the Springs a very logical location for a new headquarters for the Association.

Although the proposed Federal legislation called for the appropriation of $30,000,000 primarily for the creation of regional training centers and other facilities around the country, the principal thrust of the proposed law was to end the ongoing disputes between the National Collegiate Athletic Association (NCAA) and the Amateur Athletic Union of the United States (AAU), both of whom were seeking to control amateur athletics such as track and field, and other team sports. The winter sports really were quite aloof from all this and, even today, the question of value to them, other than in the receipt of development funds of the super body is still open to question. The proposed funding by the Federal Government never materialized and no funds were ever appropriated by Congress for the announced purposes. The United States remains today virtually the only major industrialized nation which has no direct government financial support for (amateur) sport. Despite the lack of Federal funds, the USOC was already well under way to open, by the end of 1977, three regional training centers at Squaw Valley, Calif., Colorado Springs and Lake Placid.

One direct impact of the legislation was that at least 20 percent of the membership of the governing board of each national governing body (NGB) had to consist of athletes who were either active in competition or who had competed in international competition within the past 10 years. Since this requirement was already contained in the USOC Constitution, the USFSA had to implement it on an informal basis prior to the passage of the expected legislation and the formal amendment of its By Laws. Accordingly, a task force was appointed to study ways that could be taken to restructure the Executive Committee, with immediate Past President Wright as the chairman.

Elected as Honorary Members of the Executive Committee at the meeting were John R. Shoemaker, 28 years of service; Howard G. Taylor, 21 years; Benjamin T. Wright, 20 years; Spencer E. Cram, 18 years; Frederick C. LeFevre, 17 years and Brooks Stewart, 16 years.

In financial matters, an appropriation was made to the Building Fund, funds were approved for computers to be used at the qualifying competitions and for the training of Accountants in their operation and also for the supplying of standard medals for the nine Regional Championships. It was agreed to cancel the licensing contract with Hamilton Projects, which had proven to be unproductive and to seek an agreement with another firm.

A joint meeting with representatives of the ISIA and the PSGA also took place during the Fall Meeting, as a consequence of which guidelines were approved for the holding of joint USFSA-PSGA meetings at all the qualifying competitions, leading up to a proposed joint meeting at the Nationals.

Also approved was the publication of a new edition of **Skating Through the Years**, the pictorial history of the USFSA, of which prior editions had been published in 1942 and 1957. To date, this publication has never been completed and still remains as a future project. There would be published in 1979 the **Reader's Guide to Figure Skating's Hall of Fame** which would include biographical sketches of all those persons elected to the USFSA (World) Figure Skating Hall of Fame. A second edition of the Guide was published in 1987. Another publication, which represented a contractual obligation for the permanent loan of the Grafström Collection in 1979 was an updated definitive catalog of the Collection, finally published in 1995.

Hartford, Conn., was selected as the bid city for the 1981 World Championships, which were expected to return to the United States that year, since the 1978 Worlds were to be held at Ottawa, Canada.

It is timely to take another snapshot of the level of participation in the 13 qualifying competitions, the number of entries in which for 1977-1978 were as follows:

New England	183	Eastern Great Lakes	175
North Atlantic	128	Southwestern	169
South Atlantic	80	Upper Great Lakes	192
	491		536
Central Pacific	248	Eastern	132
Northwest Pacific	146	Midwestern	118
Southwest Pacific	190	Pacific Coast	117
	584		367

National - 100

The numbers are somewhat misleading and require explanation. The totals are directly affected by the additional number of non-qualifying events included in the competitions at the option of the organizing clubs. Several Regionals, such as the Central Pacific and Northwest Pacific, have traditionally added these extra events, while other Regionals have remained lean and adhered primarily to the qualifying events. In the Central Pacifics, for example, there were the following non-qualifying events: Pre Intermediate Boys and Girls, Juvenile Girls, Preliminary Pairs and Dance, Pre Juvenile Boys and Girls, Preliminary Boys and Girls while the North Atlantics, on the other hand, had only Juvenile Boys and Girls. The Pacific Coast, with the smallest number of registered skaters, has the largest number of entries in the Regionals. This fact has led to the myth that the Pacific Coast Sectional is the hardest one to get out of to the Nationals. The obvious characteristic of all these competitions is that they were primarily for females, with just a few males and a modest number of Pairs and Dance couples, a mix which still prevails today. However, the numbers are impressive as they fully demonstrate the substantial growth which had occurred during the past 10 years, with almost 2,000 entries involved.

An event in the Central Pacific Regional from as early as 1974 was one for Drill Teams. This is the "germ" of Precision Team skating, from which would come the rapid expansion of that discipline in the 1980's. It would next appear in the Southwest Pacific Regional in 1983.

The 1978 Nationals were held at Portland, Ore., the first time in the Northwest since 1969. All the defending champions returned, except for Judy Genovesi and Kent Weigle, the 1977 champions in Dance, who had turned professional to teach. Also departed were Barbi Smith and Wendy Burge, the Silver and Bronze medalists in the Ladies in 1977. A new, yet familiar face is found in third place in the Men of Scott Hamilton, who had been the 1976 Junior Champion and who had placed ninth in his first try at the Senior Men in 1977. Scott edged out the previous Bronze medalist, Scott Cramer from the Broadmoor. Hamilton himself, while originally from Bowling Green, was now in Colorado to train. Second in the Men, once again, was David Santee from Chicago, while Charlie Tickner won his second title with first places straight across the board in all three parts.

Linda Fratianne won her second Ladies title, although she was defeated in the free skating by the runner-up Lisa-Marie Allen of Los Angeles. Lisa-Marie had been in fifth after the figures and second in the short program, to climb back up into the medals. Third was Priscilla Hill from Massachusetts, who had been fourth the year before. Priscilla had a poor short program in which she placed sixth, but rallied with third in the free to take the Bronze medal behind Allen.

The Pairs saw the unusual result of all three medalists from 1977 finishing in the exact same order in 1978. Tai Babilonia and Randy Gardner won their third title, with Gail Hamula and Frank Sweiding from the Broadmoor second, and Sheryl Franks and Michael Botticelli from Massachusetts third. In fourth were Vicki Heasley and Robert Wagenhoffer, while he placed sixth in the Men, continuing the "tradition" of skating in more than one event, which had been done so successfully by Gene Turner and Ken Shelley, also from Southern California.

With the Dance Championship open, it was anyone's guess as to who the winners would be. Michelle Ford and Glenn Patterson, the Bronze medalists from the prior year were gone, but the runners-up, Susan Kelley and Andrew Stroukoff, were back as were Stacey Smith and John Summers from Wilmington fourth, and Carol Fox and Richard Dalley from Michigan fifth in 1977. As we have seen many times, it was not the runners-up that succeeded to the title. Smith and Summers were the winners in a very close competition with Fox and Dalley by a four to three margin among the judges. Kelley and Stroukoff finished third.

In the Junior ranks, the new champions were Brian Boitano from Sunnyvale, Calif., and Jill Sawyer from Tacoma, both of whom would be heard from in the future.

The 1978 Worlds were held at Ottawa, Ontario. Vladimir Kovalev of the Soviet Union, Jan Hoffmann of GDR and Robins Cousins of Great Britain were all back among the Men, although Minoru Sano of Japan, the 1977 Bronze medalist, had retired. The event was not noted for outstanding skating and each part was won by a different skater: Vladimir Kovalev, the figures, Jan Hoffmann, the short program, and Robin Cousins, the free skating. Kovalev quickly took himself out of contention with a seventh in the short program, while Cousins faced the handicap of a fourth in figures. The final result would rest between Hoffmann and Charlie Tickner. The latter had been quietly going about his business with a third in the figures and a third in the short, so that he was close behind Hoffmann, whom everyone thought would win. As it turned out, while Jan skated well, it was not good enough, so that Tickner beat him in the free skating, to take the title on what the accountants would call a greater subsequent majority of eight seconds to five seconds. It was the first Men's title for the U.S. since Tim Wood in 1970. David Santee finished sixth after an eighth place in the short program, while Scott Hamilton placed 11th in his first Worlds, just losing ninth to Brian Pockar of Canada. It was not an auspicious start for him, especially in figures, as it was for most U.S. skaters, a negative aspect of their skating. Scott would continue to improve in them so that by the end of his career in 1984, they took him to victory. The euphoria over Tickner's unexpected victory was short lived.

It was also in the Men's event that the Triple Axel was supposedly performed successfully for the first time by Vern Taylor of Canada who finished seventh in the free skating. There was not complete agreement within the ISU that the jump had indeed been performed since Vern, in landing, indeed on one foot had to turn two threes in order to hold it. Finally, the ISU President, Jacques Favart of France declared that the jump had been done. To this day there is some doubt on the matter, since the question of whether a jump is in fact completed if it is necessary to turn threes afterwards to hold it remains open.

Linda Fratianne took third in figures in the Ladies, which put her behind. While she won both the short program and the free skating it still was not enough to overcome the lead of Anett Pötzsch of GDR. With a first in figures, a second in short and a third in the free, Anett held on to take the title away from Linda. A surprise third was Susan Driano of Italy, who edged out Dagmar Lurz of the FRG for the Bronze medal. After a disastrous start in the figures, with a 14th place, Lisa-Marie Allen placed fifth in the short and fourth in the free to climb up to seventh overall, while Priscilla Hill, after a fifth in the figures went the other direction, with an eighth in short and 10th in free to wind up ninth.

The indomitable Irina Rodnina and Alexandr Zaitsev captured their sixth title in Pairs together and her 10th, and what turned out to be their last. This time the newer pairs from East Germany who had appeared on the scene in 1977 and had not distinguished themselves in that year, had vastly improved. Manuela Mager and Uwe Bewersdorf, fifth the year before, came second, while Sabine Baess and Tassilo Thierbach who had been fifth in the 1977 Europeans, finished fifth, just behind Marina Cherkasova and Sergei Shakhrai of the Soviet Union in fourth. Tai Babilonia and Randy Gardner, after a fourth in the short program, skated well to pull up to third and win another Bronze medal for the U.S. Sheryl Franks and Michael Botticelli overturned the National result and finished in ninth place, just ahead of Gail Hamula and Frank Sweiding.

Natalia Linichuk and Gennadi Karponosov of the USSR turned the tables in the Dance event on Irina Moiseeva and Andrei Minenkov to take the title, with Krisztina Regöczy and Andras Sallay of Hungary third. Carol Fox and Richard Dalley, who had been eighth in 1977, could not improve their place and remained eighth in 1978. They did reverse the National result, and defeated Stacey Smith and John Summers, who finished ninth. So, while there were still three medals, one Gold, one Silver and one Bronze, the rest of the results were somewhat disappointing, which reflected the strength of the opposition, especially from the Eastern Bloc in Pairs and Dance. Also evident was the continued supremacy of the European skaters in the figures although the standard of them was already in decline.

The first World Junior Championships were held at Megève, France, just one week after the Senior Worlds in Ottawa and this time the USFSA did send a team. The various classes were now back up to full size and the Eastern Bloc countries were fully represented, especially in view of the fact that they had been reprimanded by the ISU for their boycott in 1977. Brian Boitano, the new National Junior Champion, after a seventh place in figures, won the short program and was third in the free skating to take third, behind Dennis Coi of Canada, the winner, and Vladimir Kotin of the USSR. Right behind Boitano was Brian Orser of Canada, in what was the first of many meetings between them culminating in the Calgary Olympics in 1988, just 10 years later.

In the Ladies it again seemed that the figures would be the death knell of the American hopes when Jill Sawyer, the National Junior Ladies champion, placed eighth in them. Amazingly, Jill won both the short program and the free skating, to win the title over Kira Ivanova of the USSR, who had won the figures, been fourth in the short and second in the free. It was not surprising, however, in view of later events, in which Kira was seen to be an excellent skater in the figures, but almost inevitably failed in the free skating. She was a member, as was Dagmar Lurz, of the Schuba school. It was the first of what would be many World Junior Championships for Ladies that the U.S. would win over the next 18 years.

Beth and Ken Flora, who had been second in the National Junior Pairs and were age-eligible, came third in the Pairs. The winners were Barbara Underhill and Paul Martini of Canada.

When they won the Senior World Championship in Pairs in 1984 they became the first World Junior Champions also to take the Senior title. The U.S. had not sent a Dance couple because of the problem of age-eligibility, since the Junior level in the United States was strictly skill based with no age limit, while the International Junior level was strictly age based, a problem which would plague the selectors of the World Junior Team members in the future. Often in Dance especially, the only age-eligible couple would be too far down domestically to merit selection. In any event, it was a good beginning in the World Junior, with three medals, one Gold and two Bronze.

The 1978 Governing Council meeting was held at Minneapolis and was a momentous one for the Association as the plans for its new Headquarters in Colorado Springs moved forward. The meeting also paused to remember and to pay respects to the memory and achievements of Theresa Weld Blanchard, who passed away in March at the age of 84. Since Tee's accomplishments are woven throughout this chronicle, it is not necessary to repeat them all here. Suffice it to say that it was hard for those who knew her, had worked with her and had been influenced by her to accept her departure. She had been the "heart and soul" of the organization since its beginnings under the leadership of her father, Winsor Weld, and was widely known and respected throughout the World. Perhaps it was fitting that she did not live to see the departure from Boston of the Association and especially of the magazine, which had been her life's work. In an unusual coincidence, the announcement was also made at the meeting of the election to the Hall of Fame of Tee's late partner, Nathaniel W. Niles, with whom she had been nine times National Pair champion, North American Pair champion and a member of three Olympic Teams in 1920, 1924 and 1928.

The construction of the new Headquarters and Museum building in Colorado Springs was approved at the meeting. With the support of the Broadmoor and Thayer Tutt, it had been possible to obtain the issuance of Industrial Revenue Bonds by El Paso County, backed by the State of Colorado in the amount of $1,000,000, with a 12-year maturity and a 6 percent interest coupon to finance the construction. The entire issue was taken by the First National Bank of Colorado Springs, the principal bank for the Broadmoor. The building was to be designed by Carlisle B. Guy, a prominent Colorado Springs architect. It was to be dual building, with the former Central Office, soon to be called the National Headquarters in the south end and the Hall of Fame and Museum in the north. Provision was made in the design and construction of the building, which had a full basement, for the future expansion of the lower level below the Museum into an added floor for that facility. This was carried out in 1985 through a generous grant from the El Pomar Foundation, then the owners of the Broadmoor. An ad hoc Construction Committee which was really a continuation of the Building Committee appointed the previous year was appointed to carry out the project, consisting of President DeMore, Vice President Joseph Serafine, Treasurer Rolf Hessler and immediate Past President Ben Wright.

Also reported to the meeting was the progress of the legislation through Congress, which would become the Amateur Sports Act of 1978. In anticipation of its enactment, four athletes and two coaches were nominated and elected to membership on the Executive Committee. Since they thereby became history as the first to serve, their names are worth mentioning: Mahlon Bradley of Boston, Randy Gardner of Los Angeles, Ken Shelley, then from Sudbury, Mass., and Charles Tickner of Littleton, Colo., the four athletes, and Carlo Fassi of Colorado Springs and Ron Ludington of Wilmington, Del., the coaches. They would be joined as athlete members in 1979 by Linda Fratianne of Los Angeles, Jacob "Jock" Kohlhas, Jr. of Philadelphia, David Santee of Chicago and Stacey Smith of Wilmington, Del.

In the summer of 1978, yet another major competition was added to what was already becoming a very busy schedule with the inauguration of the National Sports Festival, a multi-sport event sponsored by the U.S. Olympic Committee. The first Festival was held at Colorado Springs in July and included figure skating and ice hockey as the only two winter sports. Later, short track speed skating would be added. At the outset and periodically thereafter, the Association tried to make the competition a development event for the Juniors and Novices, but the USOC would have none of it and insisted upon the top Senior skaters being invited. A modest compromise was reached which provided that the Senior medal winners in each Section, plus the Junior Men and Ladies Champions from each Section, would be invited. Even this arrangement did not last very long and, in another year, the top National medalists were also included. It would take until 1994 for the original idea for a development competition for the Juniors and Novice to be allowed. The Festival was renamed the "U.S. Olympic Festival" in 1987.

In the first Festival there was a good quality of competition, even though mid-summer could not have been a worse time, since it was the period when skaters are developing and perfecting their new programs for the forthcoming season. Often last year's programs had to be used. The winners were: Men - Scott Cramer from the Broadmoor, skating in his home rink; Ladies - Linda Fratianne of Los Angeles; Pairs - Tai Babilonia and Randy Gardner from Los Angeles and Dance - Carol Fox and Richard Dalley from Michigan, who again defeated the current National Champions, Stacey Smith and John Summers from Wilmington, Del. Despite the compromise agreed upon, all of the National champions, except Charlie Tickner, were present.

It was also in May of 1978 that an important step forward in training methods was initiated with the first training camp for the elite athletes sponsored by the U.S. Olympic Committee being held at the Olympic Training Center at Squaw Valley, Calif. Participating were 54 of the top skaters, plus their coaches and a group of international officials of the USFSA, as well representatives of the USOC medical staff.

In the summer of 1978 at Lake Placid there also took place a National Judges' Seminar which was attended by the World and International Judges of the USFSA, as well as by several invited National Judges. It was actually a follow-up to an earlier ISU recognized seminar held at Colorado Springs in 1977 conducted by Donald Gilchrist of Canada, a member of the ISU Figure Skating Committee. The seminar met an ISU requirement that attendance at a seminar (then every three years) was necessary to retain an ISU appointment. The 1978 seminar was conducted by Sonia Bianchetti of Italy, the chairman of the ISU Figure Skating Committee, assisted by two members of the committee, Donald Gilchrist and Benjamin Wright. It was attended by virtually all the World and International Judges of the USFSA and was very successful. Such seminars would be a regular feature of the schedule in the future, in both Figure Skating and Ice Dancing, and have served well to keep the participants up to date and secure in their knowledge and judging.

The regular international competition season started soon thereafter, with the annual pilgrimage to St. Gervais and Oberstdorf. Once again the U.S. team did well, winning three Gold medals, five Silver and two Bronze out of fourteen possible places. The winners were Allen Schramm from New York in the Men's event in both competitions, the double yet again, with Mark Cockerell of Los Angeles second in both as well, Editha Dotson of Colorado won the Ladies at Oberstdorf and Kim Krohn and Barry Hagan of Arctic Blades the Dance at St. Gervais. The Pairs were Maria DiDomenico and Larry Schrier from Los Angeles, the 1978 National Junior Pair Champions and Tracy and Scott Prussack from Wilmington, the National Junior Pair champions of 1976, of whom each had a second and third in both competitions.

Another new competition in the schedule was the ASKO Cup of Vienna (Austria), for Men and Ladies at the end of September. There Brian Boitano won his first international competition, with Alicia Risberg from Colorado, the National Junior Ladies Silver medalist, third in the Ladies. Just two weeks later, yet another new competition in which the U.S. participated was held in England, called the Rotary Watches Ice International. Linda Fratianne won the Ladies and David Santee was second in the Men to Fumio Igarashi of Japan who trained in the United States with Linda's coach, Frank Carroll.

Two weeks later came Skate Canada with somewhat less positive results. There still were no Pairs (they would finally be added in 1984), but Lisa-Marie Allen won the Ladies and Charlie Tickner was second in the Men, again to Igarashi, an early defeat for the defending World champion, which also reflects the risk of putting it all on the line too early in the season. Scott Hamilton was fifth. Stacey Smith and John Summers placed fourth in Dance. Another week and there was the Richmond Trophy, in which Carrie Rugh from Los Angeles placed second. In another two weeks there was the Prague Skate in which Jill Sawyer won the Ladies and Vicki

Heasley and Robert Wagenhoffer won the new Pair event, with Wagenhoffer still doing his thing in two events by placing third in the Men. Finally, at the end of the line, came the Ennia Challenge Cup at the Hague in the Netherlands, at which Scott Cramer won the Men and Sheryl Franks and Michael Botticelli were second in Pairs to the new Soviet team of Irina Vorobieva and Igor Lisovski. This competition was one of the first in Singles for free skating only: that is, just the short program and free skating. It had been necessary for the Dutch federation to obtain special permission from the ISU to drop the figures in what was a distant forerunner of the situation after 1990.

The 1978 international competition season was really the first in which the level of participation was substantially escalated, with more competitions and more skaters involved. There were now eight competitions without there even being one yet held in the United States, with the total number of possible places having risen to 34. Despite the broader distribution of the resources, the medal count remained excellent: 1st - 10; 2nd -10; 3rd - five, for a total of 25.

Thayer Tutt

The fall meeting of 1978 was moved from Chicago after 24 years to Colorado Springs and the Olympic Training Center of the U.S. Olympic Committee, which provided housing, meals and meeting rooms without charge. The major event of the meeting was the ground-breaking for the new Headquarters and Museum building, which was carried out by President DeMore, assisted by Thayer Tutt of the Broadmoor, El Paso County Commissioner Charles Heim, Colorado Springs Mayor Lawrence Ochs and immediate Past President Benjamin Wright. The contractor to do the work was G.E. Johnson Construction Company, a well known Colorado Springs builder, which had and would do much work at The Broadmoor for a bid of $1,045,000. It was anticipated that the building would be completed and dedicated just a year later in October 1979. Apart from this exciting event, much business was transacted. It is at the fall meeting when the old and new committee chairmen present their initial proposals for revisions to the rules, a process which is ongoing throughout the season, leading up to the spring meeting of both the Executive Committee and the Governing Council, with many hours spent on the preparation of ballots and the specific text of the proposals.

Coupled with the ground-breaking were actions to approve the formation of a new non-profit corporation under the laws of the State of Colorado, to be the successor to the existing Massachusetts Trusts for both the Association and the Memorial Fund. On the basis of expert legal advice, it was decided to merge the Association and the Memorial Fund into the new Colorado corporation (up to then they had been separate legal entities) in order to insure that the activities of the Association in carrying out the building project were fully covered by the tax exempt status enjoyed by both of the former organizations. A special meeting of the Governing Council was accordingly called and held on Nov. 8, 1978, to authorize the transfer of the assets of the Association and the Memorial Fund to the Colorado corporation. Also approved was a review by a task force, together with F. Ritter Shumway, Chairman of the Memorial Fund Committee of the By Laws of the new corporation to insure that they would properly reflect the new status of the Association and also especially to provide that the rights and obligations pertaining to the Memorial Fund were fully covered in them. All the arrangements were to be completed, including the actual move from Boston to Colorado Springs, prior to the expiration of the lease of the Boston office at the end of January 1980, when the old Massachusetts Trusts would be dissolved.

With respect to other financial matters, an authorization to borrow at any one time up to $50,000 for working capital was approved and an increase in the subscription price for **Skating** magazine to $8.00 for 10 issues was also approved, to cover two additional issues (from the then prevailing eight issues a season) and to add color to the magazine. By this time, the total circulation of the magazine had reached 29,900.

In the competition field, it was voted to add another year to the bid process for the National Championships, so that applications would be made at the third spring meeting of the Executive Committee prior to the proposed dates to allow for proper planning and preparations well ahead of time. Also approved was a form of seeding for elimination rounds in the Regionals based on the previous record of the competitors entered. Also approved was a sanction for the Flaming Leaves International Competition, to be held at Lake Placid on Sept. 20-23, 1979. This was to be the Pre-Olympic competition to test the facilities for the 1980 Olympic Winter Games, which were returning to Lake Placid after 48 years.

A change in the names of Dance events in qualifying competitions was also adopted, dropping the old ones of Gold, Silver and Bronze and replacing them with Senior, Junior and Novice, with an Intermediate Dance event also being added. Basically, the content of the first three classes were standardized to place the compulsory dances into four groups of three dances each, with an original set-pattern dance and free dance (Senior and Junior), or an original set-pattern dance in the final round (Novice). The Intermediate Dance event consisted of two groups of three compulsory dances.

Eligibility for competition was also considered and, for the Senior events in Singles, the Eighth Figure Test and the Senior Free Skating test would now be required. For Junior Dance, it would be required that a minimum of two Pre Gold Dances and not more than three Gold Dances be passed.

Administrative changes adopted included a requirement that the three at large members of the Nominating Committee be elected by the Executive Committee at its spring meeting rather than in the fall, in order to give the committee more time to carry out its work. Another proposal was approved to provide for an annual term of office for the officers, committee chairmen and at-large members of the Executive Committee, but not to exceed four years, unless re-elected by a three-fourths vote of the Governing Council. The proposal was rejected by the Governing Council at its 1979 meeting, leaving the three year maximum term in place. Also discussed was the possibility of having a two year term with two such terms consecutively being the maximum, but this idea has never been formally proposed. The idea of correcting the existing anomaly of having appointed committee chairmen also voting members of the body without being elected has also been discussed but never formally proposed to date.

On the Olympic front it was announced that the USFSA would receive $61,700 in development funds for 1979. With the increased activity in international competitions as a means of development, the need for external sources of funds to support the effort were greater than ever.

Established as a new Special Committee was a Sports Medicine Committee with Franklin Nelson, M.D. as the chairman. This committee would become increasingly active and important over the years, as funds were made available from the USOC for research and training, as well as for the imposition of doping controls domestically. It would serve as an interface and liaison with the comparable committees of the USOC and the ISU.

Also reported was a further meeting between the representatives of the ISIA and PSGA in Chicago in September, the purpose of which was to clarify endorsements and USFSA sanctions through a joint effort of the respective Executive Directors and to develop accepted procedures for USFSA skaters to follow in participating in ISIA events. Another proposal made by the conferees was to consider the inclusion of representatives on each other's respective governing boards, ex officio. To date, this suggestion has not been implemented by any of the three organizations. It was also agreed that the Presidents of the USFSA and ISIA would draw plans for a joint promotion of ice skating by both organizations.

The 1979 Nationals were held in Cincinnati and provided some excitement for the officials. First there were the birds. There was a considerable flock of starlings inside the arena which had a tendency to swoop down on the ice in search of water. One of them even dropped a "deposit" on the head of an unwary skater! They were disposed of late at night by the mechanism of putting the Zamboni in the middle of the ice with a pool of water on the ice in front of it. The headlights were then turned on and down came the birds. Blam! They were gone. There was press coverage and some environmentalists objected, but at least the menace and distraction they represented was eliminated.

The other problem was the ice, which had been painted. With the refrigerant temperature running too high, the paint came through the ice in several places, causing difficulty for the skaters and risk to their blade edges. Eventually, with the coolant temperature lowered considerably, the surface was built up enough by the technical representative, the unperturbable Joe Serafine, to allow the competition to proceed unhindered.

The same top four competitors from the year before returned in Men to vie for the medals and a place on the World Team. With Charlie Tickner retaining his title (his third) with relative ease, the battle was really for second and third between David Santee, Scott Hamilton and Scott Cramer. When it was all over, Cramer had rebounded from his fourth place of 1978 to take the Silver medal with Santee just edging out Hamilton for third. As a result, the latter was off the team, a considerable setback and yet one that would not daunt him, when he too rebounded in 1980. Robert Wagenhoffer was in fifth spot, still doing his two event routine, adding a second place in the Pairs with partner Vicki Heasley.

As for the Ladies, Priscilla Hill was absent due to an injury, but both Lisa-Marie Allen and Carrie Rugh returned to challenge defending champion, Linda Fratianne. It was a fairly clear cut decision for the first two places, as Linda and Lisa-Marie retained their first and second places of the previous year while Carrie moved up to third in a close battle with Sandy Lenz from Wagon Wheel, the 1977 Junior Ladies Champion. Sandy was actually third in both the short program and free skating, but could not quite make up the difference in the figures in which Carrie was third.

With Gail Hamula and Frank Sweiding having retired to skate in Ice Capades, the next two couples in the Pairs would move up behind Tai Babilonia and Randy Gardner, who won their fourth title in what would turn out to be the best year of their career. Heasley and Wagenhoffer placed second, climbing over Sheryl Franks and Michael Botticelli who placed third. In seventh were Kitty and Peter Carruthers from Massachusetts.

Stacey Smith and John Summers kept their Dance title over their perennial rivals Carol Fox and Richard Dalley, against whom they had not been as successful internationally. With Susan Kelley and Andy Stroukoff retired, there was a new couple in third place, Judy Blumberg and Michael Seibert representing Los Angeles and Indianapolis. Judy had been third in the Silver Dance in 1978 with another partner, while Michael had won the Silver Dance title in 1977, also with someone else. Judy and Michael had been together less than a year and showed immediately their promise.

The winner of the Junior Ladies was 13-year-old Elaine Zayak from New York, despite a fifth place in figures. Elaine was already doing several triples with ease. Here too was Vicki Heasley doing her own double exercise, placing fifth! Of note also were the Novice Champions, Paul Wylie of Colorado in the Men and Rosalynn Sumners of Seattle in the Ladies. Paul also was doing two events, finishing fifth in Junior Pairs with Dana Graham, the daughter of Dr. Hugh C. Graham, Jr. who herself also did Singles, placing eighth in Junior Ladies. Third in the Novice Men was a young skater from Los Angeles named Christopher Bowman. It is perhaps the significant aspect of the three levels of qualifying competitions that the rising skaters of the future have usually worked their way up the ranks through diligent effort and are often spotted as comers early on, so that by the time they reach the top they have had considerable experience in competition. Added to that is what is really a further qualifying level in the International competitions, so that the skaters that finally make the World Team have all been there and have proven that they can win.

The 1979 World Championships were held at Vienna, Austria, returning to that city for the first time since 1967, this time indoors. The same three "musketeers" from Europe were back in the Men, Vladimir Kovalev, USSR, Robin Cousins, GRB and Jan Hoffmann, GDR, ready to challenge Charlie Tickner, the defending champion. Unfortunately, Charlie never really got going after placing fourth in both the figures and the short, although he made a valiant effort in the free skating to remain on the podium, finishing second in that part, but he had to accept a disappointing fourth-place finish. This is in itself a statistic since only infrequently had a defending World Champion dropped so far down in the following year, although it had actually happened to Kovalev the year before. He now rebounded spectacularly with a second in figures and a first in the short to take his second title. Robin Cousins pulled up to second with a dazzling free skating program which earned him the best marks, while Jan Hoffman, who had been first in figures, took the Bronze medal. Scott Cramer, with a second in the short program, finished fifth and David Santee who had been third in figures, but 13th in the short, finished eighth.

Happily, in the exact reverse of the result in the prior year, Linda Fratianne regained the title she had lost, despite a third in figures, defeating the defending champion Anett Pötzsch, GDR, who did win the figures but had a fifth in the short, which was her downfall. There was a new Bronze medalist in Emi Watanabe of Japan, the first lady from that country to medal, with a brilliant second in the short. Lisa-Marie Allen wound up sixth after an eighth in figures followed by a fifth in the free, while Carrie Rugh placed 11th.

The Pairs was the event for the U.S. Irina Rodnina and Alexandr Zaitsev did not appear since Irina had taken the year off to have a child, she and her partner now being married. This left the challengers for the vacant title as the two Soviet pairs, Marina Cherkasova and Sergei Shakhrai, and Irina Vorobieva with a new partner Igor Lisovski, the East German pair of Sabine Baess and Tassilo Thierbach, and Tai Babilonia and Randy Gardner. The latter skated virtually flawlessly, except perhaps for a very small error in the short program which they still did win, to take the title by a six to three margin. It was only the second World Pair title for the United States and the first since Karol and Peter Kennedy had won in 1950. Cherkasova-Shakhrai placed second and Vorobieva-Lisovski, third. Vicki Heasley and Robert Wagenhoffer were sixth and Sheryl Franks and Michael Botticelli, ninth.

The Dance event again saw the ongoing triangular fight between the two Soviet couples of Linichuk-Karponosov and Moiseeva-Minenkov with the Hungarian couple, Regöczy and Andras Sallay. This time the Hungarians came out second, with Linichuk-Karponosov the winners, setting up the classic confrontation between them that would take place in 1980. The U.S. couples were out of it and far down the line, with Stacey Smith and John Summers ninth and Carol Fox and Richard Dalley 11th. What the magic formula was to break through the heavy ranks of the European ice dancers still seemed to escape the Americans, just as it still does today. The overall results still were very encouraging for the forthcoming Olympics, with two Gold medals in hand, the first time that had been done since the Golden Age itself; when Carol Heiss and David Jenkins were the champions in 1959, just 20 years earlier.

The 1979 World Junior Championships were held at Augsburg, West Germany, in a rink which was covered but not closed, to use the ISU parlance, meaning that it had a roof but was open on three sides. The U.S. Team did very well, taking one Gold, two Silvers and a Bronze, thereby qualifying a maximum team for 1980 back in Megève. Bobby Beauchamp from Santa Monica, who had been second in the National Junior came second in the Men despite a poor start in the figures in which he was eighth, after a second in the short and a first in the free. The winner was one of the many Soviet athletes who would win in the World Junior, Vitali Egorov while Alexandr Fadeev, also from the USSR was third. Jimmy Santee, the National Junior Champion was 10th in the figures and could not recover, despite a fifth in free, placing seventh overall.

Elaine Zayak topped a very successful season by winning the Ladies, again coming from behind to do so. She had been sixth in figures, but won both the short program and the free skating. Jackie Farrell from Colorado, the National Junior Ladies' runner-up, placed third. Elaine would become in 1982 the first lady to win both the Junior and Senior World titles.

The one-two National Junior Pairs of Rosemary Sweeney and Danny Salera from Massachusetts, and Danelle Porter from California and Burt Lancon from Texas fared less well in Pairs placing eighth and fifth, respectively. The winners were Veronica Pershina and Marat Akbarov of the Soviet Union. Veronica is now the wife of Igor Shpilband, a dance coach in Detroit.

The sole U.S. entry in the Dance event were the National Silver Dance Champions, Elisa Spitz from New Jersey and Stanley Makman from Boston who placed fifth. The winners were Tatiana Durasova and Sergei Ponomarenko of the USSR.

The 1979 Governing Council Meeting was held at Pittsburgh. Despite the defeat of a proposal to permit a regular four-year term, Charles DeMore was re-elected to a fourth term as

Headquarters Building in 1979

President, only the second USFSA President to do so, the first having been Winsor Weld, from 1921 to 1925. The forthcoming shift of the Association from Boston to Colorado Springs was felt to necessitate continuity in the administration at such a critical time and since Chuck had been involved throughout the process, his guiding hand and leadership were deemed essential to the success of the transition. In an unexpected action, F. Don Stoddard of Cleveland was appointed as the Executive Director of the USFSA, effective July 1, 1979. However, Mr. Stoddard did not remain with the Association long, leaving in 1980 and Roy Winder, who served as Membership Director in the interim, reassumed the position of Executive Director in 1981 and served until 1982. As the end of the 1978-1979 season approached, everyone was poised for the transfer and the changes that it would bring to the organization, since an entirely new staff would have to be hired with no one from the Boston office going to Colorado except the Winders.

In looking back, it is indeed a credit to the administration, both old and new, that the transfer took place essentially without a hitch during the summer of 1979. Equally amazing is that it took place during a period of very high activity, including the first international competition to be organized by the Association since 1972 to be held in late September. Add to that the second National Sports Festival in July, not to mention the usual arrangements to be made for skaters to go to the St. Gervais and Oberstdorf competitions. Also there was the necessity of publishing an October issue of the magazine a month early with the new 10-issue season and of setting up the Museum exhibits, including in particular the Grafström Collection, "Skating in Art."

The acquisition of the Grafström Collection is a story in itself. This famous collection had been put together by the late Gillis and his wife Cecile (known as "Baby") beginning in the 1930's and continued by her after World War II. It had been exhibited throughout Europe and had appeared in Colorado in 1975. Two people were vital to its arrival in Colorado Springs on permanent loan to the Museum. The first was Thayer Tutt of the Broadmoor, who journeyed to Sweden with President DeMore to negotiate the terms with Mrs. Grafström and who provided through the El Pomar Foundation the funds needed to carry out the transfer. The other person who played a vital role was Dr. James Koch of Basel, Switzerland, the Honorary President of the ISU, who served as an independent advisor to both parties and whose support for the project was invaluable.

The Collection is quite unique in that it encompasses a great deal of art in all forms, such as prints, porcelain and silver, as well as a major literary archive of books, magazines and other publications. Unlike most sports-related collections, it is not just a collection of individual memorabilia, but far more than that, reflecting the sport of skating not just in a brief period of time, but across the centuries. The Collection was and remains today the centerpiece of the Museum collections.

A very special part of the Collection was not received until 1981, when Mrs. Grafström brought with her to Hartford on the occasion of the 1981 World Championships, the Swedish National costume worn by Grafström for many exhibitions that he gave in Europe, as well as in the United States in 1932. It was a very much appreciated addition to the Collection and can be seen in the Museum where skating costumes form a major part of its displays.

Mrs. Grafström and her two daughters, Louise Wriedt of Hamburg and Vera Schieckel of Berlin came to the dedication of the new Headquarters building and opening of the Museum in October 1979.

The new staff in Colorado included Ian Anderson as the Editor of Skating magazine and Jerry McGaha as Director of the Museum, with Helen ("Pat") Cataldi as the Curator. Unfortunately, Jerry did not stay long, departing in 1980 and Mrs. Cataldi ran the Museum herself until her own departure in 1990. There are, however, three employees today who have been with the Headquarters virtually from the beginning: Dalean Greenlee, the daughter of Jean Winder, Valerie Powell and Mary Ann Purpura. Much is owed to them for their loyalty and in providing continuity to the operation over the years since, with the many changes in management and staff that have taken place.

The dedication and opening took place on the occasion of the fall meeting of the Executive Committee in early October 1979 and was a gala affair, including the Army Band from Fort Carson to kick things off. Dick Button was the master of ceremonies, Thayer Tutt represented the Broadmoor, Leo Ververs, El Paso County and Mike Bird, the City of Colorado Springs. Past President Ritter Shumway gave the benediction, the National and USFSA flags were raised and the ribbon cutting was carried out with aplomb by Mrs. Grafström.

The principal business of the meeting itself was the approval of all the resolutions necessary finally to effect the transfer of all the assets and activities of "USFSA Massachusetts" to "USFSA Colorado" as well as to adopt new By Laws for the Colorado corporation. The revisions served a dual purpose and had been drafted by a task force chaired by Past President Wright. Not only did they reflect the merger of the Association and Memorial Fund, but also made the changes required in the charter and governing bodies of the organization mandated by the Amateur Sports Act of 1978 and the U.S. Olympic Committee.

The former Executive Committee was restructured and redesignated as the Board of Directors, the voting membership of which would consist of the following: the six officers, nine permanent committee chairmen (then Amateur Status, Competitions, Dance, International, Judges, Membership, Sanctions, Singles and Pairs and Tests), 15 members at large, five from each of the three Sections, nine athletes, three coaches, the immediate Past President and the ISU and Olympic Representatives for a total of 45. The Sectional Committees were abolished and five additional permanent committees with non-voting status were established: the Hall of Fame and Museum, Memorial Fund, Program Development and Rules and Sports Medicine Committees, all of which were existing special committees.

Also created was a new Executive Committee which would manage the day-to-day administrative affairs of the Association between meetings of the Board of Directors, consisting of the six officers, two athlete Board members and the immediate Past President.

The new By Laws also required that all figure skaters who were members of the member clubs of the USFSA, as well as all Board members, referees, judges and accountants and other officials, must be registered annually with the Association. This comprehensive provision was intended in part to stop the leakage that resulted when member clubs failed to register all their members, and was consistent with the provisions of the Sports Act.

The new By Laws also provided that Associate Members, Probationary and Interim Probationary Clubs could have observers present at meetings of the Governing Council who would be accorded the privileges of the floor, without a vote. The same rights were also extended to Honorary Members and members of member clubs. These broader provisions were intended to provide the opportunity to be present and to speak to the representatives of the Inter-Club associations, without diluting the voting rights of the member clubs themselves.

In a year such as 1979, the season did not start with the end of August, but instead began with the National Sports Festival, which was held at Colorado Springs for the second year. This year, many of the top skaters were on hand, but among the missing were Linda Fratianne in the Ladies, Stacey Smith and John Summers and Carol Fox and Richard Dalley in the Dance. In the Men, it was the same quartet of Tickner, Cramer, Santee and Hamilton, who finished in that order, with Cramer winning the short program. At that point, things did not look too promising for Scott Hamilton, who had disastrous short program, finishing eighth, but ultimately winding up fourth. He seemed to be locked in at that level, which would mean only an alternate for the Olympic Team. Tickner won the figures and the free skating to take the Gold.

Lisa-Marie Allen was the clear winner in Ladies, with only a second place in figures to Priscilla Hill, who had returned to competition, but wound up sixth overall. Second was Sandy Lenz from Rockford, Ill., the fourth place finisher in the last year's Nationals, while third was Jill

Sawyer from Tacoma. Tai Babilonia and Randy Gardner took their second Festival Gold in Pairs, with the surprise second being Kitty and Peter Carruthers, who had been seventh in the 1979 Nationals and fifth in the 1978 Festival, but came on strong to defeat Vicki Heasley and Robert Wagenhoffer. The latter also placed fifth in the Men.

There were but three entries in Dance, with the title going to Judy Blumberg and Michael Seibert, with Kim Krohn and Barry Hagan second, and Judy Ferris and Scott Gregory from Buffalo third.

Just a little over a month later came the St. Gervais competition, with the Nebelhorn Trophy competition usually held at Oberstdorf taking place in Garmisch-Partenkirchen due to rink renovations at the former site, which was being expanded into what the Germans called a "Bundesleistcentrum" or National Training Center. The usual dual team was sent to participate in both competitions. Brian Boitano and Jimmy Santee place third and fourth, respectively, in both events while the Ladies, Lynn Smith from Berkeley, Calif., the third place finisher in the 1979 National Junior, won both competitions, while Jackie Farrell, from Colorado, the second place finisher, placed third at St. Gervais and second at Garmisch. Kitty and Peter Carruthers again confirmed their improvement by winning both Pair competitions, a rare double indeed. Ellen Pulver and Donald Adair, who had been seventh in the National Dance, placed fourth at St. Gervais and sixth at Garmisch in Dance. With this harvest of medals, four Gold, one Silver and three Bronze, the U.S. again won handily the Coupe des Alpes Trophy for National teams, with Canada second. The success in these two competitions continued.

The next big event on the calendar was the Flaming Leaves International Competition at Lake Placid at the end of September, still rather early for most skaters, but of major importance. Originally to be called the Norton Skate because of the sponsorship of the Norton Company of Worcester, Mass., the new name was intended to convey the fall foliage found in the Adirondacks at that time of year. The pins issued for the competition were quite attractive and have become collectors items. Since it was the test competition for the Olympic facilities, with the two new rinks adjacent to the original Olympic Arena now providing a total of four surfaces, it was attended by many of the ISU officeholders, including the President, Jacques Favart from France, the ISU Vice President, Jack Shoemaker and the Chairman of the Figure Skating Committee, Sonia Bianchetti. On the same occasion, the first Judges' Examinations of the ISU were held, with six candidates, but none from the United States. It was then mostly a practical test, but later would also include a written part.

The Ladies event was again a triumph for Lisa-Marie Allen, who won with a unanimous decision over the Italian-American, Susan Driano, while third was Sandy Lenz. Jill Sawyer, the third U.S. entry, was seventh. In fourth was Denise Biellmann of Switzerland, she of the spin, while eighth was Katarina Witt of East Germany.

The Men's event was the sudden breakthrough for Scott Hamilton, who wound up on top for a major international win, with Scott Cramer second and the 1979 World Runner-up, Jan Hoffman third, who had as usual, led the figures, followed by David Santee fourth. It was a huge step for Hamilton and perhaps might be considered the launching pad for his future great career. His free skating is described in the magazine by Howard Bass as follows: "The diminutive Hamilton seized his opportunity and hardly put a foot wrong, clinching a memorable victory with a brilliant performance that included eight great triples - two salchows, three toe loops, two walleys and a lutz." Of course, under today's rules, the repetition of a triple more than once is not permitted.

Kitty and Peter Carruthers continued their strong progress in Pairs, placing second behind the winners, Sabine Baess and Tassilo Thierbach from East Germany, the 1979 World Bronze medalists. Vicki Heasley and Robert Wagenhoffer were third, while Sheryl Franks and Michael Botticelli placed sixth.

The U.S. fared less well in Dance with its three couples, Judy Blumberg and Michael Seibert, Stacey Smith and John Summers, and Carol Fox and Richard Dalley, fourth, fifth and sixth, respectively. The winners were Krisztina Regöczy and Andras Sallay of Hungary, with the rising young couple of Natalia Bestemianova and Andrei Bukin of the Soviet Union, who had been 10th in the 1979 Worlds, second. The overall result was quite acceptable: two Gold, two Silver and two Bronze medals.

By agreement with the CFSA, there was no Skate Canada in 1979, in order to avoid a conflict with the Flaming Leaves event, with this being reciprocated in 1987, with no Skate America that year, since Skate Canada was the Pre-Olympic Competition before the 1988 Calgary Olympic Winter Games.

At the 31st Richmond Trophy, which by then was the longest-running International Competition open to skaters from outside Europe (the Scandinavian Championships were older, having started in 1919, but were limited only to skaters from the four Northern countries of Denmark, Finland, Norway and Sweden), Alicia Risburg of Colorado, who had been fifth in the 1979 Nationals, was the winner, with Simone Grigorescu of New York, the seventh-place finisher in the Nationals, third, in what Dennis Bird, the reporter, described as the closest competition in the history of the event. Dennis also refers to the winners of the event from the U.S., of which there were up to that point, four, with the previous three being Dorothy Hamill (1972), Barbara Smith (1976) and Priscilla Hill (1977).

In 1979, there was a new competition added to the schedule, the NHK Trophy in Japan, which has since become a regular stop on the circuit and one of the top International Competitions in the World, and always well organized by the Japanese federation. Included in it were entries from both North and South Korea and China, for the first time. The U.S. team did well, with five medals, two Silver and three Bronze. The Men's winner was Robin Cousins, with David Santee third, ahead of Scott Hamilton fourth. The winner in the Ladies was Emi Watanabe of Japan, with Lisa-Marie Allen and Sandy Lenz, second and third, respectively. Vicki Heasley and Robert Wagenhoffer, and Sheryl Franks and Michael Botticelli were second and third in Pairs behind the winners, Irina Vorobieva and Igor Lisovsksi of the Soviet Union. Wagenhoffer was still very busy, since he would go on to compete in singles in the Ennia Cup, which followed the NHK Trophy by just two weeks. Stacey Smith and John Summers placed fourth in Dance. The winners were Irina Moiseeva and Andrei Minenkov of the USSR, while in second was the young British couple of Jayne Torvill and Christopher Dean.

The Ennia Challenge Cup followed and was again for free skating only in the Singles events. Without the figures to bother her, Elaine Zayak skated strongly and well to take second in the Ladies behind a Czech skater, Renate Baierova, while Robert Wagenhoffer, still in pursuit of his Singles goal, placed third, with Robin Cousins of Great Britain the winner. Kim Krohn and Barry Hagan were fourth in Dance, while Karen and Douglas Mankowich, representing Arctic Blades, were fifth. Lee Ann Miller and William Fauver from the Broadmoor were seventh in Pairs.

The international competition season had been reasonably successful and the patterns were beginning to form for the championship season to follow. The 1980 Nationals were held at Atlanta, Ga., the first time ever in the Southeastern portion of the country and also reflecting the growing interest in the sport in the area. With the Nationals also constituting the primary basis for selection for the Olympic and World Teams, the competition was keen.

The rigors of defending a National title when there is an Olympic berth on the line has often been arduous and 1980 was no exception in the Ladies. Linda Fratianne won the figures, with Priscilla Hill, second and Lisa-Marie Allen, third. In both the short program and the free skating, Allen was the winner ahead of Fratianne, who placed second in both parts, but had a sufficient margin to retain her title. While the ordinal placements do not show it, in the opinion of many, Linda would never have won had she not been both the defending champion and also the defending World Champion. Such is fate for the perennial runner-up. In third was Sandy Lenz. Despite third places in both the short program and the free skating by Elaine Zayak, her 10th place in the figures prevented her from making the medals. With respect to the Ladies in general, we can find Tiffany Chin of San Diego second in Junior Ladies and Debi Thomas of Redwood City, second in the Novice Ladies.

The Men were a different story in which Charlie Tickner decisively defended his title, with David Santee second. However, Scott Hamilton came third ahead of Scott Cramer, thereby landing the coveted Olympic Team berth. Brian Boitano was fifth and the indefatigable

Wagenhoffer was sixth. In the Junior Men, we find Paul Wylie in second. Paul did, also, win the Junior Pairs with Dana Graham. The Senior Pairs event reflected probably the best standard of recent years, with Tai Babilonia and Randy Gardner winning their fifth straight title followed by Kitty and Peter Carruthers topping a vary successful season up to that point with a solid second, while Sheryl Franks and Michael Botticelli easily defeated Wagenhoffer and his partner, Vicki Heasley, the runners-up the year before.

Stacey Smith and John Summers redeemed what had been so far a mixed result in Dance by defeating Judy Blumberg and Michael Seibert in a very close competition, decided by four judges to three. Third were Carol Fox and Richard Dalley. With teams chosen, things looked bright for a good showing in the Olympics and the Worlds to follow at Dortmund, West Germany.

Incredibly, the 1980 World Junior Championships were held at Megève, France, on the exact same dates as the 1980 Nationals (January 15-19), but this time, the USFSA still sent a team, unlike the decision in 1977 not to do so. For the third year in a row, the U.S. won the Ladies title, with Rosalynn Sumners of Edmonds, Wash., who had been the National Novice Ladies Champion in 1979, the winner, a quantum leap from Novice to the World Junior title. Scott Williams from Los Angeles made what would be the first of several appearances in the World Junior Men, placing fifth. Renée Roca from Rochester, N.Y., and Andrew Ouellette from Columbus, Ohio, were the Bronze medalists in the Dance. Kelly Abolt and Kevin Peaks from Berkeley, Calif., who were the 1980 Pacific Coast Junior Pair Champions, were fourth in Pairs.

The 1980 Olympic Winter Games returned to Lake Placid, the site of the IIIrd Games in 1932. The Games were held under strained circumstances, since the proposed U.S. boycott of the 1980 Summer Games in Moscow due to the Soviet Union's invasion of Afghanistan, was just then being implemented under strong pressure from the Federal Government. The Games were also beset with problems relating to transportation and housing. Despite this, the competitions at the Games were well organized and ran well. The figure skating was in the new rinks built for the Games, which were excellent and with good ice. The main arena was where the United States won the Gold medal in ice hockey for only the second time in 20 years. Just outside the main arena was the new speed skating oval on the site of the 1932 track, but artificially refrigerated this time, where Eric Heiden of the U.S. won his five Gold medals. Both feats overshadowed the somewhat disappointing results in the figure skating, where the United States came away with just two medals, one Silver and one Bronze.

The Pairs event was the story of the Games from the standpoint of the United States. With Irina Rodnina and Alexandr Zaitsev of the Soviet Union returning after a year off to defend their Olympic title and the 1979 World Champions, Tai Babilonia and Randy Gardner also entered to challenge them, it was thought that would be the battle for the title, with Marina Cherkasova and

Sergei Shakhrai also as potential challengers. Sadly, the anticipated confrontation never took place. Randy Gardner had suffered a groin injury two weeks before the Games and last minute medication just before they were to skate the short program failed. Tai and Randy actually came out to warm up and when Randy's leg clearly could not support him, as he fell twice in the practice, it was obvious that they would have to withdraw. The injury was severe enough so that they were also unable to go to the 1980 Worlds in Dortmund, Germany, following the Games, so their careers ended on a rather negative note. Happily, Randy subsequently fully recovered and he and Tai went on to a distinguished career in the Ice Capades.

The Pairs competition itself was rather predictable thereafter, with Rodnina-Zaitsev winning their second Olympic title and her third, with Cherkasova and Shakhrai second, followed by the East Germans, Manuela Mager and Uwe Bewersdorff. A positive note in the Pairs competition was the excellent showing of the other two U.S. pairs, with Kitty and Peter Carruthers placing fifth and Sheryl Franks and Michael Botticelli seventh. Also in the competition in ninth place were Barbara Underhill and Paul Martini of Canada, who would in 1984 have a classic confrontation in the Games at Sarajevo with the Carruthers.

The Men's event was also a disappointment, as many thought that Charlie Tickner would take the Gold medal. While Jan Hoffmann of East Germany won the figures as expected, with Tickner second, Charlie had a bad day in the short program, placing fifth and was thereby effectively out of the fight for the top place. Robin Cousins of Great Britain, who was the new European Champion, had placed fourth in figures and won the short program, so he moved into contention. Topping the field with an excellent free skating performance, Cousins succeeded his compatriot, John Curry, to bring his country its second Olympic Gold Medal in the Men. Jan Hoffmann placed second in free and second overall, while Tickner, who was third in the free skating had to settle for the Bronze medal. Right behind him were his teammates, David Santee, fourth and Scott Hamilton, fifth. Scott had been the flag bearer for the United States Team in the opening ceremony, a considerable honor. He placed fourth in both the short and the long, after a poor eighth in the figures, to pull up to his fifth position.

The Ladies saw once again the power of the figures. Linda Fratianne, the 1979 World Ladies champion, was the favorite and in that respect she did not disappoint in either the short program and the free skating, winning the former and placing second to Denise Biellman of Switzerland in the latter. Linda was third in the figures, which would not seem to have been a handicap, while Anett Pötzsch of East Germany, who won the figures, was fourth in the short and third in the long and yet still won the competition, with Linda second. Third was Dagmar Lurz of the FRG, with Biellmann fourth and Lisa-Marie Allen fifth. Lisa had also had a bad day in figures with an eighth place, but was third in the short and fourth in the free skating. Sandy Lenz, the other U.S. lady placed ninth, but she too had to pull up from an 11th in the figures, with a sixth and a seventh in the other two parts.

Ironically, the system of scoring in competition was changed by the 1980 ISU Congress to that in effect today, which involves the factoring of the results of each part of an event and which was designed further to reduce the exaggerated value given to the figures. If the new system had been in effect one year earlier, Linda would have been the Olympic Champion and might well have been World Champion four times instead of two!

The Dance event did not involve any of the U.S. couples in the fight for the podium, with Judy Blumberg and Michael Seibert finishing seventh and turning the tables on their perennial rivals Stacey Smith and John Summers, the National Champions, who finished ninth. The event will be remembered for the win of Natalia Linichuk and Gennadi Karponosov of the Soviet Union over Krisztina Regöczy and Andras Sallay of Hungary, with a virtual tie, caused by the failure of one judge to break a tie in free dance, while the Soviet judge naturally had awarded his second place to the second Soviet couple of Irina Moiseeva and Andrei Minekov. The result was thought by many to be a significant miscarriage of justice and this view would be vindicated at Dortmund.

So the Games ended with the summary of the places for the U.S. being: Men - third, fourth, fifth; Ladies - second, fifth, ninth; Pairs - fifth, seventh; Dance - seventh, ninth. One bright aspect of the showing was that all the U.S. skaters finished in the top 10 which was accomplished by no other country.

The 1980 World Championships were held in Dortmund, Germany, and there were only a few departures from the ranks. One was of Rodnina and Zaitsev, who were actually on site ready to skate when they were mysteriously withdrawn by the Soviet delegation and replaced with the young pair of Veronica Pershina and Marat Akbarov, the 1979 World Junior Pair Champions, who placed sixth. So, the long reign of Rodnina came to an end. In the absence also of Babilonia and Gardner, the vacant World title went to Marina Cherkasova and Sergei Shakhrai, who were now much better matched, as Marina had grown considerably and they were no longer the "Mutt and Jeff" pair that they had been a few years earlier. This time, the second and third U.S. pairs did not fare as well as they had in the Olympics, with the Carruthers placing seventh and Franks and Botticelli 10th.

The Ladies was a test of "true grit" and sportsmanship on the part of Linda Fratianne, who had suffered a painful ankle injury and knew before she ever left the United States that she would not be able to skate her best. Despite the injury, she carried out the obligation to defend her 1979 title, which will always be to her great credit and should serve as a model for those following her. With a fourth in the figures and a third in the short, Linda skated extremely well to win the free skating and finish third overall. Anett Pötzsch regained the title she had last held in 1978, despite a sixth place in the short program, but she did better in the free skating with a second, to win her second title. She and Linda had traded the title between them for the past four years, with Anett taking the rubber match in Dortmund in what had been an epic rivalry. Second in her native Germany was Dagmar Lurz, with a second in figures and despite a fourth in the short program and a fifth in free skating. It was the highest place for a skater from West Germany since 1954. The short program winner was Denise Biellmann, who had been 10th in figures and wound up sixth overall. Lisa-Marie Allen placed seventh and Elaine Zayak, who had replaced Sandy Lenz, placed 11th, with a 22nd in figures, matched with a fourth in free skating!

Jan Hoffmann turned the tables on Robin Cousins in the Men to win his second World title six years after his first one in 1974 and to deny to Robin the World title, so that he joined the ranks of those few who have been Olympic Champions but never World Champions. Charlie Tickner was again third, despite a seventh in the short program with David Santee right behind in fourth and Scott Hamilton, fifth, after an eighth in figures, but a fourth in free.

The Dance saw Regöczy and Sallay gain revenge for their Olympic defeat, when they came from behind after the compulsory dances to win the Free Dance and the World title over Linuchuk and Karponosov, with the veteran Moiseeva and Minenkov, third. Judy Blumberg and Michael Seibert remained the top U.S. couple with a sixth place, while Smith and Summers placed eighth. So the placement summary was: Men - third, fourth, fifth; Ladies - third, seventh, 11th; Pairs - seventh, 10th; Dance - sixth, eighth, a bit of a come down from 1979.

The 1980 Governing Council meeting was held at San Diego, Calif., for the first time and represented a changing of the guard, as Charles DeMore stepped down as President after four years in office and was replaced by Oscar T. Iobst, Jr., of Churchville, Pa. Chuck remained active, both in the Association, as well as on the ISU Council, to which he was elected in 1980, serving with distinction for 14 years until his retirement in 1994, when he was elected an Honorary Member of the ISU. He also served as the Representative of the USFSA to the ISU from 1990 to 1992. Chuck is also an Honorary Member of the USFSA, elected in 1980 and of the Board of Directors, elected in 1983, and today holds registration number 003. These numbers, which are held by the Past Presidents in the order of their seniority, are the only ones which change as the composition of their ranks is altered by time, while all other USFSA registrants carry a permanent number, a practice instituted in 1962.

The San Diego meeting was a large one, with 200 delegates present, perhaps a tribute to the location, which was right on Mission Bay. The meeting approved the restructuring that had been proposed by the old Executive Committee, so that the first athlete members of

Oscar T. Iobst, Jr.

the new Board of Directors were elected: Mahlon Bradley, Peter Carruthers, Randy Gardner, Jock Kohlhas, Sandy Lenz, David Santee, Ken Shelley, Stacey Smith and Charles Tickner. The three coaches elected were Don Laws, Ron Ludington and John Nicks. Bradley and Kohlhas were elected by the athletes to serve on the new Executive Committee.

The composition of the Nominating Committee was also changed. The committee, which formerly had six members, was increased to nine, with one from each Section chosen by the delegates to the Governing Council (out of which grew the Sectional Caucus), three members elected by the Board of Directors, also one from each Section and the three Vice Presidents. The membership of the committee was further revised in 1985 to provide that none of the nine members can represent the same Region.

In competition matters, the entry fee for the National Championships was eliminated to lighten a little the financial burden of participating. Also approved was a revision to permit the Sectional Junior and Novice winners to re-enter the Nationals again in the following year without having to re-qualify. In so far as judges were concerned, the passing of an annual examination would be required for the retention of their appointments. In a seemingly minor revision, but actually one of importance to them, the seating order of judges would now be drawn, rather than for them to be placed in alphabetical order.

In anticipation of the forthcoming International competition season, nine (the largest number up to that time) International Competitions in which the USFSA would participate were announced: St. Gervais, Oberstdorf, St. Ivel (England), Skate Canada, Richmond, Ennia, Golden Spin (Zagreb), NHK and Morzine (France), involving 26 officials (judges and team leaders) and 49 skaters. The St. Ivel competition in England replaced the former Rotary Watches, while Morzine was a Senior Dance competition to be held following the Worlds. A 10th competition, the Merano (Italy) Spring Trophy Competition for Junior Ladies would also be added at the last minute.

With respect to the Memorial Fund, it was noted that the assistance extended to the skaters had increased by 12-1/2 percent. The athletes asked to have included in the World team a trainer (this has since been done) and a hairdresser (this has not). The team leaders also stated that better arrangements needed to be made at International competitions especially for the coaches, with respect to whom there had been many problems of accreditation and housing, always a difficult problem and particularly at the Olympics, where the concept of individual coaches for each skater was unknown to the Olympic officials used to team sports.

At the banquet closing the meeting, the famous "Fish Award" auction, which had been inaugurated by Ritter Shumway two years earlier was conducted for the third time, with the winning bid by Cliff Kruse of Colorado Springs for the benefit of the Memorial Fund being $300, up from the $110 bid by Jack Might, also from Colorado Springs for the first year in 1978. The winning bid in 1979 had been $150 by Jim Larkin of Salt Lake City. The original award had been a fish dinner, which by the second year had become a plaque decorated with the skeleton of a fish (the prior year's dinner?). Not to be forgotten was that there actually were two dinners auctioned off in 1978, with the second one going to Tom Collins of Minneapolis for $101. The question is: where is the plaque today? No one seems to know. It has been confirmed that it is not in the Museum!

The 1980 ISU Congress was held at Davos, Switzerland, and represented the first in the new even-year cycle based on a four-year term of office, as approved in 1977. It was also one of change, although President Jacques Favart was re-elected to another term of office. It was at this Congress that Jack Shoemaker, the First Vice President for Figure Skating, retired after 13 years of distinguished service. He was elected an Honorary Vice President of the ISU, the first from Figure Skating and was succeeded by Charles DeMore of Cleveland as a member of the Council. Benjamin Wright was also re-elected to the Figure Skating Committee.

The principal action taken by the Congress was the revision of the scoring system which was not accepted by the USFSA for its competitions until 1981 for the 1982 season. The first use of the new system internationally was for the 1981 ISU Championships and the 1980-1981 International Competitions.

In addition to the increase in the number of elements in the Pair short program by the addition of a spin combination, the duration for the free skating for both Men and Pairs was reduced from five minutes to four and one-half. Also added to the rules was the requirement that the principle practice rink for Championships and the Olympics must also be covered, with the main arena also to be closed (indoor). In the Innsbruck Olympics of 1976, for example, an outdoor practice rink inside the speed skating oval had been used for practice. At least in Lake Placid, all the rinks, both competition and practice, had been indoor.

The minimum age for appointment as a Judge for International Competitions was reduced from 25 to 23 and categories of Honorary ISU Referee and Judge were created, while the category of ISU Test Judge was dropped, since the new classes were also empowered to judge ISU Tests.

On a trial basis for 1982 in the ISU Championships (World and European), a form of panel judging was to be used, with each event to be judged by two separate panels of seven judges each, with one panel doing the figures and short program of one Singles event and the free skating of the other. Two panels were also be used in Pairs and Dance as well. The trial lasted but one year since its intention, which was to reduce the possibility of bloc judging, was already addressed in the revised scoring system and the system did not have any apparent effect on the results. The judges did not like it at all, among the reasons being the resulting imbalance in assignments and conflicts with training and competition and the like. A much larger number of judges were also needed to staff it, which was a considerable increase in cost for the organizing member.

It was not possible for those present at the Congress to anticipate the unexpected death in September 1980 of President Favart and the consequent changes in the ISU that resulted. In the United States, the Association looked forward to embarking on the next quadrennium with anticipation and a new beginning at its Colorado Springs base.

As a general rule, a skating generation is about 10 years and the critical aspect of the timing for success is whether the generation matches with the Olympic cycles or quadrenniums. If a skater is lucky, he or she might be able to skate in two Olympics four years apart if their arrival at the Senior and International level has been quick enough. There is always a major

Countdown to Sarajevo
(1981-1984)

turnover right after an Olympic Games and especially in the Worlds which still follow the Games in the same season. There have been suggestions over the years that the Worlds in the Olympic year should not be held or at least be merged with the Olympics, as is the case in some sports. Because of the age of the World Championships, which reached 100 years in 1996, the ISU has been determined to maintain the integrity of the championships as the top event in the sport. From the standpoint of the media and the public, that is not really the case. The immediate post-Olympics Worlds has a definite value as it launches, as it were, instantly, the next generation into the cycle leading up to the next Olympics.

The period we are about to explore from 1981 to 1984 is a very good example of the cycle, as it was before the major changes in the sport that occurred in the 1990's.

The fall meeting of the new Board of Directors was held at Colorado Springs at the Olympic Training Center in October 1980. Reports were submitted concerning the financial situation of the Association, which was described as in good condition except for the one-time expenditures that had been necessitated by the move to Colorado. The projections, however, were for improved income. One aspect of the picture which was favorable was that a new television rights contract had been agreed to between ABC-TV and the Association near the end of the term of President DeMore. The payments for the new four year agreement for the years 1981 to 1985 were $1,865,000, a quantum increase from the predecessor agreement, on the order of almost four to one. Also under consideration was an International Senior Competition, starting in 1981, which would have television coverage.

In the technical areas there were several changes of note: one of which was to rename Veterans' Dance as Adult Dance, which it still is today. Neither name is completely satisfactory and really the best one of Seniors is not available, although there has been since 1990 a Masters category for skaters over age 50. The former Veterans Dance was originally for skaters who were over age 35, although that limit has been progressively lowered since, reaching age 25 by 1992. At the same time as the name was changed, Adult Dance Tests were included in the schedule at all levels to be skated with a partner only (i.e.; no solo being required). Otherwise, the passing requirements remained the same as for the standard Dance Tests. Masters Dance Tests would also be added in 1990, but with lower passing averages being required. Also added in 1990 were Adult Figure and Free Skating Tests, consisting of three classes, Bronze, Silver and Gold.

A report was received from Larry McCollum of the USOC indicating that while the boycott of the Moscow Games had hurt fund raising efforts, there would still be development grants to the National Governing Bodies (NGB's) over the next four years. The USFSA planning allocation was estimated at $96,000. Included in the grants would be such items as the costs of trials, team training, representation at international federation meetings and the Olympic Job Opportunities Program (a matching fund program). Also reported was that the Squaw Valley Olympic Training Center had been closed, leaving only that in Colorado Springs open, which had no rink of its own.

Approved was participation in the 1981 National Sports Festival at Syracuse, New York, to consist of 12 Men, 12 Ladies, eight Pairs and eight Dance couples, with the intention that it would be a Junior Competition (it did not happen).

The Board approved the recommendation of Ardelle K. Sanderson of Lake Placid, N.Y., as the first person to be nominated to the ISU for appointment as an Honorary ISU Judge. Ardelle had enjoyed a long and distinguished career as both a National and World Judge and had herself been an active competitor in Singles, Pairs and Fours at the National level.

The start for the forthcoming season was the participation of the top skaters in the international season which essentially ran from September though December of each year. The fall of 1980 was no exception. At St. Gervais and Oberstdorf, Vikki deVries of Los Angeles, the National Junior Ladies champion won both competitions, while Tom Dickson from the Broadmoor, the National Junior champion was fourth at St. Gervais, but won at Oberstdorf. The Pair of Dana Graham and Paul Wylie from Colorado and the dance couple of Susan Dymecki from Philadelphia and Anthony Bardin from Los Angeles did not fare as well with the latter gaining a third place at Oberstdorf, although the United States still had enough points to win the Coupe des Alpes Trophy over Canada.

The St. Ivel International at Richmond, England, which had replaced the Rotary Watches competition, saw two medals, with Sandy Lenz of Rockford the winner of the Ladies, while Scott Hamilton was second in the Men, just barely losing out to Brian Pockar of Canada by a four to three decision. The Richmond Trophy for Ladies was still alive, although 1980 would turn out to be the last competition since conflicts with other international events finally caused its demise. There was no medal this time, with Lynn Smith from Berkeley placing fourth.

At Skate Canada at Calgary there was a major break through as the representatives of the United States won all three events, the best showing ever in the competition. Scott Hamilton won the Men, with David Santee third and Brian Boitano fifth, just ahead of Brian Orser of Canada. Elaine Zayak won the Ladies, with Sandy Lenz fourth and Rosalynn Sumners fifth. Judy Blumberg and Michael Seibert won the Dance, with Elisa Spitz from New Jersey and Scott Gregory from Wilmington, Del., fourth.

The U.S. again won the Ennia Challenge Cup at the Hague, in the Netherlands, with a gold medal performance by Jackie Farrell of Colorado in the Ladies and second place finishes in the Men by Mark Cockerell of Arctic Blades and in the Pairs by Kitty and Peter Carruthers. In Dance, Elisa Spitz and Scott Gregory placed seventh.

At the NHK Trophy Competition in Japan, the U.S. won five medals: Melissa Thomas from Long Island, third in Ladies, right behind Denise Biellmann of Switzerland and Katarina Witt of the GDR; Robert Wagenhoffer of Arctic Blades second, and Allen Schramm of New York third in Men; in Pairs, Maria DiDomenico of Los Angeles, and Burt Lancon of Houston second, behind Barbara Underhill and Paul Martini of Canada, while Carol Fox and Richard Dalley of Michigan were the winners in Dance, the first win ever in that event.

A new competition added to the schedule was the Golden Spin of Zagreb, Croatia, then part of Yugoslavia, in which Priscilla Hill of Massachusetts placed second, while Jimmy Santee of Chicago won the Men. Another new competition in which U.S. skaters participated was the Merano Spring Trophy for Junior Ladies, in Italy in March 1981. Two skaters applied to go on their own and at their own expense and the International Committee agreed that they could do so on the basis of their records in the 1981 National Junior Ladies. What usually happens in this type of a situation is that the competition in question subsequently becomes a part of the schedule and is supported by the USFSA thereafter. The Merano competition was added to the schedule the next year and subsequently was transferred in 1991 to another small town in the Italian Alps, Ortisei, because the Merano rink was not covered. Under ISU rules, an international competition could no longer be held in an open rink. The record of the U.S. entrants in the competition has been outstanding over the years since. The winner in 1981 was Leslie Sikes from Atlanta, with Kelly Webster of Cleveland second.

Another competition held in April 1981 was the International Senior Dance Competition at Morzine, France, to which two couples were sent, with Kim Krohn and Barry Hagan of Southern California placing third and Nancy Berghoff and Jim Bowser of Michigan seventh. This event would basically become the competition to which the top Dance couples in the Nationals who were the World team alternates would be sent.

The World Junior Championships were finally moving back in the schedule to a time period where there would be less of a conflict with the Sectionals and the Nationals and, accordingly, were held in mid-December 1980 at London, Ontario. The usual pattern was seen in the success of the United States in the singles events, and of the Soviet Union in the Pairs and Dance events. With Paul Wylie and Tiffany Chin of San Diego, who had been the runner-up in the 1980 National Junior Ladies, the U.S. took the gold medals in both Men and Ladies. It was the fourth straight Ladies title for the U.S. and the fifth overall, while Paul's win in the Men was the first for the U.S. in the event as a World Championship and the second overall. Up to then, only the U.S. in 1976 and Canada in 1977 had won both singles titles in the same year (but in the ISU Junior Championships).

Tiffany Chin started out poorly in the figures, placing eighth, due in large measure to having an incorrect start in one figure, which she had to restart. However, she placed second in the short program, pulling up to fourth at that point, to which she added another second place in the free skating to take the title. First in the free skating was Midori Ito of Japan, who had been 20th in figures and fifth in the short program to wind up eighth overall. Maria Causey of Los Angeles placed fourth, with a third in figures. Wylie won both the short program and the free skating in the Men, added to a second in figures (to Oliver Höner of Switzerland) to win the World Junior title. Scott Williams from Arctic Blades was third. The best the U.S. could do in the Pairs was fifth and sixth, with Julie Wasserman and Robert Davenport from New York, and Deborah Lynch and Keith Green from California. In the Dance, it was eighth for Sandra Fabrocini from Massachusetts and Jim Yorke from Rye, N.Y. The Pair winners were Larisa Selezneva and Oleg Makarov of the USSR, who would subsequently have a distinguished career at the Senior level. The Dance winners for the second time were Elena Batanova and Alexei Soloviev, also from the USSR, who would become a typical example of the Soviet policy of breaking up promising Junior pairs and dance couples and assigning them new partners. The Soviets have had extraordinary success in the World Juniors, where they leave their skaters in until they are no longer age eligible. The curious fact, however, is that very few of them in Pairs and Dance have remained together and gone on to success in the Senior ranks. There are, of course, one or two obvious exceptions.

The 1981 Nationals were held at San Diego, Calif., for the first time and again, the defending champions were gone in all four Senior events, so the future of the new generation would depend on their success in the 1981 Nationals. There was a strong field in the Ladies and once again the runner-up syndrome took over, as Lisa-Marie Allen, representing the Broadmoor, was unable to capture the vacant title which went instead to Elaine Zayak of New York, fourth in 1980. After a second in figures, a surprise for her and a shaky short program with a fifth, Elaine won the free skating. Priscilla Hill of Lexington, Mass., who had won the figures, hung on with a third in the short program and a fifth in the free skating to defeat Allen and take second. With a third in figures and a second in the short, Allen had a chance to win but a fourth place in free skating prevented it. Second and third in the free skating were Vikki deVries of the Broadmoor, fourth overall and Rosalynn Sumners of Seattle, fifth overall.

The men's event had another powerful field and again the prior year's runner-up, David Santee from Chicago, could not do it, placing second. The winner across the board and showing the promise that so many had seen in him was Scott Hamilton, now representing the Philadelphia SC and HS. Robert Wagenhoffer of Arctic Blades, after years of determined effort in Singles, placed third, followed closely by Brian Boitano of California in fourth place.

Kitty and Peter Carruthers succeeded to the vacant Pair title, with Lea Ann Miller of the Broadmoor and William Fauver of Wilmington, who had been eighth in 1980, second. Sheryl Franks and Michael Botticelli of Massachusetts, who had been third in 1980, could do no better than fifth, while Vicki Heasley of Arctic Blades, who had been fourth in 1980 with Wagenhoffer, placed sixth with a new partner, Peter Oppegard of Santa Monica.

Scott Hamilton

Form prevailed in the Dance, as it usually does, with Judy Blumberg from the Broadmoor and Michael Seibert of Indianapolis, the 1980 runners-up, succeeding to the title with the 1980 Bronze medalists, Carol Fox of Michigan and Richard Dalley, now representing Wilmington second, followed by Kim Krohn and Barry Hagan from Southern California, in third.

Paul Wylie elected to remain in Junior Men, which he won, adding the National to his World title, although he did skate in the Senior Pairs with his partner Dana Graham, placing eighth.

With all the National titles vacant, three of the four new National champions had skated in their respective Sectionals, with Scott Hamilton, Elaine Zayak and the Carruthers all winning the Senior titles in the 1981 Easterns at Wilmington. Only Blumberg and Seibert passed on the opportunity. Several of the other National medalists had also entered their respective Sectionals prior to the Nationals, and experience has shown that doing so is invariably a positive event and beneficial to the skater's performance in the Nationals.

The 1981 Worlds returned to the United States and were held at Hartford, Conn., in the Civic Center there, the same building where the 1977 Nationals had been held. There had been a question whether the 1981 Worlds could even be held at the Civic Center, when its roof collapsed after a heavy snowstorm in the famous "Blizzard of 1978" but assurances had been received from the City of Hartford and the Civic Center management that the necessary repairs would be made well in advance of the 1981 event, so the award to Hartford was not disturbed.

David Santee

The highlight event of the Championships turned out to be the Men where Scott Hamilton after a shaky start in the figures, with a fourth place, won both the short program and free skating to take his first World title. Second was David Santee, who had been second in figures, for the first one-two finish by U.S. skaters since David Jenkins and Tim Brown in 1958. In third position was the new European champion, Igor Bobrin of the Soviet Union. Robert Wagenhoffer, after a 14th in the figures and a 12th in the short program, pulled up to 10th overall with an eighth in free skating. Noteworthy also was the fact that Brian Orser of Canada who placed fifth in free skating, performed a flawless triple Axel, landing as the reporter, Howard Bass of England, says, "on a sweetly smooth running edge" and if the original effort of Vern Taylor is discounted, then Orser is really the first successfully to accomplish the jump in World competition. At least in his case, the jump was absolutely clean from start to finish.

The new European Ladies champion, Denise Biellmann of Switzerland was the winner in the Ladies, with fourth in figures, a second in the short program and a first in free skating, but much to the surprise of everyone, Elaine Zayak, who had been 11th in 1980 wound up second, despite a seventh in figures. Priscilla Hill, with a fifth in figures placed seventh, but once again was not strong enough in the free skating (with a ninth) to pull up. There was no third U.S. lady due to the retirement of Linda Fratianne, who had been the third and named skater from 1980.

Both the Pairs and Dance events were very strong and the young U.S. skaters did their best. Kitty and Peter Carruthers placed fifth, with Lea Ann Miller and William Fauver 10th. The defenders, Marina Cherkasova and Sergei Shakhrai of the USSR could do no better than fourth, mainly because Marina was now "too big." The new champions were Irina Vorobieva and Igor Lisovski, also from the Soviet Union.

The Dance event was notable for the accession to the throne of Jayne Torvill and Christopher Dean of Great Britain, with the veteran Irina Moiseeva and Andrei Minenkov of the USSR second, followed by Natalia Bestemianova and Andrei Bukin, also from the USSR. Right behind in fourth were Judy Blumberg and Michael Seibert, who had been in third place in the compulsory dances while Carol Fox and Richard Dalley were sixth, an excellent showing in such a strong field.

The Hartford Championships also marked the first appearance in an official capacity in the United States of Olaf Poulsen of Norway, the new President of the ISU, who served as the ISU Representative. Also present in his capacity of Honorary Chairman of the championships was Jack Shoemaker, Past USFSA President and Honorary ISU Vice President.

The 1981 Governing Council meeting took place at New Orleans, La. There was a revision of the meeting schedule, which moved the traditional round table meeting to Friday afternoon with the Governing Council meeting itself to convene in the evening. Among the guest speakers were David Dore, the President of the CFSA, who spoke of the increase in popularity of Precision Team skating in Canada and of plans for a National Championship in the discipline. It was a look into the future, as organized Precision Team skating was just getting off the ground in the United States, although it had actually been around for awhile in the Regionals. The Competitions Committee was directed to consider and come up with rules for Precision Competitions, by the fall 1981 meeting of the Board.

Based on an impassioned plea from the World team members present, the Governing Council allocated the sum of $250,000 to the Memorial Fund for support of the expenses of the elite skaters. While popular at the time, the action reflects the risk of permitting emotion to rule in fiscal matters.

A memorial resolution was approved for the late Past President H. Kendall Kelley, who had passed away in October 1980. Also, Robert T. McLeod of Norwalk, Calif., was elected an Honorary member of the Board of Directors, the first person to be so honored under the new By Laws.

Also announced was the election to the Hall of Fame of the late Harold Hartshorne of New York and the late William O. Hickok, IV, of Harrisburg, Pa. Hartshorne, who lost his life in the 1961 airplane accident in Belgium, was many times a winner in dance events with a variety of partners and was five times the National Dance champion. He also served as member of the ISU Dance Committee and was a World Championship Judge. Hickok was a former chairman of the USFSA Dance Committee and also the first USFSA member of the Ice Dance Committee of the ISU, as well as one of the first World Championship Referees in Ice Dancing from the United States. He was a pioneer in creating modern ice dancing in the early 1950's and in obtaining its recognition as a discipline in the World Championships. He passed away in 1959.

Revisions were made to the Amateur Status rules to bring them in line with those of the ISU, under the provision of the Amateur Sports Act which prohibits a National Governing Body from having amateur status rules more restrictive than those of its international federation. The rules deleted included the monetary value limit on gifts for exhibitions and carnivals, as well as the penalties for participating in unsanctioned events.

With respect to competitions, approved was a requirement that the organizing committees for the Nationals guarantee to the USFSA the payment of $25,000 to cover the expenses for the officials, medals, trophies and accounting forms. It was also at this meeting that the original set-pattern dance was separated from the compulsory dances. Also confirmed was the commitment on the part of the Association to furnish all the medals for the Regional championships. With respect to judges, Mrs. Edith Shoemaker was recommended for nomination to the ISU for appointment as an Honorary ISU Judge. Also changed were the names of the classes of competition judges in Dance, from Intermediate, Novice and Junior, to Novice, Junior and Senior, with the National Dance Judge remaining the same, to match the structure on the figure side. Also approved was the creation of a Music Committee, with authority to develop standards for designating USFSA persons as Certified Music Technicians to serve at the qualifying competitions and the Nationals.

Announced at the meeting were the selections for no less than 14 international competitions, including the first Skate America International to be held at Lake Placid in October 1981 and also the 1981 National Sports Festival and the 1982 World Junior Championships. The 14 events now on the international schedule were: St. Gervais (France), Oberstdorf (West Germany), ASKO of Vienna (Austria), St. Ivel (England), Skate America, Skate Canada (Ottawa), Richmond (England), Prague (Czechoslovakia), Ennia (Netherlands), Golden Spin of Zagreb (Yugoslavia), NHK Trophy (Japan), Milan (Italy), a dance competition, Tours (France) and Morzine (France), another dance competition. Not included in the list was Merano (Italy), but it too would be included later. Clearly, the concept of sending quality skaters to only the best run and attended competitions had disappeared as a policy, with the word instead being quantity. Later in the season, the Competitions Committee confirmed that skaters selected for and who represented the U.S. in international competitions held after the end of October 1981 would be granted permission to go directly to their Sectional Championships in the same event without having to qualify through the Regional Championships. This was the famous "bye" rule for the members of the United States Figure Skating Team, which had been created in 1977 to include all the skaters on the World Team, plus those chosen to participate in International Senior competitions.

As had been the case in 1979, the 1981-1982 season really started with the National Sports Festival in July in Syracuse, N.Y. The title given to the report in **Skating** magazine has an appropriate sub-title: "Warming Up the Ice for 1984," certainly expressive of the view of the Festival in the minds of the USOC and the public. The Festival figure skating had been announced as being a Junior competition, but this was not the case since the USOC insisted that the top Senior skaters be there. Of the four National Senior champions, at least two were present, Scott Hamilton, who won the Men and Kitty and Peter Carruthers, who won the Pairs. The winner in the Ladies was Rosalynn Sumners, while it was Elisa Spitz and Scott Gregory in the Dance. Third in the Men was Brian Boitano, behind Mark Cockerell second, while in the Ladies, second was Jacki Farrell of Janesville, Wisconsin.

At the Coupe des Alpes competitions, the string of first places ended, but the U.S. team still did well with eight medals: five seconds and three thirds. In the Ladies, Kristy Hogan from Santa Monica and Stephanie Anderson from Boston were second and third in Ladies in both competitions. Jim White of Long Island was second at St. Gervais and John Filbig of Arctic Blades, second at Oberstdorf in the Men. Janice Kindrachuck of Skokie Valley, Ill., and Blake Hobson of Wilmington were second at St. Gervais and third at Oberstdorf in Dance.

The U.S. lost the Coupe des Alpes Trophy to Canada, and was also second to West Germany for the new team trophy for the Nebelhorn competition, which had been donated by the USFSA in memory of the late Fritz Geiger, who had been President of the Deutsche Eislauf-Union. A native of Oberstdorf, Geiger had done much to promote the St. Gervais and Oberstdorf competitions in which the U.S. had enjoyed such great success.

In late September 1981, two skaters returned to the ASKO Cup of Vienna, and one of them, Maria Causey of Los Angeles, won the Ladies event for one of the few first place medals achieved abroad in the 1981 International competition season.

The St. Ivel Ice Invitational in England followed and here too there were no first place medals, but three Silver medals were earned, with David Santee in the Men, placing second to Brian Orser of Canada, Jackie Farrell in the Ladies placing second to Tracey Wainman, also from Canada and in the Pairs, Vicki Heasley and Peter Oppegard, second to Lorri Baier and Lloyd Eisler, also from Canada.

A milestone of sorts was the first Skate America International Competition which was held at Lake Placid in early October 1981. Although the Flaming Leaves (Norton Skate) competition of 1979 has generally been regarded as the first Skate America, the 1981 event was the first of that name and also was the first permanent International Competition to be sponsored by the USFSA since the demise of the North American Championships in 1971.

With the competition being on home ice and supported by the USFSA, all the top skaters were expected to attend, especially because of anticipated television coverage. More and more, television would dictate the competitions to be held and the content of them from the standpoint of entries and Skate America 1981 was no exception to this policy. Scott Hamilton repeated his 1979 victory in the Flaming Leaves in the Men and won his first Skate America, with Robert Wagenhoffer second, despite an eighth in figures followed by Brian Boitano in third, after a seventh in figures. Scottie had a tough short program, including a fall, but actually there had been some question whether he would compete at all, as he had been ill with a high fever just before the figures, so his performance was even more remarkable. Scott has been very loyal to the Association and its events and his sportsmanship in participating in the first Skate America was greatly to his credit.

There was an upset of sorts in the Ladies when Vikki deVries of Los Angeles, who had been the National Junior Ladies champion in 1980 and fourth in the 1981 National Senior Ladies, defeated National Ladies champion Elaine Zayak in all three parts of the competition. Elaine came second, while Rosalynn Sumners was fourth.

The winners in the Pairs were Barbara Underhill and Paul Martini of Canada, with Kitty and Peter Carruthers second, after leading in the short program. Lea Ann Miller and William Fauver were fourth, and Maria DiDomenico and Burt Lancon fifth. The winners in the Dance were Judy Blumberg and Michael Seibert with Elisa Spitz and Scott Gregory fourth, and Nancy Berghoff and Jim Bowser from Michigan seventh.

All in all, it was a successful competition for the United States, with seven medals: three Gold, three Silver and a Bronze.

The Ennia Challenge Cup in the Netherlands produced another first place, when Carol Fox and Richard Dalley won the Dance event. There were also three other medals; Jimmy Santee, second in the Men; Jackie Farrell, second in the Ladies, and Vicki Heasley and Peter Oppegard, third in the Pairs. The USFSA did win the team trophy. Santee went on to Zagreb and placed second in the Men's event there, while Terry Slater from Rochester, New York and Rick Berg from Madison, Wis., were second in the Dance and Lynne and Jay Freeman from Wilmington, third in the Pairs at Prague.

For the first time, a U.S. skater entered the Grand Prize SNP held at Banska Bystrica, Czechoslovakia, again without the support of the USFSA, but approved for entry by it. The skater was Frankie Hermanson of Rockford, Ill., who had been sixth in the 1981 National Junior Ladies. The competition was one for Juniors and Hermanson was the winner. Efforts would continue in the future to find suitable Junior International competitions for the USFSA to support, but there never have been very many of them, since such competitions are not moneymakers.

The NHK Trophy competition was held at Kobe, Japan, at the end of November, and here the U.S. did have another win when Kitty and Peter Carruthers took the Pairs event, with

DiDomenico and Lancon third. Vikki deVries built on her good showing at Skate America when she placed second in the Ladies to Kristiina Wegelius of Finland. The top U.S. man was Paul Wylie in fifth, while the top U.S. Dance couple was Elisa Spitz and Scott Gregory in fourth.

With the Merano Spring Trophy now supported, two Junior ladies were sent and placed first and third. Staci McMullin from Dallas was the winner and Tracy Moore from Michigan, the Bronze medalist.

Dancers were again sent to the Morzine Dance competition in April, and Carol Fox and Richard Dalley were the winners, while in sixth place were Renée Roca from Rochester, N.Y., and Donald Adair from Michigan.

The October 1981 fall meeting of the Board of Directors was held at the Olympic Training Center in Colorado Springs for the fourth year. The deficit of **Skating** magazine was a subject for discussion as usual and a further increase in the registration fee from $8 to $10 was approved for recommendation to the Governing Council. Various ways of reducing the cost of production of the magazine were also discussed, one suggestion being a reduction in the number of color pages. The total paid circulation of the magazine had now topped 31,000, and advertising revenue had improved, but the costs of production still outweighed the income. Modest increases were also approved in the sanction fees for competitions, when admission was charged.

In competitions, a rule change was adopted to provide that test qualifications as of the date of entries for the Regional Championships would govern for the entire competition season. This date was finally pinned down in 1994 as Sept. 15 across the country, rather than a specified number of days in advance of the closing date for entries in a particular Regional, which had reached 45 days.

With respect to clubs, a revision was approved which required a club which used the Principal Skating Headquarters of another club for an event, to have the permission from the home club to do so. In sanctions, the fee for events for the benefit of a non-skating related organization (such as The Jimmy Fund) in which World or Olympic Team members appear was raised from 5 percent to 10 percent of the gross receipts received by the beneficiary of the event. In a seemingly small change, in Pair tests, it was approved that a professional could partner an amateur. Also in the membership field, a presentation was made concerning a voluntary plan for liability insurance for clubs at a group rate and an ad hoc committee was appointed, with Roger Glenn of Appleton, Wis., as the chairman, to consider insurance plans for clubs and to make recommendations to the Board. Such coverage is an important benefit of membership to the clubs.

A selection plan for the Olympic Team in 1984 was approved, which provided that the overall record of skaters in specified competitions would form the basis on which selection would be made. This was to avoid any possibility that the National championships preceding the Games would be considered as an Olympic Trial since, if that were the case, the USOC took all the revenue, including that from television. As a result, the Nationals have never been Olympic Trials in the strict sense, even though they were so advertised in 1931 and 1935. The championships included in the 1984 plan were the Worlds of 1982 and 1983; the Nationals of 1982, 1983 and 1984; the National Sports Festivals of 1982 and 1983; and the World Junior Championships of 1982, 1983 and 1984. It still remained possible for a separate trial to be held, as had been the case in 1947 and 1951.

Action was also taken to raise funds towards the expenses of coaches, in an amount not to exceed $15,000 with the funds coming from a two day exhibition tour following the Nationals, with stops at St. Louis, Mo., and Fort Wayne, Ind.

With respect to judges, a procedure for improving the performance of judges to be implemented on a trial basis was approved. The procedure would involve an experiment in the use of the referee as an independent judge and moderator for a review discussion with the judges at qualifying competitions. However, the use of the ISU system, which involves the referees as the independent evaluators of the performance of the judges has never been accepted or implemented so that there is today no system in place by which the performance of a judge in the qualifying competitions, including the Nationals, can be evaluated and appropriate disciplinary action taken. There is in place today the system operated by the Judges Education and Training Section of the Judges Committee (JETS), in which there is a review meeting following the completion of a competition. For trial judges, the acceptance of trial judging sheets from non-qualifying competitions in support of applications for appointment or promotion, was approved.

A lively discussion took place at the meeting concerning a possible ban on triple jumps to prevent injuries to skaters as contained in a report of the Sports Medicine Committee. The general view was that any such ban should start at the ISU level. Among the opinions expressed was one that "balance and beauty was more important than a series of sometimes violent jumps" and that deterring skaters from using triple jumps might help them do better jumps. Although there was and is today a body of medical information showing that multi-revolution jumps are hazardous to one's health, no action has ever been taken to ban or limit them, and the progress in their quality and expansion of their performance by more and more skaters seems to support their retention. What needs to be done is strictly to enforce the existing rules governing a well balanced program so that an excessive number of jumps in a program is in fact penalized, rather than rewarded. Further, there can be no credit given for a failed jump and this too needs to be enforced.

The 1982 World Junior Championships were held at Oberstdorf, West Germany, in the renovated arena there, with a U.S. team of three Men, two Ladies, two Pairs and one Dance couple, and once again a Gold medal was attained when Scott Williams of Arctic Blades finally won after three years of trying, since he had been fifth in 1980 and third in 1981. Scott had worked his way up the line the hard way and became a World Junior champion without having ever held a National title. He had been fourth in the 1981 National Junior Men, but did not compete in the 1980 National Junior, although he had qualified to do so in the Pacific Coasts. His success in the World Junior, with two medals, showed what could be accomplished with determination and perseverance. In second place was Paul Guerrero of Skokie Valley, Ill., who, curiously enough, had no record in the Nationals in either 1980 or 1981, but who had been fifth in the Midwestern Junior Men in 1980 and fourth in the Midwestern Senior Men in 1981. It was again the problem of finding age eligible persons to compete and in Paul's case, the selection was fully justified. Ironically, Paul would not make it to the 1982 Nationals either, placing fourth again in the Midwesterns.

In the Ladies event of the World Juniors, the two U.S. entries were a little less successful, with Jill Frost from Massachusetts, the 1981 National Junior Ladies champion, placing fourth with the National Junior runner-up, Kelly Webster from Cleveland fifth. Just ahead of them in third place was Elizabeth Manley of Canada, while just behind them in sixth was Midori Ito of Japan, who had a 19th place in figures, to which she added first places in both the short program and free skating. The figures would always be Midori's "Achilles heel."

Natalie and Wayne Seybold from Fort Wayne, Ind., who had been third in the 1981 National Junior Pairs event, placed seventh in the Pairs, while Robert Davenport from Westchester, N.Y., who had been fifth in 1981 with another partner, placed ninth with a new partner, Amy Grossman from Long Island. They were the Eastern Junior Pair champions of 1982 and would ultimately place third in the 1982 National Junior Pairs. One of the problems of the World Junior in its new time frame was that selection for it had to be based upon the prior year's record, which in the case of Pairs and Dance couples especially was complicated by the many partner changes that occurred every year. Eventually, trials for the World Juniors in the early fall would be the answer, with the first such trials being held at Colorado Springs in 1993.

The 1982 Nationals were held in Indianapolis and all the defending Senior champions were present, as was normally the case at the midpoint of a quadrennium, since the closer the next Olympics came, the more important it was to maintain or to improve one's position leading up to the Nationals. There was this year one major upset, when Rosalynn Sumners of Seattle won the Senior Ladies despite a fifth in figures, with Vikki deVries of the Broadmoor second and the defending champion, Elaine Zayak of New York third. Rosalynn won both the short and long programs, with de Vries second in both, while Elaine had three falls in her free skating to place a generous third in that part and to just retain her berth on the World Team. Little did she know, after such a disastrous performance what lay ahead for her. The figure winner, Priscilla Hill, placed

Elaine Zayak

sixth after a poor result (eighth) in the free skating. It was to be Priscilla's last Nationals in which she had competed in the Senior Ladies for every year since 1974, with the exception of 1979.

Things were more routine in the Men. Here there was a modest upset as well, when Robert Wagenhoffer from Arctic Blades took second overall ahead of David Santee of Chicago, the World Silver medalist of 1981, third and even won the short program over defender Scott Hamilton. Wagenhoffer had placed fifth in figures, which prevented him from seriously challenging Hamilton for the title, the new system of calculating the results on the basis of factored places in each part of a competition now being in effect. Scott won both the figures and the free skating to take his second title.

Kitty and Peter Carruthers won their second title in Pairs without undue difficulty, with Maria DiDomenico and Burt Lancon from Los Angeles second and Lea Ann Miller and William Fauver of Wilmington third. Form also held in Dance, with Judy Blumberg and Michael Seibert of Indianapolis winning their second title, followed by Carol Fox and Richard Dalley, now representing Wilmington and Elisa Spitz of Essex, N.J., and Scott Gregory of Wilmington third. It was straight across the board in all three parts for all three top couples, which is so typical in ice dancing, with the placings rarely if ever changing after the compulsory dances. In the Novice Men, the winner was Rudy Galindo of California, from whom much would be heard in later years.

The 1982 World championships were held at Copenhagen, Denmark, the first time in that city, although the Danish Skating Union had held the European championships there as recently as 1975. The championships were notable in two respects: the first was the use of the panel system of judging with, in the Singles, two panels of seven judges each, with one panel doing the figures and short program and the other panel doing the free skating. The U.S. fielded a rare full team of eighteen skaters: three Men, three Ladies, three Pairs and three Dance couples.

The other notable event, especially from the U.S. standpoint, was the unexpected win of Elaine Zayak in the Ladies. Although all the records have not been checked in detail, it is safe to say that Elaine came from the furthest behind to win ever recorded which would not have been possible under the old scoring system. She placed fourth in the figures and 10th in the short program in which she had fallen, so was in seventh place before the free skating. She skated before all the others ahead of her and received excellent marks, quite a contrast to her performance in the Nationals. She then had to wait to see what the six skaters ahead of her would do, since if any one of them defeated her in the free skating, she would not either top the podium or even be on it. Incredibly, all six failed to challenge her free skating marks, so she won that part of the event and with it the title, the sixth U.S. skater to become the World Ladies champion and also the first former World Junior champion to win the Senior title.

To show the problems of the others in the event, Katarina Witt of GDR won the short program but was ninth in figures and second in free, while Claudia Kristofics-Binder of Austria, the European Ladies champion, won the figures, was ninth in the short program and fourth in the free skating. Claudia Leistner of FRG, who was fourth, placed 14th in figures, second in the short and third in the free. The other two Americans, Rosalynn Sumners, who was sixth overall, was 11th in figures, fourth in the short and fifth in the free, while Vikki deVries, who finished seventh, was more consistent with an eighth in figures, a seventh in the short and a sixth in the free. To say the least, it was a very mixed up competition! Elaine performed six triple jumps, but four of them were triple toe loops and two were triple Salchows, a repetition no longer allowed. She was one of the exemplars of the jumping school among the Ladies, following in the footsteps of Barbara Smith, another early exponent of that athletic skill. In some respects, Elaine's unusual win at Copenhagen enhanced the tendency to over emphasize the jumps on the part of skaters, coaches and judges, which is not to take away from her win in any respect. It was, for her, a remarkable comeback from having lost her National title just a few weeks before and for which she deserves true credit for her determination and refusal to accept failure. We would see this spirit again, both in 1984, when she placed third in the Worlds at Ottawa and in 1994, when she returned as a reinstated skater and won the North Atlantics, placed second in the Easterns and fourth in the Nationals.

With all the uproar about Elaine's win, the equally impressive first defense of his title by Scott Hamilton almost seemed to pass unnoticed. Although Jean-Christophe Simond of France won the figures, he could do no better than fifth overall. Scott won both the short program and the free skating to take his second title, putting him on the same level as Tim Wood (1969-1970). Scott did six triples, three toe loops, two Salchows and a Lutz, which again reflects the practice seen also with Zayak of repeating triple jumps to increase content. The rules, however, also state that full credit cannot be given for the repeated element. As a consequence of the rule changes which penalize repetition today, the name of the game is triples in combination rather than alone. Scott and Elaine were the first U.S. skaters to win both singles titles in the same year since David Jenkins and Carol Heiss had done so in 1959. It was also the first time since 1979 that U.S. skaters had won two World titles in the same year. Second was Norbert Schramm of West

Germany, the new European champion, while Brian Pockar of Canada picked up another medal for North America by placing third. Robert Wagenhoffer was sixth after a ninth in figures, but with a fourth in the short and a fifth in the long. David Santee placed eighth after a third in figures and 16th in the short. Noteworthy in the event was a flawless triple Axel again performed by Brian Orser of Canada, who was third in free skating and fourth overall, after a poor 12th in figures. In those days the triple Axel was rare enough to merit comment.

The title in the Pairs went to the East German pair of Sabine Baess and Tassilo Thierbach who were also the new European Pair champions, thereby breaking the new Soviet string that had started in 1980. Second were Marina Pestova and Stanislav Leonovich of the USSR, so the Soviets were still on the podium, but not on the top step. Third were Kitty and Peter Carruthers, just ahead of Barbara Underhill and Paul Martini of Canada. Kitty and Peter had to pull up from fourth in the short program to gain the Bronze medal, the first in Pairs for the U.S. since Tai and Randy in 1979. The defending champions, Irina Vorobieva and Igor Lisovski of the USSR could do no better than fifth, after a third in the short program. Lea Ann Miller and William Fauver placed eighth, reversing the National result over Maria DiDomenico and Burt Lancon, who placed 10th.

Judy Blumberg and Michael Seibert were third in the compulsory dances and again could not hold it, this time against the ageless veterans Irina Moiseeva and Andrei Minenkov of the Soviet Union who placed third overall, with Judy and Michael fourth for the second straight year. Carol Fox and Richard Dalley were right behind in fifth position, while Elisa Spitz and Scott Gregory were eighth, so all the U.S. team placed in the top 10. The Dance winners were the incomparable Jayne Torvill and Christopher Dean of Great Britain, in a class by themselves, with Natalia Bestemianova and Andrei Bukin of the USSR a distant second.

The team places for 1982 were as follows: Men - first, sixth, eighth; Ladies - first, sixth, seventh; Pairs- third, eighth, 10th; Dance - fourth, fifth, eighth, but what was nice were two Gold medals and one Bronze, for three overall, which showed that the current new generation was well on its way at the mid-point of the quadrennium to a strong showing at the 1984 Olympics. Also rewarding was that the Soviet Union was shut out of the titles, although they did garner three medals themselves, two Silvers and a Bronze.

The 1982 Governing Council meeting was held at Hyannis on Cape Cod, Mass., with 189 delegates representing 114 clubs registered, a substantial increase over prior years and perhaps due to the resort area in which the meeting was held. There are two schools of thought about the annual meeting. One group would like to go to resorts, where there are a variety of extra-curricular activities to enjoy of a recreational nature, but with the site usually a little hard to get to. The other group favors the hotel in the big city, which is easy to fly into, but not with a lot of outside activities. In the last 20 years or so both groups have been rewarded more or less on a rotational basis while recognizing that the traditional rotation of the meeting between the Sections should be maintained. One factor is the cost to the individual delegate who travels entirely at his or her own expense in most cases, so that the sites selected need to address that aspect in so far as possible while still providing an enjoyable time. The meetings have been enough of a circus in recent years to be quite entertaining in and of themselves, so outside activities are not really as important as they might be for those that are really interested in the sport and know that they can do something to move it forward by being a part of the process.

In Massachusetts, there was even a proclamation by the Governor that May 5-8, 1982, were "USFSA Recognition Days." In his report, President Iobst noted that commercial sponsorship support was becoming more available for the Regional and Sectional championships. He also noted the increased computer capabilities of the Headquarters that permitted improved service to the member clubs.

A By Law change was approved to permit representatives of the USFSA to the ISU and USOC, athlete representatives to the USOC not otherwise members of the Board of Directors and Honorary members (of the Board) to be ex-officio members of the Board without a vote. Another change approved was to require the specific text of all amendments (of the By Laws) to be included in the Notice of the meeting. Included in the grounds for loss of membership was a failure to make timely payments of all financial obligations due to the USFSA. Further By Law revisions were made to clarify the appeals procedure and to provide for arbitration pursuant to the Amateur Sports Act of 1978 (Public Law 95-606).

Also approved were **Guidelines for Precision Team Skating**, which were published in the 1982-1983 Rulebook. They were in fact the first set of rules for the conducting of competition in Precision Team skating. Included were definitions for the divisions to be skated, the age limits to be applied and the size of teams. The divisions were Juvenile (age 11 or younger); Novice (age 15 or younger), Junior (no age limit), Senior (no age limit) and Adult (over age 25). All teams were to be between 12 and 32 skaters in size, except for Junior, for which the maximum size was 24. There would be just one program skated although elimination rounds were contemplated, and very quickly, consolation rounds would also be added. The marks to be used were for Composition and Presentation. On the basis of the Guidelines, the first Sectional championships in Precision were scheduled to be held in the 1982-1983 season. Selections of skaters were also announced for 10 International Competitions and for the 1983 World Junior Championships. The number of International Competitions approved by the International Committee is essentially a minimum number and very often, additional competitions are added as the season goes along, for example, in 1983, the World University Games.

Also announced was the creation of a Cassette Music Library at the Museum, through the generous donation by Professor Richard Stephenson of Connecticut of a substantial collection of out of print LP albums. Selections were to be put on 90 minute cassettes, to illustrate the various types of music available, as a means of assisting skaters and their coaches in finding suitable music for their programs. The required recording equipment was obtained and the project was initiated in the fall of 1982. Unfortunately, the Museum was unable to keep up with the demand due to a continuing lack of staff, and eventually the work was turned over to the Music Committee. It is regrettable that sufficient staff was never provided, as the project had merit and was a service to the membership, and would also have generated a modest income for the Museum.

The 1982 ISU Congress was held at Stavanger, Norway, and was unusual in two respects: first, it was the first Congress held that did not include general elections of officeholders, and it was also the 90th Anniversary of the ISU. The term of office had been changed by the 1977 Congress to four years starting in 1980, but Congresses were still to be held every two years, with the mid-term or off-year one being devoted to addressing the problems of the sports and the making of the necessary rule changes to reflect their development and change.

The 1982 Congress was no exception in that regard. Among the rule changes made directly affecting the sports were the following: the number of repetitions required in compulsory figures were reduced to two from three, and despite the concerns of the traditionalists, had little effect on the quality of the figures and actually made their judging easier. The real reason for the change was the substantial saving of time. Another change was to include in the rules specific definitions of the elements constituting a well balanced program in pair free skating. The definitions were important to arrest the trend towards an undue emphasis being placed upon purely athletic content (lifts and jumps) at the expense of the other elements (such as spins). Comparable definitions would be added in 1984 for single free skating. A rule change affecting the stronger countries was a reduction of the number of seeded judges in ISU Championships from five to three. In Dance, the original set-pattern dance was split off from the compulsories with its own factor of difficulty of 0.4 (20 percent). The compulsory dances were 0.6 (30 percent) and the free dance 1.0 (50 percent).

A revision in the ongoing and essential futile effort to reduce the number of entries was made to limit the number of competitors entering the final round of championships to 15, with the remaining competitors skating their own separate final round in what was called the "B" (or consolation) final. This latest revision did not last under the constant pressure from the small countries to increase the number of entries rather than reduce them.

Once again, the 1982-1983 season started with the fourth National Sports Festival at Indianapolis, and again the Senior skaters were required to participate, although the National champions were excused. The winners were Brian Boitano of California in the Men, Vikki deVries of Colorado in the Ladies, Lea Ann Miller and William Fauver of Wilmington in the Pairs and Elisa Spitz of New Jersey and Scott Gregory of Wilmington in the Dance. There was a good quality of competition in the event, which had a total of 39 entries. Actually, the absence of the National champions was a healthy aspect of the format, as it permitted skaters who were working their way up the line a chance to shine and to see if they could win.

The traditional trek to St. Gervais and Oberstdorf came next, and the U.S. Team did well with six medals, but no Golds this time. Scott Williams, the World Junior champion was second at St. Gervais, while Kelly Webster from Colorado placed second in both competitions, and Natalie and Wayne Seybold from Fort Wayne, Indiana, were third in both. James Cygan from Colorado was third at Oberstdorf for the sixth medal. The West Germans won the Coupe des Alpes trophy, with the U.S. second.

At St. Ivel Ice International in mid-September, Elaine Zayak won the Ladies, while Judy Blumberg and Michael Seibert won the Dance, a very special triumph in the home of ice dancing over the second ranked British couple at that time, Karen Barber and Nicholas Slater. Tom Dickson, the 1980 National Junior champion took third in the Men.

However, at the ASKO Cup in Vienna at the end of September, the U.S. entrants placed first and second, with Rosana Tovi from Lake Placid, the winner and Melissa Thomas from Long Island, New York, the runner-up.

Skate America '82 returned to Lake Placid, and here two of the four the National champions were present, with Scott Hamilton winning what was really his third Skate America title, if Flaming Leaves is included. Rosalynn Sumners won the Ladies. Lea Ann Miller and William Fauver were second in the Pairs, and Elisa Spitz and Scott Gregory won the Dance. It was a good sized competition, helped by the fact that air travel costs were reimbursed to the foreign skaters on a cooperative basis with Skate Canada for those going on to that competition. There were 49 entries from 17 countries. Heiko Fischer and Claudia Leistner of West Germany were the runners-up in the Men and Ladies, while the winners of the Pairs were Elena Valova and Oleg Vasiliev of the USSR, a new Soviet pair who had previously been seen in the West at the Coupe des Alpes in 1981, where they won at Oberstdorf and were second at St. Gervais. They would surprise the skating world in a few short months by winning the World title at Helsinki.

In mid-October, there was the Second Tours International Competition for the Jacques Favart Trophy, in which the U.S. had two men, Daniel Doran from Colorado, the winner and Craig Henderson from California, who took third.

Skate Canada was held at Kitchener, Ontario, which had previously held the event in 1974. This time there were 45 skaters from 13 countries, and once again the U.S. team came up with the rare sweep of all three events (Pairs still not yet having been added). Brian Boitano took the Men, defeating Brian Orser of Canada, whom he would meet again in another memorable Skate Canada in 1987. It was once again the figures (fifth) that did in Orser, who won the other two parts, but could not catch Boitano who was first in the figures. Vikki deVries won the Ladies in an upset over Kristiina Wegelius of Finland, with Rosalynn Sumners, the National Ladies champion third. DeVries had been fourth in the figures and second in the short program and won the free, while Ros had been third in the first two parts and fourth in the free. Elisa Spitz and Scott Gregory won the Dance event, defeating Tracy Wilson and Rob McCall of Canada, another couple who would make their mark in a few short years.

Just one week after Skate Canada, the Prague Skate competition took place in that city, with just one American entered, Paul Guerrero of Illinois, who placed fourth.

Just another week and the Ennia Challenge Cup was held at the Hague, the Netherlands, and here Boitano continued his steady march upwards by winning the event in which the former European champion, Igor Bobrin of the USSR, could do no better than fourth. Vikki deVries also continued her excellent skating by winning the Ladies.

Finally the NHK Trophy was held at Tokyo at the end of November, and here Scott Hamilton won the Men, while Rosalynn Sumners and Tiffany Chin, the 1981 World Junior Ladies champion were second and third, behind Katarina Witt of East Germany, a prophetic result. Lea Ann Miller and William Fauver were fourth in Pairs, while Carol Fox and Richard Dalley were second in the Dance.

As can be seen, there was an international competition somewhere in the world on virtually every weekend from the end of August to the end of November. It is a situation which has continued ever since and has put a great strain on the resources of the Association, as well as on the skaters themselves, with greater and greater demands being imposed upon those of the highest rank. This has not always been to their benefit in the major competitions. It is nice to win a Skate Canada or Skate America for example, but that will not be remembered and it is much nicer to win a World or Olympic title because that will be remembered.

The International beat did not stop at December 1982, but went on through the season with the Merano Spring Trophy at the end of March, 1983. The lone U.S. entry, Yvonne Gomez of California, the National Junior Ladies runner-up, was the winner. In early April, the Morzine Dance event took place in which Susan Wynne of Philadelphia and Joseph Druar of Seattle placed eighth, the winners being Marina Klimova and Sergei Ponomarenko of the Soviet Union. Just a month later in May 1983 was held the Wilkie Dance competition in England, in which Renée Roca of New York and Donald Adair of Michigan placed sixth. Roca and Adair had been fourth, and Wynne and Druar fifth in the National Senior Dance of 1983.

The fall meeting of the Board of Directors was held as usual at the Olympic Training Center in Colorado Springs. A variety of administrative actions were taken, some of which were of importance. For example, approved was the expenditure of up to $5,000 for an appraisal of all the fixed assets of the Association, including the Headquarters building and the Museum artifacts. Up to that time, no formal appraisal had ever been made, but now with a building and the Museum collections on the books, the need for such an appraisal for insurance and other purposes was obvious. The value of the Museum collections has ever since been an important part of the balance sheet of the Association, although accounting standards today do not contemplate the inclusion on the balance sheet of such items as assets at their fair market value.

Based on the recommendation of the ad hoc committee on insurance, the purchase of a Comprehensive Liability Insurance policy from the Travelers Insurance Company was approved, which insured the member clubs. The initial premium, which was to be paid by the Association was $1.06 per registered member. The making available to the clubs of liability insurance coverage was a major step forward in the providing of greater benefits of membership to them.

Established was a category of Emeritus Judge, to which would be appointed any judge in good standing with more than 10 years of service who wished to retire voluntarily.

Approved was a recommendation that the Association not participate in the 1983 National Sports Festival due to its early dates (late June 1983) but with the proviso that if there was television, exhibitors would be provided. Of course, this wish did not survive and when the Festival rolled around, Senior skaters were again sent, although the members of the World Team were exempted form participating. With Lake Placid now open as an Olympic Training Center, the USOC also urged the USFSA to use the facilities there, although figure skating training is not readily amenable to the use of a specified short block of time, unlike a team sport.

Announced was the appointment of Larry McCollum as the new Executive Director of the USFSA, starting in January 1983. Larry was the Assistant Director of Operations at the USOC and was to replace Roy Winder, who retired at the end of 1982.

Approved was the creation of a new Permanent Committee (as the former Standing Committees were now known since the By Law revision of 1980) known as the Athletes Advisory Committee, of which the chairman would be one of the nine athlete members of the Board of Directors. The committee was in fact a permanent non-voting committee, meaning that the chairman did not have an (additional) vote on the Board as such. In that regard, the committee was similar to the Finance Committee, of which the Treasurer is the chairman, but does not have an extra vote as the chairman of the committee.

A statement of policy was adopted to the effect that the USFSA "does not endorse or support professional figure skating competitions." This statement of policy has never been in fact rescinded (as it should be) in view of the active entry of the Association into the business of conducting "pro-am" competitions in the 1990's. It is like an old law on the books, which has been forgotten.

Approved was the sum of $41,500 (received from the Travelers Insurance Company as a sponsor of the qualifying competitions), with $33,750 allocated to the clubs organizing the Regionals ($3,750 each) and $6,000 ($2,200 each) to the Sectionals, partially to cover the expenses incurred in conducting the competitions.

Sponsorship activity was also increasing markedly, with Campbell Soup Company signing on as the sponsor of Skate America, which has always been a costly competition and which has never enjoyed the attendance by the public that it deserves. A title sponsor, as Campbell's was in this case, was an absolute necessity for its survival. Those who do not like to see a corporate name as part of the title of an amateur sports event have had to accept it as a way of life, if sponsorship funds are to be obtained to support an event. The key to it is not to sell the name too cheaply and to get for it the highest possible amount, especially if a string of conditions is attached by the sponsor, such as free tickets and other forms of exposure including participation in the awards ceremonies.

Other sponsors obtained were General Foods Corporation to sponsor the United States Figure Skating Team, with the Maxwell House (Coffee) Division making a contribution to the Memorial Fund. General Foods also agreed to sponsor the exhibition Tour, with 25 percent of the proceeds going to Tom Collins, the Tour organizer, 25 percent to the agency fee and 50 percent to the Association. A hidden cost factor in all sponsorship deals is the substantial fees to the agents, so when a big number is announced it is always wise to remember that it is a gross amount and not the net number actually received by the Association. It is an unfortunate fact of life that sponsorship contracts never seem to last long, so the search goes on constantly to find new ones. The long term relationship with one major sponsor is very hard to find, as the advertising budgets and goals of corporations constantly change.

Approved were bids for the 1985 World Junior Championships and for the 1987 World Championships, with a bid process to be implemented for the latter, so that three finalist bidders could be selected to submit proposals to the 1983 fall meeting of the Board. The World Juniors, which had not previously been held in the United States, were assigned to the Broadmoor Skating Club of Colorado Springs, the venerable site of five prior World Championships.

The 1983 World Junior Championships, the first major championship of the season were held at Sarajevo, Yugoslavia, as a test of the facilities there for the 1984 Olympic Winter Games. The team selected was a small one, consisting of two Men, two Ladies, two Pairs and two Dance couples, with the size being based on the results of the prior year under the ISU Rules. Named skaters still were able to compete only as such so that when a named skater moved on, the additional entry was lost. It would take many years of trying by the USFSA to obtain the additional entry on the basis of the places earned, without a specific skater being the only person eligible to use it. This revision would finally be approved in 1990, so that a country with an entrant in the prior year in the first three places in an event (the first five places for pairs) would earn a third entry in that event in the following year.

There were two major stories involving the U.S. team at Sarajevo. The first was a positive one: the winning of the Men's event by Christopher Bowman of California, the third World Junior title for Men won by the United States. Christopher won the figures and the free, and despite a third in the short program, took the title without undue difficulty. Philippe Roncoli of France was the runner-up and Nils Köpp of the GDR was third. Erik Larson of San Diego, the other U.S. man placed seventh after a 13th in figures, but a fourth in free skating.

First there was the withdrawal from the Ladies of Jill Frost of Massachusetts due to an injury before the team went across. Then during a practice after the draw, but before the competition started, Lorilee Pritchard, also from Massachusetts, the 1982 National Junior ladies champion, suffered an injury and had to withdraw. The alternate, Stacy McMullin of Dallas, the National Junior Ladies runner-up, was present on site and ready to skate, but was not permitted to do so under the then ISU Rules on the ground that the draw had already taken place and an alternate could not replace a skater who had been present and was already drawn, as was the case with Pritchard. So poor Stacy had to sit there and watch and could do nothing about it, while the USFSA, with no entry in the event, obviously would be able to send but one lady in the following year. It was generally unfair all around. A rule change was made by the ISU at its next Congress to permit a substitution in the case of a withdrawal due to illness or injury, right up to the start of the competition. The rule required that the alternate had to have been designated on the entry form and had to be present at the site, ready, willing and able to skate. The latter requirement of being present on site was subsequently dropped. There still has to be a medical certification by the ISU of the illness or injury which required the withdrawal of the original skater. It is, of course, known as the "McMullin" rule.

In the Pairs and Dance events, the U.S. skaters had less success, with Susan and Jason Dungjen of Detroit placing sixth, the title and the medals going to the Soviets and East Germans. The Dungjen's would go on to win the 1983 National Junior Pair title. Christina and Keith Yatsuhashi of Massachusetts were fourth in the Dance, and Colleen McGuire and Bill Lyons of Connecticut seventh. The title went to the couple of Tatiana Gladkova and Igor Shpilband of the USSR. Igor is now a top dance coach in Detroit. In the same event were Georgi Sur with Svetlana Liapina, eighth. Sur is now "Gorsha" Sur, the National champion in Dance with Renée Roca in 1993 and 1995.

It was also in the Dance event that the first case of positive doping in figure skating occurred, when Christine Chiniard and Martial Mette of France, in third place, were disqualified. The violation was really an innocent one on the part of Chiniard, who was taking a weight loss drug which happened to be on the banned list. As a consequence, the Bronze medals were subsequently awarded to the Yatsuhashi's, who were the fourth place couple.

The 1983 National Championships were held at Pittsburgh and all the champions were back, as the Olympic year approached. In the cycle, the maintaining of position in the year prior to that of the Olympics is vitally important to ultimate success as any slippage in position makes the final goal that much more difficult to attain. The quality of the competition at the top of the four Senior events was very high.

Rosalynn Sumners

Scott Hamilton won his third Men's title across the board, but Brian Boitano of California, who would be his ultimate successor, took second, thereby solidifying his position as the number two skater. He defeated Mark Cockerell, third, who was still around although David Santee had retired. Rosalynn Sumners won her second Ladies title, with Elaine Zayak climbing back up to the runner-up position. Tiffany Chin of San Diego, fifth the year before, took the Bronze medal, pushing Vikki deVries of Colorado down to fourth from the runner-up position of the prior year, despite a second place in the short program. The figures had actually been won by Melissa Thomas of Long Island who finished fifth, but Sumners was otherwise solid in winning both the short and the long to hold her title. Also in the Senior Ladies we can find Debra ("Debi") Thomas of Los Angeles in the 13th position, certainly not a portent of the future at that time, but that would soon change.

The Carruthers took their third title in Pairs, with Lea Ann Miller and William Fauver moving up to second, while Burt Lancon of Los Angeles, with his new partner, Jill Watson, took third. The musical chairs department was still going strong, since Lancon's former partner Maria DiDomenico was now skating with Peter Oppegard, who had skated in 1982 with Vicki Heasley and would in the future skate with Watson.

The Dance event seemed much more stable in the partner department, and Judy Blumberg and Michael Seibert, now representing Pittsburgh, demonstrated their superiority by easily winning their third title. Elisa Spitz of Essex and Scott Gregory of Wilmington moved up to second over Carol

Fox and Richard Dalley of Wilmington. The dance team for Worlds was a strong one. Christopher Bowman added the National Junior to his World Junior title while in the Novice Men we can find Mark Mitchell of Connecticut third and Todd Eldredge, representing Philadelphia seventh.

The World University (FISU) Games were held at Sofia, Bulgaria, in late February, and a U.S. team was present. The FISU Games were for many years the stronghold of the Eastern Bloc athletes although the degree of their commitment in fact to academic pursuits is subject to question. The Games were part of the propaganda drive of Communist society to prove that it was superior to capitalism, not only in sport, but also in education. U.S. skaters who go are generally more committed to the educational side than they are to the skating side, but they have done just as well as their peers who are not so dedicated to getting an education. The opportunity to represent their country in such an international setting is well worth the effort. The best places achieved in 1983 were fifths in the Men by Rolf Juario of Los Angeles and in the Dance by Barbara and Peter Buch of Seattle. Top U.S. place in the Ladies went to Gretchen Seller of Seattle, sixth. There was no U.S. pair. In the Men, we can find Robert Rosenbluth of Philadelphia, subsequently a National judge and in the family travel business, which is one of the largest in the country. Unknown names? Perhaps, and yet they deserve credit for representing the United States as well as they did. Three of the four titles went to representatives of the Soviet Union, while the Men was won by Takashi Mura of Japan. The Dance winners were Natalia Annenko and Genrikh Sretenski, USSR, later three time European medalists in Dance.

The 1983 Worlds were held at Helsinki, Finland, for the first time since 1934, and were a very well run event under the leadership of Jane and Aatos Erkko. Aatos was the managing director of the leading newspaper in Finland, the **Helsingin Sanomat** and as a result, the protocols for the championships were produced on time at the closing banquet with full color illustrations of the medal winners, a rare and very special feat, when the complexities of printing in color are considered. The U.S. came away from Helsinki with three medals, two of them Gold. Scott Hamilton won his third straight title, placing him on the same level as David Jenkins (1957-1959). Scott found the defense difficult, primarily in the department of concentration, since there were so many distractions for a defending champion. Second only to Jean-Christophe Simond of France in the figures, Scott won both the other parts, but coming fast was Brian Orser of Canada, second in both the short program and free skating following an eighth in figures. He pulled up to third behind Norbert Schramm of West Germany. In fourth was Alexander Fadeev of the USSR, the leading Soviet male skater of the day, who turned out to be Scott's successor in 1985. The third U.S. skater, Mark Cockerell, placed 14th and thereby below the mythical line of 10th. Tenth place is always important in World competition, since a country is entitled to a second entry in the following year if its representative is in the top 10 the year before. In the future, in ice dancing especially, 10th place would be of critical importance to the fortunes of the U.S. team.

Elaine Zayak, the defending Ladies champion, had to withdraw during the figures, due to a very painful stress fracture injury in one leg, which left it up to Rosalynn Sumners and Tiffany Chin to carry the flag. Rosalynn surprised by winning the figures and the free skating, despite a fourth in the short program and with it the Ladies title, the seventh American to become the World Ladies champion. The runner-up was Claudia Leistner of West Germany while in third was Elena Vodorezova of the Soviet Union, who had returned to competition in 1982 after several years absence due to injuries. Katarina Witt of East Germany, the new European Ladies champion, wound up fourth by reason of an eighth place in figures. She was, however, first in the short program and second in the free skating. Tiffany Chin, in her first Worlds, placed ninth, pulling up from 14th in the figures. For the first time in the Ladies, there was an elimination after the top 15 at the end of the short program, with a "B" final being skated among those eliminated. It was the initial attempt to in some way reduce the size of the event, which kept growing as more and more developing countries joined the ISU and insisted upon their one entry. The B Final was imposed only if the total number of entries in the event exceeded 24. The number of repetitions required in the figures was also reduced from three to two in another effort to shorten the time required to skate them. The number of named skaters had also been reduced from the first five in Singles and Dance to the first three. There have been many efforts since to reduce the number of entries in the ISU Championships and the various schemes tried have not proven to be satisfactory, with today elimination rounds based on the free skating only (in Singles) being used to cut the field to a total of 30 entering the short program, with 24 making it to the final free skating.

The third U.S. medal was won by Judy Blumberg and Michael Seibert in the Dance, the first medals in that discipline since Colleen O'Connor and Jim Millns in 1976. Jayne Torvill and Christopher Dean were on their inevitable march to immortality in 1984, and had not been deterred by the fact that they had to withdraw from the 1983 European championships due to an injury to Jayne. Their runners-up, Natalia Bestemianova and Andrei Bukin were in fact the European champions, temporarily, as it were. Judy and Michael were second in both the compulsory dances and the original set-pattern dance, a Rock 'n Roll rhythm, but again could not hold it with their flowing and graceful Astaire-Rogers free dance against the flamboyant and often illegal exercise of the Soviets, which seemed to be of greater appeal to the European judges, who were, after all, the majority of the panel. Spitz and Gregory placed seventh, an improvement of one place over the prior year. There were only two U.S. Dance couples in 1983, so that Fox and Dalley did not make the team.

The Pairs saw the somewhat unexpected win of Elena Valova and Oleg Vasiliev of the USSR, who defeated Sabine Baess and Tassilo Thierbach of GDR, the defending champions, who had led after the short program. Third were Barbara Underhill and Paul Martini of Canada, demonstrating their right to challenge for the Olympic title the next year, while fourth were Kitty and Peter Carruthers. Lea Ann Miller and William Fauver were seventh, with Jill Watson and Burt Lancon 11th, so another U.S. entry did slip below the line (10th).

In summary, the 1983 places were: Men - first, seventh and 14th; Ladies - first, ninth; Pairs - fourth, seventh, 11th; Dance - third, seventh.

With the 1983 Worlds history, the USFSA could turn to a different sort of history when the first Sectional championships in Precision Team skating were launched. The Midwestern Sectional had been held back in January, but the other two were held in March and that has become the traditional time for them, followed by the Nationals early in April. The growth of Precision Team skating had been explosive in the few years before the start of formal competition, and non-qualifying competitions had already been inaugurated, such as at Buffalo, where 54 teams had competed in 1982 and at Lake Placid, where 71 teams competed in 1983.

Only in the Pacific Coast, with its smaller number of clubs and registered skaters, was the beginning modest and the Pacific Coast still lags behind the rest of the country in the interest in and the number of teams participating in the discipline. Founded in the Midwest (in Michigan), although forms of team skating had been practiced in club carnivals since the early days, the discipline had grown very rapidly in such centers as Buffalo and in the Boston area. Of the three Sectionals, the Midwesterns at Wyandotte, Michigan was the largest with 26 teams in five classes - Senior, Junior, Novice, Juvenile and Adult. The Easterns at New Haven, Connecticut had 19 teams in four events (but no Juvenile), while the Pacific Coasts at San Diego could only muster four teams in two events (Junior and Novice) for a total of 49 teams, still a respectable number, when the logistics of travel and housing are considered. The teams had no financial support and the members paid their own expenses, so it was a major undertaking to put a team on the road.

One of the features of Precision team skating are the exotic names chosen for the teams, which are primarily made up of females, with only an occasional young male brave enough to join them. The Senior winners in 1983 were the "Fairfax Follies" of the SC of Northern Virginia in the East and the "Fraserettes" of the Fraser FSC of Michigan in the Midwest. The Adult teams were: in the East, the "Eis Fraus" of the Hayden Recreation Centre FSC of Lexington, Mass., the first of many titles for that club, which also won the Junior ("Haydenettes") and Novice ("Ice Mates") events as well; and in the Midwest, the "Precision Patriots" of the Midland FSC of Michigan. It should also be noted that the first true precision team, generally considered to be the founders of the discipline, the "Hockettes" of the Ann Arbor FSC of Michigan, were present and placed fourth in the Midwestern

Senior event. The referees and judges used then were regular judges for Singles and Pairs, since no categories of precision judges as yet existed. A look at the placements shows that they did well.

When one arrives at the end of the 1982-1983 season, there is almost a sense of exhaustion just writing about it. There was so much going on that would be the wave of the future, with the schedule becoming even more crowded and busy today.

Two events occurred in the 1982-1983 season that deserve to be mentioned: the Los Angeles FSC, which had joined the Association in 1933, observed its 50th Anniversary, while the Superskates exhibition in New York observed its eighth. The Los Angeles club has from the beginning of figure skating in California been the stronghold of the sport on the Coast, together with its cross town rival, the Arctic Blades FSC. The club has had almost as many champions as the old line Eastern clubs, such as the SC of Boston and the SC of New York, and is in the modern era still a dominant force in the sport, with its first USFSA President in 1995 in Morry Stillwell.

Superskates was a mammoth exhibition held in the fall at Madison Square Garden in New York City for the benefit of the U.S. Olympic Fund with all the top skaters appearing in it year after year. The idea of the late Edwin H. Mosler, Jr., and chaired by former World Ladies champion Aja Vrzanova Sandler, the event was extraordinarily successful, although unfortunately it eventually was discontinued after Mr. Mosler's untimely death in March of 1982. Mr. Mosler was the chief executive of the Mosler Safe Company, a major benefactor of the Memorial Fund and through it of the skaters.

The 1983 Governing Council meeting returned to Sun Valley, Idaho, after an absence of 21 years. There were actually 12 delegates who had been present at the earlier meeting who were in attendance. Among them were Past Presidents Ritter Shumway, Jack Shoemaker and Fred LeFevre, past Vice Presidents Bob McLeod, Betty Sonnhalter and Howard Taylor. Both outgoing President Iobst and incoming President George Yonekura of Berkeley, Calif., expressed concern with respect to flagging membership growth, rink closures and lost and expensive ice time. Among the proposals considered to address such problems were more aid to the clubs in the form of public relations assistance as a means of increasing public awareness of skating, as well as aids to help clubs increase membership ice time.

Remembered at the meeting was Past President Harry Keighley of Evanston, Ill., who had passed away earlier in the year, and for whom a memorial resolution was adopted.

Recognized by the Board for their service were Charles DeMore, Joseph Serafine and Roy Winder, who were elected as Honorary members of the Board. At the meeting, President Iobst stepped down after three years and was succeeded by George Yonekura of Berkeley,

George T. Yonekura

Calif. Oscar was elected an Honorary member of the Association and also an Honorary member of the Board in 1987. He continued his energetic and faithful service to the Association and when called upon in 1992, due to the departure of Ian Anderson, he served as Interim Executive Director until 1993. He has also served as chairman of the Long Range Planning Committee since 1993. An active National Referee and Judge, he is now involved with the organization of the 1998 Nationals, scheduled to be held in Philadelphia.

Among the rule changes approved were the following: in the competitions area, the amount to be guaranteed to the USFSA by the local sponsor of the Nationals was increased to $50,000. A procedure was also adopted for the certification of individual or personal computer programs for use in the calculation of results of competitions. Since then, several have been certified, notably those developed by Lewis Mattson of Dallas, Texas, and Robb Steinheider of Riverside, Calif., both National Accountants, which are used widely for non-qualifying competitions.

As to judges, the holding of structured review sessions before the start of qualifying competitions was approved, to be conducted by the JETS.

Also announced were the selections of skaters and officials for 11 International Competitions, including the Grand Prize SNP, a Junior competition in Czechoslovakia and the World Junior Championship, to which would be sent two Men, one Lady, two Pairs and one Dance couple.

Also announced at the meeting were the elections for 1983 to the Hall of Fame. Among them were the late George H. Browne of Cambridge, Mass., one of the founders of modern figure skating in America, the contributions of whom are well covered earlier in this work. His election was most timely since 1983 was the 100th Anniversary of the Browne and Nichols School in Cambridge, Mass., which he had founded. It was possible, as part of the Centennial celebration of the school, to present the tangible tokens of his election to his surviving daughter, Amy Browne Townsend. Also elected was Eugene Turner of California, the first National Senior champion from the Pacific Coast, two times (1940-1941) in the Men, and also in the Pairs (1941) with Donna Atwood. Gene has been a distinguished teacher of the sport and is a prolific author whose work has been published in many of the skating journals since, including "Turner's Turn" in Skating magazine.

Closing the season this time, instead of the meeting, was the fifth National Sports Festival, returning to Colorado Springs and in which the USFSA had been required to participate by the USOC. The winners were Mark Cockerell of Los Angeles in the Men, Kelly Webster of the Broadmoor in the Ladies, Natalie and Wayne Seybold of Fort Wayne, Ind., in the Pairs, and Carol Fox and Richard Dalley of Wilmington in the Dance. The latter event had an especially strong field with Renée Roca of Rochester, N.Y., and Donald Adair of Michigan, second and Susan Wynne of Philadelphia and Joseph Druar of Seattle, third. Scott Williams of California was second in the

Men, while Kathryn Adams of Berkeley, Calif., the new National Junior Ladies champion was second. Fourth in Ladies was Debi Thomas of Los Angeles.

The new season starting the Olympic year, began routinely enough with the St. Gervais-Oberstdorf competitions. The U.S. team won the Coupe des Alpes Trophy for National teams, and also the Geiger Memorial Trophy for teams at the Nebelhorn Trophy competition (Oberstdorf). The team collected a total of seven medals, one Gold, four Silvers and two Bronze. The Gold was in the Nebelhorn Ladies in which Staci McMullin made up for her inability to skate at Sarajevo by coming out on top. She also was third at St. Gervais. Katy Keeley and Gary Kemp from San Diego were second in both Pair competitions, while Eleanor DeVera and James Yorke from Boston were second in both Dance events. Scott Driscoll of Massachusetts was third at St. Gervais, but had to withdraw from Oberstdorf due to injury. Chris Bowman of California, the 1983 World Junior champion, did not fare as well as expected in his first Senior efforts, placing fifth and sixth.

In September, 1983, there was held at Wilmington, Del., the first ISU sponsored Ice Dancing Seminar in the United States, with almost all of the U.S. World and International Dance Referees and Judges present, for the purpose of earning attendance credit, as required under ISU Rules. The moderator was Roland Wehinger of Switzerland, a member of the ISU Ice Dance Committee, and several of the top U.S. Dance couples were brought in as demonstrators. It was a very well run seminar organized by the SC of Wilmington.

Also in September there took place the ASKO Cup of Vienna and here the U.S. earned the two top places in Ladies, with Leslie Sikes of Atlanta, Ga., the winner, and Maradith Feinberg of Michigan, the runner-up. Just a week later, the St. Ivel Ice International was held in England and Tiffany Chin won the Ladies, Carol Fox and Richard Dalley were second in Dance and Lea Ann Miller and William Fauver third in Pairs. Bobby Beauchamp of Massachusetts, the other U.S. entry, was fifth in the Men.

Skate America '83 was held at Rochester, N.Y., the first major competition there since the North Americans of 1959, and the U.S. team completed a sweep of its own competition. Brian Boitano won the Men, Tiffany Chin the Ladies, Kitty and Peter Carruthers the Pairs and Elisa Spitz and Scott Gregory the Dance. Bobby Beauchamp redeemed himself from his St. Ivel showing and placed third, while in the Ladies there was another sweep of all three medals, with Jill Frost second and Kelly Webster third. In Pairs, Jill Watson and Burt Lancon were second. It was a very good medal haul for the candidates for the Olympic and World teams, including four Gold, two Silver and two Bronze. There were no less than three international competitions in just under a month.

At Skate Canada just two weeks later, at the end of October, the competition was tougher and one medal, a Bronze in the Ladies by Tiffany Chin, was the total count. Brian Orser of Canada was the Men's winner, Katarina Witt of the GDR, the Ladies, and Tracy Wilson and Rob McCall of Canada, the Dance, all strong Olympic candidates. Mark Cockerell was fourth and Paul Wylie, fifth in the Men.

The 1983 fall meeting of the Board was the first under the new administration and much work was carried out. Among the decisions taken was the designation of Cincinnati as the bid city for the 1987 World Championships.

In another action, the recreation of the Finance Committee as a Permanent (non voting) Committee was also approved. The original Finance Committee, which had dated back to 1928, had disappeared in 1968 and had been replaced with a variety of temporary special and ad hoc committees, but it had become apparent with the growth of the Association and its finances that a new permanent committee was needed. Its primary function was the preparation and control of the annual budget. Under the By Law change proposed, which was subsequently approved by the Governing Council, the Treasurer served as the chairman of the committee and was not, therefore, appointed by the President.

In the competition field, approval was given for the first National Championship in Precision Team skating to be held at Bowling Green, Ohio, in May 1984. Also approved was a requirement that the execution of a proper contract be a condition precedent to the final award of the Nationals to the local organization. Also approved was the underwriting of the travel and living expenses of coaches at the 1984 Olympics. Noted was the appointment of Scott Hamilton as the USFSA athlete representative to the Athletes Advisory Council of the USOC. Scott and his predecessors and successors in that position, who have included Randy Gardner, Judy Blumberg, Paul Wylie and Richard Dalley, have been of great value in promoting the cause of figure skating within the Olympic movement.

Five more international competitions took place in November: the Prague Skate, the Ennia Challenge Cup, the Golden Spin, the Grand Prize SNP and the Critérium International du Sucre. At Prague, Jimmy Santee of Chicago took second in Men and Rosanna Tovi of Lake Placid, eighth in Ladies, which was won by Midori Ito of Japan. At Ennia in the Hague, the U.S. did not have a strong outing, with the highest place gained being a fourth in Dance by Spitz and Gregory. Jill Frost, Mark Cockerell and Miller-Fauver were all fifth in their events. The third competition was the Golden Spin at Zagreb, to which both Scott Hamilton and Rosalynn Sumners, the reigning World champions, insisted that they wished to go so that they could go on to Sarajevo and test the facilities there before the Olympics. With some misgivings, their wishes were acceded to. For Scott, it worked, as he won over his current rival Norbert Schramm of FRG, but for Rosalynn it was a disaster, as she was beaten by Sanda Dubravcic of Yugoslavia, who had placed 13th in the Worlds at Helsinki in a definitely questionable decision, although Rosalynn did not skate her best.

The risk to the highest ranked skaters in such competitions is very great especially in an Olympic year, since there is no insulation between them and the local heroes, and an upset can occur, as it did here. The adverse impact on the prospects of Sumners at Sarajevo, especially in her own loss of confidence, was readily apparent. The Association has to think very carefully in such cases, whether it is really in the best interest of the skater to take such a risk. Almost overlooked in the Golden Spin was a third place achieved in Dance by Eva Hunyadi of Cleveland and Jay Pinkerton of Indianapolis.

The fourth competition was the Grand Prize SNP for Juniors at Banska Bystrica, Czechoslovakia, on the exact same dates as Zagreb, a conflict which was becoming increasingly a problem in Europe. The one Singles entry, Christopher Mitchell of Los Angeles, the 1983 National Novice champion, placed fourth, while the pair of Kellee Murchison and David McGovern of Arctic Blades were fifth.

The fifth competition was the Critérium International du Sucre for the Jacques Favart Trophy at Tours, France, in which the U.S. took the first three places in the Men, with Danny Doran of the Broadmoor, the winner, followed by Angelo d'Agostino from Rockland, New York and Jimmy Cygan, also from the Broadmoor, third. The Ladies was won by Debi Thomas of Los Angeles, with Caroline Silby of Janesville, Wis., fourth and the unlucky National Junior Ladies champion of 1982, Lorilee Pritchard from Boston, sixth. Two U.S. pairs were also first and second, in an event in which there were but three entries, with the third place pair being a rarity, a pair from China. Sandy Hurtubise of Philadelphia and Karl Kurtz from Hershey, the National Junior Pair runners-up, were the winners, with Margo Shoup and Patrick Page from Portland, Ore., second.

The 1984 World Junior Championships were held at Sapporo, Japan, returning to the 1972 Olympic city, a strange place in winter, with incredible snow sculptures and impenetrable smog due to the use of studded tires. The championship was well run as always by the Japanese federation. Notable in the Men was the win for Viktor Petrenko of the Soviet Union, a familiar name over the next 10 years. Tom Cierniak of Chicago placed third, with Erik Larson of San Diego fourth. Also in the event was Viktor's brother Vladimir, who placed fifth. In the Ladies, two East German skaters, Karin Hendschke and Simone Koch were first and second with Midori Ito, third, the closest she would ever come to winning the event, with her performance featured by her usual low (13th) place in figures, and two first places in the short program and the free skating. In fourth was Kathryn Adams of Berkeley, Calif., the 1983 National Junior Ladies champion.

In Pairs, Susan and Jason Dungjen from Michigan, the National Junior Pair champions, placed a solid second to Manuela Landgraf and Ingo Steuer of the GDR, followed by three Soviet pairs, of whom the pair in fifth place was that of Ekaterina Gordeeva and Sergei Grinkov. In

Dance, Christina and Keith Yatsuhashi of Boston added Silver medals to the Bronze medals they had been awarded the year before, the winning couple being Elena Krikanova and Evgeni Platov of the USSR.

Finally, we arrive at the first high point of the season, the 1984 Nationals at Salt Lake City, the first time in that future Olympic city. Clearly, the highlight of the event was the skating of Scott Hamilton in winning his fourth title, with what was probably his best free skating performance ever, for which he received no less than four perfect marks. He performed five triples flawlessly (Lutz, flip, toe Walley, toe loop and Salchow) and was absolutely in total control throughout. It was a performance for the ages. Brian Boitano was again the runner-up on a less than perfect performance, which kept him ahead of Mark Cockerell, in third. Both were now veterans of the Senior ranks, being in their sixth year in the event.

While Rosalynn Sumners won the figures in the Ladies, she was second in both the short program and free skating to Tiffany Chin, who had been fourth in figures. It was a close result, 3.4 total reduced places to 3.8. In third place was Elaine Zayak, who had been second in figures and third in short and free. The Carruthers won their fourth Pairs title, with Lea Ann Miller and William Fauver second and Jill Watson and Burt Lancon third. The Dance resulted in their fourth title for Judy Blumberg and Michael Seibert. Carol Fox and Richard Dalley were second and Elisa Spitz and Scott Gregory third. It is an interesting coincidence that of the 12 medalists, all were exactly the same as in 1983. The placements in the Men and Pairs were identical, while in the Ladies and Dance, the second and third places only were reversed.

A look at the Junior and Novice results is a portent of the future. In the Junior Ladies, we find Jill Trenary of Denver in fourth and Tonya Harding of Portland in sixth. Jerod Swallow was sixth in Junior Pairs with Shelly Propson and fifth in Junior Dance with Jodie Balogh. In Novice Men, in second place was Todd Eldredge, representing Philadelphia and Kyoko Ina of New York was seventh in Novice Ladies, to name just a few of the stars of the future.

So it was on to Sarajevo for the XIV Olympic Winter Games, which today have a special poignancy, due to the destruction of the city in the Balkan wars between the Serbians and the Bosnians. The 1984 Olympics were one of the best organized Games ever and the two major facilities for the skating, "Zetra"

Caitlin and Peter Carruthers

Judy Blumberg and Michael Seibert

and "Skenderija" were modern, well equipped and run facilities. The then Yugoslav Government omitted no effort to make the Games run smoothly. When there was a major snowstorm, the army and hundreds of trucks were organized to remove the snow in a very brief period. The buses continued to run without letup and so it was. Getting in and out was the only problem, as the winter weather in the mountainous terrain is hazardous and unpredictable at best. The opening ceremony was one of the best ever, not too frilled up with gimmicks not related to sport, but an historical review of the prior Games in colorful and elegant pageantry.

In figure skating, the United States came away with three medals, one Gold and two Silver, and should really have had another medal (in the Dance). After four hard years of campaigning, Scott Hamilton finally achieved his goal of an Olympic Gold medal and he won it in the least expected way, with the figures. Scott was second in both the short program and free skating to Brian Orser of Canada, but the latter had been seventh in figures and could not make up the gap. Brian Boitano, with an eighth in figures and a third in the short, finished fifth, while Mark Cockerell placed 13th. Both by his own standard and in fact, Hamilton did not skate his best, but his all around consistency paid off for him so that he became the fourth Olympic champion in the Men from the United States.

In the Ladies the result was disappointing, as Rosalynn Sumners, after winning the figures, had a poor short program placing fifth, which took her out of the running despite a second in the free skating. The winner was Katarina Witt of East Germany, who had placed a high (for her) third in figures and had then won both the short program and the free skating to take the Olympic title, as a worthy successor to her compatriot Anett Pötzsch. In third place was Kira Ivanova of the Soviet Union, who just held off the challenge of Tiffany Chin. Tiffany had started poorly with a 12th in figures, but rebounded with a second and a third in the short and long to reach fourth place. Elaine Zayak, with also a poor figure result of 13th, placed fourth in the final free skating to finish sixth. We have seen the refrain over and over again of the poor figure places of the U.S. skaters and one can only imagine what they might have done if the figures had been abolished, as Dick Button had long ago suggested, something that would not happen until 1990.

The Pairs event was, from the U.S. standpoint, the sensation of the Games. Elena Valova and Oleg Vasiliev of the USSR won the Olympic Gold, perpetuating the Soviet supremacy, but the surprise was the Silver medal for Kitty and Peter Carruthers. Generally, going into the competition, Barbara Underhill and Paul Martini of Canada had been regarded as the principal challengers to the Soviets, but such was not the case, as they had a disastrous failure in the short program and never got out of seventh place as a result. Kitty and Peter were in an unusual tie for second after the short program with Larisa Selezneva and Oleg Makarov, USSR, with former World champions Sabine Baess and Tasilo Thierbach in fourth. They performed the free skating of their career to hold second and to win the first Silver medal in the Olympics in Pairs for the United States since Karol and Peter Kennedy in 1952. Jill Watson and Burt Lancon overturned the National result to place sixth ahead of Lea Ann Miller and William Fauver, in 10th. Fauver had been in the 1976 Games with Alice Cook and here he was in his second Games eight years later, a remarkable accomplishment.

The Dance event was once again frustrating for Judy Blumberg and Michael Seibert, who were solidly in third position throughout the compulsory dances and the original set-pattern dance, but were again passed in the free dance, this time by Marina Klimova and Sergei Ponomarenko of the Soviet Union. It had been their fate over and over again, and is not due to any inadequacy in the free dance on their part but rather to a stylistic mind-set on the part of the European judges, who did not penalize obvious violations of the rules, even at the top. Torvill and Dean made their way into the history books with their Bolero and yet it too contained violations of the then rules which went unnoticed. Ironically, it would be alleged rule violations that would cost them their second Gold medal 10 years later. Second and to the same effect were Natalia Bestemianova and Andrei Bukin, the top Soviet couple. Carol Fox and Richard Dalley did one of their best ever performances to finish fifth, while Elisa Spitz and Scott Gregory placed 10th.

So the medal count was: Men - first, fifth, 13th; Ladies - second, fourth, sixth; Pairs - second, sixth, 10th; Dance - fourth, fifth, 10th.

The 1984 World Championships were held at Ottawa, Canada, and were notable in several respects. One in particular was power failure in the main arena, which necessitated the postponement of the final round of the Dance event for six hours, while a new transformer was shipped in and installed. Another was the sudden reduction of the U.S. team, with the withdrawal of both Rosalynn Sumners and Tiffany Chin, leaving Elaine Zayak alone to carry the flag in the Ladies. Rosalynn withdrew for personal reasons and despite efforts to get her to reconsider, she did not do so. Tiffany was suffering from an ankle stress fracture. It is also a note of USFSA history that the last time that the U.S. had been represented by just one lady in a World Championship had been in 1948 by Yvonne Sherman of New York. Elaine rose to the challenge and in perhaps her finest hour, other than in Copenhagen in 1982, secured the Bronze medal giving her a complete set of Gold (1982), Silver (1981) and Bronze (1984). She was second in the free skating after a ninth in figures. Katarina Witt won the vacant title, with another Soviet, Anna Kondrashova, second.

The fallout continued in the Pairs, with the Carruthers having also withdrawn to begin their professional career, while Jill Watson and Burt Lancon had to withdraw after a disastrous fall in the short program, leaving only Miller and Fauver to represent the U.S. in the final in which they placed 10th. Scott Hamilton again won figures and also the short program in the Men to retain his title and win his fourth overall, defeating Orser, who had been seventh in figures, but won the free. Boitano place sixth and Cockerell, 13th.

Blumberg and Seibert decisively turned the tables in the Dance on Klimova and Ponomarenko to take the Bronze medal behind Torvill and Dean and Bestemianova and Bukin, some small compensation for their Olympic disappointment. Fox and Dalley placed eighth and Spitz-Gregory, 10th. The Ottawa results were somewhat disappointing for the U.S., even with two medals, a Gold and a Silver, but that is often the case when the end of the line is reached, because expectations have been built up so high by the media hype especially, that anything less than perfect is a disappointment. Now it was time to turn over the mantle to the next young generation waiting in the wings, fresh with the same hopes and dreams as their predecessors, and ready to begin the long cycle all over again.

However, the season had far from ended, even in an Olympic year. There were new and exciting events on the horizon. The second round of Sectional Championships in Precision Team skating were held and reflected an increase in the number of teams participating, although there was no Senior competition in the Easterns. The three Sectionals now had a total of 67 teams, with the Pacific Coast still the smallest with eight, and the Midwest the largest with 32. The first National Championships in Precision were held at Bowling Green, Ohio, with 38 teams in five events, and it is appropriate to list those teams which had the honor and pleasure of being the first National champions in this exciting discipline:

Senior -	Fraserettes	Fraser FSC (Michigan)
Junior -	Hot Fudge Sundaes	Buffalo SC
Novice -	Hot Fudge Sundaes	Buffalo SC
Juvenile -	Fraser Mini-ettes	Fraser FSC
Adult -	Acton Ups	Colonial FSC (Acton MA)

It should be noted that the coach of the Buffalo teams was T. "Sundae" Bafo, one of the leading Precision coaches and at the time a coach member of the Board of Directors.

While all this was going on, the spring international competition season was under way, with the Morzine and Wilkie Dance competitions and the Merano Junior Ladies event. At Morzine, Carol Fox and Richard Dalley were the delighted winners, while at the Wilkie (named after the late Reg Wilkie, a former British Dance champion and chairman of the ISU Ice Dance Committee), Susan Jorgensen and Robert Yokabaskas of Wilmington were fifth. At Merano, Jill Trenary of Denver placed second and Valory Vennes of Atlanta fifth.

The season was far from over even then, with two big events to come: the 1984 Governing Council meeting and the 1984 ISU Congress.

The Governing Council meeting was held at Colorado Springs for the third time and the first since 1975. A memorial resolution was adopted for Dr. Nelson F. Waters of Alton Bay, N.H., who had passed away earlier in the year. Dr. Waters was a former standing committee chairman, member and Honorary member of the (former) Executive Committee and the father of Claire Waters Ferguson.

With the departure at the end of the 1982-1983 season of Larry McCollum who returned to the U.S. Olympic Committee, it was necessary to appoint a new Executive Director, who was found in house in the person of Ian Anderson, the editor of Skating magazine. Ian had come to Colorado Springs from Cleveland with Don Stoddard in 1979 to become the magazine editor. He would serve in a dual capacity, both as editor and Executive Director until 1986, when he was succeeded in the editorship by Dale Mitch and would continue as Executive Director until 1993.

In addition to the By Law changes which reconstituted and re-established the Finance Committee, further By Law changes were adopted to create a Memorial Fund Operating Committee, a statutory special committee of which the three principal members were the President, the Chairman of the Memorial Fund Committee and the Chairman of the Grants and Allocations Subcommittee of the Memorial Fund Committee. The creation of the committee was to further reinforce the independent status of the Memorial Fund within the Association, its purpose being the "responsibility...to determine the policy of the Memorial Fund especially with regard to investments and operating policies."

Among the technical rule changes approved was one relating to tests. Although majority judging (i.e., two of three judges being needed to pass) in tests had been in effect since 1960, the Judges Rules had continued to specify that lower ranked judges could serve only as a minority of a test panel for certain higher tests. Since these limitations were inconsistent with the principle of a majority pass, they were deleted. Actually, the provision in the Test Rules that a mark below the minimum in any part of a test by one judge only would fail the test remained in the rules until 1995. The rule requiring that a (figure) test must be stopped in such in instance had been dropped in 1992.

For the 1984-1985 season, 11 International Competitions between August and December and three more between March and May were selected for participation and support, the same number and composition as in the prior year, except that the Ennia Challenge Cup was now the "Aegon" Cup, with a new corporate sponsor. At this point, with 15 years of experience sending skaters to International Competitions, the expenses to do so, which also included the World and World Junior teams, had increased remarkably. In the year 1974, just 10 years earlier, such expenses were $28,499 while in 1984 they were $230,915. For comparison, television revenue (rights fees) in 1974 was $35,000 and in 1984 were $630,000. Total operating revenues in 1974 were $314,702 and in 1984 were $1,908,462. Another important figure to throw into the equation was the cost of operating the National Headquarters. In the year before the move to Colorado Springs (1978-1979), the expenses of the then Central Office were $394,630, while in 1984, the expenses of the Headquarters were $642,827. Although, as a non-profit corporation there is no such thing as a "net profit," the retained earnings measure how the Association did. For the year 1974, such earnings were $28,075, while in 1984 they were $377,466. So in the major year of 1984, the Association was healthy and growing. By 1985, there would be 446 member clubs and 36,289 registered skaters. At the same time, the total paid circulation of **Skating** magazine had reached 28,375, actually down from two years earlier.

The last and a really major event of the 1983-1984 season was the 40th Ordinary Congress of the International Skating Union which was also held at The Broadmoor in Colorado Springs at the end of May, just 10 days after the Governing Council meeting. The Congress, which was the first to be held outside Europe, was originally to have been organized by the CFSA in Toronto, but when assurances could not be obtained from the Canadian Government for the free entry into the country of all the delegates, through the efforts of Charles DeMore, the U.S. member of the ISU Council, the Congress was quickly transferred to the USFSA. Once again, with the unstinting cooperation of Thayer Tutt and the Broadmoor, the Congress was wonderfully well organized, with a special treat being the usual outing, which this time was a ride up Pikes Peak on the inaugural runs of the new cog railroad trains recently obtained by Thayer from the Swiss Locomotive Works in Winterthur, Switzerland. There was also a typical Western barbeque in the area called Rotten Log Hollow, with cowboy hats very much in evidence as a trademark of all championships at the Broadmoor.

From the USFSA standpoint, another major happening was the recognition by the ISU of the Museum and Hall of Fame of the USFSA as the "World" Figure Skating Hall of Fame and Museum, which instantly transformed both the Museum and Hall of Fame into those for the entire sport worldwide, not just for the United States.

The major work of the Congress itself was the approval of an entirely new Constitution for the Union, which had been drafted by an ad hoc committee headed by Ben Wright and on which Chuck DeMore also served. The controversial issue was whether there should be a Treasurer formally required by the statutes. It is hard for North Americans to imagine any major organization without such an officer, but it was indeed true in the ISU. The idea of an elected Treasurer was rejected, but the provision for a "financial advisor" to be appointed by the Council was provided for, and eventually, in 1994, a Treasurer would finally be appointed. Proposals by the West German federation to in effect split the Union in two, with separate Councils for speed and figure skating, were also rejected.

Efforts to create alternate ways of reducing the number of entries in ISU Championships were still being considered, such as by creating an additional ("Pacific") championship, but were not implemented. However, another procedure was adopted in that regard which was to limit the final round of an event to 20 skaters only, with 17 to qualify directly after the figures and short program, and the remaining three to come from a semi-final free skating among those otherwise eliminated. This idea, like its predecessor, the A and B finals, would not last long either.

Another change made which very directly affected the USFSA was the adoption of a mandatory retirement age of 70 for referees and judges, while at the same time, the maximum age for initial appointment was reduced from age 55 to age 45. The maximum number of Judges for International Competitions was increased from 16 to 20 in order to accommodate the increasing number of International Competitions and the need of the Members to staff them. A provision for the demotion of ISU Championship ("World") judges in Singles and Pairs who were found to be incompetent or unsatisfactory was also added, with their return to that rank being based upon attendance at an official judges' seminar and the passing of the judges examination.

At long last it was mandated that the Regulations for Ice Dancing would be published in the English language. They had, up to then, been in German only, with a partial translation only of the competition rules into English. A proposal to make the second mark ("artistic impression") the tie breaker was rejected, but would ultimately be accepted in 1988.

There were many changes among the officers and committee chairmen, but Messrs. DeMore and Wright were re-elected to their respective offices of Council and Committee member, while President Olaf Poulsen of Norway was elected for the first time to a full four year term, and Josef Dedic of Czechoslovakia was elected the First Vice President.

So, yet another cycle had ended on a very high note for the U.S. and the USFSA.

One would think that there would be a period of "rest" after the whirlwind activities of an Olympic season, but such is not the case. The sport continues to function and the traditional "cycle" goes on. The season of 1984-1985 was no exception to the rule, especially because the 1985 World Junior Championships had been awarded to the USFSA, to be held at The Broadmoor for

The Road to Calgary
(1985-1988)

the sixth ISU Championship for that famous skating center. Of course, before that major event, the regular International competition season was well underway. However, as a consequence of the commitment to organize the World Juniors, Skate America was not held in 1984.

There was no National Sports Festival in 1984 since it was an Olympic year, so the first activity of the new season was St. Gervais. Once again the U.S. team proved its worth by taking seven out of a possible eight medals, including two firsts, with Craig Henderson of Stockton, Calif., winning the Men, and Debi Thomas of Los Angeles, the Ladies. Susan and Jason Dungjen of Detroit were second in Pairs, and Lois Luciani of Wilmington and Russ Witherby of Cincinnati, second in Dance.

At the following Nebelhorn Trophy competition at Oberstdorf, the team repeated its success of the previous week, with Thomas again winning the Ladies and Luciani and Witherby taking the Dance for a very satisfying win in that discipline on foreign soil. The Dungjens repeated their second place, while Henderson was second in the Men. The U.S. won both the Coupe des Alpes Team Trophy and the Geiger Memorial Trophy. The success of the team in the summer events was a very good "kickoff" for the future, with several of the skaters involved slated for greatness in the immediate future.

The next competition was the St. Ivel Ice International at Richmond, England, and the U.S. team did well, enjoying much the same level of success as in the Coupe des Alpes. Brian Boitano of California won the Men's event, and Kathryn Adams of Berkeley, Calif., won the Ladies. Katy Keeley and Joseph Mero of San Diego were second in Pairs, and Susan Wynne of Philadelphia and Joseph Druar of Seattle were third in the Dance.

With no Skate America in October of 1984, that month was relatively "quiet" except for Skate Canada at Victoria, British Columbia, at the end of the month. Most of the remaining international competitions were "squeezed" into November, as usual.

In Skate Canada, the competition was tough with the best place and the only medal being the second of Tiffany Chin of San Diego to Midori Ito of Japan, the latter winning her first Senior International. In Men, Mark Cockerell was fourth, while in Pairs Natalie and Wayne Seybold of Fort Wayne, Ind., were also fourth, as were Eva Hunyadi and Jay Pinkerton in Dance, with Susan Wynne and Joseph Druar a somewhat surprising fifth.

A week later came the Prague Skate, with Leslie Sikes of Atlanta placing second, Jimmy Cygan of Colorado, fourth. In Pairs and Dance, two third places were earned, by Maria Lako and Michael Blicharski of Michigan and Margaret Bodo of California and Rick Berg of Wisconsin, respectively. The Aegon Cup continued at The Hague, with Christopher Bowman taking third in the Men, behind the eventual winner, Petr Barna of Czechoslovakia, with Paul Wylie sixth. In Ladies, Yvonne Gomez of Berkeley, Calif., who would later represent Spain in international competition, placed third, while the Seybolds were third in Pairs. Susan Jorgensen and Robert Yokabaskas of Wilmington were fifth in Dance.

The next week was the Golden Spin of Zagreb and the Grand Prize SNP of Banska Bystrica on the same weekend. In the former, Scott Williams of California, the 1982 World Junior champion, was the winner, with Kelly Webster of Colorado second in the Ladies, and Kandi Amelon of Detroit and Alec Binnie of Des Moines, third in Dance. There was no Pair event at Zagreb. It was at the Golden Spin that a sporting gesture on the part of Amelon and Binnie captured the attention of the media and was also recognized by the Government, including the State of Delaware and President Ronald Reagan. During the warm-up for the free dance, the Hungarian couple Klara Engi and Attila Toth, who were ahead of Amelon and Binnie, suffered injuries in a collision with the West German couple Petra Born and Rainer Schönborn, and had to withdraw, with Engi injured severely enough to have to go to the hospital. At the closing banquet, Amelon and Binnie, who had mixed emotions about winning a medal as it were by default, decided to give the medal to Toth. Amelon said, "We felt badly for them. It was a hollow victory for us. That's when we decided to give the medal to the boy." The incident was widely reported and captured the imagination of the press. The State of Delaware issued a resolution recognizing them and they received a congratulatory letter from President Reagan. Subsequently they were the first recipients of the U.S. Olympic Committee's Jack Kelly Fair Play Award.

At Banska Bystrica, Rudy Galindo of Berkeley was the Men's winner of this Junior competition, while Ginger and Archie Tse of Wilmington, the 1984 National Junior Pair champions, were third in Pairs, and Jodie Balogh and Jerod Swallow of Michigan won the Dance.

In the NHK Trophy at Tokyo, again the competition was tougher. Actually, the international competitions of the time were beginning to divide themselves into "higher" and "lower" levels, with such events as Skate Canada, Skate America and the NHK Trophy drawing higher quality fields, while events such as St. Ivel, Prague, Zagreb and St. Gervais-Oberstdorf drew fields which included many newly "graduated" Junior skaters. Banska and Merano were, of course, Junior and in their own way, had quite good fields, with the U.S. success in them demonstrating the strength of the qualifying competition structure in the United States.

At NHK, Boitano was in yet another competition against Brian Orser of Canada, who this time finished ahead, but both of them were behind Alexandr Fadeev of the USSR. In the Ladies at NHK, Midori Ito won her second Senior International, defeating Debi Thomas, while in the Pairs the Dungjens were in a little over their heads, finishing fifth. In Dance, the same was true for Renée Roca and Donald Adair, who were also fifth.

The final competition on the "fall circuit" was the International competition at Tours, where David Fedor of Philadelphia was second in Men; Laura Steele of Atlanta and Tonya Harding of Portland, second and third, respectively in Ladies; and Jeannine and Tony Jones of Ohio, third in Pairs.

The Fall 1984 meeting of the Board of Directors was held at Colorado Springs. Among the actions announced was a recognition program sponsored by Travelers Insurance, with the amount of $500 going to the Memorial Fund in the name of a "Grass Roots" volunteer from each Region. In addition, $1,000 would go to the Memorial Fund for each skater chosen to receive the "Award of Merit" for Sportsmanship at each Sectional, and $2,500 for the skater chosen at the Nationals who "best exemplifies the true spirit of competition." Various recognition programs have continued since in one form of another, and have become an important part of what has come to be called "member recognition," with clubs, volunteers and officials being recognized for their efforts and service. The competitor winning the award at the 1985 Nationals was Todd Waggoner, representing Wilmington.

In the area of competition, it was decided to add Intermediate Dance events to Sectionals as well as Regional Championships. With respect to "non-funded" International competitions, the decision was made to include them in the selection process, rather than to have skaters entering them "at random" at the last minute. It was also recommended that a separate Precision Skating Committee be established as a new special committee. Since 1977, Precision had been a subdivision within the Program Development Committee. Modest grants ($500) were also made to the organizers of the Sectional championships in Precision, while it was agreed to underwrite any losses incurred up to a maximum of $2,500. Grants were also made for each of the nine Regional championships in the amount of $4,000 and in the amount of $2,500 for each Sectional Championships. The policy of making such grants and of underwriting losses has continued up to today. However, the need of adequate financial controls, in order to audit and determine the legitimacy of any losses incurred, has continued to be a problem.

The percentage assessments to be charged for exhibitions and carnivals for the benefit of non-skating related organizations in which World Team members participated (i.e., "The Jimmy Fund") continued to be an issue, but remained at 5 percent of the amount received by such organizations. A further donation of $2.00 per registered member was made to the Memorial Fund. This donation was the continuation of a practice started in 1975, when $1.00 of each registration fee was donated to the Fund. The amount was raised in 1977 to $2.00, with only 1981 being omitted due to the net loss incurred (in the amount of $85,209 for the 1979-1980 fiscal year) as a result of the move to Colorado.

The 1985 World Junior Championships were held at the Broadmoor World Arena in Colorado Springs in December 1994, and featured an unexpected Gold medal in the Men when Erik Larson of San Diego, who had been fourth the prior year, came out on top over Vladimir Petrenko of the USSR. Vladimir, the younger brother of Viktor, had been first in both the figures and short program, but failed miserably in the free skating, placing fourth. Erik, fifth in the figures and second in the short, won the free skating and the title by the narrow margin of 4.8 total factored places to 5.0, to become the fifth World Junior Men's champion for the U.S. Rudy Galindo of California was third. In the Ladies, the two U.S. entrants, Tracy Ernst from Illinois and Jana Sjodin of St. Paul, Minn., were fourth and fifth, respectively, the title going to Tatiana Andreeva of the USSR, for its first World Junior title in Ladies.

Jerod Swallow of Michigan was still doing "double duty" in Pairs and Dance as he had in the 1984 Nationals, and was fourth in both events with his two partners, Shelly Propson in Pairs and Jodie Balogh in Dance. The Championships, which were actually the first World Juniors held in the United States, were well run by the Broadmoor Skating Club and supported by the Broadmoor Hotel in their usual excellent manner. There were 17 Men, 25 Ladies, eight Pairs and 24 Dance couples from 21 countries, so the concern that the Championships would not be supported by entrants from abroad turned out to be unfounded, with only the Pairs being a small event, which at that time was generally the case. It was perhaps appropriate that the Board of Directors had voted to recommend the election of William Thayer Tutt as an Honorary member of the USFSA by the Governing Council. Tutt was the head of the hotel and the motivating force behind all the ISU Championships held at the Broadmoor, for without his unstinting support, none of the championships ever could have taken place.

The 1985 National Championships were held at Kansas City, Mo., (the first time at that site), and produced a substantial entry, especially in the Senior classes of 15 Men, 16 Ladies, 14 Pairs and 14 Dance couples, and a total of 139 entries overall. With the usual turnover of the defending Senior champions following an Olympic year, only Judy Blumberg and Michael Seibert of Pittsburgh returned. With both Singles and the Pairs titles vacant, interest was high. This time, "form" prevailed in the Singles, with the prior year's runners-up, Brian Boitano and Tiffany Chin both succeeding to the titles and both of them winning all three parts of their events. In the Men, Mark Cockerell of Los Angeles moved up to the second position from third the prior year, while Scott Williams, seventh in 1984, placed third just ahead of Christopher Bowman and Paul Wylie.

In the Ladies after Tiffany came Debi Thomas, sixth the prior year, followed by a new face in Caryn Kadavy, representing the Broadmoor. Caryn had been fifth in the 1984 Midwestern Junior Ladies and had not previously even made it to the Nationals. She had qualified by placing second in the 1985 Midwesterns, while the winner of that event, Maradith Feinberg of Michigan, placed 12th at Nationals. It was a remarkable success story and fully justified in the future.

Tiffany Chin

The Pairs also resulted in an unexpected winner, when Jill Watson and Peter Oppegard of Los Angeles took the title. Jill had been third in 1984 with Burt Lancon, while Peter had not competed at all in 1984 (he had been seventh in 1983 with Maria DeDomenico). In second were Natalie and Wayne Seybold from Fort Wayne, while Gillian Wachsman and Todd Waggoner, representing Wilmington, were third.

Judy Blumberg and Michael Seibert easily retained the Dance title, their fifth, (placing them on the same level in that regard with Judy Schwomeyer and Jim Sladky), with Renée Roca of Rochester and Donald Adair of Michigan second, followed by a new partnership of Suzanne Semanick of Pittsburgh and Scott Gregory of Wilmington.

Among the Junior and Novice winners can be found Jill Trenary in Junior Ladies, and Jodie Balogh and Jerod Swallow in Junior Dance (he was also second in Junior Pairs with Shelly Propson). In Novice Men, the winner was Todd Eldredge, representing Philadelphia. Among others were Todd Sand, third in Junior Pairs with Lori Blasko; Kristi Yamaguchi and Rudy Galindo, fifth in Junior Pairs (Kristi was also fourth in Novice Ladies); while Nancy Kerrigan was ninth in Novice Ladies (and was also 11th in Junior Pairs with Bobby Martin of Stoneham, Mass.).

An added International competition that year was the University (FISU) Winter Games, held at Belluno, Italy, in February. The U.S. Team had surprising success winning five medals: one Gold (Sandy Hurtubise and Craig Maurizi from Philadelphia in Pairs) two Silver (Robert Rosenbluth of Philadelphia in the Men and Debbie Walls of Atlanta in the Ladies), and two Bronze (David Jamison from Philadelphia in Men and Deborah Tucker from Chicago in Ladies).

The 1985 Worlds returned to Tokyo, Japan, after eight years and were again held in the Yoyogi Stadium (the swimming pool). The entry was substantial, with 27 Men, 28 Ladies, 13 Pairs and 19 Dance couples, from 23 nations. Here also, three of the four champions from the prior year (Scott Hamilton, Barbara Underhill and Paul Martini, and Jayne Torvill and Christopher Dean) were gone, with only Katarina Witt returning to defend her Ladies title.

In the Men, Alexandr Fadeev of the Soviet Union had a fairly easy time of it, winning all three parts of the competition to take a fourth Men's title for the USSR, and also repeating his win on the same ice earlier in the season in the NHK Trophy. In second was Brian Orser of Canada, the nominal favorite, who again had a low (fourth) place in figures, and surprisingly could not defeat Fadeev in the two free skating parts. Third was Brian Boitano, who recovered from a fifth in figures and a fourth in the short program to take the Bronze medal, a jump of three places from 1984. Mark Cockerell, after a disastrous 16th in figures, pulled up to eighth overall by reason of a seventh and eighth in the short and long.

In Ladies, Katarina Witt again put her title in jeopardy by a third in figures, behind Kira Ivanova of the USSR and Tiffany Chin. But with characteristic nonchalance, she took both the short and free to win her second title. Ivanova was actually second in free just ahead of Tiffany, who wound up with the Bronze medal, a substantial recovery from her withdrawal a year earlier due to injury. Debi Thomas, in her first Worlds, placed fifth with a fourth in free skating.

In the Pairs, the new champions were again from the Soviet Union, Olympic champions Elena Valova and Oleg Vasiliev, with another Soviet couple, Larisa Selezneva and Oleg Makarov, second, followed by Katherina Matousek and Lloyd Eisler of Canada. Jill Watson and Peter Oppegard were a very creditable fourth in their first Worlds, and the Seybolds were ninth.

Judy Blumberg and Michael Seibert remained on the podium in third place, as they had been in 1984, but their close rivals Marina Klimova and Sergei Ponomarenko of the USSR, wound up second behind the new champions, Natalia Bestemianova and Andrei Bukin also of the USSR. All four titles went to Eastern Bloc representatives, with three of them to the Soviet Union. It was perhaps the "height" of the Bloc dominance. Of the 12 possible medals, the West took just five (U.S. - three, Canada - two), with the other seven going to the Soviets (six) and the GDR (one).

Another International competition was "slipped" into the schedule, when "La Coupe Excellence" at Montreal was organized in mid-March (somewhat at the last minute) by the Quebec Section of the CFSA with invitations going only to skaters from Quebec, France and the United States. The competition was seen as an effort on the part of the Quebec Section to establish its own International competition as a gesture of independence from the rest of the CFSA. At that time, the movement for Quebec to seek independence from Canada was in full swing (it has not happened yet). The USFSA sent skaters and officials to the competition and won two of the four events, with Christopher Bowman taking the Men and Gillian Wachsman and Todd Waggoner the Pairs, plus three other medals. Danny Doran and Kathryn Adams were second in the Men and Ladies, while Lois Luciani and Russ Witherby were second in Dance. Christine Hough and Doug Ladret of Canada (who would later be Canadian champions) were second in Pairs, while the Dance winners were Isabelle and Paul Duchesnay, then representing Canada. (They would soon leave for France.)

The "Spring" International competition season was also a successful one for the United States. At the Morzine Dance competition, Suzanne Semanick and Scott Gregory were the winners, while at Merano, Tracey Damigella, representing Lake Placid, and Tracey Seliga from Acton, Mass., were first and third, respectively. In the closing competition of the season, the Wilkie Ice Dance International at Nottingham, England, in May, Susan Wynne and Joseph Druar were second.

The Precision "season" which comes after the regular Nationals in March and April, again demonstrated rapid growth as the number of teams participating in the second year of the Sectionals increased sharply. Most encouraging was the entry in the Pacific Coast Sectional, with 17 teams in four events, including six Junior teams, but still no Senior event. In the Midwesterns, there were 43 teams in five events, with seven Senior teams, while in the Easterns, the count was 26 teams, three in Senior.

The second National Precision championships were held at Lakewood, Ohio, and drew 50 teams in five events, with eight Senior teams. The winners of the previous year continued their dominance, with the Fraserettes of the Fraser (Michigan) FSC winning the Senior for the second time. The Hot Fudge Sundaes of the Buffalo SC took both the Junior and Novice events, while the Wyandotte Rising Stars, of the Wyandotte (Michigan) FSC, won the Juvenile. The Acton-Ups of the Colonial FSC of Acton, Mass., retained their Adult title.

The 1985 meeting of the Governing Council was held at Miami, Fla., at the Doral Resort, the first time that the meeting had been held in the Southeast and a recognition of the increased interest in and growth of skating in that area. While still a part of the South Atlantic Region, it is quite possible that in due course a separate Southeastern Region may be needed.

In a principle action, the By Laws were amended to change the composition of the Nominating Committee, to provide that none of the members shall represent the same Region. The Committee would include the three Vice Presidents, three members elected by the Board of Directors and three elected by the Governing Council. In practice, the latter election has been accomplished by the holding of Sectional caucuses during the Governing Council meeting attended by the delegates from each Section. While purportedly a "democratic" process, experience has shown that election by caucus is not the most democratic way of doing it, with "politics" inherently coming into play. Ultimately, the Nominating Committee probably should consist of nine members, one from each Region, none of whom are officers, with all nine being elected by the Governing Council annually, and a limitation of two years of continuous service. Also the inclusion of 20 percent athletes on the committee will have to be faced.

Memorial resolutions were adopted for Joseph R. Maxwell of Philadelphia and Edmund C. Bold of Seattle, who had passed away during the year. Both of them had served as Vice Presidents and chairmen of standing and special committees of the Association. Ed Bold was also an Honorary member of the Executive Committee.

Thayer Tutt of Colorado Springs was duly elected an Honorary member of the Association, only the fourth person (not a Past President) so elected.

The financial reports for the year ending in 1985 showed a total of 446 member clubs and 36,289 registered skaters. While the number of member clubs had continued to increase, registrations which had peaked in 1978 at 37,310, remained essentially flat. From the financial standpoint, the assets of the Association had reached $3,521,865; total revenues for the year $2,234,696; and total expenses $1,919,520. With respect to the Memorial Fund, its assets had reached $2,164,051; while receipts were $824,956; and disbursed amounts were $251,950. The assets of the Fund had increased enormously in the 10 years since 1976.

Added to the schedule, again under the jurisdiction of the Program Development Committee, were the first National Collegiate Championships, scheduled to be held at Lake Placid in late August 1985. The first championships were for Seniors only, without figures, which were to be added in 1986. Eligibility required full-time enrollment in a college or university degree program or to have graduated in the preceding academic year from a full-time program.

The number of International competitions to be supported was increased to 16, with three new ones being added: Danubius Thermal Trophy at Budapest, Hungary, (intended to be a companion event with the ASKO Cup of Vienna, in the same format as St. Gervais and Oberstdorf); Pokal der Blauen Schwerter, a Junior competition in East Germany; and the Prize of the Moscow News ("Moscow Skate"), which represented a return to the Soviet Union after some years absence. The increase in the cost of such support can be seen in the numbers. In 1973, $10,058 was expended. In 1983, that number had reached $200,997, while for 1984-1985, the number was $260,494. Fortunately, grants from the USOC and the increase in revenue from television had kept pace with the growth in such support. Hopefully, the reward in the form of medals would be worth the expense!

The 1985-1986 season, which would prove to be an extremely busy one, started with the National Sports Festival at Baton Rouge, La., at the end of July. Once again, all the top skaters were asked to be present. There were 46 entries in the four events, and of the National champions only Brian Boitano was on hand. Judy Blumberg and Michael Seibert had retired, and Tiffany Chin, Jill Watson and Peter Oppegard were not present. Among the 14 Men, Boitano was the winner, followed by Christopher Bowman and Daniel Doran from Colorado. In the Ladies, in which there were 13 entries, Debi Thomas was the winner, followed by Caryn Kadavy of Erie, Pa., and Leslie Sikes, representing Philadelphia. The winners of the Pairs were Gillian Wachsman and Todd Waggoner, from Wilmington, with Katy Keeley and Joseph Mero of California second, and Susan and Jason Dungjen of Michigan third, out of nine pairs. The Dance was won by Suzanne Semanick and Scott Gregory from Wilmington, with Renée Roca and Donald Adair from Michigan, second, and Kristin Lowery from Michigan and Chip Rossbach of Ohio third, out of 10 couples.

The first National Collegiate Championships were held at Lake Placid in August. The initiative for the event had come from Patricia Hagedorn of Lexington, Mass., who in 1983 had been designated to head a study group to determine the feasibility of U.S. participation in the World University (FISU) Games, and also whether a National Collegiate competition could be created to provide a basis for the selection of skaters for the FISU event. Up to that time, participation in the FISU Games had been on a "catch as catch can" basis, with anyone who met the FISU requirements able to go. Obviously, a more formal structure was needed, and with growing interest among college students in maintaining their skating skills at a competitive level, a collegiate competition was needed. There was no involvement or input by the NCAA into the activity, since figure skating was not a recognized collegiate sport.

The first championships were small in numbers but high in quality. There were just two Singles events, for Senior Men and Ladies, consisting of a short program and free skating, with no figures. There were four men, and the winner was Robert Rosenbluth, representing Emory University, with David Jamison, representing the Community College of Philadelphia, second and Thomas Zakrajsek of Denver University third. In the Ladies, in which there were 10 entrants, the winner was Kathaleen Kelly, from Harvard, with Deborah Tucker from Boston University second, and Holly Archinal from Bryn Mawr College, third.

It should be noted that Kathaleen went on to law school after college and would be the National Collegiate Ladies champion in figures in 1987 and 1989, and in free skating in 1987 and again in 1994. Kathy now serves as an athlete member of the Board of Directors and of its Executive Committee, and is also a National judge. Now married, she is a practicing attorney in a Boston law firm. She is certainly a role model for all young ladies who want to do more with their lives than just skate, but at the same time, also to achieve their goals on the ice as well.

The St. Gervais and Oberstdorf competitions resulted in six medals, two of them Gold, both at St. Gervais, with Doug Mattis from Philadelphia, the 1985 National Junior champion, winning the Men, and Tracy Damigella, representing Lake Placid, winning the Ladies. Both were second at Oberstdorf. In second place at St. Gervais was Kurt Browning of Canada. In the Dance at St. Gervais, April Sargent from California and John D'Amelio from Wilmington were third, and fourth at Oberstdorf. Maria Lako and Michael Blicharski from Michigan were fourth in Pairs at St. Gervais, but were second at Oberstdorf. The USA again won the Coupe des Alpes.

The September competitions were St. Ivel and Vienna, and in the former, there were two more Gold medals, with Debi Thomas taking the Ladies and Natalie and Wayne Seybold, the Pairs. Christopher Bowman was third in Men, and Suzanne Semanick and Scott Gregory were second in Dance. At Vienna, which had just Singles, Daniel Doran won the Men and Sara MacInnes from Los Angeles was second in Ladies.

The October competitions traditionally have been Skate America and then Skate Canada. Skate America was held at St. Paul, Minn., and, while successful operationally, suffered a significant loss, due to the failure of the local organizing committee to obtain the sponsorship support which they had assured the Association would be found, but which did not in fact materialize. It was an example of the problem that can occur between the Association and those organizing an event locally, when there is not a clear contract in advance which sets forth the obligations of the parties. In this case, the Association had to assume the loss, which was in excess of $250,000, and which resulted in an operating deficit for the year of $363,434, the largest in the history of the Association up to that time.

In the competition itself, Debi Thomas continued her winning ways to take the Ladies, while Jill Watson and Peter Oppegard won the Pairs, and Renée Roca and Donald Adair took the Dance. Brian Boitano was second in the Men behind Josef Sabovcik of Czechoslovakia, the European champion. Gillian Wachsman and Todd Waggoner were third in Pairs.

Skate Canada followed at London, Ontario, and the U.S. came away with two Golds: Caryn Kadavy in Ladies and Renée Roca and Donald Adair in Dance. Scott Williams placed second in Men, while Katy Keeley and Joseph Mero were fourth in Pairs. Second in Ladies was Elizabeth Manley of Canada.

The November competitions included Budapest, Prague, Tours, Zagreb and the NHK at Kobe, Japan, plus the new Junior competition at East Berlin. At Budapest, which was also only Singles, Yvonne Gomez of California and Angelo D'Agostino of New York won Ladies and Men, respectively, while Lois Luciani and Russ Witherby from Wilmington, were third in Dance, the winners being Maia Usova and Alexandr Zhulin of the USSR.

At Prague, Bobby Beauchamp from Massachusetts and Tonya Harding from Oregon were both fourth in the Singles, while Lori Blasko and Todd Sand from California, won the Pairs. At Tours, Christopher Bowman was the winner of the Men, while Debbie Walls from Atlanta was third in Ladies. Kristin Kriwanek and Doug Williams from California were second in Pairs, with Karen Knieriem from Colorado and Leif Erickson from California second in Dance. At Zagreb, there were two medals: John Filbig from California second in Men, and April Sargent and John D'Amelio third in Dance.

The NHK Trophy competition at Kobe was yet another win for Brian Boitano in the Men, defeating his perennial rival Brian Orser of Canada, actually in the free skating this time. Gillian Wachsman and Todd Waggoner won the Pairs, with Lako and Blicharski fourth. Ladies was less of a success story, with Kathryn Adams fifth and Leslie Sikes sixth. In Dance, always a tough event at NHK, Susan Wynne and Joseph Druar were fourth, with Marina Klimova and Sergei Ponomarenko of the USSR the winners.

In the Pokal der Blauen Schwerter ("Blue Swords") Junior competition, there were "adventures" getting into and out of East Germany, plus the attendant hardships of participating in a competition in the Eastern Bloc. The results themselves were somewhat mixed, with the best place being second for Rudy Galindo from California in the Men, behind Vladimir Petrenko of the USSR. In the Ladies, Sharon Barker from Los Angeles was fifth, while in the Pairs, Shanda and Brandon Smith from Detroit were fourth.

The return to Moscow for the Prize of the Moscow News was in one respect very successful, when Caryn Kadavy won the Ladies, defeating Anna Kondrashova and Natalia Lebedeva of the USSR, two of the top three Soviet Ladies. Perhaps it was "poetic" justice for the loss of Wendy Burge several years earlier! Christopher Bowman was fourth in the Men, which was won by Alexandr Fadeev, the reigning World champion. In Pairs and Dance, the U.S. entrants were "buried" which reflected the enormous depth then of the Soviet system in those two disciplines. For example, the World Junior champions in Pairs, Ekaterina Gordeeva and Sergei Grinkov, could do no better themselves than fourth, with the winners being Larisa Selezneva and Oleg Makarov, the 1985 World and European Silver medalists. The lone U.S. pair of Karen Courtland and Robert Daw placed ninth, with seven Soviet pairs and one East German pair ahead of them.

The same scenario was seen in the Dance, which was won by the reigning World champions Natalia Bestemianova and Andrei Bukin. Susan Wynne and Joseph Druar were also ninth, with seven USSR couples and one Austrian couple ahead of them. Discretion (and careful selection of events) was still the better part of valor in entering skaters in Moscow.

The late season events turned out to be the Morzine Dance competition and Merano Junior Ladies. The Wilkie Dance competition in England died for lack of sponsorship. At Morzine, Renée Roca and Donald Adair finished a solid second behind Usova and Zhulin. Coincidentally, in the same event in fifth place was Svetlana Liapina and Georgi (Gorsha) Sur of the USSR. (Little did he and Renée know then of their partnership in the future!)

When the "dust" had settled on the International competitions for the entire season, there had been 15 events, with a total of 69 possible places, out of which the U.S. representatives won a total of 35 medals, or 51 percent. There were 17 Gold medals, 12 Silver and six Bronze. Broken down by events, the results were:

	Men	Ladies	Pairs	Dance	Totals
Total Places	21	17	16	15	69
First	5	6	4	2	17
Second	5	2	2	3	12
Third	1	1	2	2	6
Total Medals	11	9	8	7	35

The results and medal count are representative of the general success of the U.S. skaters in the International competitions, which had two positive results for them. They gained experience in competing abroad under sometimes difficult conditions, and they also solidified their reputations and prospects with foreign judges, which would serve them well in the major championships.

The fall meeting of the Board of Directors was held as usual at Colorado Springs at the Olympic Training Center. Among the actions taken was one which permitted the acceptance by skaters of commercial sponsorship through contracts between the USFSA and the sponsor, with the money earned being placed in escrow, to go either into skater trust funds or into the restricted funds of the Memorial Fund.

The subsidies for the qualifying competitions, including the underwriting of any losses, were continued, with the National Collegiate Championships being added.

In competitions, the use of factors for the compulsory figures was dropped, and the Intermediate and Adult Dance events were made mandatory for Regional and Sectional competitions, with the former being a qualifying event and the latter not. The age limit for Adult Dance was also lowered from 35 to 30. The adoption of Adult Free Dance and International Dance Tests were also approved, while a Pre-Intermediate Dance event was added to the Regionals on an optional basis.

In the ongoing effort to increase opportunities for adult skaters to compete, a first would be seen in the 1986 Central Pacific Regional when an Adult Ladies Singles event was offered. It drew four entries with the pioneering winner being Donna Fountain from Cupertino, Calif. Another change affecting the qualifying competitions was one that required all previous winners of Regional Junior, Novice and Intermediate events to enter the Regionals again in order to qualify for the Sectionals. The same did not apply to winners of the Sectional Junior and Novice events of the prior year. The action was a modest reduction of a form of "bye." A uniform age qualification date of Oct. 1 for all qualifying competitions was also adopted.

There was also a general revision of the schedule of Pair tests, to upgrade the elements required to be performed, so that the tests would more closely approximate the same levels at competition.

With respect to exhibitions and carnivals for the benefit of a non-skating related organization, the percentages to be paid when World or U.S. Team members participated were again raised, to be based upon a scale measured by the number of such skaters involved. Much as had been the case in earlier years with such matters as skating in unsanctioned exhibitions, this seemingly minor issue, which really involved just one event, continued to take up a great deal of time and effort far in excess of its value.

In order to make room for the Precision Skating Committee as a Permanent (voting) Committee without increasing the total number of such committees, of which there were 11, it was voted to merge the Amateur Status Committee into the Sanctions Committee. The former had been in existence since 1921. The name of the latter committee would eventually be changed in 1991 to "Sanctions and Eligibility." As an example of the size to which the Association had grown, it was voted to continue the Liability Insurance coverage for the member clubs for another year at an annual premium of $275,000.

The 1986 World Junior Championships returned to Sarajevo for the second time in December, and here too, the strength of the Eastern Bloc countries, especially the USSR, was readily apparent, as the Soviets took all four titles and eight of the 12 possible medals. The best the U.S. could do was a second place in the Men by Rudy Galindo of California, the winner being Vladimir Petrenko, who finally captured the title he had "thrown away" the year before. Todd Eldredge, representing Philadelphia, was fifth. In the Ladies, the best the U.S. skaters could do was eighth by Holly Cook from Utah, and 11th by Jana Sjodin of St. Paul. The winner was Natalie Gorbenko. In the Pairs, the team of Kristi Yamaguchi and Rudy Galindo were fifth, with Ginger and Archie Tse, representing Wilmington, sixth. The winners were Elena Leonova and Gennadi Krasnitski. In the Dance, Jennifer and Jeffrey Benz from Detroit were tenth. The winners were Elena Krikanova and Evgeni Platov for the third straight year.

The growth of the Regionals had kept pace with the growth of the Association, as can be seen from the following number of entries in the 1986 competitions:

New Englands	95	Eastern Great Lakes	312	Central Pacific	134
North Atlantics	141	Southwesterns	230	Northwest Pacific	155
South Atlantics	177	Upper Great Lakes	356	Southwest Pacific	198
Easterns	149	Midwesterns	144	Pacific Coasts	135

The figures require some explanation. The relatively low entry for the New Englands, for example, reflects the fact that there was a separate competition later in the year for all the non-qualifying events. The large numbers for the Midwestern Regions can be explained by the fact that these Regions offered many non-qualifying events, which is where the bulk of the entries were. The same is true for the Pacific Coast Regions. However, the total numbers are impressive, a total of 1,798 entries. Two of the Regions on the Pacific Coast also offered events for Precision teams. As can be seen, the three Sectionals were almost equal in size, since they contained the same number of qualifying events.

The 1986 Nationals were held at Uniondale on Long Island, N.Y., and drew a total of 138 entries. All of the defending champions had returned with the exception of Judy Blumberg and Michael Seibert, who had retired. In two of the remaining three instances, two of the defenders did not succeed, so at the mid-point of the cycle leading to the 1988 Games, the cast of potential favorites was changing. In the Men, Brian Boitano defended his title with relative ease. Unfortunately, Chris Bowman, who had been fourth the prior year, had to withdraw following the short program due to injury, after a strong second place in figures and a third in the short. In the runner-up position overall was Scott Williams of California, followed by Daniel Doran of Colorado in third.

Debi Thomas

The Ladies was one of the events where the defender was upset. Debi Thomas of California, who had fully demonstrated her capability to win in the International competitions, took the title with a first in both figures and free, while second was Caryn Kadavy, representing the Broadmoor, winner of the short program. Tiffany Chin of San Diego, who had been off the ice for some months prior to the competition but had still elected to defend, had to settle for third with a third in both the short program and the free skating following a second in figures.

The other upset was in the Pairs, with Gillian Wachsman and Todd Waggoner, representing Wilmington, taking both parts of the event, to defeat Jill Watson and Peter Oppegard of Los Angeles, and Natalie and Wayne Seybold, representing Wilmington, in third. It was a close competition.

The Dance was the one open event, and here Renée Roca of Rochester and Donald Adair of Michigan took the title, defeating Suzanne Semanick and Scott Gregory, representing Wilmington. Roca and Adair won both the compulsory dances and the free dance, while Semanick-Gregory won the original set-pattern dance. In third were Lois Luciani and Russ Witherby, arriving for the first time on the podium, a place that Russ would hold on various steps with several different partners over the next several years.

In the Junior Men's event, we find Mark Mitchell of Connecticut winning, while Todd Eldredge was fifth. In Junior Ladies, the winner was Cindy Bortz of Los Angeles, while in fourth was Kristi Yamaguchi of Berkeley. Kristi and Rudy Galindo, who was also third in Junior Men, won the Junior Pairs. In Novice Men, Scott Davis of Montana was second.

The 1986 World Championships were held at Geneva, Switzerland, returning there for the first time since 1968. From the standpoint of the USFSA, the championships were notable for the three medals won, two Gold, with Brian Boitano in the Men and Debi Thomas in the Ladies, and a Bronze by Tiffany Chin in the Ladies. It was the first time since 1983 in Helsinki, when Scott Hamilton and Rosalyn Sumners had been the Singles champions, that two Americans took both titles. Both competitions were in a sense upsets, especially in the Ladies.

Debi had been fifth the previous year in her first Worlds, while Katarina Witt of East Germany was a two-time champion. As usual, Kira Ivanova of the USSR won the figures, but Debi took second, which put her ahead of Katarina, who was third, with Tiffany Chin close behind in fourth. In the short program, Witt repeated the failure of her jump combination as she had also done earlier in the Europeans and wound up fourth, with Thomas first and Chin tied for second with Anna Kondrashova of the USSR, so the free skating would be decisive. Katarina made her usual fighting comeback to win the free skating, but when Debi took second, she took the title with it, administering to Witt the major defeat of her career. Tiffany Chin, with a fourth in free skating, took third, with Ivanova fourth. Caryn Kadavy, in her first Worlds, placed eighth. It was a "huge" achievement for Thomas, making her the eighth U.S. skater to be the World Ladies champion.

In the Men, with both Alexandr Fadeev of the USSR, the defender, and Brian Orser of Canada returning, Brian Boitano, the third place finisher in 1985, was one of, but

Brian Boitano

369

not "the" favorite. The amazing thing is that after the short program, he seemed out of contention, since he had placed fourth in figures and fifth in the short program, with a missed element costing him. On the other hand, Fadeev won the figures and was second in the short, while Orser had his usual low place in figures (fifth), but won the short program. Going into the free skating, Boitano was actually fourth, with Fadeev in the lead, Josef Sabovcik of Czechoslovakia in second (he had been second in figures and fourth in the short), with Orser in third. In the free, Fadeev failed dismally, placing fifth in that part and third overall. Sabovcik, who had been suffering with a knee injury, also could not do it, and fell also, placing ninth in the free skating. It was all up to Boitano and Orser, and once again Orser the "king" of the triple Axel was frustrated, missing it on two tries. He could take only three of the nine judges and was second in the free. Boitano on the other hand was flawless throughout his performance, and accomplished successfully the only triple Axel of the competition, to win the free and become the seventh U.S. man to win the World championship. It was another "huge" triumph for him! The other two U.S. men, Scott Williams and Daniel Doran were in ninth and eighth places, respectively, although Doran did place sixth in free skating.

The U.S. Pairs and Dance couples were less successful against the strong Soviet competition. Jill Watson and Peter Oppegard redeemed themselves by placing sixth, with a fifth in the free skating after a ninth in the short program to defeat the National champions, Gillian Wachsman and Todd Waggoner, who had been fifth in the short, but dropped to seventh in the long. The latter placed seventh, while Natalie and Wayne Seybold were eighth. The title went to the young Soviet pair Ekaterina Gordeeva and Sergei Grinkov, the 1985 World Junior champions, who upset the defenders, Elena Valova and Oleg Vasiliev of the USSR, who were also the European champions. The Canadian pair Cynthia Coull and Mark Rowsom were third.

In the Dance, the battle was between the defenders, Natalia Bestemianova and Andrei Bukin and Marina Klimova and Sergei Ponomarenko, both of the USSR who finished first and second respectively, with Tracy Wilson and Rob McCall of Canada, third. Many felt that Klimova-Ponomarenko deserved better and should have won. Suzanne Semanick and Scott Gregory finished fifth, turning the tables on the National champions, Renée Roca and Donald Adair, who placed sixth.

In the final analysis the West had done much better this time, and especially North America, with six medals between the United States and Canada. The Soviets took five, with two Gold, and the remaining medal going to East Germany.

Back on the home front, the Precision season was well under way. The Pacific Coast, despite being the only Section to have Precision team competition in two of its Regionals, still was struggling to increase its numbers. The Sectional was held in Washington State and drew 12 teams in four events, a drop from the prior year. On the other hand, the Midwesterns at St. Clair Shores, Mich., had 49 teams in five events, an increase over 1985, while the Eastern Sectional at Warwick, R.I., drew 28 teams in five events, a modest increase.

The 1986 Precision Nationals were held at Boston, at the rink of Boston University and were the largest up to that time. Silver or consolation rounds were introduced for the first time. As a result, there were actually five finals (Senior, Junior, Novice, Juvenile and Adult) and five Silver or consolation finals, for a total of 10 events. In the final round, there were six teams in each event for a total of 30, while in the Silver events there were 26 teams, for a grand total of 56 teams, a big competition, in more ways than one! The "balance" shifted a little from the Midwest to the East, with Eastern teams winning four of the five titles. Buffalo SC continued its pre-eminence, winning both the Senior and Novice events. It was their first Senior title. The Acton-Ups of the Colonial FSC of Massachusetts won their third straight Adult title, with the Hamden FSA of Connecticut taking the Junior class. The lone Midwestern win was in Juvenile, by the team from the Garfield Heights FSC of Ohio. One problem cited during the championships, other than the noise in the arena, was that of sequins on the ice, which would lead to a ban on them, along with "feathers, rhinestones and jeweled trim," being imposed in the next year.

Clearly Precision was alive and well, growing and here to stay. Action had already been initiated by the Board of Directors at the fall 1985 meeting, to fund, with a grant of $12,000 three judges' schools, one in each Section to be held prior to the 1986 Sectionals. Separate categories of Precision judges were approved at the 1985 Governing Council meeting, consisting of Sectional and National Precision Judges. Separate categories of Precision Referees would be added in 1987. In due course, Precision Team skating would be recognized by the ISU and included in its regulations in 1992, with a separate Technical Committee for the discipline being created in 1994. The first chairman was Patricia French of Williamsville, N.Y. Planning is ongoing, leading hopefully to a World Championship for Precision by 1998.

Hugh C. Graham, Jr.

The 1986 Governing Council meeting was held at San Francisco, returning to that city for the first time since 1968, and was marked by the changeover of the administration. George Yonekura retired as President after three years in office and was succeeded by Hugh C. Graham, Jr., MD, of Tulsa, Okla. George was elected an Honorary member of the USFSA and an Honorary member of the Board of Directors in 1989. He has remained active as a referee and judge and was co-chairman of the 1992 World Championships at Oakland, Calif. Hugh Graham was the first

President since Joseph Savage of New York to have been a National champion (in Novice Men in 1949) and a World Team member (in 1954 and 1955).

The meeting approved a memorial resolution for Robert T. McLeod of Norwalk, Calif., who had passed away earlier in the year. Bob had served as a Vice President and was the first Honorary member of the Board of Directors in 1981. He had also served as chairman of the Competitions, Dance and Pacific Coast Committees, and had been an active referee and judge.

As a result of the deficit incurred for the year 1985-1986, the budget for International skating was substantially cut, with eleven International competitions announced as being supported: St. Gervais, Oberstdorf, St. Ivel, Skate America, Skate Canada, Budapest, Zagreb, NHK, Moscow, Morzine and Merano.

The election of F. Ritter Shumway of Rochester, N.Y., as a member of the World Figure Skating Hall of Fame was announced, an appropriate honor in his 80th year. His accomplishments and contributions to the sport have been recorded throughout this work and need not be detailed again here, but probably his finest hour was his service as acting President in 1961 at the time of the airplane accident in Belgium with the loss of the 1961 World team, out of which came the Memorial Fund, his life's work in the sport. By 1986, the Fund held assets in excess of $2,500,000, and was distributing on the order of $250,000 in grants and loans annually through its two major programs, the Competitive Skaters Education Program (CSEP), and Academic Scholarship Program (ASP).

The meeting also approved the By Law changes required to reflect the addition of Precision Skating as a Permanent Committee and the merger of the Amateur Status Committee into the Sanctions Committee, as recommended by the Board of Directors.

Announced prior to the meeting was yet another event, this time the "Goodwill Games," to be held in July 1986 at Moscow. Initially figure skating had been planned as a competitive event in the Games, but instead a series of exhibitions were held, for which the USFSA received a grant in the amount of $200,000, of which $150,000 went to the Memorial Fund. Figure skating was the only winter sport included, for obvious reasons of television coverage. The Goodwill Games were to be a summer competition in 18 sports, held every four years in the middle of the Olympic quadrennium. These Games had been negotiated by Ted Turner of Atlanta, of the Turner Broadcasting System and CNN, with the State Sports Committee of the Soviet Union. The skaters selected to go were the National champions and runners-up and World medalists in all four disciplines.

As in all such things involving the Soviet Union in those days, there were political overtones. The Games were seen as a form of protest against the boycotts that had occurred during the various Olympic Games from 1976 to 1984, including especially Moscow in 1980 and Los Angeles in 1984. The Games would be held again in the Seattle-Tacoma area in 1990 and in

St. Petersburg, Russia, in 1994, with figure skating included in both as International competitions.

The 1986 ISU Congress was held at Velden on Lake Wörth in Austria, and was the second Congress at which no general elections were held. Noted at the Congress was the passing of Georg Häsler of Switzerland, the Honorary Secretary of the ISU from 1946 to 1975, and a strong friend of the United States and of the USFSA. In 1985, the Council created the Georg Häsler medal in his memory, to be awarded either to skaters or administrators nominated by the member associations, in recognition of their contributions to the sports. So far, the only Häsler medals awarded to representatives of the USFSA have been to Ritter Shumway, who received it in 1987, and to Thayer Tutt, who received it (posthumously) in 1989. There has been one other U.S. medal awarded, to George Howie of USISA, in speed skating.

It was at the 1986 Congress that the distinction between "amateur" and "professional" was eliminated, with the terms themselves being changed to "eligible person" and "ineligible person," the changes having been requested by the International Olympic Committee.

The age limit for Juniors was increased to 18 for Men, with the minimum age of 10 and the maximum age of 16 for Ladies, and 18 for Pairs and Dance couples remaining unchanged. A further change was made in the events at Championships. The semi-final, with 17 plus three going to the final, for a total of 20, was dropped. Instead, 24 (changed to 20 in 1988 and back to 24 in 1990) would qualify directly for the final at the end of the short program, with the eliminated skaters being ranked on the basis of the combined result at that point (figures plus short).

The category of Judge for ISU Tests was revived, although the holders of appointments in that class of judge up to 1980 were not reappointed. The classes of Honorary Judge and Referee were clarified to require 15 years of service as an ISU Championship Judge or Referee, to have retired and to have served the ISU "well." Honorary officials would no longer be able to judge ISU Tests, so it was a completely retired category. The partial reimbursement by the ISU for the costs of judges nominated by the member associations for Championships, whether or not drawn, was approved. The definition of a well balanced program in pair free skating was further refined, while in ice dancing a specific schedule of deductions covering interruptions or falls in the compulsory dances and original set-pattern dance was adopted, as well as a comprehensive revision of the definitions for free dancing, one of which was to delete the limitation on the number of changes of music permitted.

The season of 1986-1987 kicked off in July of 1986 with the renamed U.S. Olympic Festival at Houston, Texas. The figure skating events were held in The Summit, with very large audiences of over 11,000 for the final events. The compulsory figures were held at the practice rink, the Sharpstown Ice Center. The competitors and officials were housed in the dormitories at Rice University. Despite the usual early dates insofar as competitive figure skaters are concerned, the quality of the competition was quite high. In the Men there were 14 entries, with the winner being Christopher Bowman of California, followed by Paul Wylie of Denver, Colo., and Angelo D'Agostino of Illinois. Bowman was third in the short program, but won the other two parts to win his first festival title.

In the Ladies, the winner was Jill Trenary, representing Colorado, followed by Cindy Bortz of California, the 1986 National Junior Ladies champion; third was Tonya Harding of Oregon, who placed second in free skating, after a seventh in figures and a sixth in the short. Bortz won the figures, while Jill won both the short and the long programs. In Pairs, the winners were Natalie and Wayne Seybold of Indiana, followed by Katy Keeley and Joseph Mero of California, second, and Kristi Yamaguchi and Rudy Galindo, the 1986 National Junior Pair champions, third. Rudy had to withdraw from the Men's event, but was able to compete in the Pairs.

In the Dance, Renée Roca and Donald Adair of Michigan began what amounted to the ultimate defense of their National title by defeating Susan Wynne of New York and Joseph Druar of Michigan, with Karen Knieriem of Colorado and Leif Erickson of Ohio third. The other National champions did not compete.

Present at the competition for an exhibition were Marina Klimova and Sergei Ponomarenko of the USSR, who came to the festival with 40 other Soviet athletes as part of a sports exchange program established between the U.S. Olympic Committee and the Soviet State Sports Committee.

The next event in late August at Lake Placid was the second National Collegiate Championships, which this time included compulsory figures as a separate event and a free skating (short program and free skating) championship for Seniors only. There were five Men and seven Ladies in the figures, won by Paul Wylie of Harvard and Eileen Groth of Central Connecticut State University. Kathaleen Kelly, also of Harvard, was second in the Ladies figures, followed by Stefanie Schmid of the University of California at Los Angeles, a Swiss citizen and later Swiss champion. In the Men, William Lawe of El Camino Community College, the National Junior champion in 1984, was second, followed by Tom Zakrajsek of the University of Denver.

In the free skating events, there were seven Men and 10 Ladies, with the winners being Wylie in the Men, followed by Zakrajsek and Lawe; and in the Ladies, Jan Bobassei of the University of Connecticut, followed by Kelly and Karen Knieriem of the University of California.

While the entry was not large, the championships appeared to be firmly established. The addition of the figures and the diversity of the entries from all across the country appeared to support its value as a viable National championship. Other events would be added in the future, including Juniors and Dance.

The Grand Prix of St. Gervais kicked off the International season at the end of August, and there was a minor "flap" when the Soviet skaters did not show up due to "visa problems." They did, however, appear at Oberstdorf. Such occurrences were often related to politics between the countries involved, having nothing to do with sport. In their absence, the U.S. Team had one of its best showings in several years, winning three events, and taking a second in the fourth. Winners in Singles were Erik Larson of San Diego, the 1985 World Junior champion, and Holly Cook of Bountiful, Utah, while Karen Knieriem and Leif Erickson won the Dance, with Ashley Stevenson and Scott Wendland of California second in the Pairs.

At Oberstdorf, the U.S. team again did well, with Larson placing second in the Men, and Holly Cook repeating her win at St Gervais in the Ladies. Stevenson and Wendland were again second in Pairs, while Knieriem and Erickson were fourth in a stronger Dance field. The combined results were good enough to enable the U.S. to win the two team trophies, the Coupe des Alpes and the Geiger Trophy for Oberstdorf.

The St. Ivel Ice International competition came next at Richmond, England, with the U.S. team winning three medals, including one Gold by Daniel Doran in the Men. Jill Trenary was second in the ladies to Elizabeth Manley of Canada, while Gillian Wachsman and Todd Waggoner were third in Pairs, behind two Canadian pairs, Christine Hough and Doug Ladret and Michelle Menzies and Kevin Wheeler. In the Dance, Susan Wynne and Joseph Druar were fourth, just behind Isabelle and Paul Duchesnay, now representing France. The winners were Kathrin and Christoff Beck of Austria.

Moving into October, back on home turf, there were Skate America and Skate Canada. Skate America journeyed to an unexpected site, Portland, Maine, where it was very well organized by the Kennebec Skating Club, headed by Priscilla Millier of Winthrop as chairman. The competition was well attended, with a total of 45 entries from 17 countries. The U.S. team enjoyed one of its best efforts, with six medals, including three Gold, two Silver and one Bronze. In the Men, Brian Boitano won for the second time, with Daniel Doran, third and Viktor Petrenko of the USSR in between, in second. In the Ladies, Tiffany Chin and Tonya Harding were one-two, with Tracy Damigella of Boston fourth. In Pairs, Katy Keeley and Joseph Mero were the winners, while Kristi Yamaguchi and Rudy Galindo were fifth and Lori Blasko and Todd Sand, sixth. Suzanne Semanick and Scott Gregory were second in Dance with the winners being the Duchesnays, representing France. Jodie Balogh and Jerod Swallow were fourth.

Skate Canada journeyed to the Far West, to Regina, Saskatchewan, and while smaller than Skate America, with 32 entries from 12 countries, was still of a high standard. The four titles were divided between Canada and the USSR, with the best U.S. places being a second in the Men by Christopher Bowman, and a second in the Dance by Suzanne Semanick and Scott Gregory. The

Men's winner was Vitali Egorov of the USSR, while the Dance winners were Natalia Annenko and Genrikh Sretenski of the USSR. The Seybolds were third in Pairs, which were won by Cynthia Coull and Mark Rowsom of Canada, defeating Ekaterina Gordeeva and Sergei Grinkov of the USSR, the reigning World champions. The Ladies winner was Elizabeth Manley of Canada, followed by Claudia Leistner of FRG. Tracey Damigella placed fourth and Kelly Szmurlo of Milwaukee, fifth. In the Ladies, there was an unfortunate accident when Natalia Lebedeva of the USSR, who was second after the short program, actually broke a leg in the free skating and had to withdraw.

The Budapest competition, which had a name change due to a change in sponsor and was now called the "Novarat" Trophy and drew quite a substantial entry in three events (there were no Pairs). Brian Orser of Canada was the Men's winner, with Doug Mattis of Philadelphia second, and Mark Mitchell of Connecticut, the 1986 National Junior champion, third. In Ladies, Cindy Bortz of Los Angeles, the 1986 National Junior Ladies champion, was the winner, with Tonia Kwiatkowski of Ohio third. In second place was Charlene Wong of Canada. The Dance was won by Tracy Wilson and Rob McCall of Canada, with Susan Wynne and Joseph Druar fourth, just behind Evgeni Platov of the USSR, with yet another partner, Larisa Fedorinova (she did not last!). The Hungarian couple of Klara Engi and Attila Toth were second. The Canadians had gone for Budapest in a big way, and it paid off with two Gold medals and one Silver, while the U.S. had one Gold, one Silver and two Bronze. It was not, however, a competition that would survive.

The other three competitions in the fall season were the Golden Spin of Zagreb, the NHK Trophy, held at Tokyo, and the Prize of the Moscow News. At the first the U.S. team had outstanding success, with Caryn Kadavy winning the Ladies, Jimmy Cygan placing third in the Men, and Susan Wynne and Joseph Druar winning the Dance. Caryn defeated Anna Kondrashova of the USSR, who had been the World Silver medalist in 1984. Viktor Petrenko was the Men's winner.

At NHK, Angelo D'Agostino was the surprise winner, with Scott Williams sixth. The Ladies winner was Katarina Witt with Midori Ito second, while Holly Cook was fourth and Yvonne Gomez, at that time still skating for the U.S., fifth. In the Pairs, Elena Valova and Oleg Vasiliev, the former World champions, were the winners, with Jill Watson and Peter Oppegard second and the Seybolds third. In the Dance, Semanick and Gregory, a very busy couple, were second to Bestemianova and Bukin, the reigning World champions.

The Moscow competition closed out the fall season in early December, and was as usual "loaded" with Soviet skaters. In the Men, Paul Wylie was fourth, after a seventh in figures, but a second in free skating. Kira Ivanova was the Ladies winner for a change, with a second place in free skating to Jill Trenary, who had been fourth in both the figures and the short program and pulled up to second. The Pairs event was comprised of the "second rank" Soviet pairs, but still Katy Keeley and Joseph Mero could do no better than fourth. The winners, Elena Kvitchenko and

Rashid Kadyrkaev, were another remade pairing, with each of them having been in the World Junior earlier with other partners. In second were Elena Bechke and Valeri Kornienko, the European Bronze medalists, another combination that would be broken up and "reorganized" in the every changing scenario of Soviet pair skating!

Two very special events took place in the fall of 1986 which were not in the normal course of events. The first was "Celebration...America on Ice," an evening to remember at the Market Square Arena in Indianapolis on Sept. 29. The benefit show was in observance of the 25th Anniversary of the Memorial Fund and the 65th Anniversary of the Association. "Celebration" was a huge family reunion, with many of the former National champions in attendance, some of them taking to the ice. The format of the show, which was choreographed by Jo Jo Starbuck and Ken Shelley, themselves former National Pair champions, was unique.

There were 32 major guest performers and two group numbers. Giant screens at each end of the arena presented still photos and film/video clips of every National titleholder from the archives of the World Figure Skating Museum. The master of ceremonies, John Powers of Evanston, Ill., well known as the announcer for "An Evening With Champions" at Harvard, was assisted by host commentators including Tenley Albright, Dick Button, Peggy Fleming, Scott Hamilton, Carol Heiss Jenkins, Hayes Alan Jenkins, David Jenkins and John Misha Petkevich. A "Currier and Ives" scene featured Donald Adair as his ancestor, Jackson Haines. Among the former champions who made appearances on the ice were 1934 Ladies champion Suzanne Davis King of Richmond and 1938-1940 Ladies champion Joan Tozzer Cave, in a duet. Others included Ken Shelley, the 1972 champion; Tim Wood, 1968-1970 champion; Charles Tickner, 1977-1980 champion; Sonya Klopfer, 1951 Ladies champion; Judy and Jim Sladky, 1968-1972 Dance champions; Scott Hamilton, 1981-1984 champion; Tiffany Chin, 1985 Ladies champion; Cindy and Ron Kauffman, 1966-1969 Pair champions; Colleen O'Connor and Jim Millns, 1974-1976 Dance champions; JoJo Starbuck and Ken Shelley, 1970-1972 Pair champions; Tai Babilonia and Randy Gardner, 1976-1980 Pair champions; Elaine Zayak, 1981 Ladies champion; Judy Blumberg and Michael Seibert, 1981-1985 Dance champions; Kitty and Peter Carruthers, 1981-1984 Pair champions; plus the current champions, and especially Ritter Shumway with his partner Harlene Lee. It was an absolutely incredible occasion, played to a full house of over 10,000 for the benefit of the Memorial Fund.

The other event was the reopening and rededication in October, at the time of the Fall meeting of the Board of Directors, of the expanded World Figure Skating Museum. Through a most generous second grant from the El Pomar Foundation, the owners of The Broadmoor Hotel, it had been possible to complete the lower level of the Museum, thereby adding another 5,000 square feet of display space, essentially doubling it in size. Among the revisions to the upper level was the creation of a separate skate gallery to house the substantial collection of skates in the Museum, to which had been added the Arthur R. Goodfellow Collection, donated by the Ice Skating Institute of America. The lower level now held the reference library and the displays of the Regional and Sectional permanent trophies and an exhibition of Sonja Henie memorabilia, donated by her former secretary Dorothy Stevens. The World Figure Skating Hall of Fame occupies the central gallery on the upper level as the centerpiece of the facility. An article in Skating magazine stated: "The newly remodeled and expanded World Figure Skating Hall of Fame and Museum, now and for years to come, assures the preservation of the heritage of our sport and the honoring of its major contributors throughout the world. It is a unique museum with priceless artifacts, a repository for precious memorabilia and memories, held in trust for future generations who will continue in the advancement and perpetuation of the sport."

The fall meeting for 1986 of the Board of Directors took place at Colorado Springs and was a busy one. Among the actions taken was one to establish an education and training section similar to the JETS within the Competitions Committee, for referees and accountants. An ad hoc committee headed by Patricia Hagedorn of Massachusetts was approved to study the development of a skating institute, which would be the means by which active competitive skaters could teach skating as a means of assisting with the their training expenses, without losing their eligibility. The Skating Institute was accordingly established in 1987, with three Governors appointed by the President.

Among the new Special Committees established in 1986 were a State Games Committee and a Special Olympics Committee, both of which have continued up to today. State Games, which are multisport events sponsored by a state, sometimes with both summer and winter versions, as in Massachusetts, had increasingly begun to include figure skating, and a committee was needed to promote the sport in the State Games programs, as well as to supervise the conducting of the competitions. Similarly, the Special Olympics program had also begun to include figure skating, and the committee was to serve as a coordinator to work with the program to develop and conduct figure skating events suitable for the Special Olympians.

The first major championship of the season was the 1987 World Junior Championships, which were held at Kitchener-Waterloo, Ontario, in December. Unfortunately, the championships were not supported by the public, with sparse audiences, but there was a large number of entries and the championships were very well organized by the CFSA. Among the skaters in the championships were representatives of China, Australia, New Zealand and (South) Korea.

One member of the U.S. team, Tonya Harding of Portland, had to withdraw due to an injury, and the alternate, Holly Cook of Utah was called upon to replace her, as was possible under the "McMullin" rule. Holly just happened to be on her way back from Japan where she had competed in the NHK Trophy, a Senior event, arriving just nine hours before the Ladies competition was to start. She had briefly practiced the Junior figures at home and had her music revised for the shorter time for the Junior free skating program. In the figures of the Ladies event, she came second to Susanne Becher of the FRG, and with a fifth in the short and a fourth in the long placed fourth overall, a very creditable showing and one carried out in the true sense of sportsmanship. The winner of the ladies was Cindy Bortz of California, the National Junior Ladies champion of 1986, who, after a third in figures, won both the short and the free skating to become the sixth U.S. lady to be the World Junior champion.

On the Men's side, the U.S. took first, second and fourth, with Rudy Galindo of California the winner, followed by Todd Eldredge of Philadelphia in second, and Cameron Birky of California, the 1986 National Novice champion, fourth. With Rudy and Cindy both winners, it was the third time overall and the first time since 1981 that the U.S. had held both World Junior singles titles at the same time. Rudy also demonstrated his versatility by placing third in the Pairs with Kristi Yamaguchi, while Ginger and Archie Tse were sixth. Two Soviet Pairs were first and second, and an East German Pair was fourth, "as usual" in those days. In the Dance, again there were two Soviet couples on top, and the U.S. was not a factor in the pursuit of medals. The first U.S. couple, Elizabeth Punsalan of Ohio and David Shirk of Michigan, was ninth. (Of course, Elizabeth would be heard from in the future.) The other U.S. couple was Jennifer Goolsbee and Peter Chupa from Detroit, who were 12th. (Jennifer would eventually skate for Germany in Dance for quite a few years with Hendryk Schamberger, and they would be the German champions.)

The U.S. came away with four medals, two Gold, a Silver and a Bronze, but still lacked strength at the Junior level in Pairs and Dance, with Kristi and Rudy the obvious exception as would be seen in the future. The highest place won by a U.S. dance couple in the World Junior remains the second of the Yatsuhashis in 1984. That title, just as is the case with the Senior World title in Dance, has continued to elude U.S. dance couples up to today.

The 1987 National Championships were held at Tacoma, Wash., in early February, returning to the Northwest Pacific Region for the first time since 1978. There was a large entry, a total of 146 in 10 events. Despite the qualifying requirements, the Senior events especially seemed to be getting larger and larger, with the inevitable byes becoming more and more of a problem. For example, in the four (Men, Ladies, Pairs, Dance) Senior events there were a total of 68 entries, while in the same four Junior events there were 54, and in the two Novice singles, a total of 24. A new sponsor for the Nationals was the NutraSweet Company, the makers of artificial sweeteners. NutraSweet, a long-time sponsor of the Professional Championships organized by Dick Button at Landover, Md., had decided to expand its involvement on the "eligible" side of the sport and had signed a three-year contract, beginning with the 1987 Nationals.

As part of its participation as sponsor, NutraSweet presented special awards called "Giving It 100%," in recognition of the quality of being "one's own best competitor." The winners were Natalie and Wayne Seybold of Marion, Ind.; Holly Cook of Bountiful, Utah; Ron Kravette of California, and Scott Kurttila of Seattle.

As the year of the Olympics neared, all the defending champions were back to try to hold on to position. As it turned out, only one was successful and three failed, although they still retained their World Team berths. Brian Boitano demonstrated his supremacy by winning all three parts of the Men's event to take his third title. Christopher Bowman made a strong comeback, despite a fifth in figures to place second, with Scott Williams third, Daniel Doran fourth and Paul Wylie fifth.

The big upset was in the Ladies, where Debi Thomas, the reigning World Ladies champion, was the defender. Although she won both the figures and the short program and seemed to be sure of her second title, it was not to be. Jill Trenary, representing the Broadmoor, was close behind in second place after the first two parts and won the free skating to take her first National Ladies title. Jill had been fifth the prior year, so it was a "quantum" jump up the ladder. Debi placed second, while Caryn Kadavy, who had a disastrous short program in which she placed ninth, held on to third and a place on the World team by a narrow margin over former champion Tiffany Chin, 8.4 total factored places to 8.6. In fourth place was Tonya Harding, with Cindy Bortz, the National Junior Ladies champion in fifth.

The Pairs event saw another rebound, with former champions Jill Watson and Peter Oppegard reclaiming the title and defeating the defenders, Gillian Wachsman and Todd Waggoner, despite being second going into the free skating. In third place were Katy Keeley and Joseph Mero of San Diego, with the Seybolds fourth and Kristi Yamaguchi and Rudy Galindo fifth in their first Senior competition.

Jill Watson and Peter Oppegard

The Wilmington "crowd" had moved on to Newark, Del., the site of the University of Delaware, where there was a new two-rink complex, and were now representing a new club there, the University of Delaware SC. Of the Pairs and Dance medalists, both Wachsman-Waggoner and Suzanne Semanick and Scott Gregory were representing the new club.

In Dance, Semanick and Gregory, after trailing in the compulsory dances, won both the original set-pattern dance and the free dance, to defeat Renée Roca and Donald Adair and take their first title. Susan Wynne and Joseph Druar were third followed by the new partnership of April Sargent and Russ Witherby, another couple training out of Newark.

In the Junior and Novice classes, the "next generation" of stars was already emerging. Todd Eldredge, now representing the Broadmoor, was the new National Junior champion, while in the Junior ladies, behind winner Jeri Campbell of California, there were Kristi Yamaguchi of Berkeley, second, Tonia Kwiatkowski of Ohio, third and Nancy Kerrigan of Boston, fourth, with Kristi moving up from fourth the prior year, Tonia from fifth and Nancy from 11th.

Between the Nationals and the Worlds, the Winter World University (FISU) Games for 1987 were held at Poprad in Czechoslovakia, and with U.S. Olympic Committee support a representative team of three Men, two Ladies, one Pair and two Dance couples was sent. In the Men, Paul Wylie, despite being ill, took a Bronze medal, the winner being Petr Barna of Czechoslovakia, with Jimmy Cygan from the Broadmoor and Scott Kurttila from Seattle, fifth and sixth, respectively. Yvonne Gomez from Berkeley placed third in Ladies, with Kathaleen Kelly of Lake Placid fifth and Michele McMahon from Detroit seventh. In Pairs, Calla Urbanski from Delaware and Michael Blicharski from Michigan won another Bronze medal, while in the Dance, Karen Knieriem from Colorado and Leif Erickson from California were fifth and Colette Huber and Ron Kravette from Los Angeles, seventh. Soviet skaters won the Ladies (Larisa Zamotina) and Pairs (Elena Kvitchenko and Rashid Kadyrkaev), while an Austrian couple, Kathrin and Christoff Beck won the Dance. In the figure skating events, there were 65 entries from 18 countries, which was a very good showing for the University Games.

The 1987 World Championships returned to the United States for the first time since 1981 and were held at the Riverfront Coliseum in Cincinnati, Ohio. They were very well run by an organizing committee from the local clubs, headed by Sharry Addison and Nancy Meiss. One innovation was the installation of a temporary rink for practice in the Sabin Convention Center near the official hotel, which worked very well except for one mishap when the Zamboni machine inadvertently cut the pipeline delivering refrigerant to the rink. This required a shut down for a part of a day and the transfer of practice to an outlying rink. The whole incident was handled well and the temporary rink was up and running again very quickly. Such temporary rinks have become more the rule than the exception, at least for championships in the U.S. and another would be seen in Oakland in 1992.

The championships were notable for the fact that competitors from Hong Kong were entered, most of whom could barely do the most elementary form of skating. There were also competitors from Chinese Taipei and Korea, some of whom were little better than their Hong Kong counterparts. Still, the number of entries was impressive, with a total of 89 from 23 countries. Since there are obviously two persons in a pair and a dance couple, the total number of competitors was 124.

From the U.S. standpoint the 1987 Worlds were disappointing, and although four medals were won, there was no Gold. The two U.S. defending champions, Brian Boitano and Debi Thomas were defeated. In the Men, Brian Orser of Canada finally fulfilled his potential and won what would be his only World title. After a third place in figures, he won both the short and the long to defeat his now perennial rival, Boitano, who was second in all three parts. The 1985 champion, Alexandr Fadeev of the USSR, was third. Christopher Bowman had a bad day in figures (11th), and another in the short (ninth), but with a fourth in free skating pulled up to seventh. Scott Williams, with a 13th in free skating, wound up 10th.

In the Ladies, there was a big negative and a big plus. Although she was only fifth in the figures, Katarina Witt won both the short and long programs to regain the title, while Debi Thomas, who had been second in figures, had a disastrous short program (seventh), which took her out of the running, despite a second in the free skating. The big plus was the Bronze medal won by Caryn Kadavy, who skated her best long program ever to reach the podium for the first time. Jill Trenary, the new National Ladies champion, had trouble in the figures, and was 11th in that part, which she followed by a fourth in the short program and a fifth in the free skating, to finish seventh overall, a complete reversal of the National results.

In the Pairs, Ekaterina Gordeeva and Sergei Grinkov of the USSR redeemed themselves (after a disastrous Europeans at Sarajevo, where they withdrew after placing third in the short program). They retained their World title. The 1984 Olympic Pair champions, Elena Valova and Oleg Vasiliev, were second, but Jill Watson and Peter Oppegard placed third, defeating the new European Pair champions, Larisa Selezneva and Oleg Makarov. Gillian Wachsman and Todd Waggoner, after a fifth in the short program, placed seventh.

In the Dance, the battle continued between the Soviet couples with Natalia Bestemianova and Andrei Bukin again retaining their title, despite the challenge of their teammates, Marina Klimova and Sergei Ponomarenko, who did manage to win the original set-pattern dance. Tracy Wilson and Rob McCall of Canada held on to their third place position, with Natalia Annenko and Genrikh Sretenski, another Soviet couple, fourth, followed by Suzanne Semanick and Scott Gregory, fifth. Susan Wynne and Joseph Druar had replaced Renée Roca and Donald Adair, who had retired after the Nationals, placed 11th in their first Worlds.

With the Worlds over, the second International competition season, was underway, with La Coupe Excellence again being held at Montreal, Quebec, for the second time. The U.S. team of six skaters came home with four medals, two Gold and two Silver. Daniel Doran won the Men and Tonya Harding the Ladies, while the Seybolds were second in the Pairs and April Sargent and Russ

Witherby second in Dance. Second to Harding was Patricia Neske of West Germany, another German-American. This year the invited countries had been expanded to include Great Britain and West Germany, in addition to Canada and the U.S. and yet curiously no French skaters were on hand.

The Merano Spring Trophy was held at the end of March, and was won by Kristi Yamaguchi, who could be said to be beginning to make her statement in Singles, after several years of activity primarily in Pairs.

The Precision qualifying competitions were again held in late March, leading up to the 1987 National Championships at Tulsa, Okla. The championships were continuing to grow, with 64 teams in six final events and six Silver or Consolation events. This year also, the Pacific Coast broke through to take a National championship, with the Fabulous Forties of the Los Angeles FSC winning the Adult division. The Fraserettes of the Fraser FSC regained the Senior title they had last won in 1985. The Hot Fudge Sundaes of the Buffalo SC won their fourth straight Novice title, while another Fraser FSC team, the Miniettes, won the Juvenile Division. In Junior, the Superettes of the Warwick (R.I.) Figure Skaters were the winners. In Intermediate, the first title for the Hayden Recreation Centre FSC of Lexington, Mass., was won by their Ice Mates. The six final round titles were divided between the Sections: two Midwestern, three Eastern and one Pacific Coast. In the Silver round events, the Midwest took five firsts and the Pacific Coast one.

The 1987 Governing Council meeting was held at Milwaukee, Wis., and was very well attended. Among the actions taken, a memorial resolution was adopted for Delaplaine McDaniel of Narberth, Pa., who had died during the year. Delly had been a USFSA Vice President, Honorary member of the Executive Committee elected in 1967, an active referee and judge, and chairman of Dance, Eastern, Finance and Judges Committees, as well as a long-time member of the Executive Committee.

With the improvement in the financial picture (the retained earnings had returned to the black and the operating revenues had reached in excess of $2,079,000), greater support for participation in International competitions was forthcoming. In that regard, the revenue from television over the years had successively increased. For 1973-1974 it was $70,000; for 1975-1977, $202,500; for 1978-1980, $376,000; for 1981-1984, $1,530,000; and for 1985-1987, $2,400,000. Obviously, without such revenue, plus that from sponsorships the Association could not carry out its external programs and especially competition abroad. In any event, the number of International competitions to be supported during 1987-1988 was increased to 11 at the beginning of the season.

Another activity which required sponsorship and Olympic funding were the Elite Sports Science and Sports Medicine Developmental Camps, of which the first for Juniors had been held in 1986 and the second at Colorado Springs in May 1987, with 17 skaters participating in the latter year. The on-going studies conducted included follow-up testing on some skaters from the prior year's camp, as well as initial testing of new skaters. In addition to the medical and physiological aspects of the testing, special attention was also given to examination of the skating boot and blade and injury prevention. In that regard, it can be said that the quality of boots manufactured has continued to decline over the years, with more injuries resulting, not all of them being attributable to the greater difficulty of free skating, but directly to improperly fitting boots. Research in the area of boots and blades continues to be vital to the future success of American skaters.

The new season kicked off in July with the 1987 U.S. Olympic Festival at Greensboro, N.C. Instead of a conventional competition, the organizers, the North Carolina Amateur Sports Corporation, proposed that there be a team competition, a format which had been used in other sports involved in the Festival in the past. The competitors were divided into four teams - North, South, East and West, with the competitors assigned to the teams on the basis of their standings at the 1987 Nationals, in order for the teams to be as equally balanced as possible. Each team consisted of three Men, three Ladies, two Pairs and two Dance couples. Together with the team concept, a different system of scoring was used. The total points of each competitor on each team were added together and averaged in each event. These were then added together to obtain final, overall scores for each team.

In Singles, there were no figures, while in Dance, two compulsory dances plus the original set-pattern dance were skated. For the free skating and free dance, either competition programs, programs in development or experimental numbers within the time limits of the long program were allowed. With the Festival coming as it does at the very beginning of the new season, it is sometimes difficult for skaters to participate when preparing for the International season and when new programs are still in development. The team concept removed some of the pressures usually associated with early season individual competitions and offered the opportunity for some new programs to be premiered. There was no let up in the quality of performance nor in the intensity of the competition, which the team format enhanced among the skaters themselves. The event was enjoyed by the skaters and was accepted by the audiences, which were the largest in Festival history. Over 42,000 spectators filled the Greensboro Coliseum to witness what was the first major figure skating competition ever held in North Carolina. The team concept obviously did not "sell" on television, since there were no individual winners, and the format would not be used again. Curiously, in recent years, efforts to promote "team" competitions among the professional ranks have also been attempted with only mixed success. In the end, it was the North team that came out on top, consisting of Paul Wylie, Steven Rice of Lake Placid, Tom Zakrajsek of Denver, Jill Trenary, Rory Flack of San Diego, Kristi Yamaguchi, Katy Keeley and Joseph Mero, Lori Blasko and Todd Sand, Karen Knieriem and Leif Erickson, and Jill Heiser and Michael Verlich of California. It was a close competition, as the total points for the winning team were 638.18, to 636.69 for the East Team (which was second), with the North having to come from behind to overtake a fairly substantial East lead after the initial round.

The 1987 National Collegiate Championships had moved on from Lake Placid to Colorado Springs in August, with events for Senior Pairs and Junior Dance being added to the separate figure and free skating events for Seniors. There were 28 entries in six events. In the Senior figures, the winners were Steven Rice of Pierce College and Kathaleen Kelly of Harvard, with both also winning the free skating competitions as well. For Kathy, it was her second and third Collegiate titles, and she was far from finished. In the new Pair event, the winners were Lori Blasko and Todd Sand of California State University at Northridge, while the winners of the new Junior Dance event were Holly Robbins and Jonathan Stine of the Pikes Peak Community College.

The International competition season started, as usual with St. Gervais and Obertsdorf, and good success, especially in the Men's events. Todd Eldredge and Patrick Brault of Los Angles, who just happened to be first and second in the 1987 National Junior, were also first and second in both of the Coupe des Alpes events. In the Ladies, Rory Flack of San Diego was second at St. Gervais and fifth at Oberstdorf. In Pairs, Michelle Laughlin and Mark Naylor of Delaware were third at St. Gervais and fourth at Oberstdorf, while in Dance, Dorothi Rodek of Dallas and Robert Nardozza of Detroit were second at St. Gervais and third at Oberstdorf. Jennifer and Jeffrey Benz from Detroit, the National Junior Dance champions, were fifth at St. Gervais and seventh at Oberstdorf. The U.S. team also won the Couple des Alpes.

The U.S. success continued at the St. Ivel Ice International in England, where Paul Wylie and Caryn Kadavy won the Singles events. Gillian Wachsman and Todd Waggoner placed third in the Pairs, and April Sargent and Russ Witherby, fifth in the Dance. The runner-up in the Men was Kurt Browning of Canada. The dance winners were Maia Usova and Alexandr Zhulin of the USSR, while in the Pairs the winners were Denise Benning and Lyndon Johnston of Canada.

The "ASKO" Cup of Vienna had lost its sponsorship and had been replaced with a new competition sponsored directly by the Austrian federation, called the "Karl Schäfer Gedächtnislaufen," a competition in memory of the legendary Austrian skater. Schäfer was twice Olympic champion (1932, 1936) and seven times World champion (1930-1936), and later was a teacher in the United States as well as in his native Vienna. In the inaugural competition, Rudy Galindo won the Men, while Holly Cook was second in the Ladies, won by Natalie Gorbenko of the USSR, the World Junior Ladies champion in 1986.

There was no Skate America in 1987, as had originally been agreed between the USFSA and the CFSA at the time of the 1980 Olympic Winter Games. Skate Canada was the major competition in North America and was the pre-Olympic event held at Calgary using the facilities for the Games. As a result many of the top officials of the ISU were present, and the competition drew many of the potential challengers for the Olympic medals. In the Ladies, Debi Thomas was the winner, defeating Elizabeth Manley of Canada, and stamping herself as a principal contender for Olympic Gold. In the Men, the top three on the podium would be the same three as would be there in the Games, but in a different order. Brian Orser of Canada won the event, with Brian Boitano second, Viktor Petrenko of the USSR third, and Kurt Browning of Canada fourth. With both Brians doing their planned Olympic programs, they both had misses in the short program and Orser just barely edged Boitano in the free skating. A reporter of the event said, "When scores are that close, school is far from out between these two friendly rivals in the months ahead." How true that would be!

The Pairs event at Skate Canada did not draw the top contenders, but was still of high quality, won by Christine Hough and Doug Ladret of Canada, with Elena Kvitchenko and Rashid Kadyrkaev of the USSR second, followed by Katy Keeley and Joseph Mero. The Dance winners were Tracy Wilson and Rob McCall of Canada, on course for their moment of destiny in the Olympics, with Susan Wynne and Joseph Druar placing a somewhat disappointing sixth. Skate Canada that year was an excellent test of the Olympic sites and was conducted by the CFSA (led by Joyce Hisey of Toronto, who would be in charge during the Games), in its usually efficient manner. Over the years, it can be said that Skate Canada has probably been the best run of all the International competitions, and has usually had the strongest fields as a result.

Another event in November 1987 demonstrated the value of active sponsorship, which goes beyond merely the advertising value to the sponsor, but which demonstrates the support a conscientious sponsor can give to the sport in a sound working relationship. "NutraSweet National Ice Skating Awareness Week" was held from Nov. 5-12 as a joint venture of the USFSA, the ISIA and the PSGA, together with NutraSweet. Dorothy Hamill consented to serve as national spokesperson, with the week beginning at the Wollman Rink in New York City. Rinks nationwide were encouraged to lend their support in promoting ice skating and its benefits at the local level. Over 100 rinks held "NutraSweet Skate Days" with free ice time, skate rentals and skating lessons offered to the public. The three skating organizations, the USFSA, ISIA and PSGA provided support in the form of club volunteers, rink time and free coaching. Members of the World Team promoted the week on a regional level in several major cities across the country. Public service announcements featuring Dorothy Hamill were broadcast on many radio and television stations throughout November, and a commemorative poster of Dorothy was also issued. All in all, it was a very successful promotion and did in fact increase interest and participation in the sport.

The November competitions occurred almost weekly, and U.S. skaters spread around the world did reasonably well in them. At Prague, Renée Roca with new partner James Yorke of

Boston won the Dance event, while Julie Wasserman of New York was third in the Ladies. In Pairs, Ginger and Archie Tse of Delaware were fifth, in a competition in which Natalia Mishkutenok and Arthur Dmitriev of the USSR were second, Isabelle Brasseur and Lloyd Eisler of Canada, third, and Evgenia Shishkova and Vadim Naumov of the USSR, fourth, all future World or European champions. The winners were Mandy Wötzel and Axel Rauschenbach of East Germany. In the Men, James Cygan of Colorado was fifth, behind winner Petr Barna of Czechoslovakia.

The USFSA was still supporting the Golden Spin of Zagreb, and it proved worthwhile in 1987, as Scott Kurttila of Seattle and Jeri Campbell of California, the 1987 National Junior Ladies champion, were the winners of the Men and Ladies, while Jodie Balogh and Jerod Swallow of Michigan, the 1986 National Junior Dance champions, were second behind Stefania Caligari and Pasquale Camerlengo of Italy.

The new French competition was the "Grand Prix International de Paris" the former Tours competition having been discontinued. Here the four U.S. entries won two Gold and two Silver medals: Jill Trenary, first in the ladies; Natalie and Wayne Seybold, first in the Pairs; Angelo D'Agostino of New York, second in the Men to Petr Barna; and Susan Wynne and Joseph Druar, second in the Dance to Lia Trovati and Roberto Pelizzola of Italy. As can be seen, the Italian dancers were beginning to re-emerge on the international scene as a force to be reckoned with.

At the Prize of the Moscow News, a U.S. entry again managed to win the Ladies, with Cindy Bortz of California, the 1987 World Junior Ladies champion, coming out on top over Gorbenko, the 1986 champion. In the Men, Daniel Doran was second to Alexandr Fadeev, the former World champion, while in the Pairs, Calla Urbanski and Michael Blicharski of Delaware were 11th, with eight Soviet Pairs, one East German Pair (seventh) and one Canadian Pair (eighth) in the top 10. It just did not "pay" to go in Pairs (or Dance, for that matter) at Moscow, regardless of what the real qualities of the foreign entrants were. In the Dance, in fact, Karen Knieriem and Leif Erickson were sixth, with five Soviet couples ahead of them, the winners being Marina Klimova and Sergei Ponomareko, with Maia Usova and Alexandr Zhulin, second.

The German competition for 1987 was the "Fuji Film" Trophy at Frankfurt. The U.S. team won two Gold medals and one Silver. Unfortunately, Suzanne Semanick and Scott Gregory had to withdraw, but Christopher Bowman won the Men and Jill Watson and Peter Oppegard won the Pairs, while Jill Trenary placed second in the Ladies to Midori Ito. There were no figures included in the Singles events.

At the Novarat Trophy in Budapest, Brian Boitano won the Men and Tracey Damigella, from Colorado, won the Ladies, while April Sargent and Russ Witherby were a somewhat disappointing sixth in Dance, which was won by the Hungarian couple Klara Engi and Attila Toth.

The NHK Trophy competition was held at Kushiro on the Northern island of Hokkaido, with the U.S. team collecting six medals, including one Gold by Christopher Bowman with Paul Wylie a close second. In the Ladies, Tonya Harding was third behind Katarina Witt of East Germany and Midori Ito of Japan with Nancy Kerrigan in fifth. In Pairs, Gillian Wachsman and Todd Waggoner were second, with Katy Keeley and Joseph Mero third. The winners were a Soviet pair, Elena Leonova and Gennadi Krasnitski. In Dance, Susan Wynne and Joseph Druar placed third, the winners being Natalia Bestemianova and Andrei Bukin, with Svetlana Liapina and Georgi Sur second.

The fall meeting of the Board of Directors was held as usual at Colorado Springs at the Olympic Training Center. A memorial resolution was adopted for Roy Winder, who had passed away earlier in the year. Roy was Executive Secretary and the first Executive Director of the USFSA, and had been elected an Honorary member of the Board of Directors in 1983. He also served as chairman of the Amateur Status and Sanctions Committees, and, together with his wife Jean, had been an active National Accountant. He had been named an Honorary Accountant in 1985.

Among the rule changes adopted with respect to competitions, Adult Dance events at qualifying competitions were divided into two classes: Senior, for couples of which one or both partners had passed the Silver Dance Test or higher; and Junior for couples of which neither partner had passed a Silver Dance.

In the membership area, a resolution was adopted which directed the Membership Committee to allow a second member club to establish its principal skating headquarters in a rink which was already the headquarters of another member club, as long as ice time was available for both clubs.

In the area of tests, a decision was made to require professionals who wished to take USFSA Tests to be current members of the USFSA at the time of testing. At the same time, the separate professional test fee ($5.00) was dropped.

In sports medicine, mandatory education on the subject of drug testing was approved, starting with the Nationals of 1989 and thereafter, with the costs of any actual drug testing to be borne by the USOC.

The cancellation of the existing loan program and the conversion of the current loan program funds into grants were approved for the Memorial Fund. Experience with the loan program had shown that very few of the recipients of loans had met their obligations for repayment after they had finished competing and were gainfully employed, a somewhat disappointing result.

With respect to the administration of the meetings of the Board and Governing Council, it was voted to abolish the requirement that matters and proposals must first be declared "urgent" before they could be presented to the Spring meeting of the Board of Directors.

Immediately following the Board meeting, a Judges' Seminar in Singles and Pairs, which was recognized by the ISU, was held at the Broadmoor World Arena, with Sonia Bianchetti of Italy, the chairman of the ISU Figure Skating Committee, as the moderator. ISU rules required that the holders of ISU appointments as judges and referees must attend within a specified period of time (then three years) a sponsored or recognized seminar, in order to retain such appointments. As a consequence, almost all of the World and International judges and referees in figure skating of the USFSA, a total of 30 in all, were present. Assisting Mrs. Bianchetti in conducting the seminar were Benjamin T. Wright, a member of the ISU Figure Skating Committee, and Charles A. DeMore, a member of the ISU Council. There were also 12 demonstrators from among the skaters training at the Broadmoor, who made a material contribution to the success of the seminar.

The World Junior Championships were held at Brisbane, Australia, in December, 1987, the first time an ISU Championship had been held in Australia. Brisbane is a wonderful place to visit in December, since it is summer there then, although Christmas decorations were very much in evidence. There were many and varied recreational opportunities available for those not actually competing, especially along the "Gold Coast," south of the city. The U.S. team did very well in Brisbane, in all the events except the Dance, and actually won three of the four events, including a very rare "double-double" by Kristi Yamaguchi and Rudy Galindo in the Ladies and Pairs. In the Men, Todd Eldredge won over Viacheslav Zagorodniuk, then of the USSR, who would later be one

of his principal rivals in the Senior Worlds. Shepherd Clark of Atlanta and Cameron Birky of California were fourth and fifth, respectively.

In the Ladies, Kristi Yamaguchi was the winner, with Elizabeth Wright of Colorado, sixth. Kristi defeated two Japanese girls, Junko Yaginuma and Yukiko Kashihara. In 14th place was Surya Bonaly of France in her first World Junior. It was in the Pairs, however, that the "big" win of the championships took place, when Kristi and Rudy won, defeating three Soviet Pairs and breaking the string of Soviet and (one) East German wins in the World Junior Pairs that went back to 1979. Actually, the "box score" in the Pairs was at that time: USSR - 15; Canada - three; GDR - one; USA - one. The three Canadian wins were in the first three championships, 1976 to 1978.

Kristi Yamaguchi and Rudy Galindo

Kristi and Rudy were the "double-double." He had been the Men's champion in the prior year and no one, before or since, has won both a World Junior Singles and the Pair title in the same year. The only other time it was ever done was in the Senior Worlds in 1927, when Herma Szabo of Austria did it with her partner Ludwig Wrede. Kristi was the seventh U.S. lady to be World Junior Ladies champion, and Todd Eldredge, coincidentally, was the seventh U.S. man.

In the Dance, the best the U.S. couples could do was ninth with Rachel Mayer and Peter Breen from Boston, and 10th with Jeannine Jones and Michael Shroge of Ohio. Nonetheless, however, it was still the best overall result ever for the U.S. in the World Juniors.

The 1988 Nationals were held at Denver and constituted the principal championship, on the basis of which the Olympic and World Teams were chosen, in accordance with the selection procedure approved by the USOC, which allocated a value to it of 75 percent, with the 1987 Worlds at 10 percent, the 1987 Nationals at 5 percent, the Olympic Festival at 5 percent, and the International competitions at 5 percent. The weight of 5 percent given the Festival (especially when it was a team event in 1987), seems somewhat out of balance with the International competitions being rather under valued.

The 1988 Nationals had various operational problems, due in part to a lack of communication between the local (and inexperienced) organizing committee with the (experienced) officials responsible for the actual running of the event. One example was a traffic jam of epic proportions at the Sunday exhibitions, with people trying to get to McNichols Arena at the same time as the crowd was leaving an NFL playoff game at Mile High Stadium across the street. Happily, since the Denver Nationals, the communication and co-ordination has been much better, thanks in large measure to Valerie Powell, the Director of Competitions at the National Headquarters, who provides that essential communications "link," and who also works hard to keep the local organizing committee from "re-inventing the wheel" each year!

In the championships themselves, "form" held up quite well, with all four of the defending champions at the Senior level retaining their titles. Brian Boitano was a clear Men's winner, but Paul Wylie surprised by coming up from fifth place in the prior year to take the runner-up position over Christopher Bowman, by placing second in free skating. It was the first of several such "cliffhanger" finishes that Paul would experience over the next few years!

In the Ladies, Debi Thomas regained the title she had lost in 1987 (for her second), with Jill Trenary, the defender, second, and Caryn Kadavy third. In 10th was Kristi Yamaguchi and in 12th was Nancy Kerrigan, so the future was already in evidence. In Pairs, the first two places remained the same as 1987, with Jill Watson and Peter Oppegard winning their second title, and former champions Gillian Wachsman and Todd Waggoner once again the runners-up. In third place this time were Natalie and Wayne Seybold, who placed over Katy Keeley and Joseph Mero, the Bronze medalists in 1987. Kristi Yamaguchi and Rudy Galindo were again fifth, as they had been in the prior year.

In the Dance, Suzanne Semanick and Scott Gregory retained their title, with Susan Wynne and Joseph Druar now second, and April Sargent and Russ Witherby, third. Former champion Renée Roca, with new partner Jim Yorke, was fourth.

With the U.S. having qualified three Men, three Ladies, three Pairs and two Dance couples, almost a full team, all the Bronze medalists were on the team, except in Dance.

The XVth Olympic Winter Games were held at Calgary, Alberta, the first time the Winter Games had been held in Canada, the site of the Summer Games of 1976 at Montreal. Calgary is a "Western" city on the plains facing the Rocky Mountains in a spectacular setting. It can be very cold in winter but also quite warm when the "chinook" wind comes across the mountains from the West. Happily, the skaters were very comfortable, having the brand new Saddledome for the finals, and the older, but still very well maintained arena, the Corral, for the preliminary rounds. The speed skaters were also indoors for the first time, in the magnificent indoor 400-meter oval on the campus of the University of Calgary, where virtually all the World and Olympic records were broken during the Games.

The two Singles events were the major ones of the figure skating competitions, with the Men at the beginning and the Ladies at the end. The Men's event was called by the media the "Battle of the Brians," since it represented the culmination of that vigorous and yet friendly rivalry between Brian Orser of Canada and Brian Boitano of the U.S. Strictly speaking, Orser was the "favorite." He was the current World champion, had defeated Boitano in Skate Canada and was skating in his own country. Other factors in the equation were former World champion Alexandr Fadeev and the rising young star and former World Junior champion Viktor Petrenko, both from the USSR.

In the competition itself, Fadeev won the figures with Boitano and Orser second and third. Fadeev had a disastrous short program, in which he placed ninth, but was still third going into the final free skating, with Petrenko right behind him in fourth. Between Orser and Boitano there was a margin of only 0.2 reduced points (with Boitano leading at 2.0, since he had been second in the short and Orser in second at 2.2, since he had won the short), so whoever won the free skating would win the Gold medal.

Christopher Bowman and Paul Wylie were not in the medal hunt, and ultimately finished seventh and 10th overall, respectively. In the free skating, Boitano had to skate first in the final group, and did so flawlessly in what he himself described as his best performance ever in a major championship, with seven triples, plus two triple axels, one of them in combination. He received somewhat cautious marks from the judges, which in hindsight were relatively low. Orser, on the other hand, with it all at stake and knowing exactly what was required, did not skate cleanly, stepping out of a triple flip and reducing his second triple axel to a double. Although he received one perfect mark, in the end he lost the free skating and with it the Gold medal by a five to four margin. In retrospect, Boitano probably should have won the free skating by all nine judges. Petrenko skated last and overtook Fadeev to win the Bronze medal.

The Ladies event, which came at the end of the Games, was another "battle," this time the "Battle of the Carmens," since both Katarina Witt and Debi Thomas were skating to music from the opera "Carmen" in the free skating. The Ladies event was not as exciting as that of the Men and the standard of the skating was lower, with more mistakes being made in general. The figures were won "as usual," by Kira Ivanova of the Soviet Union, but with a tenth in the short program and a ninth in the free skating, she was quickly out of medal contention and wound up seventh overall, a long way from her Bronze medal in 1984. Thomas was second in figures with Witt in third, a higher position for her than was usually the case. Katarina won the short program with Thomas second, so that the latter was actually leading going into the free skating by that same 0.2 margin, 2.0 factored points for Thomas to 2.2 for Witt.

In the free skating, Katarina skated a somewhat cautious program, with no serious errors, although her technical merit marks were low as the difficulty of the program was a little thin. Still, she received high marks for artistic impression. Thomas, who skated last, never really got going and suffered a fall among other mistakes, to finish fourth in the free skating. The two sensations of the free skating were Elizabeth Manley of Canada and Midori Ito of Japan, both of whom skated all out, having nothing to lose, so that Manley, who had been fourth in figures and third in the short, won the free and captured the Silver medal, with Thomas winning the Bronze. Ito, who had been tenth in the figures, fourth in the short and third in the free, placed fifth overall, just behind Jill Trenary, in the fourth position who had a fifth, sixth and fifth in the three parts. Caryn Kadavy, who had been seventh in the figures and fifth in the short program, was forced to withdraw due to a severe case of the flu.

In the Pairs it was no "contest" as Ekaterina Gordeeva and Sergei Grinkov of the USSR continued the Soviet domination of the Pairs discipline, to win their first Olympic Gold medal and seventh for the USSR at the expense of the defending champions, Elena Valova and Oleg Vasiliev, also from the USSR. Jill Watson and Peter Oppegard demonstrated that U.S. Pair skating was still a force to be reckoned with, in two solid performances to take the Bronze medal, only the fourth medal for the U.S. in Pairs since 1948. In fourth place were Larisa Selezneva and Oleg Makarov of the USSR, the European Silver medalists, while in fifth with two more good performances were Gillian Wachsman and Todd Waggoner. The Seybolds finished 10th, right behind Isabelle Brasseur and Lloyd Eisler of Canada, in their first Olympics together.

The Dance resulted in the "inevitable" win of Natalia Bestemianova and Andrei Bukin of the USSR, the World champions since the retirement of Jayne Torvill and Christopher Dean of Great Britain in 1984. Their flamboyant style and unorthodox music were often questioned, but never in the marks! Second were Marina Klimova and Sergei Ponomarenko, also of the Soviet Union, moving up just as "B and B" did by one color of medal from 1984. Such is the "pecking order" of ice dancing! In third were Tracy Wilson and Rob McCall of Canada, who easily took the Bronze medal with their sparkling free dance to "The Entertainer" by Scott Joplin and earned the first Olympic medal in Dance for Canada, and a well deserved one. The two U.S. couples did their best, with Semanick and Gregory in sixth place and Susan Wynne and Joseph Druar in 11th, but the results reflected the decline that had been ongoing in U.S. Dance since the Bronze medal of Colleen O'Connor and Jim Millns in 1976.

Overall, the U.S. team produced three medals, one Gold and two Bronze, not a bad showing, and the same total as the speed skaters, who had 10 events and 30 possible medals to the four events and 12 possible medals of the figure skaters. Brian Boitano became the fifth American man to be Olympic champion since Dick Button won the first time in 1948.

In an Olympic year, there is little rest for the weary, with the World championships at Budapest, Hungary, still to come. The big question always being who will drop out? The U.S. team remained intact except for Suzanne Semanick and Scott Gregory, who elected to retire after the Games and were replaced at the Worlds by April Sargent and Russ Witherby. In the actual competition, practically all the other leading skaters were present, which had not been the case in 1984. There were, however, some upsets in the results.

In the Men, Brian Boitano, after a third in figures won the short program, and with a second in the free skating regained the World title that he had last held in 1986. Orser, on the other hand, reverted to type as it were, with a fifth in figures and a second in the short program; he placed second overall once again, despite the fact that he won the free skating in an excellent performance. The figures were once again his downfall. Fadeev had won the figures, but had to withdraw due to an injury before the short program. As a result, Viktor Petrenko was third and in a good position to contend for the World title in 1989. Chris Bowman improved on his Olympic performance to place fifth overall, with a fourth in the free skating, while Paul Wylie, who had been 13th in figures, eighth in the short and sixth in the free skating, wound up ninth, so both he and Bowman improved their positions for the future.

One of the notable events in the Men's competition was the performance of Kurt Browning of Canada in the free skating, in which he placed third, and in which he successfully completed the first quadruple jump in skating history in competition, a quadruple toe loop. Kurt's quad had a three turn after the landing. although he landed on one foot and remained upright. Thus he made history, joining a third compatriot, Donald Jackson of the triple Lutz in 1962, in the annals of "firsts" in the sport. Dick Button had done the first triple jump of all, the loop in 1952, and Vern Taylor of Canada the first triple axel in 1978.

The Ladies was also an unusual event, with the same protagonists as in Calgary contending for the medals. What was unexpected was the first place of Katarina Witt in figures, which was described by some as "impossible" but probably correct, as she was fully capable of doing good figures when she wanted to. Also surprisingly, Elizabeth Manley of Canada was second in figures, with Debi Thomas third. Debi then proceeded to win the short program, with Manley fourth and Katarina second, so Debi was still within striking distance of the Gold, but again she could not bring off the free skating, placing fourth, to finish third overall. Manley, by reason of a second place in free skating held on to second, with Katarina winning the free skating and her fourth title. Jill Trenary, who had been fourth in figures, had a bad day in the short program (11th). A fifth in free skating held her in fifth position just ahead of Midori Ito, who had her usual low place (14th) in figures, and two thirds in the other two parts to place sixth, ahead of the recovered Caryn Kadavy, in seventh. In fourth place was Claudia Leistner of West Germany.

The Pairs result was really "topsy turvy", with Elena Valova and Oleg Vasiliev upsetting Gordeeva and Grinkov to win their third title, going back to 1983. Then, Selezneva and Makarov took the third spot, with Wachsman and Waggoner in fourth, while Watson and Oppegard, with a seventh in the free skating, wound up sixth. Their performance had been adversely affected by a collision in warmup with Vasiliev, and Jill fell twice in the program. The second fall caused a 35 second lapse before they were able to pick up the program again, omitting both a lift and a death spiral. It was a disappointing finish to their careers together, as it was their last competition. Natalie and Wayne Seybold, the third U.S. Pair, placed 10th, just behind Christine Hough and Doug Ladret of Canada.

In Dance, with Semanick and Gregory gone, the weight of finishing in the top 10 (in order to insure two entries for the following year) fell upon Susan Wynne and Joseph Druar, and they did not fail, placing ninth overall, an improvement of three places over 1987. April Sargent and Russ Witherby, in their first Worlds, were 13th.

Back at home, the Precision season was on, with the National Championships being held at Reno, Nev., in the Reno/Sparks Convention Center, which had one regular ice surface with another temporary surface being installed for practice and warmup. Since an Intermediate event was added in 1987, there were now six final round classes, with matching Silver or consolation events in all classes except Novice. Only four Novice teams entered, all from the Midwestern Section as there were no Novice competitions in either the Eastern or Pacific Coast Sectionals. This can perhaps best be explained by the simple fact that the team members were growing up and the ranks had not yet been filled up from below. There still were 28 teams in the final rounds and 25 in the Silver finals. The Haydenettes from Lexington, Mass., won the Senior event, to begin a "dynasty" which has continued up to today. They defeated the defending champions, the Fraserettes of Michigan. The Hot Fudge Sundaes from Buffalo won their third Junior title, while the Fabulous Forties from Los Angeles won their second-straight Adult crown. Hayden also took another title, with the Ice Cubes winning the Juvenile event. The Novice event went to the Fraserettes of Michigan (ending the four-year reign of Buffalo), and the Intermediate event went to Buffalo.

The Spring International competition season was also going on, with a late addition to the schedule in England of the "Skate Electric" competition, sponsored by the National Energy Council. A team was sent and did very well, with Daniel Doran of Colorado winning the Men, and Jeri Campbell of California, who like Doran had been fourth in the Nationals, winning the Ladies. Kristi Yamaguchi and Rudy Galindo won the Pairs, while April Sargent and Russ Witherby were third in the Dance, which was won by Svetlana Liapina and Georgi Sur of the USSR.

The Morzine Dance competition for the Challenge Lysiane Lauret (a French Dance judge) was transferred to Grenoble and for some unknown reason carried the name "Grand Prix de Paris," typical French confusion! Renée Roca and Jim Yorke were only able to complete the single compulsory dance (in which they placed sixth), and had to withdraw due to an ankle injury suffered by Renée.

The Merano Spring Trophy for Junior Ladies was again held in that Italian mountain village on outdoor (artificial) ice, with Lisa Cornelius of Minnesota and Shenon Badre of Illinois the entries. Lisa finished second to Surya Bonaly of France, with Badre finishing sixth. Third in the competition was Yuka Sato of Japan.

The 1988 Governing Council meeting was held at Bethesda, Md., just outside Washington, D.C., 12 years after the last meeting in the National Capital area, with 300 delegates in attendance. As Kristin Matta of the Headquarters staff wrote most effectively in the report of the meeting in **Skating** magazine:

"The 1988 Governing Council meeting offered a far different scenario than that of the 1976 meeting. Today, the event spans almost an entire week and has a greatly expanded agenda which includes separate committee meetings, seminars and social events. Although membership in the Association has not increased over the years since the Washington DC meeting, the activities of the Association have more than doubled. With the awareness of figure skating expanding throughout the general public and the media, and with the growing demand for more exhibitions and shows, skating business is booming."

There was much discussion at the meeting of ways and means of increasing membership. One example which had already met with some success was the Basic Skills program, for which a separate special committee had been set up in 1987, with Cindy Geltz of New Jersey as the chairman.

Another active issue at the meeting was the announced intention of the ISU to eliminate compulsory figures in ISU Championships (World, World Junior, European and the Olympics), which would be acted upon at the 1988 ISU Congress. The determination of the USFSA to oppose the proposal was confirmed.

The first group of persons who had 50 or more years of service as judges for the USFSA was recognized. The group included Leonore Drake of New York, Margaretta Drake (no relation) of Glencoe, Ill., Ardelle Sanderson of Lake Placid, Roger F. Turner of Walpole, Mass., Lyman E. Wakefield, Jr., of Minneapolis, and the late Grace Madden Ward. This event was the beginning of annual recognition at the meeting of volunteers and officials for their long and faithful service to the Association.

As we have progressed through this narrative, little has been said about the working officials, the referees and judges, who are responsible for conducting competitions and tests. This is probably as it should be, since as a group of around a 1,000, they perform their duties in relative anonymity. Many of them, of course, have served in other capacities or have been champion skaters. Lyman Wakefield and Roger Turner, for example, were both former officers of the Association, while Roger as well, had been seven times National champion. The dedication of the "JETS" in conducting seminars for the education of the working officials is also outstanding, and in recent times, such efforts have more and more become cooperative efforts fully involving the coaches. The most recent and perhaps best example of such cooperation has been the development of the "Moves in the Field" Tests to replace figures.

A memorial resolution was adopted for John R. Shoemaker of San Francisco, who passed away at the end of April, just before the meeting. Jack had been President, Vice President and Treasurer, chairman of the International, Nominating, Pacific Coast, President's Planning and Skating Standards Committees, ISU Representative, an Honorary member of the USFSA and of the Executive Committee and a National Accountant. He also had been a Vice President of the ISU, and was an Honorary Vice President at the time of his death.

Among the By Law and rule changes adopted at the meeting was one creating an additional category of membership for rink management members. A general revision of the objects article of the By Laws was also adopted, based upon the recommendations of the Long Range Planning Committee, by way of an update and to more accurately reflect the role of the Association as the recognized National Governing Body (NGB) under the Amateur Sports Act of 1978.

There were also continuing discussions of the importance of providing more assistance to skaters through the Memorial Fund or other sources, and the need for a marketing or resource director at National Headquarters, as well as the expansion of fund raising efforts, subjects which have remained current right up to the present time.

For the next International competition season, 13 competitions in the fall were supported, with the Budapest and Vienna competitions finally being combined as the "Donaupokal" or "Danube Cup." The British competition was now "Skate Electric," replacing St. Ivel, so there would be two competitions by that name in the same year! It was also expected that the late season competitions would be supported, if they were held.

The second NutraSweet National Ice Skating Month for October 1988, was also announced with Dorothy Hamill and Christopher Bowman as the national spokespersons. The event, which had been very successful the first time, had been the idea of President Graham, working with Robert Shapiro, the CEO of NutraSweet. NutraSweet had also continued their "Giving it 100%" Awards at the 1988 Nationals, with four skaters being honored, Archie Tse, Paul Wylie, Susan Wynne and Joseph Druar.

The 1988 ISU Congress was held at Davos, Switzerland, and was a momentous one for the sport. Despite the opposition of both North American associations, the proposal was accepted to drop compulsory figures from the ISU Championships and the Olympics after the 1989-1990 season. For the two years 1988-1989 and 1989-1990, there would be two compulsory figures skated in Singles worth 20 percent, together with the "Original" (formerly "short") program worth 30 percent, and free skating worth 50 percent. Effective July 1, 1990, the Singles classes would consist of the original program worth 33.3 percent and free skating worth 66.7 percent, with the same weight being applied to the analogous parts in Pairs. As the author stated in the ISU History, "the die was cast and the sport, in Singles skating at least, was changed forever."

The former short program was also increased from seven to eight elements and renamed the "original" program. The four separate groups which had been drawn in rotation over a four year period were abolished and one group of categories of elements was created, with the elements within each category (with one exception in Senior) being left to the choice of the skater. It was actually a format similar to that followed in the first Pair short program in 1964. The program length was increased to two minutes and forty seconds. The only fixed element was the double axel for Seniors, and the principal other difference was the addition of a solo jump (triple for Men and double for Ladies) preceded by connecting steps or other free skating movements.

The Pair short (now original) program was also increased to eight elements, with a pair spin combination added. Its length was also increased. Similar changes were made in Dance, with the number of compulsory dances being reduced to two (from three), so that the value or weight assigned to each part became: compulsory dances - 20 percent; original set-pattern dance - 30 percent; and free dance - 50 percent.

Another important change was to make the second mark (composition and style in the United States, artistic impression elsewhere) the "tie breaker" in free skating and free dancing. The costume rule was also revised and expanded to define more specifically what constituted suitable costumes for competition, with a penalty for violations of 0.1 to 0.2, to be applied in the second mark.

The number of competitors in the final rounds of ISU Championships was reduced from 24 to 20. At the same time, the so-called "seeded" judges were also eliminated, with a free draw to be made for each panel from among those judges present with competitors entered in the competition.

The age limit for Juniors was again changed, to 17 for Ladies, up from 16, with a minimum age of 12 (up from 10).

Participation in the Olympic Winter Games was also redefined to limit entrants to those belonging to ISU member associations, thereby eliminating the anomaly of there being skaters in the Games from countries without an ISU member, which had actually happened in the past.

The elections in 1988 resulted in some changes in the composition of the governing bodies, with Sonia Bianchetti of Italy joining the Council as its first woman member. Charles DeMore was re-elected as the substitute member of the Council. With the election of Mrs. Bianchetti to the Council, a new chairman of the Figure Skating Committee was elected in the person of Benjamin T. Wright, who had been a member of the Committee since 1973. He thereby became the first ISU Officeholder representing the USFSA to serve as a chairman of a technical committee and actually, when he was elected in 1973, he had been the first U.S. representative to serve on the Figure Skating Committee, although no less than four persons, Bill Hickok, Ritter Shumway, Harold Hartshorne and Ken Kelley, had served as members of the Ice Dance Technical Committee. In 1994, Ronald Pfenning of Hyannis, Mass., would be elected the second U.S. member of the Figure Skating Committee, while also in that year Patricia French of Williamsville, N.Y., would be elected as the first chairman of the new Precision Team Skating Technical Committee, a rare distinction indeed to chair a new committee. Pat is also only the third woman to serve as a committee chairman, the others being Mrs. Bianchetti and Sally-Anne Stapleford of Great Britain, who succeeded Ben Wright in 1992 as chairman of the Figure Skating Committee.

So the long Road to Calgary came to an end, after many twists and turns during the four-year journey by the great skaters of the day. With change rapidly coming to the sport, a new road lay ahead to be traveled by anyone with the determination to succeed and the endurance to accept the challenge.

Following the 1988 Olympic Winter Games, the usual turnover among the top skaters took place, as happens every four years. Among those that seemed to be permanently departing were Brian Boitano, Debi Thomas, Jill Watson and Peter Oppegard, and Scott Gregory, among the current National Senior champions. Only Suzanne Semanick, of the University of Delaware SC,

The Calm Before the Storm
(1989-1992)

one half of the National Dance champions, would return with a new partner, Ron Kravette of Los Angeles.

However, the absence of the champions in a sense is a positive thing, as it energizes those coming behind them to strive harder for the top spot, and often produces excellent competition and sometimes unexpected results.

There was an important non-competitive event in the summer of 1988, the 50th Anniversary summer ice review of the Broadmoor Skating Club, which included as guest stars six members of the Olympic team, including Boitano, Watson and Oppegard, Jill Trenary, and Susan Wynne and Joseph Druar. The show has been an enduring tradition in Colorado Springs, now, of course, no longer being held in the former Broadmoor Ice Palace, as it was originally called, later the World Arena, but in a new rink not on the Broadmoor property.

There was no Olympic Festival in 1988, it being an Olympic year, so the new competitive season kicked off with the National Collegiate Championships at Colorado Springs in August. There were seven events: Senior Men's and Ladies' Figures, Senior Men's and Ladies' Free Skating, Senior Pairs, Junior Pairs, a new event, and Junior Dance.

In the figures, there were just three Men, with the win going to Troy Goldstein of California State University at Long Beach. In the Senior Ladies figures there were 10 entries, with the title going to Kelly Szmurlo of Marquette University, followed by the defender Kathaleen Kelly of Harvard, and Nancy Kerrigan of Emmanuel College, in third place. In the Senior Men's Free Skating the winner was Steven Rice of Pierce College, with Goldstein second. In the Senior Ladies Nancy Kerrigan was the winner, defeating Szmurlo.

In the Senior Pairs, Calla Urbanski and Mark Naylor of the University of Delaware won, while in the Junior Pairs the winners were Jocelyn and Brad Cox of the University of Delaware. The Junior Dance was won by Wendy Millette and James Curtis of the University of Delaware. As can readily be seen, the integration of Ron Ludington's training center into the athletic program of the University of Delaware, provided unique opportunities for the top skaters to pursue both an education and achievement in the sport. The total entries in 1988 were 40.

The Coupe des Alpes, the usual start of the Fall International season, came at the end of August, and had more significance for the participating skaters as every event they entered leading up to the 1989 Nationals at Baltimore would be of importance to their future chances. The team sent in 1988 was a mixture of Senior and Junior skaters, including the 1988 National Junior champions. At St. Gervais in the Men, Christopher Mitchell of Los Angeles, the National Junior champion, placed second to Marcus Christensen of Canada. He also was third at Oberstdorf. The other Men's entrant, Aren Nielsen of Kansas City, the National Junior runner-up, was third in France and won in Germany. In the Ladies the two entrants were Tonia Kwiatkowski of Ohio, a National Senior competitor, and Dena Galech of Seattle, the National Junior Ladies champion. Tonia accomplished the rare "double," winning at both St. Gervais and Oberstdorf. Dena was less successful, which is sometimes the case with the Junior skaters moving up to the Senior ranks for the first time, placing sixth at St. Gervais and 17th at Oberstdorf.

In Pairs, the National Junior Pair champions, Kenna Bailey of Utah and John Denton of California, were third in both competitions. The other Pair entry, Ginger and Archie Tse of Delaware, National Senior competitors, were fourth at St. Gervais and seventh at Oberstdorf, while Elizabeth Punsalan of Los Angeles and Shawn Rettstatt of Pittsfield, Massachusetts, the National Junior Dance champions, were third in France and fourth in Germany, with Elizabeth McLean and Ari Lieb of Massachusetts, second in both Dance competitions. The U.S. team won the Coupe des Alpes trophy for national teams. The medal count was: three Gold, three Silver and five Bronze, out of a possible 24, not a bad showing. It was the sixth year in a row that the U.S. team had won the trophy and the 10th time out of the last 12.

The next competition in early October was the new Skate Electric UK International competition, with one entry in each discipline. Christopher Bowman placed second in Men to Kurt Browning of Canada, the beginning of what could well be called the "Browning era." Kelly Szmurlo was fourth in Ladies, which was won by Charlene Wong of Canada. Katy Keeley and Joseph Mero, the fourth ranked National Senior Pair, were fifth in their event, which was won by Peggy Schwarz and Alexander König of the GDR. In Dance Suzanne Semanick and new partner Ron Kravette were third, with the winners being Maia Usova and Alexandr Zhulin of the USSR.

The next two weeks in October were taken up with the Donaupokal competitions in Budapest and Vienna, with the same small team of one Man, one Lady and one Dance couple being sent. Mark Mitchell of Connecticut won the Men's event at the Novarat Trophy in Budapest, and was third in the Schäfer Memorial competition at Vienna, which was won by Viacheslav

Zagorodniuk of the USSR. In the Ladies Nancy Kerrigan of Massachusetts accomplished a double by winning both competitions. Jodie Balogh and Jerod Swallow of Michigan were second in Dance at Budapest and third at Vienna, with a Soviet couple, Larisa Fedorinova and Evgeni Platov, the winners of both competitions. As can be seen, this was yet another new Soviet combination and it would not be the last for Platov (who would eventually be World and Olympic champion with Oksana Ghitschuk).

The remaining two October competitions were Skate America, returning to Portland, Maine, for the second time, and Skate Canada at Thunder Bay, Ontario. Skate America drew a fairly good field with a total of 46. There was a sweep of the medals by the U.S. Men, an unusual occurrence even for the Americans in their own competition. The winner was Christopher Bowman, followed by Daniel Doran and Todd Eldredge. In the Ladies, the winner was Claudia Leistner of West Germany, with Midori Ito second, but first in the free skating after her usual low (eighth) place in figures. The three Americans were next in order, with Kristi Yamaguchi of California third, Holly Cook of Utah fourth and Jeri Campbell of California fifth.

In Pairs, Natalie and Wayne Seybold of Fort Wayne, Ind., the third ranked U.S. Pair in 1988 but now in effect number "one" since Gillian Wachsman and Todd Waggoner, the 1988 runners-up, had also retired, were third, with the winners being the new Soviet pair of Natalia Mishkutenok and Arthur Dmitriev, who had been fourth in the 1988 Europeans.

In Dance, Susan Wynne and Joseph Druar were the winners, with Svetlana Liapina and Georgi Sur of the USSR second, followed by Renée Roca and Jim Yorke in third place. Who knew then that Sur and Roca would soon become a team, first as professionals and then as reinstated amateurs?

Skate Canada was at Thunder Bay, at the top of Lake Superior, a small city noted principally for being a shipment point for grain from the Great Plains. As is always the case with Skate Canada, the competition was a well run and friendly one with great local support. Here Browning continued to assert his claim to the top ranking by winning the Men and defeating the Olympic Bronze medalist Viktor Petrenko of the USSR, theoretically the top ranked man in the World following the retirement of Boitano and Orser. Third was Angelo D'Agostino, with Jimmy Cygan seventh.

In the Ladies, Natalia Lebedeva of the USSR returned from the disaster of two years before, when she was injured and could not finish, to win the Ladies, defeating Jill Trenary in the free skating. Jill had led throughout the earlier two parts of two figures and the original program. Tracey Damigella was fifth. The Pairs winners were Isabelle Brasseur and Lloyd Eisler of Canada, who also were beginning to make their claim to top ranking. The Seybolds placed fourth, behind Schwarz-König of the GDR and an unknown Soviet pair in third, by the names of Murugova and Torgashov.

April Sargent and Russ Witherby, now the number two U.S. Dance couple, placed a solid second to yet another Soviet couple, Natalia Annenko and Genrikh Sretenski. Balogh and Swallow were fifth.

The competitions in November always come in rapid succession, usually a week apart and sometimes on the same weekend, so resources are spread thin and far. There still has never been an effort on the part of the ISU to organize the various International competitions into an orderly sequence and spacing. Perhaps the new Champions Series circuit started in 1995 will be a step in that direction.

The leadoff event in the month was the Prize of the Moscow News where Tonya Harding of Portland had quite a success, winning the Ladies over Lebedeva, Gorbenko and Kondrashova, the top Soviet Ladies, who placed in that order. In the Men the surprise winner was Vladimir Petrenko, younger brother of Viktor, with Alexandr Fadeev, the former World champion third just ahead of Doug Mattis. Fadeev had won both figures and original, but was seventh in free. As usual in Moscow the U.S. Pair and Dance couples were well down the results, with Sharon Carz and Doug Williams of California 11th in the former, and Tracey Sniadach and Leif Erickson, a new combination, eighth in the latter.

At Zagreb, which the USFSA continued to support, Erik Larson of San Diego was fourth in the Men, Kelly Szmurlo, second in the Ladies, and Dorothi Rodek and Robert Nardozza of Texas, second in the Dance.

The Pokal der Blauen Schwerter Junior competition organized by the East German association at Berlin took place at the same time as Zagreb, and there were just two U.S. entrants. Scott Davis of Montana was second in Men to Zagorodniuk, while Tisha Walker of California was second in the Ladies to Tanja Krienke of the GDR.

The French competition, now called the "Lalique Trophy" followed by just a few days at Paris, with Paul Wylie the winner of the Men. Jeri Campbell was fourth in Ladies, which was won by Claudia Leistner of FRG. Katy Keeley and Joseph Mero redeemed themselves by taking third in Pairs, behind Elena Bechke and Denis Petrov of the USSR, while Susan Wynne and Joseph Druar won the Dance, an event in which Oksana Ghitschuk, with Alexandr Tchitchkov as the partner of the day, was third.

The final competition of November has usually been the NHK Trophy in Japan. Amazingly (after his defeat at Moscow), Alexandr Fadeev was the winner over Petr Barna of Czechoslovakia, with Kurt Browning third, a bit of a temporary setback for him. Daniel Doran was fourth and Todd Eldredge, fifth. The Eastern Bloc countries had always supported the NHK Trophy and usually have sent their better skaters there.

Midori Ito was the winner in the Ladies in her own country, while Kristi Yamaguchi was second. She was fascinating to the Japanese, being a Japanese-American, but she did not speak Japanese, which confused them no end! Kristi and Rudy Galindo also skated in Pairs at Tokyo and placed third, the winners being Larisa Selezneva and Oleg Makarov of the USSR. In the Dance the Soviet "big guns" were there, with Marina Klimova and Sergei Ponomarenko the winners, followed by Maia Usova and Alexander Zhulin. April Sargent and Russ Witherby were a good third in a strong field. To do well at the NHK competition was a very positive thing for one's career! As far away as it is, it is still highly respected as an excellent event and one of the competitions included in the Champions Series.

So the International competition season of 1988 had come to an end, and just as in former years one almost feels a sense of "exhaustion" in simply chronicling it!

For a change, the fall meeting of the Board of Directors was held at Indianapolis, at the invitation of the new Indiana/World Skating Academy there, marking the first time in 10 years that the meeting was not held at Colorado Springs. The Olympic Training Center in the Springs had and would in the future continue to serve well for the meeting. With its proximity to the Headquarters and Museum, the facilities at the OTC had continually been improved over the years, although living in the "dorms" (former barracks of the Ent Air Force Base) was a little "spartan." With its spectacular views of the Front Range and Pikes Peak, the OTC was a nice place to visit. Of course its major advantage was cost, or rather the lack of it, since at least in the earlier years there housing and meals were free.

The size and cost of the two meetings a year of the Association have long been a subject for discussion from the cost standpoint, and despite various proposals to reduce cost, they remain essentially the same. Arguments can well be made, especially with the existence of the Executive Committee created in 1980, that the Board could be reduced in size and perhaps even eliminated altogether! It is indeed a cumbersome body and difficult to control. It was suggested many years ago that there be only one meeting a year instead of two, and that concept may well have to be revisited if the OTC is no longer available or if charges are made for its use in the future. The size and cost of the spring meeting has continued to escalate as the Association has grown. It is a vital part of the life of the organization, but there also, cost reductions are possible. The Association seems to be one of the most active NGB's in the holding of meetings, and the cost of all this does not really benefit the skaters that much, despite the good intentions of the participants. With greatly improved means of communication available, such as e-mail, the number of meetings could be substantially reduced.

In any event, Indianapolis in 1988 was a pleasant change of scene with its excellent facilities not only for the practice of the sport, such as the new two rink skating/science facility of the I/WSA but also for meetings in the Capitol Center. Among the actions taken at the meeting was the selection of San Francisco/Oakland as the bid city for the 1992 World Championships. The 1989 Skate America was awarded to Indianapolis, with the I/WSA being granted at the same time Associate membership in the USFSA, and the 1990 event was awarded to Buffalo, N.Y.

In the financial area the Association continued to make major commitments of funds in support of its competitions, including Skate America, the Regionals and Sectionals. A budget of $100,000 for development and fund raising programs was approved. The President's Excellence Fund was granted the sum of $50,000. This was a discretionary resource for use in support of skaters. It was also voted to place 10 percent of the proceeds of the 1988 World Tour in the Memorial Fund.

In the technical field, among the changes approved were the addition of an Intermediate Pairs event to the Regionals and Sectionals, and a rule giving competitors the option of progressing directly to Sectionals if there were less than three entries in their event at Regionals. The old rule was that a competition must be held if there were at least two entries, so the new rule had the effect of eliminating some events from the Regionals, especially at the Senior level. It was then and still remains controversial, with those clubs organizing Regionals objecting to the potential loss of events, although the motivation for it, of saving expenses for the skaters, seemed to be praiseworthy.

In the area of tests, a Bronze Free Dance Test was added to the structure. Also, the Singles and Pairs and Tests Committees were directed to work with the Competitions Committee on any new requirements that might be instituted as a result of the change of status of compulsory figures in competitions. Also approved was the development of a program for notifying skaters' schools with letters of recognition for the passing of USFSA Tests.

The passing of Frank Zamboni, the inventor of the ice resurfacer and the father of former National Dance champion Joan Zamboni was noted. In its way the "Zamboni" (which has now become a recognized noun in the language), has done as much to revolutionize the making of ice and thereby the sport itself as any other change over the last half century. Today there are even propane and electric powered machines, which substantially reduce or remove the hazard of carbon monoxide fumes, which despite various catalytic scrubbing devices for their removal, still have caused health problems in some rinks.

In initial observance of the 65th anniversary of the publication of **Skating** magazine, the first annual "Readers' Choice Amateur Figure Skater of the Year Award" was announced. It was to be voted upon and selected by the readers of the magazine, with the first recipient of the award to be announced at the 1989 Governing Council meeting at Anaheim, Calif. The only requirement was that the skater must be a qualified eligible amateur competitor who skated in the current season and represented the United States.

At the end of November, the 1989 World Junior Championships were again held at Sarajevo, Yugoslavia, the last major competition to use the Olympic facilities, which have since been destroyed in the ongoing Balkan War between the Serbs and the Bosnians. It is a tragedy, really, as the rinks were excellent and well maintained for the events held in them after the 1984 Olympics. There was an unexpected result in the World Juniors when Jessica Mills of Northfield, Ill., won the Ladies. The sister of Phoebe Mills, an Olympic Bronze medalist in gymnastics, and also of Nathaniel and Hillary, both speed skaters, Jessica was 14 and actually had been an alternate for the team. Starting out in fourth place in the figures, she moved up with a second in the original program and won the free skating to take the title, defeating Junko Yaginuma of Japan and Surya Bonaly of France. It was a remarkable success story, from fourth in the National Junior Ladies to World Junior champion. The other U.S. entrant, Jennifer Leng of Boston, who had been the 1988 National Junior runner-up, placed sixth after winning the figures, but managed only seventh and eighth in the other two parts. Jessica thus became the eighth U.S. lady to be World Junior Ladies champion.

In the Men the U.S. also achieved a Silver medal when Shepherd Clark of Atlanta placed second to Zagorodniuk of the USSR. The other U.S. entrant, Alex Chang of Los Angeles, placed ninth. In Pairs the strength of the Eastern Bloc nations remained evident, with three Soviet Pairs, one East German Pair and one Canadian Pair in the first five. Ann-Marie and Brian Wells, representing Delaware, were sixth, with Jennifer Heurlin of the Broadmoor and John Frederiksen of Delaware, the National Junior Pair runners-up, placing seventh. The Dance results were somewhat disappointing, with the two U.S. Dance couples, Holly Robbins from Colorado and Kyle Schneble from Delaware (a new combination), and Katherine and Ben Williamson from Colorado, placing ninth and 10th, respectively. Again, there were two Soviet couples on top. The perennial problem with the U.S. entrants in Junior Pair and Dance events has always been finding those who are "age eligible" since the Junior events in the United States did not then or later have an age criteria. The men are almost invariably too old. Efforts to solve this problem have so far not reached the Junior level, which internationally is still governed by the age driven ISU Rules, not so far adopted in the United States.

The 1989 National Championships were held at Baltimore, Md., the first time in that city and actually for the first time in the Capital area since 1950. An unusual feature of the championships was the presence of the United States Army Band, which gave the premiere performance of a newly composed USFSA Championships Fanfare. Written by Sergeant Major James Kessler, USA, Ice Champions was specially commissioned for the championships. The theme was recorded by the band and used for all medal ceremonies, and is expected to be used for official awards ceremonies in the future. The presence of the band was due in no small measure to the efforts of band member Joseph Inman, a member of the SC of Northern Virginia and an International Judge.

Although there was a slightly smaller entry (183) than in former years, the length of the championships was extended by one day, including the last Sunday, on which the Senior events were broadcast live by ABC Sports. The championships now last a full week, Monday through Sunday.

The longtime controversy over whether to drop or move the Novice events out of the main Nationals continues to be an unresolved issue. In 1989 there were still only the Novice Singles classes, but in 1991 Novice Pairs and Dance, and an Open Dance event in 1996 would be added, thereby further compounding the problem. The Novice events in Singles have been in the Nationals since 1932, so they seem to be permanent, so far as least.

In 1989 there were four skaters doing double duty: Kristi Yamaguchi in Senior Ladies and Pairs with Rudy Galindo; Troy Goldstein in Senior Men and Junior Pairs with his sister, Dawn; Natasha Kuchiki in Junior Ladies and Pairs, with Richard Alexander; and John Frederiksen in Novice Men and Junior Pairs with Jennifer Heurlin.

The championships had their share of drama, controversy and upsets, along with a special kind of "epidemic" called "lace-itis." Surely, it was the Nationals with the greatest number of instances of boot lace problems, loosened, broken or untied! There was at least one or more of each in most events. (The author himself had no less than five such incidents in the events on which he served.)

With all the Senior titles undefended, it was anybody's ball game! In the Men Christopher

Jill Trenary

Bowman of California realized his potential by winning the title after a shaky fourth place start in figures, followed by first in both the original program and free skating. Daniel Doran of Colorado, with a first in figures, a second in original, and a fifth in free skating, held on to second, with Paul Wylie of Boston, sixth in figures but second in the free, placing third.

Jill Trenary recaptured the Ladies title she had last held in 1987, with solid performances in all three parts, losing the free skating only to Kristi Yamaguchi. The latter however had been eighth in figures, which with a second in the original program held her in second ahead of Tonya Harding of Portland. Nancy Kerrigan placed fifth.

With the top two pairs both having departed, the unexpected winners were Kristi Yamaguchi and Rudy Galindo, who defeated Natalie and Wayne Seybold in the free skating to take their first title. Kristi's "double," with a Silver and a Gold medal, was comparable to the success of Ken Shelley back in 1972. Returning to the Bronze medal position were Katy Keeley and Joseph Mero of California. The Seybolds suffered from the dreaded "lace-itis" midway through their free skating program, and were allowed to continue from where they left off, rather than to reskate the program. This was, strictly speaking, not in accordance with the existing rules, which permit a reskate in the cases of an equipment failure on a "no fault" basis. Obviously, their performance was adversely affected, by both the delay and the decision.

Dance ran more true to form, with Susan Wynne, representing the Broadmoor, and Joseph Druar, representing Seattle, succeeding to the vacant title, followed by April Sargent and Russ Witherby, representing Delaware. Suzanne Semanick of Delaware, the defending champion, with her new partner, Ron Kravette of Los Angeles, placed third.

In the Junior ranks, Jessica Mills could not win the National Junior Ladies title, placing second to Kyoko Ina of New York, a Japanese-American who briefly had represented Japan before returning to the United States. Jessica had problems in the original program in which she placed fifth, which cost her the chance to add the National title to her World one. It has not been unusual for a U.S. World Junior champion never to win the comparable National Junior title, again that "age" factor sometimes coming into play. Of the nine ladies (up through 1995) who have won the World Junior Ladies, only three (Jill Sawyer, Elaine Zayak and Cindy Bortz) have won the National Junior Ladies, while of the eight men who have won the World Junior, only four (Paul Wylie, Christopher Bowman, Todd Eldredge and Michael Weiss) have won the National Junior.

In March the 1989 World University (FISU) Games were held in Sofia, Bulgaria, and since a substantial degree of support was available from the U.S. Olympic Committee, a representative team was sent, with the National Collegiate Championships of 1988 as one of the principal bases for selection. James Cygan of Colorado was second in the Men's event to Makoto Kano of Japan, with Craig Heath of California sixth and Stephen Rice of New York tenth. In the Ladies Nancy Kerrigan of Massachusetts was third, followed by Kathaleen Kelly in fourth and Kelly Szmurlo in fifth place.

Sharon Carz and Doug Williams of California were second in Pairs to Natalia Mishkutenok and Arthur

Christopher Bowman

Dmitriev of the USSR, with Maria Lako of Delaware and Rocky Marval of New York fourth. In the Dance Tracy Sniadach of Delaware and Leif Erickson of California were third, and Regina Woodward of Philadelphia and Charles Sinek of Delaware, fourth. The winners of the Dance were none other than Svetlana Liapina and Georgi Sur of the USSR.

In a non-Olympic year, the World Championships are usually the principal highlight of the season, and 1989 was no exception, especially since all the titles were vacant. The championships were held at Paris, France, the first in that city since 1958. The problems of the competition related more to such matters as housing and transportation than they did to the actual event, which ran well. There was a loss of ice for practice in the main arena, which required transporting the skaters to an outlying rink for one day, a not uncommon occurrence at Worlds. The U.S. had one of its smaller teams, since it had lost entries by reason of the retirement of its named skaters, under the then ISU rules. There were only two Men, two Ladies, two Pairs and two Dance couples. Still, the team did well, bringing home two medals, a Silver in the Men by Christopher Bowman and a Bronze in the Ladies by Jill Trenary.

In the Men, both Kurt Browning of Canada with a fifth, and Bowman with a fourth, got into the hole early in the figures, won by Alexandr Fadeev of the USSR, the 1985 champion. Both of them recovered in the original program, placing first and second, with the title still up for grabs between them and Grzegorz Filipowski of Poland, the European Silver medalist behind Fadeev.

In the end Browning pulled it out by winning the free skating, to take his first title and only the second for Canada in the Men since Donald McPherson in 1963. Bowman held on to second over Filipowski, by just 5.8 reduced points to 6.2. Daniel Doran, with an 11th in the original program to go with a sixth in figures and a seventh in the free skating, wound up seventh.

The Ladies had another close competition between Claudia Leistner of West Germany, Jill Trenary and Midori Ito, who had finished in that order (in fourth, fifth and sixth) the year before. Midori also got off to a slow start by placing sixth in figures (not bad for her actually), but won both the original and the free skating programs to narrowly win the title, the first ever for Japan. There had been one Japanese medalist in the Ladies in the past, the Bronze of Emi Watanabe in 1979. Leistner made a run for it, having won the figures and being second in the free skating, but a third in the original program was just enough to deny her the title, by a factored placement of 4.0 for Ito to 4.2. Jill Trenary was also in the hunt, with second places in both the figures and the original program, but a third in free put her in that final position at 5.0 factored placements. It was one of the closest Ladies championships of recent times. Kristi Yamaguchi, in her first Senior Worlds, had trouble in figures with a 12th place, but with a fifth in the original program and a fourth in free skating, pulled up to sixth behind the German-American, Patricia Neske and Natalia Lebedeva of the USSR.

In the Pairs, Kristi and Rudy Galindo reconfirmed their National win by placing fifth in a strong field, with the Seybolds eighth. The winners were the former champions, Ekaterina Gordeeva and Sergei Grinkov of the USSR, who had stayed on for at least another year, with the Canadian pair of Cindy Landry and Lyndon Johnston breaking the Soviet barrier to take second over Elena Bechke and Denis Petrov.

Susan Wynne and Joseph Druar demonstrated that they were indeed of world class in Dance, by placing fifth behind the two Soviet couples, Klimova-Ponomarenko and Usova-Zhulin, with Isabelle and Paul Duchesnay of France third, and Klara Engi and Attila Toth of Hungary fourth. Unfortunately, April Sargent was injured in training after the compulsory dances in which she and Russ Witherby had placed 10th, and they had to withdraw.

The late season International competitions in which the USFSA had entered skaters had shrunk a little, and now consisted of the Challenge Lysiane Lauret at Grenoble, France, for Senior Dance and the Merano Spring Trophy for Junior Ladies.

At Grenoble, Suzanne Semanick and Ron Kravette, the World Team first alternates, finished second to Engi and Toth, with (guess who?), Liapina and Sur, third, and Ghitschuk-Tchitchkov, fourth! Of the first five places, three were Soviets. At Merano, Geremi Weiss of Washington, D.C. who had been fourth in National Junior Ladies, was the winner over Laetitia Hubert of France and Tanja Krienke of the GDR.

The 1989 National Precision Championships were held at Providence, R.I., with the same format as in the prior year of six final round events and five Silver events. Curiously Novice teams were still in short supply, with seven entrants, so that the decision was made that there would be no Novice Silver event for just one team, the cut off point being at six in the other events. There were now 64 teams in the championships, the largest entry so far.

The Haydenettes of Lexington, Mass., reconfirmed their supremacy by taking the Senior title over the Goldenettes of Garfield Heights, Ohio. The Shoreliners of the St. Clair Shores FSC of Michigan won the Junior division, while the Fraserettes of Michigan retained their Novice title; the Ice Mates from the Hayden Recreation Centre FSC regained their Intermediate title, while the Ice Cubes, also from Hayden, retaining their Juvenile title. The Fabulous Forties from Los Angeles won their third straight Adult crown to uphold the presence of the Pacific Coast by winning one title, with the Midwest taking two and the East three.

In February, there was an external event which would have a direct impact on the USFSA. Charles U. ("Chuck") Foster of Duxbury, Mass., was elected Secretary of the U.S. Olympic Committee. Foster was the third figure skater to hold the position, the other two having been Tenley Albright Gardiner of Boston and E. Newbold Black, IV, of New York. Chuck was serving at the time as the Eastern Vice President of the USFSA and also as its Olympic Representative. He first had to step down from the latter position and was replaced by Paul E. George of Wellesley, Mass., a former National Junior Pair champion with his sister Elizabeth. George was serving at the time as chairman of the USFSA's Long Range Planning Committee. With President Hugh Graham, Jr.'s term coming to an end in 1989, Chuck was one of the obvious candidates for that position, but under USOC rules, he had to take his name out of consideration since a person cannot serve as both an NGB officer and USOC officer at the same time. It was a loss to the continued leadership of the Association. Chuck has remained active as a referee and judge and has been a most effective representative of both figure skating and the other winter sports within the Olympic Movement. He served as the Chef de Mission for the U.S. Olympic Team at Albertville in 1992.

Also in February, the death of Lois Waring McGean of Norwich, Vt., was recorded, a five time National champion in Dance with two different partners, Walter H. ("Red") Bainbridge, Jr., and her husband, Michael McGean with whom she won the first recognized International competition in Ice Dancing in London in 1950. Her father, H. Glenn Waring, had also served as USFSA Secretary.

Prior to the 1989 annual meeting of the Governing Council, President Graham outlined in **Skating** magazine the proposed reorganization of the structure of the Association recommended by the Long Range Planning Committee. "The overall intent [of the proposals] is to provide greater efficiency and focus with more emphasis on policy by the Board [of Directors] and on rules by the suggested Administrative Council, to increase financial planning, to include [in the Association] two important constituencies (coaches and rink operators), and to encourage continuity of competent leadership." President Graham also pointed out that the Vice Presidents had each been assigned "oversight" responsibility for a group of committees, with this policy later being extended to all the (six) officers. Also noted were proposals for the use of the neutral gender term of "chair" instead of "chairman," and the addition of a new category of membership for Professional members.

Contemplated were the creation of three Councils: Administrative, Rink Management and Professional, and the reduction of the size of the Board of Directors to 35 voting members (from the present 45), with emphasis on policy making and planning, as opposed to rule making. The Administrative Council was to be made up of the chairmen of the Permanent Committees, for the coordination of rules formulation and enforcement. The Rink Management and Professional Councils would consist of representatives of their respective constituencies, the numbers being calculated in a manner similar to those of a member club. A new Vice President for Finance, in addition to the three (Sectional) Vice Presidents, was also proposed, as was the creation of the position (as an officer) of a President Elect, to achieve greater continuity in the top position. The proposals were very forward looking and represented the best thinking available from the Long

Range Planning Committee. They really reflected the "legacy" of President Graham, but unfortunately hit the "buzz saw" of the Governing Council, and were referred back to committee. It probably is time again to revisit them or something like them, as the unwieldy state of the Association "bureaucracy" is readily apparent to anyone who has to deal with it, and the leaving of policy decisions to the Executive Committee has not proven to be the best policy either!

The 1989 Governing Council meeting returned to Anaheim, Calif., for the first time since 1965. Quite a few who had been delegates at the earlier meeting in 1974 were also present in 1989, 25 years later. Memorial resolutions were adopted for Honorary member Thayer Tutt; John F. Groden, former Secretary and Treasurer and chairman of the Memorial Fund Committee; and Kenneth L. Brown, Past President, Vice President, Honorary member of the both the USFSA and the Executive Committee, and chairman of the Amateur Status, Competitions, Museum, and Nominating Committees. All had passed away earlier in the year.

The first annual **Skating** magazine "Reader's Choice Athlete of the Year Award" was presented by the magazine's editor, Dale Mitch, to Kristi Yamaguchi of California, the National Senior Ladies Silver medalist and the National Senior Pair champion with Rudy Galindo. Dale had become the editor of the magazine in 1986, succeeding Ian Anderson in that position, and would subsequently become the Director of the Museum in 1989, serving in that position until 1993.

The hottest issues at the meeting had to do with the determination of the changes in figures in the USFSA test and competition structures, with the principal question being at what point or level would the integration between figures and free skating be separated. In the end, the decision was to leave the Juvenile level as a combined event, while at the Intermediate and Novice levels for 1989-1990 the events would be combined, but separate awards would be made for figures and free skating.

For 1990-1991, figures were to be separate events at the Novice through Senior levels. The question of the separation of the figures from the free skating in competition would remain a controversial issue for the next several years, right up to 1995, when complete separation of the two "streams" would finally be achieved. Looking back on it, the heat and light and energy expended on the issue far out weighs its importance, but it was very difficult for an essentially conservative organization to face reality, just as was the case with the rejection of the proposals of the Long Range Planning Committee. It has been said that there is no more conservative governing body in sport than the ISU and within the United States, than the USFSA!

At the meeting, the recognition program was continued with respect to those judges (12), referees (12) and accountants (13) with more than 25 years of service. Also recognized were the charter member clubs (five) and clubs with 50 or more years of membership (39) and with 25 years or more of membership (65).

In the President's column in **Skating** magazine, a policy which President Graham established, and which has been continued by his successors, he sums up some of the achievements and events of his three years in office. Referred to was the effort to improve the service to the member clubs by National Headquarters, and also to increase sponsorship support, as well as to implement a member recognition program. Also cited was the policy of rotating the vice-chairmen and members of committees to give more USFSA members a chance to participate. The success of the Basic Skills Program "Skate With U.S." was also cited. Grants to eligible skaters though the Memorial Fund programs were more than doubled, while the President's Excellence Fund issued grants with primary consideration being given to help develop Pairs and Dance couples.

In his closing remarks to the Governing Council, Hugh concludes by saying: "We should cherish our heritage, love our traditions and honor our past. But we must not dissipate our energies in nostalgia. If we are to progress and succeed, we must take a bold vision of the future [and] have [a] strong and cohesive structure with vigorous leadership." So President Graham stepped down and was succeeded by Franklin S. Nelson, M.D., also from Tulsa. Hugh was elected an Honorary member of the USFSA and also an Honorary member of the Board of Directors in 1992. He has continued his active service as a referee and judge as well as the chairman of the Electors for the United States Figure Skating Hall of Fame which he inaugurated in 1991.

Franklin S. Nelson

In his acceptance of office as the 23rd President of the USFSA, Dr. Nelson spoke as well of four major topics: NutraSweet Skating Awareness Month (October), as an opportunity to bring skating to those who have never experienced it; the new structure for competitions in view of the changed role of compulsory figures internationally; open competitions, which he indicated were definitely coming, stating further that "We must consider how to position ourselves to accommodate the inclusion of eligible performing professionals while accommodating our own skaters as well;" and the restructuring of the Board of Directors. Franklin concluded by saying: "As we proceed into the last decade of the 20th Century, we must be attentive to our position as a leader among the figure skating members of the ISU and a responsible national governing body for our sport. We must work together to make things happen to promote programs for our competitors and increasingly for our grass roots members. We must give increasing guidance and support to our clubs. We must actively seek to establish new programs to promote our sport and discard ones which have outlived their usefulness."

The season of 1989-1990 would be the last for compulsory figures in International competition. In the USFSA qualifying competitions for that season, all the Senior and Junior Singles events were still three part combined events (figures-original program-free skating). For the Novice and Intermediate, the events were no longer combined and consisted of separate competitions for figures and free skating. The Pre-Intermediate and Juvenile events, which were non-qualifying events in the Regionals, were still combined.

The 1989-1990 season may well have been the busiest ever from the standpoint of the number of International competitions in which USFSA entrants participated, with no fewer than 16 being supported, to which were added the World Juniors, back at Colorado Springs and the Worlds at Halifax, Nova Scotia. The season began, however, with the 1989 Olympic Festival at Oklahoma City. The competitors were again divided into four teams (North, South, East and West), but this time individual placements in each discipline were also announced, so that there were in effect both a team competition and individual competitions. The East Team was the overall winner (with 319 points to 300 for the South Team) and included: Paul Wylie of Boston (2), Troy Goldstein of California (8), Christopher Mitchell of California (10), Tonia Kwiatkowski of Ohio (2), Kelly Szmurlo of Milwaukee (8), Geremi Weiss of Washington, D.C., (7), Calla Urbanski and Mark Naylor of Delaware (1), Wendy Weston of Massachusetts and Alexander Enzmann of California (7), Elizabeth McLean and Ari Lieb of Boston (3), and Tiffany Vetre and Duane Greenleaf of California (6). (The numbers in parentheses represent the individual places of the team members in their respective events.)

In the individual events, the winners were: Men - Mark Mitchell of Connecticut, with Wylie second and Shepherd Clark of Atlanta third; Ladies - Kristi Yamaguchi of California, with Kwiatkowski second and Nancy Kerrigan of Massachusetts third; Pairs - Urbanski and Naylor, with Sharon Carz and Doug Williams of California second, and Elaine Asenakis of Delaware and Joel McKeever of Texas third; Dance - April Sargent and Russ Witherby of Delaware, with Jeanne Miley and Michael Verlich of California second, and McLean and Lieb third. There were 41 entries in the four events.

The National Collegiates returned to Lake Placid at the end of August. As has been seen, the Collegiate championship had adopted the "split" concept in 1986, with separate events for figures and free skating. In 1989, figure events were finally added for Junior Men and Ladies, so there were actually four figure events held with a total of five Men and 15 Ladies. The winners were: Senior Men - Eddie Shipstad of the University of Southern Colorado, from that famous skating family, the grandson of Hall of Fame member, Eddie, Sr.; Senior Ladies - Kathaleen Kelly of Harvard, regaining the title she had previously held in 1987; Junior Men - Glenn Ziehnert of Adirondack Community College; and Junior Ladies - Lisa Floreck, University of Delaware.

The free skating events drew 27 entries, and the winners were: Senior Men - Shipstad; Senior Ladies - Michelle Millekan of Indiana University, with Kelly, second; Junior Men -Edmund Nesti of Northwestern University; Junior Ladies - Floreck. There was also a Senior Pair event with five entries, which was won by Calla Urbanski of Delaware Technical & Community College and Mark Naylor of the University of Delaware, with Maria Lako and Rocky Marval of the University of Delaware, second. The two dance events (which were both Junior), were also "split," with the compulsory dances being won by Beth Buhl and Neal Smull of the University of Delaware, who also won the free dance event. There were five entries in the dance. For some reason, it appeared that Senior Dance couples did not go to college and there was, as yet, no Senior Dance event competed for in the championships.

The normal International competition season kicked off as usual, with the Coupe des Alpes, with the United States team doing very well in the Singles events with a "double-double." At St. Gervais two Atlantans, Colin Van der Veen and Shepherd Clark were one-two in the Men, while at Oberstdorf Clark was the winner with Van der Veen fifth. In the Ladies Kyoko Ina of New York was the winner at both competitions, with Jessica Mills of Chicago fifth in both. Second in both was Surya Bonaly of France. The U.S. Pairs were out of the medals, with Elaine Asenakis and Joel McKeever fifth in both competitions, and Jennifer Heurlin and John Frederiksen of Colorado, the National Junior Pair champions, sixth in France and seventh in Germany. Both events were won by the Soviet pair of Elena Leonova and Gennadi Krasnitski. In the Dance, however, Lisa Grove of Pittsburgh and Scott Myers of Delaware were second in both competitions, with a Soviet couple winning at St. Gervais and a French couple winning at Oberstdorf. The second U.S. Dance couple, Wendy Millette and James Curtis, were seventh at St. Gervais and fifth a Oberstdorf. The U.S. did win the Coupe des Alpes once again and also the Geiger Memorial Trophy for the Nebelhorn competition (Oberstdorf).The two summer competitions have continued to be a very successful proving ground for the U.S. skaters moving up to the Senior ranks.

The next competition was Skate Electric UK International early in October, actually the first of two such competitions by that name, with a second one scheduled for the Spring. In the autumn, the U.S. did well, with two Gold and two Silver medals. Todd Eldredge won the Men, defeating Grzegorz Filipowski and Vladimir Petrenko, while Tonia Kwiatkowski won the Ladies. Kellie Creel and Bob Pellaton from California were second in Pairs to Isabelle Brasseur and Lloyd Eisler of Canada, and Jeanne Miley and Michael Verlich, also from California, were second in Dance to yet another unknown Soviet combination of Angelica Krylova and Vladimir Leliukh.

The Donaupokal came next, with the Novarat Trophy in Budapest first, in which Daniel Doran placed second to the ubiquitous Zagorodniuk. Fourth in the event was Elvis Stojko of Canada. In the Ladies Holly Cook of Utah was third, behind Josée Chouinard of Canada and Tanja Krienke of the

GDR. In the Dance (there was no Pair event), Elizabeth McLean and Ari Lieb of Boston placed second to another Soviet couple, Liudmila Berezova and Vladimir Fedorov. There was then and still is an apparently endless supply of Soviet (Russian since 1992) Dance couples.

In the second competition in Vienna, the Schäfer Memorial, Zagorodniuk was again the winner with Stojko now second. Doran finished fifth. Cook was again third to the same two skaters as in Budapest, while McLean and Lieb were fourth, the same Soviet couple winning again.

On this side of the Atlantic, Skate America took place at Indianapolis, and here the U.S. team did well also, with five medals including Golds in both Singles events. Chris Bowman won the Men, defeating Viktor Petrenko and Kurt Browning of Canada, with Mark Mitchell fourth and Erik Larson sixth. In the Ladies, Tonya Harding won her second major International, defeating Jill Trenary and overturning the 1989 National result. Jill placed second and Nancy Kerrigan fifth. The top foreign skater was Simone Koch of the GDR in third, followed by Junko Yaginuma of Japan.

The winners in the Pairs were Natalia Mishkutenok and Arthur Dmitriev of the USSR, the third ranked European pair, but Kristi Yamaguchi and Rudy Galindo placed second ahead of Peggy Schwarz and Alexander König of the GDR. Karen Courtland of New Jersey, with a new partner, David Goodman of Delaware, were sixth. In Dance, April Sargent and Russ Witherby were second to Maia Usova and Alexandr Zhulin of the USSR, with Miley and Verlich sixth, and the new couple of Elizabeth Punsalan of Ohio and Jerod Swallow of Michigan, seventh.

Skate Canada was held at Cornwall, Ontario and was unique in several respects. Firstly, an event for Fours was included, and also two Singles events for "artistic" skating. At the suggestion of the CFSA, artistic free skating was included in Skate Canada on an experimental basis, with the approval of the ISU, which would have an observer at the competition (the author) for the purpose of determining the possible inclusion of rules for such events in the ISU Regulations. As eventually approved by the ISU in 1992, the event became know as the "interpretive" program, and consisted of a "variety of skating moves selected for their value in enhancing the skater's interpretation of the music and artistry rather than for their technical difficulty." No triple or double jumps were permitted, although the single axel was allowed. The program was to be "an integrated exploration of the chosen music, not merely a collection of pleasing or spectacular moves assembled to entertain an audience with emphasis still being placed on skating skills," to paraphrase the rules. The interpretive event has been held at Skate Canada ever since (up through 1995), but, unfortunately, has not been accepted for inclusion in International competitions elsewhere, so far as is known. Such a program (which was of two and one-half minutes duration), could well be the common ground on which an "open" competition could be built for both eligible (amateur) and ineligible (professional) skaters.

The early problem with the event was the tendency of the skater to try to "tell a story," with acting and even some props, which was not the idea at all. In the first "artistic" events, Daniel Weiss of West Germany won the Men, with Paul Wylie second, and Yukiko Kashihara of Japan won the Ladies, with Jenni Meno of Ohio third.

The Fours discipline had long since died, but the CFSA tried to revive it and the event at the 1989 Skate Canada, and there were actually two Canadian Fours and one U.S. Four which participated. The Canadian Four of Christine Hough, Cindy Landry, Lyndon Johnston and Doug Ladret were the winners, while the U.S. Four of Elaine Asenakis, Calla Urbanski, Joel McKeever and Mark Naylor were third. Sadly the event lasted for only two years and has since "died" once more.

In the main events, Petr Barna of Czechoslovakia was the winner in the Men over Paul Wylie, while in the Ladies, Kristi Yamaguchi was the winner over Simone Lang of the GDR and Natalia Lebedeva of the USSR, the defender. In the Pairs, the winners were Elena Leonova and Gennadi Krasnitski, another Soviet pair which had considerable success in International competitions but were never quite good enough to make the World team. Such was often the case with Soviet Pairs and Dancers. The new team of Natasha Kuchiki and Todd Sand from California, placed fifth, with Urbanski and Naylor sixth. Suzanne Semanick and Ron Kravette were the winners in Dance over two Canadian couples, with the inevitable Soviet couple in fourth for a change.

Just a week later, it was back to Europe for the Prague Skate, to which the USFSA was returning after several years absence. Originally Singles only, the competition had expanded to include Pairs and Dance. The U.S. entered a Pair, Maria Lako of Delaware and Rocky Marval of New York, but no Dance couple participated. In the Pairs Lako and Marval were fourth, the winners being a new Czech combination of Radka Kovarikova and René Novotny. In the Ladies, which had 20 entries, Tisha Walker of California was the winner, defeating Simone Koch of the GDR. In the Men a French skater, Nicolas Petorin, won, with Scott Davis of Montana, fourth, just ahead of Sebastien Britten of Canada.

The U.S. also went back to Zagreb for the Golden Spin, with two skaters. Craig Heath of California, placed second to a Soviet, Sergei Dudakov. Kelly Szmurlo of Wisconsin, perhaps better known for her figures, won the Ladies over Dianne Takeuchi of Canada. Actually, the skater who won the free skating, Tatiana Malinina of the USSR, had been 21st in figures and finished sixth.

The Pokal der Blauen Schwerter, a Junior competition, was again held in East Berlin, being organized by the East German federation, and the team of a Man, a Lady and a Pair were witnesses to history, since while they were there the Berlin Wall came down. The process then began which would lead to the eventual merger of the two Germanies and the disappearance of the Soviet supported state in that country. From a skating standpoint, the two skating federations were quite quickly merged as well, and the confusing designations of the "FRG" and the "GDR" also disappeared and were replaced by 1992 with the old "GER." Under ISU Rules, all member countries have a three letter designation in English, which is therefore different from the acronyms used by the IOC, which are based on French. The competition itself was affected by the event, as most of the volunteers connected with it disappeared, but it still went on to a successful conclusion.

In the Ladies competition, Robin Petrosky of Minnesota was the winner over Tanja Krienke of the GDR, while John Baldwin, Jr. of California was seventh in the Men, won by Mirko Eichhorn of the GDR. In Pairs, Aimee Offner and Brian Helgenberg of Delaware were second to another pair from the Soviet "stable," Elena Vlasenko and Sergei Ostry.

At practically the same time, the Trophée Lalique was being held at Paris with another team of Senior skaters entered. In Men the winner was Zagorodniuk (known as "Zaggy"), with Filipowski second. Daniel Doran was fourth. In the Ladies Surya Bonaly of France won what must have been one of her first Senior Internationals, defeating Holly Cook, with Laetitia Hubert, also of France, third. Most of the International competitions in Europe had already dropped the figures, so the handicap they represented to someone like Surya, who was not very good at them, was no longer a deterrent to her success. In Pairs, Sharon Carz and Doug Williams were fourth, the winners being Mandy Wötzel and Axel Rauschenbach of the GDR, with Brasseur and Eisler of Canada second, and Kovarikova and Novotny third, a very strong event. In Dance Sargent and Witherby were second to Krylova and Leliukh.

The Nations Cup at Gelsenkirchen, Germany, was a new competition which included prize money for the national teams participating. Gelsenkirchen is a small industrial city in Northwest Germany where the German federation had found local sponsorship, so the competition was established there and has continued since at that site.

Because of the possibility of prize money, which was not then distributed directly to the skaters but rather to their associations, the competition has had strong fields over the years since its inauguration. In 1989, the Men's winner was Petr Barna of Czechoslovakia, then the European Bronze medalist, with Viktor Petrenko of the USSR second, and Paul Wylie third. In the Ladies Tonya Harding added another International Gold medal to her collection, defeating Marina Kielmann of the FRG, second, and the German-American, Patricia Neske, third. In Pairs, which was won by Elena Bechke and Denis Petrov of the USSR, Calla Urbanski and Mark Naylor finished third, while in Dance, which was won by Usova-Zhulin, Suzanne Semanick and Ron Kravette were second.

The NHK Trophy returned to Kobe, Japan, with the Soviets sending a strong team except in Ladies, which they did not enter at all. In Men the U.S. had only Erik Larson of California, who placed fourth, with Viktor Petrenko and the veteran Alexandr Fadeev being first and second. Kurt

Browning was third, a surprise, since he was the reigning World champion, but he had a very poor original program, in which he finished seventh; a second in the free skating pulled him to third, there being no figures.

Midori Ito again won the Ladies at home, with Kristi Yamaguchi and Tonia Kwiatkowski right behind in second and third. Kristi and Rudy Galindo also did pairs at NHK and placed fifth, the winners being Gordeeva and Grinkov in what was thought then to be their last season in competition.

In the fall of 1989, two anniversaries were observed at the National Headquarters at Colorado Springs. The Museum celebrated its 10th anniversary, with its curator Pat Cataldi (who had joined the Museum staff in 1979) also observing her own 10th anniversary. The Museum had grown substantially since its inauguration in Colorado, with such collections as the Arthur R. Goodfellow skates having been added.

The other anniversary was the 10th of several staff members, including Pat Cataldi, Valerie Powell, the Director of Competitions, and Mary Ann Purpura, then in charge of advertising and production for Skating magazine. While Pat left the Museum in 1990, Valerie and Mary Ann are still with the Headquarters staff, and their loyalty and hard work as well as the continuity they provide to the operation deserves much credit.

Another anniversary celebrated during the 1989-1990 season was the 50th of Ice Capades, which had been started in 1940 by a group of Eastern rink managers to keep their buildings busy and to compete with the more well known and firmly established Ice Follies, founded in 1936. Ice Capades had an outstanding life during its years under the management of John Harris of Pittsburgh, and while it has changed hands several times in recent years it still survives, although on a greatly reduced scope from the standpoint of production costs, going more towards the smaller skating company. The Ice Capades "alumni" continue to meet at an annual reunion, and the list of stars who have skated in the show over the years reads like a "Who's Who" of the skating world.

In September 1989, the death at age 42 of John Carrell of Seattle occurred. John and his partner, Lorna Dyer, had been National and North American Dance champions in the 1960's, and twice Bronze and once Silver medalists in the World Championships.

The NutraSweet Ice Skating Month was again observed for the third year, starting this time at Indianapolis. The first year, in 1987, the kickoff had been in New York City, and in 1988 in Los Angeles, so it rotated nicely in 1989 to the Midwest. Dorothy Hamill and Christopher Bowman were still on board as co-spokespersons. A quick tour to publicize the sport included stops at New York, Greenwich, Conn., (near the original home of Dorothy Hamill in Riverside), Boston, Chicago, Minneapolis and St. Louis.

It is a curious fact that no report of the 1989 fall meeting of the Board of Directors can be found in **Skating** magazine, one of the few times this oversight occurred. However, the magazine published a most informative summary of the sources and amounts of the monies available for elite skaters (World and National Teams and National Competitors), compiled by the Olympic Representative, Paul E. George:

1. U.S. Olympic Committee.

Level I Basic Grants: $45,000 (30 skaters eligible; top 5 in National Senior)

Operation Gold: $15,000 (6 eligible; 6th place or better in Worlds)

Level II Special Assistance Grants: up to $150,000 (30 skaters eligible for up to $5,000 each)

2. **USFSA Memorial Fund.** The Fund expended approximately $383,200 through June 30, 1989 for grants, scholarships and special awards to skaters. The budget for 1989-1990 was $395, 400.

Level of Skater		CSEP (Avg.)	ASP (Avg.)
Novice -	Singles	$ 765	
	Pairs	575	
	Dance	575	
Junior -	Singles	925	$ 650
	Pairs	1,050	650
	Dance	915	650
Senior -	Singles	1,500	650
	Pairs	1,410	650
	Dance	1,360	650
World Team Members -	Singles	7,500	650
	Pairs	6,000	650
	Dance	6,000	650

3. **USFSA General Fund** - In 1988-1989, the World Tour generated $250,000 for skaters' training. An additional $250,000 from the Tour was set aside for 1989-1990, with distribution estimated as follows:

Level of Skater	World Tour Grant
Novice (Singles, Pairs, Dance)	$ 270
Junior (Singles, Pairs, Dance)	1,875
Senior (Singles, Pairs, Dance)	1,089
World Team Members	4,200

4. Summary - With respect to direct training support on an individual basis, a World Team Member who placed in the top six in Singles at the Worlds could expect to receive a total of approximately $16,500, before any special assistance or private funding. The total of USOC and USFSA direct assistance monies amounted to $705,400. Among other sources of support were the USFSA (Vice) Presidents' Excellence Fund, for which a total of $45,000 was budgeted for 1989-1990. Many skaters are also the beneficiaries of restricted funds within the Memorial Fund and others have trust funds into which monies may be deposited for participation in exhibitions and other promotional activities.

The foregoing is probably the clearest exposition ever made of the support given to the elite skaters (at that time, of course), and is included here to demonstrate the importance of such a summary being included in the annual reports, as too little is known within the general membership of the amount and distribution of the funds of the Association in the form of aid to the elite skaters. It is a source of regret that such financial information has not been generally made available. The published reports in the magazine of the annual meetings in modern times have been singularly lacking in any specifics of the financial reports. Like any sizable corporation, an annual report should be published which contains all such information in a simplified form, not just in the very complicated account by account form now used in the reports to the meetings.

The 1989 fall meeting of the Board of Directors returned to Colorado Springs, and while relatively routine in nature, insofar as such meetings ever are routine, there were several actions of importance taken. Approved was the addition to the Nationals of Novice Pairs and Dance events, starting in 1991, for a significant increase in the number of entries at Nationals. Also approved was the addition of Senior Fours to the Nationals as a non-qualifying event. In the competitions area, the Vice Chairman of the Competitions Committee for Special Projects was authorized to certify all competition results software, a seemingly unimportant revision, but one of great value to the integrity of the computerized scoring system. It was also provided that the Judges Committee, instead of the referees, would make trial judging assignments at the qualifying competitions, including the Nationals, another minor and yet important decision to the progress of judges. The award of the 1991 National Precision Championships to Anchorage, Alaska, was approved, if the issue of transportation costs could be resolved. Also approved was the creation of Adult Figure and Free Skating Tests and the minimum age for adult skaters of 25.

The 1990 World Junior Championships returned to the Broadmoor for the second time, and once again the Soviet Junior skaters demonstrated their superiority by taking three of the four titles and a total of six out of the 12 medals, with the others going to: USA - 2; Canada - 1; France - 1; GDR - 1, and Japan - 1. The first two Men's places were taken by Igor Pashkevich and Alexei Urmanov, with

John Baldwin, Jr., third just ahead of Philippe Candeloro of France, who was closely followed by Scott Davis in fifth place. In the Ladies, Jessica Mills made a valiant attempt to defend her title but it was not to be, as she could finish only sixth in the free skating, after a second in figures and third in the original program. The winner was Yuka Sato of Japan (who would become the fourth lady to win both the Junior and Senior titles in 1994), with Surya Bonaly second, despite a 12th in figures. Sato had dominated the event in the first two parts, but could do no better than fifth in the free; Surya could not overtake her, being too far behind. Kyoko Ina, with a third in free after two eighth places, finished fifth, while Tisha Walker, after an eleventh in figures, finished seventh.

The Soviets took first and second in the Pairs, but a courageous performance by Jennifer Heurlin and John Frederiksen of Colorado in the free skating earned them the Bronze medal and prevented a Soviet sweep. The winners were Natalia Krestianinova and Alexei Torchinski. The second U.S. pair, Aimée Offner and Brian Helgenberg, placed sixth. It was much the same in the Dance, with the couples from the USSR taking the first two places, with Marina Anisina and Ilia Averbukh the surprise winners. (However, they were not the "top" Soviet couple in the eyes of the Eastern Bloc judges.) The best the U.S. could do was seventh by Beth Buhl of Seattle and Neal Smull of California, and tenth by Katherine and Ben Williamson of Colorado.

Despite the distance that had to be traveled from Europe, the championships were large, with 81 entries in the four events for a total of 110 persons, and were well run by the Broadmoor Skating Club and the hotel.

The 1990 Nationals were held at Salt Lake City, Utah, and were growing ever larger. In the four Senior events there were 60 entries, while in the Junior events there were 51. Somewhat as a forerunner of the complete separation of the figures from the free skating, the Novice Singles in 1990 were split into separate figure and free skating events, with the winners in the Men being: Free skating - Ryan Hunka of Ohio; Figures - Michael Weiss of Delaware; Ladies Free Skating - Lisa Ervin of Ohio; Figures - Natalie Thomas of Colorado. All of the entrants skated in both parts, which for the Men were 18 in both figures and free, and for the Ladies, 22 in figures and in free skating. The differences in places in the two parts were striking. For example in the Novice Ladies, Storey Ellis of Virginia was third in figures and 22nd in free skating, while Natalie Thomas of Colorado, the winner of the figures, was 19th in free skating, and so it went. Ryan Hunka of Ohio, the winner of the Novice Men's free skating, was 15th in figures.

The unwieldy size of the championships as a whole was obvious, especially to the officials, some of whom had to race from one rink to another to do back to back events, and yet, up to today, nothing has been done to address the problem.

All the Senior champions were back to defend, but Christopher Bowman, who was suffering from a back injury, unfortunately had to withdraw after a fourth in figures and a fifth in the

Todd Eldredge

original program, in which he had a hard fall on his triple Axel. This of course opened the door for the challengers, with Todd Eldredge of Massachusetts in the lead, having won both the figures and the original program. Paul Wylie had the dubious (in the view of some) honor of skating the last figure in a U.S. Championship, to place third in that part. He pulled up, however, with second in the original and first in free skating, to take the runner-up spot over Mark Mitchell of Connecticut, who had worked his way up from a sixth place in figures.

The Ladies was a little more routine, with Jill Trenary making a successful defense of her title (for her third overall), although she had a fall in the original program, placing third in that part. Kristi Yamaguchi, who had been fifth in figures, won the original program and was second in free skating to wind up second, with Holly Cook of Utah third, after a second in figures. Nancy Kerrigan finished fourth, with a seventh in figures and a third in free. Tonya Harding, who had been third in figures and second in the original, had a shot at the title, but had a disastrous free skating, being able to complete just one triple jump cleanly (of six planned), to finish 10th in free skating and seventh overall. She had been suffering from the flu for two weeks and it took its toll on her stamina in the long program.

Kristi Yamaguchi and Rudy Galindo successfully defended their Senior Pair title, but the sensation of the event was 13-year-old Natasha Kuchiki with Todd Sand, second in their first season. In third place were Sharon Carz and Doug Williams - so it was a California sweep. Kuchiki-Sand had a vocal in their free skating music, an excerpt from "Madame Butterfly." Vocal music is not permitted under the rules, but it did not seem to have much of an effect on their marks! Since Natasha was under the revised minimum age of 14 for entry in the Senior Worlds, an appeal was made to the ISU and permission was granted for her to skate, based on prior precedents. The rule had been changed from 12 to 14 at the previous Congress in 1988.

In Dance, as usual, form held, with the same three medalists as in 1989 retaining their positions. Susan Wynne and Joseph Druar won their second title, with April Sargent and Russ Witherby again second, and Suzanne Semanick and Ron Kravette third. In fifth were Elizabeth Punsalan and Jerod Swallow, a new combination since the prior year, when both of them had skated in Senior Dance with different partners.

Looking at the Junior and Novice events, some of the stars of the future were already progressing up the ladder. Scott Davis won the Junior Men, with Michael Chack of New York second, while Nicole Bobek, representing Colorado, was fourth in Junior Ladies.

The 1990 World Championships were held at Halifax, Nova Scotia, perhaps an unlikely site, but they were run by the CFSA with its usual efficiency and were a very well attended championship, with 93 entries, including 146 persons. The two Singles classes had 31 Men and 29 Ladies entries, while the Dance event had 27. Here too the defenders were all returning, and in three of four cases they were successful in retaining their titles. It was in the Ladies, with figures being done for the last time, that an upset occurred when Midori Ito failed in her defense, the figures once again being her downfall. With a very poor loop, Midori could do no better than tenth in the figures and, despite being first in both the original program and the free skating, finished no better than second overall. The winner was Jill Trenary, third in 1989, who had won the figures and placed second in free skating, despite a fifth in the original program. The surprise for the U.S. was Holly Cook who finished third. Kristi Yamaguchi had figure problems, finishing ninth, so a second in the original and a third in the free were not enough to elevate her to the podium. Cook, on the other hand, was fourth in figures, third in the original and fourth in the free, which earned her the Bronze medal with 7.4 factored placements to 7.8 for Kristi.

Kurt Browning was successful in the Men in his first defense, by virtue of winning the free skating together with seconds in the other two parts. The figure winner was Richard Zander of West Germany, another German-American who had competed earlier in the U.S. qualifying competition structure, but he could not hold his position, finishing seventh. Viktor Petrenko won the original program, which coupled with a third in figures and a second in free earned him the Silver medal. Christopher Bowman, recovered from his injury at the Nationals, and despite a sixth in figures, pulled off one of his best free skating performances to take the Bronze medal. Todd Eldredge, the new National champion, finished fifth, although he was third in the original program. Paul Wylie did not have his best day, with a 14th in the original program, winding up 10th overall.

In the Pairs Ekaterina Gordeeva and Sergei Grinkov of the USSR successfully defended their title, to win their fourth overall, but Isabelle Brasseur and Lloyd Eisler of Canada, despite a fourth in the original program, won the Silver medal. The younger pair of Natalia Mishkutenok and Arthur Dmitriev, also of the USSR, and the European Bronze medalists, took third ahead of their compatriots Larisa Selezneva and Oleg Makarov. Kristi Yamaguchi and Rudy Galindo were again fifth, as they had been in 1989. The "bubble" burst for Kuchiki-Sand, who were 11th, while Carz and Williams were 13th.

In Dance it was the Soviet-French confrontation, as Isabelle and Paul Duchesnay moved up to second behind the successful defenders, Marina Klimova and Sergei Ponomarenko, with Maia

Usova and Alexandr Zhulin third. Although they had been fifth in the compulsory dances, Susan Wynne and Joseph Druar showed their class by placing fourth, just ahead of Oksana Gritschuk and Evgeni Platov, yet another Soviet team. April Sargent and Russ Witherby placed eighth.

So the U.S. came away with three medals, a Gold and two Bronze. The USSR had its usual crop of five (but none in the Ladies), while Canada had two, Japan one and France one.

Efforts to obtain sponsors for USFSA events were being actively pursued, and among new sponsors was Creamette, a subsidiary of Borden, makers of the first and only nationally distributed pasta in America. Campbell's Soups and NutraSweet had also renewed their contracts, so the group of major sponsors was increasing. Even the 1990 National Precision Championships at Houston, Texas, had a title sponsor in Gilda Marx Industries, a national designer and manufacturer of exercise apparel, as well as additional sponsors in Shell Oil, Conoco, Panhandle Eastern, Continental Airlines and two public accounting firms, Deloitte and Touche, and Ernst and Young.

The Nationals in Precision returned in 1990 to the format of separate Sectional Championships, which in 1989 had been held at the same site and just before the Nationals. Although the idea of combining the competitions had been carried out successfully in Canada for many years, in the interest of reducing travel costs, it did not seem to work well in the U.S. and was therefore abandoned. The three Sectionals were held: Easterns - Stone Mountain, Georgia; Midwesterns - Edina, Minnesota; and Pacific Coasts - Burbank, California, so the travel costs were indeed high. The Easterns had 30 teams in six events, the Midwesterns had 56 teams in six events, while the Pacific Coasts had only 14 teams in four events.

The Nationals, however, drew 58 teams in six finals and four consolation rounds, now called "Sterling" instead of "Silver." In the Senior event the Goldenettes of the Garfield Heights FSC of Ohio upset the Haydenettes of Massachusetts to take the title, but the Ice Mates, which was now a Novice team, took that title for Hayden. The Ice Cubes, the defending Juvenile champions, were also defeated by a team from Garfield Heights, the Angelettes. The Junior title went to the Royalettes, yet a third Garfield Heights team; while the Detroit Royals won the Adult division, upsetting the Fabulous Forties of Los Angeles who were trying for their fourth straight. The Hot Fudge Sundaes of Buffalo regained the Intermediate crown they had last held in 1988. So the championships were most successful for the Midwest with four of the six titles, and three of them going to Ohio.

The spring International competition season started with the Merano Spring Trophy once again, with two entries, Charlene von Saher of Rye, N.Y., placing second behind Claudia Unger of West Germany, and Dana McDonald of Fraser, Michigan, the National Junior Bronze medalist, placing fourth. Von Saher would soon be representing Great Britain, the land of her birth.

The Challenge Lysiane Lauret dance event was again at Grenoble, France, with three Soviet couples in the first three places. Elizabeth Punsalan and Jerod Swallow were ninth, while Elizabeth McLean and Ari Lieb had to withdraw due to injury.

The added spring event was the second Skate Electric at the end of April, with Craig Heath winning the Men, Nancy Kerrigan third in the Ladies (the winner being Surya Bonaly), Calla Urbanski and Mark Naylor third in Pairs, with the USSR pair of Evgenia Shishkova and Vadim Naumov the winners, and Jeanne Miley and Michael Verlich second in Dance to Susanna Rahkamo and Petri Kokko of Finland. There was also a team prize which went to "Europe," with the USA second.

The 1990 Governing Council meeting was held at Indianapolis for the first time at what had become a major training center with the Indiana/World Skating Academy. Again for some reason there was no report of the meeting published in **Skating** magazine, but recourse to the Reports of Action provided information concerning the actions taken. Recognition was again made of those judges who had attained 50 or more years of service. In 1990 they included Dorothy Burkholder of Hazel Crest, Ill.; LeRoy Lindgren of Winchester, Mass.; Allen Lomax of Grosse Pointe Farms, Mich.; Sally Rial of Buffalo, N.Y., and Mary Louise Wright of Belmont, Mass. Dorothy Burkholder had been a World judge and was a National judge. Allen Lomax and Sally Rial were both National judges, while Mary Louise Wright was both a World and National judge.

In addition, notice was taken of the deaths during the past year of several long-time judges: Kathy Sackett of Palo Alto, Calif., who had been a World judge in both figure skating and ice dancing; Tom Easton of Calif., a former dance competitor and National Dance judge; and Lou Bodek of Aspen, Colo., a former International judge and also the first chairman of the Singles and Pairs Committee. Kathy had been appointed an Honorary National Judge in 1973, and Tom and Lou were posthumously appointed as Honorary National judges in 1989 and 1990, respectively.

At the meeting the announcement was made of the election of Scott Hamilton, Olympic champion in 1984, four-time World champion (1981-1984) and four-time National champion in the same years, to the World Figure Skating Hall of Fame, the ninth U.S. skater elected to that body, and a well deserved honor. Scott was also elected to the U.S. Olympic Hall of Fame in the same year.

The winner of the **Skating** magazine Readers' Choice Award was announced at the meeting by outgoing editor Dale Mitch to be Jill Trenary, the current World and National Ladies champion. With Dale moving on to the position of Director of the World Figure Skating Museum, a new editor for the magazine was appointed in Kim Mutchler, who joined the Headquarters staff from U.S. Swimming and would serve until 1994, when she was succeeded in turn by Jay Miller.

In the area of competitions there were many minor rule changes, among them being one which required a skater to compete in the Region in which his or her home club was located. Also approved was the final abolition of the Modified Open Judging system, so that in the future only the Closed system (no marks displayed) or the Open system (all marks displayed), would be used, as appropriate. Also established was the position of a National Vice Chairman for Referees and Accountants Education and Training, by way of further implementation of the creation in 1988 of that subcommittee, to promote greater knowledge and training among the referees and accountants.

The requirement for judges to attend a sanctioned judges' school was changed to one in every four years. At the suggestion of Sally Rial, judges with 50 years or more of service were exempted from taking the annual judges' examination.

One significant change made was the adoption of interim eligibility rules to apply to skaters who desired to teach, exhibit or use their likeness for compensation. Essentially, such activities were permitted provided the skater registered with the USFSA, obtained contractual approval from it and established a trust fund to hold the monies received. There was also a restriction on such activities two weeks before and during USFSA and International competitions (in which the skater was participating). The interim rules were to be effective for one year, pending the development of permanent ones based on the action of the 1990 ISU Congress.

In Precision skating, the USFSA set aside funds to support the first "Snowflake" International competition in the discipline which was to be held at Boston at the end of December, 1990.

The 1990 ISU Congress can finally be said to have achieved the objectives sought for the mid-term Congress, as originally contemplated by the late President Jacques Favart. It was held in a new part of the skating world (New Zealand), in a very pleasant environment (Christchurch). There were no elections, everyone was healthy, there was a large enough agenda (182 proposals) for some positive work to be done and to keep the delegates busy, and everyone had a good time.

Among the matters considered and acted upon of interest to figure skating in the United States was the transfer of the U.S. television contract for the ISU Championships (which would include those in 1992) from CBS to NBC, at a substantially increased price. Provision was made to enable the ISU itself to carry out random "out of competition" doping control tests of skaters belonging to the members. Also added to the doping regulation was an arbitration procedure permitting the appeal of sanctions to the Court of Arbitration for Sport (CAS), an IOC endorsed tribunal at Lausanne, Switzerland.

The eligibility rules were formally liberalized, essentially reflecting those adopted by the USFSA on an interim basis at the 1990 Governing Council meeting. Also adopted was a more specific definition of commercial advertising permitted to be displayed on equipment or clothing by competitors or officials, which was limited to one dignified trademark, not larger than 13 square centimeters.

Once again the age limits for Juniors were changed, this time to use the calendar year (within which the maximum age is reached), instead of the former July 1st, with a consequent increase of one year in the maximums, to 18 for Ladies and 19 for Men, Pairs and Dance couples. The revised rule would apply to competitions being held during the same calendar year in which the maximum age was reached. Another revision was to be permit partners of different nationalities in Pairs and Dance to skate together internationally for the member of either partner.

A definition of group skating was restored to the Regulations to cover Fours and Precision Team skating. At the same time the Congress appointed an ad hoc committee to prepare proposals for the next Congress in 1992, to cover international competitions in precision team skating, as it was called. The committee included Donald Gilchrist and Doug Steele of Canada, Chuck DeMore and Pat French representing the U.S. and Margaretha Alerius of Sweden. Donald and Chuck represented the ISU Council on the committee, and were in effect its co-chairmen.

The final deletion of compulsory figures from International competitions was also approved, so that only separate competitions in figures alone could be held. Also approved was a requirement in the original program that the jumps included in the jump combination had to be different from the solo jumps, as well as the complete prohibition of the use of vocal music for the original program and the free skating in Singles and Pairs.

Insofar as judges and referees were concerned, the same requirements already imposed on World officials with respect to activity and attendance at judges' seminars were extended to include International Officials as well. It was also clarified that the maximum age (45) for a first appointment applied separately to the two disciplines (figure skating and ice dancing). In dance, each compulsory dance was to be a separate part of the competition, with a separate result being calculated. Accordingly, the multiplying factor for one compulsory dance was defined as 0.2 (10 percent). The original set-pattern dance was changed to an "Original dance," with no repetitive set pattern being required, becoming in effect a "mini" free dance. For free dance, greater freedom in the choice of music was to be permitted, with the requirement that it "be suitable of ice dancing" being deleted. This would result in an explosion of somewhat exotic and far out music, and the Ice Dance Technical Committee would be forced in future years to rein it all back in again, a reflection of the on-going "churning" of the rules for dance that seemed to be the norm rather than the exception.

Finally, after many years of trying on the part of the USFSA, the proposal to permit a third entry in championships to a member with a competitor placed among the top three (five in pairs) in the prior year, without specific designation by name, was accepted. The final round size for ISU Championships and the Olympics was returned to 24 (from 20). The ISU Tests in Figure Skating (compulsory figures and free skating) were replaced with a new schedule of free skating tests and Pair skating tests.

Claire W. Ferguson

Just as the 1990-1991 season began, there occurred an event which was unique in the history of the Association up to that time. President Franklin Nelson, a surgeon in private life, practicing in his home town of Tulsa, Okla., earlier in the year had rejoined the United States Navy as a Lieutenant Commander in the Medical Corps, and was assigned to the Oakland (California) Naval Hospital. At the outset of the war against Iraq in the Persian Gulf, he was posted in August, 1990, to the hospital ship USS Mercy which was sent to the Gulf. Franklin would remain with the ship until the following March (1991), so in his absence, the duties of the Presidency devolved upon the First Vice President, Claire Ferguson of Jamestown, R.I. It was the first and so far the only time that a USFSA President has been unable to carry out his or her duties for any measurable period of time. With the administrative structure which had been put into place in 1980, of an Executive Committee and an Executive Director to conduct the daily operations of the Association, the season itself was conducted without incident and turned out to be a very successful one for the Association.

The first major event of the new season, in early July, was the Olympic Festival, held this time in Minneapolis and once again a combination of a four team event with individual winners in the four events. The West Team, consisting of Troy Goldstein of Los Angeles, Craig Heath of Berkeley, Doug Mattis of Los Angeles, Richard Sears of Massachusetts and Steven Smith of California, in the Men; Jodi Friedman of Colorado, Dena Galech of Seattle, Tonya Harding of Oregon and Meredith Vaughn of Colorado in Ladies; Dawn and Troy Goldstein, and Natasha Kuchiki and Todd Sand of Los Angeles in Pairs; and Cheryl Demkowski of California and Jeffrey Czarnecki of Delaware, Jennifer Goolsbee of Detroit and Shawn Rettstatt of Colorado, Jeanne Miley and Michael Verlich of Los Angeles and Wendy Millette of Boston and James Curtis of Wissahickon, in Dance, were the winners of the team prize.

The individual winners were Erik Larson of San Diego in the Men, Nancy Kerrigan of Massachusetts in the Ladies, Angela Deneweth of Michigan and John Denton of California in the Pairs, and Jeanne Miley and Michael Verlich of Los Angeles in the Dance. There were 54 entries in the four events.

Just a month later the 1990 Goodwill Games were held at Tacoma, Wash., it being an International Senior Competition held for the first time, with 46 skaters from six countries participating. This "made for television" event, the creation of Ted Turner of Atlanta, offered substantial appearance fees for participation, an early example of what would become a common practice in just a few years. As a consequence, quite a strong field was on hand, despite the fact that it was the middle of the summer. No figures were included.

In the Men, the reigning World champion Kurt Browning of Canada was the winner, with the Olympic Bronze medalist Viktor Petrenko of the USSR second, followed by Todd Eldredge and Paul Wylie in third and fourth, with Christopher Bowman sixth. The winner in the Ladies was Kristi Yamaguchi, who defeated the reigning World Ladies champion, Jill Trenary. Nancy Kerrigan finished fifth.

The Pairs event was a Soviet sweep, with Ekaterina Gordeeva and Sergei Grinkov the winners, followed by Natalia Mishkutenok and Artur Dmitriev second, and Elena Bechke and Denis Petrov third. Natasha Kuchiki and Todd Sand finished fourth, with Sharon Carz and Doug Williams sixth, and Calla Urbanski and Mark Naylor seventh.

In the Dance it was one-two for the Soviets, with Marina Klimova and Sergei Ponomarenko the winners over Maia Usova and Alexandr Zhulin. Finishing a strong third in what was announced as their last competition in the amateur ranks were Susan Wynne and Joseph Druar, and there were many present who wished that it was not so. April Sargent and Russ Witherby were sixth. In fourth were Oksana Ghitschuk and Evgeni Platov of the USSR. Even with its obvious commercial overtones, the competition was quite successful, the principal difficulty being the long delays imposed between skaters for television commercials. Although the top skaters are now used to it and are allowed to "orbit" the ice before being called, the general unwillingness of television, with the exception of ABC, to cooperate in that regard continues to be an ongoing problem.

Just two weeks later at Lake Placid, the 1990 National Collegiate Championships were held with quite a large field of 99 entries in 12 events. Separate figure events were still held for Senior and Junior Men and Ladies; these attracted 35 entries with 18 of them in the Senior Ladies, in which the winner was Jennifer Leng of Tufts. Troy Goldstein of California State won the Senior Men, while in Juniors, Glenn Ziehnert of Adirondack Community College won the Men and Janet Lynn Melville of the University of Delaware the Ladies.

In the free skating events, Troy Goldstein repeated his figure win for his third National Collegiate gold medal. In the Senior Ladies, with 25 entries, the winner was Leanna Naczynski of Indiana University. In the Junior Men Glenn Ziehnert also repeated his figure win to take his third Collegiate gold medal. In Junior Ladies the winner was Dana Chinn of North Virginia Community College.

There were two Pairs events, with Laura Murphy and Brian Wells of the University of Delaware winning the Senior class over the Goldsteins, and Dawn Piepenbrink and Nick Castaneda of Arizona State University taking the Junior title.

In the two Dance events, Rachel Mayer and Peter Breen of Boston University won the Senior title, and Laura Gayton of Boston College and Peter Abraham of Boston the Junior event.

So, as can be seen, three major competitions had already been held before the regular International Competition season had even started. The idea that figure skating was a winter sport certainly could no longer be accepted, and in the years ahead it would get even busier during the summer.

In 1990-1991, the USFSA continued to support participation in 11 International Competitions between August and December, plus the World Junior at Budapest in December, the World University Games at Sapporo, Japan, and the World Championships in March at Munich, to which would be added two or three more competitions following the Worlds. Unfortunately, the criteria of excellence and reward has never really been a primary factor in the selection of competitions or skaters in the International realm, with apparent "political" reasons often being a greater motivation. Included in the roster were Prague, Zagreb and Moscow.

The Coupe des Alpes kicked off the season as usual at the end of August, with the National Junior champions having the priority. In Men, Michael Chack of New York, the National Junior Silver medalist, won at Oberstdorf and was second at St. Gervais, while National Junior champion, Scott Davis, now of Tacoma, was less successful, with a fourth at Oberstdorf and a sixth at St. Gervais. In the Ladies, Alice Sue Claeys of Minnesota, the National Junior Ladies champion, was sixth at St. Gervais and eighth at Oberstdorf, while Geremi Weiss, the National Junior Silver medalist, was twelfth at St. Gervais and fifteenth at Oberstdorf.

In the Pairs, Tristen Vega and Richard Alexander of Los Angeles, the National Junior Pair champions, were third at the Grand Prix and fourth at the Nebelhorn, with Susan Purdy and Scott Chiamulera of Detroit fifth in both competitions. In Dance Beth Buhl and Neal Smull of California, the National Junior Dance champions, were fifth at St. Gervais and fourth at Oberstdorf, with Krista Schulz and Jonathan Stine of Colorado, ninth and tenth, respectively. In the team trophies, the U.S. was third, for one of its poorest showings in the Coupe des Alpes in many years.

Skate Electric in England followed in early October, and here the U.S. representatives did better, with Holly Cook of Utah winning the Ladies, Erik Larson of San Diego placing third in Men, Sharon Carz and Doug Williams seventh in Pairs and Elizabeth Punsalan and Jerod Swallow of Colorado fourth in Dance.

Skate America followed at Buffalo, N.Y., with the "big guns" on board, producing a haul of four medals in Singles, but none in Pairs and Dance, the prevailing pattern. In the Men the winner was Viktor Petrenko of the USSR, with Chistopher Bowman second and Todd Eldredge third. Craig Heath was fifth. Kristi Yamaguchi was the winner in the Ladies, defeating Midori Ito of Japan, with Tonia Kwiatkowski of Ohio third, and Jeri Campbell of Los Angeles sixth. In Pairs, the best U.S. place was a fourth for Natasha Kuchiki and Todd Sand of California, with the winners being Marina Eltsova and Andrei Bushkov of the USSR. Calla Urbanski and new partner Rocky Marval were seventh, with Angela Deneweth and John Denton 10th. The winners in Dance for once were not Soviet, but Stefania Calegari and Pasquale Camerlengo of Italy. The best U.S. place was a sixth for Jeanne Miley and Michael Verlich of California, with Amy Webster of Boston and Leif Erickson of Wilmington tenth and Wendy Millette and James Curtis 11th.

One dance couple, Kimberly Callahan and Robert Peal, of Illinois, who had been 11th in the 1990 National Junior Dance, was sent to an "add-on" Junior competition held in Rome, Italy, at the same time as Skate Canada, the "Autumn Trophy Mezzaluna," in which they placed seventh.

Skate Canada was held at Lethbridge, Alberta, in accordance with the CFSA policy of moving the competition to the smaller Canadian centers of skating. It again included the Interpretive events for Men and Ladies, as well as Fours. The Ladies interpretive event was won by Joanna Ng of Los Angeles, while Larry Holliday of Indianapolis was fifth in Men. In Fours, there were actually four entries, the largest in modern times, with the Canadian four of Stacey Ball, Isabelle Brasseur, Lloyd Eisler and Jean-Michel Bombardier the winners. Elaine Asenakis, Calla Urbanksi, Rocky Marval and Joel McKeever from Delaware were third.

Kurt Browning was the Men's winner, with Grzegorz Filipowski of Poland second and Mark Mitchell of Connecticut third. In Ladies Holly Cook of Utah was also third behind the winner, Josée Chouinard and Lisa Sargeant of Canada, second. Brasseur-Eisler were the Pair winners, with Jennifer Heurlin and John Frederiksen fourth and with Asenakis-McKeever seventh. In Dance Rachel Mayer and Peter Breen of Boston were seventh, with a Canadian couple, Jacqueline Petr and Mark Janoschak, the winners over a Soviet couple. Skate Canada has always been a "tough nut" to crack, and the U.S. team did well, with three medals.

The next three competitions were Prague, Zagreb and the Trophée Lalique at Paris, with the latter two on the same weekend. At Prague the U.S. was represented in the Ladies by Dena Galech of Seattle, who placed eighth, and in the Pairs by Karen Courtland of New Jersey and Jason Dungjen of Michigan, a new combination, who pulled off a surprising win over pairs from Canada, the USSR and Germany.

At the Golden Spin of Zagreb, Aren Nielsen of Kansas City was the winner, while Tisha Walker of California gained a third place in the Ladies. In the Dance Elisa Curtis of Wissahickon and Robert Nardozza of Texas were the winners, so the three U.S. entries all earned medals. The 1990 competition would turn out to be the last at Zagreb, with the onset of the breakup of

Yugoslavia and the resulting Balkan war. Although the event was reinstated in 1994, the U.S. has not sent skaters to it, in view of the general unrest and conditions, not only in Croatia but also in Bosnia.

At the Trophée Lalique at Paris, the U.S. was represented by Christopher Bowman, Nancy Kerrigan and Jeanne Miley and Michael Verlich. Bowman placed first in his event, defeating Viacheslav Zagorodniuk of the USSR and Elvis Stojko of Canada. Fifth was Philippe Candeloro of France. In the Ladies, Nancy finished third, the winner being Surya Bonaly of France. Miley and Verlich were sixth in Dance, which was won by Calegari and Camerlengo of Italy.

Just a week later came the Nations Cup at Gelsenkirchen, Germany, with Todd Eldredge placing second to Kurt Browning of Canada. Kristi Yamaguchi won the Ladies, defeating Evelyn Grossmann of Germany, who was then the reigning European Ladies champion. In the Pairs, Sharon Carz and Doug Williams were fourth, with Mishkutenok and Dmitriev of the USSR the winners. April Sargent and Russ Witherby placed second in Dance to another Soviet couple, Irina Romanova and Igor Jaroshenko.

Just a week after Paris, the NHK Trophy competition took place at Asahikawa on Hokkaido, Japan, which had become one of the regular stops on the circuit. Viktor Petrenko of the USSR won the Men, while Paul Wylie finished fourth and Daniel Doran, sixth. Midori Ito of Japan was again the Ladies winner, with Tonya Harding second and Kyoko Ina, a Japanese-American, sixth. In the Pairs, which was won by Elena Bechke and Denis Petrov of the USSR, Natasha Kuchiki (another Japanese-American) and Todd Sand were fifth, while in Dance, which was won by Maia Usova and Alexandr Zhulin of the USSR, Elizabeth Punsalan and Jerod Swallow were sixth, and Lisa Grove from Pittsburgh and Scott Myers from Delaware were seventh.

The Moscow Skate, an event that the U.S. had entered sporadically, usually with disastrous results was canceled for lack of a sponsor and was replaced by the GosTeleRadio Prize at Odessa in Ukraine, and was supported with one U.S. entry in each event. Doug Mattis was fifth in Men, which was won by Alexei Urmanov of the USSR, while Stacy Rutkowski of Illinois was second in Ladies to Olga Markova of the USSR. In Pairs Katie Wood and Todd Reynolds, a new team, were seventh.

It was here that Wood suffered a severe fall in the exhibitions following the competition, going down from full extension in a "helicopter" type lift and sustaining a fractured skull and punctured ear drum. The medical facilities available were quite primitive, and had it not been for the help given by Viktor Petrenko and his coach, Galina Smievskaia, who lived in Odessa, the outcome could well have been quite different. Katie's coach, Bob Young, now at Simsbury, Conn., (where Galina is also a coach), remained with her. Assistance was also provided to the team in Moscow by the husband of Natalia Dubova (a former Soviet Dance coach now in Lake Placid), who assisted in the coordination with the U.S. Embassy of the arrangements for Katie's evacuation via Germany and then back to the U.S. It was an example of the good fellowship and friendship that exists among the skaters themselves and their coaches around the world. Happily, Wood recovered and even resumed activity as a Pair skater. In the Dance Jeanne Miley and Michael Verlich placed fourth.

Another competition added to the schedule was the Oslo Piruetten at the end of November at Oslo, Norway. Shepherd Clark of Atlanta, the only U.S. entry, placed second in Men. There was also a Junior Men's event which was won by Ilya Kulik of the USSR, a future star.

A notable first in the International Competition schedule was the Snowflake Invitational Precision competition which was held at Boston at the end of December, 1990. Since there were as yet no International rules for Precision, the competition was held under USFSA rules, but drew a representative field of 36 teams from Canada, Japan, Mexico, Norway, Sweden and the USA. The Canadians demonstrated their supremacy in the discipline by taking three of the four final round events, with the Team Surprise from Sweden "surprising" everyone by winning the Junior class.

In the Senior event the winners were Les Pirouettes de Laval from Quebec, with a team from the same club winning the Novice and the team Les Coccinelles de Charlesbourg, also from Quebec, winning the Juvenile class. The best U.S. showing was in the Senior event with the Goldenettes from Garfield Heights, Ohio, second and the Haydenettes from Lexington, Mass., third. The Ice Mates, also from Lexington, were second in the Novice class, and the Angelettes, also from Garfield Heights, were second in the Juvenile event. It was a major kickoff of International competition for Precision. Soon other competitions abroad followed, to which the U.S. would send teams, and there has now grown up a regular International Competition season for Precision teams, just as has been the case for figure skating and Ice Dancing.

The October, 1990, meeting of the Board of Directors was held at Colorado Springs as usual, with Acting President Claire Ferguson presiding in the absence of President Franklin Nelson, who was in the Persian Gulf. Noted was the death earlier in the year of Robert Sackett of Palo Alto, Calif. Bob had served in many capacities in the Association, including Vice President and Chairman of the Figure Judges and Judging Standards Committees, an area in which he had a special interest and a strong influence. He really can be considered as one of the founders of the JET's. He also served as a member of the Executive Committee, of which he was elected an Honorary member in 1967. His greatest contribution, however, was as a four-time Chairman of the Nominating Committee, in which position he played a major role in finding and bringing along the leadership of the Association for 20 years. To many at the time (in the 1950's) he was the "power behind the throne!"

Among the rule changes adopted by the Board was one which would enable recognized Inter-Club Associations (of three or more clubs) to serve as hosts for competitions. Until the change, sanctions for competitions could be issued only to a USFSA Member club, and the recognition of the Inter-Club Associations in this regard was an important step forward.

With respect to bids for the holding of the National Precision Championships, it was decided that the Sectional rotation applied to the regular Nationals was not to be followed, with bids to be entertained on a nation-wide basis.

In the Judging rules, a minimum age of 16 for trial judges was adopted, which gave a two year period before eligibility for appointment at age 18. Previously there had been no minimum age specified.

In the area of International Competitions and exhibitions, it was decided that money received for exhibitions would go directly to the exhibitor, but that prize money received for competitions would be divided equally among all international competition skaters. At the time, most prize money, as for example in the case of the Nations Cup competition in Germany, was given to the participating member and not to the skaters, for distribution as the receiving member saw fit.

Also approved was the creation of a United States Figure Skating Hall of Fame, with 15 Electors including the President, the three Vice Presidents, three coaches, the Vice Chairman of the Hall of Fame and Museum Committee and seven members at large. A two-thirds vote would be required for election in the same categories as for the World Figure Skating Hall of Fame: (1) skaters; (2) administrators; (3) professionals - show and coaches; and (4) "old-timers" - 1940 and earlier.

A significant action was the approval of a proposal made by the New York Regional Council of Figure Skating Clubs for the creation of a National Championship for Juvenile and Intermediate skaters, with the first such event to be held in the spring of 1991. A budget for the championships of $25,000, plus a 20 percent override if necessary was also approved. Remarkably, the "J-I" Nationals, as they came to be called, were indeed held for the first time in April, 1991, at Monsey, N.Y.

With the advent of the separation of compulsory figures from free skating in Singles, the qualifying competitions were significantly different, with separate figure events being offered. It was also voted by the Board that the existing permanent trophies for the former combined events would be assigned to the new free skating events, unless otherwise directed by the original donors. Also to be included, especially at the Regional level, were Adult free skating and figure events. The Pacific Coast had been the first Section to offer Adult free skating events, with mixed success, some 10 years earlier. Such events would now be found in the Sectionals as well. Of course Adult (originally Veterans) Dance events had been in place for many years, with the event first appearing in the Easterns in 1950, largely due to the efforts of Harold Hartshorne of New York and Ritter Shumway of Rochester, both of them many time winners with a variety of partners.

The origin of the Veterans Dance events can probably be attributed to the Middle Atlantic Championships, with its special exemption from the conventional rules, since a Veterans Waltz was held in that competition as early as 1939, won by Mr. and Mrs. Joseph K. Savage of New York, and a regular Veterans Dance event by 1949, won by Ann Walsh and Carl Sorenson of the Metropolitan FSC. With the resulting expansion of the content of the qualifying competitions, it is worthwhile to look once again at the numbers of entries in the 1991 Regionals, Sectionals and Nationals:

Regionals	Number of Events	Total Entries	Totals
New Englands	23	326	
North Atlantics	21	296	
South Atlantics	29	273	895
Eastern Great Lakes	39	490	
Southwesterns	28	419	
Upper Great Lakes	18	254	1,163
Central Pacific	41	305	
Northwest Pacific	24	244	
Southwest Pacific	26	237	786
Sectionals			
Eastern	29	256	
Midwestern	29	286	
Pacific Coast	28	256	798
Nationals	19	229	
J-I Nationals	9	114	

The wide variation of the numbers needs some explanation. In general, the differences depend upon the number and size of the non-qualifying events offered. Several of the Regions, especially the Central and Northwest Pacific, have always had many events for Juvenile and lower Singles, while others, such as New England have generally adhered to the standard events. The Central Pacific Region, for example, offered 11 artistic Singles events in 1991, which drew 81 entries.

What is not readily apparent from the totals is the lack, especially at the Regional level, of any significant number of Pair and Dance events. In the nine Regions there were only 14 Pair events with a total of 41 entries, and 19 Dance events with 59 entries. There were no Senior events at all in the Regionals in Pairs and Dance. The decline of these disciplines is readily apparent, and it is quite possible that they may eventually disappear altogether from the Regionals. In the three Sectionals, of course, the picture looks better. There were 12 Pair events with a total of 77 entries and 12 Dance events with 90 entries. In the Nationals there were three

Pair events with 39 entries and three in Dance, also with 39 entries. In the J-I Nationals, there was one Pair event with 11 entries and one Dance event with 12.

Despite the weakness in Pairs and Dance, the increase in the number of events and entries was exponential, when compared with prior years. But what of the judges to service them? In 1991, there were 921 judges on the lists, divided as follows: East - 291; Midwest - 356; Pacific Coast - 274, a smaller number than in prior years, when there were over 1,000 as long ago as 20 years before. To put the numbers even more in focus, the numbers of judges qualified to judge competitions (as distinguished from tests) is even smaller: Singles and Pairs - 420; Dance - 221; and Precision - 138. The number of judges has remained essentially flat or in decline ever since World War II.

The state of the judging corps is a hidden crisis in the making. It is an aging and shrinking group, and unless drastic steps are taken without delay to increase the ranks with a substantial number of younger and qualified persons, the time will arrive when the structure simply will collapse because there will not be enough judges to do the job. At that point, we may well see professional (i.e. paid) judges as the only alternative.

The bureaucracy of the system is overwhelming and intimidating to younger persons interested in judging, and the costs are substantial. Somehow progress must be expedited and made simpler if new judges are to be found in sufficient number to meet the ever growing demand.

The 1991 World Junior Championships were held at Budapest, Hungary, at the end of November 1990, with the U.S. team coming away with two medals: a Silver for Lisa Ervin of Ohio, the 1990 National Novice Ladies champion in free skating and a bronze in the Pairs for Jennifer Heurlin and John Frederiksen of Colorado, the 1989 National Junior Pair champions. In the Men, Scott Davis of Great Falls, Mont., was fourth, Ryan Hunka of Ohio, the 1990 National Novice champion in free skating, ninth, and John Baldwin, Jr., of California, 10th. In the Ladies, which was won by Surya Bonaly of France (who would also win the European Ladies title in the same year), Nicole Bobek of Colorado was fourth, while in the Pairs, Aimee Offner and Brian Helgenberg of Delaware were fifth and Nicole and Gregory Sciarrotta, Jr., of California were sixth. Kimberly Callahan and Robert Peal of Illinois were ninth, and Laurie Baker of Delaware and David Kastan of Ohio were 14th in Dance. The apparent inability of the U.S.A. to field pairs and dance couples with medal potential at the Junior level remained an ongoing problem.

The 1991 Nationals were held at Minneapolis in the new Target Center, an unusual arena with the ice surface elevated above the arena floor. The championship was the biggest ever, with the separate figure events which were held in the arena of Augsburg College, the home of the St. Paul FSC. The six figure events drew 69 entries and it is appropriate to list the first National champions in figures at the Senior and Junior levels.

Senior Men - Craig Heath, St. Moritz ISC, California

Senior Ladies - Kelly Ann Szmurlo, Broadmoor SC, Colorado

Junior Men - Laurent Massé, Hayden Recreation Centre FSC, Massachusetts

Junior Ladies - Casey Link, Las Vegas FSC, Nevada

The Novice events were in fact the second championship for figures, since the split format had been applied to those events in 1990, as we have seen.

With Fours having been revived in Skate Canada, the event had been restored to the list of National events and a National Championship was held for the first time in 41 years. Two of the judges were themselves former members of winning National Championship Fours: Mary Louise Wright, from the "first" St. Paul Four, winners in 1940, and Janet Allen, from the

1991 National Champion Four
(L to R) Joel McKeever, Rocky Marval, Calla Urbanski and Elaine Asanakis

"second" St. Paul Four, winners in 1947, 1948 and 1950. The new champions were Elaine Asanakis and Calla Urbanski of the University of Delaware FSC, with Rocky Marval of the SC of New York and Joel McKeever of the Dallas FSC. Much of the credit for the revival of the discipline was due to Ron Ludington, who put together two fours from the pairs in his training center to make a competition. Unfortunately, the revival did not last and the discipline has once again disappeared into the mists of history. But for that one brief moment, it was exciting to see Fours skate again at the National level, and it can be said that the winners compared favorably with their predecessors, and of course did some elements not known in the past, such as the "double" death spiral!

The major event of the championships was the Senior Ladies, with Tonya Harding taking the vacant title (Jill Trenary being out of action due to injury) in an upset over Kristi Yamaguchi, winner of the original program. In her free skating program, Tonya completed the first triple axel jump ever by a U.S. Lady in competition. The only other lady ever to do the jump in competition was Midori Ito of Japan. Nancy Kerrigan placed third, so Tonya, Kristi and Nancy would be the U.S. entries in the 1991 Worlds at Munich. In Senior Men Todd Eldredge retained his title, defeating Christopher Bowman and Paul Wylie, with the latter just edging out Mark Mitchell of Connecticut in the free skating. In the Pairs, with Kristi Yamaguchi and Rudy Galindo having retired as a pair

Nancy Kerrigan

although they both continued as single skaters, the new champions were Natasha Kuchiki and Todd Sand of California, with Calla Urbanski and Rocky Marval second, and Jenni Meno of Ohio and Scott Wendland of California third.

In Senior Dance, with Susan Wynne and Joseph Druar having retired, the title went in an upset to Elizabeth Punsalan and Jerod Swallow, representing the Broadmoor SC, who came from behind in the free dance with their unusual and unique program, "The Race," to defeat April Sargent and Russ Witherby, representing Delaware. In third place were Jeanne Miley and Michael Verlich of California, but only two Dance couples would go to the Worlds.

Lisa Ervin of Ohio, the World Junior Silver medalist, added the Junior title to her Novice title of the prior year, with Aimee Offner and Brian Helgenberg of Delaware taking the Junior Pairs, and Kimberly Callahan of Delaware and Robert Peal of Illinois, the Junior Dance, demonstrating the value of the experience they had gained by their participation in the World Junior Championships.

For the first time Novice Pair and Dance events were included in the schedule of the Nationals, with the winners being Andrea Catoia and Paul Dulebohn of Delaware in Pairs and in the Dance, Nicole Dumonceaux and John Reppucci of Minnesota.

The 1991 World Championships were held at Munich, Germany, in the Olympiahalle, the gymnastics venue for the 1972 Summer Olympics and also the site of the 1974 Worlds. They were organized very well as usual by the German Federation and were very memorable from the standpoint of the U.S. team, which had its best results since prior to 1960, with five medals: one Gold, one Silver and three Bronze. Several records were set, the most notable being the sweep of the medals in the Ladies by the three U.S. entrants. Kristi Yamaguchi reversed the National result to become the new World Ladies champion, Jill Trenary still being out with her injury. Kristi was the 10th U.S. lady to be World champion, and just as had been the case with Carol Heiss in 1956, she was a World champion without being the National champion of her own country, an omission which she would rectify in 1992.

Tonya Harding's triple axel failed her but she took second, while Nancy Kerrigan was fifth in the original program and pulled up to take the Bronze medal with a third in the free skating.

Midori Ito of Japan was fourth and she too could not bring off the triple axel. Ito had a most unusual problem in the original program, when she did her jump combination too close to the boards and wound up outside the rink, going through the opening for the low television camera. She hopped up apparently none the worse for wear, but it was too late. Earlier in the warmup she also had a collision with a French skater, Laetitia Hubert, which obviously threw off her timing. Surya Bonaly of France, who placed fifth, attempted a quadruple toe loop in the free skating and stood up, but was short a half turn on the rotation, and immediately afterwards, in celebrating, caught her toe pick and "belly flopped" forward. That and other errors took her out of contention.

Kristi Yamaguchi

There never had been a sweep of the medals before in a World Championship for Ladies, although there had been four in the Men, two by Austria in 1927 and 1928 and two by the U.S. in 1955 and 1956 (Hayes Alan Jenkins, Ronnie Robertson and David Jenkins). Sweeps had also been achieved in Pairs by the USSR and in the Dance by the British, but never in the Ladies. It is probably a record that will stand for a long time!

Not to be outdone by the Ladies, Todd Eldredge rose to the challenge in the Men to take the bronze medal behind the defender, Kurt Browning of Canada and Viktor Petrenko of the USSR. Todd pulled up from fifth in the original to gain the medal. Chris Bowman placed fifth, while Paul Wylie did not have one of his better days and finished 11th, after a disastrous original program in which he was 20th and just qualified for the final round in the last spot. A seventh in the free skating, however, pulled him up to his final place.

In the Pairs, there was another sensational achievement, when Natasha Kuchiki and Todd Sand took the Bronze medal, pulling up from fourth in the original program. The winners were Natalia Mishkutenok and Artur Dmitriev of the USSR, with Isabelle Brasseur and Lloyd Eisler of Canada second, so North America took two of the three medals. The other two Soviet Pairs, Bechke-Petrov and Shishkova-Naumov were fourth and fifth. Calla Urbanski and Rocky Marval placed ninth and Jenni Meno and Scott Wendland, 10th.

In the Dance, it was as usual tough going, and April Sargent and Russ Witherby reversed the National result, placing ninth, with Elizabeth Punsalan and Jerod Swallow 11th. Elizabeth and Jerod had a problem in the second compulsory dance, in which they placed 17th, but were ninth in the free dance, with Sargent-Witherby, 10th in that part of the competition. The Dance winners were, surprisingly, the somewhat controversial French-Canadian couple of Isabelle and Paul Duchesnay, who defeated the defenders, Marina Klimova and Sergei Ponomarenko, by winning both the original dance and the free dance. The third place couple, Maia Usova and Alexandr Zhulin, also of the USSR, won both compulsory dances, so it was a very close competition.

Other events during the season included the NutraSweet Ice Skating Month in October 1990, with Dorothy Hamill and Chris Bowman again serving as spokespersons for the events. This promotion did much to promote the interest in and awareness of the sport which ultimately "exploded" in 1994. The NutraSweet "Giving It 100%" awards were presented at the 1991 Nationals, with the recipients being Elaine Asanakis of Delaware, who persevered over an injury and still participated in the Fours competition, Scott Davis of Montana, Troy and Dawn Goldstein of California, and Kelly Ann Szmurlo of Colorado. Another award presented by a sponsor was the "Unexpected Twist" award by Diet Sprite, which went to Elizabeth Punsalan and Jerod Swallow.

Sandwiched in between the Nationals and the Worlds were the World University (FISU) Games at Sapporo, Japan, in which a U.S. team sponsored by the U.S. Olympic Committee performed very well, winning four medals: two Gold, one Silver and one Bronze. The Golds were won by Tonia Kwiatkowski of Ohio in the Ladies and Michael Chack of New York in the Men. Kyoko Ina of New York won the Silver medal in the Ladies, while Troy and Dawn Goldstein of California were third in Pairs. The Gold medals were the first for the U.S. in the University Games since 1985, and actually were the only Gold medals won by any U.S. athletes in the multi-sport games. Scott Davis placed fourth in the Men, while Leana Naczynski of Indiana was fifth in Ladies. In Dance, Amy Webster of Boston and Leif Erickson of Wilmington, were fourth, Lisa Grove of Pittsburgh and Scott Myers of Delaware, seventh, and Wendy Millette of Delaware and James Curtis of Indianapolis, eighth.

The two usual spring events also were supported by the USFSA, with Elizabeth McLean of Delaware and new partner Ron Kravette of California placing second in the Challenge Lysiane Lauret at Grenoble, France, with Amy Webster and Leif Erickson fifth. The winners were a Soviet couple with the unpronounceable names of Aliki Stergiadu and Yuri Razguliaiev, the 1991 World Junior champions in Dance.

The Merano Spring Trophy for Junior Ladies was transferred to Ortisei/St. Ulrich, a town nearby in the Dolomites of Northern Italy, because ISU Rules no longer permitted International Competitions to be held on outdoor (uncovered) rinks. While Merano had been granted an exemption for two years, they had still failed to cover their rink. The new name was the Gardena Spring Trophy, and the U.S. Junior Ladies once again proved their supremacy in the event.

Joanna Ng of California, the National Junior Ladies Silver medalist, was the winner and Tamara Kuchiki, the older sister of Natasha, was ninth in a field of 20. The competition has remained in Ortisei since 1991.

While all this was going on, the Precision season was in full swing. The level of participation was down a little, especially on the Pacific Coast, where only three events, Junior, Intermediate and Adult were held, with 12 teams participating. The Easterns had all six events (Senior, Junior, Novice, Intermediate, Juvenile and Adult), with 38 teams in competition. The Midwesterns also had all six events, with 48 teams entered.

The 1991 National Precision Championships were held at Anchorage, Alaska, and despite the long and very expensive travel involved were quite successful, with 55 teams participating. The Haydenettes of Lexington, Mass., regained the Senior title they had lost the year before, with the Ice Cubes, also of Hayden, doing the same in the Juvenile class. However, the third Hayden team, the Ice Mates, lost their Novice title to the Starlettes of Garfield Heights, Ohio. The Junior title went to Team Elan from St. Clair Shores FSC, in Michigan, with another Team Elan from the Detroit SC winning their first title in the Adult class. The fourth Hayden team, the Esprit de Corps, was second in Adult. The Intermediate title went to the Munchkins from the Warwick (Rhode Island) Figure Skaters, for their first title.

The first National Juvenile and Intermediate Championships were held at Monsey, N.Y., in April, with 114 entries in nine events. There was a good quality of skating and, despite the relatively short time available to organize the championships, they were an unqualified success, with much credit due to the New York Regional Council and especially to Anne Gerli and Lucy Brennan of New York. In order to qualify for the championships, a skater at the Intermediate level had to have placed in the top four in a Sectional Championship. Juveniles, who competed in Singles only, had to have placed first in one of the nine Regional Championships. It is entirely appropriate to list the first "J-I" National champions as follows:

Intermediate Men Free Skating - Derrick Delmore, Washington FSC, D.C.

Intermediate Men Figures - Paul Binnebose, SC of Rockland, New York

Intermediate Ladies Free Skating - Sonia Kim, Arctic Blades FSC, California

Intermediate Ladies Figures - Laurie Kaufmann, Rye FSC, New York

Intermediate Pairs - Danielle and Steven Hartsell, Garden City FSC, Michigan

Intermediate Dance - Kara Thornham and Jonathan Magalnick, Arizona FSC

Juvenile Boys - Jonathan Keen, Orange County FSC, California

Juvenile Girls - Stephanie Stiegler, Los Angeles FSC, California

The 1991 Governing Council meeting was held at Orlando, Fla., and featured a visit to the East Coast Disney World, to match the two meetings which had been held at Anaheim, Calif., near the West Coast Disneyland. President Franklin Nelson was back from the Gulf War to preside.

The meeting was well attended, as is usually the case on the East Coast, with over 400 delegates present. The Florida resort location was no deterrent to the accomplishment of a lot of good work, as is usually the case with the Governing Council Meeting, where the level of interest and involvement of the delegates has always been enthusiastic and high. There is probably no governing body in sport that works harder.

Several By Law changes of a procedural nature were adopted, among them one to clarify that the two athlete members of the Executive Committee would be recommended by the Athletes Advisory Committee. Also added to the Board as non-voting ex officio members were three Substitute Athlete Representatives, who would act and vote in the order of their designation in the absence of any of the nine Athlete Representatives. Since 1980 when athletes became members of the Board, often their commitments prevented them from attending meetings, so the additional Athlete Representatives were intended to keep the representation of the athletes at the meeting up to full strength, if at all possible.

The fact that two additional special committees had been created, to recognize the concerns of important constituencies within the sport, and the chairmen made their first reports to the Board of Directors and Governing Council. The first, for Coaches had been established in 1990, with Ron Ludington of Newark, Del., as the first chairman. It was a lineal descendant of a Professionals Committee which had originally been created in 1937 and continued until 1953. That original committee's primary purpose had been to serve as a "placement" bureau for coaches but had also provided a means of transmitting their concerns to the then Executive Committee. The new committee would become a permanent voting committee in 1994.

The other special committee, also created in 1990, was a Parents Advisory committee, with Ann Morton Neale of Troy, Ohio, as the first chairman. Renamed the Parents Committee in 1991, the committee has provided a vital link for the communication of the concerns and recognition of parents of skaters competing at major competitions, an often ignored group. The committee provides volunteer parents to assist with the needs of parents at major competitions, such as a hospitality room, housing, transportation and the like.

Service recognition was made of many referees, judges and accountants with 25 years or more of service. Fifty year judges recognized included Wilhelm Appeltofft of Kennebunk, Maine; Janet French of Williamsville, N.Y.; Elisabeth Hickok of Wynnewood, Pa.; and Eugene Maeder of Los Angeles. Bill Appeltofft was a former International judge and current National judge. Elisabeth Hickok was a former International judge and current National judge, and Eugene Maeder had been a National judge.

As has become a tradition at the meetings, the members of the World Team were present and were recognized for their accomplishments. Also recognized were the members of the World Junior Team and the members of the World University Games Team.

An issue of the use of a member club's ice surface by an inter-club association for a sanctioned event was referred to the appropriate committees, with the sanctioning officers in the interim being directed to take into consideration the wishes of a home club when issuing a sanction to an inter-club association.

One small change in the By Laws was made to transfer Colorado to the Pacific Coast Section for the purpose of Precision team skating only, a decision based both on geography and also in an effort to strengthen the discipline on the Coast. Coincidentally, Colorado had originally been in the Pacific Coast Section up until 1948.

Tonya Harding was announced as the recipient of the 1991 **Skating** magazine "Readers' Choice Award." The award was voted by the readers of the magazine, and the tangible token of it was a silvered antique skate mounted on an ice-like Lucite surface, from the collection of Dale Mitch, then Director of the World Figure Skating Hall of Fame and Museum and a contributing editor to the magazine.

The fact that 30 years had passed since the loss of the 1961 World team at Brussels, Belgium, was remembered, with the anniversary date of Feb. 15 having occurred during the 1991 Nationals at Minneapolis. The efforts and accomplishments of the USFSA Memorial Fund in the period since were cited in an article in **Skating**, which concludes with the following statement. "The activities of the Memorial Fund, intended to serve as a living memorial, rather than a plaque, a statue, or even a building, have allowed these victims immortality by helping generations of competitive skaters who have succeeded them. The 1961 World Team will live forever in our memories through the continuing activities of the Memorial Fund."

With the season of 1991-1992 being an Olympic year, the International Competitions in which the USFSA would participate became of greater importance, since the results in them were part of the building process for the skaters involved, leading towards the 1992 qualifying competitions, culminating in the 1992 Nationals, at which the Olympic and World teams would finally be selected. For the season 12 competitions prior to the Nationals were selected, many of them familiar ones: St. Gervais, Oberstdorf, Skate America, Vienna, UK International (England), Mezzaluna (Italy), Skate Canada, Trophée Lalique (which would be held at Albertville, as the Pre-Olympic competition), Zagreb, Nations Cup (Germany), Oslo Piruetten and NHK Trophy (Hiroshima, Japan).

Before that, however, there was the 13th Olympic Festival, this time held in a large city for the first time, Los Angeles, Calif. The first Festival in 1978 drew 1,900 athletes to Colorado Springs, while in 1991 there were over 3,000 in 38 sports.

Despite the interest that had been shown in the 1984 Olympic Games at Los Angeles, the 1991 Festival was not supported by the public, drawing a low turnout of only 200,000 spectators, the lowest figure in 10 years. There was a lack of promotion locally, so that even figure skating, usually a tough ticket to get at a Festival, had plenty of seats available. Despite the poor attendance, the figure skating events were excellent competitions, and while the 1991 World Team members were not generally in attendance (with some notable exceptions), there was a high standard shown throughout.

In the Men, Todd Eldredge of Massachusetts, his real home state, the World Bronze medalist, was the winner in a field of 10. The Ladies event, with nine entrants, was won by Nicole Bobek of Colorado, defeating Tonia Kwiatkowski of Ohio. Nicole had been eighth in the 1991 Nationals and Tonia, fourth, so it was a big step forward for Nicole. Joanna Ng of California was third and Lisa Ervin of Ohio, fourth.

In the Pairs, the World Bronze medalists, Natasha Kuchiki and Todd Sand of California were the winners, with Calla Urbanski of Illinois and Rocky Marval of New Jersey second, followed by Tristen Vega and Richard Alexander of California, third, and Jenni Meno of Ohio and Scott Wendland of California, fourth. There were 12 pairs.

The Dance event was won by Elizabeth Punsalan of Ohio and Jerod Swallow of Michigan, who defeated Jeanne Miley and Michael Verlich of California, with Elizabeth McLean of Massachusetts and Ron Kravette of California third, in a field of 11.

The 1991 National Collegiate Championships returned to Lake Placid, N.Y., with the largest entry ever of 67. The turnout was disappointing in the Senior Men's event, with just two entries, and in Junior Pairs with three, and Junior Dance also with three. However, in the Ladies figures there were 22 entries and in the free skating, 39. The free skating events included the original program and the free skating. In the Senior Men, the winner was Alex Chang from Harvard, and in the Senior Ladies, Dena Galech of Shoreline Community College, while the Junior Ladies winner was Shiri Cattani of Penn State. The figure winners were: in Senior Ladies, Samantha Hawks of Boston College, and in Junior Ladies, Cathleen Reynolds of Villanova. The Junior Pairs were won by Andrea Catoia of West Chester University and Paul Dulebohn, while the Junior Dance title went to Sian Matthews and Jeremy Williams of the University of Texas. Under the eligibility rules for the championships then in effect, only one partner of a pair or dance couple needed to be a college student.

The International Competition season kicked off as usual with the Coupe des Alpes, with the same team still being sent to the two competitions which formed the cup, the Grand Prix at St. Gervais, France, and the Nebelhorn Trophy at Oberstdorf, Germany. The many years of unique co-operation between the French and the German skating federations had made the two competitions a permanent fixture on the circuit and they were very well attended, with 73 entries at St. Gervais and 76 at Oberstdorf. Actually, the Singles classes were getting "too big," with 28 Ladies at St. Gervais the largest event. Ryan Hunka of Ohio, the 1991 National Junior Bronze medalist, placed third at St. Gervais (which was won by Philippe Candeloro of France), and was the winner at Oberstdorf, with Damon Allen of Illinois, the National Junior champion, sixth in both competitions. In the Ladies Lisa Ervin of Ohio, the National Junior Ladies champion, was second at St. Gervais to Surya Bonaly of France, and sixth at Oberstdorf. The other U.S. skater, Karen Gooley of Delaware, the National Junior Ladies Bronze medalist, was seventh in France and tenth in Germany.

In the Pair events Aimée Offner and Brian Helgenberg of Delaware, the National Junior Pair champions, were fifth at St. Gervais and tenth at Oberstdorf, with the other U.S. pair of Laura Murphy of Delaware and Brian Wells of California sixth in both competitions. There were three Soviet Pairs on top in France and a Canadian Pair won at Oberstdorf.

The two U.S. entries in Dance were Elisa Curtis of Pennsylvania and Robert Nardozza of Texas, with a sixth place in France and a ninth in Germany; and Mimi Wacholder of Utah and Collin Vail Sullivan of Colorado, eighth at St. Gervais and 10th at Oberstdorf. Again Soviet and Canadian Dance couples were on the podium. The inability of the U.S. to place Pairs and Dance couples on the podium continued to be disappointing.

The 1992 World Championships had been awarded to the USFSA, to be held at Oakland, Calif. It was appropriate that Skate America '91 also be held at the same venue, but a month earlier than its normal October dates, in mid-September. Also held in conjunction with it was an official ISU Judges Seminar for the World and International Judges of the USFSA, together with several invited from Canada, who needed to attend a seminar either for retention or promotion. The seminar was conducted by Jürg Wilhelm of Switzerland, a member of the ISU Figure Skating Committee.

With the competition so early, appropriately referred to as "On the Road to Albertville," there were some unexpected results among the U.S. skaters. In the Men Christopher Bowman surprised by winning the event, with Petr Barna of Czechoslovakia, the 1991 European Silver medalist second, followed by Todd Eldredge, the National champion, third, and Michael Chack of New York fourth. As it turned out, Eldredge had a foot injury which forced him out of his second International assignment, the Trophée Lalique. In the Ladies there was an upset of sorts, when Tonya Harding defeated Kristi Yamaguchi, the reigning World champion, who suffered a fall in the free skating to place second, with Surya Bonaly third, and Tisha Walker of California sixth.

In the Pairs, there was another surprise, where Calla Urbanski and Rocky Marval won the event, while Natasha Kuchiki and Todd Sand could do no better than sixth. The latter had a disastrous free skating program, in which they finished seventh, so that in the end they placed behind Jennifer Heurlin and John Frederiksen, who were fifth. In Dance Elizabeth Punsalan and Jerod Swallow were fourth, Rachel Mayer and Peter Breen sixth, and Beth Buhl and Neale Smull ninth.

In an Olympic year, the relatively poor performances of the National champions were not a favorable portent for Olympic success. Many reasons could be advanced for the apparent low quality of the performances. One was the long post-World Tour, followed by the Olympic Festival along with the demands of many other commitments of the leading skaters of a commercial nature, all of which cut in to training time. This would be the pattern in the future as well, as the sport has become increasingly more "open" and commercial. It takes a rare skater to be able to handle all of the various obligations and at the same time remain competitive.

A return was made to the Pokal der Blauen Schwerter, the Junior competition held in the former East Germany, this time at Chemnitz in mid-October. John Bevan of Washington, the National Novice champion, was the winner, with Tanya Street of Illinois, the National Novice Ladies champion, fourth in the Ladies. In Pairs Nicole and Gregory Sciarrotta, Jr. of California were third.

Skate Canada was held as usual at the end of October, at London, Ontario, and was notable for the return to competition of Jill Trenary, after 15 months of absence due to an ankle injury and surgery which had kept her out of the 1991 Nationals and Worlds. She had elected, following her recovery, to make a try for the Olympic team in 1992, and Skate Canada was her first test. Unfortunately, it was not a successful return, as Jill could do no better than fourth, with Surya Bonaly of France, the winner.

Paul Wylie wound up third in Men, with Elvis Stojko of Canada the winner. Paul, too, had injury problems, but elected to skate with mixed success. In Pairs the best U.S. places were a fifth by Jenni Meno and Scott Wendland and a sixth by Tristen Vega and Richard Alexander, while in Dance Jeanne Miley and Michael Verlich were sixth. Interpretive events were held again and in the Ladies, Leana Naczynski of Indiana was third. Skate Canada still remained a difficult competition for the U.S.

The Trophée Lalique was held at the Olympic venue at Albertville, France, in early November, as the Pre-Olympic competition, and again, the U.S. results were not promising. In Men Paul Wylie could do no better than fifth, the event being won by Kurt Browning of Canada. (Who could imagine the reversal that would be seen between them a few short months later?) In Ladies the winner was Midori Ito of Japan, with Kristi Yamaguchi second and Nancy Kerrigan third, the best U.S. places of the competition. In Pairs Calla Urbanski and Rocky Marval were fourth, the title going to Natalia Mishkutenok and Arthur Dmitriev; while in Dance April Sargent and Russ Witherby also were fourth, the winner being a Soviet couple, Angelika Krylova and Vladimir Fedorov.

At the Nations Cup at Gelsenkirchen, Germany, a week after Lalique, things began to look up, with the U.S. taking both the Men with Mark Mitchell the winner, and the Ladies with Nancy Kerrigan the winner. Another medal was added by April Sargent and Russ Witherby taking third in the Dance, while in the Pairs, Calla Urbanski and Rocky Marval were fourth.

The Oslo Piruetten was another competition to which the U.S. sent skaters, this time to the future 1994 Olympic venue of Lillehammer. Scott Davis won the Men, while Kyoko Ina was second in Ladies to Lisa Sargeant of Canada. Junior Singles events also were held and in those, Paul Dulebohn of Delaware was third in the Men and Teresa Aiello of New York was fourth in the Ladies.

The last major International competition prior to Nationals was the NHK Trophy, held at Hiroshima, Japan, with the first string' not present. Craig Heath was eighth in Men, Tonia Kwiatkowski, eighth in Ladies, Jenni Meno and Scott Wendland, fourth and Susan Purdy and Scott Chiamulera of Michigan, eighth in Pairs. In Dance, Jeanne Miley and Michael Verlich were seventh and Elizabeth McLean and Ron Kravette, ninth.

In general, the 1991 International Competition season was at best a mixed bag, with a few exceptions.

The fall meeting of the Board of Directors was held at Colorado Springs as usual. The deaths of two well known skaters form the past were noted: Pierre Brunet, a former Olympic and World champion in Pairs with his wife Andrée, and the coach of Carol Heiss, who passed away in August at the age of 89; and Suzanne Davis King Bradshaw, the National Ladies champion in 1934 and an Olympic team member in 1932, who passed away in July at the age of 79. Also noted was the induction of Dorothy Hamill, the 1976 Olympic and World Ladies champion into the U.S. Olympic Committee Hall of Fame. Since the USOC Hall of Fame was inaugurated in 1979, Dick Button, Tenley Albright, Peggy Fleming and Scott Hamilton had previously been elected from figure skating.

Among the rule changes adopted was a recommendation that two ice surfaces be used for Regional and Sectional Championships "whenever possible," due to the ever increasing number of entries and the need for additional practice ice. Also approved was the payment by the USFSA of the entry fees of qualified competitors to the Sectionals. Approved was that Intermediate and Juvenile events be combined (that is, figures and free skating) at the Juvenile-Intermediate Nationals, with the latter to retain that name pending negotiation with the U.S. Olympic Committee for the use of the designation "Junior Olympics." Prior to the 1992 championships, the decision to combine the Singles events was reversed, with the events to be for free skating only, with no separate figure events. Also dropped was the so-called "Silver Round," which had been held for Juvenile Girls in 1991.

Another matter clarified within the International Committee rules was the basis for the reimbursement of the expenses of coaches traveling to International events with their skaters. The policy stated that coaches were also part of the teams to which their skaters belonged and would therefore be included in team activities and be expected to assist the team leaders as needed. In general, the integration of the coaches into the family of skaters and officials had been ongoing with recognized success, which the new rules and policies simply reflected.

The 1992 World Junior Championships were held at Hull, Quebec, across the river from Ottawa, with the U.S. Team coming home with two medals. For the second year in a row, Lisa Ervin of Ohio was the Silver medalist in the Ladies, again second to a French skater, this time Laetitia Hubert. After a first in the original program, a fourth in the free skating prevented Lisa from taking the Gold medal. Joanna Ng of Los Angeles, who had been second in the original program, was 19th in the free skating to wind up 14th, while the third U.S. skater, Tamara Kuchiki of Los Angeles, with a 13th and a 20th in the two parts, finished 19th.

In the Men Damon Allen came third behind two Soviet skaters, Dmitri Dmitrenko and Konstantin Kostin, while Ryan Hunka finished eighth. The 1992 World Junior Championships were the last ISU Championship in which there would be skaters representing the Union of Soviet Socialist Republics (USSR), since the rapid breakup of the Soviet Union occurred in late 1991; it was succeeded by a loose group of the former Soviet republics, initially called the "Commonwealth of Independent States" (CIS). In Pairs, with three U.S. entries, Aimée Offner and Brian Helgenberg of Delaware were fourth, Nicole and Gregory Sciarrotta, Jr., sixth and Tristan Colell and John Baldwin, Jr., of California, ninth. The best the U.S. could do in Dance was 10th, with Christina and Mark Fitzgerald of New Jersey and Delaware tenth, and the National Novice Dance champions, Nicole Dumonceaux and John Repucci of Minnesota, 19th. Once again, the weakness in Pairs and Dance at the Junior level was evident.

A major new event for the Precision discipline was an International Competition at Helsinki, Finland, held just after the New Year, at which the Haydenettes from Lexington, Mass., won the Senior Gold final; Team Elan from Detroit took the Silver medal in the Junior Gold final, and the Superettes from Warwick, R.I., the Bronze medal; and the Ice Mates, also of Lexington, won the Gold medal in the Novice Gold Final. With four medals, two of them Gold, it was certainly the most successful foray up to then into the new International scene of Precision team skating for the United States.

The 1992 National Championships went to Florida for the first time at Orlando, early in January, and were the scene at which the World and Olympic teams were selected. There were many unusual happenings at the Championships, the first of which was the withdrawal of Todd Eldredge, the defending Men's champion, due to injury. A quandary facing the International

Committee was whether, based upon his record and depending upon his medical situation, he should be selected for the teams. Also fanning the flames were allegations against Christopher Bowman, involving drugs, which ultimately required the USFSA to issue a statement to the effect that "the USFSA has no basis at this time to believe that Mr. Bowman is engaging in any type of activity which would adversely affect his eligibility to compete."

In the competition itself, Bowman claimed the vacant title, his second, with Paul Wylie second, again just edging out Mark Mitchell. In the selections for the teams, Eldredge was selected for both, while Mitchell was selected for the World Team in the place of Wylie, a compromise that had been used in the past on several occasions.

Paul Wylie

There was also "turmoil" in the Ladies, with two potential team members, Holly Cook and Jill Trenary, electing not to compete. Jill had changed coaches and was troubled by ongoing injury problems, while Cook had also changed coaches. Jill did not close the door on future competition, while Cook elected to pursue a career in the professional ranks. Jill was of course the 1990 World Ladies champion, while Cook was the Bronze medalist the same year. As a result, the battle for their places on the teams was primarily in the hands of the three medalists from 1991, Kristi Yamaguchi, Tonya Harding and Nancy Kerrigan. In the end, they finished in that order, with Lisa Ervin, the World Junior Silver medalist, in fourth. Harding had a slight injury suffered in practice, and her triple axel deserted her, never to be seen again in competition. She just held on to take the third spot on the teams.

In Pairs there was another reversal, as Calla Urbanski and Rocky Marval took the title, defeating Jenni Meno and Scott Wendland, with the defenders, Natasha Kuchiki and Todd Sand third. Calla and Rocky pulled up from third in the original program to win, with Kuchiki and Sand dropping from first to third. In the Dance April Sargent-Thomas (she was now married to John Thomas of Canada) and Russ Witherby finally won the title which they had long sought. The surprise second place winners were Rachel Mayer of Boston and Peter Breen of the Broadmoor, with Elizabeth Punsalan and Jerod Swallow, the defending champions, third. Since the U.S. was entitled to only two entries in the Olympics and the Worlds, Mayer and Breen were selected for the teams.

April and Russ were also the recipients, quite appropriately, of the 1991 NutraSweet

"Giving It 100%" Award. April had undergone emergency surgery a few days before Christmas, but had overcome the obvious obstacles involved through sheer determination and perseverance, to go on to win the couple's first National title.

The 1992 National Championship was a large competition, which necessitated the holding of the Novice events outside the main arena, a necessary but unpopular decision, since the practice rinks used were less than the best. The inability properly to showcase the lower classes at Nationals continues to be a controversial problem, with one view being that the Novice events should be separated from the main Nationals and included in the Juvenile-Intermediate Nationals. The Canadians, which have equally as large, if not larger, Nationals, have solved the problem by using at least three rinks, with separate venues being dedicated to each level and Seniors only in the main arena. This is fine if the rinks can be found, but it inherently limits the available sites for the Nationals, which would affect the traditional rotation between the Sections. There are some who feel that the rotation should be dropped and the Nationals awarded to the best possible venue regardless of Section. That too remains an unresolved issue.

The 1992 Nationals had 253 entries in 18 events, broken down as follows: Senior - 97; Junior - 78; and Novice - 72. In the six figure events, there were 71 entries. The separation of the figures from the main Nationals is another problem which so far remains unresolved. Essentially, there is no real will to streamline the Nationals, despite the many good reasons for doing so.

Unfortunately, the 1992 Nationals had an unpleasant aftermath, with the alleged failure of the local organizing committee to account properly for the net proceeds and the ultimate removal from the Association of the sponsoring club, the Orlando FSC. The issue remains unsettled more than three years later.

The results of the first elections to the United States Figure Skating Hall of Fame were announced at the 1992 Nationals and the inductions made of those present. Those elected were:

Ardelle K. Sanderson of Lake Placid, a long time World and National judge and a former National competitor in Singles, Pairs and Fours;

The late William Thayer Tutt of Colorado Springs, the head of The Broadmoor Hotel and the promoter and organizer of the World Championships of 1957, 1959, 1965, 1969 and 1975, the World Junior Championships of 1985, and the ISU Congress of 1984;

Karol Kennedy and Peter Kennedy of Seattle, World Pair champions 1950, North American Pair champions 1949, 1951, National Pair champions 1948-1952, Olympic Silver medalists 1952;

Yvonne Sherman Tutt of Colorado Springs, North American Ladies champion 1949, National Ladies champion 1949-1950, World Ladies Silver medalist 1949 and World Ladies Bronze medalist 1950, National Pair champion (with Robert Swenning) in 1947;

The late Lois Waring McGean and her husband J. Michael McGean of Norwich, Vt., National Dance champions 1950 and 1952, winners of the first International Competition in Ice Dancing in 1950. Lois was also National Dance champion with Walter H. Bainbridge, Jr. in 1947-1949;

James D. Grogan of California, World Silver medalist 1951-1954, Olympic Bronze medalist 1952, North American Silver medalist 1947,1949,1951, National Silver medalist 1948-1949, 1951-1952;

Judy Schwomeyer Sladky of Indianapolis and James Sladky of Rochester (N.Y.), North American Dance champions 1971, National Dance champions 1968-1972, World Dance Silver medalists 1970, World Dance Bronze medalists 1969,1971-1972;

Dorothy Hamill of Connecticut, World Ladies champion 1976, Olympic Ladies champion 1976, National Ladies champion 1974-1976, World Silver medalist 1974-1975;

Charles Tickner of California, World champion 1978, National champion 1977-1980, World Bronze medalist 1980, Olympic Bronze medalist 1980;

Tai Babilonia and Randy Gardner of California, World Pair champions 1979, National Pair champions 1976-1980, World Pair Bronze medalists 1977-1978, Olympic Team members 1976 and 1980.

At the same time, by a vote of the Electors, 14 U.S. persons who had originally been elected to the USFSA Hall of Fame prior to 1984 were transferred to the United States Figure Skating Hall of Fame. They were (with the year of their original election shown in parentheses) as follows:

The late Irving Brokaw (1976), of New York, Champion of America 1906, the first U.S. competition in the Olympic Games of 1908, Honorary President of the USFSA, author of the definitive work **The Art of Skating**;

The late A. Winsor Weld (1976), of Boston, the first President of the USFSA 1921-1925, President of The Skating Club of Boston 1913-1924, Honorary President of the USFSA, the "founder" of the USFSA;

The late Theresa Weld Blanchard (1976), of Boston, the first National Ladies champion 1914, 1920-1924, the first North American Ladies champion 1923, National Pair champion (with Nathaniel W. Niles) 1918,1920-1927, North American Pair champion (with Niles) 1925, long-time editor of **Skating** magazine;

The late Sherwin C. Badger (1976), of New York and Boston, North American champion 1923, National champion 1920-1924, National Pair champion (with Beatrix Loughran) 1930-1932, Olympic Pair Silver medalist (with Loughran) 1932, World Pair Bronze medalist (with Loughran) 1930,1932;

The late Maribel Vinson Owen (1976), of Boston, North American Ladies champion 1937, National Ladies champion 1928-1933,1935-1937, North American Pair champion (with George Hill) 1935, National Pair champion (with Thornton Coolidge) 1928-1929, (with George Hill) 1933,1935-1937, World Silver medalist 1928, Olympic Bronze medalist 1932, World Bronze medalist 1930;

Eddie Shipstad (1976) and the late Oscar Johnson (1976), of St. Paul, a legendary comedy team, who with Roy Shipstad (elected in 1995) were the founders of the Ice Follies professional touring ice show;

The late Heaton R. Robertson (1977), of New Haven, President of the USFSA 1940-1943, Honorary Vice President of the USFSA, long-time judge and referee;

The late Nathaniel W. Niles (1977), of Boston, National champion 1918, 1925, 1927, National Pair champion (with Theresa Weld Blanchard) 1918, 1920-1927, North American Pair champion (with Blanchard) 1925, the first editor of **Skating** magazine;

The late Harold Hartshorne (1981) of New York, National Dance champion (with Nettie Prantel) 1937-1938, (with Sandy McDonald) 1939-1941, World Championship judge and member of the ISU Dance Committee;

The late George H. Browne (1983) of Cambridge, the first Secretary of the USFSA, Honorary President of the Cambridge Skating Club, prolific student and author of the sport, organizer of the first exhibition of the International Style of skating in America in 1908, and an active judge;

Eugene Turner (1983) of California, the first National Senior champion from the Pacific Coast, National champion 1940-1941, National Pair champion (with Donna Atwood) 1941, show skater and long-time teaching professional.

With the Olympic and World teams selected, the stage was set for the XVI Olympic Winter Games, to be held at Albertville in the Savoy region of France, the first Winter Games in that country since Grenoble, just down the road, in 1968, and the third overall. The first Winter Games were held at Chamonix, also nearby, in 1924.

Probably the overriding aspect of the Games was the fact that the Soviet Union was no longer represented, but at the insistence of the International Olympic Committee, the former Soviet republics had agreed to send a team (under the banner of the IOC), which was called the "Unified Team," or as the acronym was in French: "EUN." The three Baltic republics, Estonia, Latvia and Lithuania, having all declared their total independence and not being a part of the EUN, were all very quickly elected to membership in the IOC and ISU before the Games, quite appropriately, since all three countries had been ISU members before their occupation by the Soviet Union in World War II. Also, with the simultaneous breakup of the former Yugoslavia, it had been necessary for the ISU to take quick action, again at the insistence of the IOC, to admit as members the new independent nations of Croatia and Slovenia, since IOC rules now provided that entrants had to belong to a member of their International Federation in order to be eligible to participate in the Games.

The number of entrants in the Games was the largest up to that time, with 31 Men, 29 Ladies, 18 Pairs and 19 Dance couples, for a total of 97 entries and 134 skaters. The event which created the greatest surprise and excitement from the standpoint of the Americans was the Men, with both the expected and the unexpected happening.

As one of the pre-Olympic favorites, Viktor Petrenko of the EUN, the 1988 Olympic Bronze medalist, was the winner, but the unexpected was the Silver medal finish of Paul Wylie. In third place, winning the Bronze medal was Petr Barna of Czechoslovakia, the 1992 European champion. Paul and Petr had stood third and second after the original program, with Paul taking second in the free skating. There were many who felt that Paul should have won the free skating, which would have given him the Gold medal, since he skated a generally clean program while Petrenko, who started out and did well for most of his program, "ran out of gas" near the end, with some minor technical errors. For Paul, it was a complete vindication of his dedication and hard work and a well deserved medal.

In another unexpected result, Kurt Browning of Canada, the reigning World champion, could do no better than sixth in the free, after a fourth in the original, to finish sixth overall. Curiously, it was his double axel that deserted him in his hour of need. Christopher Bowman performed very well after a seventh in the original program to take fourth. Todd Eldredge, skating by reason of his "bye," was still not in top form and finished 10th.

In the Ladies "form" held up better, with Kristi Yamaguchi the winner as expected, to become the fifth U.S. lady to become an Olympic Ladies champion. Nancy Kerrigan let Midori Ito slip "off the hook," after she was fourth in the original program, but was second in the free skating, to take the Silver medal. Nancy, who was second in the original program, placed third in the free skating to take the Bronze medal, with Tonya Harding, who had been sixth in the original program, finishing fourth, still without the triple axel.

In Pairs Natasha Kuchiki and Todd Sand could not repeat their performance of Munich in 1991 and were sixth. The winners were Natalia Mishkutenok and Artur Dmitriev of the EUN, with only Isabelle Brasseur and Lloyd Eisler of Canada, who took the Bronze medal, breaking the Eastern grip on the top five places. Calla Urbanski and Rocky Marval, the National Pair champions, found themselves in 10th place after an 11th in the free skating, while Jenni Meno and Scott Wendland, after a 12th in the original program, redeemed themselves with a ninth in the free skating (which might well have been higher as they were clearly undermarked), to take 11th.

The Dance event went to Marina Klimova and Sergei Ponomarenko of the EUN, who completed their set of three medals started in 1984. Isabelle and Paul Duchesnay of France, skating before their home audience, never really seemed to get going, and were not a threat to the winners, although they did defeat Maia Usova and Alexander Zhulin of the EUN for the Silver medal. April Sargent-Thomas and Russ Witherby placed 11th and Rachel Mayer and Peter Breen 15th.

Despite the somewhat disappointing result in Pairs and Dance, the U.S. came away with three medals, one of them Gold, equaling the number of medals earned in 1988.

The 1992 World Championships were held at Oakland, Calif., and represented the eighth time the championships had been held in the United States, as seen from the following list of the venues:

New York - 1930; Colorado Springs - 1957, 1959, 1965, 1969, 1975; Cincinnati - 1987; Oakland - 1992.

Once the "ice was broken," as it were, after World War II, with the first North American Worlds being those of 1957, the scheduling of the Worlds outside Europe, either in Asia or North America, was fairly well recognized and accepted. The first Worlds in Canada had been at Montreal in 1932, with the first post-war championships being those at Vancouver in 1960; while the first Worlds in Asia had been those at Tokyo, Japan, in 1977. The Oakland Worlds were the first held on the Pacific Coast and were well organized through the efforts of the San Francisco Bay Area clubs. Despite Paul Wylie's Olympic Silver medal, the prior selection decision which replaced him at Worlds with Mark Mitchell remained in effect and was not reversed. Another absentee was Midori Ito, who elected not to compete and subsequently announced her retirement from competition. The Soviet skaters were listed as being from "CIS," the acronym for the designation of the "Commonwealth of Independent States," and skated under the banner of the ISU.

Viktor Petrenko of CIS repeated his Olympic win to take the Men's World title away from Kurt Browning of Canada, the defending champion, who did redeem himself somewhat for his poor Albertville showing by placing second; his teammate, the rising star Elvis Stojko, took the Bronze medal, just ahead of Christopher Bowman. Mark Mitchell did well in his first Worlds, placing fifth after an eighth in the original program and a fourth in free skating. Todd Eldredge, with two sixth places in the two parts, curiously wound up seventh.

In the Ladies Kristi Yamaguchi retained her title, while Nancy Kerrigan took the Silver medal although her performance was not distinguished. In third was Lu Chen of China, another rising star, who had been Bronze medalist in the World Juniors in both 1991 and 1992. So at least two of the three medals were retained by the U.S. Tonya Harding, with a sixth in the free skating, ended up in that position.

The results in Pairs and Dance were about what one would have expected after the Olympics. This time Calla Urbanski and Rocky Marval placed seventh, just edging out Natasha Kuchiki and Todd Sand, while Jenni Meno and Scott Wendland were 11th. In the Dance April Sargent-Thomas and Russ Witherby got into the top 10 at ninth place, which meant a second entry in 1993, with Rachel Mayer and Peter Breen placing 15th. The winners were Klimova and Ponomarenko, with Usova-Zhulin second, the Duchesnays having elected not to enter, so in third place were Oksana Ghitschuk and Evgeni Platov. As a result, the medal count was just the two earned by Yamaguchi and Kerrigan.

The Basler Cup Dance competition was held in February in Basel, Switzerland, with one U.S. entry, Wendy Millette and Jason Tebo of Boston, placing second to an Italian couple. The two post-Worlds competitions were also held as usual, with the first alternate Dance couple being sent to the Challenge Lysiane Lauret dance event, this time at Morzine once again. Elizabeth Punsalan and Jerod Swallow were fourth behind one CIS couple, a Latvian couple and an Italian couple. In the Gardena Spring Trophy at Ortisei, Italy, there were two U.S. entries, with Lefke Terzakis of Texas taking third and Lisa Matras of Michigan, fifth.

The 1992 National Precision Championships were held at Portland, Maine, the same site that had been used twice for Skate America. A new event was added, a separate original program for the Senior class. The championships continued to grow with 67 teams participating in 22 events, since elimination and Silver rounds were held in all classes except Senior. In the Senior class, the Haydenettes of Lexington, Mass., continued their dominance, winning their second straight and fourth overall title. Team Elan of Detroit, their closest rivals, were second in the Gold final and won the Senior original program, in which the Haydenettes placed third. A new team, the Crystallettes of Michigan won the Junior Gold title, while the Esprit de Corps from Hayden won their first Adult Gold title. The Ice Mates, another Hayden team, regained the Novice title they had previously held in 1990, while in Intermediate, the Munchkins of Warwick, R.I., retained their Intermediate crown, as did the Ice Cubes from Hayden, their Juvenile title. The championships represented an outstanding effort by the teams from the Hayden Recreation Centre FSC, which won four of the six final round events.

One downside event in what was otherwise an upbeat year, was the death in March, 1992, of F. Ritter Shumway, at the age of 85. Ritter was the senior Past President of the USFSA at the time of his death and was still serving as Chairman of the USFSA Memorial Fund Committee, a position he had held since 1971. He was an active competitor and champion in Veterans Dance, but will always be remembered for his wholehearted dedication to the cause of the Memorial Fund since its inception in 1961.

The second Juvenile-Intermediate National Championships were held at St. Clair Shores,

Michigan, in April, 1992, and were again a large competition, with 116 entries in seven events. Although there was no Juvenile Pair event, what was encouraging was the size of the entry in the Intermediate Pairs, with 13 entries, and in the Intermediate (12) and Juvenile (17) Dance events with a total of 29 entries. The champions were as follows:

Intermediate Men - Dwayne Parker, Philadelphia SC and HS

Intermediate Ladies - Melissa Paul, Los Angeles FSC

Intermediate Pairs - Whitney Gaynor, Peninsula FSC, and Thomas Branch, St. Moritz ISC

Intermediate Dance - Mica Darley, All Year FSC, and Casper Young, Los Angeles FSC

Juvenile Boys - Jered Guzman, Los Angeles FSC

Juvenile Girls - Jacqueline Redenshek, Mentor FSC

Juvenile Dance - Christie Moxley and Thomas Gaasbeck, University of Delaware FSC

It is worth mentioning these young champions, as hopefully among them are the top skaters of the future.

The 1992 Governing Council meeting was held at Anchorage, Alaska, a first for the Association, just as it had been for the National Precision Championships the year before. Despite the distance from the "lower 48," the meeting was well attended. Among the highlights of the meeting every year are the honors and awards, and this time a most popular one was the selection of Paul Wylie to receive the fourth "Reader's Choice Award" of **Skating** magazine. Also honored was another group of 50 year judges: Margaret Marshall Berglund of the Chicago FSC, a High Test and former Silver Dance judge; Paul W. Church of the Duchess FSC of Poughkeepsie, New York, a Silver Dance judge; Doris Tufts Heinold of The SC of Boston, a National judge and Virginia Vale of the Los Angeles FSC, a National judge. Very special among such honorees are those who have never, for one reason or another reached the National level, but have continued to labor faithfully in the vineyards (read: ice rinks) for all those years. They truly are the dedicated ones.

The member recognition program was also continued with the recognition of member clubs which had reached 25 and 50 years of membership. The membership of the Association from a club standpoint has been remarkably stable, with many clubs in the 25 year range and quite a few at 50.

The meeting also represented a change in administration, with President Franklin Nelson of Oakland, Calif., stepping down after three years, including his Persian Gulf stint, and being replaced by the first woman President, Claire W. Ferguson, of Jamestown, R.I. Franklin has continued his activities as a Medical Advisor to the ISU, as well as serving on the Executive Committee, in his capacity as immediate Past President until 1995. He was elected an Honorary member of the USFSA upon his retirement from office and an Honorary member of the Board of Directors in 1995.

An appropriate memorial resolution was adopted for F. Ritter Shumway. In addition, the usual resolutions of congratulations for the Olympic, World and World Junior teams were also adopted.

In the legislation considered and acted upon by the meeting, there were several matters of importance. One was an ongoing effort to refine, clarify and improve the procedures for the handling of grievances. Further, the mandate of the Membership Committee, as contained in the By Laws, was expanded to include the development of programs designed to provide growth in all categories of membership.

A procedural rule was adopted which required that all actions or motions presented to the Governing Council resulting in increased expenditures must be presented together with a financial analysis. Also approved was the removal of all references to gender in the By Laws and Rules.

In the technical field, an ad hoc committee was to be appointed to consider how and in what way compulsory figures could be retained as a viable part of the sport. The concept of a "Pro-Am" Dance competition was approved, and another special committee was to be appointed to deal with protocol and sponsors. At the same time, the separate Basic Skills and Competitions Committee was discontinued and its functions transferred to a subcommittee of the Membership Committee. The committee had begun in 1987 and had done much useful and progressive work in expanding the "learn to skate" programs offered by the USFSA, under its long-time chairman, Cindy Geltz of New Jersey. The registration program for Basic Skills skaters started with a total of 28,653 in 1988-1989, and had increased by 1991-1992 to 57,135, or almost 100 percent increase. The curve would continue upward until the total of 74,023 was reached at the end of 1993-1994, while for 1994-1995 there was a slight drop to 70,223, still a significant total for the programs, of which "Skate With U.S." is a part.

The final major event of the 1992 season, while not having a direct impact on the USFSA, was still of importance to it, was the observance of the 100th Anniversary of the ISU at Davos, Switzerland, in June, followed by the 44th Congress. As part of the Jubilee observance many of the former World champions were invited to attend. Among those from the United States were Carol Heiss Jenkins and Hayes Alan Jenkins, while from Canada there were Frances Dafoe, Donald Jackson, Barbara Wagner and Robert Paul, and Barbara Ann Scott King. Several books were published in observance of the Anniversary and which were "unveiled" during the Jubilee, including **Skating Around the World, the 100th Anniversary History of the ISU** by Benjamin Wright, the ISU Historian; **ISU Officeholders Through the Years**, originally prepared by the late Dr. James Koch of Switzerland, Honorary President of the ISU, and updated and finished by Benjamin Wright; as well as books containing the results of all the major ISU Championships from 1968, when the 75th Anniversary was held, up through 1991, compiled by committees for the respective disciplines.

The elections in 1992 were once again for a two year term only, as an interim measure to realign by 1994 the elections and terms of the ISU Officeholders to the Olympic cycle. President Olaf Poulsen of Norway was returned to office, as was the Vice President for Figure Skating, Josef Dedic of Czechoslovakia. There was, however, a considerable turnover among the other officeholders. Among those retiring were Donald Gilchrist of Canada, a Council member, and Benjamin Wright, Chairman of the Figure Skating Committee, both of whom were elected Honorary members of the ISU. As a consequence the formal representation of the USFSA in the ISU was down to just three persons: Charles DeMore, as a Council member, Franklin Nelson, a Medical Advisor, and Patricia French, who continued to serve as a member of the ad hoc committee for Precision Team skating, which was continued to the next Congress in 1994.

The principal action taken was a further liberalization of the eligibility rules to permit the reinstatement with the right to compete of formerly ineligible persons. Member associations would also be able to organize and conduct purely "professional" competitions. The impact of this change would soon be felt, with the next Olympic Winter Games being just two years away in 1994, as a result of the shift in the cycle between the Summer and Winter Games mandated by the IOC.

In the sports themselves, special rules were adopted for the new discipline of Precision Team skating, as well as for the Interpretive free skating program, while in ice dancing, rules revisions were accepted reconfirming and emphasizing the relationship of the discipline to its ballroom dancing origins.

In ISU Championships, a qualifying round consisting of free skating only was accepted for Singles, with 24 skaters to enter the final round, which would be a complete competition in itself. A form of seeding, based upon the ranking earned in the prior year, was also accepted for both the qualifying and final rounds.

The changes in rules accepted would have a significant impact in the years to come, but perhaps not as foreseen by those who voted for them.

The countdown to the 1994 Games in Norway began almost immediately, under the temporary two-year cycle mandated by the IOC. Coupled with this was the revision of the eligibility rules adopted by the 1992 ISU Congress, which permitted the reinstatement of an ineligible (professional) person to full eligibility (including the right to compete), with such a

The Winds of Change Begin to Blow (1993-1995)

reinstatement to be permitted only once. For reinstatement Internationally, the deadline was April 1, 1993, while for domestic purposes, the deadline was Sept. 1, 1992.

Almost immediately after the adoption of the reinstatement rule revision, interest was expressed by several prominent skaters including, among others, Brian Boitano, Elaine Zayak, Christopher Bowman, Renée Roca, Susan Wynne, Judy Blumberg and Joseph Mero from the United States, Katarina Witt of Germany, Jayne Torvill and Christopher Dean of Great Britain, Viktor Petrenko, now of Ukraine, Ekaterina Gordeeva and Sergei Grinkov, and Natalia Mishkutenok and Arthur Dmitriev, now of Russia, and Georgi (Gorsha) Sur, formerly of the Soviet Union, the partner of Renée Roca, who would be reinstated by the USFSA. Not all of those reinstating actually returned to eligible competition, and some eventually again became ineligible. The leader of the movement to permit reinstatement with the right to compete was Boitano, and he did indeed follow through, as will be seen.

At the same time, following the collapse of the Soviet Union and the breakup of East Germany, an effort was made by quite a few coaches, from the former Soviet Union especially, to emigrate to the United States to find work. The coaches often brought with them former Soviet dance couples and pairs to train in the United States, although the latter did not in most cases, if Internationally-ranked, renounce their former allegiance to the successor republics of the USSR for the purpose of competition. There were a few, however, who came before 1991 by defecting, notably in 1989, Igor Shpilband, who wound up in Detroit as a coach, and Gorsha Sur, who went to Colorado, where he teamed up with Renée Roca, first as coaches and a non-eligible dance team, and then as eligible competitors in 1993.

Despite the liberal immigration policy of the United States toward former Soviet citizens and its long history of accepting foreigners, there has been a controversy over the arrival of the former Soviet coaches and athletes, and a considerable "backlash," which at least in so far as the latter are concerned, has resulted in a considerable tightening up of the eligibility rules for competition.

With respect to the coaches, it should be noted that historically, virtually all the top coaches in the United States from the earliest days of the sport have been foreign-born. The number of native-born Americans achieving the highest rank in the coaching profession is very few, for example, Howard Nicholson, Frank Carroll, Ron Ludington, Eugene Turner, William Swallender and Maribel Vinson Owen. Among the foreign coaches, on the other hand, are George Muller, Willi Frick, Montgomery Wilson and Cecilia Colledge in Massachusetts, Bror Meyer, Willi Böckl and Pierre Brunet in New York, Gustave Lussi in Pennsylvania and Lake Placid, Walter Arian in Ohio, Edi Scholdan in Massachusetts and Colorado, Eugen Mikeler and John Nicks in California, Carlo and Christa Fassi in Colorado and California, Hans Gerschwiler in New Jersey, Cliff Thaell, Fritz Dietl and Peter Burrows in New York, Otto Gold, who also taught in the United States, and Werner Rittberger in Canada, and many others.

The presence of the former Soviet coaches in the country needs to be put into a long-term perspective. In general, foreign-born coaches are nothing new and collectively they have made a tremendous contribution to the development of the sport in the United States. Those who have arrived in recent years, from the former Eastern Bloc nations, have had a difficult time making the adjustment to the way of teaching in the West, as distinguished from the East, but they still have begun to make a material contribution to the improvement of American skating, especially in Pairs and Dance.

It is also a curious fact that among the skaters arriving from the East in recent years, almost all of them have been male ice dancers. Virtually no Singles or Pair skaters have appeared here, although in some of the countries outside the U.S., Pair skaters at least can be found.

Prior to 1991, the rules in the U.S. were the same as those of the ISU, which basically required merely one year of residence in the host country, plus the consent of the two federations involved, for a skater to compete in a foreign country of which he/she was not a citizen. There were some former Soviet skaters who qualified under these rules and were "grandfathered" under the more restrictive rules which have been adopted since 1991. Today, the rules basically require an entrant in qualifying competition to be either a U.S. citizen or the holder of an Alien Registration Card (permanent resident). For non-U.S. citizens, the old one year of residence rule still applies, if the skater has no record and is not a member of a foreign association. For those under 18 who have a competitive record ("National or higher"), the consent of the foreign association is required, as is residence in the United States for one year, while residing with one or both parents or a legal guardian who is "legally employed" in the United States. The rules effectively prevent skaters from abroad from competing in the U.S. on any short-term (one year or less) basis, at least until they acquire their Alien Registration Cards, unless they have no prior competitive record.

Why are the majority of the incoming skaters male ice dancers, one might ask? Simply speaking, because of the lack of sufficient male American ice dancers, and a majority of lady ice dancers without partners. In the case of Gorsha Sur, efforts to obtain U.S. citizenship for him on an accelerated basis through special legislation (a private bill) in Congress, in order to enable him to compete in the 1994 Olympic Winter Games, further "fanned the flames," although in the end, the effort failed. Olympic rules require citizenship in the country to be represented in order to be eligible to compete.

The 1992-1993 season started conventionally enough. There was no Olympic Festival in the summer of 1992 since it was an Olympic year, with the Summer Games in Barcelona, Spain. However, the 1992 National Collegiate Championships were again held at Lake Placid, at the end of August, with a somewhat reduced entry, and unfortunately, no Men's or Dance events, and just one pair event for Juniors with two entries, with the winners being Erin Covington and Brandon Powell of Clackamas Community College. In the Senior and Junior Ladies Figures there were 17 entries, while in the Senior and Junior Ladies Free Skating there were 27 entries. The winner of the Senior Ladies Figures was Sarah Gendreau of Pierce College, and in the Junior Ladies Figures the winner was Desirée Toneatto of West Chester University. In the Senior Ladies Free Skating, the winner was Sara Kastner of the University of St. Thomas, and in the Junior Ladies the winner was Amy Ross of Boston University.

The International season included nine competitions prior to the end of the year 1992: St. Gervais, Oberstdorf, Vienna, Skate America (Atlanta, Georgia), Prague, Skate Canada (Victoria, British Columbia), Nations Cup (Gelsenkirchen, Germany), Trophée Lalique (Paris), Piruetten (Lillehammer, Norway) and NHK Trophy (Tokyo). To these would be added the World University (FISU) Games in Zakopane, Poland, in February 1993, the Basler Cup (Basel, Switzerland) in Ice Dancing and the Gardena Spring Trophy (Ortisei, Italy) for Junior Ladies.

Another major International event would be the Snowflake International Precision Competition to be held at Minneapolis in early January 1993. Perhaps the most unusual development was the scheduling of two "Pro-Am" competitions, between eligible and ineligible skaters, the first in Hershey, Pa., in November 1992, and the second in April 1993, in Los Angeles, with the payment of prize money to those participating. The competitions were open only to U.S. skaters, since they were conducted under USFSA and not the ISU rules, the ISU, as yet, not having permitted the holding of such competitions with International skaters participating. The permission to conduct Pro-Am competitions had been granted by the ISU as a "clarification" of its rule change permitting the Member associations to conduct purely "professional" competitions.

The first competitions of the International season were the Coupe des Alpes events at St. Gervais, France, and Oberstdorf, Germany. The results were mixed, with two medals at St. Gervais and none at Obertsdorf. In the former, Daniel Hollander of Michigan, the 1992 National Junior Silver medalist, placed third in the Men, and Tamara Kuchiki and Neale Smull of California, a new combination, placed third in the Dance. Coincidentally, the same skaters placed fourth in their respective events at Oberstdorf. In Ladies, Caroline Song, the 1992 National Junior Ladies champion, was sixth in France and 10th in Germany. Also competing in the Men was John Baldwin, Jr., of California, sixth in France and 11th in Germany.

In Pairs, Nicole and Gregory Sciarrotta of California, the 1992 National Junior Pair champions, were fifth and fourth, while Dawn Piepenbrink of Arizona and Nick Castaneda of California, the National Junior Pair Silver medalists, were seventh and sixth, respectively, in the two competitions. Also in the Dance were Cheryl Demkowski of Delaware and Sean Gales of Indiana, the National Junior Dance Silver medalists, who were fifth and seventh in their events.

The USFSA was not in the running for the Coupe des Alpes, placing third, with Canada the overall winner. Among the winners in the two competitions were Surya Bonaly in the Ladies at St. Gervais and David Liu of Chinese Taipei, second in the Men at St. Gervais and the winner at Oberstdorf. In Dance, the first International success of Shae-Lynn Bourne and Victor Kraatz of Canada can be seen, winning both Dance events.

At the end of September 1992, the Vienna Cup was held, with one man, one lady and one Dance couple being entered from the U.S. The best place achieved was the sixth of Ryan Hunka of Ohio, the 1992 National Junior champion. The winner was the ultimate European champion, Dmitri Dmitrenko of Ukraine. Jennifer Itoh of California could do no better than 13th in the Ladies, while in Dance, Mimi Wacholder of Utah and Collin Vail Sullivan of Colorado were seventh.

Skate America, or "Sudafed Skate America International," to name its title sponsor, was held at Atlanta, Ga., at the end of October, with the "first" team on hand, so the results were better. U.S. Men made a sweep of the medals by Todd Eldredge, Scott Davis and Mark Mitchell, in that order, defeating among others, Viacheslav Zagorodniuk of Ukraine and Philippe Candeloro of France. In the Ladies, Nancy Kerrigan was second, losing to Yuka Sato of Japan, with Nicole Bobek sixth and Lisa Ervin eighth. The winners in Pairs were Marina Eltsova and Andrei Bushkov of Russia, with the U.S. Pairs, Calla Urbanski and Rocky Marval, Tristen Vega and Richard Alexander of California, and Karen Courtland of Delaware and Todd Reynolds of Texas, fourth, fifth and sixth respectively. A fourth U.S. Pair, Laura Murphy and Brian Wells of Colorado, were ninth.

The Dance was won by Maia Usova and Alexandr Zhulin of Russia (now training in Lake Placid with their coach Natalia Dubova, who was a resident there), Elizabeth Punsalan and Jerod Swallow of Colorado, who had just announced their engagement, were third, with Wacholder and

Sullivan ninth. So the medal count for the home forces was five: one Gold, two Silver and two Bronze.

At Prague just a week later, Rudy Galindo continued his remarkable career by placing second in Men, to Masakazu Kagiyama of Japan. The Pairs produced a win for the new team of Jenni Meno and Todd Sand of California, while in Dance another new combination of Jennifer Nocito and Michael Verlich of California were third.

Sunlife Skate Canada International (to give it its full name, including that of the title sponsor), was held in just another week at Victoria, British Columbia, with the U.S. team coming away with one medal, that of Scott Davis, second in the Men to Elvis Stojko of Canada. In Ladies, Tonya Harding-Gillooly was fourth after a poor original program, the eventual winner being a Russian, Maria Butyrskaia, with Alice Sue Claeys, formerly of the U.S. now representing Belgium, second, and Josée Chouinard of Canada third.

The results in Pairs and Dance were less inspiring. In Pairs, Katie Wood and Joel McKeever of Delaware were seventh, and Murphy and Wells were eighth. In Dance, the best U.S. place was that of Punsalan and Swallow, fifth. The winners were Susanna Rahkamo and Petri Kokko of Finland.

The next competition was the Nations Cup again held at Gelsenkirchen, Germany, with two medals being won. Todd Eldredge of Massachusetts, took the Men's event over a future star, Alexei Urmanov of Russia, with the ever-present Viacheslav Zagorodniuk of Ukraine third. In Ladies, Tonia Kwiatkowski of Ohio placed fifth, just behind Oksana Baiul of Ukraine. Surya Bonaly of France won the event. In Pairs, Kyoko Ina of New York and Jason Dungjen of Delaware placed second to Mandy Wötzel and Ingo Steuer of Germany, a new combination. In Dance, Amy Webster and Ron Kravette, another new combination, placed fifth just behind a Canadian couple, Jacqueline Petr and Mark Janoschak, fourth. The winners were from Russia, Krylova and Fedorov.

Following the Nations Cup by just another week (as was the case in November each year, with a competition on each weekend throughout the month), was the Trophée Lalique at Paris. Here the U.S. enjoyed another success when Mark Mitchell of Connecticut won the Men's event, defeating both the top Frenchmen, Eric Millot, second, and Philippe Candeloro, fourth. In the Ladies, Tisha Walker of California was eighth, with Surya Bonaly winning. Alice Sue Claeys of Belgium was fifth. In Pairs, Karen Courtland of Delaware and Todd Reynolds of Texas, were third behind the winners Evgenia Shishkova and Vadim Naumov of Russia, and Radka Kovarikova and René Novotny of Czechoslovakia second, a very strong event. Rachel Mayer and Peter Breen of Massachusetts were eighth in Dance, the winners being Sophie Moniotte and Pascal Lavanchy of France.

While all this was going on, the "Chrysler Concorde Pro-Am Figure Skating Challenge," the first-ever competition for eligible and ineligible skaters, was held at Hershey, Pa., on Nov. 23 and 24. Such events featured limited fields and this first competition was for Men and Ladies only, with prize money being awarded for the top four places (Gold - $50,000; Silver - $30,000; Bronze - $25,000; and Fourth - $20,000). Modifications were made to the standard rules covering the technical program (the former original program, which had been renamed in 1992), which would be worth one-third of the total score, and free skating, called the "artistic" program, worth two-thirds, with time limits for the programs being lifted, vocal music being permitted, and with no penalties to be imposed for elements not strictly in accordance with the standard rules. The judges were all holders of ISU appointments as International or World judges, while the referees were either World or National.

Two ineligible (professional) and two eligible (amateur) skaters competed in each event. The strength of the fields was excellent, with Scott Hamilton, Paul Wylie, Todd Eldredge and Mark Mitchell in the Men; and Rosalynn Sumners, Nancy Kerrigan, Tonya Harding-Gillooly and Caryn Kadavy in the Ladies. The competition was aptly described by the ever-articulate Paul Wylie: "This was a breakthrough event – unprecedented. It's a new way to see skating. It was important for the gap to be bridged between amateurs and professionals."

Nancy Kerrigan won both parts in the Ladies to easily take the first prize, with Harding-Gillooly second, Kadavy third and Sumners fourth. In the Men, Wylie was the winner, by pulling up in the free skating to overtake Mitchell, who had led after the technical program. Scott Hamilton was third, and Todd Eldredge, fourth. Paul did his dramatic number to music from the movie "JFK," and it was, as is noted in the report "vintage Wylie." He surpassed his Olympic performance and actually received six perfect marks for artistic impression.

Despite the problems of the standard and level of difficulty to be required, and the rather broad differences between the eligible and ineligible skaters in athletic difficulty on the one hand and in artistic development on the other, the relative success of the event resulted in its permanent inclusion in the schedule in the future (as long as title sponsorship could be maintained, since the revenue from gate receipts was nominal). When a new contact was signed with ABC Sports in 1994, the National Championships, Skate America, two Pro-Am competitions and one show of the Tom Collins Tour of World Champions would be included in the package, in order to insure television coverage for them. While achieving that goal, this agreement has locked Skate America and the Pro-Ams into the schedule-making adjustments or revisions of the three events difficult. It also presents a degree of commercial risk, if in the future public interest in such events and therefore the ratings decline.

The next event on the International schedule was the Piruetten, at Lillehammer, Norway. Michael Chack of New York, was the winner of the Men's event, while Michelle Cho of California, the 1992 National Novice Ladies champion, was the winner of the Ladies. Tristen Vega and Richard Alexander of California were fourth in Pairs. The winners were Mandy Wötzel and Ingo

Steuer of Germany. In Dance, Amy Webster of Massachusetts and Ron Kravette of California were fourth, the winners being Susanna Rahkamo and Petri Kokko of Finland. The fields in the competition were large and quite strong, since Lillehammer was the site for the forthcoming 1994 Olympic Winter Games, although the figure skating events were actually to be held in the city of Hamar, south of Lillehammer.

As usual, the last International competition in the pre-Nationals season was the NHK Trophy at Tokyo, Japan, early in December, 1992. (NHK, incidentally, is the acronym for the National Japanese television network, which is the title sponsor.) The best the U.S. team could do was one medal in Pairs by Calla Urbanski and Rocky Marval who placed third, with Shishkova-Naumov and Eltsova-Bushkov of Russia, first and second. Tracey Damigella, formerly of Boston and now in California after a sojourn in Australia and a ranked singles skater of some years earlier, was now skating Pairs with Doug Williams, and they placed sixth. Fourth in the event were Isabelle Brasseur and Lloyd Eisler of Canada, to give an idea of the strength of the field.

Philippe Candeloro and Surya Bonaly were the winners of the Men and Ladies, to take two Gold medals for France. Aren Nielsen of Ohio was fifth in the Men, and Craig Heath of California, 11th, Kyoko Ina of New York, in her Singles "mode," was eighth in the Ladies, with Lisa Ervin of Ohio 10th. Among those seen in the events were Elvis Stojko of Canada, second, and Alexei Urmanov of Russia, third, in the Men, while in the Ladies, Yuka Sato of Japan was third and Chen Lu of China was fourth, certainly a preview of things to come!

The Snowflake International Precision Competition, just after the New Year, was run under the new ISU rules in Minneapolis and was a very successful event, with 24 teams from eight countries represented (Canada, Finland, Great Britain, Italy, Japan, South Africa, Switzerland and USA). The Senior Canadian team from Quebec "Les Pirouettes de Laval" continued to demonstrate their excellence by winning the Senior Free Skating Final Round, as they had in Snowflake I at Boston, but the gap between them and the rest of the World was clearly closing. Second in the event were the Rockettes from Finland, with the Haydenettes of Massachusetts third. Happily, however, in the new Senior technical program held as a separate event, the Haydenettes were the winners with the Rockettes second.

Junior and Novice events were also offered. The Crystallettes of Michigan won both the Junior technical program and final round free skating, with two Finnish teams, "Step By Step" and "Team Fintastic," in the other two places. There were only two U.S. teams in the Novice free skating event, with the "Windjammers" of Minnesota the winners.

The Fall 1992 meeting of the Board of Directors was held as usual in Colorado Springs. One matter in the financial field was the plan to explore the establishment of a separate, "universal," non-profit entity for the annual running of major events such as Skate America. This exploration is still going on, with an ultimate objective of the formation of a "subsidiary," under which all the income derived from the holding of major events can be sheltered from the other revenues and income of the Association and the Memorial Fund.

The return to competition of those reinstated was recognized, by providing that skaters with uninterrupted eligibility would not be displaced by formerly ineligible skaters. At the same time, those reinstatees who were former World or U.S. Team members would have to qualify for the Nationals through the Sectionals, but were exempted from having also to enter Regionals to qualify for the Sectionals.

Approved for qualifying competitions was the classification of "Announcing Coordinator," to match the earlier designation of Music Coordinators and to complete the support staff for competitions with persons who were qualified and recognized as such.

The Board also recommended an increase in registration fees for members of member clubs, from $10.00 to $20.00, with the year for the payment of dues and fees to start on Oct. 1, rather than July 1. In the end the Governing Council, at its 1993 meeting, would approve an increase to $15.00. At the same time the annual fee for Basic Skills members was set at $4.00. The Basic Skills membership has become an increasingly important part of the constituency of the Association, as previously noted. For example, the tally as of September 1992, was 57,135 registered in the "Skate With U.S." program. At the same time, the number of regular registered members was 45,311 in September 1992, with the total membership reaching 102,446, representing an increase of 14,313 over the prior year, including the Basic Skills members.

In the area of figure tests, in which the High tests (Fifth through Eighth) had been split in 1992, so that the tests could be taken in halves, test fees for the split tests were established, at $1.00 less than the fee for the complete test. Also approved was the awarding of the Gold lapel pin to skaters passing the Gold Free Dance, Adult Gold Free Dance or Masters Gold Free Dance Test.

The meeting recognized the state of ice dancing and the general decline in standards and places in competition. The formation of a joint Dance Committee project was approved to improve the competition standings of U.S. dance couples, by identifying the reasons for their lack of success, designing a program to introduce the new ISU dances; to provide training materials and to publish information for judges, coaches and skaters. This project has been ongoing since, and much useful work has been done and information disseminated, but so far an improved standard of U.S. ice dancing with the consequent increase in the number of medals earned has been slow to materialize.

The 1994 World Junior Championships were held for the first time in Seoul, South Korea, at the beginning of December 1993. The U.S. was represented by a team of three Men, three Ladies, two Pairs and once Dance couple, and managed to return with two Silver medals. Michael

Weiss of Washington placed second in the Men, behind Evgeni Pliuta of Russia, with John Bevan of Spokane, Washington fourth, and Ryan Hunka of Ohio, the 1992 National Junior champion, a somewhat disappointing ninth. The results were really a reversal of the National places, since Weiss had been fifth in Orlando, Bevan fourth and Hunka first.

In the Ladies Lisa Ervin of Ohio was second for the third year in a row, losing this time to Kumiko Koiwai of Japan. Lisa actually was fourth in the technical program, and had to place second in the free to make it to the podium. While a Silver medal in a World championship is a high reward, it is still not the Gold, and the failure of Lisa to win the World Junior Ladies title after three tries was obviously a disappointment for her and the Association. The other two U.S. entrants did not fare very well, with Nicole Bobek of Colorado placing sixteenth and Caroline Song of California, the 1992 National Junior Ladies champion, placing nineteenth. Nicole had been seventh in the technical program, but finished eighteenth in free skating, while Song was twentieth in the free skating.

Two young U.S. pairs did well, finishing fourth and fifth, with two Russian and a Canadian pair ahead of them. In fourth were Robin Heckler of New York and Jeff Tilley of Delaware, with the 1992 National Junior Pair champions, Nicole and Gregory Sciarrotta of California, fifth. The winners, with the usual unpronounceable names were Inga Korshunova and Dmitri Savaliev of Russia.

It was the same in the Dance, with a Russian couple, Ekaterina Svinina and Sergei Sakhovski winning. In second was a very promising young couple from Poland, Sylwia Nowak and Sebastian Kolasinksi, which was not unexpected, since there has been a good tradition of ice dancing in Poland. The lone U.S. couple, Christina Fitzgerald of New Jersey and her brother Mark from Delaware, were seventh.

It is in the World Juniors that the competitors from the former Soviet republics can be seen, such as Estonia, Latvia, Ukraine and Uzbekistan. Representation from them would continue to increase over the following years, although in many cases the skaters were themselves ethnic Russians residing in the newly independent republics. The same would also be seen with the former Soviet judges, many of whom would be found in the future in republics other than those of their original representation.

An unexpected event occurred at the end of November 1992, when the Memorial Fund received the sum of $116,302.12 (to give the exact amount), from the Hettie and Ritter Shumway Community Fund of the Rochester (New York) Area Foundation. The title of the report of the donation is most appropriate: "A Generosity Without End," and reflects the ongoing legacy of Ritter and Hettie. It was during his long-time leadership of the Memorial Fund that the assets had grown from $100,000 to over $3,000,000. With the arrival of such events as the Pro-Ams with prize money involved, the focus of the Memorial Fund could now be redirected more towards the lower and grassroots levels of skating. This was something that Ritter had always wanted to do, but had never been able to carry out completely in the past. It was now possible, not only because of this most generous donation in his memory, but also because of the greater amounts of funds for the World Team skaters available from other sources.

The 1993 National Championships journeyed to Phoenix, Ariz., and the America West Arena there – another first for the championships to be held in the sunny Southwest. It was a very large competition, with 254 entries in 18 events, reflecting 344 individual skaters. The Senior free skating events alone had 77 entries and 116 skaters in four events. The Figures, with six events in all, had 71 entries and was really a major championship in itself. (The merits of holding the figure events at another time and place remains a controversial issue, as yet unresolved.)

The Senior Singles events are, of course, the ones that catch the attention of the public and 1993 was no exception. Scott Davis, representing the Broadmoor SC, became the new National Men's Champion, succeeding to the title vacated by Christopher Bowman. Scott had to come from behind in the free skating to overtake Mark Mitchell, who had won the technical program. Scott could be proud to bring back to his home town of Great Falls, Mont., another National title, just as his predecessor John Misha Petkevich had done in 1971. Todd Eldredge, the former champion now representing Detroit, was still not fully recovered from the various injuries and problems that had plagued him in 1992, and could do no better than sixth after a third in the technical program, and was off the World Team. The third-place finisher was Michael Chack of Rockland, N.Y., coming up from a seventh place the year before but could be no more than an alternate to the Worlds, since the U.S. was entitled to only two entries.

In the Ladies, with Kristi Yamaguchi no longer present, the title was open, and Nancy Kerrigan, representing the Colonial FSC of Massachusetts, rose to the challenge to win her first (and what would turn out to be her only) National Ladies title, by winning both parts. The surprising result was the failure of Tonya Harding-Gillooly of Portland, to make the World Team. Tonya was second in the technical program, but placed fourth in the free skating (her triple Axel no longer being there), and was passed by two young skaters from Winterhurst, Ohio (pupils of Carol Heiss Jenkins), Lisa Ervin, who took second after being fifth in the technical program, and Tonia Kwiatkowski, fourth in the technical program and third in the free skating. Since the U.S. would have three entries in the forthcoming Worlds at Prague, the team would be Kerrigan, Ervin and Kwiatkowski.

The Pairs event saw another close fight for the title, with Calla Urbanski of Delaware and Rocky Marval of New York, successfully defending the title they had won the year before, the only Senior champions to repeat. Second was the new team of Jenni Meno of Ohio and Todd Sand of California, with Karen Courtland of Delaware and Todd Reynolds of Texas, third. Only the top two Pairs would go to Prague.

In Dance, Renée Roca and Gorsha Sur, representing the Broadmoor SC, won the title by placing first in all four parts (two compulsory dances, the original dance and free dance), defeating a new combination of former champions Susan Wynne of Philadelphia and Russ Witherby of Wilmington, Del., (Russ was actually the defending champion), with the 1991 champions, Elizabeth Punsalan, representing the Broadmoor and Jerod Swallow of Detroit, placing third. Amy Webster of Boston and Ron Kravette of California were fourth, with the 1992 Olympians, Rachel Mayer of Boston and Peter Breen of the Broadmoor, fifth. It has been said that Gorsha was the first foreign-born skater to win a National championship, but, of course, this was not true. That distinction went to Norman Scott and Jeanne Chevalier of Canada, the first National champions in Men and Pairs, respectively, in 1914. Someone in the media is always trying to come up with some new angle without checking the past, which perhaps is one reason for this history having been written! Actually, there was another foreign-born champion in the person of Rosemary Beresford of Great Britain, who was the National Ladies champion in 1918.

Noteworthy in the Figures competition was the third straight win in the Senior Ladies by Kelly Ann Szmurlo of the Broadmoor. Michael Weiss of Washington was the winner of the Junior Men's free skating, and Michelle Cho of California added the Junior Ladies free skating title to her Novice win of the prior year, one of those rare doubles. In the Junior Dance, there was yet another foreign born winner in Michael Sklutovsky, formerly of Russia, with Kimberly Hartley, representing the Indiana/World Skating Academy. Michael was one of the "grandfathered" former Soviet ice dancers; others were Max Sevostianov, representing Delaware, 12th in Senior Dance with Galit Chait, representing New York; and Oleg Fediukov, representing Providence, third in Novice Dance with Julieanna Sacchetti, representing Boston.

Altogether, there were seven foreign skaters in the championships, four from Russia, and one each from Australia, Canada and Great Britain. As already mentioned, the USFSA rules in 1993 were more restrictive than those of the ISU, requiring an "application" for permanent resident status by a non-citizen, in addition to having been a resident for one year.

Another issue surrounding the foreign skaters was the level at which they should enter the U.S. qualifying structure. There was a case of a Russian ice dancer with experience at the International Senior level, who competed with an American girl at the Novice level. This issue was addressed and the rules changed in 1993 to provide that a determination would be made by the Chairman of the Competitions Committee of the competition level for the skater to enter the system, based upon the prior record of the skater abroad. So bit by bit, as such issues were raised and controversy arose among the "natives," the rules were gradually tightened to make it increasingly difficult for foreign skaters to participate in the U.S. qualifying structure. Broader questions involving the families of the American partner providing complete financial and other support to the foreign partner are issues that remain unresolved.

Ironically, in one case an American lady and a Russian man who competed in the U.S. subsequently moved on to represent Israel, and the original Russian partner who came to the U.S. was replaced with yet another Russian. There is another example of the strange twists that can occur, in which an American girl who went to Germany to skate with a German partner has now changed partners, and is representing Germany with a partner from Belarus, who is a Russian! The stories are endless. An American man who skated in Pairs for Greece and an American lady who skated in Dance for Hungary, and so on. In every case, the combinations were permitted by the existing ISU rules. There is really no solution to the phenomenon of Americans skating for other countries and of foreigners skating for America. Still, the issue has always generated "heat" in both directions.

Several outstanding champions and "builders" of the Association were duly inducted into the United States Figure Skating Hall of Fame at the 1993 Nationals: the late Past Presidents Walter S. Powell and Harry N. Keighley; the legendary former World Pair champion and long-time coach, John Nicks; Nancy Rouillard Graham and Ronald Ludington, Olympic Bronze medalists in 1960 and four-time National Pair champions; Tim Wood, two-time World champion in 1969-1970, Olympic Silver medalist in 1968, World Silver medalist 1968, and three-time National champion 1968-1970. Tim was also North American champion in 1969; Colleen O'Connor and Jim Millns, Olympic Bronze medalists in 1976, and three-time National Dance champions 1974-1976; and Linda Fratianne Maricich, two-time World Ladies champion, 1977, 1979; Olympic Silver medalist 1980, World Silver medalist 1978 and Bronze medalist 1980, and four-time National Ladies champion 1977-1980.

Following the Nationals, the 1993 World University (FISU) Games took place in February at Zakopane, Poland, a very well known ski resort in the High Tatra Mountains along the border with Slovakia. With the support of the U.S. Olympic Committee, a representative team was fielded, which did well. In the Men, Damon Allen of Colorado placed second, after a third in the technical program, with the winner being Yueming Liu of China. Craig Heath of California placed fourth. Kyoko Ina of New York, showed her skill as a Single skater was still there by placing second in the Ladies to Junko Yaginuma of Japan, also after a third in the technical program. The second U.S. skater, Andrea Catoia of Delaware, placed sixth.

In Pairs, there were just three entries. The U.S. took first and third, with Dawn Piepenbrink of Arizona and Nick Castaneda of California taking a first-ever Pair Gold medal in the Games for the U.S., while Dawn and Troy Goldstein of California placed third. The Dance was almost as successful, as Wendy Millette and Jason Tebo of Massachusetts took third, the winning couple being Katerina Mrazova and Martin Simecek of Czechoslovakia. As for other Americans, Mimi Wacholder of Utah and Collin Vail Sullivan of Colorado were fifth, and Ann-Morton Neale of Delaware and Robert Peal of Illinois were ninth in Dance. With five medals, one Gold, two Silver and two Bronze, it was the most successful result for the U.S. in the University Games since the five medals won at Lake Placid in 1972.

Also held in February was the Basler Cup Dance Competition at Basel, Switzerland, which had temporarily replaced the Challenge Lysiane Lauret Dance competition in France on the schedule. The one U.S. couple, Jennifer Nocito and Michael Verlich of California, placed second behind Irina Lobacheva and Ilia Averbukh of Russia. Averbukh had been the World Junior Dance champion in 1990 with another partner, a typical case for a Soviet World Junior champion.

The 1993 World Championships were held at Prague, Czechoslovakia, which shortly thereafter would become the Czech Republic when the Slovak Republic separated from the original "dual" country and became an independent state. The Championships were well organized, although ISU Vice President Josef Dedic (who was the general chairman) became ill just as the competition started and later that same year passed away. Fortunately, Dr. Gerry Bubnik, a lawyer who had attended Harvard Law School, took over and ran an excellent event.

From the U.S. standpoint, the championships were the lowest point in the fortunes of the Team since just after the air accident in 1961. The U.S. won no medals at all for the first time since 1964! The best place earned by an American skater in the championships was a fourth place in the Men by Mark Mitchell, in his first Worlds. Scott Davis, the National champion, after a seventh in the technical program, finished sixth. In the Pairs, Meno and Sand overturned the National result by placing fifth, with Urbanski and Marval, the National champions, eighth. Roca and Sur were 11th and Wynne-Witherby, 15th in Dance.

The big disappointment, however, was in the Ladies, where Nancy Kerrigan, after winning the technical program, could do no better than ninth in the free skating to finish fifth overall. The Ladies winner was the young, seemingly fragile Ukrainian, Oksana Baiul, while in the Men Kurt Browning of Canada redeemed himself by winning decisively, with his compatriot Elvis Stojko second. The Canadians also took the Pair title with Isabelle Brasseur and Lloyd Eisler, the first for Canada since 1984, while in the Dance, Maia Usova and Alexandr Zhulin of Russia finally captured the title that had eluded them in the past.

Also in the Ladies, Lisa Ervin placed 13th, while Tonia Kwiatkowski was 16th in her elimination round group and did not make the final round. The new system of elimination rounds involved the free skating only and were used to reduce the field to a final 24 (which, after 1994, would be changed to provide for 30 to enter the short program, with a subsequent reduction to 24 for the final free skating).

The elimination rounds are held at the beginning of the week of the championships, with everyone performing their long free skating in two groups. The final round, consisting of both the technical program and free skating, then commences a day or two later, depending upon which event goes first, Men or Ladies. It is a very stressful situation for the competitors, much like the pressure of the technical program, and the elimination rounds have not proven to be the best solution to the ever-increasing number of entries in the World Championships.

The final competition of the season was the Gardena Spring Trophy for Junior Ladies at Ortisei, Italy, in April, at which Michelle Kwan of California won her first International competition, representing yet another win in this competition for a future star. Jenna Pittman of Delaware was second.

Following the Worlds, the Precision season was in full swing, culminating in the National Precision Championships at Detroit at the end of March, the 10th anniversary of the event. It was the largest ever, with 1,700 skaters on 73 teams being entered in seven final events, seven Silver or consolation events and no less than 14 elimination rounds. In Senior and Junior, a technical program was skated as a separate medal event. The new program was similar to those required in Singles and Pairs, and of the same duration of two minutes and 40 seconds, with five required elements: a circle, line, block, wheel and intersecting maneuver.

The Haydenettes (Senior team)

The teams from the Hayden Recreation Centre FSC of Lexington, Mass., continued their domination of the championships by again winning the Senior (Haydenettes), Novice (Ice Mates), Adult (Esprit de Corps) and Juvenile (Ice Cubes) final round events, with the Senior team also winning the technical program. The remaining final round events were the Junior, won by the Miami (Ohio) University team (which also won the technical program), and the Intermediate final round, which was won by the Munchkins of the Warwick Figure Skaters of Rhode Island. All in all, it was a most successful championship and a bright future for the discipline seemed obvious.

The second Pro-Am competition, the Hershey's Kisses Pro-Am Figure Skating Championships, was held at Los Angeles early in April, with leading eligible and ineligible skaters again competing against each other for total prize money of $310,000. In the Men, it was Scott Hamilton, Brian

Boitano and Paul Wylie as the ineligibles, with Scott Davis, Mark Mitchell and Michael Chack as the eligibles; while in the Ladies, it was Jill Trenary and Caryn Kadavy versus Nancy Kerrigan, Lisa Ervin and Tonia Kwiatkowski. Rosalynn Sumners had to withdraw due to an injury. The six eligible skaters represented one Olympic and two World medals, and two National championships, but the ineligibles represented two Olympic titles, seven World titles and 11 National titles. When all was said and done, the ineligibles had swept the Men's division and won both Pro-Am titles, and deservedly so. Brian Boitano, one step removed from his return to regular eligible competition, was the Men's winner, taking the $40,000 first prize, although there were many present who could make a good case for Scott Hamilton, who placed second, followed by Wylie, Mitchell, Chack and Davis, in that order. Even Davis in last place took home $20,000. Wylie was fifth in the technical program, but pulled up in the free skating to take third place. Under the rules for the event, Hamilton was allowed to do his back flip, to which he added three triples, earning him one perfect mark and only losing out by four judges to five.

In the Ladies, a very popular win was that of Caryn Kadavy over Nancy Kerrigan. Nancy suffered three falls in her free skating, but still was able to finish second and take home $30,000 (since she had won the technical program) with Ervin third, Trenary fourth and Kwiatkowski fifth. Caryn's comment on winning was, "This was like the Olympics I never had." This win in the second Pro-Am launched her on a very successful career in such competitions, as well as in those strictly for the professionals, where she continues to demonstrate her classic and elegant style.

In summing up the first two Pro-Ams, a report stated: "For spectators, they present a chance to see the nation's top skaters, regardless of eligibility, go head-to-head. For the professionals, they give the opportunity to once again compete, pitting the benefits of maturity against the limits of age. And for the eligible skaters, the Pro-Ams offer a chance for the athletes to see how they compare to figure skating's past heroes. What seems to be unique about the Pro-Am concept is that each skater brings something different to the competition, whether it's the ability to play to the crowd, display graceful and fluid movements, or showcase extraordinary athletic ability, a Pro-Am puts it all out in one competition." The real risk of the event, as previously noted, is its commercial viability and the willingness of sponsors to assume the substantial financial risk that goes with it. Whether the Pro-Ams will last remains an unanswered question.

One phenomenon of the increased public interest in the sport and heightened television coverage was a significant increase in the number of major sponsors. In her message in January 1993, President Ferguson summarized the situation. "The largest contributors to our sport are event title sponsors and presenting sponsors who make a significant financial contribution to the Association and underwrite a specific competition. Other sponsors...provide print advertising and discounts on air travel for USFSA skaters and officials in addition to a financial contribution...(or) provide the USFSA and its athletes, officials or USFSA functions with products, as well as financial support throughout the year...Our gross corporate sponsorship dollars are 20 times what they were five years ago."

A large part of the sponsorship scene has also been the Tom Collins Tour of World Figure Skating Champions, which has become a major undertaking with many shows in cities across the country, and which has provided funding to the participating eligible skaters, as well as direct financial support to the USFSA. The Tour probably has done more to promote public interest in the sport than any other continuing activity, apart from television, at least in North America, and its success is in large measure due to the entrepreneurial skill and energy of Tom Collins himself.

The third Juvenile-Intermediate Championships were held in mid-April in Great Falls, Mont., with 132 entries in 11 events. For the first time "A" and "B" events were held in Pairs and Dance, a division based upon age, with the "B" event being for the older skaters. The Singles events still were combined and included figures. The Intermediate Dance events were compulsory dances and an original set-pattern dance, while the Juvenile Dance events were compulsory dances in both an initial and final round, with all couples skating in both rounds. Once again the entry in Pairs and Dance was encouraging, with a total of 12 Intermediate and 20 Juvenile Pairs and 15 Intermediate and 24 Juvenile Dance, among the various divisions. The 1993 championships were the first in which Juvenile Pairs were included. The first winners were:

Juvenile Pairs "A" - Meredith Ward and James A. Ward III, Tampa Bay FSC

Juvenile Pairs "B" - Christina Connally and Arnold Myint, Nashville FSC

The 1993 Governing Council meeting was held at Cleveland, a return to that city after 21 years. There were 217 clubs represented by delegates and proxies, which made the meeting one of the largest ever. The appointment of Jerry Lace of Colorado Springs as the new Executive Director of the USFSA was announced, succeeding Ian Anderson who had resigned in August 1992, after eight years of service as Executive Director. Past President Oscar Iobst had willingly stepped in to serve as Interim Executive Director for the 1992-1993 season, until a permanent replacement could be found. Oscar did an outstanding job for nine months and was "rewarded" with a new wife in the person of Maggie Heimbecker, who was serving as the Office Manager at Headquarters. They were married in April just before the meeting.

Jerry came to the USFSA from the comparable position with the U.S. Cycling Federation, which he had joined in 1987 after serving since 1973 with the U.S. Olympic Committee as Assistant Executive Director and Director of Operations. Joining Jerry in a new position, Executive Business Director was Robert T. Crowley of Philadelphia, where he had served as Executive Director of the Indiana/World Skating Academy. Previously, he had been Skating Director and Head Coach of the Great Falls (Montana) FSC and of the St. Lawrence FSC in

Canton, New York. Bob was a USFSA Gold Medalist and former National competitor, and had also served as a Vice President and Treasurer of the Professional Skaters Guild of America (PSGA).

As President Ferguson stated in her message: "Jerry Lace is recognized as a leader within the Olympic Movement and we feel his experience in running a successful national governing body will make him an excellent addition to the USFSA. Bob Crowley will bring vast figure skating experience to the Association. I am confident that we have two of the best people in the sports industry to join our federation." President Ferguson further went on to define the duties and responsibilities of the two new Directors. As Executive Director, Lace would be responsible for all business-related matters, including the negotiation of sponsorship contracts for the Association, the overseeing of all marketing and sponsorship programs and the coordination of all major events. Crowley would be responsible for the overall management and operation of the USFSA Headquarters in Colorado Springs and would implement all policies adopted by the Board of Directors and the Governing Council. He would also be responsible for the implementation and administration of the USFSA's annual budget and would be in charge of the selection and recruitment of all paid personnel.

The fifth annual Readers' Choice Award of **Skating** magazine went to Scott Davis, the current National champion. The award is voted on by the readers of the magazine, which had by 1992-1993 reached a paid circulation of 32,800.

There was a lot of detailed legislation carried out at the meetings, with that of the Board of Directors preceding the Governing Council meeting. In the area of competitions, the effort to restructure the National Championships was still on the agenda, with a further task force to be appointed to review the possible separation of the Novice events from the Senior and Junior events. The extension of the use of the standard USFSA contract for the Nationals to the National Precision Championships, Skate America International and the Snowflake International Precision Competition was also approved, as these events have become larger and more important in the overall schedule.

With the 1993-1994 Olympic season just ahead, the selection of International Competitions was critical to the strategy of providing the best opportunities for qualified skaters seeking to make the team to participate. Included were the Coupe des Alpes (St. Gervais and Obertsdorf); Skate America at Dallas, Texas; Piruetten at Hamar, Norway, the Olympic venue; Skate Canada at Ottawa; Trophée Lalique at Paris; Nations Cup at Gelsenkirchen; and NHK Trophy at Chiba, Japan, the venue for the 1994 Worlds. Competitions for the spring season included the Basler Cup (Dance) at Basel, Challenge Lysiane Lauret (Dance) at Morzine, and Gardena Spring Trophy (Junior Ladies) at Ortisei, with a Precision International Competition at Helsinki in January – 12 in all. Competitions originally selected and later dropped included Budapest, Vienna, Prague, Mezzaluna (Dance) and Chemnitz (Junior). As can be seen, the selection was of the major International competitions, which, while providing exposure for potential team members, also gave them time to train.

In the area of judging, the ongoing problem of the apparent conflict of interest for competitors who were both judges as well as teachers in the Eligible Skater Instructor Program (ESIP) was addressed, with a proviso that such persons could either coach or judge/trial judge at a test session or competition, but not both at the same time. It was also at this meeting that Dorothy Burkholder of Chicago was appointed an Honorary National Judge.

In membership matters, a restriction was included in the rules to permit only one ineligible or restricted person to serve as a director of a member club. Also approved was a directive to the Executive Committee to prepare amendments to the By Laws to remove the dues structure from Articles XXIV and XXV and to incorporate them into the Membership Rules, with the necessary amendments to be presented to the 1994 Governing Council meeting. This proposal would simplify the revision of the dues structure, although any changes would still be subject to the review of the Governing Council. Over the years the member clubs had jealously guarded their right to keep dues down, even when need otherwise dictated an increase. On the other hand, when an increase did not directly affect the clubs, they would quickly vote for it, such as the increases in the dues of Individual Members already referred to.

In Precision, the technical program and the free skating program were retained as separate events for another year, except that teams seeking consideration for International competition would have to enter both categories and a combined result would be calculated, to be used in the selection process. Also established was a Collegiate Precision division. Following the leadership of the Miami (Ohio) University team, which was, in 1993, the National Junior champion, and with Precision team skating subsequently being recognized by the University as an official varsity sport, interest in Precision skating in colleges and universities had grown rapidly.

Among those reinstated as eligible persons could be found the name of Scott Hamilton. He had requested no publicity for his application and said afterwards that he wanted to show his support for the USFSA. "I didn't reinstate for publicity reasons. I have no formal plans as far as reinstatement is concerned. I just wanted to leave my options open. And this is a good way to remain involved in the organization and to continue to promote the sport."

The Long Range Planning Committee and the Sponsorship Committee were added as permanent committees, making a total of 17 in all, with 10 voting and seven non-voting. The mandate of the Long Range Planning Committee was deceptively simple: "To develop a workable plan to ensure the future programs and stability of the Association in all areas of its involvement." For the Sponsorship Committee, the mandate was: "To formulate policy with respect to commercial sponsors to be approved by the Board of Directors, to assist in the maintenance of sponsorship agreements and to monitor the efforts on behalf of the USFSA to obtain sponsors."

Probably the highlight of the meeting, and an innovation of President Ferguson, was the consolidation of all the awards and recognitions made each year into a gala banquet. This first such banquet was an outstanding affair and has set the pattern for the future, enabling the Association to recognize properly its skaters, officials, clubs and volunteers in a suitable and dramatic setting. A large part of the success of the banquets has been due to the permanent master of ceremonies, Harry Gleeson, now of Cleveland and the son-in-law of Past President Chuck DeMore. Harry has orchestrated an increasingly sophisticated format, assisted by the Tom Collins audio-visual crew, so that the affair is now really the major event of the meeting.

Among those honored at the meeting were Scott Hamilton, the first recipient of the "Spirit of Giving" award, which is presented to a skater who has excelled, not only on the ice, but also by giving back to the figure skating community. Also recognized were the living Past Presidents, of whom there were then eight, with six of them present, headed by Frederick LeFevre of Williamsburg, Va. The Past Presidents were thanked for their distinguished service, and received a very special gift, which included an annual invitation, tickets and accreditation to the National Championships for life.

Others recognized included Joe Serafine of Chicago, best known as the "Ice Technician" at many National and International events held in the United States over 20 or more years. Another dedicated volunteer recognized was Nancy Meiss of Cincinnati, a long-time World and National Judge, who in 1987 had been co-chairman of the organizing committee for the Worlds. Tom Collins of Minneapolis also was recognized as a benefactor and friend of the figure skating community through his Tour of World Champions.

During the Governing Council meeting, Ben Wright received the F. Ritter Shumway Award of the PSGA, which is presented to individuals distinguished for their contribution to the world of figure skating. Appropriately, the winner of the award in the prior year, Joe Serafine, was also present. At the banquet, Ben was also honored as a 50 year judge and his wife Mary Louise as a 50 year National judge, the latter a quite unique distinction. The only other person known to have achieved that plateau was the late Roger Turner of Boston.

The USFSA Coaches Committee announced the recipient of the 1993 Paul McGrath Award for Choreography, Sarah Kawahara of California. The award is given to a coach who has excelled in choreography for a specific work or a body of work in figure skating. The award is made in memory of Paul McGrath of Boston, a National Junior and professional champion and a long-time coach who was well known for his innovative choreography and outstanding program design. The award had first been presented in 1992, with the first recipient being Sandra Bezic of Canada.

Also announced at the meeting were the results of the annual elections to the World Figure Skating Hall of Fame, which included two Americans, Ronnie Robertson and Richard Dwyer of California. Robertson had been an Olympic Silver medalist in 1956 and a two-time World Silver medalist in 1955 and 1956. He is perhaps best remembered for his outstanding spins, one of which was called the "blur." He was probably one of the best ever in that lost art. Richard Dwyer had a very brief but successful competitive career, having been both National Novice (1948) and Junior (1949) champion and National Senior Bronze medalist (1950); Dwyer had enjoyed an outstanding professional career ever since, including 32 years with the Ice Follies, in which he was the successor to the late Roy Shipstad as "Mr. Debonair."

Also noted was the death of Andrée Brunet. (With her late husband Pierre, she was twice Olympic champion in 1928, 1932, and four-time World champion in Pairs in 1926, 1928, 1930, 1932.) She passed away at the end of March at her home in Boyne City, Mich., at the age of 91. The Brunets were elected to the World Figure Skating Hall of Fame in the first election held in 1976. Through the good offices of Hayes and Carol Jenkins, the Museum was able to obtain the World and Olympic medals and certificates emblematic of the championships won by the Brunets, as well as some very rare film of their skating, which now form part of a significant display for this legendary pair in the Museum.

Created in mid-1993, as a follow-up to discussions at the meetings, were two new special committees: Collegiate Program and Ethics. The former, with Patricia Hagedorn of Lexington, Mass., as its first chairman, represented a transfer from the Program Development Committee of responsibility for the promotion of the sport in colleges and universities. As figure skating programs in educational institutions had grown and matured, the need for a permanent committee to provide liaison and support for them had become evident. Thus, the new committee was formed, just as had been the case when other developmental programs were in due course transferred from Program Development to the mainstream of the administration of the Association.

The Ethics Committee, with Nancy Piro of Danville, Calif., as the first chairman, reflected the need that had been recognized by President Ferguson for the updating and streamlining of the USFSA Code of Ethics, including the procedures under it for the handling of grievances. The process (which had begun before the Kerrigan-Harding affair in 1994 emphasized the urgent need for it), would take two years to be fully implemented. Finally in 1995, the Ethics Committee and a new Grievance Committee both became permanent committees, together with a completely new Article in the By Laws covering grievance and disciplinary proceedings, including suspension, expulsion and the loss of membership privileges. The entire effort can be considered one of the major achievements of President Ferguson's administration.

With the Governing Council meeting, the 1992-1993 season officially came to an end, but one season soon becomes another and there is really no seasonal break as there used to be in the days of outdoor skating. The season ahead would turn out to be either "earthshaking" or "cataclysmic," whichever adjective one wishes to apply to it!

Another major impact on the face of the Association would be seen in the fall of 1993, when Skating magazine again returned to the "full" size (8-1/2 by 11 inches) format that had been in effect from 1966 to 1969. This time, however, there were to be six issues of the magazine each year, with a supporting bimonthly newsletter; in fact, there would really be 12 issues a year, with the volume and issue numbering remaining the same. The newsletter would quickly become much more than that, lacking only the coated paper stock and color, but otherwise being a complete magazine. Added to the magazine were several new departments, including "Beginner's Edge," a layman's column answering a spectrum of questions that a beginner might have; "Ask the Experts," where technical questions would be responded to; and "Center Ice," a guest editorial or parting word, just to name three of them, plus, for the first time, a "Letters to the Editor" department.

Appropriately, the feature article in the first large size issue of October 1993, (Volume 70, Number 8), covered the 1993 Olympic Festival, the first major event of the new season held at San Antonio, Texas. Skating was the first major event in the brand new Alamodome, which drew over 25,000 spectators, for the largest audiences ever to watch Festival figure skating. In hindsight, 1993 may well have been the height of Festival success from the figure skating standpoint, especially in view of the anticipated demise of the event in its original form, with the Festival of 1995 presumably being the last.

The events in 1993 were still at the Senior level and included 34 entries in the four disciplines. The team format of the previous Festivals was abandoned, with individual prizes only being awarded. In the Ladies, Michelle Kwan of California was the winner. Just 13 years old, Michelle became the youngest figure skating Gold medalist in the Festival up to that time. Coincidentally, Jenna Pittman of Delaware was second to Michelle, just as she had been at Ortisei a few months earlier.

The Men's winner was Michael Chack of New York, for his first Senior title. The durable Rudy Galindo of California, still skating very well in Singles, placed second, pulling up from fourth in the technical program to overtake Damon Allen and Aren Nielsen.

In the Pairs, Karen Courtland of Delaware and Todd Reynolds of Texas, the National Senior Pair Bronze medalists, took the Festival title over Kyoko Ina and Jason Dungjen of New York. In Dance, the winners were Amy Webster of Boston and Ron Kravette of California, who defeated Tamara Kuchiki of California and Neale Smull of New York. Despite the early dates (July 24-25) for the Festival in the new season, the performances in general were of a high quality, with a minimum of errors, a somewhat unusual occurrence for the time of year and much to the credit of the skaters.

Following in late August were the 1993 National Collegiate Championships, which had moved to Colorado Springs from Lake Placid. While there was a good turnout for the Senior and Junior Ladies free skating, Men's and Pair events were still lacking, and the only Dance competition was for Junior Dance, with just three entries. However, there were 22 Senior Ladies and 11 Junior Ladies. The number of entries in the Senior and Junior figures had also declined, with eight in Senior and seven in Junior. In the Senior Ladies free skating, Sara Kastner from St. Paul, Minn., representing the University of St. Thomas, retained her title by coming from behind after a third place in the technical program to overtake Shirl Marie Cattani of Pennsylvania, representing Temple University. Cattani was also the winner of the Senior figures.

In the Junior Ladies free skating, the winner was Wendy Budzynski, also from St. Paul, representing Augsburg College, with Michelle Lindberg of Minneapolis, representing the College of St. Catherine, second. In third place was Elin Gardiner of Boston, representing the University of Massachusetts, the daughter of former Olympic champion Tenley Albright. The Junior figures were won by Elisa Goldberg, representing the University of Delaware. The Junior Dance was won by Daniela and Andras Lopez of California, representing West Valley College.

The National Collegiate Championships were now a permanent fixture on the calendar, and had also proven useful in the selection process for the Winter University Games. They still need greater promotion and publicity, especially as figure skating grows as a recognized sport within the college and university community, which is, after all, where many of the rinks are. The sport also fits the Title IX directives, with its preponderance of women participants.

The International competition season kicked off as usual with the Coupe des Alpes at St. Gervais, followed by Oberstdorf, with the Single team still doing both competitions as had been the pattern for many years. Michael Weiss of Washington was second in the Men in both competitions. The winner in St. Gervais was Michael Shmerkin of Israel, a story in itself.

His win was the first ever for a skater representing that country. Shmerkin had represented the Soviet Union in the World Junior Championships from 1985 through 1988, with his best place being fourth in 1986. He then went to Israel under the limited Soviet policy allowing Russian citizens of Jewish extraction to emigrate to that country, and he literally had to bide his time until an Israeli federation could be formed and join the ISU, which took several years. He finally made it to the 1993 Worlds in Prague, placing 19th. So his St. Gervais win was the culmination of a long effort and speaks well for his determination to keep skating, despite the long odds against him.

In Oberstdorf, the winner was Jeffrey Langdon of Canada, who had been third at St. Gervais.

Matt Kessinger of Indiana, who was the National Junior Silver medalist of 1993, placed 10th in both competitions.

In the Ladies, Jenna Pittman, the 1993 National Junior Ladies Silver medalist, continued her excellent efforts internationally by winning at St. Gervais, defeating Susan Humphreys of Canada. She could do no better than sixth at Obertsdorf, which was won by Irina Slutskaia of Russia, with Humphreys second. In Pairs, Stephanie Stiegler and Lance Travis from California, the 1993 National Junior Pair champions, were second in St. Gervais and third at Oberstdorf, with the Canadian pair of Caroline Haddad and Jean-Sébastien Fecteau the winner in both instances. The second U.S. Pair of Robin Heckler of New York and Jeff Tilley of Delaware, the National Junior Pair Silver medalists, were fourth at St. Gervais and seventh at Oberstdorf.

The Dance event at St. Gervais saw the withdrawal due to injury of Rachel Mayer of Boston and Peter Breen of Colorado, but they recovered enough to be able to compete at Oberstdorf. There they placed a solid and close second to the winners, Martine Patenaude and Eric Massé of Canada, who had been second at St. Gervais to a Russian couple. It has often been the pattern in the Coupe that the Soviet/Russian entries are usually only in one of the two competitions, and generally that was St. Gervais. The second U.S. couple, Christina and Mark Fitzgerald, the National Junior Dance Silver medalists from Delaware and Massachusetts, were fifth at St. Gervais and 10th at Oberstdorf.

The three medals at St. Gervais and three at Oberstdorf (for a total of six, consisting of one Gold, four Silver and two Bronze) spoke well not only for the efforts of the skaters but also for the future. The success in the Coupe, in which the U.S. placed second to Canada, was a return to some of the achievements of the past in these two most popular competitions. The Canadian team with its total of 10 medals, consisting of four Gold, three Silver and three Bronze, was clearly the strongest team present.

At the end of September two U.S. skaters, Michael Chack and the newly reinstated Elaine Zayak (the 1982 World Ladies champion), elected to participate in the Vienna Cup, actually the Karl Schäfer Memorial Competition, an event which was not supported by the USFSA. Chack of New York, won the Men's event, while in the Ladies, in what was her return to International competition after almost 10 years, Elaine did not have an auspicious start, placing 13th in a field of 19. However, she fully redeemed herself in the subsequent competitions, by winning the 1994 North Atlantic Senior Ladies, placing second in the 1994 Easterns and fourth in the Nationals. The winner of the Ladies at Vienna was Krisztina Czako of Hungary, followed by Tanja Szewczenko of Germany and Olga Markova of Russia, a strong field of rising young stars.

In prior years, the members of the World Junior Team had been selected primarily on the basis of the placements of the age eligible skaters in the preceding Nationals, together with certain selected summer non-qualifying competitions. This system (much as had been the case many years before, when the Nationals followed the Worlds and the Senior team was selected on the basis of the prior year's record), was far from satisfactory. The rapidity with which the young skaters matured and moved up, plus the never ending changes in partnerships in Pairs and Dance, made a more up-to-date competition for selection a must. As a result, the first selection competition for the World Junior Championships team was held in Colorado Springs, just after the fall 1993 meeting of the Board of Directors. This enabled Board members who were also referees and judges to be utilized. The 1994 World Junior Championship itself was returning to the Broadmoor World Arena just two months later, the third World Juniors to be held at that venerable venue.

The selection competition proved to be a successful innovation which was well accepted by the skaters and officials, and it has been continued since as a permanent fixture in the schedule.

There were 25 entries (34 skaters) in the selection competition, and a good quality of skating was seen. In the Men, those making the team, in the order of their finish in the competition, were Jere Michael of Colorado, Michael Weiss of Washington, D.C., and Johnnie Bevan of Spokane, Wash. In the Ladies, the qualifiers were Michelle Kwan of California and Jenna Pittman of Delaware. In Pairs, those making the team were Sara Ward of New Jersey and J. Paul Binnebose of Delaware, Danielle and Steve Hartsell of Michigan, and Ali Blank and Jeb Gerth of Nashville. In Dance the successful couples were Eve Chalom and Mathew Gates of Michigan, and Jayna Cronin of California with Jonathan Nichols of Delaware.

Sudafed Skate America International followed in the latter half of October, in Dallas, Texas, with a good-sized field of 38 entries, representing 57 skaters. It was in this competition that Brian Boitano made his return to International competition under ISU Rules. The Men had a strong field, with the ultimate winner being Viktor Petrenko, another reinstated skater, now representing his native Ukraine. Viktor was third in the technical program, but took first in the free skating to win, while Boitano, who had won the technical program, placed second. In third was Alexei Urmanov of Russia, with Todd Eldredge fourth. The other two U.S. skaters, Aren Nielsen and Michael Chack, were sixth and seventh, respectively.

The three U.S. entrants for the Ladies were Tonya Harding (no longer Gillooly), Lisa Ervin and Michelle Kwan, with Nancy Kerrigan not being present due to her commitment to the Piruetten competition in Norway. Tonya won the technical program but could not hold the lead, with a fourth in free skating to finish third. The winner was the reigning World Ladies champion Oksana Baiul of Ukraine, with Surya Bonaly of France second. Lisa Ervin placed sixth and Michelle Kwan, seventh.

The Pair title went to Evgenia Shishkova and Vadim Naumov of Russia, the World Bronze medalists, but right behind them were two of the three U.S. Pairs, with Kyoko Ina and Jason

Dungjen taking second and Karen Courtland and Todd Reynolds, third. The other U.S. Pair, a new combination, of Tristen Vega and Joel McKeever, placed sixth.

In the Dance, a popular win was that of Sophie Moniotte and Pascal Lavanchy of France, with Katerina Mrazova and Martin Simecek of the Czech Republic second, followed by Renée Roca and Gorsha Sur third. Elizabeth Punsalan and Jerod Swallow were fourth. The third U.S. couple, Rachel Mayer and Peter Breen were eighth. Roca and Sur had been sixth in each of the two compulsory dances, but were second in the original dance and third in the free dance, to pull up to the podium and earn the Bronze medal. On the other hand, Punsalan and Swallow had been third and second in the two compulsory dances, but fifth in the original dance and fourth in the free dance, to finish fourth. It was almost as if the two couples were passing each other in elevators, with one going up and the other going down!

The next competition on the schedule was the Piruetten at Hamar, Norway, held in the Northern Lights Arena where the Olympic figure skating events would be held. Both National champions in Singles, Scott Davis and Nancy Kerrigan, opted to go to Hamar instead of Dallas. Amazingly, Kyoko Ina and Jason Dungjen and Karen Courtland and Todd Reynolds both did Skate America and less than a week later were in Norway for the Piruetten. Scott Davis was third behind Elvis Stojko of Canada and Philippe Candeloro of France in the Men. Scott won the technical program, but dropped to third in the free skating. In the Ladies, Kerrigan was the winner, defeating Josée Chouinard of Canada and Chen Lu of China, with the European Ladies champion, Surya Bonaly, fourth.

The Pairs were won by the newly reinstated Natalia Mishkutenok and Arthur Dmitriev, with Isabelle Brasseur and Lloyd Eisler, the 1993 World Pair champions, second, the peripatetic Americans Ina and Dungjen were third, and Courtland and Reynolds, fifth; truly an excellent showing in two back-to-back competitions. The Dance event was won by Susanna Rahkamo and Petri Kokko of Finland, with the U.S. entry of Susan Wynne and Russ Witherby fourth.

Skate Canada, which followed immediately at Ottawa, was also notable for the return to competition of the reinstated Ekaterina Gordeeva and Sergei Grinkov, in their pre-European Championship warm up. They easily won the Pair event, with Radka Kovarikova and René Novotny of the Czech Republic second. The U.S. entry of Jennifer Perez and John Frederiksen of Colorado placed 10th.

In the Men, Kurt Browning of Canada was the winner, with Mark Mitchell second. Mark had trouble in the technical program, but came back strongly in the free skating to take the only U.S. medal. The Ladies was a triumph for Chen Lu of China, who topped the field with two graceful and classical programs. It was a major win for her. Olga Markova of Russia was the runner-up, while the lone U.S. entry, Michelle Cho of California, placed 10th. The Dance saw the very popular French couple of Sophie Moniotte and Pascal Lavanchy come out on top, with the young and rising Canadian couple of Shae-Lynn Bourne and Victor Kraatz third. The U.S. entry of Amy Webster of Boston and Ron Kravette of California was ninth. So, apart from Mark Mitchell's Silver medal, it was not one of the better Skate Canadas for the U.S.

Going into November, the scene moved back to Europe with the Nations Cup in Germany and the Trophée Lalique in Paris, actually on the same dates, an unusual conflict not normally permitted by the ISU. In the Nations Cup, Scott Davis continued his solid skating to take second behind the reinstated Viktor Petrenko of Ukraine in his pre-European warm-up. Scott led after the technical program but was overtaken in the free skating. Rudy Galindo was also in the event and performed well to take fourth, after a third in the technical program. In the Ladies (which was won by Tanja Szewczenko of Germany), Tonia Kwiatkowski was the only U.S. entry and placed seventh after a fifth in the technical program. In Pairs, the indomitable Kyoko Ina and Jason Dungjen, in their third major International competition, took third behind Shishkova and Naumov of Russia, the winners, and Mandy Wötzel and Ingo Steuer of Germany. Tracy Damigella and Doug Williams, the second U.S. Pair, placed seventh. In the Dance, which was won by Irina Romanova and Igor Yaroshenko of Ukraine, Susan Wynne and Russ Witherby continued their European tour by taking a fourth place. As can be seen, some of the members of the Hamar team had moved on to Germany, although presumably they went home in between the two competitions, which were two and a half weeks apart.

At the Trophée Lalique, the U.S. garnered a Gold medal when Todd Eldredge won the Men's event, the first sign of his resurgence after two years in the doldrums, defeating Philippe Candeloro and the ubiquitous Viacheslav Zagorodniuk of Ukraine, who came third. The Ladies was won by Surya Bonaly with Nicole Bobek, the only U.S. entry, fifth. She had been eighth in the technical program, but was fourth in the free skating to pull up three places.

The Pairs were won by Mishkutenok and Dmitriev, in another warm-up in anticipation of the 1994 European Championships (where the decisions would be made as to the Russian representatives in the Olympic Winter Games), with the 1993 European Pair champions, Maria Eltsova and Andrei Bushkov, also of Russia, second. Jenni Meno and Todd Sand solidified their claim to the top spot in the U.S. (Urbanski and Marval, the 1993 champions, having split up), by placing third, with Karen Courtland and Todd Reynolds right behind them in fourth. Dance was won by Irina Lobacheva and Ilia Averbukh of Russia. Elizabeth Punsalan and Jerod Swallow were a solid second, so the Lalique was a very successful competition for the U.S. Team, at the critical stage of the pre-Olympic campaign, with three medals, one of them Gold.

The 1993 NHK Trophy competition at Chiba, Japan, wound up the International season prior to the Nationals, and with the top skaters not there due to their conflicting commitments elsewhere, it was a tough event for the U.S. Philippe Candeloro of France, another inveterate traveler on the circuit, won the Men. The best the U.S. could do was an eighth place by Damon Allen of Colorado. In the Ladies, which was won by Surya Bonaly, Tonya Harding took fourth after a seventh in the technical program. In the Pairs, won by Isabelle Brasseur and Lloyd Eisler of Canada, the sole U.S. team of Jennifer Perez and John Frederiksen of Colorado, were seventh. The Dance event had no U.S. entry and went to Oksana Gritschuk and Evgeni Platov of Russia, perhaps a forecast of the future.

Early in January, 1994, there were two International Precision competitions in Sweden and Finland, just four days apart. The first was at Soldertälje, Sweden, with just one U.S. entry, the Crystallettes of Michigan, who placed second in the Senior event to Team Surprise of Sweden. The latter, as a Junior team had won that event in the first Snowflake competition at Boston in 1990. There were 19 teams from eight countries in the Swedish competition. The second event was held at Turku, Finland, with three U.S. teams present: The Haydenettes of Lexington, Mass., who placed third in the Senior event, won by the Laval, Quebec, team "Les Pirouettes"; the Crystallettes, who were eighth in the Senior event; and the Superettes of Rhode Island, who won the Junior event. The competition drew 39 teams from 12 countries, certainly the largest number of nations to participate in an International Precision competition up to that time.

The International season for Precision was still far from over, with two more competitions being held in France in February and in England in March. The French competition, which was held at Louviers, drew 21 teams from eight countries including Russia. The Goldenettes from Ohio were fourth in the Senior class, which was won by Team Surprise of Sweden, while the Colonials from Massachusetts were second in the Junior class to a French team, Les Chrysalides. The London competition in England drew 17 teams from eight countries. The Haydenettes returned to Europe and won the Senior event, while the Ice Mates, also from the Hayden Recreation Centre FSC, won the Novice class.

All this activity took place before the Sectional and National Championships in Precision for 1994, and gave a strong impetus to the growth of the discipline around the world. It should be borne in mind that while some financial support was forthcoming from the USFSA, it did not cover the expenses entirely and the teams had to raise their own funds to a large extent in order to participate in the foreign competitions. The scope of funding for International Precision competitions has been expanded since, with, for example, $119,600 budgeted for 1993-1994 and $160,300 for 1994-1995. Precision team skating is rapidly becoming a major part of the competition activity of the Association, involving as it does more skaters than any other discipline. The build-up to a possible World Championship in 1998 needs to be fully supported, with as much International exposure as possible.

While all the intense activity leading up to the Olympics was going on, there was the curious and sad occurrence of the deaths within a very few months in the latter part of 1993 and early 1994 of many well known skaters, coaches and administrators, many of whom had made an enormous contribution to the sport. Among them were: George W. Eby of California, who passed away in June at the age of 79. He had been the long-time President of Ice Capades and was always a friend of the amateur side of the sport. Josef Dedic of the Czech Republic, who passed away in June at the age of 69, had been the First Vice President of the ISU, a World Referee and a prolific author and student of the sport, as well as a key administrator at the highest level. Gustave Lussi of Lake Placid, who passed away in June at the age of 95, was a truly great teacher and the inventor of many of the jumps and other elements seen in the programs of his skaters, the leader of whom was two-time Olympic champion, Dick Button. Frederick C. LeFevre of Williamsburg, Va., who passed away in September at the age of 80, was USFSA President from 1970 and 1973 and served the USFSA in many other key positions. He was a strong and effective leader of the Association in his time. Roger F. Turner of Massachusetts, who passed away in October at the age of 92, was seven-times National champion 1928-1934 and twice a World Silver medalist 1930-1931, as well as a National judge for over 50 years. Evelyn Chandler Mapes, who passed away in January 1994 at the age of 87, while only a National Junior Ladies champion in the amateur ranks in 1929, was the leading star of the Ice Follies during the 1930s and early 1940s and did much to popularize figure skating as a form of entertainment. She was probably the originator of the "Arabian" cartwheel and was well known for her huge open Axel jump. These departed giants will not be forgotten by the sport they loved!

The fall 1993 meeting of the Board of Directors was held at Colorado Springs, as usual, with more legislation involving rule changes than ever. It was voted to move the compulsory figure events of the National Championships from the practice rinks of the current Nationals and to hold them at another venue that would provide to the participants optimal conditions and exposure starting in 1995. Despite this mandate, the separation has yet to take place and the compulsory figure events are still part of the main Nationals.

Also approved were rules which strengthened the status of the approved budget as the sole authority for the disbursement of Association funds, with the authority to terminate with the end of the fiscal year, and only the Governing Council to have the power to change a budget after adoption. The Treasurer was charged with the responsibility for the preparation of the annual budget, a switch from prior years when the Finance Committee had that duty. The Treasurer was also the officer charged with the responsibility for authorization of expenditures in excess of the budget amounts, but only to the extent not considered material by the accountants in the most recent audit. All these rules were designed to strengthen the fiscal reporting, accounting and control of the assets of the Association, essentially under one officer. The Finance Committee became primarily an advisor and assistant to the Treasurer and not an independent entity, in order to avoid any potential conflicts between them, which had occurred on occasion in the distant past before the committee was abolished in 1968 and revived in 1984.

In the competition area, it was voted that the winners of events in the Juvenile-Intermediate Nationals would have to move up and could not defend their titles, as had always been the case with the Junior and Novice events. It was at this meeting that the uniform deadline of Sept. 15 for entries in the Regionals was adopted. The so-called "bye" rules were also redrafted and clarified from a procedural standpoint, requiring unanimous decisions for their granting by the officials concerned. A deadline for the application for byes was also adopted. Perhaps the key provision of the revisions was that one requirement for the granting of the bye was that the competitor in question would have a reasonable chance of placing in the first four in the higher level (Sectional or National) competition in which the competitor would participate if the bye were granted, instead of in the competition (Regional or Sectional) for which the bye was granted, a much tougher standard to meet.

Another change approved was to limit the number of qualifying skaters from Regional to Sectional and from Sectional to National to three instead of four, and to permit only the defending National champion to qualify automatically without having to go through Sectionals. Of the two proposals, which were designed to have a modest effect in reducing the number of entries, the former one did not stick and was subsequently overturned. The latter, however, did survive and is in the rules today.

The test requirements for qualifying competitions were also recodified, which meant in simplest terms that skaters must have passed the appropriate tests for their level. The revisions also reflected the first effort to set forth suitable requirements for Adult Singles events, with at that time no test requirements for either Senior or Junior, and in the case of the Junior level, the reverse, that is, competitors could not have passed the Intermediate Free Skating or higher test. As Adult Singles skating grew, leading up to the first Nationals in 1995, the need for standards and eligibility requirements for the various levels of Adult free skating was readily apparent and is still being worked on in 1995.

The addition of an Intermediate technical program starting in 1995 was also approved. Also revised was the extension to the lower Dance events (below Junior) of the requirement to calculate the results of compulsory dances individually and separately, as was already the case for the Senior and Junior Dance events. The merits of this requirement at any level is still the subject of strong differences of opinion, especially at the International level, and there are many who believe the results of the compulsory dances should once again be combined. The object of the split was to try to enhance the judging of the dances independently of one another, so that more accurate results could be achieved. That has not proven to be the case, with the second dance invariably being judged exactly the same as the first, barring some serious error or failure on the part of the Dance couples.

With respect to skaters enrolled in the Eligible Skater Instructor Program (ESIP), a requirement for them to have competed within the past five years, in order to remain in the program was adopted. Also approved was a prohibition of those enrolled in the program from judging tests or competitions, although they could still trial judge.

As proposed by the Athletes Advisory Committee, a detailed Code of Ethics for participants in competitions, exhibitions and training camps was adopted, which contained a specific provision relating to engaging in criminal activity, and also provided that any disciplinary proceedings would be conducted in accordance with Article XXVII of the By Laws. While the Code was approved in the fall of 1993, it was not effective until one year later. In the light of the Kerrigan-Harding affair, the irony is readily apparent!

Reported in the new **Skating** magazine were two articles of considerable interest, which reflected a review of the judges "corps" by the new chairman of the Judges Committee, Eleanor Curtis of California. Among the statistics cited were that 26 percent of all judges were over the age of 60 and that 79 percent of Singles and Pair judges and 83 percent of Dance judges were over 40. Also mentioned was that the average Low Figure test judge has nine years of experience and the average Bronze Dance Test judge has 10 years of experience, which clearly reflects the apparent inability of the system to move people up the line and to add new and younger persons at a rate sufficient to meet the ever increasing demand. The fact that there were 903 figure judges and 505 dance judges available was noted, both numbers lower than in prior years, confirming the shrinkage and aging of the judging corps.

In her second article, Mrs. Curtis, herself a World Dance and International Figure judge and a former National competitor, commented on the uneven workload for judges across the country. For example, in the New England Region each judge is expected to do 27 free skating tests per year, while on the Pacific Coast eight or nine is the rule. For the Upper Great Lakes Region, it is 25 per person, and in the South Atlantic Region, 15 per person. Insofar as competitions are concerned, 92 percent of all judges serve in them. Low judges average three competitions per year and Gold judges nine. The workload also varies among the qualifying competitions. In New England, it was five entries per official (including the referees, judges and accountants), while at Upper Great Lakes, the workload was 13 entries per official. Mrs. Curtis asked some thought-provoking questions: "Who will be the judges of the future, providing an equal and fair standard for the next generation of skaters?" As to the workload: "Why so much variation? Does it mean we need a better balance of judges for the workload?"

During the fall of 1993 there were two events of significance which deserve mention. The first was a unique exhibition held at Boston Garden at the end of October, produced by Jim Spence, a former Vice President of ABC Sports, called "Skates of Gold" (with IBM as the sponsor and with television by ABC as part of its pre-Olympic coverage), to which were invited all the living Olympic Gold medalists. The show was divided into four segments for the four disciplines (Ladies, Men, Pairs and Dance) and featured "cameo" appearances by the early medalists and performances by the recent winners. The numbers of former Gold medalists who came was truly remarkable, comparable only to those who were present for the ISU Anniversary in 1992, but this time with real skating, as well. Among the U.S. Gold medalists present were: Ladies - Tenley Albright, Peggy Fleming and Kristi Yamaguchi; Men - Dick Button, Scott Hamilton and Brian Boitano. The oldest medalist present (at the age of 87) was Ernst Baier of Germany, who with his partner Maxi Herber (who was not well enough to attend), were the Olympic Pair champions in 1936. They are the Senior living former Olympic champions.

The other major event was the second East Coast Pro-Am competition and the third overall, held in early December at Philadelphia. With AT&T as the title sponsor of what was called the "AT&T Pro-Am Figure Skating Challenge," a total of $359,000 in prize money was on the line. Invited were Ladies - Lisa Ervin, Caryn Kadavy, Nancy Kerrigan, Rosalynn Sumners and Jill Trenary; and Men - Brian Boitano, Michael Chack, Scott Hamilton, Mark Mitchell and Paul Wylie. Pairs and Dance were now added to the program, with the following invitees: Pairs - Karen Courtland and Todd Reynolds, Jenni Meno and Todd Sand, Natalie and Wayne Seybold, and Anita Hartshorn and Frank Sweiding; Dance - Judy Blumberg and James Yorke, Elizabeth Punsalan and Jerod Swallow, Renée Roca and Gorsha Sur, and Susan Wynne and Russ Witherby.

The competition was not an easy one, especially for the participating eligible skaters, and in particular for Brian Boitano, and imposed the pressure of the build-up to the Nationals and Olympics. Brian met the challenge and the pressure as the true champion he is, to win the competition over Paul Wylie and Scott Hamilton, his friendly rivals from the previous Pro-Am in Los Angeles, with Todd Eldredge and Aren Nielsen, fourth and fifth, they having replaced Chack and Mitchell in the starting field. Brian won $40,000 for his efforts. In the Ladies, Nancy Kerrigan was the winner and recipient of the $40,000 first prize, and was certainly on track for her return to Hamar after the Nationals. Second was Nicole Bobek, who had replaced Jill Trenary, with Caryn Kadavy third, followed by Rosalynn Sumners and Lisa Ervin.

Jenni Meno and Todd Sand

In the Pairs, and taking a $20,000 prize, were Jenni Meno and Todd Sand, who prevailed over Karen Courtland and Todd Reynolds, with the Seybolds third, and Hartshorn and Sweiding fourth. Roca and Sur were the winners in the Dance of the $20,000 first prize over Punsalan and Swallow, with Wynne and Witherby third and Blumberg and Yorke fourth. The Pro-Am, as a part of the pre-Olympic build-up, was successful and saw a high standard of skating from all the entrants.

The 1994 World Junior Championships returned to the Broadmoor World Arena in Colorado Springs in early December 1993 for the third and last time. The championships previously had been held there in 1984 and 1989. It was truly a "sentimental journey" for many of those present. This was the last major championship to be held in the building which was slated for demolition in March 1994, to be replaced with additional hotel rooms. Originally built by Spencer Penrose (the founder of the modern Broadmoor Hotel) as a riding hall and turned into a skating rink in 1938, the old building had seen five Senior World Championships, three World Junior Championships, six National Championships and many Sectional and Regional events. It was probably the only arena in the country to have held both a Pacific Coast Sectional Championship (in 1941 and 1947, when Colorado was in the Pacific Coast section) and a Midwestern Sectional Championship (after Colorado was transferred to the Midwest Section) less than five years later (in 1951 and again in 1953).

While the old building admittedly had seen better days and was no longer suitable for a major championship, due in part to its limited seating capacity and ventilation problems, still the ice was always good and it carried such an aura of tradition and history as to more than overcome the technical difficulties.

Happily, the U.S. World Junior team acquitted itself very well, taking three medals, two of them Gold, to give the venerable venue a good sendoff into the "heaven" where all such buildings go, just as would be the case with Boston Garden in 1995!

In the Men's event, Michael Weiss of Washington, D.C., overturned the result of the selection competition to take the Gold medal, stepping up from his Silver medal position of the prior year, to be one of the few U.S. skaters to win more than one medal in the World Junior. Jere Michael of Colorado, in his home rink and the winner of the selection competition, won the Bronze medal, with Naoki Shigematsu of Japan the Silver medalist. For once, the Russian men were shut out of the medals. The leading Russian, Ilya Kulik, the Bronze medalist in 1993, after a second in the technical program, dropped all the way down to 11th place in the final result with a 16th in the free skating. On the other hand, Johnnie Bevan of Spokane, Wash., placed sixth, after a truly disastrous technical program (in which he was 15th), but he placed second in the free skating to pull up nine places! So, the "elevator" principle seemed to be in operation again.

Michelle Kwan of California was the clear winner in the Ladies. It was the first time since 1988 (Todd Eldredge and Kristi Yamaguchi) that the U.S. had taken both Singles titles in the same year, and the third time overall, the other instance having been in 1981 (Paul Wylie and Tiffany Chin). Jenna Pittman of Delaware did not meet the potential she had showed in her prior competitions and finished 17th.

In Pairs and Dance, the results for the U.S. were less distinguished. Among the three U.S. Pairs, Danielle and Steve Hartsell of Michigan were eighth, Sara Ward of New Jersey and Paul Binnebose of Delaware were ninth, and Ali Blank and Jeb Gerth of Nashville, 15th.

The 1994 National Championships were held at Detroit in early January, using the Joe Louis Arena as the main venue and the adjacent Cobo Hall as the second competition and practice rink. The twin rinks of the Detroit Skating Club, some miles away to the North, served as the third competition and practice rink. It was a big operation, with 245 entries in 18 events, representing 331 skaters. In the six figure events, there were 70 entries, while in Pairs there were 44 entries, a very good number, with 15 and 13, respectively, in the Junior and Novice Pair events. The official hotel was nearby and when severe winter weather arrived, the transportation system was outstanding and never faltered in carrying the skaters, their coaches and others to and from the three rinks.

It was at the 1994 Nationals that further inductions were made into the United States Figure Skating Hall of Fame:

The late Maribel Vinson and George Hill of Boston, four-time National Pair champions, 1933, 1935-1937, North American Pair champions, 1935, and 1936 Olympians. Maribel has now been elected twice, previously as a Singles champion in 1976;

Jo Jo Starbuck and Ken Shelley, formerly of California, three-time National Pair champions, 1970-1972, North American Pair champions, 1971, World Pair Bronze medalists, 1971-1972;

Janet Lynn Salomon, formerly of Illinois, five-time National Ladies champion, 1969-1973, North American Ladies champion, 1969, World Silver medalist, 1973, World Bronze medalist, 1972, Olympic Bronze medalist 1972.

The championships were well organized and there was a high level of competition, but unfortunately all of the positive aspects were lost in the incredible publicity and media attention resulting from the assault at Cobo Hall during a practice session on the defending Ladies champion, Nancy Kerrigan.

Another unfortunate injury that was almost overlooked, was the fractured left wrist suffered by Renée Roca, also in a practice session, which ultimately forced her withdrawal with her partner Gorsha Sur before the free dance in the Senior Dance event.

What should have been the lead story of the championships was the return to National competition of Brian Boitano, in his effort also to return to the Olympic Games, six years after his success at Calgary in 1988. After the technical program, Brian was the leader and it seemed likely that he would win his fifth National title, to go with the four that he had won between 1985 and 1988. His closest rival, the defending champion Scott Davis, was not intimidated by Brian's presence and skated an outstanding performance, as he always seemed to do in the Nationals, to win the free skating and to retain his title. In third place, after a fifth in the technical program, was Aren Nielsen, who placed third in the free skating to take the Bronze medal over former champion Todd Eldredge fourth and Mark Mitchell, fifth. With no third entry, due to the poor results the prior year in Prague, only Davis and Boitano would be going to Hamar.

The Pair event saw the return of Todd Sand to the top spot of the podium and his second National Pair title. Todd and his partner, Jenni Meno, won decisively over Kyoko Ina and Jason Dungjen, second, with Karen Courtland and Todd Reynolds third. Based on the fifth place of Todd and Jenni in 1993 at Prague, all three would be going to Norway. Todd joined a very select group of skaters who had won the Pair title with two different partners: Maribel Vinson, in 1928-1929 with Thornton Coolidge, and in 1933, 1935-1937 with George Hill; and Melissa Militano in 1973 with her brother Mark, and in 1974-1975 with Johnny Johns. Todd is the only man to do so.

In the Dance, prior to the injury to Renée Roca, she and Sur had been tied with Elizabeth Punsalan and Jerod Swallow at the end of the compulsory dances. Despite the injury, Roca-Sur did their original dance, in which they placed second, but the strain on the injury was too great and they were forced to withdraw. Due to Sur's lack of U.S. citizenship they were not eligible for the Olympics, but still had hoped to be able to go the Worlds. Elizabeth and Jerod, newly married, won their second title, with Susan Wynne and Russ Witherby as the Silver medalists, and Amy Webster of Boston, with Ron Kravette of California, third. Only one couple would go to the Olympics, since the U.S. had finished out of the top 10 at Prague.

Not to be overlooked in the 1994 Nationals were those in the Junior and Novice classes, who did their "thing" and did it well despite all the distractions of the Kerrigan affair. Among them were Jere Michael of Colorado, the World Junior Bronze medalist, who won the Junior Men; Laura Gayton of Boston and Oleg Fediukov of Providence, R.I. (one of the Russian emigres), who won the Junior Dance; Timothy Goebel of Ohio, who won the Novice Men; and Jessica Joseph and Charles Butler, Jr., of Michigan, the winners of the Novice Dance, all future stars, just to name a few of them.

We must now turn to the Senior Ladies. With the leg injury to Nancy Kerrigan, clubbed just above the right knee of her landing leg by an unidentified assailant who escaped, she was forced to withdraw from the competition, which was to start the next day. Almost immediately, she began an intense period of rehabilitation under the guidance of Dr. Mahlon Bradley (an orthopedic surgeon and himself a former National competitor and athlete member of the Board of Directors of the Association), in an effort to be physically fit and ready for the Olympics. She was selected for the team by the International Committee at its meeting in Detroit, with the understanding that her progress would be closely monitored and her ability to compete certified by both the medical side and the official representatives of the Association. Happily, as we all know, Nancy recovered well, returned to the ice and was readily approved for her participation in the Games.

In her absence, the undefended title was easily won by former champion Tonya Harding of Oregon, with the surprising Michelle Kwan of California, the World Junior champion, second. Michelle pulled up over Nicole Bobek of Colorado, with the returned Elaine Zayak of New York a solid fourth. Two medalists of 1993, Lisa Ervin and Tonia Kwiatkowski, both of Ohio, could not sustain their previous form and finished seventh and fifth respectively. With just two entries for the Olympics, those to go were Kerrigan and Harding, with Kwan the first alternate, on standby as it were. Michelle was actually sent to Norway by the Association and trained in Oslo during the Games, in the event that she would have to step in should Kerrigan not be able to compete.

While all this was going on, the authorities in Michigan and Oregon diligently sought to identify and apprehend the actual perpetrators of the assault on Kerrigan. This was successfully accomplished when Shawn Eckardt, the "bodyguard" of Harding, admitted that he and her former husband, Jeff Gillooly, had planned the assault and that two others were also involved, the getaway driver Derrick Smith, and the actual assailant Shane Stant.

Eventually Gillooly, Eckardt, Stant and Smith all confessed to their roles in the crime and were convicted in the Oregon courts, which assumed jurisdiction although the crime had taken place in Michigan. They also implicated Harding herself in the planning and subsequent coverup, although Harding steadfastly denied that she had any prior knowledge of the plan or the attack.

As a result of the findings of the authorities, the USFSA and the USOC were into uncharted territory. For the first time, the Association had to deal with the possibility that one of its own skaters had participated in a plot to injure another skater. The Association also had to protect the rights of the skater involved in the criminal investigation. The Association very promptly initiated an investigative action under its own rules to determine if its Code of Ethics had been violated, with the object of making a ruling which either would remove Harding from the World and Olympic Teams and impose other penalties, or find her innocent of any violation of the Code. Unfortunately, the USOC did not permit the USFSA to proceed with its own action, properly conducted under its own rules, but insisted that it, the Olympic Committee, would take whatever action was necessary, since, insofar as the Olympics were concerned, the Olympic Committee exercised the sole jurisdiction with respect to entry in the Games.

Time constraints prevented the USOC Administrative Board from taking any action until the arrival in Norway before the Games of the members of the hearing body. Harding, in the meantime, had filed suit against the USOC in Oregon seeking damages of $20,000,000 if she were excluded from the Games, and also obtained a temporary restraining order preventing the USOC from taking any action to prevent her from participating in the Games. As a result the USOC, in an unpopular decision in the U.S., reached an agreement with Harding in which they would permit her to skate in the Games and she would drop the damage suit.

As stated in the excellent article published in Skating magazine by Mike Spence of the Colorado Springs Gazette Telegraph: "U.S. courts prevented a timely resolution of the problem, and in protecting the rights of Harding, they denied the rights of the USFSA and the USOC to enforce their own rules."

Following the Games, the hearing panel of the USFSA (which was headed by William Hybl, Esq., a former President of the USOC and Chairman of the El Pomar Foundation in Colorado Springs), which had found probable cause for the holding of a disciplinary hearing before the Games, convened the hearing in early March. Once again, a temporary restraining order was obtained by Harding in Oregon, which prevented the hearing from proceeding on the ground that Harding had not had sufficient time to prepare a defense. At the same time, however, the investigation by the authorities in Oregon had been continuing, with the ultimate outcome that Harding, in a plea bargain, pleaded guilty to one felony charge of conspiring to hinder the investigation into the attack, in exchange for no jail time, a suspended sentence and three years of supervised probation and a $100,000 fine. As part of the agreement with the court, she also agreed to resign from the USFSA, and to forfeit her place on the World Team, to undergo psychiatric examination, to provide 500 hours of community service, to donate $50,000 to the Portland (Oregon) Special Olympics and to pay $10,000 in court costs.

Despite the plea bargain agreement, the Association continued with its disciplinary hearing, which was actually held at the end of June 1994, once the restraining order had been lifted by the court in Oregon, and stripped Harding of the 1994 National Ladies title (which was declared "vacant"), and also banned her from membership in the USFSA for life. The statement of Mr. Hybl sets forth the decision clearly:

> "The hearing panel concluded that Ms. Harding's felony plea to the crime of conspiracy to hinder the prosecution and other evidence, including her actions prior to the attack demonstrated a clear violation of the (USFSA's) Code of Ethics. Such conduct intentionally undermines the concept of sportsmanship and fair play embodied in the USFSA By Laws and Rules and amateur sportsmanship in general."

Mr. Hybl also stated that the panel further concluded "by a preponderance of the evidence," that Harding had prior knowledge of the assault. Harding did not appear before the hearing and did not send any representatives. The removal of Harding's tainted title and the ban on membership for life were unprecedented in the history of the USFSA, but Sharon Watson, Chairman of the USFSA's Sanctions and Eligibility Committee and a member of the hearing panel, perhaps wrote the best "finis" to the affair. "The decisions we have reached today are the correct and necessary ones given the volume of the evidence before us."

The effects of the affair have been far reaching, especially as the drama was played out in Norway under the close scrutiny of the media. The country was as taken up by it in 1994 as it was in 1995 by the O.J. Simpson murder trial. Ironically, the affair had the effect of vastly increasing the interest of the public in the sport, resulting in explosive growth during the 1994-1995 season. Many additional competitive and non-competitive events for eligible and non-eligible skaters suitable for television broadcast were developed, for which the ratings were extraordinary. They obviously greatly increased the interest of commercial organizations in becoming involved in the sport.

In hindsight, the figure skating competitions of the 1994 Olympic Winter Games were a bit anticlimactic from the standpoint of the USFSA. The Games were beautifully organized by the Norwegian Olympic Committee, with excellent facilities. While not involved with figure skating, one deserves mention: the incredible "Vikingskapet" or "Viking Ship" in Hamar, for the speed skating, a giant building holding 12,000 spectators and a 400-meter speed skating track. What was amazing about the 1994 Games was that during the two months preceding the Games, there were over 50 inches of snowfall, but on the day the Games started the sun came out and it did not snow again until the Games were over, although it was bitterly cold but sunny throughout.

The Northern Lights Hall for the figure skating held two surfaces, one for practice, which itself was a problem. Under ISU Rules governing the competition, the practice groups for each discipline put all the competitors from the same country in the same group, which automatically put Harding and Kerrigan in the same session, and in which they remained, despite requests from the U.S. Team to separate them. One had to have been there to imagine the furor which occured at the first practice session when both of them took to the ice in the small practice rink, with over 500 cameramen and journalists hanging from the walls. It is to the credit of both Kerrigan and Harding that they handled the media pressure outwardly very well, and did their best to carry out their training, which included run throughs of their programs, despite the incredible media pressure on them. Much credit must also go to the team leaders and support staff for enabling them to do so, but inevitably one has to wonder how they would have skated if the assault had never taken place.

The first figure skating event of the Games was the Pairs, with the head-to-head competition between the reinstated Ekaterina Gordeeva and Sergei Grinkov, the 1988 champions, the reinstated Natalia Mishkutenok and Artur Dmitriev, the 1992 champions, both of Russia, and Isabelle Brasseur and Lloyd Eisler of Canada, the 1993 World Pair champions, who finished in that order. Gordeeva and Grinkov had won the 1994 European Pair championship in Copenhagen before the Games, in which Mishkutenok and Dmitriev had finished third after a disastrous technical program. Although Gordeeva and Grinkov had a minor bobble in the free skating, their incredible pair unison, style and speed gave them their second Olympic Gold medal. It is safe to say that, of all the reinstated skaters, they were the ones who fully demonstrated that their skills had not diminished during the intervening years, and they set a very high standard in their event for which they deserve great credit. The U.S. Pairs did well, but not spectacularly so. Jenni Meno and Todd Sand were fifth, just behind Evgenia Shishkova and Vadim Naumov of Russia, the European Silver medalists. Kyoko Ina and Jason Dungjen, after a poor technical program in which they placed 15th, redeemed themselves in the free skating, in which they placed seventh to finish ninth overall, while Karen Courtland and Todd Reynolds placed 14th.

The Dance event started next, and featured the return to competition of the reinstated Jayne Torvill and Christopher Dean of Great Britain. They too had won the preceding European Championship, but just barely so after falling behind in the compulsory dances. Dance would be a "triangular" competition, much like the Pairs, involving Oksana Gritschuk and Evgeni Platov of Russia, the European Silver medalists, Maia Usova and Alexandr Zhulin of Russia, the 1993 World champions, and Torvill and Dean, the 1984 Olympic champions. In the Olympics, Torvill and Dean were again behind after the compulsory dances, but won the original dance, which was vintage "T and D." It all came down to the free dance, with the judges preferring the rock and roll of Gritschuk and Platov by a narrow margin, giving them the Gold medal, with Usova and Zhulin second and Torvill and Dean third. For many, a case could be made that Torvill and Dean should have been the winners, especially when the performances of the couples were strictly measured by the applicable rules. All had some violations for which they were not necessarily penalized. The best the lone U.S. couple of Elizabeth Punsalan and Jerod Swallow could do was 15th, which was, unfortunately, the lowest place for the United States since the Olympic Dance event started in 1976. Insofar as Elizabeth and Jerod were concerned, it should be noted that just before the Games her father was killed by her brother, which put an enormous strain on them. Yet they took solace from each other and were strengthened by it, so that they performed as true Olympians, with no complaints or any excuses for their performances, which were, in fact, up to their usual excellent standard. Their fortitude in the face of such adversity is to be greatly admired.

The Men's event followed, and for a brief time the attention of the public turned from Kerrigan and Harding to the anticipated battle between the reinstated Brian Boitano; the 1994 European champion, the reinstated Viktor Petrenko of Ukraine; and the 1993 World champion, Kurt Browning of Canada. Surprisingly, none of them reached the podium. All three experienced serious failures in the technical program, in which Boitano was eighth, Petrenko ninth, and Browning 12th. They all did far better in the free skating, with Browning third, Petrenko fourth, and Boitano sixth, but it was too late and they were shut out of the medals, with Petrenko finishing fourth overall, Browning fifth and Boitano sixth.

The surprise winner of the Gold medal was Alexei Urmanov of Russia, the European Bronze medalist, followed by Elvis Stojko of Canada for the Silver medal, and Philippe Candeloro of France for the Bronze – a result for the latter reminiscent of the Bronze medals won by Patrick Pera of France in 1968 and 1972, and just as unexpected! The other U.S. man, Scott Davis, was in the hunt after the technical program, in which he finished fourth, but he could not sustain his success and was eighth in the free skating, to finish eighth overall.

Finally, after two weeks of build-up, the Ladies event, which is traditionally at the end of the Games, arrived, and was actually somewhat of an anticlimax from the standpoint of the U.S. Suffice it to say that Nancy Kerrigan performed extremely well and to the best of her ability, winning the technical program and skating a clean free skating program, in which her only error was the doubling of a triple flip. The surprise winner was Oksana Baiul of Ukraine, the 1993 World champion and 1994 European Silver medalist, who, despite two mistakes in the free skating and the squeezing in of a belated and unscheduled jump combination at the end, still won the free skating by a five to four margin, to take the Gold medal. Baiul actually had skated with a back injury incurred by a collision with Tanja Szewczenko of Germany, which both of them overcame, but as a result of which neither of them skated as well as they might have. For Nancy, it was the cruel hand of fate and she deserved better, with many of the opinion that she should have won.

There was a "flap" over the awards ceremony which was completely misreported. The delay in it, which was upsetting to the participants, was due to the lack of availability of the Ukrainian national anthem, which had to be obtained by the team leader from his hotel, and had nothing to do with Oksana herself. Since the Games, Nancy has comported herself very well in regard to the result despite endless pressure from the media, which is much to her credit. At the end of the competition, she stated it very well: "I don't think this (the Silver medal) takes away from what I planned to do or what I did out there. I was really proud of myself and to watch the American flag raised for the efforts that I've put in for the year was thrilling. I knew I was capable of doing just what I did."

In third place in the competition was Chen Lu of China, while Surya Bonaly, the European Ladies champion, was fourth, followed by Yuka Sato of Japan in fifth place. Tonya Harding had nothing but problems throughout the training and in the free skating, with a shoe lace difficulty in the latter which resulted in her having to skate at the end of her group. She had been 10th in the technical program, so was not in the final group to skate in any event. In the free skating, she placed seventh to wind up eighth overall, a rather dismal end to her eligible career, especially after the promise she had shown in 1991.

Another sidebar to the Ladies event was the return to competition of Katarina Witt of Germany, who skated well, especially in the technical program, in which she was sixth, but could not equal the difficulty of the younger contemporary skaters in the free skating, placing seventh overall, just ahead of Harding.

Despite all the attention directed to the Games, there were other activities and events that continued. One such event was the Basler Cup for Senior Dance, held early in February at Basel, Switzerland. Appropriately, the winners were a Swiss couple, Diane Gerencser with yet another Russian emigre, Alexandr Stanislavov, a very rare win for the Swiss in a major International Dance event. The lone U.S. couple of Tamara Kuchiki and Neale Smull of California, placed fourth.

The USFSA supported participation in the Challenge Lysiane Lauret once again; the event had returned to Morzine, France, from Grenoble, and was held at the end of April. Entered were the third- and fourth-placed couples from the Nationals, Amy Webster of Boston and Ron Kravette of California, who placed fourth, and Wendy Millette and Jason Tebo of Boston, who placed ninth. The winners were Irina Lobacheva and Ilia Averbukh of Russia.

The third spring competition was the Gardena Spring Trophy for Junior Ladies at Ortisei, Italy, and once again the U.S. representative came away the winner, with Jennifer Karl of Minnesota taking the Gold medal. The success over the years of the U.S. Junior Ladies in the Ortisei competition and its predecessor event at Merano has been outstanding.

Once the Olympics were over, the "fallout" began, with 13 of the 18 Olympic medalists, and especially the reinstated skaters, electing not to go on to Japan for the 1994 World Championships. It remains a perennial problem after every Olympics. Dropping out, among others, in the Men, were Boitano, Petrenko and Browning; in the Ladies, Baiul and Kerrigan, and, of course, Harding. Chen Lu also had to withdraw due to an injury. In the Pairs, it was Gordeeva-Grinkov and Mishkutenok-Dmitriev, and in the Dance, Usova-Zhulin and Torvill and Dean. This left the U.S. Team quite decimated in Singles, with the ranks being filled in the Ladies by Michelle Kwan and Nicole Bobek, the second- and third-place finishers at the Nationals, replacing Kerrigan and Harding. Scott Davis remained on the Men's team, and Boitano was replaced by Aren Nielsen, the third-place finisher in Detroit. All three U.S. Pairs went to Japan as did the Dance couple.

The 1994 Worlds were held at Makuhari in Chiba Prefecture, in an incredible industrial development across the bay from Tokyo, with many hotels, the main arena and the practice rink close by. Already the talk was of "establishing the forerunners on the road to Nagano" (in 1998). In the Pairs, with every expectation that Isabelle Brasseur and Lloyd Eisler would retain their title, they were surprisingly beaten by Evgenia Shiskova and Vadim Naumov of Russia, the European Silver medalists. What was not generally known was that Isabelle had aggravated a cracked rib injury in practice and skated in pain. Actually, the free skating performance of Isabelle and Herbie was probably their finest effort ever, to take the Silver medal. In third place was another Russian Pair, Marina Eltsova and Andrei Bushkov. The U.S. Pairs did not quite equal their Olympic efforts, with Jenni Meno and Todd Sand placing sixth, which surprisingly turned out to be the highest place achieved by the U.S. Team in the 1994 Worlds. Kyoko Ina and Jason Dungjen were 12th and Karen Courtland and Todd Reynolds, 17th. Kyoko and Jason had an incredible run of bad luck in the draws for the technical programs, having to skate first at both Olympics and Worlds. Their performance in Japan deserved far better than the 14th place that they received.

With the title open, Elvis Stojko of Canada confirmed his right to the highest position by winning both parts of the Men's competition decisively and thereby succeeding Kurt Browning as the World champion. He soundly defeated in the process the new Olympic champion, Alexei Urmanov of Russia, who could do no better than fourth. In second was the irrepressible Philippe Candeloro of France, with the ever present Viacheslav Zagorodniuk of Ukraine taking the Bronze. Scott Davis turned in a disappointing effort, placing seventh, while Aren Nielsen, after an excellent sixth in the technical program, fell apart in the free skating, placing 16th and finishing 13th overall.

The Dance event was won by Gritschuk-Platov, for their first World title, with Sophie Moniotte and Pascal Lavanchy of France second, and Susanna Rahkamo and Petri Kokko of Finland third. The U.S. entry, Elizabeth Punsalan and Jerod Swallow skated much better than they had in Hamar, but still could not make the top 10 (to earn a second entry in 1995), placing 12th.

The Ladies event, which had a total of 42 entries, had to go through elimination rounds consisting of the long free skating at the start of the championships. Nicole Bobek had replaced Harding just a very few days before the start of the championships, due to the delay in the final resolution of the Harding case and her withdrawal. Nicole just barely made it to Japan in time and had little opportunity to practice before having to face the elimination round, which in itself can be as traumatic as the technical program. She did her best, but placed 13th in her group, thereby missing the final, for which the cut off was at 12th place. This left Michelle Kwan to carry the entire weight and attention of the United States public on her back, as she remained the sole

U.S. lady in the final round. She did not disappoint. After placing 11th in the technical program, it seemed that she would not make the top 10, but she came back strongly to finish eighth in the free skating and eighth overall, insuring the U.S. of two entries in 1995.

Yuka Sato of Japan was the surprise winner of the Gold medal, with flawless performances in both parts. One can imagine the pressure on her skating before her own countrymen. Surya Bonaly of France was once again second, and made a scene at the awards ceremony, in which she first refused to mount the podium and then removed her medal. The French federation later issued an apology to the ISU for her conduct. In third place was Tanja Szewczenko of Germany, a rising young star, who had placed sixth at Hamar.

The results in the 1994 Worlds for the USFSA were the poorest since the sending of full teams had been implemented following World War II, and even including the three post-crash years (1962-1964). The results also meant that the U.S. World Team in 1995 would be reduced to two Men, two Ladies, two Pairs and one Dance couple. Still the seeds of future improvement could be seen, not only in the Worlds, but also in the World Juniors, the Nationals and the Olympic Festival.

The fourth Pro-Am competition and the second at the Los Angeles Memorial Sports Arena was held in early April 1994, with the new name of "Hershey's Kisses Pro- Am Championships." The competition was in the same format as in the prior year, with Pairs and Dance being added, as had been the case in Philadelphia. It was still a domestic event, with U.S. eligible and ineligible skaters only. Paul Wylie was the Men's winner and Caryn Kadavy successfully defended her Pro-Am Ladies title of 1993, thereby maintaining the supremacy of the ineligibles. Todd Eldredge was second in the Men, followed by Aren Nielsen, with Scott Davis (who did not seem to find Pro-Ams to his liking), fourth. In the Ladies, Michelle Kwan was second, followed by Rosalynn Sumners and Nicole Bobek.

The Pair event included just one ineligible pair, Natalie and Wayne Seybold, who placed third behind Jenni Meno and Todd Sand and Kyoko Ina and Jason Dungjen. In Dance, Renée Roca and Gorsha Sur were the winners, followed by Elizabeth Punsalan and Jerod Swallow, Susan Wynne and Russ Witherby (now the ineligibles), and Amy Webster and Ron Kravette. Clearly, it would be necessary to achieve a better balance between the two categories of skaters in the future, if the events were to continue to be worthwhile.

With the 1993-1994 season winding down, there were still two important non-skating events to take place, the Annual Meeting of the Governing Council and the 45th ISU Congress. The former took place at Newport, R.I., in the home state of President Ferguson, early in May 1994. It was another very well attended meeting at that most pleasant Colonial city and maritime community on Narragansett Bay.

Although much work was accomplished, the issues generating the "heat" included such items as the level of integration for singles events in which both figures and free skating would still be combined and the matter of an increase in dues for members of member clubs. As previously mentioned, two new permanent committees were created, one voting - Coaches, and one non-voting - Collegiate Program, making a total of such committees of 19 in all, with nine voting and 10 non-voting. Also, as previously mentioned, the dues of Individual Members were doubled, while those for members of clubs were unchanged, an increase to $20.00 recommended by the Board of Directors being defeated. This action took place despite an excellent article which appeared in **Skating** magazine designed to educate the constituency on the matter of fees in general, out of which two essential facts emerged. The first was that the membership dues collected did not cover the cost of the services provided to the members. For 1993, for example, such revenue was $272,749, while expenses, consisting of membership services and Club liability insurance, totaled $474,246. The second fact was that the dues structure of the USFSA was generally lower than the average of 26 other national governing bodies that responded to a survey taken in December 1993.

The International Committee was extensively restructured, to include an Athlete Development Program Subcommittee and a Management Team within the committee responsible for the selection of skaters for International competitions. Also added to the rules was one to the effect that entry in competition was a "privilege" and not a "right" and was subject to the signing of an appropriate contract with the USFSA by the skater, thereby agreeing to abide by the USFSA's rules and regulations. This was an obvious effort to tighten up the control of the Association over those representing it, in view of the Kerrigan-Harding affair.

In the competition area, the action was finally taken to separate figure and free skating events completely at all levels of single skating. Also in Precision team skating, initial and Silver rounds at the Nationals were eliminated and the technical program was made mandatory for Senior and Junior teams, thereby creating a combined event of two parts, to be effective for 1994-1995.

Insofar as eligibility to compete was concerned, the dual requirement of having to have passed both a figure test and a free skating test was retained, with the former being the Third test for Intermediate and above and the Second Test for Juveniles. This duality would come under attack in 1995 and be eliminated as well, thereby finally ending the only remaining link between figures and free skating in competition. Curiously, the addition of an Intermediate technical program was defeated, but it too would be approved in 1995. In the 1994-95 qualifying competitions, including the Juvenile-Intermediate Nationals, the Juvenile "B" Pairs and Dance events would carry the age restriction for either partner of being at least 13 years of age or older, but under 16 years of age.

The problem of age limitations for competitive classes in the qualifying structure below Senior continued to be a controversial and confusing issue, with the matter of whether or not the ISU age requirements for Junior skaters and, as a consequence, age limitations for the levels below Junior should be adopted. Historically, the only age limitations for many years had been Veteran (later Adult), originally over age 35, and Juvenile, under age 13. Age limits were set for Intermediate and Juvenile categories in both Singles free skating and Pairs and Dance at the meeting, but only in Dance for the Junior and Novice levels. These rules are still evolving and are far from permanent today. The eventual outcome would appear to be a two-path structure, with age limited events on the one hand and matching non-age limited events on the other, for all classes of competition below Senior.

One small rule change was made in an effort to speed up the appointment of judges, by which the Regional Vice Chairmen of the Judges Committee were granted authority to appoint the lowest two levels of judge (Low and Intermediate Test, Bronze and Silver Dance Test). Certification would also be required of all judges, reflecting attendance at a seminar before being eligible to serve on the Moves in the Field portion of the Free Skating tests.

The new Free Skating tests including the Moves in the Field tests were also adopted, which added two new tests to the structure, a Pre-Preliminary and a Pre-Juvenile Free Skating Test. The matching Moves in the Field Test had to be passed before the test candidate could take the comparable free skating test. The new tests were the product of a huge cooperative effort on the part of judges, coaches and others, under the leadership of Margaret Anne Wier of Utah and Christine Haigler Krall of Colorado Springs. They are an enormous step forward for the sport and could well provide the basis for better skating and much improved free skating programs at all levels. The volume of such tests has risen very rapidly and has presented a problem to Headquarters in keeping up with the processing of them, which is a nice one to have!

The gala banquet at Newport was equally as successful as the first one at Cleveland. The recipient of the "Reader's Choice Award" of Skating magazine was Michelle Kwan, the youngest recipient at just under 14. Recognized as a special honoree was Anne Gerli of New York, a National judge and former Board member, who had been instrumental in the founding of the Juvenile-Intermediate Nationals, and a long-time and vigorous advocate of many causes at the Governing Council meetings as a representative of the New York Regional Council of Figure Skating Clubs. Recognized for their achievements as coaches were Ron Ludington and John Nicks, both of them former champion skaters themselves in Pairs and the long-time coaches of many Pair and Dance champions too numerous to mention. Recognized as 50 year judges were Nancy D'Wolf of Bristol, R.I., a High Test judge; Marie Church of Boiceville, N.Y., a Silver Dance judge, and Anne Gerli of New York, a National judge. A very special award was presented to Haik

Gharibians, of Vancouver, British Columbia, a world-class physiotherapist, for his long-time association with the USFSA as a team trainer, including many Olympic Games and World Championships.

Two clubs, the Arctic Blades FSC of Paramount, Calif., and the Dallas FSC of Texas, were recognized for their 50 years of membership in the USFSA. Honored as exceptional volunteers were Al and Joan Brown of Massachusetts, for their special services in running the copy center at major competitions. Without them, bulletins would not have been issued and protocols never would have been ready in time for distribution. Also at the Gala, the late Roger Turner was inducted into the U.S. Figure Skating Hall of Fame. Also noted was the naming of Brian Wright of Indianapolis (the artistic director of the Indiana/World Skating Academy) by the USFSA Coaches Committee as the recipient of the Paul McGrath Award for Choreography. The award was duly presented to him by the PSGA at its annual meeting.

An appropriate memorial resolution was adopted for the late Past President, Frederick C. LeFevre of Williamsburg, Va., as well as resolutions honoring the members of the World, Olympic and World Junior Teams.

The new editor of **Skating** magazine, Jay Miller of Colorado Springs, who had replaced Kim Mutchler, was present at the meeting. He came to the USFSA from his prior position of Director of Communications for USA Boxing, and, of course, was the recipient of many comments concerning the obvious comparisons between boxing and figure skating, which he fielded good naturedly. In fact there were many similarities between the two associations.

The 45th Ordinary Congress of the ISU was held at Boston in June 1994, the second Congress to be held in the United States, just 10 years after the first one at Colorado Springs in 1984. A major undertaking, the Congress was very well organized under the sponsorship of the New England Council of Figure Skating Clubs, with E. Newbold Black IV, of Boston as the chairman of the local organizing committee. He was ably assisted by Judy Edmunds, Oscar and Maggie Iobst, Shirley Taylor, David Wallis, Mary Louise and Benjamin Wright, George Yonekura and Sally Zeghibe. Also assisting greatly with the arrangements were members of the Headquarters staff, headed by Executive Director Jerry Lace. The site of the Congress was the venerable Copley Plaza Hotel in the Back Bay area of Boston.

Despite the long distances traveled by the delegates from Europe and Asia, the Congress was very well attended, with 49 countries being represented by 64 Members and 181 delegates, plus 39 ISU Officeholders and eight Honorary members. Since the ISU is a "dual" federation governing both speed and figure skating, in many countries there are two separate national associations for each sport, hence the larger number of members than countries. Notable among the delegates were no less than five former Olympic champions, Terry McDermott and Lidia

Skoblikova Polozkova in speed skating, Carol Heiss Jenkins and Scott Hamilton in figure skating and Alexandr Gorshkov in ice dancing. Former World champions included Igor Zhelezovski and Boris Stenin in speed skating, Carol Heiss Jenkins and Scott Hamilton in figure skating, and Lawrence Demmy, Courtney Jones and Alexandr Gorshkov in ice dancing. The ISU has always been proud to have among its officeholders and delegates the former champions in the sports.

The main items topping the agenda were questions of eligibility and the elections. As to the former, the previously open door permitting ineligible skaters to be reinstated with the right to compete was once again closed, with one last opportunity for reinstatement being permitted with a deadline of April 1, 1995. It was really a retroactive move, and a return to the more strict eligible rules of the past up to 1992. Also permitted were fixed payments to competitors, officials and others in connection with preparation for and participation in ISU activities. This would mean, for example, that judges and referees could be paid, and that eligible skaters could receive prize money. Also permitted would be open International competitions between eligible and ineligible skaters, provided the organizing national associations controlled the entries and conducted the competitions in accordance with ISU Rules.

The technical program returned to its old name of "short" program, with a concurrent increase in the difficulty of some of the elements, for example, no double/double jump combination being permitted for Men. The Ladies finally were allowed a triple in the jump preceded by connecting footwork. Major deductions were slightly reduced and would now be the same for jump combinations, solo jumps and spins at 0.1 to 0.4 for failures and 0.5 for omissions. New deductions of 0.1 to 0.2 in both marks for lying or kneeling on the ice or excessive turning on the knees or boots were added. For Juniors, a second step sequence was added for Men and a step sequence for Ladies.

In the Pair short program, a solo triple jump was now permitted, and the twist lifts now specified that the lady be caught in the air around the waist. For Junior Pairs, there was a return to the former format of (three) groups of the required elements, to be drawn for the three years, 1994-1997. The Senior Pair free skating would now require two death spirals, and the twist lift was now to be a minimum requirement. In Ice Dancing, four new dances would be introduced, the Austrian Waltz and Silver Samba in 1995-1996, and the Golden Waltz and Cha Cha Congelado in 1996-1997.

Further refinements of the Precision Team skating rules were made to reflect the continuing progress and growth of the discipline, to the end that with the advent of formal International competition, the necessary rules were there and comprehensive enough to cover all eventualities. One change also for all disciplines was that of the name of the second mark from "artistic impression" to "presentation."

Yet another revision was made in the rules covering clothing, which required that ladies wear a skirt, men wear full-length trousers (no more tights) and have sleeves (no bare arms).

Another rule change of interest to the U.S. was one in Ice Dancing which provided that the first appointment of a Judge for International Competitions would be on a probationary basis for the first two years, and thereafter such judges would become permanent International judges, provided they had at least one satisfactory judging report during the probationary period. A five-year "window" was also opened to permit judges between the ages of 45 and 50, who had been appointed in one discipline prior to age 45, to be appointed a judge in the other two disciplines (there are three altogether - figure skating, ice dancing and precision) if they were otherwise qualified.

Also approved was a change in the marking of the compulsory dances to use two marks, with the first being for "technique" (accuracy, placement, style and unison), and the second for "timing/expression." Another change was also made with respect to the singles events at the World (and European) Championships, which was to "bye" through to the final round the top 10 from the previous year, but by name only with no substitutions, with the top 10 from each qualifying round (Groups A and B) making the final round, for a maximum starting number of 30. Seeding was therefore eliminated.

One unusual aspect of the Congress was the processing of the rule changes by computer. This effort, led by Charles DeMore, assisted by Benjamin Wright, together with the unstinting cooperation of the several drafting committees, enabled the General Secretary, Beat Häsler of Switzerland, to take back with him to Davos the complete draft of all the rules, fully revised and ready to go to the printer.

The elections at the Boston Congress were quite "earthshaking." First, Olaf Poulsen of Norway retired as President after serving 14 years in that office and 23 years overall as an ISU Officeholder. He was duly elected an Honorary President, the sixth person so honored. Charles A. DeMore, a member of the ISU Council for 14 years, also retired and was elected an Honorary member of the ISU, the fourth from the United States so honored, the others being Walter S. Powell, John R. Shoemaker and Benjamin T. Wright.

With the Presidency open, a very closely contested election between Lawrence Demmy of Great Britain, the Figure Skating Vice President, and Ottavio Cinquanta of Italy, the Speed Skating Vice President took place, in which Ottavio prevailed by the narrow margin of 52 to 46 votes. Claire Ferguson was elected as the fourth member of the Council for Figure Skating, thereby continuing the unbroken representation of the United States on that body since 1947. Lawrence Demmy was re-elected Vice President for Figure Skating and also was elected First Vice President. Gerhard Zimmerman of Germany was elected the Speed Skating Vice President.

A new Technical Committee was established for Precision Team Skating, making three committees in figure skating, with Patricia French of Williamsville, N.Y., elected as its first chairman, a singular honor, but also a well deserved recognition of her work on the ad hoc committee for Precision for four years since 1990. Happily also, Ronald Pfenning of Hyannis, Mass., was elected as a member of the Figure Skating Committee, returning a U.S. representative to that important committee after a two-year hiatus. Franklin Nelson of Oakland, Calif., was re-appointed as a Medical Advisor, a position in which he is the Senior ISU Officeholder for the United States, having been originally appointed in 1976. As a result of the elections, the representation of the USFSA in the ISU was doubled, from two to four, a quantum jump, which speaks well for the high regard in which the USFSA is held among its peer associations. It should also be noted that there are U.S. representatives on two of the Speed Skating Technical Committees: Eugene Sandvig of Minneapolis on Speed Skating (long track) and William Markland of Champaign, Ill., on Short Track, while James Hawkins of St. Louis serves on the Appeals Commission.

The social events of the Congress were highlighted by a Boston Harbor cruise on a luxury vessel, the Odyssey, and a gala banquet. At the latter, the tangible tokens of the election to the World Figure Skating Hall of Fame of the late Jacques Favart of France, President of the ISU from 1967 to 1980, were presented by Benjamin Wright to ISU Honorary Vice President and Honorary President of the French Federation, Jean Heckly of Paris, to take back to France for the family of Mr. Favart.

So it was that the "cataclysmic" season of 1994-1995 came to an end on a very high note.

A commentary on the way in which one season becomes another almost unnoticed can be seen on the cover of the August 1994 issue of **Skating** magazine, which had a large headline at the bottom, "U.S. Olympic Festival -'94 • 45th I.S.U. Congress." While the two events were reversed on the cover, the Congress represented the end of the 1993-1994 season, while the Festival represented the start of the 1994-1995 season!

At long last, the USOC finally permitted the Festival figure skating events to be for Junior skaters, which had been an objective of the USFSA practically since the beginning (1976). As it turned out, it was a good decision, as the young Juniors participating did just as well as their elders and were just as pleasing to the audience. As the first competition following the Olympic year, the Festival was indeed a kick-off for the future stars, who might be competing at Nagano in 1998. Instead of there being a separate selection competition for the 1995 World Junior Championships, the Festival results were used for that purpose, with three Men, three Ladies, two Pairs and one Dance couple to be selected.

The 1994 Festival was held at St. Louis, Mo., in the St. Louis Arena, which has a considerable history of skating in that city. There were a total of 29 entries, representing 42 skaters in the competition. The winner in the Ladies was 12-year-old (just a month before) Tara

Lipinski of Texas (trained at Newark, Delaware), who won decisively over Teresa Aiello of New York, almost a Festival veteran herself, since she had been third in the 1993 Senior event. Third was Chrisha Gossard of Delaware, while the best the reigning National Junior Ladies champion, Jennifer Karl of Minnesota, could do was fifth, which shows the meteoric speed with which young skaters mature and advance.

In the Men, there was a popular win by Derrick Delmore of Maryland, who defeated the 1994 National Novice champion, Timothy Goebel of Ohio, second. Johnnie Bevan of Washington was third. In Pairs, Danielle and Steve Hartsell of Michigan were the winners, continuing their promising and successful march up the ladder. They defeated Erin Elbe and Jeffrey Weiss of California, with Jacki Davison of Torrance, Calif., and J. Paul Binnebose, formerly of Delaware (a new partnership), third.

The Dance event winners were Jayna Cronin of Maryland and Jonathan Nichols of Delaware, with Jessica Joseph and Charles Butler, Jr., of Michigan, the 1994 National Novice Dance champions, second, and Kristina Feliciano and Alex Jacoby of California third.

Not to be overlooked as a regular fixture early in each season is the Figure Skating Sports Medicine and Science Program, conducted by the USFSA's Sports Medicine Committee in conjunction with the U.S. Olympic Training Center's Sports Science and Technology Division in Colorado Springs, better known, despite all the fancy names, as the Summer Training Camps. In recent years, the camps have been for Junior and Novice skaters. Among the areas covered and evaluations made of the skaters are musculoskeletal, medical, nutrition, psychology, physiology and biomechanics.

Much useful information has been obtained by the camps on an ongoing basis, one finding of which, for example, is that skaters who work at their on-ice and off-ice conditioning will improve their performances. It is a well known fact that figure skaters generally are not well conditioned throughout their bodies, and that few of them carry out any comprehensive program of conditioning, or even of proper warm-up prior to going on to the ice. Much information has been learned directly relating to actual skating techniques, especially such elements as jumps and spins for Singles and Pair skaters. In 1993, there began a study of the speed and lean angles for ice dancers and Pair skaters. The camps are an important part of the preparation of skaters for competition, and perhaps have not received the publicity and awareness within the skating community that they deserve. The Sports Medicine Committee deserves much credit for its continuing efforts in the field.

The next competition during the summer of 1994 was the third Goodwill Games, returning to Russia and St. Petersburg, for the second actual competition. There were many problems with the arenas to be used, with one, the Yubileiny Ice Palace's ice-making machinery breaking down completely and the competition being temporarily transferred to what was in fact the practice rink. It was simply not possible to hold the ice in the summer (the competition being held in early August), with no real air conditioning available to properly cool the building. Ultimately, a refrigeration expert was brought in, who devised a way to use liquid nitrogen as a freezing agent, so that the competition could continue. The problems clearly reflected what was happening in Russia, with the virtually complete "evaporation" of any central government support for sports and their facilities, leaving the local governments who were responsible for them to struggle on their own as best they could.

A representative U.S. team was sent, including Todd Eldredge, Michael Weiss and Aren Nielsen in the Men; Michelle Kwan, Nicole Bobek and Elaine Zayak in the Ladies; Stephanie Stiegler and Lance Travis, the 1993 National Junior Pair champions, and Calla Urbanski and Rocky Marval, the former National Pair champions back together again, in the Pairs; and Tamara Kuchiki and Neale Smull in Dance. There were 29 entries and 42 skaters from five countries (Russia, USA, France, Ukraine and Latvia) in the four events.

In the end, the U.S. came away with two Silver medals, Todd Eldredge in the Men, behind Alexei Urmanov of Russia, the 1994 Olympic champion; and Michelle Kwan, who recovered from a sixth in the short program, by winning the free skating, to place second behind Surya Bonaly of France. Michael Weiss placed sixth and Aren Nielsen, seventh in Men; Nicole Bobek placed seventh and Elaine Zayak eighth in Ladies.

The Pair title went to Natalia Mishkutenok and Arthur Dmitriev, who were followed by Marina Eltsova and Andrei Bushkov and Evgenia Shishkova and Vadim Naumov, all of the Russian "big guns." Stephanie Stiegler and Lance Travis were sixth and Calla Urbanski and Rocky Marval seventh. The Dance event was won by Irina Romanova and Igor Yaroshenko of Ukraine, followed by two Russian couples, a Ukrainian couple and another Russian couple and then Tamara Kuchiki and Neale Smull bringing up the rear in sixth place.

The competition once again raised the old question of the value of participating in competitions in Pairs and Dance inside Russia, which goes back to the Moscow Skate. Inherently, the question of fair judging under such circumstances has to come into play, since the judging panels usually consist of a majority of judges from the former Soviet republics. Of course, the value of the experience is considerable, even if the results are not.

The next competition was the 1994 National Collegiates, which had become an important event in the summer schedule, returning once again to Colorado Springs. There were 54 entries in just four events: Senior Ladies Figures and Free Skating and Junior Ladies Figures and Free Skating. The Senior Ladies Free Skating actually had 28 entries, while the Junior Ladies Free Skating curiously had only four. There were no Men's or Dance events.

The championships were very special in one respect, which was the return, in what was her last year of eligibility as a collegian, of Kathaleen Kelly, now Cutone, representing Northeastern Law School. Kathaleen had been an active singles competitor at all levels up to 1990, including being the North Atlantic Ladies champion. Educational demands then intervened, with college and law school, so she had not actively competed for three years. It was a triumphant return, as she won her third National Collegiate Senior Ladies title, her third in all, the others having been in 1985 (a combined event) and 1987. She had also won the Senior Figures event twice, in 1987 and 1989. Kathy was third after the short program, but pulled up to win. In second was Amanda Farkas of Boston University, while the defending champion, Sara Kastner of the University of St. Thomas, was fourth.

Kathy did not stop with the Collegiates. She went on to the 1995 New Englands, where she placed second to Patricia Mansfield of Acton, Mass.; and the 1995 Easterns, where she was also second, this time to Kyoko Ina of New York, thereby qualifying for the 1995 Nationals at Providence, R.I. In the Nationals, Kathy placed 11th overall, after an eighth in the short program. She still qualified, however, for one of her ultimate goals, a return to the World Winter University (FISU) Games, in which she had last competed in 1989, placing fourth. The 1995 University Games were held at Jaca, Spain, where Kathy placed a creditable sixth after a fourth in the short program. Today she is married, an associate in a prominent law firm in Boston, a member of the USFSA Board of Directors and its Executive Committee as an athlete representative and an active judge. She continues to skate very well and to compete. She certainly is a role model, and her enthusiasm and love for the sport is very evident. She comes from the "skating" Kelly family of New Jersey and Lake Placid, with two sisters who also competed, Noreen and Aileen.

In the Collegiates, the winners of the Senior Ladies Figures were Lisa Bryson of the University of Colorado and Janette Lynn Lewis of Denver University, in a unique tie, which results from the fact that the placements on each figure are calculated separately and then factored. Bryson had a third and two seconds in the three figures, for a factored total of 7.0, while Lewis had two firsts and a fifth, for a factored total also of 7.0. Whether the marks for the figures should again be added together and an overall result taken from the total of the marks for each judge seems to remain a controversial issue for some reason.

In the Junior Ladies, the winner was Amy Lynn Love of the University of Kansas, while the winner of the Junior Ladies Figures was Sonja Castaneda of the University of Alaska.

On the International competition circuit, for the first half up to the Nationals, the events chosen by the Association included nine competitions: the Coupe des Alpes (St. Gervais and Oberstdorf), the Karl Schäfer Memorial (Vienna), Skate America (Pittsburgh), the Pokal der Blauen Schwerter for Juniors (Chemnitz, Germany), Skate Canada (Red Deer, Alberta), the

Trophée de France (Lyon), the Nations Cup (Gelsenkirchen, Germany), and the NHK Trophy (Morioka, Japan). The number of International Precision competitions was also growing, with Precision Canada International (Toronto), Snowflake International (Dearborn, Mich.), and the French Cup (Rouen).

Added competitions on the domestic scene included the first Adult Nationals at Wilmington, Del., and an Intercollegiate Team competition at MIT, Cambridge, Mass., the first Intercollegiate competition to be held in the United States other than the Nationals. Added to these were the regular events, such as the nine Regionals, three Sectionals, the Nationals, two Pro-Am competitions, the new Kodak Junior Olympics (the former Juvenile-Intermediate Nationals), plus three more International competitions in the spring, the Basler Cup (Basel, Switzerland), the Challenge Lysiane Lauret (Morzine, France), both Senior Dance events, and the Gardena Spring Trophy for Junior Ladies (Ortisei, Italy). As can readily be seen, when compared with just 20 years before, the volume of competition activity, not to mention the many non-qualifying competitions held throughout the year, had increased a hundredfold, and involved probably thousands of skaters, compared with just a few hundred in the past. That certainly is one of the major accomplishments of the Association during its 75-year history!

The 1994-1995 International season kicked off as usual with the return to St. Gervais and Oberstdorf. The competitions were, from the standpoint of the U.S. entries, split for the first time with separate teams going to each. This was a significant change from past practice, going back to the early 1970s, when a joint or dual team was sent to the two competitions, just a week apart. Part of the considerable success of the U.S. Team in the Coupe des Alpes over the years can be attributed to the same skaters performing twice in two back-to-back competitions, as often the problems encountered at St. Gervais were worked out by Oberstdorf, especially by the young and inexperienced Junior skaters moving up. Whether two separate teams will do as well remains to be seen.

The first year of the new system probably is not a good criterion, as generally the U.S. skaters did reasonably well, but with just three medals among them; as usual, these came only in Singles, with none in Pairs or Dance. At St. Gervais, Amanda Ward of New York, the 1994 National Junior Ladies Silver medalist, was the winner, with her teammate, Teresa Aiello of New York, seventh. In the Men, John Bevan of Washington was fifth, and Jason Sylvia of Massachusetts, the National Junior Silver medalist, 10th. In Pairs, the highest place was a fifth by Cheryl Marker and Todd Price of Minnesota, the National Junior Pair Silver medalists, with Nicole Bateson-Rock of Delaware and Keith Tindall of Washington, the 1994 National Junior Pair champions, eighth. In Dance it was the same story, with the best place being a seventh by Julia Bikbova and Robert Peal of Illinois, with Eve Chalom and Mathew Gates of Michigan 10th. The winners in the Pairs and Dance were a French pair and an Italian couple, respectively, the

Eastern skaters from the former Soviet Union having decided to skip St. Gervais for a change. Actually, it had been at St. Gervais in 1991 that Oleg Fediukov, who would be skating at Oberstdorf with Laura Gayton, had been second in the Dance with Ekaterina Proskurina, representing the USSR.

The Russians and Ukrainians were very much in evidence at Obertsdorf, however, apparently having switched their allegiance, with Ilya Kulik winning the Men and Irina Slutskaia, the Ladies. Shepherd Clark of Georgia was second, with Damon Allen of Colorado fifth in Men. In the Ladies, Jennifer Karl, the 1994 National Junior Ladies champion, was third. Curiously, the French again prevailed in the Pairs at Oberstdorf, and also in the Dance; and although there were Russians and Ukrainians in the fields, they did not do well. In Pairs, the best U.S. place was ninth by Aimée Offner and Brad Cox of Delaware, while in the Dance the best U.S. place was seventh by Wendy Millette and Jason Tebo of Massachusetts, with Laura Gayton of Massachusetts and Oleg Fediukov of Rhode Island, the 1994 National Junior Dance champions, ninth. In the Coupe des Alpes itself, the two teams combined to take second place overall, behind France but ahead of Canada.

The Karl Schäfer Memorial competition at Vienna, Austria, took place at the end of September, with one Man, one Lady and one Dance couple representing the U.S. There was no Pair event. Rudy Galindo of California added another important milestone to his long and distinguished career by winning the Men's event, defeating, among others, Ilya Kulik of Russia, who later in the season would be both the World Junior and the European champion. In the Ladies, Chrisha Gossard of Delaware was seventh, the winner being Szusanna Szwed of Poland. In the Dance, which was won by Michelle Fitzgerald and Vincent Kyle, for a rare British triumph, Nicole Dumonceaux and John Reupucci of Minnesota, the 1991 National Novice Dance champions, were tenth.

A revisit was made to the Pokal der Blauen Schwerter (Blue Sword) for Juniors, being held at Chemnitz (formerly Karl-Marx-Stadt) at the end of October. The U.S. did well in the competition, which is virtually the only major Junior competition before the World Junior Championships, the one usually attended by the leading contenders from both East and West. Two Gold medals were earned. Tara Lipinski of Texas won the Ladies in a field of 29, while Timothy Goebel of Ohio was fourth in the Men, with Gabriel Monnier of France the winner. Derrick Delmore, the Olympic Festival winner had a bad day and finished 17th out of 29 entries, with an 18th in free skating.

In Pairs, Danielle and Steve Hartsell of Michigan were winners over a Russian and a Ukrainian Pair, in a field of 10. Erin Elbe and Jeffrey Weiss of California were seventh. The Dance was won by a Russian couple, Olga Sharutenko and Dmitri Naumkin. The two U.S. couples,

Jessica Joseph and Charles Butler, Jr., of Michigan, and Kristina Feliciano and Alex Jacoby of California, were eighth and 11th respectively.

The next big competition was Sudafed Skate America International 1994 held at Pittsburgh, Pa., the site of the 1983 Nationals, at the end of October. There was a representative field of 33 entries from 10 countries, with the U.S. taking three medals, including a rare Gold in Dance. Prize money was again offered at Skate America, as it had been in 1993, but at a substantially increased level, $10,000, $7,500 and $5,000 for first through third respectively. Todd Eldredge clearly confirmed that he "was back," by winning the Men's event over Philippe Candeloro and Eric Millot of France. Aren Nielsen finished sixth. Seventh was Michael Shmerkin of Israel, the first time a representative of that country had participated in Skate America.

Surya Bonaly of France pulled up from third after the Ladies short program to win, defeating Michelle Kwan and Irina Slutskaia of Russia, who had won the short program. Nicole Bobek was seventh. In Dance, Elizabeth Punsalan and Jerod Swallow of Michigan were the winners over a good field, with Marina Anissina (another Russian emigre) and Gwendal Peizerat of France second, and Elisaveta Stekolikova and Dmitri Kazarliga of Kazakhstan third. In sixth place were Amy Webster of Massachusetts and Ron Kravette of California.

The Pairs was "loaded," with Marina Eltsova and Andrei Bushkov of Russia, the 1993 European Pair champions, the winners, followed by Evgenia Shiskova and Vadim Naumov of Russia, the 1994 World Pair champions, second, and Radka Kovarikova and René Novotny of the Czech Republic, who would become the 1995 World Pair champions, third. The fourth place Pair was Elena Berezhnaia and Oleg Shliakov of Latvia, with Kyoko Ina and Jason Dungjen fifth, and Stephanie Stiegler and Lance Travis sixth.

Sunlife Skate Canada International followed just a week later, as it usually does, this time in Alberta, at the small city of Red Deer, halfway between Calgary and Edmonton. This continued the policy of the CFSA to send the competition to small urban centers as a means of promoting the sport. This has generally been successful for them, with sellout crowds in the smaller buildings. The Canadians sent their top man, Elvis Stojko, who won the Men's event, and their third man, Sebastien Britten, who would become the Canadian champion later in the season when Stojko had to withdraw due to an injury. The U.S. sent its middle-rank skaters, as has been the practice in recent years. In the Men, Michael Chack was the lone U.S. entry, and he finished fifth, just behind Dmitri Dmitrenko of Ukraine, the 1993 European champion.

The winner of the Ladies was Krisztina Czako of Hungary, followed by Laetitia Hubert of France, the 1992 World Junior Ladies champion, with Jessica Mills of Illinois, the 1989 World Junior Ladies champion, third. Amanda Farkas of Massachusetts was seventh, but skated with an injury which prevented her from doing her best. The Pairs was a good, but not top, World-class event, and was won by Kristy Sargeant and Kris Wirtz of Canada, with Berezhnaia and Shliakov of Latvia second. The only U.S. Pair, Cheryl Marker and Todd Price of Minn., were seventh.

The Dance saw a major win in their home International competition for Shae-Lynn Bourne and Victor Kraatz of Canada, with a Lithuanian couple Margareta Drobiazko and Povilas Vanagas second. Renée Roca and Gorsha Sur were third, for the second U.S. medal. The interpretive free skating events were still being offered, the only International competition to do so, and Daniel Hollander of Michigan was fifth, the winner for the third time being Daniel Weiss of Germany. Weiss actually received one perfect mark for presentation from the French judge, the first-ever awarded in the Interpretive events. At the same time, the Danish judge gave him just 4.5!

The 1994 Trophée de France was held at Lyon (the same site as for the 1971 Worlds and 1982 Europeans), a pleasant city on the Rhine River in Southern France, well known for its cuisine. Here the U.S. team did well, with four medals including one in Dance. The Men's event was won by Philippe Candeloro of France, with his teammate Eric Millot second, followed by Michael Chack, who slipped a little after having been second in the short program. The Ladies were was won once again by Surya Bonaly of France, who herself also had to pull up from third in the short program. The surprise from the U.S. standpoint was the second place by Tonia Kwiatkowski at the expense of Michelle Kwan, who had been fourth in the short.

In Pairs, Eltsova and Bushkov of Russia were the winners, with the ever-present Berezhnaia and Shliakov of Latvia second, followed by Mandy Wötzel and Ingo Steuer of Germany, and Radka Kovarikova and René Novotny of the Czech Republic, another loaded event. In fifth were Kyoko Ina and Jason Dungjen. The Dance event was won by Marina Anissina and Gwendal Peizerat of France, with Elizabeth Punsalan and Jerod Swallow second, defeating Katerina Mrazova and Martin Simecek of the Czech Republic. Drobiazko and Vanagas of Lithuania were third, in the constant shuffling that is usually seen in the International Dance competitions, but which is never found in the later ISU Championships.

The next competition a week later was the Nations Cup at Gelsenkirchen, Germany, with a mixed team of experienced and inexperienced skaters being sent. In the Men, Shepherd Clark was again second, reconfirming his progress towards the podium in the United States. He had, however, to recover from a fifth in the short program, by taking second in the free skating to earn the Silver medal. The winner was Elvis Stojko of Canada, with Dmitri Dmitrenko of Ukraine third. In 10th place was Michael Weiss, the 1994 World Junior champion. The Ladies winner was Marina Kielmann of Germany, with the two U.S. entrants, Lisa Matras sixth, and Tanya Street seventh. The Pairs was won by Wötzel and Steuer of the home country, but Stephanie Stiegler and Lance Travis were third, just ahead of Sargeant and Wirtz of Canada. In Dance, which was won by Anissina and Peizerat of France, Christina and Mark Fitzgerald were 10th.

The ninth competition was the NHK Trophy, held in early December in Morioka, Japan, a Northern city on the main island of Honshu. Here again, Todd Eldredge made his statement and challenge for World supremacy by winning the Men, coming from behind to defeat Candeloro of France and Zagorodniuk of Ukraine. Scott Davis placed fourth after a sixth in the short program. The Ladies was won by Chen Lu of China, who made her own statement by defeating Surya Bonaly of France; the only U.S. entrant, Michelle Cho of California, the 1993 National Junior Ladies champion, placed 10th. The Pair title was won by Eltsova and Bushkov of Russia, with Kovarikova and Novotny of the Czech Republic second, and Wötzel and Steuer of Germany third, followed by the new rising young pair of Berezhnaia and Shliakov of Latvia, a field quite typical of the strong pair competitions usually seen at NHK, where the Eastern countries would often send their skaters. Jenni Meno and Todd Sand, the National Pair champions of 1994, could not crack the Eastern bloc and finished fifth. In Dance, the winners were Sophie Moniotte and Pascal Lavanchy of France, followed by Tatiana Navka and Samuel Gezolian of Belarus, Marina Anissina and Gwendal Peizerat of France, and Katerina Mrazova and Martin Simecek of the Czech Republic, essentially the middle of the top 10 in the world. As in the Pairs, the National champions Renée Roca and Gorsha Sur could not break through to the medals, placing fifth.

At the end of November in Philadelphia, the "Thrifty Car Rental International Challenge" was held, the fall Pro-Am competition, but this time open to International skaters, as had been decreed by the ISU at the 1994 Congress. So, the competition was conducted under ISU Rules. The "balance" between the eligibles and the ineligibles was really lost in this event, with just three ineligibles overall in the four events, out of a total of 17 entries: Viktor Petrenko and Mark Mitchell in the Men, and Caryn Kadavy in the Ladies. The continued viability of the Pro-Am type event held under ISU Rules has to be very much in doubt if the ineligibles do not elect to participate. It would be better to merge it with Skate America in such a case. In the Men, Todd Eldredge once again came out on top, defeating Alexei Urmanov of Russia. Petrenko, who had been fifth in the short program, won the free skating to wind up third, followed by Mark Mitchell, fourth, and Scott Davis, fifth. In the Ladies, Surya Bonaly of France was the winner, with Olga Markova of Russia, second, followed by Michelle Kwan (who had been fourth in the short program, but second in free skating). Caryn Kadavy was fourth, and Nicole Bobek fifth.

The Pair event was won by Shishkova and Naumov of Russia, with Meno-Sand second and Ina-Dungjen third, and a Pair from Ukraine, Elena Beloussovskaia and Sergei Potalov fourth. In Dance, there were just three entrants, with Angelika Krylova and Oleg Ovsiannikov of Russia the winners, followed by Irina Romanova and Igor Yaroshenko of Ukraine, with Renée Roca and Gorsha Sur, third. As can readily be seen, the event was essentially one between the U.S. and the former Soviet skaters from Russia and Ukraine, with only Bonaly representing a third country.

In the fall of 1994 and early in 1995, there was another occurrence of the deaths of several persons who had been much involved with and who had made a substantial contribution to the sport. Among them were Walter Probst of California, who passed away at the end of September at the age of 79. Walter, with his wife, Carol, had been the founder of the Ice Castle Training Center at Lake Arrowhead, Calif., and had also instituted the Foundation for International Ice Skating Advancement, which provided financial assistance to international skaters.

Another death during the summer was that of Megan Taylor of Great Britain, at the age of 73. Megan had been World Ladies champion in 1938 and 1939, and was the daughter of the late Phil Taylor, a renowned exhibition skater and instructor before World War II. She had been a member of the 1932 British Olympic Team at the age of 12. After the War, she had come to the United States, where she had been an instructor for many years.

Coincidentally, a contemporary of Taylor who passed away in January 1995, at the age of 77, was Graham Sharp of Great Britain, the World and European champion in 1939. He was a member of both the 1936 and 1948 British Olympic teams, making a return to competition after long service during the War. He was the first Englishman to win both the World and European titles.

Passing away in January at the age of 97 in Hamburg, Germany, was Cécile ("Baby") Grafström, the widow of the late three-time Olympic champion, Gillis Grafström of Sweden and a great-granddaughter of the composer Felix Mendelssohn. It was she who ultimately gave to the World Figure Skating Museum in Colorado Springs in 1979 the unique collection she and her late husband had put together, known as "Skating in Art."

Another death was that of Virginia Fratianne of California in October at the age of 63. The mother of former World champion Linda Fratianne-Maricich, Virginia was a Gold Test and Senior Competition judge, and active for many years in the Los Angeles FSC.

The fall meeting of the Board of Directors for 1994 was held at Colorado Springs at the Olympic Training Center, probably for the last time at that facility, since in the future charges were to be imposed by the USOC for its use. In the October 1994, issue of **Skating** magazine, there was an excellent summary of the budget of the Association by Executive Director Jerry Lace, which was really supplemental to his report to the meeting. In it, Jerry pointed out the breakdown of the expenditures and revenue, as follows:

Expenditures	Revenue
Governance - 6%	Membership - 14%
Membership - 13%	ABC - fundraising, TV, sponsorship - 53%
Fundraising - 5%	USOC - 9%
Athlete support - 28%	Events - 9%
Technical - 4%	Other - 15%

Events - 16%

Operations - 15%

Other - 13%

Jerry states that: "The U.S. Figure Skating Association – in meeting its responsibilities to the various constituencies of the Association – needs to continually review its resources of income in order to meet those obligations. Knowing full well that the requirements of USFSA constituents far exceeds the money available, there needs to be a balance of allocation of resources to reflect the goals established by the Governing Council. This is not an easy task, but one that can be accomplished with good decision-making and resourcefulness on the part of the individuals responsible for implementing the programs."

Also pointed out in the article was that in an ideal revenue-generating scenario, approximately one-third of the revenues should come from television and sponsorship, one-third from events and one-third from membership. The vulnerability of the organization to downward trends in sponsorship and television was readily apparent, and Lace was firmly of the opinion, and rightly so, that the dependency on television and sponsorship for revenue had to be reduced.

He also stated that the Association could not become complacent because of the favorable television contract with ABC. Areas for increasing revenue mentioned included new events, increased local sponsorship, expansion of licensing and merchandising and increasing of membership. These were wise words, made despite the incredible explosion of media interest in the sport.

In spite of the enormous increase in activity and participation that we have seen throughout this history, the core membership of the Association remains surprisingly static or flat. The total paid subscriptions for the magazine, for example, for the season of 1993-1994 were at an average of 35,400, not substantially greater than they had been over the prior years. The one big change in the membership picture, which does not impact the magazine, is the Basic Skills membership, which, as has already been noted, had peaked around 74,000 in 1993-1994.

Another article in the December 1994 issue of the magazine, by President Ferguson and Executive Director Lace, recounted the extraordinary exposure and resulting volatility of the media marketplace insofar as the sport was concerned. Some of the factors for this were outlined, including the addition of a fourth broadcast network and the proliferation of cable networks, which created an unprecedented demand for programming. Also cited was the unfortunate fact that all of the commercial activity had not generated any revenue to go back into the development of grassroots programs, with no programs for clubs, officials, coaches or beginning skaters being funded from outside the Association as a result.

The two articles are cited as an example of the forward thinking that must be implemented by the Association administration in a time of extreme turmoil. The second article ends with a cogent statement: "The USFSA leadership and membership should recognize that although the organization has been pro-active in this area, it is incumbent upon us to take greater control of the sport, to guide its development in a direction that will further foster and promote growth of the sport instead of helping to line the pockets of individual entrepreneurs. Because long after our recent promoter acquaintances have packed up their money bags and headed for the next venture, the USFSA will be here developing the sport and providing programs for the thousands of figure skaters, coaches and officials across the United States."

It is also appropriate to take another look at the financial status of the Association at mid-1994. The report of the fall meeting showed that the assets of the Association, including the Memorial Fund, had reached $11,088,703 by the end of the fiscal year (June 30th), with actual revenue for the year at $10,100,905 and expenses of $8,157,205, and a transfer to reserves of $1,943,700 (net income). The largest revenue items were fundraising at $4,708,343, or 46.6 percent, and championships/events at $2,337,351, or 23.1 percent. On the expense side, the largest item at $1,820,831, or 18.0 percent, was operations, followed by championships/events at $1,466,862, or 14.5 percent, and fundraising at $1,428,390, or 14.2 percent. Athlete program expense stood at $1,160,378, or 11.5 percent.

The membership registration totals for the same date (June 30th) were 50,176, which can be compared with the figure for the same date in 1991 of 44,818. In 1995, the number would reach 52,111. There is another view of the membership numbers that is revealing. In the Eastern Section, there were 204 clubs with 21,499 members; in the Midwestern Section, there were 191 clubs with 20,414 members; and in the Pacific Coast Section, there were 61 clubs with 7,018 members. The totals, therefore, were 456 clubs with 48,931 members, a number slightly lower than the number registered. It should be remembered that there is, as a practical matter, no direct control over the number of members a club either reports or registers, so the figures are inherently inaccurate.

Another measure of size and activity that is most relevant is the number of tests taken, which on June 30, 1994, was at 26,414 (for the year), compared with 16,677 in 1991. The number would reach 45,750 in 1995, reflecting the addition of the Moves in the Field tests.

At the meeting itself, in the area of competitions, an amendment was approved to permit former World and Olympic medalists to enter the Nationals without having to qualify at the Regionals and Sectionals. The meeting also approved the change in name of the Juvenile-Intermediate Nationals to the "U.S. Junior Olympic Championships." In the area of tests, it was voted to drop the Preliminary Figure test, the various components of it having been incorporated into the Moves in the Field Tests. Also approved was the elimination of the "below minimum" fail by one judge.

Also approved was a grant of $60,000 to the Memorial Fund, to be allocated equally to the three Vice Presidents, who would make recommendations to the Memorial Fund for grants to skaters in their respective Sections. In the area of Member Recognition, 40 year pins were established to be awarded to all persons who have served as USFSA Judges, Referees and Accountants for more than 40 years.

Approved were a Set of Principles of Ethical Behavior and Conflict of Interest, and an appropriate Conflict of Interest Disclosure Form, to be signed by all officers, special assistants, members of the Executive Committee, committee chairmen and key staff personnel.

The next major event in the schedule was the 1995 World Junior Championships, which returned to Budapest, Hungary, where they previously had been held in 1991. Apart from one Silver medal earned by Danielle and Steve Hartsell of Michigan in the Pairs, the results in the Championships were somewhat disappointing, especially in Singles. Unfortunately, Johnnie Bevan of Washington had to withdraw from the Men due to an injury. The best U.S. place in the Men was that of Derrick Delmore of Washington, in 10th place, which thereby earned the U.S. a second entry in 1996. Timothy Goebel of Ohio was 14th. The title went to Ilya Kulik of Russia, as previously noted, with Thierry Cerez of France second and Seichi Suzuki of Japan third.

Tara Lipinski of Texas came in fourth in the Ladies, behind two Russians, Irina Slutskaia and Elena Ivanova, with Krisztina Czakjo of Hungary third. The other U.S. Ladies, Chrisha Gossard of Delaware and Teresa Aiello of New York, were 16th and 18th respectively. In the Pairs, in addition to the Hartsells, Erin Elbe and Jeffrey Weiss of California placed ninth. The winners of the Pairs were Maria Petrova and Anton Sikharulidze of Russia. The Dance event also was won by a Russian couple (as usual), Olga Sharutenko and Dmitri Naumkin, with the only U.S. couple, Jessica Joseph and Charles Butler, Jr., of Michigan 17th, out of 26 couples, which meant but one entry for the U.S. in 1996.

The International season for Precision team skating was held right around the New Year, as usual, to coincide with time out of school for many members of the teams. The first such competition, Precision Canada International at the end of December 1994, was held at Toronto and drew 26 teams from 10 countries. In the Senior event, Team Surprise of Sweden continued to show their improvement and mastery by winning the Gold medal, defeating the team which had been generally considered the "power" in the discipline, les Pirouettes de Laval from Canada. In third was another Canadian team, also from Quebec, Les Etincelles, with the Haydenettes of Lexington, Mass., finishing fourth. The Crystallettes of Michigan were eighth and the Miami University (Ohio) team was 13th. In the Junior event, the Canadians made a clean sweep of the top three places. The Colonials from Massachusetts were seventh and the Ice Liners also from Massachusetts were ninth.

The third Snowflake International competition was held at Dearborn, Mich., just five days later, with 27 teams from nine countries. Once again, Team Surprise of Sweden won the Senior event with a Canadian team second and a Finnish team third. Team Elan of Michigan was ninth and the Crystallettes 11th. The Junior event was won by the Burlington Ice Image of Canada, with Starlets of Illinois eighth and Team Elan of Michigan ninth.

The third International Precision competition was held at the end of February in Rouen, France, the International French Cup. There were 17 teams from seven countries. One U.S. team, the Superettes of Rhode Island, placed third in the Junior event, which was won by an Italian team.

The 1995 National Championships were held at Providence, R.I., in the home state of President Ferguson, in the same building, the Civic Center, in which they were held in 1974. An additional practice rink was set up in the adjoining and brand new Convention Center, which, with the official hotel on the other end, made going back and forth very easy. There were 224 entries in 18 events.

At the 1995 Nationals, additional inductions were made into the United States Figure Skating Hall of Fame:

Robin Lee of Minneapolis, five-time National champion, 1935-1939, North American Silver medalist, 1935, 1939 and 1936 Olympian, and a long-time coach;

Cynthia Kauffman Marshall and Ron Kauffmann of Seattle, National Pair champions, 1966-1969, North American Pair champions, 1967, 1969, and World Pair Bronze medalists, 1966-1968;

The late Roy Shipstad, a founder and long-time star of the Ice Follies, the first "Mr. Debonair."

Just as the year before there were three new champions in the four Senior events. However, in the case of Todd Eldredge, it was a case of a veteran returning to the top. Todd's comeback was truly remarkable. He had been the National champion in 1990 and 1991 and was then completely off the podium for three years, 1992-1994. There was only one comparable instance in early USFSA history, that of Nathaniel Niles of Boston, the National champion in 1918 and then again in 1925. His case is not quite the same, however, as during the intervening years, 1920-1924 (there was no championship in 1919), he was the Silver medalist three times, in 1920, 1921 and 1924.

Scott Davis, the defending champion, won the short program and made a strong effort to retain his title, but could not hold off Eldredge. In third once again was Aren Nielsen of

Nicole Bobek

Ohio. In the Ladies, it had been generally expected that Michelle Kwan of California, the 1994 Silver medalist, would prevail, but such was not the case as Nicole Bobek of California became the new National Ladies champion. Tonia Kwiatkowski of Ohio had won the short program, with Bobek second, and Kwan third. While Michelle was second in the free skating, she could do no better than that place. Tonia was third, with Kyoko Ina fourth. Once again, the U.S. finally had a genuine champion, after two years. The winners of the Senior Figure events were John Baldwin, Jr., of California, a veteran competitor who had been the Novice champion in 1987, and Lisa Bryson of Colorado.

In the Pairs, Jenni Meno and Todd Sand successfully defended their title, for their second and Todd's third. Runners-up were Kyoko Ina and Jason Dungjen of New York, with Stephanie Stiegler and Lance Travis of California third. In the Dance, Renée Roca and Gorsha Sur of Colorado regained the title that they had to abandon in 1994, for their second, with Elizabeth Punsalan and Jerod Swallow of Michigan, the defenders, second. Amy Webster and Ron Kravette of Boston were third. In fourth were a new combination of Kate Robinson and Peter Breen of Colorado.

There was a mild surprise in the Junior Ladies, when Sydne Vogel of Anchorage, Alaska, took the title, defeating Tara Lipinski of Texas. It was the first major National title for a representative of Alaska, although actually the second overall, the first having been the win in Novice Men's Figures of Danny Clausen of Anchorage in 1992. Danielle and Steve Hartsell of California added the Junior Pair title to their World Junior Silver medal, while the winners of the Junior Dance were Eve Chalom and Mathew Gates of Michigan. Also notable was the win in Novice Pairs of Tiffany and Johnnie Stiegler of California, two more members of the talented Stiegler family.

Following the Nationals, there were the usual Spring International Competitions, with the Association now supporting two Senior Dance competitions, the Basler Cup at Basel, Switzerland, at the end of February, and the Challenge Lysiane Lauret at Morzine, France, at the end of March. In the Basler Cup, there was a very nice and unexpected win by Kate Robinson and Peter Breen, with a German and an Italian couple in the other two places. There were no Eastern bloc dance couples present at Basel, but they were very much present at Morzine. In the latter competition, Amy Webster and Ron Kravette were sixth, and Robinson and Breen, eighth. The winners were Drobiasko and Vanagas from Lithuania, with an Italian couple second, and a Russian couple third. Amy and Ron were fourth after the compulsory dance, but dropped to sixth in the original dance.

The third spring competition was the Gardena Spring Trophy at Ortisei, Italy, in early April, and once again, a U.S. Junior lady was the winner. This time it was Brittney McConn of

Georgia, who was the National Junior Ladies Bronze medalist. The National Junior Ladies champion, Sydne Vogel of Alaska, was fourth, after a second in the short program. A Finnish skater, Alisa Drei, won the free skating and pulled up to second from fourth in the short.

The Sectional Precision championships were held during February, and there were some changes in the composition of the events. The standard divisions were still present (Senior, Junior, Novice, Intermediate and Juvenile), but the Adult division was divided into an Open class, for teams of 12 to 24 skaters, over age 21, with 75 percent over age 25, and a Masters class, for teams of 8 to 20 skaters, over age 25, with 75 percent over age 35. These were added to the additional non-qualifying divisions that had been established earlier: Preliminary (1992), for teams of 8 to 16 skaters, with 75 percent over age 9 and 25 percent between 9 and 11; Youth (1993) for teams of 8 to 12 skaters, age 11 or younger; Teen (1993) for teams of 8 to 12 skaters, age 18 or younger; and Adult (1993) for teams of 8 to 12 skaters, age 19 or older. The latter three categories were revised in 1994 to add "Introductory" to their names.

The increase in the number of teams participating in the Sectionals can be seen as a result of the broadening of the number of categories available for participation. It was also necessary to run elimination rounds in the Intermediate and Juvenile divisions in both the Eastern and Midwestern Sections. In the Easterns, which were held at Fitchburg, Mass., there were 67 teams in 10 events. In the Midwesterns at Chicago, there were 74 team in nine events. The Pacific Coasts, which were held at Las Vegas, Nev., were still small, with only 23 teams in six events. What is notable about the Coasts was the presence of three Adult events, including Adult Introductory, with 11 teams. The Coast still lacked a Senior competition.

1995 World Team

The 1995 World Championships were held at Birmingham, England, at the National Exhibition Center (NEC), which had been the site of the 1989 European Championships. The main hotel, the Metropole, was within walking distance of the complex. A temporary practice rink was installed and worked well this time (it broke down in 1989). The U.S. was represented by its smallest team in quite a few years, of just 10 skaters: two Men (Eldredge, Davis), two Ladies (Bobek, Kwan), two Pairs

(Meno-Sand, Ina-Dungjen), and one Dance couple (Roca-Sur). A full team would be 18, with three entries in each category. Happily, based on the results, the 1996 team will be much larger, missing the maximum by just two skaters.

The U.S. came home with three medals, its best haul since 1991, consisting of one Silver (Eldredge) and two Bronze (Bobek, Meno-Sand). In the Men, Eldredge came close to winning, but not quite. He won the short program, but had one fall in the free skating on a triple Axel, from which he quickly recovered and put in another one near the end of the program. This, of course, laid him open to a mandatory deduction for repeating a triple, but it is doubted that the judges did much if anything about it, the retry being far more positive. As a result, he wound up second to defending champion Elvis Stojko of Canada, who had his own problems, including a fall on an attempted quadruple jump. Stojko was still suffering from the ankle injury that had taken him out of the Canadian Championships, and his too was a very gutsy performance. One can only anticipate the future competitions between these two fighters. In third place was Philippe Candeloro of France, who always seems to bounce "right side up," having placed fifth in the short program. His programs are short on choreography, footwork and the like, but long on showmanship and he does seem to pull off the jumps when he has to. Alexei Urmanov of Russia, the Olympic champion, was fourth, and still frustrated from his effort to achieve the podium in a World Championship. The second U.S. man, Scott Davis, placed seventh, after a third in the short program, from which he collapsed to an eighth place in the free skating.

Nicole Bobek established her claim to a medal early in the Ladies by winning the short program in the final round. She had previously won her elimination round group, defeating Chen Lu of China in the process. Neither of them were seeded into the final round, due to their 1994 positions. Bobek had been eliminated and Lu had to withdraw. After the short, Olga Markova of Russia was second, with Lu third. Michelle Kwan skated early in the short and was fifth, while Surya Bonaly of France was fourth. It almost seemed as if the "form charts" were upside down. Unfortunately, Bobek could not sustain her place in the free skating, making several mistakes to place fourth and just hang on for the Bronze medal against the charging Kwan, who, skating all out, was third in the free skating to place fourth overall. Bonaly, as usual, was overmarked, placing second in the free skating to take the Silver medal for the third year in a row, while Chen Lu won the free skating to win the first World championship ever for China. Markova dropped to fifth in the final result.

The Pairs was a tough fight also, with the apparent favorites, Radka Kovarikova and René Novotny of the Czech Republic, seeking to overcome a second place in the European Championships to Mandy Wötzel and Ingo Steuer of Germany. The Czech pair quickly established their claim to the crown by winning the short program, with the defending champions, Evgenia

Shishkova and Vadim Naumov of Russia, in third place behind Wötzel and Steuer. The fourth-place Pair was former European Pair champions Marina Eltsova and Andrei Bushkov of Russia. The top U.S. Pair of Jenni Meno and Todd Sand were in fifth place after the short, a similar situation to what Todd had experienced in 1991 with his former partner, Natasha Kuchiki, when they were fourth in the short program and came out with the Bronze medal.

With the top Pairs generally not skating cleanly, Jenni and Todd skated flawlessly (almost up to their incredible performance at Providence), and climbed on to the podium to take the Bronze medal away from Eltsova-Bushkov. Kovarikova and Novotny won the free skating, despite a flawed performance, to win the first-ever World championship in Pairs for the Czech Republic. Shishkova and Naumov had to settle for second.

In the Dance, the "form chart" essentially remained unchanged, with Oksana Gritschuk and Evgeni Platov of Russia winning all parts, and even the compulsory dances, to take their second title. The slight reshuffling that occurred was the Silver medal of Susanna Rahkamo and Petri Kokko of Finland, who edged out Sophie Moniotte and Pascal Lavanchy of France, in both cases straight across the board, that is, by taking all four parts. It is typical of Dance. The rising young Canadian stars, Shae-Lynn Bourne and Victor Kraatz, had to settle for fourth, while the best Renée Roca and Gorsha Sur could do was 10th. They had to fight for it, having been sitting in 11th place throughout the compulsory dances and the original dance (behind the German-American Jennifer Goolsbee and Hendryk Schamberger of Germany), but finally overtaking them in the free dance, to earn that valuable second entry for 1996.

All in all, it was a most successful Worlds for the U.S. and the 1995 team deserves a lot of credit for winning the medals and places that they did.

One more major International event remained to be skated, the Hershey's Kisses International Challenge, at Los Angeles at the end of March, the second of the International Pro-Ams. Once again the competition was essentially a dual meet between U.S. and Russian skaters, plus one Czech entry and three French entries. There was but one ineligible skater in the entire competition, Caryn Kadavy, who placed fifth in Ladies. In the Men, Todd Eldredge continued to demonstrate his winning ways, although he was again behind in the short program. Second overall was Ilya Kulik of Russia, the European champion, followed by Eric Millot of France. Scott Davis placed fourth, while Alexei Urmanov of Russia, who had been second in the short program, finished fifth.

In Ladies, Michelle Kwan was the winner, finally defeating Surya Bonaly of France, with Olga Markova of Russia third, and the National Ladies champion, Nicole Bobek, fourth. Radka Kovarikova and René Novotny of the Czech Republic, confirmed their World win in Pairs, defeating Evgenia Shishkova and Vadim Naumov, with Kyoko Ina and Jason Dungjen third. In the Dance, Oksana Gritschuk and Evgeni Platov of Russia did the same, defeating Sophie Moniotte and Pascal Lavanchy, second, with Angelika Krylova and Oleg Ovsiannikov of Russia third. Amy Webster and Ron Kravette were fourth.

The 1995 United States Postal Service National Precision Championships were held at San Diego, Calif., in early April, and drew 79 teams, representing more than 1,700 skaters in seven events. There were quite a few firsts. It was the first Championships to have a title sponsor and the first to be televised nationally (on cable). The short program for the Senior and Junior events was now mandatory, and there were no qualifying rounds or consolation finals.

In the Senior division, which had 10 teams, there was an upset when Team Elan of Michigan became the new champions, dethroning the Haydenettes of Massachusetts. The defenders had suffered a fall in the new short program, which put them fourth and out of the running, although they did win the long program to wind up second, ahead of the Miami (Ohio) University team, which placed third. The Starlets of Wagon Wheel, Ill., won the Junior event, followed by the Crystallettes of Michigan and the Colonials of Massachusetts. The Ice Mates of Lexington, Mass., retained their Novice crown for the fourth straight year and fifth overall.

In the Intermediate division, the Magic Edges of North Dakota were the winners, a first for that state, defeating the Colonials of Acton, Mass., and thereby ending the long reign of the Munchkins of Rhode Island, who did not defend their title. Team Elan of Michigan won the Juvenile class for the second straight year, with two Massachusetts teams, the Colonials and the Ice Cubes of Hayden, second and third, respectively.

The Adult division was now divided into two classes. In the Open class, the Esprit de Corps from Hayden came back to win their third title, with the former champions, the Fabulous Forties from Los Angeles second and Team Elan of Detroit third. In the new Masters class, which drew six teams, the Ice Classics of the Lloyd Center ISC of Portland, Oregon, won a rare title for the Pacific Coast, by taking the first National title to be contested in the event, and actually the first Coast title, since those won by the Fabulous Forties between 1987 and 1989.

With the main Nationals and the Precision Nationals now over, it is hard to believe that two more National events were still to come. The first was the new Kodak U.S. Junior Olympic Championships, to give it its full name, the former Juvenile-Intermediate Nationals, now in their fifth year, and with a title sponsor to boot. Limited television coverage on cable was also achieved for the first time.

The championships were held at Indianapolis, Ind., and included a change, with the Novice qualifiers from the main Nationals being invited to participate. The inclusion of Novice events in the new Junior Olympics was with a view to their ultimate deletion from the main Nationals, although it now appears that neither their deletion from the main Nationals nor their inclusion in the Junior Olympics will take place, and that the Junior Olympic events will revert to the former Juvenile and Intermediate divisions only, with Open Juvenile and Open Intermediate events for Pairs and Dance being added for 1996. These additional events will be for older skaters qualified, by test but not by age, with the Open Intermediate entry age being over 15, but not over 25, and for Open Juvenile, over 13 and not over 16.

With the addition of the Novice events, the entry was very large, which added another dimension to the events. The championship is essentially supported entirely by the Association, other than for entry fees, since there is little gate and as yet no television, as noted above. There was a total of 218 entries in 18 events, representing a total of 303 skaters. The Novice events drew only 27 entries, and it is interesting that not one of the champions from the main Nationals showed up. The Men's winner was Justin Dillon of Washington, who had been second at Providence. The Ladies winner was Shelby Lyons of New York (actually a Senior Pair skater with Brian Wells of Colorado), who had been fourth in Providence. The Pair winners were Lauren Carpenter and Brad Russi of Indiana, who had been ninth in Providence, while in the Novice Dance the winners were Kerrie O'Donnell and Brandon Forsyth of Massachusetts, who were third at Providence. Obviously, the experiment did not prove successful.

The 1995 Junior Olympics still included Intermediate and Juvenile "A" and "B" events which would become the "Open" events in the future, and also separate figure events returned after a four-year absence, since all the events were now split. The entries for the figure events are of interest: Intermediate - Men: 12, Ladies: 12; Juvenile - Boys: 11, Girls - 18. So, even among male skaters, an interest in figures remained, especially if it would lead to medals. The "B" Pair and Dance events at the Juvenile level were also large: Pairs - 11, and Dance - 13. There were no "B" events in the Intermediate division.

Clearly the composition and size of the Junior Olympics were still evolving, with further changes to come, but the success of the championships was readily apparent by the degree of interest and participation.

However, the biggest impact on the season and the future was the inaugural Adult Nationals, which were held at Wilmington, Del., in April, just five days after the Junior Olympics. A significant miscalculation was made in anticipating the size of the competition, which had, therefore, to be continually expanded and extended, so that it eventually wound up covering four full days. Because the championships were essentially a "non-qualifying" competition, had no minimum standards, and did not require qualifying from the Regionals and Sectionals, especially for the lower classes, the competition was in effect open to everyone! Essentially, what had to be done was to divide the classes and the entries in two different ways: first, by age, and second by test level.

Accordingly, three classes according to age were created: Class I - 25 to 35; Class II - 36 to 45; and Class III - 46 and over. It was necessary to specify both a minimum and a maximum test level. For example, for 1996, an entrant in Adult Gold Free Skating, must have passed the Adult Silver Free Skating Test and no higher than the Adult Gold Free Skating Test, the standard Intermediate Free Skating Test and the Third Figure Test (prior to 1977) or the ISIA Freestyle 6 Test, certainly a complicated set of requirements! Adult Bronze Free Skating will require no higher than the Adult Bronze Free Skating Test, the standard Preliminary Figure Test (prior to 1977), the Preliminary Free Skating Test or the ISIA Freestyle 4 Test, and so on. The requirements for the Pair and Dance events were similar. The credit for the completion of a reasonably orderly schedule of events for the championships must go largely to the ad hoc Adult Skaters Advisory Committee and its first chairman, Joseph Kaplenk of Illinois; the Program Development Committee, chaired by Phyllis Howard of Virginia, and the Skating Club of Wilmington organizing committee, chaired by D.J. Tindall.

In any event, in the end there were 41 events, seven of which required qualifying rounds, with the largest being the Ladies Interpretive Skating I, with five qualifying groups and 64 entries. Right behind it in size was Ladies Interpretive Skating II, with four groups and 50 entries. There were 529 entries, representing 581 skaters from 37 states. It is impossible to list all 41 winners, but some of them were:

Gold Men's Free Skating I - John-Patrick Hull, The SC of Boston

Gold Men's Free Skating II - Ken DeBit, San Diego FSC

Gold Men's Free Skating III - Michael Barsotti, Lloyd Center ISC

Gold Ladies Free Skating I - Colleen Conroy, Highland SC

Gold Ladies Free Skating II - Terry Walters, SC of Northern Virginia

Gold Ladies Free Skating III - Priscilla Rushing, Nashville FSC

Masters Senior Men's Free Skating - David Hilliard, Diamond Edge FSC

Masters Senior Ladies Free Skating - Sherry Dowlen, Alpine SC

Adult Pairs - Karen Cook, Baltimore FSC and Paul Capiobianco, Individual Member

Adult Senior Dance -Sandra and Mike Ricigliano, St. Moritz ISC

Men's Interpretive Skating I - Stephen Crago, Seattle SC

Men's Interpretive Skating II - Randy Faria, Individual Member

Ladies Interpretive Skating I - Didi Marquez, Highland SC

Ladies Interpretive Skating II - Terrie Kerth, Peninsula FSC

With all the "dust" beginning to settle, there was still one more major event in the season of a non-skating nature, the 1995 Governing Council meeting. It too would be a very large affair, being held at the Ritz-Carlton Hotel in Phoenix, Ariz., the first time in that Southwest city, at which the 1993 Nationals were held. The same group of faithful volunteers from the Phoenix clubs carried out the organization in a very efficient manner, so that the many delegates were very well taken care of and had a good time.

A very sad event occurred at the meeting, when Bill Brennan of New York, a former Vice President, Secretary and Honorary member of the Board of Directors, passed away unexpectedly. Bill had been a faithful worker for the Association and skating for many years, and especially as Chairman of the Television Committee from 1968 to 1992, in which position he had been very much involved in all of the critical negotiations with the networks for television coverage.

The gala closing banquet was again an outstanding success. Honored for his dedicated service was Al Beard of Portland, formerly of Phoenix, the creator of the Association's computerized scoring system. Al had also served as Secretary, Chairman of Sanctions and as a member of the Board of Directors. Honored for their roles in creating and implementing the Moves in the Field Tests were Bobbie Parkinson of Pennsylvania, Christine Haigler Krall of Colorado and Margaret Anne Wier of Utah.

A very special award was presented to Doug Wilson of ABC Sports, whose association with the USFSA, and especially its Nationals, began in 1964. A 50 year judge honored was Ramona Allen McIntyre of Hawaii, a long-time World Judge, and a former Senior competitor and National Junior Ladies champion. Betty Sonnhalter of California was honored, not only for being the first woman officer of the Association but also for her long service in many positions; Betty had earlier been elected an Honorary member of the Board of Directors. Jo Lawless, another Southern Californian, was also honored, not only as the first woman to serve as the chief referee of the Nationals, but also for her dedicated service, including Chairman of the Competitions Committee and Chairman of the World Hall of Fame Electors.

Special recognition was also extended to Frank Carroll of California, one of the leading U.S. coaches, who was surprised to be greeted by his former pupil, Linda Fratianne Maricich of Sun Valley, Idaho, a two-time World Ladies champion and Olympic Silver medalist. The banquet ended with a special presentation, including a video of her three years in office, to outgoing President Claire Ferguson of Rhode Island.

The election of the late William Thayer Tutt of Colorado Springs as a member of the World Figure Skating Hall of Fame was announced at the meeting. Thayer is the only person to have been elected an Honorary member of the USFSA and a member of both the United States and World Figure Skating Halls of Fame, a triple honor which reflects the esteem in which he was held by all who have had anything to do with the Broadmoor.

A great deal of work was carried out by the meeting, as well as at the Board of Directors Meeting preceding it. Among the most significant legislation adopted were new grievance procedures, including, as previously mentioned, the establishment of an Ethics and a Grievance Committee as permanent committees of the Association; and a change to the By Laws increasing the representation at the Governing Council meeting for the larger clubs, so that, for example, a club with 650 or more members would be entitled to nine delegates and nine votes. The previous maximum was five delegates for clubs with more than 250 members.

In the area of competitions, the bye rule was further clarified to require an application 21 days in advance, and that a competitor is automatically withdrawn from a competition in the case of a medical bye, once such an application is submitted. A rule was also adopted which requires all members of the U.S., World, World Junior and Olympic Teams to be U.S. citizens.

The meeting overturned the Board decision to drop the Preliminary Figure Test, and also approved the judging of Adult Bronze Figure and Free Skating Tests by one judge, Intermediate or higher. The Intermediate short program was finally accepted, to include six elements: an Axel, double Salchow or double loop, one jump combination (single and double or two doubles), spin, spin combination and one step sequence.

The Judges Review Committee, a statutory committee within the Judges Committee, was given authority to act upon complaints against judges involving their marks, a mental or physical inability to perform effectively and reliably as a judge, repeated actions unbecoming a judge and ineligibility under other rules, with the power to reprimand, demote, suspend or remove. This essentially replaced the former and long-standing rules requiring the convening of special panels in such cases, and set up a permanent tribunal to do so.

The composition of the Selections Committee, a statutory committee within the Competitions Committee for the selection of officials for qualifying and International competitions, was revised to add athlete representatives comprising at least 20 percent of the membership, but providing that no athlete competing in the current season or who had competed in the immediately prior season could serve on the committee.

As noted, the below minimum failing mark by one judge was eliminated in all tests, so that a strict majority only pass or fail rule applies.

An ad hoc committee was also to be appointed to review once again the By Laws, which has to be done from time to time. Ongoing amendments made each year sometimes do not fit in properly and the entire document needs to be reconfigured periodically. The last major revision of that sort took place prior to 1980.

Another action taken in recognition of the uncertainties of the sources of revenues was to establish the principle that the financial reserves of the Association should be increased to $15,000,000 over the next five years.

The meeting marked the end of the three-year term of President Claire Ferguson, who actually had served almost four years, due to having to step in as acting President during the sojourn of Franklin Nelson in the Persian Gulf during the last year of his term of office. In her remarks to the meeting and also in an article in Skating magazine, President Ferguson commented upon some of the major events of her administration, which also reflect some of its accomplishments:

The Kerrigan-Harding incident and the chain of events which forced the Association to review and revise their codes of conduct and disciplinary procedures;

The restructuring of the USFSA Headquarters operation, with the bringing in as Executive Director of Jerry Lace, which helped place the organization on solid financial ground;

The signing of new television contracts, to insure greater visibility for the sport and to provide financial security for several years to come;

The development and success of the International Pro-Am competitions, with the goal of bringing all skaters together in the competition for prize money;

Abandoning the athlete trust funds and drafting new athlete contracts, and the implementation of a new system that works better for the athletes, with the Association no longer in the role of monitoring the expenditures of the earnings of an athlete;

Maintaining a position of strength within the ISU, through the election of additional officeholders. Also noted was the presence of a coach and athlete in the U.S. delegation to the Congress for the first time;

The repackaging of the Juvenile-Intermediate Nationals into the U.S. Junior Olympics, with resulting corporate sponsorship and television in the future to promote awareness of the event;

The development and institution of the Moves in the Field Free Skating Tests, a joint effort with the PSGA, which had been well received by the membership as a replacement for the figures;

Precision team skating being designated as an official ISU discipline, the fastest-growing one in the United States, which is attracting more attention, not only from participants, but also from sponsors and television;

The creation of the Adult Nationals, an event which appeared to have a strong future;

The steady growth of the USFSA's Basic Skills program, which had continued to grow very rapidly, with over 70,000 members enrolled.

With President Ferguson stepping down, she was duly elected an Honorary member of the Association, joining her seven living predecessors as a Past President, and was succeeded by Morry Stillwell

Morry Stillwell

of California, the third President from the Pacific Coast and the first from the Southwest Pacific Region. The other two (Ken Brown and George Yonekura) both came from the Central Pacific Region. Morry had served as a Vice President, Chairman of the Competitions, Long Range Planning, Membership and Sanctions Committees, and as an active National Referee and Judge.

The Association seems to be well positioned as the new administration takes up its duties to meet the challenges ahead for the sport in the extremely volatile environment that is the hallmark of the 1990s. Obviously, it must guard its financial resources and constantly seek new sources of revenue, while at the same time continuing to expand its programs and support, especially for its clubs and skating members at the grassroots level. The new leaders, however, can look forward to the challenge with confidence.

While all good things must come to an end, including this History, the Association and the sport go on just as they have for the past 75 years.

It is appropriate, however, to provide a brief summary of the events that occurred at the beginning of the 1995-1996 Anniversary season, as well as those planned during the rest of the season.

Epilogue
(1995-1996)

Early in July, the "USA vs. the World Team Challenge" was held at Kennewick, Wash., an all-eligible international event. The winners were: Men - Todd Eldredge; Ladies - Nicole Bobek; Pairs - Elena Berezhnaia and Oleg Shliakov of Latvia, with the "World" Team winning the team competition. There was no Dance event.

The Olympic Festival was held at Denver at the end of July and, as was subsequently announced, was the last in the present form. The next Festival for 1997 was canceled. Whether a Festival-type event with many sports involved will be organized in the future remains to be seen. The possibility of such a competition open to foreign athletes training in the United States is being considered. The entries in the figure skating events in the last Festival were from the Junior and Novice ranks, with the winners being:

Men - Trifun Zivanovic, All Year FSC

Ladies - Erin Sutton, Plymouth FSC

Pairs - Nicole Perry, Palomares FSC and Paul Dulebohn, University of Delaware FSC

Dance - Jessica Joseph and Charles Butler, Jr., Detroit SC

The 1995 National Collegiate Championships were held at Colorado Springs in mid-August, and consisted of the four Senior and Junior Ladies events (Figures and Free Skating), plus a return of the Junior Dance, with just two entries. There were a total of 50 entries in the four Singles events. The winners and their colleges were:

Senior Ladies Free Skating - Angela Meduna, Mount Hood Community College

Senior Ladies Figures - Jessica Rainey, Knox College

Junior Ladies Free Skating - Tiffany Scott, Regis College

Junior Ladies Figures - Nicole Buckles, Arizona State University

Junior Dance - Azumi Sagara, Whittier College, and Jonathan Magalnick,

California State University

The Coupe des Alpes took place as usual at St. Gervais, France, and Oberstdorf, Germany, with separate teams being sent to the two competitions, as had been instituted in 1994. There was just one U.S. medal out of the two competitions, the Silver medal of Sydne Vogel of Alaska, the 1995 National Junior Ladies champion, in the Ladies event at St. Gervais, behind Elena Ivanova of Russia. The next best place was the fourth of Tara Lipinski of Texas in the Ladies at Oberstdorf, which was won by Shizuka Arakawa of Japan.

The Association conducted an additional International Open competition, the "Best of the Best" at the Meadowlands in New Jersey in September, in which Scott Hamilton and Paul Wylie came out ahead of Todd Eldredge in the Men. Nicole Bobek was the winner in the Ladies over Michelle Kwan and Chen Lu of China; while in Pairs, Jenni Meno and Todd Sand defeated the reigning World Pair champions, Radka Kovarikova and René Novotny of the Czech Republic. There was no Dance event.

A second International Open competition, the "Starlight Challenge," was scheduled at the end of October in New York City, just after Skate America at Detroit.

Early in October the Selection competition for the 1996 World Junior Team was again held at Colorado Springs, just after the Fall Board of Directors Meeting, with the following results and team being selected:

Men -   1. Jere Michael of Colorado

2. Timothy Goebel of Ohio

Ladies - 1. Shelby Lyons of Colorado

2. Tara Lipinski of Texas

Pairs -   1. Danielle and Steve Hartsell of Michigan

2. Natalie Vlandis and Jered Guzman of California

3. Erin Elbe and Jeffrey Weiss of California

Dance - Jessica Joseph and Charles Butler, Jr., of Michigan

A competition on the International circuit, which was supported by the USFSA was the Finlandia Trophy at Helsinki in early October. The best U.S. place earned was a fourth in the Men by Trifun Zivanovic of California. The event was won by Igor Pashkevich of Russia, with Ilya Kulik of Russia, the European and World Junior champion, second.

The USFSA also returned to the Karl Schäfer Memorial competition in Vienna, Austria, in mid-October, and there was a pleasant surprise when Daniel Hollander of Michigan won the Men's event, defeating Patrick Meier of Switzerland and Roman Ekimov of Russia.

During the summer of 1995, the USFSA established a "forum" on America Online, one of the on-line services which provides access to the Internet through a computer and modem. Hopefully, the next step of a World Wide Web page will soon follow, which will permit access to the information posted for all those on the Internet who do not subscribe to an on-line service. The immense value of the site is obvious, with much faster communication to the skating public, such as results and other information about the USFSA and its programs. President Stillwell deserves the credit for this innovative step.

Early in September, a license agreement was announced between the USFSA and ABC Sports under which a series of products will be created featuring the ABC Sports and USFSA logos. The agreement should provide a greater opportunity to generate valuable exposure for the Association and its (trade)marks, while also providing a new source of revenue. The licensed products are expected to be available in retail stores and through direct mail purchase early in 1996.

The agreement reflects a further implementation of the marketing agreement entered into in March, 1994, by the USFSA and ABC Sports, for the marketing of Association events, including the creation of joint promotional opportunities for sponsors and the television and print media.

In his remarks to the fall meeting of the Board of Directors which was held at Colorado Springs in early October, 1995, as well as in an article published in the August issue of **Skating** magazine, President Stillwell commented upon the state of the sport and the fact that "amateur" sport had changed "forever," with the return of the ineligible skaters and also the opening of sanctioned events to them. He also made clear that internally generated funds could not provide the support needed to encourage skaters to remain eligible, and pointed out that USFSA income does not even provide enough funds to support all the services demanded by member clubs, much less funds directly to athletes. The new ABC contract, however, he noted, would provide additional skater support through 1999, while the International Challenge series (the "Pro-Ams") would provide additional funds to the U.S. Team skaters.

Also cited was a significant development from the ISU, which included Skate America as one of five of the ISU-sponsored "Champions Series" competitions, the others being Skate Canada, Trophée de France, Nations Cup (Germany) and NHK Trophy (Japan). A newly created Champions Series Final will be held at Paris in mid-February 1996. Invited skaters were required to designate which two of the five events they choose to count for points towards the Champions Series final.

Also approved by the ISU were a greater number of International "Open" competitions, of which the "Best of the Best" and the "Starlight Challenge" were examples, in addition to the two USFSA Pro-Ams, which were to be returned to a domestic format only. In summary, President Stillwell's own words are relevant: "Skating continues to evolve under pressures brought on by increasing popularity...While this popularity brings on new challenges and responsibilities, I believe that the USFSA will continue to benefit from this popularity. We should continue our leadership role in the evolution of skating."

At the fall meeting, among the actions taken was the approval for an expansion of the office space at the National Headquarters building in Colorado Springs, with a second floor being added. Funding will come from sources other than the general fund.

The problems of additional events in the qualifying structure based on age continued to be addressed, with the withdrawal of Open Intermediate Pair and Dance events from the Junior Olympics and of the Open Novice Dance event from the Nationals after 1996. Open Juvenile Single events when held at Regionals will not be a qualifying event for Junior Olympics.

Also approved was a rule that eligibility for competition in Singles would be based upon the free skating tests only, without regard to the level attained in the Moves in the Field Tests. The marks for Dance Tests were renamed to match the comparable divisions in competition, of technique and timing/expression. Also approved in principle was a two-track system for Dance Tests, one for competitive dancers and one for standard dancers, which would include the introduction of Moves in the Field to the competitive structure.

In the International Committee rules, a provision was added giving the Management Team the right to withhold or withdraw selection for a failure to abide by the applicable training rules, policies and procedures, or for conduct in violation of the Code of Ethics or for any false statements, misrepresentations, contracts and/or agreements or acts not deemed appropriate for a member of the U.S. Team.

Also amended was the schedule of sanction fees for exhibitions, to include Precision Teams.

The preparation of job descriptions and budgets, where appropriate, for all (permanent) committees (Board positions) within one year was approved.

Among the events announced to be held during the 1995-1996 season were, of course, the regular qualifying competitions; the U.S. Junior Olympics at Northbrook, Ill., the Adult Nationals at Lake Placid and an additional International event for Precision Teams, the World Challenge Cup, to be held at Boston in early April 1996.

Among the International competitions to be supported, in addition to the Champions Series, were the Coupe des Alpes (St. Gervais, France, and Oberstdorf, Germany), the Finlandia Trophy (Helsinki), Vienna Cup (Austria), Autumn Trophy Mezzaluna for Junior Dance (Italy), Pokal der Blauen Schwerter for Juniors (Chemnitz, Germany), Basler Cup for Senior Dance (Basel, Switzerland), 100th Anniversary (St. Petersburg, Russia), Polish Trophy (Gdansk), Challenge Lysiane Lauret (Morzine, France), and Gardena Spring Trophy (Ortisei, Italy), for a total of 11. When the five events for the Champions Series are added, the total of 16 becomes the largest number of international competitions ever to be participated in by USFSA skaters in one season.

International Precision competitions to be supported, in addition to the World Challenge Cup, included the Swedish International at Goteborg, the International French Cup at Rouen, and the Italian International at Milan.

The 1996 World Junior Championships will return to Brisbane, Australia, while the 1996 World Championships will be held at Edmonton, Alberta, Canada.

Insofar as the 75th Anniversary is concerned, the principal event in celebration of the milestone will be held at the 1996 Governing Council Meeting at Colorado Springs, with a gala banquet, at which many former World, Olympic and National champions and other invited dignitaries will be present. There will also be articles in **Skating** magazine by some of the former champions, reflecting skating as they knew it. The 75th Anniversary History of the USFSA, "Skating in America" by Benjamin Wright, is also scheduled to be available at the meeting.

At the 1996 Nationals at San Jose, Calif., the annual inductions into the United States Figure Skating Hall of Fame will be carried out, as part of the observance. The Anniversary theme will also be used in the opening ceremony, as well as at other activities during the championships.

The possibility of an Anniversary ice show in the fall of 1996, with television coverage by ABC, is still being explored at the time of writing. The 75th Anniversary logo will be the basis for pins and other memorabilia.

As Jo Lawless, Chairman of the 75th Anniversary Committee states in her report to the fall meeting of the Board of Directors, "During the coming year, we will all have the opportunity to learn about the history of skating in the United States. It will be a rewarding experience, a chance to reminisce, a chance to learn, a chance to enjoy, and a chance to reflect on what lies in the future of figure skating."

Champions of the United States

The Championships held in 1914, 1918, 1920 and 1921 under the auspices of the International Skating Union of America were open to Canadians, although they were considered to be United States Championships. Beginning in 1922, the Championships have been held under the auspices of the United States Figure Skating Association. In 1991, singles competition was split into two separate events, Figures and Free Skating, each with its own champion.

MEN

FREE SKATING

1995 Todd Eldredge, Detroit SC
1994 Scott Davis, Broadmoor SC
1993 Scott Davis, Broadmoor SC
1992 Christopher Bowman, Los Angeles FSC
1991 Todd Eldredge, Los Angeles FSC

COMBINED

1990 Todd Eldredge, Los Angeles FSC
1989 Christopher Bowman, Los Angeles FSC
1988 Brian Boitano, Peninsula FSC
1987 Brian Boitano, Peninsula FSC
1986 Brian Boitano, Peninsula FSC
1985 Brian Boitano, Peninsula FSC
1984 Scott Hamilton, Philadelphia SC & HS
1983 Scott Hamilton, Philadelphia SC & HS
1982 Scott Hamilton, Philadelphia SC & HS
1981 Scott Hamilton, Philadelphia SC & HS
1980 Charles Tickner, Denver FSC
1979 Charles Tickner, Denver FSC
1978 Charles Tickner, Denver FSC
1977 Charles Tickner, Denver FSC
1976 Terry Kubicka, Arctic Blades FSC
1975 Gordon McKellen, Jr., SC of Lake Placid
1974 Gordon McKellen, Jr., SC of Lake Placid
1973 Gordon McKellen, Jr., SC of Lake Placid
1972 Kenneth Shelley, Arctic Blades FSC
1971 John Misha Petkevich, Great Falls FSC
1970 Tim Wood, City of Colorado Springs
1969 Tim Wood, Detroit SC
1968 Tim Wood, Detroit SC
1967 Gary C. Visconti, Detroit SC
1966 Scott Ethan Allen, The SC of New York
1965 Gary C. Visconti, Detroit SC
1964 Scott Ethan Allen, The SC of New York
1963 Thomas Litz, Hershey FSC
1962 Monty Hoyt, Broadmoor SC
1961 Bradley R. Lord, The SC of Boston
1960 David Jenkins, Broadmoor SC
1959 David Jenkins, Broadmoor SC
1958 David Jenkins, Broadmoor SC
1957 David Jenkins, Broadmoor SC
1956 Hayes Alan Jenkins, Broadmoor SC
1955 Hayes Alan Jenkins, Broadmoor SC
1954 Hayes Alan Jenkins, Broadmoor SC
1953 Hayes Alan Jenkins, Cleveland SC
1952 Richard T. Button, The SC of Boston
1951 Richard T. Button, The SC of Boston
1950 Richard T. Button, The SC of Boston
1949 Richard T. Button, Philadelphia SC & HS
1948 Richard T. Button, Philadelphia SC & HS
1947 Richard T. Button, Philadelphia SC & HS
1946 Richard T. Button, Philadelphia SC & HS

1944-1945 No Competitions
1943 Arthur R. Vaughn, Jr., Philadelphia SC & HS
1942 Robert Specht, Chicago FSC
1941 Eugene Turner, Los Angeles FSC
1940 Eugene Turner, Los Angeles FSC
1939 Robin H. Lee, St. Paul FSC
1938 Robin H. Lee, Chicago FSC
1937 Robin H. Lee, Skating Club, New York
1936 Robin H. Lee, Skating Club, New York
1935 Robin H. Lee, Skating Club, New York
1934 Roger F. Turner, The SC of Boston
1933 Roger F. Turner, The SC of Boston
1932 Roger F. Turner, The SC of Boston
1931 Roger F. Turner, The SC of Boston
1930 Roger F. Turner, The SC of Boston
1929 Roger F. Turner, The SC of Boston
1928 Roger F. Turner, The SC of Boston
1927 Nathaniel W. Niles, The SC of Boston
1926 Chris I. Christenson, Twin City FSC
1925 Nathaniel W. Niles, The SC of Boston
1924 Sherwin C. Badger, The SC of Boston
1923 Sherwin C. Badger, The SC of Boston
1922 Sherwin C. Badger, The SC of Boston
1921 Sherwin C. Badger, The SC of Boston
1920 Sherwin C. Badger, The SC of Boston
1919 No Competition
1918 Nathaniel W. Niles, The SC of Boston
1915-1917 No Competitions
1914 Norman M. Scott, WC of Montreal

FIGURES

1995 John Baldwin, Jr., Los Angeles FSC
1994 Gig Siruno, St. Paul FSC
1993 Gig Siruno, St. Paul FSC
1992 Brian Schmidt, Broadmoor SC
1991 Craig Heath, St. Moritz ISC

LADIES

FREE SKATING

1995 Nicole Bobek, Los Angeles FSC
1994 Vacant
1993 Nancy Kerrigan, Colonial FSC
1992 Kristi Yamaguchi, St. Moritz ISC
1991 Tonya Harding, Carousel FSC

COMBINED

1990 Jill Trenary, Broadmoor SC
1989 Jill Trenary, Broadmoor SC
1988 Debi Thomas, Los Angeles FSC
1987 Jill Trenary, Broadmoor SC
1986 Debi Thomas, Los Angeles FSC
1985 Tiffany Chin, San Diego FSC
1984 Rosalynn Sumners, Seattle SC
1983 Rosalynn Sumners, Seattle SC
1982 Rosalynn Sumners, Seattle SC

1981 Elaine Zayak, The SC of New York
1980 Linda Fratianne, Los Angeles FSC
1979 Linda Fratianne, Los Angeles FSC
1978 Linda Fratianne, Los Angeles FSC
1977 Linda Fratianne, Los Angeles FSC
1976 Dorothy Hamill, The SC of New York
1975 Dorothy Hamill, The SC of New York
1974 Dorothy Hamill, The SC of New York
1973 Janet Lynn, Wagon Wheel FSC
1972 Janet Lynn, Wagon Wheel FSC
1971 Janet Lynn, Wagon Wheel FSC
1970 Janet Lynn, Wagon Wheel FSC
1969 Janet Lynn, Wagon Wheel FSC
1968 Peggy Gale Fleming, Broadmoor SC
1967 Peggy Gale Fleming, Broadmoor SC
1966 Peggy Gale Fleming, City of Colo. Springs
1965 Peggy Gale Fleming, Arctic Blades FSC
1964 Peggy Gale Fleming, Arctic Blades FSC
1963 Lorraine G. Hanlon, The SC of Boston
1962 Mrs. Barbara Roles Pursley, Arctic Blades FSC
1961 Laurence R. Owen, The SC of Boston
1960 Carol E. Heiss, The SC of New York
1959 Carol E. Heiss, The SC of New York
1958 Carol E. Heiss, The SC of New York
1957 Carol E. Heiss, The SC of New York
1956 Tenley E. Albright, The SC of Boston
1955 Tenley E. Albright, The SC of Boston
1954 Tenley E. Albright, The SC of Boston
1953 Tenley E. Albright, The SC of Boston
1952 Tenley E. Albright, The SC of Boston
1951 Sonya Klopfer, The Junior SC of NY
1950 Yvonne Claire Sherman, The SC of NY
1949 Yvonne Claire Sherman, The SC of NY
1948 Gretchen Van Zandt Merrill,
    The SC of Boston
1947 Gretchen Van Zandt Merrill,
    The SC of Boston
1946 Gretchen Van Zandt Merrill,
    The SC of Boston
1945 Gretchen Van Zandt Merrill,
    The SC of Boston
1944 Gretchen Van Zandt Merrill,
    The SC of Boston
1943 Gretchen Van Zandt Merrill,
    The SC of Boston
1942 Mrs. Jane Vaughn Sullivan, Philadelphia
    SC & HS
1941 Mrs. Jane Vaughn Sullivan, Philadelphia
    SC & HS
1940 Joan Tozzer, The SC of Boston
1939 Joan Tozzer, The SC of Boston
1938 Joan Tozzer, The SC of Boston
1937 Maribel Y. Vinson, The SC of Boston

1936 Maribel Y. Vinson, The SC of Boston
1935 Maribel Y. Vinson, The SC of Boston
1934 Suzanne Davis, The SC of Boston
1933 Maribel Y. Vinson, The SC of Boston
1932 Maribel Y. Vinson, The SC of Boston
1931 Maribel Y. Vinson, The SC of Boston
1930 Maribel Y. Vinson, The SC of Boston
1929 Maribel Y. Vinson, The SC of Boston
1928 Maribel Y. Vinson, The SC of Boston
1927 Beatrix Loughran, New York SC
1926 Beatrix Loughran, New York SC
1925 Beatrix Loughran, New York SC
1924 Mrs. Theresa Weld Blanchard, The SC of Boston
1923 Mrs. Theresa Weld Blanchard, The SC of Boston
1922 Mrs. Theresa Weld Blanchard, The SC of Boston
1921 Mrs. Theresa Weld Blanchard, The SC of Boston
1920 Theresa Weld, The SC of Boston
1919 No Competition
1918 Mrs. Rosemary S. Beresford, New York SC
1915-1917 No Competitions
1914 Theresa Weld, The SC of Boston

FIGURES

1995 Lisa Bryson, Rocky Mountain FSC
1994 Melanie Dupon, Los Angeles FSC
1993 Kelly Ann Szmurlo, Broadmoor SC
1992 Kelly Ann Szmurlo, Broadmoor SC
1991 Kelly Ann Szmurlo, Broadmoor SC

PAIRS

1995 Jenni Meno, Winterhurst FSC
Todd Sand, Los Angeles FSC
1994 Jenni Meno, Winterhurst FSC
Todd Sand, Los Angeles FSC
1993 Calla Urbanski, University of Delaware SC
Rocky Marval, SC of New York
1992 Calla Urbanski, University of Delaware SC
Rocky Marval, SC of New York
1991 Natasha Kuchiki, Los Angeles FSC
Todd Sand, Los Angeles FSC
1990 Kristi Yamaguchi, St. Moritz ISC
Rudi Galindo, St. Moritz ISC
1989 Kristi Yamaguchi, St. Moritz ISC
Rudi Galindo, St. Moritz ISC
1988 Jill Watson, Los Angeles FSC
Peter Oppegard, Los Angeles FSC
1987 Jill Watson, Los Angeles FSC
Peter Oppegard, Los Angeles FSC
1986 Gillian Wachsman, SC of Wilmington
Todd Waggoner, SC of Wilmington
1985 Jill Watson, Los Aneles FSC
Peter Oppegard, Los Angeles FSC
1984 Caitlin Carruthers, SC of Wilmington
Peter Carruthers, SC of Wilmington
1983 Caitlin Carruthers, SC of Wilmington
Peter Carruthers, SC of Wilmington
1982 Caitlin Carruthers, SC of Wilmington
Peter Carruthers, SC of Wilmington
1981 Caitlin Carruthers, SC of Wilmington
Peter Carruthers, SC of Wilmington
1980 Tai Babilonia, Los Angeles FSC
Randy Gardner, Santa Monica FSC
1979 Tai Babilonia, Los Angeles FSC
Randy Gardner, Santa Monica FSC
1978 Tai Babilonia, Los Angeles FSC
Randy Gardner, Santa Monica FSC
1977 Tai Babilonia, Los Angeles FSC
Randy Gardner, Los Angeles FSC

1976 Tai Babilonia, Los Angeles FSC
Randy Gardner, Los Angeles FSC
1975 Melissa Militano, The SC of New York
Johnny Johns, Detroit SC
1974 Melissa Militano, The SC of New York
Johnny Johns, Detroit SC
1973 Melissa Militano, The SC of New York
Mark Militano, The SC of New York
1972 Alicia Jo Starbuck, Arctic Blades FSC
Kenneth Shelley, Arctic Blades FSC
1971 Alicia Jo Starbuck, Arctic Blades FSC
Kenneth Shelley, Arctic Blades FSC
1970 Alicia Jo Starbuck, Arctic Blades FSC
Kenneth Shelley, Arctic Blades FSC
1969 Cynthia Kauffman, Seattle SC
Ronald Kauffman, Seattle SC
1968 Cynthia Kauffman, Seattle SC
Ronald Kauffman, Seattle SC
1967 Cynthia Kauffman, Seattle SC
Ronald Kauffman, Seattle SC
1966 Cynthia Kauffman, Seattle SC
Ronald Kauffman, Seattle SC
1965 Vivian Joseph, Chicago FSC
Ronald Joseph, Chicago FSC
1964 Judianne Fotheringill, Broadmoor SC
Jerry J. Fotherigill, Broadmoor SC
1963 Judianne Fotheringill, Broadmoor SC
Jerry J. Fotheringill, Broadmoor SC
1962 Dorothyann Nelson, Village of Lake Placid
Pieter Kollen, Village of Lake Placid
1961 Maribel Y. Owen, The SC of Boston
Dudley S. Richards, The SC of Boston
1960 Mrs. Nancy Rouillard Ludington,
Commonwealth FSC
Ronald Ludington, Commonwealth FSC
1959 Mrs. Nancy Rouillard Ludington,
Commonwealth FSC
Ronald Ludington, Commonwealth FSC
1958 Mrs. Nancy Rouillard Ludington,
Commonwealth FSC
Ronald Ludington, The SC of Boston
1957 Mrs. Nancy Rouillard, Commonwealth FSC
Ronald Ludington, The SC of Boston
1956 Carole Ann Ormaca, St. Moritz ISC
Robin Greiner, St. Moritz ISC
1955 Carole Ann Ormaca, St. Moritz ISC
Robin Greiner, St. Moritz ISC
1954 Carole Ann Ormaca, The SC of Fresno
Robin Greiner, The SC of Fresno
1953 Carole Ann Ormaca, The SC of Fresno
Robin Greiner, The SC of Fresno
1952 Karol Kennedy, Broadmoor SC
Peter Kennedy, Broadmoor SC
1951 Karol Kennedy, Broadmoor SC
Peter Kennedy, Broadmoor SC
1950 Karol Kennedy, Broadmoor SC
Peter Kennedy, Broadmoor SC
1949 Karol Kennedy, Seattle SC
Peter Kennedy, Seattle SC
1948 Karol Kennedy, Seattle SC
Peter Kennedy, Seattle SC
1947 Yvonne Claire Sherman, The SC of New York
Robert J. Swenning, The SC of New York
1946 Donna Jeanne Pospisil, The SC of New York
Jean-Pierre Brunet, The SC of New York
1945 Donna Jeanne Pospisil, The SC of New York
Jean-Pierre Brunet, The SC of New York

1944 Doris Schubach, Springfield Ice Birds
Walter Noffke, Springfield Ice Birds
1943 Doris Schubach, Springfield Ice Birds
Walter Noffke, Springfield Ice Birds
1942 Doris Schubach, Springfield Ice Birds
Walter Noffke, Springfield Ice Birds
1941 Donna Atwood, Mercury FSC
Eugene Turner, Los Angeles FSC
1940 Joan Tozzer, The SC of Boston
M. Bernard Fox, The SC of Boston
1939 Joan Tozzer, The SC of Boston
M. Bernard Fox, The SC of Boston
1938 Joan Tozzer, The SC of Boston
M. Bernard Fox, The SC of Boston
1937 Maribel Y. Vinson, The SC of Boston
George E.B. Hill, The SC of Boston
1936 Maribel Y. Vinson, The SC of Boston
George E.B. Hill, The SC of Boston
1935 Maribel Y. Vinson, The SC of Boston
George E.B. Hill, The SC of Boston
1934 Grace E. Madden, The SC of Boston
James L. Madden, The SC of Boston
1933 Maribel Y. Vinson, The SC of Boston
George E.B. Hill, The SC of Boston
1932 Beatrix Loughran, Skating Club, NY
Sherwin C. Badger, Skating Club, NY
1931 Beatrix Loughran, Skating Club, NY
Sherwin C. Badger, Skating Club, NY
1930 Beatrix Loughran, Skating Club, NY
Sherwin C. Badger, Skating Club, NY
1929 Maribel Y. Vinson, The SC of Boston
Thornton L. Coolidge, The SC of Boston
1928 Maribel Y. Vinson, The SC of Boston
Thornton L. Coolidge, The SC of Boston
1927 Mrs. Theresa Weld Blanchard, The SC of Boston
Nathaniel W. Niles, The SC of Boston
1926 Mrs. Theresa Weld Blanchard, The SC of Boston
Nathaniel W. Niles, The SC of Boston
1925 Mrs. Theresa Weld Blanchard, The SC of Boston
Nathaniel W. Niles, The SC of Boston
1924 Mrs. Theresa Weld Blanchard, The SC of Boston
Nathaniel W. Niles, The SC of Boston
1923 Mrs. Theresa Weld Blanchard, The SC of Boston
Nathaniel W. Niles, The SC of Boston
1922 Mrs. Theresa Weld Blanchard, The SC of Boston
Nathaniel W. Niles, The SC of Boston
1921 Mrs. Theresa Weld Blanchard, The SC of Boston
Nathaniel W. Niles, The SC of Boston
1920 Theresa Weld, The SC of Boston
Nathaniel W. Niles, The SC of Boston
1919 No Competitions
1918 Theresa Weld, The SC of Boston
Nathaniel W. Niles, The SC of Boston
1915-1917 No Competitions
1914 Jeanne Chevalier, WC of Montreal
Norman M. Scott, WC of Montreal

DANCE

1995 Renée Roca, Broadmoor SC
Gorsha Sur, Broadmoor SC
1994 Elizabeth Punsalan, Broadmoor SC
Jerod Swallow, Detroit SC
1993 Renée Roca, Broadmoor SC
Gorsha Sur, Broadmoor SC
1992 April Sargent-Thomas, Ogdensburg FSC
Russ Witherby, University of Delaware FSC
1991 Elizabeth Punsalan, Broadmoor SC
Jerod Swallow, Broadmoor SC

1990 Susan Wynne, Broadmoor SC
   Joseph Druar, Seattle SC
1989 Susan Wynne, Broadmoor SC
   Joseph Druar, Seattle SC
1988 Suzanne Semanick, University of Delaware SC
   Scott Gregory, University of Delaware SC
1987 Suzanne Semanick, University of Delaware SC
   Scott Gregory, University of Delaware SC
1986 Renée Roca, Genesee FSC
   Donald Adair, Academy FSC
1985 Judy Blumberg, Pittsburgh FSC
   Michael Seibert, Pittsburgh FSC
1984 Judy Blumberg, Pittsburgh FSC
   Michael Seibert, Pittsburgh FSC
1983 Judy Blumberg, Pittsburgh FSC
   Michael Seibert, Pittsburgh FSC
1982 Judy Blumberg, Broadmoor SC
   Michael Seibert, ISC of Indianapolis
1981 Judy Blumberg, Broadmoor SC
   Michael Seibert, ISC of Indianapolis
1980 Stacey Smith, SC of Wilmington
   John Summers, SC of Wilmington
1979 Stacey Smith, SC of Wilmington
   John Summers, SC of Wilmington
1978 Stacey Smith, SC of Wilmington
   John Summers, SC of Wilmington
1977 Judy Genovesi, SC of Hartford
   Kent Weigle, Charter Oak FSC
1976 Colleen O'Connor, Broadmoor SC
   Jim Millns, Broadmoor SC
1975 Colleen O'Connor, Broadmoor SC
   Jim Millns, Broadmoor SC
1974 Colleen O'Connor, Broadmoor SC
   Jim Millns, City of Colorado Springs
1973 Mary Karen Campbell, Lansing SC
   Johnny Johns, Detroit SC
1972 Judy Schwomeyer, WC of Indianapolis
   James Sladky, Genesee FSC
1971 Judy Schwomeyer, WC of Indianapolis
   James Sladky, Genesee FSC
1970 Judy Schwomeyer, WC of Indianapolis
   James Sladky, Genesee FSC
1969 Judy Schwomeyer, WC of Indianapolis
   James Sladky, Genesee FSC
1968 Judy Schwomeyer, WC of Indianapolis
   James Sladky, Genesee FSC
1967 Lorna Dyer, Broadmoor SC
   John Carrell, Broadmoor SC
1966 Kristin Fortune, Los Angeles FSC
   Dennis Sveum, Los Angeles FSC
1965 Kristin Fortune, Los Angeles FSC
   Dennis Sveum, Los Angeles FSC
1964 Darlene Streich, WC of Indianapolis
   Charles D. Fetter, Jr., WC of Indianapolis
1963 Sally Schantz, The SC of Boston
   Stanley Urban, Buffalo SC
1962 Yvonne N. Littlefield, Arctic Blades FSC
   Peter F. Betts Paramount, Calif.
1961 Diane C. Sherbloom, Los Angeles FSC
   Dallas (Larry) Pierce, WC of Indianapolis
1960 Margie Ackles, Los Angeles FSC
   Charles W. Phillips, Jr., Arctic Blades FSC
1959 Andrée Anderson Jacoby, Buffalo SC
   Donald Jacoby, Buffalo SC
1958 Andrée Anderson, Buffalo SC
   Donald Jacoby, Buffalo SC
1957 Sharon McKenzie, Los Angeles FSC
   Bert Wright, Los Angeles FSC

1956 Joan Zamboni, Arctic Blades FSC
   Roland Junso, Arctic Blades FSC
1955 Mrs. Carmel Bodel, St. Moritz ISC
   Edward L. Bodel, St. Moritz ISC
1954 Mrs. Carmel Bodel, St. Mortiz ISC
   Edward L. Bodel, St. Moritz ISC
1953 Carol Ann Peters, Washington FSC
   Daniel C. Ryan, Washington FSC
1952 Lois Waring, Baltimore FSC
   Michael McGean, Baltimore FSC
1951 Mrs. Carmel Bodel, St. Moritz ISC
   Edward L. Bodel, St. Moritz ISC
1950 Lois Waring, Baltimore FSC
   Michael McGean, Baltimore FSC
1949 Lois Waring, Baltimore FSC
   Walter H. Bainbridge, Jr., Washington FSC
1948 Lois Waring, Baltimore FSC
   Walter H. Bainbridge, Jr., Washington FSC
1947 Lois Waring, Baltimore FSC
   Walter H. Bainbridge, Jr., Washington FSC
1946 Anne Davies, Washington FSC
   Carleton C. Hoffner, Jr., Washington FSC
1945 Mrs. Kathe Mehl Williams, The SC of New York
   Robert J. Swenning, The SC of New York
1944 Marcella May, Skate & Ski Club
   James Lochead, Jr., Skate & Ski Club
1943 Marcella May, Skate & Ski Club
   James Lochead, Jr., Skate & Ski Club
1942 Edith B. Whetstone, Philadelphia SC & HS
   Alfred N. Richards, Jr., Phila. SC & HS
1941 Sandy MacDonald, The SC of New York
   Harold Hartshorne, The SC of New York
1940 Sandy MacDonald, The SC of New York
   Harold Hartshorne, The SC of New York
1939 Sandy MacDonald, The SC of New York
   Harold Hartshorne, The SC of New York
1938 Nettie C. Prantel, SC, New York
   Harold Hartshorne, SC, New York
1937 Nettie C. Prantel, SC, New York
   Harold Hartshorne, SC, New York
1936 Marjorie Parker, SC, New York
   Joseph K. Savage, SC, New York
1935 Waltz
   Nettie C. Prantel, SC, New York
   Roy Hunt, SC, New York
1934 Waltz
   Nettie C. Prantel, SC, New York
   Roy Hunt, SC, New York
   Original
   Suzanne Davis, The SC of Boston
   Frederick Goodridge, The SC of Boston
1933 Waltz
   Ilse Twaroschk, Brooklyn FSC
   Frederick F. Fleishmann, Brooklyn FSC
   Original
   Suzanne Davis, The SC of Boston
   Frederick Goodridge, The SC of Boston
1932 Waltz
   Mrs. Edith C. Secord, SC, New York
   Joseph K. Savage, SC, New York
   Original
   Mrs. Clara Rotch Frothingham, The SC
   of Boston
   George E.B. Hill, The SC of Boston

1931 Waltz
   Mrs. Edith C. Secord, SC, New York
   Ferrier T. Martin, SC, New York
   Original
   Mrs. Theresa Weld Blanchard, The SC of Boston
   Nathaniel W. Niles, The SC of Boston
1930 Waltz
   Mrs. Edith C. Secord, SC, New York
   Joseph K. Savage, SC, New York
   Original
   Mrs. Clara Rotch Frothingham, The SC
   of Boston
   George E.B. Hill, The SC of Boston
1929 Waltz and Original Dance combined
   Mrs. Edith C. Secord, SC, New York
   Joseph K. Savage, SC, New York
1928 Waltz
   Rosaline Dunn, New York SC
   Joseph K. Savage, New York SC
   Fourteenstep
   Mrs. Ada Bauman Kelly, New York SC
   George T. Braakman, New York SC
1927 Waltz and Fourteenstep
   Rosaline Dunn, New York SC
   Joseph K. Savage, New York SC
1926 Waltz
   Rosaline Dunn, New York SC
   Joseph K. Savage, New York SC
   Fourteenstep
   Sydney Goode, New York SC
   James B. Greene, New York SC
1925 Waltz and Fourteenstep
   Virginia Slattery, New York SC
   Ferrier T. Martin, New York SC
1924 Waltz
   Rosaline Dunn, New York
   Frederick Gabel, New York SC
   Fourteenstep
   Sydney Goode, New York SC
   James B. Greene, New York SC
1923 Waltz
   Mr. & Mrs. Henry W. Howe, New York SC
   Fourteenstep
   Sydney Goode, New York SC
   James B. Greene, New York SC
1922 Waltz
   Beatrix Loughran, New York SC
   Edward M. Howland, The SC of Boston
   Fourteenstep
   Mrs. Theresa Weld Blanchard, The SC of Boston
   Nathaniel W. Niles, The SC of Boston
1921 Waltz and Fourteenstep
   Mrs. Theresa Weld Blanchard, The SC of Boston
   Nathaniel W. Niles, The SC of Boston
1920 Waltz
   Theresa Weld, The SC of Boston
   Nathaniel W. Niles, The SC of Boston
   Fourteenstep
   Mrs. Gertrude Cheever Porter, New York SC
   Irving Brokaw, New York SC
1915-1919 No Competitions
1914 Waltz
   Theresa Weld, The SC of Boston
   Nathaniel W. Niles, The SC of Boston

iii

FOURS

1991 Elaine Asanakis, University of Delaware FSC
   Calla Urbanski, University of Delaware FSC
   Rocky Marval, SC of New York
   Joel McKeever, Dallas FSC
1951-1990 No Competitions
1950 Janet Gerhauser, St. Paul FSC
   Marilyn Thomsen, St. Paul FSC
   John Nightingale, St. Paul FSC
   Marlyn Thomsen, St. Paul FSC
1949 No Competition
1948 Janet Gerhauser, St. Paul FSC
   Marilyn Thomsen, St. Paul FSC
   John Nightingale, St. Paul FSC
   Marlyn Thomsen, St. Paul FSC
1947 Janet Gerhauser, St. Paul FSC
   Marilyn Thomsen, St. Paul FSC
   John Nightingale, St. Paul FSC
   Marlyn Thomsen, St. Paul FSC
1946 Jacqueline Dunne, Chicago FSC
   Joan Yocum, Chicago FSC
   Edward Van Der Bosch, Chicago FSC
   Larry Van Der Bosch, Chicago FSC
1945 Jacqueline Dunne, Chicago FSC
   Joan Yocum, Chicago FSC
   Edward Van Der Bosch, Chicago FSC
   Larry Van Der Bosch, Chicago FSC
1941-1944 No Competitions
1940 Mary Louise Premer, St. Paul FSC
   Janette Ahrens, St. Paul FSC
   Robert Uppgren, St. Paul FSC
   Lyman E. Wakefield, Jr., St. Paul FSC
1939 Nettie C. Prantel, SC, New York
   Marjorie Parker, SC, New York
   Joseph K. Savage, SC, New York
   George Boltres, SC, New York
1936-1938 No Competitions
1935 Nettie C. Prantel, SC, New York
   Ardelle V. Kloss, SC, New York
   Joseph K. Savage, SC, New York
   Roy Hunt, SC, New York
1934 Suzanne Davis, The SC of Boston
   Mrs. Theresa Weld Blanchard, The SC of Boston
   Frederick Goodridge, The SC of Boston
   Richard L. Hapgood, The SC of Boston
1926-1933 No Competitions
1925 Clara Hartman, New York SC
   Grace Munstock, New York SC
   Paul Armitage, New York SC
   Joel B. Liberman, New York SC
1924 Clara Hartman, New York SC
   Grace Munstock, New York SC
   Paul Armitage, New York SC
   Joel B. Liberman, New York SC

JUNIOR MEN

FREE SKATING

1995 Matthew Kessinger, Indiana/World SA
1994 Jere Michael, Broadmoor SC
1993 Michael Weiss, Washington FSC
1992 Ryan Hunka, Winterhurst FSC
1991 Damon Allen, FSC of Rockford
COMBINED
1990 Scott Davis, Lakewood WC
1989 Shepherd Clark, Broadmoor SC
1988 Christopher Mitchell, Los Angeles FSC
1987 Todd Eldredge, Broadmoor SC
1986 Mark Mitchell, SC of Hartford

1985 Doug Mattis, Philadelphia SC & HS
1984 William Lawe, Broadmoor SC
1983 Christopher Bowman, Los Angeles FSC
1982 James Cygan, Broadmoor SC
1981 Paul Wylie, Colorado SC
1980 Tom Dickson, Broadmoor SC
1979 James Santee, Chicago FSC
1978 Brian Boitano, Silver Edge FSC
1977 Robert Wagenhoffer, Arctic Blades FSC
1976 Scott Hamilton, Bowling Green SC
1975 Tim Zink, Charleston FSC
1974 Randy Gardner, Los Angeles FSC
1973 John Carlow, Jr., Arctic Blades FSC
1972 Terry Kubicka, Arctic Blades FSC
1971 David Santee, Chicago FSC
1970 Richard Ewell, III, All Year FSC
1969 John Baldwin, Broadmoor SC
1968 Kenneth Shelley, Arctic Blades FSC
1967 Roger Bass, Arctic Blades FSC
1966 John Misha Petkevich, Great Falls FSC
1965 Paul McGrath, Commonwealth FSC
1964 Tim Wood, Detroit SC
1963 Billy Chapel, Los Angeles FSC
1962 Thomas Litz, Hershey FSC
1961 Monty Hoyt, Broadmoor SC
1960 Douglas Ramsay, Detroit SC
1959 Gregory E. Kelley, The SC of Boston
1958 James Short, Los Angeles FSC
1957 Bradley R. Lord, The SC of Boston
1956 Robert Lee Brewer, Blade & Edge Club
   of Pasadena
1955 Tom Moore, Lakewood WC
1954 Tim Brown, Los Angeles FSC
1953 David Jenkins, Cleveland SC
1952 Ronald Robertson, Broadmoor SC
1951 Dudley S. Richards, The SC of Boston
1950 Donald E. Laws, Washington FSC
1949 Richard Dwyer, Los Angeles FSC
1948 Hayes Alan Jenkins, Cleveland SC
1947 Robert J. Swenning, The SC of New York
1946 John Lettengarver, St. Paul FSC
1945 Richard T. Button, Philadelphia SC & HS
1944 James Lochead, Jr., Skate & Ski Club
1943 Edward LeMaire, The SC of New York
1942 Walter Sahlin, FSC of Minneapolis
1941 William H. Grimditch, Jr., Philadelphia SC & HS
1940 Robert Specht, Chicago FSC
1939 Arthur R. Vaughn, Jr., Philadelphia SC & HS
1938 Eugene Turner, Los Angeles FSC
1937 Ollie E. Haupt, Jr., St. Louis SC
1936 M. Bernard Fox, The SC of Boston
1935 Erle Relter, Twin City FSC
1934 George R. Boltres, SC, New York
1933 William Swallender, FSC of Minneapolis
1932 Robin H. Lee, Twin City FSC
1931 Joseph K. Savage, SC, New York
1930 Gail Borden II, SC, New York
1929 George E.B. Hill, The SC of Boston
1928 James L. Madden, The SC of Boston
1927 Frederick Goodridge, The SC of Boston
1926 Roger F. Turner, The SC of Boston
1925 Ferrier T. Martin, New York SC
1924 Egbert S. Cary, Jr., Philadelphia SC & HS
1923 George T. Braakman, New York SC
1922 Louis Van N. Washburn, The SC of Boston
1921 George Greenslet, The SC of Boston
1920 Oscar L. Richard, New York SC
1919 No Competition
1918 Sherwin C. Badger, The SC of Boston

FIGURES

1995 Christopher Malato, SC of Vail
1994 Erik Schulz, Broadmoor SC
1993 Everett Weiss, Denver FSC
1992 Jay Cochon, DuPage FSC
1991 Laurent Massé, Hayden Recreation Centre FSC

JUNIOR LADIES

FREE SKATING

1995 Sydne Vogel, Anchorage FSC
1994 Jennifer Karl, St. Paul FSC
1993 Michelle Cho, Orange County FSC
1992 Caroline Song, Los Angeles FSC
1991 Lisa Ervin, Winterhurst FSC
COMBINED
1990 Alice Sue Claeys, Braemar-City of Lakes FSC
1989 Kyoko Ina, SC of New York
1988 Dena Galech, Seattle SC
1987 Jeri Campbell, All Year FSC
1986 Cindy Bortz, Los Angeles FSC
1985 Jill Trenary, Broadmoor SC
1984 Allison Oki, SC of New York
1983 Kathryn Adams, St. Moritz ISC
1982 Lorilee Pritchard, The SC of Boston
1981 Jill Frost, Silver Blades SC
1980 Vikki de Vries, Los Angeles FSC
1979 Elaine Zayak, SC of New York
1978 Jill Sawyer, Lakewood WC
1977 Sandy Lenz, Wagon Wheel FSC
1976 Carrie Rugh, Los Angeles FSC
1975 Lisa-Marie Allen, City of Burbank, Cal.
1974 Barbara Smith, Arctic Blades FSC
1973 Laurie Brandel, Arctic Blades FSC
1972 Wendy Burge, Los Angeles FSC
1971 Melissa Militano, City of New York, N.Y.
1970 Juli McKinstry, Santa Rosa FSC
1969 Louise Vacca, Long Island FSC
1968 Barbara Ray, City of Burlingame, Calif.
1967 Julie Lynn Holmes, Arctic Blades FSC
1966 Janet Lynn, Wagon Wheel FSC
1965 Sharon Bates, St. Moritz ISC
1964 Carol S. Noir, Essex SC of New Jersey
1963 Albertina N. Noyes, The SC of Boston
1962 Christine Haigler, Broadmoor SC
1961 Lorraine G. Hanlon, The SC of Boston
1960 Karen E. Howland, Sun Valley FSC
1959 Laurence R. Owen, The SC of Boston
1958 Barbara Ann Roles, Arctic Blades FSC
1957 Carol Joyce Wanek, The SC of New York
1956 Joan Schenke, Lakewood WC
1955 Nancy E. Heiss, The SC of New York
1954 Catherine Machado, Los Angeles FSC
1953 Patricia Firth, Lakewood WC
1952 Carol E. Heiss, The Junior SC of N.Y.
1951 Frances Dorsey, Seattle SC
1950 Tenley E. Albright, The SC of Boston
1949 Sonya Klopfer, The Junior SC of N.Y.
1948 Virginia Bxter, Chicago FSC
1947 Yvonne Claire Sherman, The SC of N.Y.
1946 Barbara Jones, Philadelphia SC & HS
1945 Eileen Seigh, Philadelphia SC & HS
1944 Madelon Olson, St. Paul FSC
1943 Hildegarde Balmain, The SC of New York
1942 Dorothy Goos, The SC of New York
1941 Donna Atwood, Mercury FSC
1940 Ramona Allen, Oakland SC
1939 Gretchen Van Zandt Merrill, The SC of Boston
1938 Charlotte Walther, SC, New York
1937 Joan Tozzer, The SC of Boston

1936 Katherine Durbrow, SC, New York
1935 Polly Blodgett, The SC of Boston
1934 Valerie Jones, SC, New York
1933 Estelle Weigel, Buffalo SC
1932 Louise Weigel, Buffalo SC
1931 Margaret Bennett, FSC of Minneapolis
1930 Dr. Hulda Berger, Winter Sports Club, N.Y.
1929 Mrs. Evelyn Chandler Mapes, Brooklyn FSC
1928 Virginia Badger, The SC of Boston
1927 Suzanne Davis, The SC of Boston
1926 Julia E. Honan, New York SC
1925 Ada Bauman, New York SC
1924 Maribel Y. Vinson, The SC of Boston
1923 Rosalie Knapp, New York SC
1922 Helen Stantial, The SC of Boston
1921 Beatrix Loughran, New York SC
1920 Rosaline Dunn, New York SC
1919 No Competition
1918 Mrs. Clara Rotch Frothingham, The SC of Boston

FIGURES

1995 Jamie Wunderlich, Rocky Mountain FSC
1994 Jennifer Clark, Highland SC
1993 Leah Hardy, Denver FSC
1992 Jessica Posada, Los Angeles FSC
1991 Casey Link, Las Vegas FSC

JUNIOR PAIRS

1995 Danielle Hartsell, Garden City FSC
     Steve Hartsell, Detroit SC
1994 Nicole Bateson-Rock, Univ. of Delaware FSC
     Keith Tindall, SC of Wilmington
1993 Stephanie Stiegler, Los Angeles FSC
     Lance Travis, Los Angeles FSC
1992 Nicole A. Sciarrotta, Orange County FSC
     Gregory G. Sciarrotta, Jr., Orange County FSC
1991 Aimée Offner, University of Delaware FSC
     Brian Helgenberg, University of Delaware FSC
1990 Tristen Vega, Los Angeles FSC
     Richard Alexander, Los Angeles FSC
1989 Jennifer Heurlin, Broadmoor SC
     John Frederiksen, Broadmoor SC
1988 Kenna Bailey, Utah FSC
     John Denton, Arctic Blades FSC
1987 Kellie Lynn Creel, Los Angeles FSC
     David McGovern, Arctic Blades FSC
1986 Kristi Yamaguchi, St. Moritz ISC
     Rudy Galindo, St. Moritz ISC
1985 Deveny Deck, Detroit SC
     Luke Hohmann, Buffalo SC
1984 Ginger Tse, SC of Wilmington
     Archie Tse, SC of Wilmington
1983 Susan Dungjen, Detroit SC
     Jason Dungjen, Detroit SC
1982 Natalie Seybold, Fort Wayne ISC
     Wayne Seybold, Fort Wayne ISC
1981 Deborah Lynch, Santa Monica FSC
     Keith Green, Arctic Blades FSC
1980 Dana Graham, Colorado SC
     Paul Wylie, Colorado SC
1979 Rosemary Sweeney, Colonial FSC
     Daniel Salera, North Shore SC
1978 Maria DiDomenico, Los Angeles FSC
     Larry Schrier, All Year FSC
1977 Vicki Heasley, Arctic Blades FSC
     Robert Wagenhoffer, Arctic Blades FSC
1976 Tracy Prussack, Los Angeles FSC
     Scott Prussack, Los Angeles FSC
1975 Lorene Mitchell, Long Island FSC
     Donald Mitchell, Long Island FSC

1974 Lisa Carey, Los Angeles FSC
     Douglas Varvais, Los Angeles FSC
1973 Tai Babilonia, Los Angeles FSC
     Randy Gardner, City of Burbank, Calif.
1972 Michelle McCladdie, City of Santa Monica, Calif.
     Richard Ewell, III, City of Santa Monica, Calif.
1971 Cynthia Van Valkenburg, City of
     Paramount, Calif.
     James Hulick, Arctic Blades FSC
1970 Barbara Brown, Denver FSC
     Doug Berndt, Denver FSC
1969 Jannat Thompson, City of Colorado Springs
     John Baldwin, Broadmoor SC
1968 Annetta Baird, Philadelphia SC & HS
     Richard Inglesi, Town of Ardmore
1967 Alicia Jo Starbuck, Arctic Blades FSC
     Kenneth Shelley, Arctic Blades FSC
1966 Betty Jean Lewis, The SC of Boston
     Richard Gilbert, The SC of Boston
1965 Page Paulsen, Arctic Blades FSC
     Larry Dusich, Arctic Blades FSC
1964 Barbara Yaggi, Troy SC
     Gene Floyd, Troy SC
1963 Cynthia Kauffman, Seattle SC
     Ronald Kauffman, Seattle SC
1962 Elizabeth George, The SC of Boston
     Paul George, The SC of Boston
1961 Vivian Joseph, Chicago FSC
     Ronald Joseph, Chicago FSC
1960 Laurie Hickox, The SC of San Francisco
     William Hickox, The SC of San Francisco
1969 Judianne Fotheringill, Lakewood WC
     Jerry J. Fotheringill, Lakewood WC
1958 Mrs. Gayle Freed, Queen City FSC
     Karl Freed, Queen City FSC
1957 Ila Ray Hadley, Seattle SC
     Ray E. Hadley, Seattle SC
1956 Nancy Rouillard, Commonwealth FSC
     Ronald Ludington, North Shore SC
1955 Maribel Y. Owen, The SC of Boston
     Charles U. Foster, The SC of Boston
1954 Dawn May, Seattle SC
     David Hertz, Seattle SC
1953 Norma McCullagh, Rye FSC
     Robert E. Goodfellow, Jr., Rye FSC
1952 Sharon Choate, Seattle SC
     Richard Bromley, Lakewood WC
1951 Caryl Johns, Baltimore FSC
     Jack Jost, Baltimore FSC
1950 Janet Gerhauser, St. Paul FSC
     John Nightingale, St. Paul FSC
1949 Lois Waring, Baltimore FSC
     Walter H. Bainbridge, Jr., Washington FSC
1948 Anne Davies, Washington FSC
     Carleton C. Hoffner, Jr., Washington FSC
1947 Harriet Sutton, St. Paul FSC
     John Lettengarver, St. Paul FSC
1946 Yvonne Claire Sherman, The SC of N.Y.
     Robert J. Swenning, The SC of N.Y.
1945 Betty Jean Higgins, The SC of Boston
     Lyman E. Wakefield, Jr., The SC of Boston
1944 Donna Jeanne Pospisil, The SC of N.Y.
     Jean-Pierre Brunet, The SC of N.Y.
1943 Betty Schalow, St. Paul FSC
     Arthur F. Preusch, Jr., St. Paul FSC
1942 Dorothy Goos, The SC of New York
     Edward LeMaire, The SC of New York
1941 Doris Schubach, Springfield Ice Birds
     Walter Noffke, Springfield Ice Birds

1940 Dorothy L. Glazier, The SC of Boston
     Stephen B. Tanner, The SC of Boston
1939 Betty Lee Bennett, Seattle SC
     John Kinney, Seattle SC
1938 Mrs. Annah M. Hall, Philadelphia SC & HS
     William P.G. Hall, III, Philadelphia SC & HS
1937 Ardelle V. Kloss, The SC of New York
     Roland Janson, The SC of New York
1936 Joan Tozzer, The SC of Boston
     M. Bernard Fox, The SC of Boston
1935 Jeanne Schulte, St. Louis SC
     Ollie E. Haupt, Jr., St. Louis SC
1934 Polly Blodgett, The SC of Boston
     Roger F. Turner, The SC of Boston
1933 Eva Schwerdt, Winter Sports Club, N.Y.
     William H. Bruns, Jr., Winter Sports Club, N.Y.
1932 Mrs. Virginia S. Martin, SC, New York
     Ferrier T. Martin, SC, New York
1931 Nancy Follett, Quincy, Mass.
     Fred A. Parmenter, The SC of Boston
1930 Mrs. Helen Herbst, Winter Sports Club, NY
     William J. Nagle, Winter Sports Club, N.Y.
1929 Dorothy Weld, The SC of Boston
     Richard L. Hapgood, The SC of Boston
1928 Grace E. Madden, The SC of Boston
     James L. Madden, The SC of Boston
1927 Maribel Y. Vinson, The SC of Boston
     Thornton L. Coolidge, The SC of Boston
1926 Beatrix Loughran, New York SC
     Raymond Harvey, New York SC
1925 Sydney Goode, New York SC
     James B. Greene, New York SC
1924 Ada Bauman, New York SC
     George T. Broakman, New York SC
1923 Mrs. Ruth Chapman, Philadelphia SC & HS
     Joseph Chapman, Philadelphia SC & HS

JUNIOR DANCE

1995 Eve Chalom, Detroit SC
     Mathew Gates, Detroit SC
1994 Laura Gayton, SC of Boston
     Oleg Fediukov, Pawtucket & Providence FSC
1993 Kimberly Hartley, Indiana/World SA
     Michael Sklutovsky, Indiana/World SA
1992 Christine Fowler, Broadmoor SC
     Garrett Swasey, Broadmoor SC
1991 Kimberly Callahan, University of Delaware FSC
     Robert Peal, Skokie Valley SC
1990 Beth Buhl, Seattle SC
     Neale Smull, Peninsula FSC
1989 Rachel Mayer, SC of Boston
     Peter Breen, SC of Boston
1988 Elizabeth Punsalan, Los Angeles FSC
     Shawn Rettstatt, Pittsfield FSC
1987 Jennifer Benz, Detroit SC
     Jeffrey Benz, Detroit SC
1986 Colette Huber, Los Angeles FSC
     Ron Kravette, Rim of the World FSC
1985 Jodie Balogh, Academy FSC
     Jerod Swallow, Detroit SC
1984 Christina Yatsuhashi, SC of Boston
     Keith Yatsuhashi, SC of Boston
1983 Suzanne Semanick, Pittsburgh FSC
     Alexander Miller, III, Academy FSC
1982 Amanda Newman, South Mountain FSC
     Jerry Santoferrara, Buffalo SC
1981 Anne Spiewak, The SC of Boston
     Keith Lichtman, SC of Wilmington

1980 Terri Slater, Genesee FSC
  David Lipowitz, So. Mountain FSC
1979 Elisa Spitz, Essex SC of New Jersey
  Stanley Makman, The SC of Boston
1978 Judy Ferris, Buffalo SC
  Scott Gregory, Buffalo SC
1977 Kelly Morris, Lincoln Center FSC
  Michael Seibert, ISC of Indianapolis
1976 Bonnie Burton, The SC of Boston
  William Burton, The SC of Boston
1975 Deborah Mansfield, Charter Oak FSC
  Frederick Maynard, III, Charter Oak FSC
1974 Jennifer Young, SC of Hartford
  David Young, SC of Hartford
1973 Judy Genovesi, SC of Hartford
  Kent Weigle, Charter Oak FSC
1972 Michelle Ford, SC of Phoenix
  Glenn Parriott, SC of Phoenix
1971 Cathleen Casey, SC of Hartford
  Francis X. Cassella, SC of Hartford
1970 Mary Bonacci, Rye FSC
  Gerard Lane, The SC of Boston
1969 Candace Johnstone, Essex SC of New Jersey
  Bruce Bowland, Essex SC of New Jersey
1968 Joan Bitterman, Seattle SC
  Brad Hislop, Seattle SC
1967 Debbi Gerken, The SC of Lake Placid
  Keith Galgot, Town of Watertown
1966 Dolly Rodenbaugh, Pittsburgh FSC
  Thomas Lescinski, Pittsburgh FSC
1965 Kathy Flaherty, Los Angeles FSC
  Roger Berry, Los Angeles FSC
1964 Kristin Fortune, Los Angeles FSC
  Claude Sweet, Los Angeles FSC
1963 Carole MacSween, Los Angeles FSC
  Raymond Chenson, Los Angeles FSC
1962 Susan Bright, Cleveland SC
  Robert Munz, Cleveland SC
1961 Rosemary McEvoy, Metropolitan FSC
  Ralph Owen, Metropolitan FSC
1960 Mrs. Patricia Dineen, The SC of Lake Placid
  Robert Dineen, The SC of Lake Placid
1959 Marilyn Meeker, WC of Indianapolis
  Dallas (Larry) Pierce, WC of Indianapolis
1958 Judy Ann Lamar, The SC of Boston
  Ronald Ludington, The SC of Boston
1957 B. Claire O'Neill, Baltimore FSC
  John J. Bejshak, Jr., Baltimore FSC
1956 Aileen Kahre, St. Moritz ISC
  Charles W. Phillips, Jr., Arctic Blades FSC
1955 Barbara Stein, Los Angeles FSC
  Ray Sato, Los Angeles FSC
1954 Sidney Ann Foster, The SC of Boston
  Franklin S. Nelson, The SC of Boston
1953 Katrine D. Neil, The SC of New York
  William Neil, Jr., The SC of New York
1952 Mrs. Elizabeth Chambers, Buffalo SC
  Roger J. Chambers, Jr., Buffalo SC
1951 Caryl Johns, Baltimore FSC
  Jack Jost, Baltimore FSC
1950 Carol Ann Peters, Washington FSC
  Daniel Ryan, Washington FSC
1949 Vera Ruth Elliott, Metropolitan FSC
  Rex Cook, Metropolitan FSC
1948 Mary C. Firth, Seattle SC
  Donald Laws, Washington FSC
1947 Renée Stein, Los Angeles FSC
  Sidney J. Moore, Los Angeles FSC

1946 Vivian H. Queisser, Washington FSC
  Richard C. Queisser, Washington FSC
1945 Patsy Jones, Washington FSC
  Walter H. Bainbridge, Jr., Washington FSC
1944 Marilyn Grace, St. Moritz ISC
  William Hoyt, St. Moritz ISC
1943 Dorothy L. Glazier, The SC of Boston
  Lyman E. Wakefield, Jr., The SC of Boston

NOVICE MEN
FREE SKATING
1995 James Yoo, Colorado SC
1994 Timothy Goebel, Winterhurst FSC
1993 Ryan Jahnke, St. Clair Shores FSC
1992 Roman Fraden, Los Angeles FSC
1991 John Bevan, Lilac City FSC
1990 Ryan Hunka, Winterhurst FSC
COMBINED
1989 Philip R. Dulebohn, Baltimore FSC
1988 Chris Browne, Dallas FSC
1987 John Baldwin, Jr., Los Angeles FSC
1986 Cameron Birky, St. Moritz ISC
1985 Todd Eldredge, Philadelphia SC & HS
1984 Patrick Brault, Los Angeles FSC
1983 Christopher Mitchell, Los Angeles FSC
1982 Rudy Galindo, Mission Valley ISC
1981 Thomas Cierniak, Chicago FSC
1980 James Cygan, Broadmoor SC
1979 Paul Wylie, Colorado SC
1978 Karl Kurtz, Hershey FSC
1977 James Santee, Broadmoor SC
1976 Robert Taylor, Los Angeles FSC
1975 Reggie Stanley, Town of Lexington
1974 Shane Douglas, Broadmoor SC
1973 Scott Carson, Los Angeles FSC
1972 David Kirby, Arctic Blades FSC
1971 Terry Kubicka, Arctic Blades FSC
1970 Glen Schulke, Glacier Falls FSC
1969 James Demogines, Los Angeles FSC
1968 Dean Hiltzik, Metropolitan FSC
1967 John Baldwin, Broadmoor SC
1966 Atoy Wilson, Los Angeles FSCR
1965 Roger Bass, Arctic Blades FSC
1964 Robert L. Black, The SC of Boston
1963 Johnny Moore, Arctic Blades FSC
1962 Tim Wood, Detroit SC
1961 Peter J. Meyer, Buffalo SC
1960 Robert Madden, Lakewood WC
1959 Monty Hoyt, Broadmoor SC
1958 Harvey Balch, Blade & Edge Club of Pasadena
1957 Gregory E. Kelley, The SC of Boston
1956 Bob Hubbard, Capital City FSC
1955 James Short, Los Angeles FSC
1954 Robert Lee Brewer, Blade & Edge Club of Pasadena
1953 J. Barlow Nelson, Tulsa FSC
1952 Tim Brown, Baltimore FSC
1951 Noel T. Ledin, Chicago FSC
1950 Ronald Robertson, Arctic Blades FSC
1949 Hugh C. Graham, Jr., Tulsa FSC
1948 Richard Dwyer, Los Angeles FSC
1947 Marlyn Thomsen, St. Paul FSC
1946 Dudley S. Richards, The SC of Boston
1945 John Lettengarver, St. Paul FSC
1944 Richard T. Button, Philadelphia SC & HS
1943 G. Austin Holt, St. Moritz ISC
1942 Richard W. More, Buffalo SC
1941 Walter Sahlin, FSC of Minneapolis
1940 William H. Grimditch, Jr., Philadelphia SC & HS

1939 Robert Specht, Chicago FSC
1938 Arthur R. Vaughn, Jr., Philadelphia SC & HS
1937 Robert Scott, St. Moritz ISC
1936 Edward Berkson, Manhattan FSC
1935 M. Bernard Fox, The SC of Boston
1934 Ollie E. Haupt, Jr., St. Louis SC
1933 Wilfred MacDonald, Winter Sports Club, N.Y.
1932 Samuel Ferguson, SC, New York
FIGURES
1995 Scott Sarbacker, Atlanta FSC
1994 Brad Russi, Lincoln Center FSC
1993 Kurt Fromknecht, Westminster FSC of Erie
1992 Danny Clausen, Anchorage FSC
1991 Kevin Donovan, Chicago FSC
1990 Michael Weiss, University of Delaware FSC

NOVICE LADIES
FREE SKATING
1995 Erin Sutton, Plymouth FSC
1994 Cohen Duncan, Los Angeles FSC
1993 Amanda Ward, SC of Rockland New York
1992 Michelle Cho, Orange County FSC
1991 Tanya Street, SC of Lake Forest
1990 Lisa Ervin, Winterhurst FSC
COMBINED
1989 Casey Link, Las Vegas FSC
1988 Caroline Lee, DuPage FSC
1987 Amy Holmberg, Rocky Mountain FSC
1986 Liane Moscato, The SC of Boston
1985 Katie Wood, Skokie Valley SC
1984 Sharon Barker, Los Angeles FSC
1983 Suggie Oh, Santa Barbara FSC
1982 Kathryn Adams, St. Moritz ISC
1981 Kathleen Haines, Arctic Blades FSC
1980 Joan Campbell, Los Angeles FSC
1979 Rosalynn Sumners, Seattle SC
1978 Michelle Schelske, Los Angeles FSC
1977 Jill Sawyer, Lakewood WC
1976 Kelsy Ufford, FSC of Minneapolis
1975 Sandy Lenz, Wagon Wheel FSC
1974 Jeanne Chapman, Los Angeles FSC
1973 Barbara Smith, Arctic Blades FSC
1972 Kim McIsaac, South Bay FSC
1971 Laurie Brandel, Arctic Blades FSC
1970 Dorian Shields, Glacier Falls FSC
1969 Dorothy Hamill, Rye FSC
1968 Pegeen Naughton, Long Island FSC
1967 Wen-An Sun, Broadmoor SC
1966 Dawn Glab, Arctic Blades FSC
1965 Julie Lynn Holmes, Arctic Blades FSC
1964 Gail Newberry, Buffalo SC
1963 Taffy Pergament, Westchester FSC
1962 Pamela Schneider, Garden State FSC
1961 Albertina N. Noyes, The SC of Boston
1960 Carol S. Noir, The SC of New York
1959 Mary Batdorf, Hershey FSC
1958 Rhode Lee Michelson, Arctic Blades FSC
1957 Diana Jean Lapp, Denver FSC
1956 Barbara Ann Roles, Blade & Edge Club
  of Pasadena
1955 Carol Wanek, The SC of New York
1954 Patricia Kilgore, Arctic Blades FSC
1953 Janice Marie Crappa, Los Angeles FSC
1952 Mary Ann Dorsey, St. Paul FSC
1951 Carol E. Heiss, The Junior SC of N.Y.
1950 Patricia Quick, St. Moritz ISC
1949 Tenley E. Albright, The SC of Boston
1948 Josephine Barnum, The SC of Boston

1947 Joanne Scotvold, Chicago FSC
1946 Gloria Peterson, Seattle SC
1945 Barbara Jones, Tulsa FSC
1944 Eileen Seigh, Brooklyn FSC
1943 Ann Robinson, New Haven SC
1942 Mabel MacPherson, Philadelphia SC & HS
1941 Dorothy Goos, The SC of New York
1940 Caroline Brandt, Cleveland SC
1939 Betsy C. Nichols, The SC of Boston
1938 Gretchen Van Zandt Merrill, The SC of Boston
1937 Marcia Zieget, Philadelphi SC & HS
1936 Jane Vaughn, Philadelphia SC & HS
1935 Mary Weigel, Buffalo SC
1934 Joan Tozzer, The SC of Boston
1933 Polly Blodgett, The SC of Boston
1932 Valerie Jones, SC, New York

FIGURES
1995 Rhea Sy, Arctic Blades FSC
1994 McKenzie Savidge, Univ. of Delaware FSC
1993 Jessica Austin-Hashimoto, Florida Suncoast FSC
1992 Melanie Dupon, Rim of the World FSC
1991 Bethany Quintin, SC of Boston
1990 Natalie Thomas, Rocky Mountain FSC

NOVICE PAIRS
1995 Tiffany Stiegler, Los Angeles FSC
     Johnnie Stiegler, Los Angeles FSC
1994 Brie Teaboldt, Indiana/World Skating Academy
     John Zimmerman, Indiana/World Skating
     Academy
1993 Sara Katherine Ward, South Mountain FSC
     J. Paul Binnebose, Univ. of Delaware FSC
     1992 Nicole Bateson-Rock, Univ. of Delaware FSC
     J. Paul Binnebose, SC of Rockland NY
1991 Andrea Catoia, SC of Wilmington
     Paul Dulebohn, Univ. of Delaware FSC

NOVICE DANCE
1995 Naomi Lang, Detroit SC
     John Lee, Detroit SC
1994 Jessica Joseph, Detroit SC
     Charles Butler, Jr., SW Michigan SC
1993 Eve Chalom, Detroit SC
     Mathew Gates, Detroit SC
1992 Kate Black, Indiana/World Skating Academy
     Kevin Spada, Indiana/World Skating Academy
1991 Nicole Dumonceaux, Braemar-City of Lakes FSC
     John Reppucci, Braemar-City of Lakes FSC

HARNED TROPHY
Awarded to the club earning the most points in the
National Championships.
1975 Los Angeles FSC
1974 Los Angeles FSC
1973 Los Angeles FSC
1972 Arctic Blades FSC
1971 Arctic Blades FSC
1970 Arctic Blades FSC
1969 Detroit SC
1968 Detroit SC
1967 Broadmoor SC
1966 Arctic Blades FSC
1965 Arctic Blades FSC
1964 The SC of Boston
1963 The SC of Boston
1962 Arctic Blades FSC
1961 The SC of Boston
1960 Broadmoor SC
1959 Broadmoor SC

1958 The SC of Boston
1957 Los Angeles FSC
1956 The SC of Boston
1955 Broadmoor SC, Los Angeles FSC (tie)
1954 Los Angeles FSC
1953 Los Angeles FSC, The SC of Boston (tie)
1952 Broadmoor SC
1951 The SC of Boston
1950 Washington FSC
1949 The SC of Boston
1948 Washington FSC
1947 St. Paul FSC
1946 Washington FSC
1945 The SC of New York
1944 The SC of New York
1943 The SC of New York
1942 Philadelphia SC & HS
1941 Philadelphia SC & HS
1940 The SC of Boston
1939 The SC of New York

NATIONAL INTERMEDIATE MEN
FREE SKATING
1995 Curt Doten, Colonial FSC
1994 Braden Overett, Denver FSC
1993 Travis Perkins, Arctic Blades FSC
1992 Dwayne Parker, Philadelphia SC & HS
1991 Derrick Delmore, Washington FSC
FIGURES
1995 Shaun Blase, Los Angeles FSC
1991 J. Paul Binnebose, SC of Rockland, New York

NATIONAL INTERMEDIATE LADIES
FREE SKATING
1995 J. J. Matthews, Anchorage FSC
1994 Amy Evidente, Los Angeles FSC
1993 Dena Darland, Las Vegas FSC
1992 Melissa Paull, Los Angeles FSC
1991 Sonia Kim, Arctic Blades FSC
FIGURES
1995 Leigh-Ann Hruz, Univ. of Delaware FSC
1991 Laurie Kaufmann, Rye FSC

NATIONAL INTERMEDIATE PAIRS
1995 "A" Brandi Seabol, Tampa Bay SC
          Cheyne Coppage, Tampa Bay SC
1994 Lauren Carpenter, Lincoln Center FSC
     Brad Russi, Lincoln Center FSC
1993 "A" Tiffany Stiegler, Los Angeles FSC
          Johnnie Stiegler II, Los Angeles FSC
1992 Whitney Gaynor, The Peninsula FSC
     Thomas Branch, St. Moritz ISC
1991 Danielle Hartsell, Garden City FSC
     Steven Hartsell, Garden City FSC

NATIONAL INTERMEDIATE DANCE
1995 "A" Cheri Whitney, Detroit SC
          Justin Pekarek, Detroit SC
1994 "A" Annalise Swanson, Univ. of Delaware FSC
          James Swanson, Univ. of Delaware FSC
1993 "A" Karen Ferrara, SC of Boston
          Brandon Forsyth, SC of Boston
     "B" Emily Rossman, St. Moritz ISC
          Robert Eads, St. Moritz ISC
1992 Mica Darley, All Year FSC
     Casper Young, Los Angeles FSC
1991 Kara Leigh Thornham, Arizona FSC
     Jonathan Magalnick, Arizona FSC

NATIONAL JUVENILE BOYS
FREE SKATING
1995 Parker Pennington, Winterhurst FSC
1994 Sean Calvillo, Golden State FSC
1993 Fitzhugh Middleton, Lincoln Center SC
1992 Jered Guzman, Los Angeles FSC
1991 Jonathan Keen, Orange County FSC
FIGURES
1995 Stephen Demarest, St. Joseph FSC

NATIONAL JUVENILE GIRLS
FREE SKATING
1995 Naomi Nam, All Year FSC
1994 Jacqueline Hernandez, Arctic Blades FSC
1993 Caitlin Marino, Pilgrim SC
1992 Jacqueline Redenshek, Mentor FSC
1991 Stephanie Stiegler, Los Angeles FSC
FIGURES
1995 Hilary Glovack, Jamestown SC

NATIONAL JUVENILE PAIRS
1995 "A" Courtney Michalak, Dallas FSC
          Matthew Quon, Dallas FSC
     "B" Carey Floyd, Nashville FSC
          David Tankersley, Nashville FSC
1994 Megan Sierk, Huntsville FSC
     Dustin Sierk, Huntsville FSC
1993 "A" Meredith Ward, Tampa Bay SC
          James A. Ward III, Tampa Bay SC
     "B" Christina Connally, Nashville FSC
          Arnold Myint, Nashville FSC

NATIONAL JUVENILE DANCE
1995 "A" Christine Hall, SC of Southern
          New England
          Bruce Hutchings, SC of Southern
          New England
     "B" Kristyn Starr, Lone Star FSC
          Nick Traxler, Lone Star FSC
1994 "A" Natalia Maxwell, Lone Star FSC
          Michel Klus, Lone Star FSC
     "B" Kimberly Navarro, Santa Rosa FSC
          Matthew Tinney, St. Moritz ISC
1993 "A" Erin Williams, Dallas FSC
          Caleb Heaton, Dallas FSC
     "B" Melissa Anne Gratta, SC of Mt. Lebanon
          David Paul Gratta, SC of Mt. Lebanon
1992 Christie Moxley, Univ. of Delaware FSC
     Thomas Gaasbeck, Univ. of Delaware FSC

NATIONAL COLLEGIATE SENIOR MEN
FREE SKATING
1991 Alexander Chang, Harvard University
1990 Troy Goldstein, Calif. State Univ., Long Beach
1989 Eddie Shipstad, University of Southern Colorado
1988 Steven Rice, Pierce College
1987 Steven Rice, Pierce College
1986 Paul Wylie, Harvard University
COMBINED
1985 Robert G. Rosenbluth, Emory University
FIGURES
1990 Troy Goldstein, Calif. State Univ., Long Beach
1989 Eddie Shipstad, University of Southern Colorado
1988 Troy Goldstein, Calif. State Univ., Long Beach
1987 Steven Rice, Pierce College
1986 Paul Wylie, Harvard University

NATIONAL COLLEGIATE SENIOR LADIES

FREE SKATING
1995 Angela Meduna, Mt. Hood Community College
1994 Mrs. Kathaleen Kelly Cutone, Northeastern University Law School
1993 Sara Kastner, University of St. Thomas
1992 Sara Kastner, University of St. Thomas
1991 Dena Galech, Shoreline Community College
1990 Leana Naczynski, Indiana University-Purdue University, Indianapolis
1989 Michelle Millikan, Indiana University
1988 Nancy Kerrigan, Emmanuel College
1987 Kathaleen Kelly, Harvard University
1986 Jan Bombassei, University of Connecticut

COMBINED
1985 Kathaleen Kelly, Harvard University

FIGURES
1995 Jessica Rainey, Knox Collegee
1994 Lisa Bryson, Univ. of Colorado-Boulder (tie)
    Janette Lynn Lewis, Denver University (tie)
1993 Shirl Marie Cattani, Temple University
1992 Sarah Gendreau, Pierce College-Puyallup
1991 Samantha Hawks, Boston College
1990 Jennifer Leng, Tufts University
1989 Kathaleen Kelly, Harvard University
1988 Kelly Szmurlo, Marquette University
1987 Kathaleen Kelly, Harvard University
1986 Eileen Groth, Central Conn. State University

NATIONAL COLLEGIATE SENIOR PAIRS

1990 Laura Murphy, Univ. of Delaware
    Brian Wells, Univ. of Delaware
1989 Calla Urbanski, Delaware Technical & Community College
    Mark Naylor, University of Delaware
1988 Calla Urbanski, Univ. of Delaware
    Mark Naylor, Univ. of Delaware
1987 Lori Blasko, Calif. State Univ., Northridge
    Todd Sand, Calif. State Univ., Northridge

NATIONAL COLLEGIATE SENIOR DANCE

1990 Rachel Mayer, Boston University
    Peter Breen, Boston University

NATIONAL COLLEGIATE JUNIOR MEN

FREE SKATING
1990 Glenn Ziehnert, Adirondack Community College
1989 Edmund Nesti, Northeastern University Figures

FIGURES
1990 Glenn Ziehnert, Adirondack Community College
1989 Glenn Ziehnert, Adirondack Community College

NATIONAL COLLEGIATE JUNIOR LADIES

FREE SKATING
1995 Tiffany E. Scott, Regis College
1994 Amy Lynn Love, University of Kansas
1993 Wendy Budzynski, Augsburg College
1992 Amy Ross, Boston University
1991 Shirl Cattani, Pennsylvania State University
1990 Dana Chinn, North Va. Community College
1989 Lisa Floreck, Univ. of Delaware

FIGURES
1995 Nicole Buckles, Arizona State University
1994 Sonja Castaneda, Univ. of Alaska-Fairbanks
1993 Elisa M. Goldberg, Univ. of Delaware
1992 Desiree V. Toneatto, West Chester University
1991 Cathleen Reynolds, Villanova University
1990 Janet Lynn Melville, Univ. of Delaware
1989 Lisa Floreck, Univ. of Delaware

NATIONAL COLLEGIATE JUNIOR PAIRS

1992 Erin Covington, Clackamas Comm. College
    Brandon Powell, Clackamas Comm. College
1991 Andrea Catoia, West Chester University
    Paul Dulebohn, West Chester University
1990 Dawn Piepenbrink, Arizona State University
    Nick Castaneda, Arizona State University
1988 Jocelyn Cox, Univ. of Delaware
    Brad Cox, Univ. of Delaware

NATIONAL COLLEGIATE JUNIOR DANCE

1995 Azumi Sagara, Whittier Collegee
    Jonathan Magalnick, Calif. State Univ., Long Beach
1993 Daniela Lopez, West Valley College
    Andras Lopez, West Valley College
1991 Sian Matthews, Univ. of Texas Arlington
    Jeremy Wyndham, Univ. of Texas Arlington
1990 Laura Gayton, Boston College
    Peter Abraham, Los Angeles FSC
1988 Wendy Millette, Univ. of Delaware
    James Curtis, Univ. of Delaware
1987 Holly Robbins, Pikes Peak Community College
    Jonathan Stine, Pikes Peak Community College

DANCE COMPULSORIES
1989 Beth Buhl, Univ. of Delaware
    Neale Small, Univ. of Delaware

FREE DANCE
1989 Beth Buhl, Univ. of Delaware
    Neale Small, Univ. of Delaware

NATIONAL SENIOR PRECISION

1995 Team Elan, Detroit SC
1994 Haydenettes, Hayden Recreation Centre FSC
1993 Haydenettes, Hayden Recreation Centre FSC
1992 Haydenettes, Hayden Recreation Centre FSC
1991 Haydenettes, Hayden Recreation Centre FSC
1990 Goldenettes, Garfield Heights FSC
1989 Haydenettes, Hayden Recreation Centre FSC
1988 Haydenettes, Hayden Recreation Centre FSC
1987 Fraserettes, Fraser FSC
1986 Hot Fudge Sundaes, Buffalo SC
1985 Fraserettes, Fraser FSC
1984 Fraserettes, Fraser FSC

NATIONAL JUNIOR PRECISION

1995 Starlets, Wagon Wheel FSC
1994 Team Elan, Detroit SC
1993 Miami University Precision Team, Miami Univ.
1992 Crystallettes, Great Lakes FSC
1991 Team Elan, St. Clair Shores FSC
1990 Royalettes, Garfield Heights FSC
1989 Shoreliners, Saint Clair Shores FSC
1988 Hot Fudge Sundaes, Buffalo SC
1987 The Supremes, Warwick Figure Skaters
1986 The Figurettes, Hamden FSA
1985 Hot Fudge Sundaes, Buffalo SC
1984 Hot Fudge Sundaes, Buffalo SC

NATIONAL ADULT PRECISION

1995 Esprit de Corps, Hayden Rec. Centre FSC (Open)
1995 Ice Classics, Lloyd Center ISC (Master)
1994 Team Elan, Detroit SC (Open)
1993 Esprit De Corps, Hayden Recreation Centre FSC
1992 Esprit De Corps, Hayden Recreation Centre FSC
1991 Team Elan, Detroit SC
1990 Detroit Royals, Detroit SC
1989 Fabulous Forties, Los Angeles FSC
1988 Fabulous Forties, Los Angeles FSC
1987 Fabulous Forties, Los Angeles FSC
1986 Acton-Ups, Colonial FSC
1985 Acton-Ups, Colonial FSC
1984 Acton-Ups, Colonial FSC

NATIONAL NOVICE PRECISION

1995 Ice Mates, Hayden Recreation Centre FSC
1994 Ice Mates, Hayden Recreation Centre FSC
1993 Ice Mates, Hayden Recreation Centre FSC
1992 Ice Mates, Hayden Recreation Centre FSC
1991 Starlettes, Garfield Heights FSC
1990 Ice Mates, Hayden Recreation Centre FSC
1989 Fraser Juniorettes, Fraser FSC
1988 Fraser Juniorettes, Fraser FSC
1987 Hot Fudge Sundaes, Buffalo SC
1986 Hot Fudge Sundaes, Buffalo SC
1985 Hot Fudge Sundaes, Buffalo SC
1984 Hot Fudge Sundaes, Buffalo SC

NATIONAL INTERMEDIATE PRECISION

1995 Magic Edges, Magic City FSC
1994 Munchkins, Warwick Figure Skaters
1993 Munchkins, Warwick Figure Skaters
1992 Munchkins, Warwick Figure Skaters
1991 Munchkins, Warwick Figure Skaters
1990 Hot Fudge Sundaes, Buffalo SC
1989 Ice Mates, Hayden Recreation Centre FSC
1988 Hot Fudge Sundaes, Buffalo SC
1987 Ice Mates, Hayden Recreation Centre FSC

NATIONAL JUVENILE PRECISION

1995 Team Elan, Detroit SC
1994 Team Elan, Detroit SC
1993 Ice Cubes, Hayden Recreation Centre FSC
1992 Ice Cubes, Hayden Recreation Centre FSC
1991 Ice Cubes, Hayden Recreation Centre FSC
1990 Angelettes, Garfield Heights FSC
1989 Ice Cubes, Hayden Recreation Centre FSC
1988 Ice Cubes, Hayden Recreation Centre FSC
1987 Fraser Mini-ettes, Fraser FSC
1986 Angelettes, Garfield Heights FSC
1985 Wyandotte Rising Stars, Wyandotte FSC
1984 Fraser Mini-ettes, Fraser FSC

World Championships – U.S. Medalists

MEN

	Gold	Silver	Bronze
1930		Roger F. Turner	
1931		Roger F. Turner	
1947		Richard T. Button	
1948	Richard T. Button		
1949	Richard T. Button		
1950	Richard T. Button		Hayes Alan Jenkins
1951	Richard T. Button	James D.Grogan	
1952	Richard T. Button	James D.Grogan	Hayes Alan Jenkins
1953	Hayes Alan Jenkins	James D.Grogan	
1954	Hayes Alan Jenkins	James D.Grogan	
1955	Hayes Alan Jenkins	Ronald Robertson	David Jenkins
1956	Hayes Alan Jenkins	Ronald Robertson	David Jenkins
1957	David Jenkins	Tim Brown	
1958	David Jenkins	Tim Brown	
1959	David Jenkins		Tim Brown
1965		Scott E. Allen	
1966			Gary Visconti
1967			Gary Visconti
1968		Tim Wood	
1969	Tim Wood		
1970	Tim Wood		
1978	Charles Tickner		
1980			Charles Tickner
1981	Scott Hamilton	David Santee	
1982	Scott Hamilton		
1983	Scott Hamilton		
1984	Scott Hamilton		
1985			Brian Boitano
1986	Brian Boitano		
1987		Brian Boitano	
1988	Brian Boitano		
1989		Christopher Bowman	
1990			Christopher Bowman
1991			Todd Eldredge
1995		Todd Eldredge	

LADIES

	Gold	Silver	Bronze
1924			Beatrix Loughran
1928		Maribel Y. Vinson	
1930			Maribel Y.Vinson
1938			Hedy Stenuf
1939		Hedy Stenuf	
1947			Gretchen Merrill
1949		Yvonne C. Sherman	
1950			Yvonne C. Sherman
1951			Sonya Klopfer
1952		Sonya Klopfer	Virginia Baxter
1953	Tenley E. Albright		
1954		Tenley E. Albright	
1955	Tenley E. Albright	Carol E. Heiss	
1956	Carol E. Heiss	Tenley E. Albright	
1957	Carol E. Heiss		
1958	Carol E. Heiss		
1959	Carol E. Heiss		
1960	Carol E. Heiss		Barbara Ann Roles
1965			Peggy G. Fleming
1966	Peggy G. Fleming		
1967	Peggy G. Fleming		
1968	Peggy G. Fleming		
1970			Julie Lynn Holmes
1971		Julie Lynn Holmes	
1972			Janet Lynn
1973		Janet Lynn	
1974		Dorothy Hamill	
1975		Dorothy Hamill	
1976	Dorothy Hamill		
1977	Linda Fratianne		
1978		Linda Fratianne	
1979	Linda Fratianne		
1980			Linda Fratianne
1981		Elaine Zayak	
1982	Elaine Zayak		
1983	Rosalynn Sumners		
1984			Elaine Zayak
1985			Tiffany Chin
1986	Debi Thomas		Tiffany Chin
1987		Debi Thomas	Caryn Kadavy
1988			Debi Thomas
1989			Jill Trenary
1990	Jill Trenary		Holly Cook
1991	Kristi Yamaguchi	Tonya Harding	Nancy Kerrigan
1992	Kristi Yamaguchi	Nancy Kerrigan	
1995			Nicole Bobek

PAIRS

Year	Gold	Silver	Bronze
1930			Beatrix Loughran / Sherwin C. Badger
1932			Beatrix Loughran / Sherwin C. Badger
1947		Karol Kennedy / Peter Kennedy	Anne Davies / Carleton.C.Hoffner, Jr.
1949		Karol Kennedy / Peter Kennedy	
1950	Karol Kennedy / Peter Kennedy		
1951		Karol Kennedy / Peter Kennedy	
1952		Karol Kennedy / Peter Kennedy	
1959			Nancy R. Ludington / Ronald Ludington
1965		Vivian Joseph / Ronald Joseph	
1966			Cynthia Kauffman / Ronald Kauffman
1967			Cynthia Kauffman / Ronald Kauffman
1968			Cynthia Kauffman / Ronald Kauffman
1971			Alicia Jo Starbuck / Kenneth E.Shelley
1972			Alicia Jo Starbuck / Kenneth E.Shelley
1977			Tai Babilonia / Randy Gardner
1978			Tai Babilonia / Randy Gardner
1979	Tai Babilonia / Randy Gardner		
1982			Caitlin Carruthers / Peter Carruthers
1987			Jill Watson / Peter Oppegard
1991			Natasha Kuchiki / Todd Sand
1995			Jenni Meno / Todd Sand

DANCE

Year	Gold	Silver	Bronze
1952			Carol Ann Peters / Daniel C. Ryan
1953			Carol Ann Peters / Daniel C. Ryan
1954			Carmel W. Bodel / Edward L. Bodel
1957			Sharon McKenzie / Bert Wright
1958			Andrée Anderson / Donald Jacoby
1959		Andrée A. Jacoby / Donald Jacoby	
1965			Lorna Dyer / John Carrell
1966		Kristin Fortune / Dennis Sveum	Lorna Dyer / John Carrell
1967	Lorna Dyer / John Carrell		
1969			Judy Schwomeyer / James Sladky
1970		Judy Schwomeyer / James Sladky	
1971			Judy Schwomeyer / James Sladky
1972			Judy Schwomeyer / James Sladky
1975		Colleen O'Connor / James Millns	
1976			Colleen O'Connor / James Millns
1983			Judy Blumberg / Michael Seibert
1984			Judy Blumberg / Michael Seibert
1985			Judy Blumberg / Michael Seibert

Olympic Winter Games – U.S. Medalists

MEN

	GOLD	SILVER	BRONZE
1948	Richard T. Button		
1952	Richard T. Button	James D. Grogan	
1956	Hayes Alan Jenkins	Ronald Robertson	David Jenkins
1960	David Jenkins		
1964			Scott E. Allen
1968		Tim Wood	
1980		Charles Tickner	
1984	Scott Hamilton		
1988	Brian Boitano		
1992		Paul Wylie	

LADIES

	GOLD	SILVER	BRONZE
1920			Theresa Weld
1924		Beatrix Loughran	
1928			Beatrix Loughran
1932			Maribel Y. Vinson
1952		Tenley E. Albright	
1956	Tenley E. Albright	Carol E. Heiss	
1960	Carol E. Heiss		Barbara Ann Roles
1968	Peggy G. Fleming		
1972			Janet Lynn
1976	Dorothy Hamill		
1980		Linda Fratianne	
1984		Rosalynn Sumners	
1988			Debi Thomas
1992	Kristi Yamaguchi		Nancy Kerrigan
1994		Nancy Kerrigan	

PAIRS

	GOLD	SILVER	BRONZE
1932		Beatrix Loughran Sherwin C. Badger	
1952		Karol Kennedy Peter Kennedy	
1960			Nancy R. Ludington Ronald Ludington
1984		Caitlin Carruthers Peter Carruthers	
1988			Jill Watson Peter Oppegard

DANCE

	GOLD	SILVER	BRONZE
1976			Colleen O'Connor James Millns

World Junior Championships[1] – U.S. Medalists

MEN

	GOLD	SILVER	BRONZE
1976	Mark Cockerell		
1978			Brian Boitano
1981	Paul Wylie		Scott Williams
1982	Scott Williams	Paul Guerrero	
1983	Christopher Bowman		
1984			Thomas Cierniak
1985	Erik Larson		Rudy Galindo
1986		Rudy Galindo	
1987	Rudy Galindo	Todd Eldredge	
1988	Todd Eldredge		
1989		Shepherd Clark	
1990			John Baldwin, Jr.
1992			Damon Allen
1993		Michael Weiss	
1994	Michael Weiss		Jere Michael

LADIES

	GOLD	SILVER	BRONZE
1976	Suzie Brasher		
1978	Jill Sawyer		
1979	Elaine Zayak		Jackie Farrell
1980	Rosalynn Sumners		
1981	Tiffany Chin		
1987	Cindy Bortz		
1988	Kristi Yamaguchi		
1989	Jessica Mills		
1991		Lisa Ervin	
1992		Lisa Ervin	
1993		Lisa Ervin	
1994	Michelle Kwan		

PAIRS

	GOLD	SILVER	BRONZE
1976		Lorene Mitchell Donald Micthell	
1978			Beth Flora Ken Flora
1984		Susan Dungjen Jason Dungjen	
1987			Kristi Yamaguchi Rudy Galindo
1988	Kristi Yamaguchi Rudy Galindo		
1990			Jennifer Heurlin John Frederiksen
1991			Jennifer Heurlin John Frederiksen
1995		Danielle Hartsell Steve Hartsell	

DANCE

	GOLD	SILVER	BRONZE
1980			Renée Roca Andrew Ouellette
1982			Lynda Malek Alexander Miller
1983			Christina Yatsuhashi Keith Yatsuhashi
1984		Christina Yatsuhashi Keith Yatsuhashi	

[1] For the years 1976-1977, designated as ISU Junior Championships.

Sites of the National Championships and Governing Council Meetings

	NATIONALS	GOVERNING COUNCIL		NATIONALS	GOVERNING COUNCIL
1914	New Haven, CT	–	1958	Minneapolis, MN	Boston, MA
1918	New York, NY	–	1959	Rochester, NY	Seattle, WA
1920	New York, NY	–	1960	Seattle, WA	Colorado Springs, CO
1921	Philadelphia, PA	New York, NY	1961	Colorado Springs, CO	New York, NY
1922	Boston, MA	New York, NY	1962	Boston, MA	Sun Valley, ID
1923	New Haven, CT	New York, NY	1963	Long Beach, CA	Rockton, IL
1924	Philadelphia, PA	New York, NY	1964	Cleveland, OH	Philadelphia, PA
1925	New York, NY	New York, NY	1965	Lake Placid, NY	Anaheim, CA
1926	Boston, MA	New York, NY	1966	Berkeley, CA	Denver, CO
1927	New Haven/New York	New York, NY	1967	Omaha, NE	Buffalo, NY
1928	New Haven, CT	New York, NY	1968	Philadelphia, PA	San Francisco, CA
1929	New York, NY	New York, NY	1969	Seattle, WA	Tulsa, OK
1930	Providence, RI	New York, NY	1970	Tulsa, OK	New York, NY
1931	Boston, MA	New York, NY	1971	Buffalo, NY	Santa Monica, CA
1932	New York, NY	New York, NY	1972	Long Beach, CA	Cleveland, OH
1933	New Haven, CT	New York, NY	1973	Minneapolis, MN	Boston, MA
1934	Philadelphia, PA	New York, NY	1974	Providence, RI	Seattle, WA
1935	New Haven, CT	New York, NY	1975	Oakland, CA	Colorado Springs, CO
1936	New York/Boston	New York, NY	1976	Colorado Springs, CO	Washington, DC
1937	Chicago, IL	New York, NY	1977	Hartford, CT	Oakland, CA
1938	Philadelphia, PA	New York, NY	1978	Portland, OR	Minneapolis, MN
1939	Saint Paul, MN	New York, NY	1979	Cincinnati, OH	Pittsburgh, PA
1940	Cleveland, OH	New York, NY	1980	Atlanta, GA	San Diego, CA
1941	Boston, MA	New York, NY	1981	San Diego, CA	New Orleans, LA
1942	Chicago, IL	New York, NY	1982	Indianapolis, IN	Hyannis, MA
1943	New York, NY	New York, NY	1983	Pittsburgh, PA	Sun Valley, ID
1944	Minneapolis, MN	New York, NY	1984	Salt Lake City, UT	Colorado Springs, CO
1945	New York, NY	New York, NY	1985	Kansas City, MO	Miami, FL
1946	Chicago, IL	New York, NY	1986	Uniondale, NY	San Francisco, CA
1947	Berkeley, CA	Chicago, IL	1987	Tacoma, WA	Milwaukee, WI
1948	Colorado Springs, CO	Chicago, IL	1988	Denver, CO	Bethesda, MD
1949	Colorado Springs, CO	Chicago, IL	1989	Baltimore, MD	Anaheim, CA
1950	Washington, DC	Chicago, IL	1990	Salt Lake City, UT	Indianapolis, IN
1951	Seattle, WA	Chicago, IL	1991	Minneapolis, MN	Orlando, FL
1952	Colorado Springs, CO	Chicago, IL	1992	Orlando, FL	Anchorage, AK
1953	Hershey, PA	Pasadena, CA	1993	Phoenix, AZ	Cleveland, OH
1954	Los Angeles, CA	Chicago, IL	1994	Detroit, MI	Newport, RI
1955	Colorado Springs, CO	Buffalo, NY	1995	Providence, RI	Phoenix, AZ
1956	Philadelphia, PA	Berkeley, CA	1996	San José, CA	Colorado Springs, CO
1957	Berkeley, CA	Chicago, IL			

United States Figure Skating Association Officers

PRESIDENT

NAME	RESIDENCE	YEARS IN OFFICE
*A. Winsor Weld	Boston, MA	1921-1925
*Henry W. Howe	New York, NY	1925-1928
*Charles T. Church	New York, NY	1928-1930
*Sherwin C. Badger	New York, NY	1930-1932; 1934-1935
*Charles M. Rotch	Boston, MA	1932-1934; 1935-1937
*Joseph K. Savage	New York, NY	1937-1940
*Heaton R. Robertson	New Haven, CT	1940-1943
*Walter S. Powell	Saint Louis, MO	1943-1946
*Henry M. Beatty	Cleveland, OH	1946-1949
*Harry M. Keighley	Evanston, IL	1949-1952
*H. Kendall Kelley	Cleveland Heights, OH	1952-1955
*Kenneth L. Brown	Berkeley, CA	1955-1958
*Howard D. Herbert	Moorestown, NJ	1958-1961
*F. Ritter Shumway	Rochester, NY	1961-1964
*John R. Shoemaker	San Francisco, CA	964-1967
Spencer E. Cram	Hendersonville, NC	1967-1970
*Frederick C. LeFevre	Troy, OH	1970-1973
Benjamin T. Wright	Belmont, MA	1973-1976
Charles A. DeMore	Cleveland, OH	1976-1980
Oscar T. Iobst, Jr.	Churchville, PA	1980-1983
George T. Yonekura	Berkeley, CA	1983-1986
Hugh C. Graham, Jr.	Tulsa, OK	1986-1989
Franklin S. Nelson	Oakland, CA	1989-1992
Claire W. Ferguson	Jamestown, RI	1992-1995
Maurice W. Stillwell	Malibu, CA	1995-

NAME	RESIDENCE	YEARS IN OFFICE
George T. Yonekura	Berkeley, CA	1976-1977; 1980-1983
E. Newbold Black, IV	New York, NY	1977-1978
Joseph L. Serafine	Lake Forest, IL	1978-1980
Hugh C. Graham, Jr.	Tulsa, OK	1983-1986
Anne H. Gerli	New York, NY	1986-1988
Frederick D. Meyers	Columbus, OH	1988-1989
Claire W. Ferguson	Jamestown, RI	1989-1992
Carolyn Y. Kruse	Colorado Springs, CO	1992-1993
Joan H. Gruber	Wyomissing, PA	1993-1995
John F. LeFevre	McLean, VA	1995-

FIRST VICE PRESIDENT

NAME	RESIDENCE	YEARS IN OFFICE
*Irving Brokaw	New York, NY	1921-1922; 1923-1924
*Hugh A. Whytock	Salt Lake City, UT	1922-1923
*Alfred R. Whitney, Jr.	New York, NY	1924-1925
*Nathaniel W. Niles	Boston, MA	1925-1928
*Sherwin C. Badger	New York, NY	1928-1930; 1932-1934
*Arthur M. Goodridge	Cambridge, MA	1930-1932; 1943-1946
*Charles M. Rotch	Boston, MA	1934-1935
*Joseph K. Savage	New York, NY	1935-1937
*Charles Myers	Philadelphia, PA	1937-1940
*Walter S. Powell	Saint Louis, MO	1940-1943
*Joseph R. Maxwell	Philadelphia, PA	1946-1948
*George B. Jenkinson, Jr.	Tulsa, OK	1948-1949
*William O. Hickok, IV	Harrisburg, PA	1949-1951
*Robert Sackett	Omaha, NE	1951-1952
Allen M. Lomax	Grosse Pointe, MI	1952-1953
*Robert R. Kierland	Rochester, MN	1953-1955
*Gerald J. Hurley	Tacoma, WA	1955-1956
*T. Elliott Pugh	Alameda, CA	1956-1957
*John P. Hart	Tacoma, WA	1957-1958; 1963-1964; 1965-1966
*Delaplaine McDaniel	Narberth, PA	1958-1959; 1966-1967
*F. Ritter Shumway	Rochester, NY	1959-1961
*Henry R. Heebner	Wynnewood, PA	1961-1962
*John R. Shoemaker	San Francisco, CA	1962-1963
Spencer E. Cram	Chagrin Falls, OH	1964-1965
*William R. Haigler	Colorado Springs, CO	1967-1968
*Frederick C. LeFevre	Troy, OH	1968-1970
Benjamin T. Wright	Belmont, MA	1970-1973
*Robert T. McLeod	Norwalk, CA	1973-1975
Brooks Stewart	Southampton, PA	1975-1976

SECOND VICE PRESIDENT

NAME	RESIDENCE	YEARS IN OFFICE
*Hugh A. Whytock	Salt Lake City, UT	1921-1922 ; 1923-1924
*Alfred R.Whitney, Jr.	New York, NY	1922-1923
*Chris I. Christenson	Saint Paul, MN	1924-1925
*Carl R. Engel	Chicago, IL	1925-1928
*Ashley C. Bennett	Minneapolis, MN	1928-1930
*Roger F. Turner	Boston, MA	1930-1932
*Joseph K. Savage	New York, NY	1932-1934
*Edgar S. McKaig	Philadelphia, PA	1934-1935
*Bedell H. Harned	New York, NY	1935-1937
*Walter S. Powell	Saint Louis, MO	1937-1940
*Alex Young, Jr.	San Francisco, CA	1940-1943
*Rudolf C. Gingg	Berkeley, CA	1943-1946
*Bradford H. Miller	Los Angeles, CA	1946-1947 ; 1948-1949
*Edmund C. Bold	Seattle, WA	1947-1948
*Henry F. Swift	San Francisco, CA	1949
*Otto Dallmayr	Los Angeles, CA	1949-1951
*Eli E. Dorsey	Seattle, WA	1951-1952
*Kenneth L. Brown	Berkeley, CA	1952-1953
*Gerald J. Hurley	Tacoma, WA	1953-1955
*Abbot P. Mills	Washington, DC	1955-1956
*Delaplaine McDaniel	Narberth, PA	1956-1958 ; 1965-1966
*Harry N. Keighley	Evanston, IL	1958-1959
*George B. Jenkinson, Jr.	Tulsa, OK	1959-1962
*Henry R. Heebner	Wynnewood, PA	1962-1964
*John P. Hart	Tacoma, WA	1964-1965
*William R. Haigler	Colorado Springs, CO	1966-1967
Norman E. Fuller	La Mirada, CA	1967-1968
*Carl W. Gram, Jr.	New York, NY	1968-1970
Howard G. Taylor	Walnut Creek, CA	1970-1972
*Gordon C. Brown	Ann Arbor, MI	1972-1973
Brooks Stewart	Southampton, PA	1973-1975
Charles A. DeMore	Cleveland, OH	1975-1976
E. Newbold Black, IV	New York, NY	1976-1977
Joseph L. Serafine	Lake Forest, IL	1977-1978
Elvira Sonnhalter	Seal Beach, CA	1978-1980
*William J. Brennan, Jr.	New York, NY	1980-1983
Ronald T. Pfenning	Hyannis, MA	1983-1985
Anne H. Gerli	New York, NY	1985-1986
Ida S. Tateoka	South Jordan, UT	1986-1987
Frederick D. Meyers	Columbus, OH	1987-1988
Joseph D. Driano	Edmonds, WA	1988-1990
Carolyn Y. Kruse	Colorado Springs, CO	1990-1992
Harland L. Burge, Jr.	Laguna Hills, CA	1992-1993
Maurice W. Stillwell	Malibu, CA	1993-1995
Anne L. Klein	Wayzata, MN	1995-

THIRD VICE PRESIDENT

Name	Residence	Years in Office
*Theodore G. Patterson	Weston, MA	1952-1953
*Abbot P. Mills	Washington, DC	1953-1955
*Robert R. Kierland	Rochester, MN	1955-1956
*Harry N. Keighley	Evanston, IL	1956-1958
*John P. Hart	Tacoma, WA	1958-1960
*John R. Shoemaker	San Francisco, CA	1960-1962
Spencer E. Cram	Chagrin Falls OH	1962-1964
*Delaplaine McDaniel	Narberth, PA	1964-1965
*William R. Haigler	Colorado Springs, CO	1965-1966
Norman E. Fuller	Paramount, CA	1966-1967; 1968-1969
*Carl W. Gram, Jr.	New York, NY	1967-1968
Howard G. Taylor	Walnut Creek, CA	1969-1970
*Gordon C. Brown	Ann Arbor, MI	1970-1972
*Robert T. McLeod	Norwalk, CA	1972-1973
Hugh C. Graham, Jr.	Tulsa, OK	1973-1974
Charles A. DeMore	Cleveland, OH	1974-1975
George T. Yonekura	Berkeley, CA	1975-1976
Joseph L. Serafine	Lake Forest, IL	1976-1977
Elvira Sonnhalter	Seal Beach, CA	1977-1978
Oscar T. Iobst, Jr.	Churchville, PA	1978-1980
Franklin S. Nelson	Tulsa, OK	1980-1983
Eleanor G. Schultz	Burbank, CA	1983-1985
Ida S. Tateoka	South Jordan, UT	1985-1986
Frederick D. Meyers	Columbus, OH	1986-1987
Joseph D. Driano	Edmonds, WA	1987-1988
Charles U. Foster	Duxbury, MA	1988-1989
Carolyn Y. Kruse	Colorado Springs, CO	1989-1990
Harland L. Burge, Jr.	Laguna Hills, CA	1990-1992
Joan H. Gruber	Wyomissing, PA	1992-1993
Anne L. Klein	Wayzata, MN	1993-1995
Gloria Earnhardt	Scottsdale, AZ	1995-

SECRETARY

Name	Residence	Years in Office
*George H. Browne	Cambridge, MA	1921-1923
*Joseph Chapman	Philadelphia, PA	1923
*Joel B. Liberman	New York, NY	1924-1928; 1931-1932
*Joseph K. Savage	New York, NY	1928-1930
*William S. Bird	New York, NY	1930-1931
*Richard L. Hapgood	Cambridge, MA	1932-1934; 1935-1940
*Bedell H. Harned	New York, NY	1934-1935
*Edgar S. McKaig	Philadelphia, PA	1940-1943
*Harry N. Keighley	Evanston, IL	1943-1947
Lyman E.Wakefield, Jr.	Minneapolis, MN	1947-1948
*H. Glenn Waring	Baltimore, MD	1948-1950
*Joseph P. Gibson, Jr.	New York, NY	1950-1951
*John P. Hart	Tacoma, WA	1952-1954
*Otto Dallmayr	Los Angeles, CA	1954-1956
*Theodore G. Patterson	Boston, MA	1956-1957
*Harold T. Leroux	Tulsa, OK	1957-1960
*Harold G. Storke	Hull, MA	1960-1961
*John F. Groden	Boston, MA	1961-1964
*Henry R. Heebner	Wynnewood, PA	1964-1966
Benjamin T. Wright	Belmont, MA	1966-1969
Brooks Stewart	Southampton, PA	1969-1972
*Eugene W. Harvey	Concord, CA	1972-1975
*William J. Brennan, Jr.	New York, NY	1975-1978
Albert L. Beard	Phoenix, AZ	1978-1981
Elvira Sonnhalter	Seal Beach, CA	1981-1984
Carolyn Y. Kruse	Colorado Springs, CO	1984-1987
Maribel A. Leiter	Wichita, KS	1987-1989
Robert S. Watson	Santa Ana, CA	1989-1992
J. Ronald Hershberger	Redwood Shores, CA	1992-1995
Patricia K. Hagedorn	Lexington, MA	1995-

TREASURER

Name	Residence	Years in Office
*John L. Evans	Philadelphia, PA	1921-1925; 1927-1928
*Joseph Chapman	Philadelphia, PA	1925-1927
*Heaton R. Robertson	New Haven, CT	1928-1940
*Bedell H. Harned	New York, NY	1940-1943
*John B. Thayer	Philadelphia, PA	1943-1945
*H. Kendall Kelley	Cleveland Heights, OH	1945-1948
*T. Elliott Pugh	Alameda, CA	1948-1951
*Howard D. Herbert	Buffalo, NY	951-1954
*Harold T. Leroux	Tulsa, OK	1954-1957
*Theodore G. Patterson	Boston, MA	1957-1960; 1967-1970
*Carl W. Gram, Jr.	New York, NY	1960-1963
*John R. Shoemaker	San Francisco, CA	1963-1964
*John F. Groden	Boston, MA	1964-1967
John W.W. Wood	Wilmington, DE	1970-1973
* Rolf E. Hessler	Cleveland Heights, OH	1973-1981
* Harold Hiltzik	Westbury, NY	1981-1986
John H. Holdsworth	Lexington, MA	1986-1993
Jack W. Curtis	Granada Hills, CA	1993-

*deceased

Honorary Officers, Members of the USFSA, Members of the Executive Committee and Board of Directors

HONORARY PRESIDENT

Name	Residence	Year of Election
*Irving Brokaw	New York, NY	1922
*A. Winsor Weld	Boston, MA	1925

HONORARY VICE PRESIDENT

| *Oscar L. Richard | New York, NY | 1941 |
| *Heaton R. Robertson | New Haven, CT | 1951 |

HONORARY MEMBERS OF THE USFSA

*Herbert J. Clarke	London, England	1949 [1]
*H. Kendall Kelley	Cleveland Heights, OH	1955
*Kenneth L. Brown	Berkeley, CA	1958
*Sherwin C. Badger	Boston, MA	1960
*Henry M. Beatty	Cleveland, OH	1960
*Harry N. Keighley	Evanston, IL	1960
*Walter S. Powell	Saint Louis, MO	1960
*Heaton R. Robertson	New Haven, CT	1960
*Charles M. Rotch	Boston, MA	1960
*Joseph K. Savage	New York, NY	1960
*A.Winsor Weld	Boston, MA	1960
*Theresa W.Blanchard	Brookline, MA	1962 [2]
*Harry E. Radix	Chicago, IL	1963
*F. Ritter Shumway	Rochester, NY	1964
*John R. Shoemaker	San Francisco, CA	1967
Spencer E. Cram	Hendersonville, NC	1970
*Frederick C. LeFevre	Troy, OH	1973
Benjamin T. Wright	Belmont, MA	1976
Charles A. DeMore	Cleveland, OH	1980
Oscar T. Iobst, Jr.	Churchville, PA	1983
*W. Thayer Tutt	Colorado Springs, CO	1985
George T. Yonekura	San Leandro, CA	1986
*Henry W. Howe	New York, NY	1989
*Charles T. Church	New York, NY	1989
*Howard D. Herbert	Moorestown, NJ	1989
Hugh C. Graham, Jr.	Tulsa, OK	1989
Franklin S. Nelson	Oakland, CA	1992
Claire W. Ferguson	Jamestown, RI	1995

HONORARY MEMBERS OF THE EXECUTIVE COMMITTEE

Name	Residence	Year of Election
*Edmund C. Bold	Seattle, WA	1965
*Harry E. Radix	Chicago, IL	1965
*Nelson F. Waters	Alton Bay, NH	1965
*Henry M. Beatty	Tacoma, WA	1966
*Kenneth L. Brown	Fort Bidwell, CA	1966
*Harry N. Keighley	Evanston, IL	1966
*H. Kendall Kelley	Cleveland Heights, OH	1966
*John P. Hart	Tacoma, WA	1967
*George B. Jenkinson, Jr.	Tulsa, OK	1967
*Delaplaine McDaniel	Narberth, PA	1967
*Theodore G. Patterson	Boston, MA	1967
*Robert Sackett	Palo Alto, CA	1967
*F. Ritter Shumway	Rochester, NY	1970
Spencer E. Cram	Hendersonville, NC	1977
*Frederick C. LeFevre	Troy, OH	1977
*John R. Shoemaker	San Francisco, CA	1977
Brooks Stewart	Southampton, PA	1977
Howard G. Taylor	Walnut Creek, CA	1977
Benjamin T. Wright	Belmont, MA	1977

HONORARY MEMBERS OF THE BOARD OF DIRECTORS [3]

*Robert T. McLeod	Norwalk, CA	1981
Charles A. DeMore	Cleveland, OH	1983
Joseph L. Serafine	Lake Forest, IL	1983
*Roy Winder	Colorado Springs, CO	1983
*William J. Brennan, Jr.	New York, NY	1987
Oscar T. Iobst, Jr.	Churchville, PA	1987
George T. Yonekura	San Leandro, CA	1989
Hugh C. Graham, Jr.	Tulsa, OK	1992
Franklin S. Nelson	Oakland, CA	1995
Elvira Sonnhalter	Seal Beach, CA	1995

*deceased
[1] First elected by the Executive Committee in 1949. Re-elected by the Governing Council in 1952.
[2] Elected by the Executive Committee in October 1962.
[3] The original Executive Committee was redesignated as the Board of Directors in 1980.

World Figure Skating Hall of Fame (U.S. Members)

MEMBERS	ELECTED
*Jackson Haines	1976
*Howard Nicholson	1976
Richard T. Button	1976
Hayes Alan Jenkins	1976
Tenley E. Albright	1976
Carol Heiss Jenkins	1976
David Jenkins	1976
Peggy Fleming Jenkins	1976
*William O. Hickok, IV	1981
*F. Ritter Shumway	1986
Scott Hamilton	1990
Richard Dwyer	1993
Ronald Robertson	1993
*William Thayer Tutt	1995

*deceased

United States Figure Skating Hall of Fame Members

MEMBERS	ELECTED
*Irving Brokaw	1976
*A. Winsor Weld	1976
*Theresa Weld Blanchard	1976
*Sherwin C. Badger	1976
*Maribel Vinson Owen	1976
Eddie Shipstad and *Oscar Johnson	1976
*Heaton R. Robertson	1977
*Beatrix Loughran Harvey	1977
*Henry M. Beatty	1977
*Nathaniel W. Niles	1978
*Harold Hartshorne	1981
*George H. Browne	1983
Eugene Turner	1983
Ardelle K. Sanderson	1992
*William Thayer Tutt	1992
Karol Kennedy and Peter Kennedy	1992
Yvonne Sherman Tutt	1992
*Lois Waring McGean and J. Michael McGean	1992
James Grogan	1992
Judy Schwomeyer Sladky and James F. Sladky	1992
Dorothy Hamill	1992
Charles Tickner	1992
Tai Babilonia and Randy Gardner	1992
*Walter S. Powell	1993
*Harry N. Keighley	1993
John A.W. Nicks	1993
Nancy Rouillard Graham and Ronald E. Ludington	1993
Tim Wood	1993
Colleen O'Connor and James G. Millns	1993
Linda Fratianne Maricich	1993
*Roger F. Turner	1994
*Maribel Vinson Owen and *George E.B. Hill	1994
Alicia Jo "JoJo" Starbuck and Kenneth E. Shelley	1994
Janet Lynn Salomon	1994
*Roy Shipstad	1995
Robin H. Lee	1995
Cynthia Kauffman Marshall and Ronald Kauffman	1995

*deceased

Honorary Officials – Referees, Accountants, National Judges

HONORARY WORLD REFEREE [1]

ELECTED	NAME	RESIDENCE
1993	Benjamin T. Wright	Belmont, MA

HONORARY WORLD JUDGE

ELECTED	NAME	RESIDENCE
1981	Ardelle V. Sanderson	Lake Placid, NY
	*Edith M. Shoemaker	San Francisco, CA
1993	Mary Louise Wright	Belmont, MA

HONORARY WORLD DANCE REFEREE

ELECTED	NAME	RESIDENCE
1993	Benjamin T. Wright	Belmont, MA

HONORARY WORLD DANCE JUDGE

ELECTED	NAME	RESIDENCE
1981	*Edith M. Shoemaker	San Francisco, CA
1993	Mary Louise Wright	Belmont, MA

HONORARY REFEREE

ELECTED	NAME	RESIDENCE
1978	*Harry N. Keighley	Evanston, IL
	*Delaplaine McDaniel	Narberth, PA
1979	*Edmund C. Bold	Seattle, WA
1980	*J.N. Bower Keebler	Philadelphia, PA
1981	*Edith M. Shoemaker	San Francisco, CA
1985	*Jerome Ross	Port Chester, NY
1987	*Fred W. Amery	Pueblo, CO
	Spencer E. Cram	Hendersonville, NC
	Margaretta S. Drake	Winnetka, IL
	J. Bert Drew	Denver, CO
1991	Brooks Stewart	Newtown, PA

HONORARY ACCOUNTANT

ELECTED	NAME	RESIDENCE
1978	John S. Edwards	Punta Gorda, FL
	*Harry N. Keighley	Evanston, IL
	*Delaplaine McDaniel	Narberth, PA
	*Herman Meyle	Ardmore, PA
1982	Jane W. Stewart	Southampton, PA
1984	*Eugene W. Harvey	Daly City, CA
1985	Spencer E. Cram	Hendersonville, NC
	*Roy Winder	Colorado Springs, CO
1987	*Fred W. Amery	Pueblo, CO
	J. Bert Drew	Denver, CO
1989	Jean C. Winder	Colorado Springs, CO
1990	*E. Leonard Arnoff	Cincinnati, OH
1991	Charles A. DeMore	Cleveland, OH
	*Harold Hiltzik	Jericho, NY
1995	Merton R. Gundry	Pinehurst, NC
	E. Gail Munns	Concord, CA

HONORARY NATIONAL JUDGE [2]

ELECTED	NAME	RESIDENCE
1952	*Sherwin C. Badger	Boston, MA
	*Stanley W. Dwinnell	Minneapolis, MN
	*Carl R. Engel	Chesterton, IN
	Phebe T. Everson [3]	Pine Orchard, CT
	*Roy W. McDaniel	Minneapolis, MN
	Margaret Parker	Washington, DC
	*Charles M. Rotch	Milton, MA
1954	M. Bernard Fox	West Los Angeles, CA
	*Clara R. Frothingham [4]	Chestnut Hill, MA
	*Joel B. Liberman	New York, NY
	*Barbara Ann Skerry	Mountain View, CA
1955	Carmel W. Bodel	Orinda, CA
	Edward L. Bodel	Orinda, CA
1965	J. Howard Bobbitt	San Diego, CA
	*Charles A. McCarthy	Chicago, IL
1967	*Alex J. Krupy	Chicago, IL
1972	*Otto Dallmayr	Los Angeles, CA
	*H. Kendall Kelley	Cleveland Heights, OH
1973	*Mary N. Meredith	New York, NY
	*Katherine Sackett	Laguna Hills, CA
1974	Jane C. Russell	Delray Beach, FL
1976	Norman E. Fuller	Chino, CA
	*Myrtle Girten	Los Angeles, CA
	Mabel Graham	Cuyahoga Falls, OH
	Sanford A. Lindstrom	Mercer Island, WA
	*John W.C. Rogers	San Francisco, CA
1977	*Edith H. Preusch	Denver, CO
1978	*Theresa Weld Blanchard	Boston, MA
	*Mrs. H.L. (Peg) Garren	Troy, NY
	*Frank E. Holcombe	Denver, CO
	Katherine Y. Monnier	Santa Rosa, CA
	*Edward F. Page	Scarsdale, NY
	*Margaret G. Ridgely	Baltimore, MD
1979	*Edmund C. Bold	Seattle, WA
	*Wilhelmine Timm	Spokane, WA
1980	*Marguerite Holcombe	Denver, CO
1981	*Edith M. Shoemaker	San Francisco, CA
1982	*Delaplaine McDaniel	Narberth, PA
	*Roger F. Turner	Walpole, MA
1983	Jane V. Sullivan	Tubac, AZ
1984	Lorraine R. Cruikshank	Cleveland Heights, OH
1986	*Jerome Ross	Port Chester, NY
	Marcella M. Willis	Lafayette, CA
1987	*Fred W. Amery	Pueblo, CO
	Margaretta S. Drake	Winnetka, IL
	*Ferne M. McEntire	San Diego, CA
1988	Ardelle V. Sanderson	Lake Placid, NY
	Lyman E. Wakefield, Jr.	Miinneapolis, MN
1989	*Thomas W. Easton	Shadow Hills, CA
	Janet Maeder	Los Angeles, CA
1990	*Louis Bodek	Aspen, CO
1991	Brooks Stewart	Newtown, PA
1992	Blanche Horsman	Buck Hill Falls, PA
1993	Dorothy M. Burkholder	Hazel Crest, IL

* deceased

[1] Appointments as Honorary ISU (World) Referees and Judges are made annually by the ISU, upon the receipt of nominations by the member concerned.

[2] Including Honorary National Dance Judges.

[3] First election. Re-elected 1982.

[4] First election. Re-elected 1967.

Representatives and Staff

ISU DELEGATE

NAME	RESIDENCE	YEARS
*Walter S. Powell	St. Louis, MO	1947-1961
*Henry M. Beatty	Menlo Park, CA	1961-1965

ISU REPRESENTATIVE

*Henry M. Beatty	Tacoma, WA	1965-1967
*John R. Shoemkaer	San Francisco, CA	1967-1980
Benjamin T. Wright	Belmont, MA	1980-1983
Franklin S. Nelson	Tulsa, OK	1983-1989
Charles U. Foster	Duxbury, MA	1989-1990
Charles A. DeMore	Cleveland, OH	1990-1992
John F. LeFevre	McLean, VA	1992-1995
Joan H. Gruber	Wyomissing, PA	1995-

OLYMPIC FIGURE SKATING COMMITTEE [1] – CHAIRMAN

*Carl W. Gram, Jr.	New York, NY	1971-1973
E. Newbold Black, IV	New York, NY	1973-1976

OLYMPIC REPRESENTATIVE

Charles U. Foster	Duxbury, MA	1977-1980; 1984-1989
Anne H. Gerli	New York, NY	1980-1983
Oscar T. Iobst, Jr.	Churchville, PA	1983-1984
Paul E. George	Wellesley, MA	1989-1994
Carol Heiss Jenkins	Akron, OH	1994-

ATHLETES ADVISORY COUNCIL [2]
USFSA REPRESENTATIVE (SINCE 1982)

Randy Gardner	Marina del Rey, CA	1982-1984
Scott Hamilton	Denver, CO	1984-1985
Judy Blumberg	New York, NY	1985-1990
Paul Wylie	Cambridge, MA	1990-1993
Richard Dalley	Grosse Ile, MI	1993-

EXECUTIVE SECRETARY [3]

*Roland G. Janson	New York, NY	1947-1949
Irene W. Baldwin	Chicago, IL	1949-1950
*Virginia B. Bremer	Boston, MA	1952-1953
*Gerard B. Crook	Boston, MA	1961-1962
Robert Y. Ellis	Boston, MA	1966-1967
*Roy Winder	Boston, MA	1974-1977

EXECUTIVE DIRECTOR

NAME	RESIDENCE	YEARS
*Roy Winder	Boston, MA	1977-1979; 1981-1982
F. Don Stoddard	Colorado Springs, CO	1979-1980
Larry McCollum	Colorado Springs, CO	1983
Ian A. Anderson	Colorado Springs, CO	1984-1992
Oscar T. Iobst, Jr.	Churchville, PA	1992-1993 (interim)
Jerry Lace	Colorado Springs, CO	1993-

ASSISTANT SECRETARY

Virginia B. Bremer	Boston, MA	1950-1952; 1961-1963
Jean C. Winder	Boston, MA	1974-1979

BUSINESS MANAGER

Robert Y. Ellis	Boston, MA	1962-1966
Virginia K. Burnham	Boston, MA	1971-1974

EXECUTIVE BUSINESS DIRECTOR

Robert T. Crowley	Colorado Springs, CO	1993-

EDITOR, SKATING MAGAZINE

*Nathaniel W. Niles	Boston, MA	1923-1924; 1926-1932
*Theresa W Blanchard	Boston, MA	1924-1926; 1926-1963
Robert Y. Ellis	Boston, MA	1963-1966
Marjorie Martin	Boston, MA	1966-1970
Laura J. Kaplan	Boston, MA	1970
Karen S. McDonald	Boston, MA	1971-1972
Barbara R. Boucher	Boston, MA	1972-1976
Gregory R. Smith	Boston, MA	1976-1979
Ian A. Anderson	Colorado Springs, CO	1979-1986
E. Dale Mitch	Colorado Springs, CO	1986-1990
Kimberly Mutchler	Colorado Springs, CO	1990-1994
Jay Miller	Colorado Springs, CO	1994-

WORLD FIGURE SKATING MUSEUM DIRECTOR [4]

Jerry L. McGaha	Colorado Springs, CO	1979-1980
E. Dale Mitch	Colorado Springs, CO	1989-1993

WORLD FIGURE SKATING MUSEUM CURATOR

Helen E. Cataldi	Colorado Springs, CO	1980-1990
Beth Davis	Colorado Springs, CO	1990-

* deceased

[1] A committee of the USOC, of which the Chairman was a voting member of the Executive Committee.

[2] A committee of the USOC.

[3] No one held the title of Executive Secretary from 1950 to 1952, 1953 to 1961, 1962 to 1966 or 1968 to 1974.

[4] There was no Museum Director between 1980 and 1989 and none since 1993.

Permanent Committees (Voting) – Chairs [1]

PROFESSIONALS [2]

Name	Residence	Years in Office
*Theresa Weld Blanchard	Boston, MA	1937-1943; 1945-1947
Ernest E. Hall	Sioux City, IA	1947-1949
*Joseph R. Maxwell	Phildelphia, PA	1949-1951
*H.L. Garren	Lake Placid, NY	1951-1953

COACHES

Ronald E. Ludington	Newark, DE	1990-1992
Robert A. Mock	Pittsburgh, PA	1992-

COMPETITIONS AND RULES

*James A. Cruikshank	New York NY	1921-1925
*Heaton R. Robertson	New Haven, CT	1925-1928
*Charles M. Rotch	Boston, MA	1928-1930
*Richard L. Hapgood	Cambridge, MA	1930-1932
*Bedell H. Harned	New York, NY	1932-1934; 1935-1940
*Frederick Goodridge	Cambridge, MA	1934-1935
*Joseph K. Savage	New York, NY	1940-1945
*Henry M. Beatty	Cleveland, OH	1945-1946; 1949-1950; 1954-1955
*Walter S. Powell	Saint Louis, MO	1946-1947
*Harry N. Keighley	Evanston, IL	1947-1949
*Harold G. Storke	Allerton, MA	1951-1952

COMPETITIONS

*Harold G. Storke	Allerton, MA	1952-1954
*H. Kendall Kelley	Cleveland, OH	1955-1957
*George B. Jenkinson, Jr.	Tulsa, OK	1957-1958; 1962-1965
*Howell Janes	Lafayette, CA	1958
*Kenneth L. Brown	Berkeley, CA	1958-1959
Spencer E. Cram	Shaker Heights, OH	1959-1962
*Robert T. McLeod	Norwalk, CA	1965-1968
*William R. Haigler	Colorado Springs, CO	1968-1971
Charles U. Foster	Worcester, MA	1971-1974
Hugh C. Graham, Jr.	Tulsa, OK	1974-1977
George T. Yonekura	Berkeley, CA	1977-1980
Joseph L. Serafine	Lake Forest, IL	1980-1983
Howard G. Taylor	Walnut Creek, CA	1983-1986
Josephine Lawless	Canoga Park, CA	1986-1989
John F. LeFevre	McLean, VA	1989-1992
Maurice W. Stillwell	Malibu, CA	1992-1993
Ronald T. Pfenning	Hyannis, MA	1993-1995
Nancy H. Bizzano	Long Lake, MN	1995-

DANCE [3]

*Maribel Y. Vinson	Winchester, MA	1936-1937
Nettie C. Prantel	New York, NY	1937-1938
*Harold Hartshorne	New York, NY	1938-1941
*William O. Hickok, IV	Harrisburg, PA	1941-1946
*Clarence L. Parker	Washington, DC	1946-1948
*William E. Wardman	Colorado Springs, CO	1948-1949

Name	Residence	Years in Office
*H. Kendall Kelley	Cleveland Heights, OH	1949-1950; 1962-1965
*Delaplaine McDaniel	Narberth, PA	1952-1955
*Harry N. Keighley	Evanston, IL	1955-1956; 1959-1962
*F. Ritter Shumway	Rochester, NY	1956-1959; 1972-1975
Norman E. Fuller	Paramount, CA	1965-1966
Howard G. Taylor	Walnut Creek, CA	1966-1969
*Robert T. McLeod	Norwalk, CA	1969-1972; 1978-1981
Franklin S. Nelson	Tulsa, OK	1975-1978
Charles W. Dillie, Jr.	Washington, PA	1981-1984
Ida S. Tateoka	South Jordan, UT	1984-1985; 1989-1992
John F. LeFevre	McLean, VA	1985-1989
Eleanor B. Curtis	Granada Hills, CA	1992-1993
Warren D. Maxwell	Dallas, TX	1993-1995
Robert J. Horen	New Hope, PA	1995-

INTERNATIONAL SKATING [4]

*Walter S. Powell	Saint Louis, MO	1946-1949

INTERNATIONAL

*Walter S. Powell	Saint Louis, MO	1949-1952
*Harry N. Keighley	Evanston, IL	1952-1955
*Henry M. Beatty	Cleveland, OH	1955-1957
*John R. Shoemaker	San Francisco, CA	1957-1960
*H. Kendall Kelley	Cleveland Heights, OH	1960-1962
James M. Earle	Philadelphia, PA	1962-1965
Spencer E. Cram	Chagrin Falls, OH	1965-1967; 1970-1971
*F. Ritter Shumway	Rochester, NY	1967-1970
*William R. Haigler	Colorado Springs, CO	1971
Charles A. DeMore	Cleveland, OH	1971-1974
*Frederick C. LeFevre	Troy, OH	1974-1977
Brooks Stewart	Southampton, PA	1977-1980
Howard G. Taylor	Walnut Creek, CA	1980-1983
Claire W. Ferguson	Jamestown, RI	1983-1987
Joan H. Gruber	Wyomissing, PA	1987-1990
Margaret Faulkner	Ann Arbor, MI	1990-1993
James W. Disbrow	Cincinnati, OH	1993-

JUDGES

*Henry W. Howe	New York, NY	1928-1931
*Charles M. Rotch	Boston, MA	1931-1932

JUDGES AND JUDGING

*Charles M. Rotch	Boston, MA	1932-1937
*Sherwin C. Badger	New York, NY	1937-1939; 1947-1948
*Joel B. Liberman	New York, NY	1939-1945
*Heaton R. Robertson	New Haven, CT	1945-1947
*Charles Myers	Philadelphia, PA	1948-1950
*Joseph K. Savage	New York, NY	1950-1951
*Henry M. Beatty	Cleveland, OH	1951-1954
*John P. Hart	Tacoma, WA	1954-1957
*H. Kendall Kelley	Cleveland Heights, OH	1957-1958

FIGURE JUDGING

Name	Residence	Years in Office
*H. Kendall Kelley	Cleveland Heights, OH	1958-1960
*Henry R. Heebner	Wynnewood, PA	1960-1961
*Robert Sackett	Palo Alto, CA	1961-1964
*Frank E. Holcombe	Denver, CO	1964-1966

FIGURE JUDGES

Name	Residence	Years in Office
*Frank E. Holcombe	Denver, CO	1966-1967

DANCE JUDGING

Name	Residence	Years in Office
*Robert R. Kierland	Rochester, MN	1956-1959
*Deane E. McMinn	Lomita, CA	1959-1961
Norman E. Fuller	Long Beach, CA	1961-1964
*Arthur F. Preusch	Minneapolis, MN	1964-1966

DANCE JUDGES

Name	Residence	Years in Office
*Gordon C. Brown	Ann Arbor, MI	1966-1967

JUDGES

Name	Residence	Years in Office
*Delaplaine McDaniel	Narberth, PA	1967-1968
*Harry N. Keighley	Evanston, IL	1968-1971
Norman E. Fuller	Chino, CA	1971-1974
Howard G. Taylor	Walnut Creek, CA	1974-1977
*Frederick C. LeFevre	Troy, OH	1977-1980
Brooks Stewart	Southampton, PA	1980-1983
Anne H. Gerli	New York, NY	1983-1985
Susan A. Johnson	Atlanta, GA	1985-1988
Gale H. Tanger	Wauwatosa, WI	1988-1991
Ronald T. Pfenning	Hyannis, MA	1991-1993
Eleanor B. Curtis	Granada Hills, CA	1993-1995
Margaret Anne Wier	Park City, UT	1995-

Membership

Name	Residence	Years in Office
*Charles E. F. McCann	New York, NY	1921-1923
*Joseph Chapman	Philadelphia, PA	1923-1925; 1928-1931
*John L. Evans	Philadelphia, PA	1925-1928
*Edward M. Howland	Boston, MA	1931-1932
*Ferrier T. Martin	New York, NY	1932-1934
*Joel B. Liberman	New York, NY	1934-1938
*Charles A. McCarthy	Chicago, IL	1938-1945
*Rollett A. Carson	Shaker Heights, OH	1945-1946
*George B. Jenkinson, Jr.	Tulsa, OK	1946-1948
*Evar T. Cedarleaf	Saint Paul, MN	1948-1951
*Harold T. Leroux	Tulsa, OK	1951-1954
*Forrest M. Burke	Portuguese Bend, CA	1954-1957
*Carl W. Gram, Jr.	New York, NY	1957-1960
Howard G. Taylor	Walnut Creek, CA	1960-1963
*Frederick C. LeFevre	Troy, OH	1963-1966
Brooks Stewart	Southampton, PA	1966-1969
George T. Yonekura	Berkeley, CA	1969-1972
Joseph L. Serafine	Lake Forest, IL	1972-1975
Oscar T. Iobst, Jr.	Churchville, PA	1975-1978
*Eugene W. Harvey	Daly City, CA	1978-1981
Joan I. Burns	Millbrae, CA	1981-1984
Marie Pearce	Gladwyne, PA	1984-1987
Maurice W. Stillwell	Malibu, CA	1987-1990
Richard C. Gold	Tulsa, OK	1990-1993
Cheryl H. Wood	Trenton, NJ	1993-

PRECISION SKATING [5]

Name	Residence	Years in Office
Ronald T. Pfenning	Hyannis, MA	1985-1986
Ann T. Fauver	Gorham, ME	1986-1989
Patricia S. French	Williamsville, NY	1989-1993
Margaret Faulkner	Ann Arbor, MI	1993-

CARNIVAL AND EXHIBITION SANCTIONS [6]

*Richard L. Hapgood	Cambridge, MA	1937-1942
*Sherwin C. Badger	Boston, MA	1942-1943
*H. Jay Raymond	Cleveland, OH	1943-1947
*Henry F. Swift	San Francisco, CA	1947-1949
*Kenneth L. Brown	Berkeley, CA	1949-1950
*Edmund C. Bold	Seattle, WA	1950-1952

SANCTIONS

*Edmund C. Bold	Seattle, WA	1952-1953
*Walter B. Moore	Seattle, WA	1953-1954
*Howard D. Herbert	Buffalo, NY	1954-1957
*Nelson F. Waters	East Lansing, MI	1957-1960
*Francis B. Turner	Boston, MA	1960-1963
Howard G. Taylor	Walnut Creek, CA	1963-1966
*Roy Winder	Seattle, WA	1966-1969
William K. Munns	Concord, CA	1969-1972
George T. Yonekura	Berkeley, CA	1972-1975
Elvira Sonnhalter	Seal Beach, CA	1975-1977
Robert L. Houk	Seattle, WA	1977-1980
Ruth L. Jackson	Greensboro, NC	1980-1983
Albert L. Beard	Phoenix, AZ	1983-1984
Maurice W. Stillwell	Malibu, CA	1984-1987
Carolyn Y. Kruse	Colorado Springs, CO	1987-1989
Gloria Earnhardt	Scottsdale, AZ	1989-1991

SANCTIONS AND ELIGIBILITY

Gloria Earnhardt	Scottsdale, AZ	1991-1993
Sharon G. Watson	Los Angeles, CA	1993-

SINGLES AND PAIRS

*Louis Bodek	Birmingham, MI	1975-1977
Anne H. Gerli	New York, NY	1977-1980
Eleanor G. Schultz	Burbank, CA	1980-1983
Roger A. Glenn	Appleton, WI	1983-1985
Joan H. Gruber	Wyomissing, PA	1985-1987
Janet G. Allen	Minnetonka, MN	1987-1990
Margery L. Schleh	Sacramento, CA	1990-1993
Margaret Anne Wier	Park City, UT	1993-1995
William M. Fitzpatrick	Bethlehem, PA	1995-

[5] A special committee from 1985 to 1986.

[6] A special committee from 1937 to 1938.

Permanent Committees (Non-Voting) – Chairs

ATHLETES ADVISORY

NAME	RESIDENCE	YEARS IN OFFICE
Hal E. Marron, Jr.	Phoenix, AZ	1983-1986
Mahlon A. Bradley	Weymouth, MA	1986-1988
Scott Kurttila	Seattle, WA	1988-1990
Richard J. Dalley	South Rockwood, MI	1990-1993
Jeffrey G. Benz	San Francisco, CA	1993-

COLLEGIATE PROGRAM

Patricia K. Hagedorn	Lexington, MA	1993-1995
Kathaleen Kelly-Cutone	Lexington, MA	1995-

ETHICS [1]

Nancy M . Piro	Danville, CA	1993-

GRIEVANCE

Christine Mayer	Wellesley Hills, MA	1995-

FINANCE [2]

*A. Winsor Weld	Boston, MA	1928-1931
*Edgar S. McKaig	Philadelphia, PA	1939-1940
*Anthony Forbes	Greenwich, CT	1940-1941
*John B. Thayer	Philadelphia, PA	1941-1943
Joseph P. Gibson, Jr.	Rye, NY	1943-1946
*Arthur M. Goodridge	Cambridge, MA	1946-1947
*H. Glenn Waring	Baltimore, MD	1947-1948
*Howard D. Herbert	Buffalo, NY	1948-1951
*T. Elliott Pugh	Alameda, CA	1951-1953
*Theodore G. Patterson	Weston, MA	1953-1956; 1968-1971
*Abbot P. Mills	Washington, DC	1956-1959
Winston L. Molander	Minneapolis, MN	1959-1961
James M. Earle	Philadelphia, PA	1961-1962
*Delaplaine McDaniel	Narberth, PA	1962-1964
*Carl W. Gram, Jr.	New York, NY	1964-1967
*Thomas H. Miller	Rochester, NY	1967-1968
*Harold Hiltzik	Jericho, NY	1984-1985
John H. Holdsworth	Lexington, MA	1986-1993
Jack W. Curtis	Granada Hills, CA	1993-

MUSEUM [3]

*Kenneth L. Brown	Fort Bidwell, CA	1964-1965
*William R. Haigler	Colorado Springs, CO	1965-1970
Gregory M. Kelley	Santa Fe, NM	1970-1971
Benjamin T. Wright	Belmont, MA	1971-1973; 1976-1977
Theodore M. Buck	Waban, MA	1973-1976

HALL OF FAME AND MUSEUM

Benjamin T. Wright	Belmont, MA	1977-

* deceased

[1] A special committee from 1993 to 1995.
[2] A special committee from 1939 to 1942.
[3] A special committee from 1964 to 1980.
[4] A special committee from 1964 to 1993.
[5] A special committee from 1961 to 1980.
[6] A special committee from 1966 to 1980.
[7] A special committee from 1963 to 1980.

LONG RANGE PLANNING [4]

NAME	RESIDENCE	YEARS IN OFFICE
*F. Ritter Shumway	Rochester, NY	1964-1965
Paul E. George	Wellesley, MA	1986-1989
Maurice W. Stillwell	Malibu, CA	1989-1990
Howard M. Silby	Potomac, MD	1990-1993
Oscar T. Iobst, Jr.	Churchville, PA	1993-

PRESIDENT'S PLANNING

*F. Ritter Shumway	Rochester, NY	1965-1967
*John R. Shoemaker	San Francisco, CA	1967-1968

1961 U.S. WORLD FIGURE SKATING TEAM MEMORIAL FUND [5]

*Henry M. Beatty	Menlo Park, CA	1961-1962
*Harry N. Keighley	Evanston, IL	1962-1963
*John F. Groden	Boston, MA	1963-1968
Patrick J. Donnelly	Seattle, WA	1968-1970

USFSA MEMORIAL FUND

*Theodore G. Patterson	Boston, MA	1970-1971
*F. Ritter Shumway	Rochester, NY	1971-1980

MEMORIAL FUND

*F. Ritter Shumway	Rochester, NY	1980-1992
J. Barlow Nelson	Tulsa, OK	1992
Carolyn Y. Kruse	Colorado Springs, CO	1992-1995
George B. Ludlow, Jr.	Venice, FL	1995-

CO-ORDINATING CHAIRMAN'S [6]

*John W. McNair	Baltimore, MD	1966-1967

LIAISON AND PROGRAM DEVELOPMENT

*John W. McNair	Baltimore, MD	1967-1969

PROGRAM DEVELOPMENT

Ruth L. Jackson	Greensboro, NC	1972-1980
Sally Warfield	Kirkwood, MO	1980-1983
Walter H. Lupke, Jr.	Fort Wayne, IN	1983-1987
George B. Ludlow, Jr.	Kent, CT	1987-1991
Joanne Schillinger	Marquette, MI	1991-1994
Phyllis F. Howard	Falls Church VA	1994-

RULES-DRAFTING [7]

Benjamin T. Wright	Belmont, MA	1963-1970

RULES

Benjamin T. Wright	Belmont, MA	1970-1973
Spencer E. Cram	Hendersonville, NC	1973-1978
Ronald T. Pfenning	Newport, NH	1978-1980
Elvira Sonnhalter	Seal Beach, CA	1980-1983; 1987-1990
J. Barlow Nelson	Tulsa, OK	1983-1984
Carolyn Y. Kruse	Colorado Springs, CO	1984-1986
Maribel A. Leiter	Wichita, KS	1986-1987
Virginia S. Luttenton	Shaker Heights, OH	1987-1988
Gay Barnes	Boulder, CO	1990-1993; 1995-
Marcha L. Pipes	Overland Park, KS	1993-1995

PROTOCOL AND SPONSORSHIP ADVISORY

NAME	RESIDENCE	YEARS IN OFFICE
Anthony C. Morici	San Jose, CA	1992-1993

SPONSORSHIP

Anthony C. Morici	San Jose, CA	1993-1995
Andrew A. Paterson	Bloomfield Hills, MI	1995-

SPORTS MEDICINE [*]

Franklin S. Nelson	Tulsa, OK	1978-1983
Howard M. Silby	Potomac, MD	1983-1989
Morton G. Rosenstein	Fresno, CA	1989-1992
Craig H. McQueen	Salt Lake City, UT	1992-1994
Angela D. Smith	Cleveland, OH	1994-

[*] A special committee from 1978 to 1980.

Special Committees – Chairs

MEMORIAL FUND OPERATING

Name	Residence	Years in Office
*F. Ritter Shumway	Rochester, NY	1984-1992
J. Barlow Nelson	Tulsa, OK	1992
Carolyn Y. Kruse	Colorado Springs, CO	1992-1995
George B. Ludlow, Jr.	Venice, FL	1995-

MUSIC

*F. Ritter Shumway	Rochester, NY	1982-1986
Walter H. Lupke, Jr.	Fort Wayne, IN	1986-1991
Eugene Thielman	Rancho Palos Verdes, CA	1991-1994
C. Peter Zurlinden, III	La Crescenta, CA	1994-

NOMINATING (not a complete listing)

*Alfred R. Whitney, Jr.	New York, NY	1922
*John L. Evans	Philadelphia, PA	
*Ralph G. Van Name	New Haven, CT	
*Arthur M. Goodridge	Cambridge, MA	1925
*John L. Evans	Philadelphia, PA	
*Stowe Phelps	New York, NY	1926
*Joseph K. Savage	New York, NY	
*A. Winsor Weld	Boston, MA	1927
*Paul Armitage	New York, NY	
*A. Winsor Weld	Boston, MA	1928
*Charles M. Rotch	Boston, MA	
*Charles M. Rotch	Boston, MA	1930
*Joseph K. Savage	New York, NY	1931
*Frederick Goodridge	Cambridge, MA	1932; 1933-1935
*Joel B. Liberman	New York, NY	1932-1933
*Sherwin C. Badger	New York, NY	1936-1938
*Joseph K. Savage	New York, NY	1940-1942
*Walter S. Powell	Saint Louis, MO	1942-1943
*Thomas A. Dean	Chicago, IL	1946-1947
*Dallas W. Dort	Washington, DC	1947-1948
*Robert Sackett	Omaha, NE	1948-1949; 1952-1953; 1954-1955; 1956-1957
*George B. Jenkinson, Jr.	Tulsa, OK	1949-1950
*Kenneth L. Brown	Berkeley, CA	1950-1952; 1958-1960; 1964-1965
*Robert R. Kierland	Rochester, MN	1953-1954; 1957-1958
*John P. Hart	Tacoma, WA	1961-1962; 1965-1967
Spencer E. Cram	Chagrin Falls, OH	1963-1964; 1970-1974
*William R. Haigler	Colorado Springs, CO	1967-1969
*John R. Shoemaker	San Francisco, CA	1969-1970
*Frederick C. LeFevre	Troy, OH	1974-1977
Benjamin T. Wright	Belmont, MA	1977-1981
Elvira Sonnhalter	Seal Beach, CA	1981-1982
*William J. Brennan, Jr.	New York, NY	1982-1983
Eleanor G. Schultz	Burbank, CA	1983-1984
Susan A. Johnson	Altanta, GA	1984-1985
Gale H. Tanger	Wauwatosa, WI	1985-1986
Anne H. Gerli	New York, NY	1986-1987
Charles U. Foster	Duxbury, MA	1987-1988
Franklin S. Nelson	Tulsa, OK	1988-1989

Name	Residence	Years in Office
Joseph D. Driano	Edmonds, WA	1989-1990
Harland L. Burge, Jr.	Laguna Hills, CA	1990-1991
J. Ronald Hershberger	Palo Alto, CA	1991-1992
Ronald T. Pfenning	Hyannis, MA	1992-1993
Anne L. Klein	Wayzata, MN	1993-1994
Patricia K. Hagedorn	Lexington, MA	1994-1995
John F. LeFevre	McLean, VA	1995-1996

PARENTS ADVISORY

Ann M. Neale	Troy, OH	1990-1991

PARENTS

Ann M. Neale	Troy, OH	1991-1993
Carole Yamaguchi	Fremont, CA	1993-

PROTOCOL [1]

Carolyn Y. Kruse	Colorado Springs, CO	1993-

RINK COOPERATION

John R. Harris	San Francisco, CA	1948-1951
Keith L. Moshier	Los Angeles, CA	1951-1953
Wilfred S. Bigelow	Berkeley, CA	1953-1954
*Deane E. McMinn	Lomita, CA	1954-1956
Oscar T. Iobst, Jr.	Churchville, PA	1975-1978
*Eugene W. Harvey	Daly City, CA	1978-1980

RINK MANAGEMENT ADVISORY

Richard Potticary	Dallas, TX	1987-1989

RINK OPERATIONS LIAISON

Richard F. Hooper	Littleton, CO	1989-1991
Ann P. Bullock	Dallas, TX	1992-1995
Peter G. Martell	Hollywood, CA	1995-

RINK OPERATIONS

Richard F. Hooper	Littleton, CO	1991-1992

SKATING STANDARDS

*Sherwin C. Badger	Boston, MA	1941-1942
*T. Elliott Pugh	Alameda, CA	1953-1956
*Deane E. McMinn	Lomita, CA	1956-1959
Norman E. Fuller	North Long Beach, CA	1959-1961
*H. Kendall Kelley	Cleveland Heights, OH	1961-1965
Spencer E. Cram	Chagrin Falls, OH	1965-1967; 1975-1978
*John R. Shoemaker	San Francisco, CA	1967-1975
Benjamin T. Wright	Belmont, MA	1978-1983
Charles U. Foster	Duxbury, MA	1983-1984
Franklin S. Nelson	Tulsa, OK	1984-1989
Josephine Lawless	Canoga Park, CA	1989-1992
Bette Snuggerud	Minnetonka, MN	1992-1993
John F. LeFevre	McLean, VA	1993-1995
Joan H. Gruber	Wyomissing, PA	1995-

SPECIAL OLYMPICS

Ida S. Tateoka	South Jordan, UT	1986-1989
Alma Jim Larkin, III	Salt Lake City, UT	1989-1992
Robert S. Watson	Santa Ana, CA	1992-1995
Sandra S. Lamb	Indianapolis, IN	1995-

[1] A special "ad hoc" committee from 1993 to 1995.

STATE GAMES

Judith A. Edmunds	West Yarmouth, MA	1986-1992
Edward G. Picken	Chevy Chase, MD	1992-1994
Elizabeth Stark	Coral Springs, FL	1994-

WORLD FIGURE SKATING HALL OF FAME ELECTORS

Theodore G. Clarke	North Weymouth, MA	1975-1989
Josephine Lawless	Canoga Park, CA	1989-

UNITED STATES FIGURE SKATING
HALL OF FAME ELECTORS

Hugh C. Graham, Jr.	Tulsa, OK	1991-

Permanent Committees (discontinued) – Chairs

AMATEUR STATUS

NAME	RESIDENCE	YEARS IN OFFICE
*A. Winsor Weld	Boston, MA	1921-1928
*Joel B. Liberman	New York, NY	1928-1939
*Charles Myers	Philadelphia, PA	1939-1945
*Joseph K. Savage	New York, NY	1945-1948
*H. Kendall Kelley	Cleveland Heights, OH	1948-1949
*Eli E. Dorsey	Seattle, WA	1949-1951
*Otto Dallmayr	Los Angeles, CA	1951-1953
*Kenneth L. Brown	Berkeley, CA	1953-1955
*William O. Hickok, IV	Harrisburg, PA	1955-1957
*Harold G. Storke	Allerton, MA	1957-1960
*Nelson F. Waters	East Lansing, MI	1960-1963
*Thomas H. Miller	Rochester, NY	1963-1966
*Frederick C. LeFevre	Troy, OH	1966-1968
Charles A. DeMore	Cleveland, OH	1968-1971
*Roy Winder	Seattle, WA	1971-1974
Elvira Sonnhalter	Seal Beach, CA	1974-1975
*Eugene W. Harvey	Park City, CA	1975-1978
Hugh C. Graham, Jr.	Tulsa, OK	1978-1981
Carolyn Y. Kruse	Colorado Springs, CO	1981-1984
Maribel A. Leiter	Wichita, KS	1984-1986
	(Discontinued 1986)	

EASTERN [1]

NAME	RESIDENCE	YEARS IN OFFICE
*Sherwin C. Badger	Boston, MA	1942-1943
*Heaton R. Robertson	New Haven, CT	1943-1945
*Clarence L. Parker	Washington, DC	1945-1946
Ernest E. Hall	Washington, DC	1946-1947
*Dallas W. Dort	Washington, DC	1947-1950
*Theodore G. Patterson	Weston, MA	1950-1951
*Abbot P. Mills	Washington, DC	1953-1956
*Delaplaine McDaniel	Narberth, PA	1956-1959; 1964-1967
*F. Ritter Shumway	Rochester, NY	1959-1961
*Henry R. Heebner	Wynnewood, PA	1961-1964
*Carl W. Gram, Jr.	New York, NY	1967-1970
Benjamin T. Wright	Belmont, MA	1970-1973
Brooks Stewart	Southampton, PA	1973-1976
E. Newbold Black, IV	New York, NY	1976-1978
Oscar T. Iobst, Jr.	Churchville, PA	1978-1980
	(Discontinued 1980)	

EXECUTIVE COMMITTEE [2]

NAME	RESIDENCE	YEARS IN OFFICE
*Paul Armitage	New York, NY	1921-1925
*Charles M. Rotch	Boston, MA	1925-1928
*John L. Evans	Philadelphia, PA	1928-1929
*Arthur M. Goodridge	Cambridge, MA	1929-1930
*M. Lester Madden	Boston, MA	1930-1931
	(Discontinued 1931)	

MIDWESTERN [3]

NAME	RESIDENCE	YEARS IN OFFICE
*Walter S. Powell	Saint Louis, MO	1941-1943
*Henry M. Beatty	Cleveland, OH	1943-1945
*Thomas A. Dean	Chicago, IL	1945-1947
*Robert Sackett	Omaha, NE	1947-1949
*George B. Jenkinson, Jr.	Tulsa, OK	1949-1950; 1959-1962
Allen M. Lomax	Grosse Pointe, MI	1950-1953
*Robert R. Kierland	Rochester, MN	1953-1956
*Harry N. Kieghley	Evanston, IL	1956-1959
Spencer E. Cram	Chagrin Falls, OH	1962-1965
*William R. Haigler	Colorado Springs, CO	1965-1968
*Frederick C. LeFevre	Troy, OH	1968-1970
*Gordon C. Brown	Ann Arbor, MI	1970-1973
Hugh C. Graham, Jr.	Tulsa, OK	1973-1974
Charles A. DeMore	Cleveland, OH	1974-1976
Joseph L. Serafine	Lake Forest, IL	1976-1980
	(Discontinued 1980)	

PACIFIC COAST [4]

NAME	RESIDENCE	YEARS IN OFFICE
*Henry F. Swift	San Francisco, CA	1938-1945; 1946-1947
*Alex Young, Jr.	Healdsburg, CA	1945-1946
Bradford H. Miller	Los Angeles, CA	1947-1948
*Edmund C. Bold	Seattle, WA	1950-1953
*Gerald J. Hurley	Tacoma, WA	1953-1956
*T. Elliott Pugh	Alameda, CA	1956-1957
*John P. Hart	Tacoma, WA	1957-1960; 1963-1966
*John R. Shoemaker	San Francisco, CA	1960-1963
Norman E. Fuller	Paramount, CA	1966-1969
Howard G. Taylor	Walnut Creek, CA	1969-1972
*Robert T. McLeod	Norwalk, CA	1972-1975
George T. Yonekura	Berkeley, CA	1975-1977
Elvira Sonnhalter	Seal Beach, CA	1977-1980
	(Discontinued 1980)	

PUBLICITY AND PUBLICATIONS

NAME	RESIDENCE	YEARS IN OFFICE
*Irving Brokaw	New York, NY	1921-1922
*Paul Armitage	New York, NY	1922-1923
*Theresa Weld Blanchard	Boston, MA	1923-1924; 1932-1944
*Nathaniel W. Niles	Boston, MA	1924-1932

PUBLICATIONS

NAME	RESIDENCE	YEARS IN OFFICE
*Theresa Weld Blanchard	Boston, MA	1944-1947
	(Became a special committee in 1947)	

PUBLIC RELATIONS [5]

NAME	RESIDENCE	YEARS IN OFFICE
*Thomas A. Dean	Chicago, IL	1944-1949
*William E. Wardman	Colorado Springs, CO	1949-1950
Lester J. Will	Chicago, IL	1950-1953
*Gerald J. Hurley	Tacoma, WA	1953-1954
Allen M. Lomax	Grosse Pointe, MI	1954-1957
*Howard D. Herbert	Moorestown, NJ	1957-1958

[1] A special committeee from 1942 to 1943.

[2] A separate Executive Committee of the Board of Directors was established in 1980, of which the President is the Chair.

[3] A special committee from 1941 to 1943.

[4] A special committee from 1938 to 1943.

[5] A special committee from 1944 to 1964.

PUBLIC RELATIONS [5] (continued)

NAME	RESIDENCE	YEARS IN OFFICE
*Charles H. Vilas	Branford, CT	1958-1959
Douglas O. Woodruff	Salt Lake City, UT	1959-1962
*Palmer Hoyt	Denver, CO	1962-1965
*Oscar Dystel	New York, NY	1965-1968
*Lawrence C. Shire, Jr.	New York, NY	1968-1969
*John W. McNair	Baltimore, MD	1969-1973
Jack L. Might	Colorado Springs, CO	1973-1976
Charles W. Dillie, Jr.	Washington, PA	1976-1980

(Became a special committee again in 1980)

RECORDS

*Rosalie Knapp	New York, NY	1922-1925
*Richard L. Hapgood	Cambridge, MA	1925-1928
*James L. Madden	Boston, MA	1928-1937
*Edward E. Denniston	Germantown, PA	1937-1942

(Became a special committee in 1942)

STANDARDS AND TESTS

*Joel B. Liberman	New York, NY	1921-1928
*Bedell H. Harned	New York, NY	1928-1932
*Howard J. Meredith	New York, NY	1932-1934
*Roger F. Turner	Walpole, MA	1934-1940
*Rollett A. Carson	Shaker Heights, OH	1940-1943
*Arthur F. Preusch	Minneapolis, MN	1943-1944
*Edward E. Denniston	St. Davids, PA	1944-1946
*C.E. Lindstrom	Boston, MA	1946-1948
*Heaton R. Robertson	New Haven, CT	1948-1951
Benjamin T. Wright	Cambridge, MA	1951-1952

TESTS

Benjamin T. Wright	Cambridge, MA	1952-1953
*T. Elliott Pugh	Alameda, CA	1953-1956
*Deane E. McMinn	Lomita, CA	1956-1959
Norman E. Fuller	Long Beach, CA	1959-1961

FIGURE TESTS

NAME	RESIDENCE	YEARS IN OFFICE
*George W. Fisk	Buffalo, NY	1961-1964
*Frank M. Petkevich	Great Falls, MT	1964-1967
*Gordon C. Brown	Ann Arbor, MI	1967-1970
E. Newbold Black, IV	New York, NY	1970-1973
*Louis Bodek	Birmingham, MI	1973-1975

TESTS

*Robert T. McLeod	Norwalk, CA	1975-1978
Claire W. Ferguson	Jamestown, RI	1978-1981
Janet G. Griffiths	Saint Paul, MN	1981-1984
Paula M. Naughton	Portland, OR	1984-1987
Bonnie P. McLauthlin	Denver, CO	1987-1990
Susan A. Johnson	Atlanta, GA	1990-1993

(Discontinued 1993)

SUMMER SKATING SESSIONS [6]

*Rollett A. Carson	Shaker Heights, OH	1941-1942

SUMMER SESSIONS STANDARDS

Helen Barrett	Detroit, MI	1942-1943

SUMMER SKATING

*Minerva S. Burke	Baltimore, MD	1944-1946
*Howard D. Herbert	Buffalo, NY	1946-1948
Lyman E. Wakefield, Jr.	Minneapolis, MN	1948-1950
*Abbot P. Mills	Washington, DC	1950-1953
Carl E. Lovett	Baltimore, MD	1953-1954
*Nelson F. Waters	East Lansing, MI	1954-1957
Howard M. Odel	Rochester, MN	1957-1958
Spencer E. Cram	Shaker Heights, OH	1958-1959
Charles E. Ingersoll	Philadelphia, PA	1959-1962
*William R. Haigler	Colorado Springs, CO	1962-1964

(Discontinued 1964)

---

* deceased

[6] A special committee from 1941 to 1957.

Special Committees [1] (discontinued) – Chairs

BASIC SKILLS AND BASIC COMPETITIONS

Name	Residence	Years in Office
Cindy H. Geltz	Califon, NJ	1987-1992
(Discontinued 1992)		

CENTRAL OFFICE ADVISORY

*Theresa W. Blanchard	Boston, MA	1950-1953

CENTRAL OFFICE

*Theodore G. Patterson	Weston, MA	1953-1956; 1957-1960; 1962-1970
*Harold G. Storke	Allerton, MA	1956-1957; 1960-1961
*Carl W. Gram, Jr.	New York, NY	1961-1962
Spencer E. Cram	Hendersonville, NC	1970-1974
Gerald G. Gearheart	Framingham, MA	1974-1976
Benjamin T. Wright	Belmont, MA	1976-1977

NATIONAL HEADQUARTERS

Charles U. Foster	Duxbury, MA	1986-1988
(Discontinued 1988)		

COLLEGE FIGURE SKATING

Hubert L. Perry	Buffalo, NY	1950-1951
Mary Louise Premer	Saint Paul, MN	1951-1953
Ainslie C. Whyman	Denver, CO	1953-1955
*F. Ritter Shumway	Rochester, NY	1955-1956
Douglas O. Woodruff	Salt Lake City, UT	1956-1959
Howard G. Taylor	Walnut Creek, CA	1959-1960
*Dudley S. Richards	Boston, MA	1960-1961
Mary F. Maroney	Summit, NJ	1961-1962

SCHOOL & COLLEGE FIGURE SKATING

Mary F. Maroney	Summit, NJ	1962-1967
(Discontinued 1967)		

CONSTITUTION

*Joel B. Liberman	New York, NY	1928-1929; 1937-1938
*John K. Ewing, III	Philadelphia, PA	1940-1942
*Joseph K. Savage	New York, NY	1948-1950
*Henry F. Swift	San Francisco, CA	1950-1951
John R. Harris	San Francisco, CA	1951-1953
*Harold G. Storke	Hull, MA	1960-1961
(Discontinued 1961)		

BY LAWS

Maurice W. Stillwell	Malibu, CA	1989-1990
(Discontinued 1990)		

JUDGING STANDARDS

*Heaton R. Robertson	New Haven, CT	1943-1945
*Robert Sackett	Palo Alto, CA	1963-1964
E. Newbold Black, IV	Haverford, PA	1964-1966
*H. Kendall Kelley	Cleveland Heights, OH	1966-1967
(Discontinued 1967)		

MAJOR GRANTS AND ACQUISITIONS

Name	Residence	Years in Office
Marilyn K. Palik	New York, NY	1987-1989
(Became a subcommittee of the Memorial Fund Committee in 1989)		

MEMBER RECOGNITION

Barbara D. Holland	Columbus, OH	1987-1992
Carolyn W. Grimditch	Hillsboro Beach, FL	1992
(Became a subcommittee of the Membership Committee in 1992)		

PUBLIC RELATIONS

Robert N. Briley	Spokane, WA	1980-1983
Lou Sherman	Wilmette, IL	1983-1985
Pam Robinson	Noblesville, IN	1985-1987
(Discontinued 1987)		

PUBLICATIONS

*Theresa W. Blanchard	Boston, MA	1947-1957
*Henry M. Beatty	Tacoma, WA	1966-1967
Brooks Stewart	Southampton, PA	1967-1977
(Discontinued 1977)		

PUBLICATIONS ADVISORY

*Theresa W. Blanchard	Boston, MA	1957-1963
(Discontinued 1963)		

RECORDS

*Edward E. Denniston	Gladwyne, PA	1942-1948
(Discontinued 1948)		

SCHOLASTIC REQUIREMENTS

M. Bernard Fox	Brookline, MA	1946-1950
*Forrest M. Burke	Portuguese Bend, CA	1950-1954
Leonard H. Bruce	Cleveland, OH	1954-1956
(Discontinued 1956)		

TELEVISION

*Henry M. Beatty	Cleveland, OH	1949-1950
*Carl W. Gram, Jr.	New York, NY	1961-1968
*William J. Brennan, Jr.	New York, NY	1968-1978
*William J. Brennan, Jr.	New York, NY	1987-1992
(Discontinued 1992)		

TELEVISION AND COMMERCIAL SPONSORSHIP

*William J. Brennan, Jr.	New York, NY	1978-1987
(Discontinued 1987)		

COMMERCIAL SPONSORSHIP

John W. Powers	Evanston, IL	1987-1989
(Discontinued 1989)		

---

[1] The special committees listed as discontinued do not include all such committees known to have been established. Those special committees which had a limited existence for a minor specific purporse or were not listed either in the Rulebook or in Skating magazine (prior to 1940) have been omitted.

TROPHY

Name	Residence	Years in Office
Ardelle V. Sanderson	New York, NY	1946-1947
*Harry E. Radix	Chicago, IL	1947-1949
*Robert H. MacMurphey	New York, NY	1949-1952
Mabel Graham	Cuyahoga Falls, OH	1952-1957
	(Discontinued 1957)	

USFSA-ISIA LIAISON

Spencer E. Cram	Chagrin Falls, OH	1963-1967
	(Discontinued 1967)	

USFSA-PSGA LIAISON

*Harry N. Keighley	Evanston, IL	1964-1967
	(Discontinued 1967)	

USFSA OLYMPIC

*Harry E. Radix	Chicago, IL	1955-1965
*Harry N. Keighley	Evanston, IL	1965-1976
	(Discontinued 1976)	

Board of Directors [1] (Including Executive Committee)

MEMBERS [2]

A

Name	Residence		Years in Office
*Paul Armitage	New York, NY		1921-1928
*William Arthur	New Haven, CT		1924-1927
*John J. Allen, Jr.	Oakland, CA		1942-1945
*Hollis L. Albright	Newton Centre, MA		1954-1957
Milton W. Anderson	Minneapolis, MN		1962-1964
Robert S. Aamodt	Garden Grove, CA		1971-1974
Raymond C. Alperth	San Francisco, CA		1981-1984
Mary-Lucile Ager	Lake Placid, NY		1985-1988
Lisa Marie Allen Lucie	Huntington Station, NY	(A)	1985-1988
Robert Allen	Lake Placid, NY		1992-1994

B

Name	Residence		Years in Office
*Charles J. Beck, Jr.	Lake Placid, NY		1925-1938
*Theresa Weld Blanchard	Brookline, MA		1925-1938
*Sherwin C. Badger	New York, NY		1927-1928; 1935-1938; 1939-1946; 1948-1951
*Henry M. Beatty	Cleveland, OH		1940-1943; 1957-1967 [3]
*Eileen Bigelow	Saint Paul, MN		1942-1945; 1947-1950
*Edmund C. Bold	Seattle, WA		1943-1946; 1953-1956; 1957-1962; 1963-1965
*Forrest M. Burke	Los Angeles CA		1945-1948; 1962-1963
*Dorothy Ballantine	Berkeley, CA		1951-1954
J. Howard Bobbitt	San Diego, CA		1951-1954
*Ruth Babbit	Tacoma, WA		1955-1958
*Kenneth L. Brown	Berkeley, CA		1959-1962; 1963-1967
*Gordon C. Brown	Ann Arbor, MI		1964-1966; 1973-1975
E. Newbold Black, IV	New York, NY		1966-1970; 1973-1976 [4]
*William J. Brennan, Jr.	New York, NY		1968-1975; 1978-1979
*Louis Bodek	Birmingham, MI		1969-1973; 1977-1979
F. Alfred Beeler	Tacoma, WA		1971-1974
Harland L. Burge, Jr.	Tarzana, CA		1972-1975; 1983-1984; 1987-1990
Albert L. Beard	Phoenix, AZ		1974-1978; 1981-1983
Robert N. Briley	Spokane, WA		1977-1981
Mahlon A. Bradley	Chestnut Hill, MA		1978-1980; (A) 1980-1981; (A) 1984-1988; (EC) 1980-1981

(continued — right columns)

Name	Residence		Years in Office
James E. Browning	Indianapolis, IN		1980-1981
Judy Ann Blumberg	Colorado Springs, CO	(A)	1981-1990; (EO) 1985-1990
Brian Boitano	Sunnyvale, CA	(A)	1982-1985; 1987-1989
T. Sundae Bafo	Buffalo, NY	(C)	1983-1986
Joan I. Burns	Millbrae, CA		1984-1987
*Jo Anne Bryan	Syvania, OH		1985-1989
Gay Barnes	Boulder, CO		1986-1989
Jeffrey G. Benz	Bloomfield Hills, MI	(A)	1989-1992; (SA) 1992-1993; (A) 1993- ; (EC) 1993-
Christopher Bowman	Santa Monica, CA	(A)	1989-1990
Lucy J. Brennan	New York, NY		1989-1992
Tod A. Bartholomew	Bay Village, OH	(C)	1991-1992
Peter Burrowes	Monsey, NY	(C)	1992-1994
Barret Brown	Cambridge, MA	(C)	1994-

C

Name	Residence		Years in Office
*Joseph Chapman	Philadelphia, PA		1921-1925; 1930-1932
*James A. Cruikshank	New York, NY		1922-1923
*Ruth Chapman	Philadelphia, PA		1925-1927
*Chris I. Christenson	Saint Paul, MN		1928-1936
*Charles T. Church	New York, NY		1930-1937
William R. Cady	Saint Louis, MO		1936-1937
William C. Coleman	Baltimore, MD		1937-1941
Herbert E. Cook	Detroit, MI		1937-1939
*Rollett A. Carson	Cleveland, OH		1944-1945
*Carl W. Chamberlin	Colorado Springs, CO		1948-1951; 1953-1956
*Vernon Campbell	Seattle, WA		1949-1950
John Cotton	San Diego, CA		1949-1952
*Evar T. Cedarleaf	Saint Paul, MN		1951-1954
*Gerald B. Crook	Baltimore, MD		1961-1962
William V. Colway	Omaha, NE		1967-1970
Jack W. Curtis	Granada Hills, CA		1969-1972
Spencer E. Cram	Hendersonville, NC		1971-1973; [5] 1973-1977
*Dora Mae Coy	Lakebay, WA		1971-1975
Peter Carruthers	Wilmington, DE	(A)	1980-1983
Roy H. Cofer	Walnut Creek, CA		1986-1989
Kathy Casey	Steilacoom, WA	(C)	1987-1990
James Cygan	Colorado Springs, CO	(A)	1989-1992
Sharon A. Carz	North Hollywood, CA	(A)	1990-1993
D. Bradley Cox	Newark, DE	(A)	1993-
Karen Courtland	Newark, DE	(A)	1994-
Deborah D. Currie	Fairview, PA		1994-
Gary A. Clark	Ypsilanti, MI		1995-

[1] The Executive Committee from 1921 to 1980.

[2] (A) Athlete member; (SA) Substitute athlete member; (C) Coach member; (EC) Athlete member of the (new) Executive Committee after 1980; (EO) ex officio (non-voting) member.

[3] As ISU Representative from 1962 to 1967.

[4] As Chairman, Olympic Figure Skating Committee (of the USOC) from 1973 to 1976.

[5] As immediate Past President 1971-1973

D

Name	Residence	Years in Office
*Russell Doubleday	Locust Valley, NY	1926-1928; 1930-1935
*Allen R. Diefendorf	New Haven, CT	1932-1939
*Edward E. Denniston	Germantown, PA	1937-1938
*Stanley W. Dwinnell	Minneapolis, MN	1940-1942; 1944-1947
*Thomas A. Dean	Chicago, IL	1941-1944
*Dallas W. Dort	Washington, DC	1946-1947; 1950-1951
*Otto Dallmayr	Los Angeles, CA	1948-1949; 1953-1954; 1956-1957; 1959-1961
*Eli E. Dorsey	Seattle, WA	1948-1949; 1952-1955: 1956-1957
*Hugh Dean	Farmington, MI	1951-1954
Margaretta S. Drake	Glencoe, IL	1952-1955
Joseph N. DuBarry, IV	Philadelphia, PA	1956-1957
*Oscar Dystel	New York, NY	1963-1965
Patrick J. Donnelly	Seattle, WA	1965-1971
Charles A. DeMore	Cleveland, OH	1966-1968; 1971; 1980-1983;[6] (EO) 1983-1994
Charles W. Dillie, Jr.	Washington, PA	1975-1976; 1980-1981; 1984-1986
Richard J. Dalley	Wilmington, DE	(A) 1981-1985; 1990-1993; (EC) 1983-1985; 1990-1993; (EO) 1993-
Joseph D. Driano	Bothell, WA	1982-1985; 1990-1993
James W. Disbrow	Haworth, NJ	1990-1992
Avonia Dondero	Orinda, CA	1990-1993
Joseph H. Druar	Boston, MA	(SA) 1991-1992

E

Name	Residence	Years in Office
*John L. Evans	Philadelphia, PA	1925-1927; 1928-1930
*Howard P. Eells, Jr.	Cleveland, OH	1937-1940
*John K. Ewing, III	Philadelphia, PA	1939-1942
James M. Earle	Philadelphia, PA	1959-1961
Rutherford L. Ellis, Jr.	Atlanta, GA	1977-1980
William B. Estey, Jr.	Wyandotte, MI	1989-1992
Gloria Earnhardt	Scottsdale, AZ	1993-1995

F

Name	Residence	Years in Office
Robert H. Fenn	New York, NY	1936-1940
M. Bernard Fox	Boston, MA	1941-1944; 1945-1948; 1949-1952
*George W. Fisk	Buffalo, NY	1956-1958; 1959-1961; 1964-1966
Norman E. Fuller	North Long Beach, CA	1957-1959; 1964-1965; 1969-1971; 1974-1975
Dick P. Fullerton	New York, NY	1961-1963
Charles U. Foster	Worcester, MA	1967-1971; 1977-1980;[7] 1984-1989;[8] 1989-1990[9]
Claire W. Ferguson	Jamestown, RI	1975-1978; 1981-1982; 1987-1989; 1995-[10]; (EO) 1994-
Ronald F. Fry	Portland, OR	1975-1978
Carlo Fassi	Denver, CO	1978-1980
Linda Fratianne	Northridge, CA	1979-1980
William B. Fauver	Claymont, DE	(A) 1982-1985
Patricia S. French	Williamsville, NY	1987-1989; 1993-1995; (EO) 1994-
William M. Fitzpatrick	Bethlehem, PA	1992-1995

G

Name	Residence	Years in Office
*Edward W. Gray	Minneapolis, MN	1921-1922
*Arthur M. Goodridge	Cambridge, MA	1927-1929; 1932-1939; 1940-1943
*Frederick Goodridge	Boston, MA	1932-1938
*Joseph P. Gibson, Jr.	Rye, NY	1940-1943; 1946-1949; 1951-1953
William H. Grimditch, Jr.	Rydal, PA	1948-1950
*Frank J. Goodwin	Philadelphia, PA	1954-1957
*Carl W. Gram, Jr.	New York, NY	1955-1957; 1963-1964; 1970-1971; 1971-1973[11]
*John F. Groden	Boston, MA	1967-1968
Hugh C. Graham, Jr.	Tulsa, OK	1969-1973; 1977-1978; 1989-1992[12]
Gerald G. Gearheart	Framingham, MA	1973-1976
*Edward A. Glenn	Rockford, IL	1973-1976
Anne H. Gerli	New York, NY	1975-1977; 1980-1983[13]
Randy Gardner	Los Angeles, CA	1978-1980; (A) 1980-1981; (EO) 1982-1984
Roger A. Glenn	Appleton, WI	1980-1983
Janet G. Griffiths	Saint Paul, MN	1980-1981
Sherie Grimson	Santa Ana, CA	1980-1983
Joan H. Gruber	Wyomissing, PA	1983-1985; 1995-[14]
Wanda Mae Guntert	Venice, CA	(C) 1984-1987
Scott C. Gregory	Wilmington, DE	(A) 1985-1989
Richard C. Gold	Tulsa, OK	1987-1990
Paul E. George	Wellesley, MA	1989-1994[15]
Darlene S. Gilbert	Signal City, CA	(C) 1992-1994
Troy Goldstein	Culver City, CA	(A) 1992-1994

[6] As immediate Past President 1980-1983.

[7] As Olympic Representative 1977-1980.

[8] As Olympic Representative 1984-1989.

[9] As ISU Representative 1989-1990.

[10] As immediate Past President 1995-.

[11] As Chairman, Olympic Figure Skating Committee (of the USOC) 1971-1973.

[12] As immediate Past President 1989-1992.

[13] As Olympic Representative 1980-1983.

[14] As ISU Representative 1995-.

[15] As Olympic Representative 1989-1994.

NAME	RESIDENCE	YEARS IN OFFICE	NAME	RESIDENCE	YEARS IN OFFICE

H

NAME	RESIDENCE	YEARS IN OFFICE		NAME	RESIDENCE		YEARS IN OFFICE
*Henry W. Howe	New York, NY		1921-1925;	*Howell Janes	San Francisco, CA		1950-1953
			1928-1931	*Richard Jackson	Cambridge, MA		1957-1959
*Charles P. Hobbs	Lake Placid, NY		1923-1925	Ruth L. Jackson	Greensboro, NC		1977-1980
*Bedell H. Harned	New York, NY		1930-1934;	Susan A. Johnson	Atlanta, GA		1981-1984
			1937-1938	Carol H. Jenkins	Akron, OH	(C)	1986-1989;
*Edward M. Howland	Boston, MA		1930-1932				1994-[18]
*Mary B. Howe	New York, NY		1934-1938				
*Richard L. Hapgood	Cambridge, MA		1934-1935		**K**		
*William O. Hickok, IV	Harrisburg, PA		1939-1942;	*Rosalie Knapp	New York, NY		1925-1934
			1946-1949;	*Robert R. Kierland	Rochester, MN		1951-1952;
			1951-1954				1959-1962
*Howard D. Herbert	Akron, OH		1945-1948;	*Harry N. Keighley	Evanston, IL		1962-1968;
			1957-1958				1971-1977
John R. Harris	San Francisco, CA		1947-1950	*H. Kendall Kelley	Cleveland Heights, OH		1965-1967
*Harold Hartshorne	New York, NY		1949-1950;	John Klindworth	Minneapolis, MN		1975-1977
			1952-1955;	Jacob J. Kohlhas, Jr.	Cambridge, MA	(A)	1979-1983;
			1959-1961			(EC)	1980-1983
Thomas Hocking	Alameda, CA		1949-1951	Carolyn Y. Kruse	Colorado Springs, CO		1980-1981
*John P. Hart	Tacoma, WA		1949-1951;	Scott Kurttila	Seattle, WA	(A)	1986-1990;
			1960-1963;			(EC)	1988-1990
			1966-1967	Joyce Komperda	Milwaukee, WI		1987-1990
*Gerald J. Hurley	Tacoma, WA		1950-1953	Robert L. Kaine	Philadelphia, PA	(C)	1989-1992
W.R. Holloway	Dallas, TX		1956-1958	Kathaleen A. Kelly	Lake Placid, NY	(A)	1990- ;
*Henry R. Heebner	Wynnewood, PA		1957-1960;			(EC)	1991-
			1966-1968	Linda J. Kola	Colorado Springs, CO		1990-1991
*William R. Haigler	Colorado Springs, CO		1959-1962;	Ronald I. Kravette	Newark, DE	(SA)	1991-1992;
			1964-1965			(A)	1992-1995;
*Frank E. Holcombe	Denver, CO		1959-1960;			(SA)	1995-
			1967-1969	Anne L. Klein	Wayzata, MN		1992-1993
*Palmer Hoyt	Denver, CO		1960-1964	Tonia S. Kwiatkowski	Broadview Height, OH		1992;
*Eugene W. Harvey	San Francisco, CA		1961-1963;			(SA)	1993-
			1969-1972	Larry Kriwanek	Manhattan Beach, CA		1993-
*Rolf E. Hessler	Cleveland Heights, OH		1970-1973	Vicki L. Korn	Oxford, OH	(C)	1994-
Robert L. Houk	Seattle, WA		1974-1977	Christine H. Krall	Colorado Springs, CO	(C)	1994-
*Harold Hiltzik	Westbury, NY		1980-1981				
Scott Hamilton	Denver, CO	(A)	1981-1987;		**L**		
		(EO)	1984-1985;	*Beatrix S. Loughran	New York, NY		1925-1938
		(EC)	1985-1986	*Joel B. Liberman	New York, NY		1928-1938;
Priscilla Hill	Lexington, MA	(A)	1981-1982				1941-1943;
Barbara D. Holland	Columbus, OH		1983-1986				1945-1948
Monty Hoyt	Englewood, CO		1983-1986	*David T. Layman, Jr.	New York, NY		1938-1941
John H. Holdsworth	Lexington, MA		1983-1985	Frederic C. Lee	Baltimore, MD		1942-1945
Robert J. Horen	Haddonfield, NJ		1985-1987	Sanford A. Lindstrom	Seattle, WA		1946-1949
Patricia K. Hagedorn	Lexington, MA		1986-1989;	*Harold T. Leroux	Tulsa, OK		1949-1951
			1992-1995	*Carl E. Lovett	Baltimore, MD		1952-1955
J. Ronald Hershberger	Palo Alto, CA		1989-1992	Allen M. Lomax	Grosse Pointe, MI		1953-1956
Phyllis F. Howard	Falls Church, VA		1990-1993	Frederick C. LeFevre	Troy, OH		1961-1963;
							1973-1976;
	I						1980-1982 [19]
Charles E. Ingersoll	Philadelphia, PA		1957-1959	J. Keith Louden	Lancaster, PA		1961-1963
Oscar T. Iobst, Jr.	Churchville, PA		1971-1975;	Alvin A. Lais	Los Angeles, CA		1965-1968
			1983-1984;[16]	Alma Jim Larkin, III	Salt Lake City, UT		1974-1977
			1984-1986 [17]	Walter H. Lupke, Jr.	Fort Wayne, IN		1977-1980
				Ronald E. Ludington	Wilmington, DE		1978-1980;
	J					(C)	1980-1981;
Thomas B.L. Jordan	Seattle, WA		1938-1939			(C)	1983-1986
*George B. Jenkinson, Jr.	Tulsa, OK		1943-1946;	Donald E. Laws	Denver, CO	(C)	1980-1983
			1950-1953;	George B. Ludlow, Jr.	Kent, CT		1980-1983;
			1955-1957;				1984-1985;
			1965-1968				1986-1987
*Robert R. Jenks	Pawtucket, RI		1944-1946	Sandra Lenz	Rockford, IL	(A)	1980-1981
				Maribel A. Leiter	Wichita, KS		1981-1984
				John F. LeFevre	McLean, VA		1982-1985;
							1992-[20]
				Josephine Lawless	Canoga Park, CA		1984-1986
				Julie F. Lobo	Cleveland, OH		1989-1992
				Gerard V. Lane	Plano, TX	(C)	1992-1994

[16] As Olympic Representative 1983-1984.
[17] As immediate Past President 1984-1986.
[18] As Olympic Representative 1994-.
[19] As immediate Past President 1973-1976.
[20] As ISU Representative 1992-1995.

NAME	RESIDENCE		YEARS IN OFFICE
M			
*Charles E.F. McCann	New York, NY		1922-1925
*M. Lester Madden	Newton, MA		1927-1938
*Charles Myers	Philadelphia, PA		1927-1928;
			1932-1936;
			1945-1947;
			1950-1951
*Edgar S. McKaig	Philadelphia, PA		1935-1939
*Roy W. McDaniel	Minneapolis, MN		1936-1940
*James L. Madden	Newton, MA		1937-1940
William A. More	Buffalo, NY		1941-1944
Bradford H. Miller	Beverly Hills, CA		1942-1945
*Howard J. Meredith	New York, NY		1945-1946;
			1948-1951
*Charles A. McCarthy	Chicago, IL		1945-1948
*Keith L. Moshier	Los Angeles, CA		1950-1951
*Abbot P. Mills	Washington, DC		1951-1952
*Deane E. McMinn	Lomita, CA		1954-1956
*Delaplaine McDaniel	Philadelphia, PA		1951-1952;
			1955-1956;
			1959-1962
Winston L. Molander	Minneapolis, MN		1958-1959;
			1961-1963
William N. Moritz, Jr.	Pomona, CA		1960-1962
*Thomas H. Miller	Rochester, NY		1961-1963;
			1966-1967
*Sidney A. MacSween	Glendale, CA		1962-1964
*John W. McNair	Baltimore, MD		1963-1969
*Robert T. McLeod	Norwalk, CA		1964-1965;
			1968-1969
*C. Dallas Mauk, Jr.	Denver, CO		1964-1971
William K. Munns	Concord, CA		1967-1969;
			1984-1985
Jack L. Might	Colorado Springs, CO		1972-1973;
			1976-1977;
			1981-1983
Nancy Meiss	Cincinnati, OH		1973-1976
Hal E. Marron, Jr.	Colorado Springs, CO	(A)	1981-1987;
		(EC)	1982-1987
Nancy A. Meyer	Lake Placid, NY		1981-1984
Grace A. Moore	Spring Lake, NJ		1981-1984
Frederick D. Meyers	Columbus, OH		1982-1985
Gordon McKellen, Jr.	Rockford, IL	(A)	1983-1986
Bonnie P. McLauthlin	Denver, CO		1984-1987
Janet R. McLeod	Norwalk, CA		1984-1987
Peggy McDonald	Warren, MI		1986-1989
Bruce McNally	Katonah, NY		1988-1990
Ronald J. Millier	Winthrop, ME		1989-1992
Mark D. Mitchell	Wellesley, MA	(SA)	1991-1992;
		(A)	1992-1994;
		(SA)	1994-
Lee Ann Miele	Narragansett, RI		1993-
Virginia B. Mount	Boulder, CO		1993-
Rachel L. Mayer	Wellesley, MA	(A)	1994-
Priscilla Millier	Winthrop, ME		1995-
Jessica S. Mills	Vail, CO	(SA)	1995-
Lawrence G. Mondschein	East Brunswick, NJ		1995-
Anthony C. Morici	San Jose, CA		1995-

NAME	RESIDENCE		YEARS IN OFFICE
N			
*Nathaniel W. Niles	Boston, MA		1922-1925;
			1928-1932
*William J. Nagle	Brooklyn, NY		1930-1936
Franklin S. Nelson	Tulsa, OK		1972-1975;
			1978-1980;
			1983-1989 [21];
			1992- [22]
J. Barlow Nelson	Tulsa, OK		1976-1978;
			1981-1983
John A.W. Nicks	Santa Monica, CA	(C)	1980-1983;
		(C)	1989-1992
Paula M. Naughton	Portland, OR		1981
O			
Nelse F. Ockerblad	Kansas City, MO		1937-1938
Alice Cook O'Connell	Boston, MA	(A)	1983-1985
P			
George W. Pepper, Jr.	Philadelphia, PA		1934-1936
*Gertrude Cheever Porter	New York, NY		1937-1938
Grattan Phillips	San Francisco, CA		1943-1946
*Clarence L. Parker	Washington, DC		1944-1945;
			1948-1950
Edward A. Peterson	Indianapolis, IN		1945-1947
*Walter S. Powell	Saint Louis, MO		1947-1949;
			1952-1955;
			1957-1961
Hubert L. Perry	Buffalo, NY		1949-1951
Latham Pollock	Los Angeles, CA		1949-1950
*Arthur F. Preusch	Excelsior, MN		1955-1958
Harold C. Payne	Omaha, NE		1957-1959
*Theodore G. Patterson	Boston, MA		1960-1967;
			1971-1975
*Frank M. Petkevich	Great Falls, MT		1962-2964;
			1967-1969
James H. Poyner	New York, NY		1970-1972
Ronald T. Pfenning	Newport, NH		1976-1979;
			1980-1981;
			1985-1987;
		(EO)	1994-
John R. Phelps	Marietta, GA		1980-1981
John W. Powers	Evanston, IL		1986-1987
Roberta Parkinson	McMurray, PA		1987-1990
Marcha L. Pipes	Overland Park, KS		1990-1992
Andrew A. Paterson	Bloomfield Hills, MI		1992-1995
R			
*Heaton R. Robertson	New Haven, CT		1924-1925;
			1927-1929;
			1947-1948
*Charles M. Rotch	Boston, MA		1925-1932;
			1937-1941
Robert Reed	Brooklyn, NY		1930-1935
*Harry E. Radix	Chicago, IL		1935-1941;
			1942-1945;
			1946-1949;
			1950-1953;
			1954-1957;
			1959-1965
Robert B. Ridder	Minneapolis, MN		1954-1957
*John W.C. Rogers	San Francisco, CA		1957-1959
*Dudley S. Richards	Boston, MA		1960-1961
*Jerome Ross	Port Chester, NY		1962-1963;
			1972-1975
Robert E. Reed	Tulsa, OK		1966-1969
Renée Roca	Saint Claire Shores, MI	(A)	1985-1987
Morton G. Rosenstein	Fresno, CA		1992-1995
Edward J. Reisman	Spokane, WA		1993-

[21] As ISU Representative 1883-1989.
[22] As immediate Past President 1992-1995.
[23] As immediate Past President 1964-1965.
[24] As immediate Past President 1967-1968.
[25] As ISU Representative 1967-1980.

S

Name	Residence	Years in Office
*Joseph K. Savage	New York, NY	1924-1928; 1930-1932; 1934-1935; 1943-1945; 1951-1954
*Henry F. Swift	San Francisco, CA	1940-1943
*Robert Sackett	Omaha, NE	1949-1951; 1952-1955; 1956-1958; 1964-1967
*F. Ritter Shumway	Rochester, NY	1953-1956; 1964-1965[21]; 1965-1967; 1970-1972; 1975-1978
*John R. Shoemaker	San Francisco, CA	1956-1957; 1967-1968[24]; 1967-1980[25]; 1980-1982
Lyndon E. Snow	Salt Lake City, UT	1962-1964
Brooks Stewart	Southampton, PA	1962-1966; 1972-1973; 1976-1977
*Raymond Satterwhite	Dallas, TX	1963-1966; 1971-1972
Joseph L. Serafine	Lake Forest, IL	1968-1972; 1975-1976
Elvira Sonnhalter	Seal Beach, CA	1971-1974; 1980-1981
Ardelle K. Sanderson	Lake Placid, NY	1972-1978
Eleanor G. Schultz	Burbank, CA	1975-1979; 1985-1986
Les Seale	Playa del Rey, CA	1975-1978
Kenneth E. Shelley	Sudbury, MA	1978-1980; (A) 1980-1981
Harry F. Spuehler	San Diego, CA	1978-1980
David Santee	Park Ridge, IL	1979-1980; (A) 1980-1982
Stacey Smith	Wilmington, DE	1979-1980; (A) 1980-1982; (EC) 1981-1982
Evy Scotvold	Janesville, WI	(C) 1981-1984
Rosalyn Sumners	Edmonds, WA	(A) 1982-1984
Wayne Seybold	Newark, DE	(A) 1987-1990
Margery L. Schleh	Sacramento, CA	1987-1990
Jerry Sisson	Manchester, MO	1987-1990
Howard M. Silby	Potomac, MD	1989-1992
Robb Steinheider	Riverside, CA	1989-1992
Jerod J. Swallow	Colorado Springs, CO	(A) 1990-1995; (SA) 1995-
Lou Sherman	Wilmette, IL	1990-
Bette Snuggerud	Minnetonka, MN	1990-1992
Reiko Seger	Portland, OR	1991-1994
Caroline Silby	Charlottesville, VA	(A) 1991-1994
Kathy Slack	Troy, OH	1992-1995
Todd Sand	Costa Mesa, CA	(SA) 1993-
Janice Serafine	Lake Forest, IL	1993-
William S. Smith	Tulsa, OK	1993-

T

Name	Residence	Years in Office
*Roger F. Turner	Milton, MA	1928-1930; 1932-1938
*John B. Thayer	Philadelphia, PA	1938-1941
Warren A.Throop	Spokane, WA	1939-1940
Glenn H. Terwilliger	Oakland, CA	1946-1949
Howard G. Taylor	Walnut Creek, CA	1957-1960; 1972-1974; 1977-1980
*Francis B. Turner	Weston, MA	1959-1960
*Kenneth O. Turner	Palos Verdes Estates, CA	1965-1971
*Ralph W. Talley	Buffalo, NY	1968-1972
Yvonne S. McGowan	Colorado Springs, CO	1976-1980
Charles Tickner	Littleton, CO	1978-1980; (A) 1980-1981
Gale H. Tanger	Wauwatosa, WI	1983-1987
Ida S. Tateoka	Riverton, UT	1983-1984
Melissa J. Thomas	Massapequa, NY	(A) 1987-1989; (EC) 1987-1989
Charlene A. Tagas	Issaquah, WA	1988-1991
Jill Trenary	Colorado Springs, CO	1988-1989
Archie Tse	Newark, DE	(A) 1990-
Kanae Tagawa	San Carlos, CA	1995-
Newton T. Todd	Indianapolis, IN	1995-

U

Name	Residence	Years in Office
Stanley T. Urban	Portland, OR	1980-1981

V

Name	Residence	Years in Office
*Ralph G. Van Name	New Haven, CT	1922-1936
*Maribel Y. Vinson	Winchester, MA	1930-1937
*Charles H. Vilas	Branford, CT	1956-1959
*Howard Van Camp	East Lansing, MI	1977-1978

W

Name	Residence	Years in Office
*Hugh A. Whytock	Salt Lake City, UT	1921-1924
*Alfred R. Whitney, Jr.	New York, NY	1925-1926
Lyman E. Wakefield, Jr.	Saint Paul, MN	1939-1942; 1949-1950
*William E. Wardman	Colorado Springs, CO	1941-1944; 1947-1948; 1951-1952
*Fred H. Wiley	Colorado Springs, CO	1944-1947
*H. Glenn Waring	Baltimore, MD	1950-1953
Benjamin T. Wright	Cambridge, MA	1953-1956; 1963-1966; 1969-1970; 1976-1980[26]; 1980-1983[27]; (EO) 1982-1992
Arthur W. Wiley	Los Angeles, CA	1954-1956
Marcella M. Willis	Oakland, CA	1954-1957
Douglas O. Woodruff	Salt Lake City, UT	1955-1958; 1959-1962
Robert F. Wilkins	Playa del Rey, CA	1959-1960
*Nelson F. Waters	Alton Bay, NH	1963-1964
*Roy Winder	Seattle, WA	1963-1966; 1969-1971
John W.W. Wood	Wilmington, DE	1967-1970
Kent Weigle	Salt Lake City, UT	(A) 1985-1987
Steve Winkler	Copalis Beach, WA	1985-1988; 1994-
Robert S. Watson	Santa Ana, CA	1986-1989
Susan E. Wynne	Camillus, NY	(A) 1987-1990; (EC) 1989-1990

[26] As immediate Past President 1976-1980.

[27] As ISU Representative 1980-1983.

Name	W (continued) Residence	Years in Office
Paul S. Wylie	Weston, MA	(A) 1988-1992;
		(EC) 1990-1991;
		(EO) 1992-1993
Cheryl H. Wood	Trenton, NJ	1992-1993
Sharon G. Watson	Los Angeles, CA	1992-1993
Scott Wendland	Costa Mesa, CA	(SA) 1992-1994;
		(A) 1994-
Sharon D. Wiggins	Atlanta, GA	1995-

Y

*Alex Young, Jr.	San Francisco, CA	1936-1937; 1938-1940
George T. Yonekura	Berkeley, CA	1967-1969; 1986-1989[28]

Z

Matthew H. Zats	Saint Paul, MN	1968-1971

[28] As immediate Past President 1986-1989.